Common Writing Assignments

Free Writing .... pp. 5–7
Journal Keeping .... pp. 7–8
Writing for an Audience .... pp. 36–43
Analyzing Voice in Writing .... pp. 57–80
Journalistic Writing .... pp. 62–69
Expository Writing .... pp. 93–124
Paragraph Writing .... pp. 121–161
Sentence Combining .... pp. 167–194
Narrating and Describing .... pp. 199–235
Imitating Sentences .... pp. 237–258
Writing About Language .... pp. 293–367
Writing to Fixed Forms .... pp. 411–421
Writing Business Letters .... pp. 416–417
Creating a Resume .... pp. 418–419
Creating the Formative Idea .... pp. 421–432
Writing Essay Examinations .... pp. 436–446
Writing the Investigative Paper .... pp. 446–488
Writing Argumentative Papers .... pp. 493–519
Writing Definition Papers .... pp. 533–539
Writing Classification Papers .... pp. 539–543
Writing Illustration Papers .... pp. 543–545
Writing Comparison and Contrast Papers .... pp. 545–548
Inventing Ideas for Writing .... pp. 554–578
Revising Writing .... pp. 581–599
Writing About Literature .... pp. 600–609

College Reading Skills

Reading Fluently .... pp. 13–22
Reading the Code of Print .... pp. 49–50
Reading for Tone .... pp. 80–83
Creating Coherence in Reading .... pp. 93–107
Reading Textbook Chapters .... pp. 124–127
Outlining as a Reading Skill .... pp. 161–163
"Chunking" Meaning in Sentences .... pp. 167–187
Readability .... pp. 187–197
Reading Descriptions and Narrations .... pp. 199–235
Reading for Style .... pp. 237–258
Recognizing Parody .... pp. 258–260
Reading Punctuation Signals .... pp. 262–280
Recognizing Devices of Language .... pp. 293–325
Analyzing Figurative Language .... pp. 303–310
Building Vocabulary .... pp. 328–334
Using a College Dictionary .... pp. 334–359
Grasping the Spelling System .... pp. 368–394
Grasping Form in Reading .... pp. 401–421
Identifying Main Ideas .... pp. 421–431
Reading Examination Questions .... pp. 436–446
Using Library Skills .... pp. 446–460
Taking Notes from Reading .... pp. 460–464
Reading Analytically .... pp. 493–519

OPEN TO LANGUAGE

OPEN TO LANGUAGE

A New College Rhetoric

PATRICK HARTWELL
Indiana University of Pennsylvania

with

ROBERT H. BENTLEY
Lansing Community College

New York   Oxford
OXFORD UNIVERSITY PRESS
1982

Copyright © 1982 by Oxford University Press, Inc.

Library of Congress Cataloging in Publication Data

Hartwell, Patrick.
  Open to language.

  Includes index.
  1. English language—Rhetoric.   I. Bentley,
Robert H.   II. Title.
PE1408.H3925   808'.042   81-18853
ISBN 0-19-503080-X   AACR2

Cover design by Egon Lauterberg

Printing (last digit):   9 8 7 6 5 4 3

Printed in the United States of America

Acknowledgments

James Agee and Walker Evans. From *Let Us Now Praise Famous Men,* by James Agee and Walker Evans. Copyright 1939 and 1940 by James Agee and Walker Evans. Copyright renewed © 1960 by Walker Evans, copyright renewed © 1969 by Mia Fritsch Agee.

Peter Albersheim. From "The Walls of Growing Plant Cells," in *Scientific American,* April 1975. Reprinted by permission of W. H. Freeman and Company, Publishers.

American Heritage Dictionary. Entries "anvil" to "anxious," copyright © 1981 Houghton Mifflin Co. Reprinted by permission from *The American Heritage Dictionary of the English Language.*

Quentin Bell. From *Virginia Woolf: A Biography,* copyright © 1972, by Quentin Bell. Reprinted by permission of Harcourt Brace Jovanovich, Inc.

John D. Bransford and Marcia K. Johnson. "Consideration of Some Problems of Comprehension," from *Visual Information Processing,* copyright © 1973 by Academic Press. Reprinted by permission of the authors and the publisher.

Daniel Calhoun. From *The Intelligence of a People.* Copyright © 1973 by Daniel Calhoun. Reprinted by permission of the author and Princeton University Press.

Vine Deloria, Jr. From *Custer Died For Your Sins,* copyright © 1969 by Vine Deloria, Jr. Reprinted by permission of Macmillan Publishing Co., Inc.

Joan Didion. Excerpt from *Play It As It Lays,* by Joan Didion. Copyright © 1970 by Joan Didion. Reprinted by permission of Farrar, Straus and Giroux, Inc.

E. L. Doctorow. From *Ragtime.* Copyright © 1975 by E. L. Doctorow. Reprinted by permission of Random House, Inc.

Robert L. Ebel. "Standardized Tests: They Reflect the Real World," reprinted from *The New York Times,* May 1, 1977. Copyright © 1977 by The New York Times Company. Reprinted by permission.

Peter Elbow. From *Writing Without Teachers.* Copyright © 1973 by Oxford University Press, Inc. Reprinted by permission.

Funk & Wagnalls Standard College Dictionary. Entries from "anvil" to "anxious." Reprinted from *Funk & Wagnalls Standard College Dictionary,* © 1966 by Harcourt, Brace, and World, by permission of the publisher.

Walker Gibson. Excerpt from *The Limits of Language,* by Walker Gibson. Copyright © 1962 by Walker Gibson. Reprinted by permission of Farrar, Straus and Giroux, Inc.

Robert M. Gorrell and Charlton Laird. "Chart of the Indo-European Language Family," from *Modern English Handbook,* 6th edition, copyright © 1976, p. 278. Reprinted by permission of Prentice-Hall, Inc., Englewood Cliffs, New Jersey.

Dan Greenberg. "Catch Her in the Oatmeal," by Dan Greenberg. Reprinted from *Esquire* (February, 1958). Copyright © 1958 by Esquire Publishing Inc. Used by permission.

Ronald Gross. "Yield," from *Pop Poems.* Copyright © 1967 by Ronald Gross. Reprinted by permission of Simon & Schuster, a Gulf and Western Corporation.

Donald Hall. "Introduction: An Ethic of Clarity," from *The Modern Stylists.* Copyright © 1968 by Donald Hall. Reprinted with permission of Macmillan Publishing Company, Inc.

David G. Hays. From the essay, "Language and Interpersonal Relationships," which appeared in Einar Hauger and Morton Bloomfield (eds.), *Language As a Human Problem* (1974). Reprinted by permission of W. W. Norton & Co.

Jay Hall. *NASA Moon Survival Task,* from *Psychology Today* 5 (November 1971). Special permission for reproduction of this material is granted by the author, Jay Hall, Ph.D. and the publisher, Teleometrics International. All rights reserved.

Ernest Hemingway. From "The Undefeated," in *Men Without Women.* Copyright 1927 by Charles Scribner's Sons; copyright renewed. Reprinted with the permission of Charles Scribner's Sons.

Ernest Hemingway. From *The Sun Also Rises.* Copyright 1926 by Charles Scribner's Sons; copyright renewed. Reprinted with the permission of Charles Scribner's Sons.

Ernest Hemingway. From *A Farewell to Arms.* Copyright 1929 by Charles Scribner's Sons; copyright renewed. Reprinted with the permission of Charles Scribner's Sons.

Gerard Manley Hopkins. "God's Grandeur," from *Poems of Gerard Manley Hopkins,* Fourth Edition, edited by W. H. Gardner and N. H. MacKenzie. Copyright © 1967 by the Society of Jesus. Reprinted by permission of Oxford University Press, Inc.

Lou Kelly. From *From Dialogue to Discourse.* Copyright © 1972 by Lou Kelly, published by Scott, Foresman and Company.

Jack Kerouac. From *On the Road*. Copyright © 1956 by Jack Kerouac. Reprinted by permission of The Sterling Lord Agency, Inc.

Phillip Knightley. From *The First Casualty*, copyright © 1975 by Phillip Knightley. Reprinted by permission of Harcourt Brace Jovanovich, Inc.

Richard A. Lanham. From *Motives of Eloquence: Literary Rhetoric in the Renaissance*, copyright © 1976. Reprinted by permission of Yale University Press.

C. F. Main. Questions from College Entrance Examination Board in *Grading the Advanced Placement Examination in English Composition and Literature, 1977 and 1978*. Reprinted by permission of Educational Testing Service, the copyright owner.

Oxford English Dictionary. Entries from "Anvil" to "Anxious." Reproduced from *The Oxford English Dictionary* by permission of Oxford University Press. Copyright © 1933 by Oxford University Press.

Sylvia Plath. From "The Colossus," by Sylvia Plath. Copyright © 1961 by Sylvia Plath. Reprinted from *The Colossus and Other Poems*, by Sylvia Plath, by permission of Alfred A. Knopf, Inc.

Ezra Pound. "In a Station of the Metro," from *Personae*. Copyright 1926 by Ezra Pound. Reprinted by permission of New Directions Publishing Corporation.

Jim Quinn. "Hopefully, They Will Shut Up," from *Newsweek* Feb. 23, 1981, copyright © 1981, Newsweek, Inc., all rights reserved. Reprinted by permission.

Random House College Dictionary. Entries from "Anvil" to "Anxious," reprinted by permission from the *Random House College Dictionary, Revised Edition*, copyright © 1982 . . . 1975 by Random House, Inc.

Reader's Guide to Periodical Literature. Vol. 81, No. 3 (April 10, 1981), entries "Civil Rights—Continued" through "Cladocera." Copyright © 1981 by the H. W. Wilson Company. Material reproduced by permission of the publisher.

Alain Robbe-Grillet. From *The Erasers*, copyright 1964 by Grove Press. Reprinted by permission of Grove Press, Inc. Translated by Richard Howard from the French.

Bertrand Russell. "How I Write," from *Autobiography of Bertrand Russell*, Vol. 1, copyright © 1951, 1952, 1953, 1956 by Bertrand Russell. Reprinted by permission of George Allen & Unwin (Publishers) Ltd.

Gertrude Stein. From *Lectures in America*, by Gertrude Stein. Copyright 1935 and renewed 1963 by Alice B. Toklas. Reprinted by permission of Random House, Inc.

Martha Stephens. From *Cast A Wistful Eye*. Copyright © 1976, 1977 by Martha Stephens. Reprinted with permission of Macmillan Publishing Company, Inc.

Edwin P. Taylor. "Standardized Tests: They Don't Measure Learning," reprinted from *The New York Times*, May 1, 1977. Copyright © 1977. Copyright © 1977 by The New York Times Company. Reprinted by permission.

Studs Terkel. From *Working: People Talk About What They Do All Day and How They Feel About What They Do*. Copyright © 1972, 1974 by Studs Terkel. Reprinted by permission of Pantheon Books, a Division of Random House, Inc.

John Updike. From *Assorted Prose*, by John Updike. Copyright © 1959 by John Updike. Reprinted by permission of Alfred A. Knopf, Inc. Originally appeared in the *New Yorker*.

Webster's New Collegiate Dictionary. Entries from "Anvil" to "Anxious." From *Webster's New Collegiate Dictionary* © 1981 by G. & C. Merriam Co., publishers of the Merriam-Webster Dictionaries. Reprinted by permission.

Webster's New World Dictionary. Entries from "anvil" to "anxious," reprinted with permission of *Webster's New World Dictionary*, Second College Edition. Copyright © 1980 by Simon & Schuster, Inc.

A. Whimbey and J. Lochhead. Reprinted by permission of The Franklin Institute Press from *Problem Solving and Comprehension*, by A. Whimbey and J. Lochhead, copyright 1980.

Martin Williams. From *Where's the Melody? A Listener's Introduction to Jazz*, by Martin Williams. Copyright © 1966 by Martin Williams. Reprinted by permission of Pantheon Books, a Division of Random House, Inc.

Raymond Williams. "Introduction," from *The Pelican Book of English Prose*, Vol. II. Copyright © 1969 by Raymond Williams. Reprinted by permission of Penguin Books Ltd.

William Carlos Williams. "This Is Just To Say," from *Collected Earlier Poems*. Copyright 1938 by New Directions Publishing Corporation. Reprinted by permission of New Directions.

Tom Wolfe. Excerpt from *The Kandy-Kolored Tangerine-Flake-Streamline Baby*, copyright © 1963, 1964, 1965 by Thomas K. Wolfe, Jr. Copyright © 1963, 1964, 1965 by the New York Herald Tribune, Inc. Reprinted by permission of Farrar, Straus & Giroux.

Tom Wolfe. From "The New Journalism" (pp. 17–18) in *The New Journalism* edited by Tom Wolfe and E. W. Johnson. Copyright © 1973 by Tom Wolfe and E. W. Johnson. Reprinted by permission of Harper & Row, Publishers, Inc.

To the Instructor

This text treats rhetoric as a coherent body of interdisciplinary knowledge, with suggestions for further reading at the end of each chapter, and it encourages inductive learning, asking the student to participate actively as learner and as writer.

We've kept the best of the standard college rhetoric text—a solid range of examples from the work of modern writers, workable final assignments that test the student's ability to learn from chapter discussions, and full handbook treatment of common errors (though our discussions appear at appropriate points in the text rather than in a separate handbook). The text will support the instructor in many ways, and it should be useful, over a two-semester period, in a number of different program sequences.

On the other hand, we have not hesitated to depart, at times maximally, from what E. D. Hirsch, Jr., calls "the collected wisdom of the textbooks." We have done so whenever our own experience, supported by our reading in composition, reading theory, psychology, and linguistics, suggests that traditional practices are limited in utility. This is an invention-centered text, with a strong focus on the writing process, and it stresses the active involvement of the learner. It offers advice on mastering the many codes of literate print discourse, but without trivializing the subject or patronizing the learner. In particular, it refines the traditional recognition that reading and writing are interrelated abilities, by treating at several points the reading skills that parallel, and support, specific writing skills.

A text such as this one is never simply the work of two authors. We owe abundant thanks to our students, who have allowed us to watch them learn and to learn from their learning, and to our own teachers—Ronald E. Freeman, Robert M. Gorrell, and Charlton Laird. We owe much to other researchers and theorists in composition—as the references in the text and in the *Instructor's Manual* will attest. We owe special thanks to readers of our early drafts—particularly to Andrea Lunsford and to Diane Menendez—for their general support as well as their specific suggestions. Debbie Thompson of IUP prepared the index. To our colleagues at Oxford University Press, we owe particular gratitude—to Ellen Fuchs, who supported this project from its inception, to John Wright, whose tact and patience (and confidence and encouragement) helped us to complete this project, and to Nancy Amy, whose care and wisdom as textual editor improved our manuscript on every page, and did so with wit and grace.

<table>
<tr><td>*Indiana, Pa.*</td><td>Patrick Hartwell</td></tr>
<tr><td>*East Lansing, Mich.*</td><td>Robert H. Bentley</td></tr>
<tr><td>*January 1982*</td><td></td></tr>
</table>

To the Student

This text asks you to be an active learner and, from the first page, an active writer. It presents you with problems within chapters, problems that ask you to grapple actively, in thinking and writing, with the subjects we discuss, and it presents you, at the end of each chapter, with suggestions for further reading and with longer writing assignments that follow from the subjects discussed in each chapter.

You'll want to note several special features of this text. The correction chart on the inside back cover will lead you to boxed inserts which offer suggestions and examples for correcting common mistakes, and two chapters, chapters Nine and Twelve, deal with punctuation and spelling as features of what we call the *code of print*. Chapter Fourteen offers advice on two common college writing tasks, the essay examination and the investigative paper.

The "Brief Glossary of Usage," on pages 611–614, should help with questions of usage in writing, and answers to several problems in the text are given in a second appendix, "Answers to Selected Problems," pages 615–629. The index, at the end of the book, should guide you to pages that provide help with other questions.

Contents

UNIT I   STARTING-POINTS

1   Writing Fluently   3

A STARTING-POINT   4
  Problem One. A minute of writing   4
Free Writing   5
  Problem Two. Experiments in fluency   7
The Journal   7
Brainstorming   9
  Problem Three. Brainstorming, Incorporated   9
THE WRITING PROCESS   10
  Problem Four. How students write   12
THE LANGUAGE YOU USE   13
  Problem Five. Writing nonsense   13
Knowing How and Knowing About   14
  Problem Six. Knowing how and knowing about   15
  Problem Seven. Exercising competence   17
Language Competence   17
  Problem Eight. Kinds of nonsense   18
Reading Competence   20
  Problem Nine. A proverb from Trinidad   22
SUMMARY   22
IMPLICATIONS FOR THE WRITER   22
FINAL WRITING ASSIGNMENTS
  I. Starting Your Journal   22

II. From Free Writing to a Finished Paper   23
III. The Writing Process   23
FOR FURTHER READING   25

2 The Dimensions of Rhetoric   27

Problem One. The word **rhetoric**   29
THE USES OF RHETORIC   30
BUILDING A DYNAMIC MODEL OF WRITING   31
Problem Two. A static model of writing?   31
Rhetorical Choice   34
Rhetorical Contexts   35
Problem Three. A first exercise in rhetorical
choice   36
The Rhetorical Triangle as Context   36
Problem Four. Appeals in advertising   39
Problem Five. The rhetorical triangle as a generative
model   42
The Larger Contexts of Rhetoric   43
Communication Codes   45
Purposes and Goals in Writing   45
Purpose in Writing   45
Truth and Harmony as the Writer's Goals   47
SUMMARY   48
IMPLICATIONS FOR THE WRITER   48
The Code of Print   49
School as a Context   51
The "Offices" of Rhetoric: Invention, Arrangement, and
Style   52
FINAL WRITING ASSIGNMENTS
I. Programming Director   53
II. Political Campaign   53
III. Direct Mail, Incorporated   53
IV. The Facts of Life in Midville   54
V. Working with Goals and Codes   55
FOR FURTHER READING   55

3 Voice, Tone, and the Writer's Stance   57

THE WRITER'S STANCE   57
TRYING ON SOME VOICES   58
The Bubblegum Voice   59
Problem One. The bubblegum voice   61
The Neutral Voice of Journalism   62
Problem Two. Journalist for a day   64

The Voice of the "New Journalism"   66
   Problem Three. The new journalism   68
The Bureaucratic Voice   69
   Problem Four. Reading the bureaucratic voice   71
   Problem Five. Writing the bureaucratic voice   72
   Problem Six. Bureaucrat for a day   73
VOICES TO AIM FOR   74
The Detached Discursive Voice   74
The Committed Personal Voice   77
   Problem Seven. Reading personal voices   77
READING FOR TONE   80
   Problem Eight. Recognizing parody   82
SUMMARY   83
IMPLICATIONS FOR THE WRITER   84
FINAL WRITING ASSIGNMENTS
   I. An Identifiable Voice   84
   II. A First-Person Voice   85
   III. Reading for Tone   85
   IV. The Right Voice?   87
FOR FURTHER READING   89

UNIT II   SMALLER ELEMENTS OF ARRANGEMENT

4   From Talk to Written Discourse   93

THE COMPLEXITIES OF COHERENCE   94
   Problem One. Creating coherence   94
Coherence Is a Pattern of Meaning   95
   Problem Two. Logical connection   96
Incoherence Measures Coherence   98
   Problem Three. An exercise in incoherence   100
COHERENCE IN SPEAKING AND WRITING   101
"TALKING ABOUT" IS STRUCTURED   102
SUMMARY   106
IMPLICATIONS FOR THE WRITER   107
   Problem Four. Evaluating coherence   107
Repetition   110
   Repeat Key Words   110
   Repeat Sentence Patterns   111
   Problem Five. Repetition in word and sentence pattern   112
Logical Connection: Transition   113
   Problem Six. Sentence-to-sentence connections   119
   Problem Seven. Creating coherence   120

Frameworks of Meaning   122
    Problem Eight. Frameworks of meaning   123
IMPLICATIONS FOR READERS: SQRRM   124
Survey   125
Question   125
Read   125
Review   126
Map   126
    Problem Nine. Experiments in mapping   126
FINAL WRITING ASSIGNMENTS   127
FOR FURTHER READING   128

5 The Discursive Paragraph   129

    Problem One. When Is a paragraph?   129
A NEW VOCABULARY: COMMITMENT AND
RESPONSE   133
A Commitment Is a Topic Plus a Comment   134
Commitments Guide Paragraphs   135
    Problem Two. Commitment sentences   136
LEVELS OF GENERALITY IN THE PARAGRAPH   136
The Three-Sentence Paragraph   138
    Problem Three. The three-sentence paragraph   140
Expanding Coordinate Frameworks   142
    Problem Four. The simple coordinate framework   143
Simple Subordinate Frameworks   144
    Problem Five. Simple subordinate frameworks   146
Mixed Paragraph Frameworks   147
    Problem Six. The master paragraph   151
Fudge Factors   152
    Introductory and Concluding Sentences   152
    Sometimes You Can't Tell   153
    Stress the Rhetoric of a Paragraph, Not Its Logic   153
    Some Paragraphs Are Anomalous   154
SUMMARY   155
IMPLICATIONS FOR WRITERS   155
Punctuate by the Paragraph   155
Breaking the Paragraph Barrier   157
    Problem Seven. Topic sentences in magazines   157
    Problem Eight. Breaking the paragraph barrier   160
IMPLICATIONS FOR READERS: THE OUTLINE   161
Informal Outlines   161
Formal Outlines   161
    Problem Nine. The sentence outline   162

FINAL WRITING ASSIGNMENTS
    I. From Paragraph to Theme   163
    II. Reparagraphing   163
FOR FURTHER READING   164

UNIT III STYLE

6 Sentence Choices: Clarity and Directness   167

SENTENCE COMBINING   168
    Problem One. Sentence combining   169
MEANING CHUNKS   170
Ambiguity: Mischunking   171
    Problem Two. Ambiguity   172
The Dumb Reader   173
    Problem Three. Chunking headlines   175
    Problem Four. The rewrite desk   175
A DRAM OF GRAMMAR   178
The Sentence Base   178
    Problem Five. Asking questions in German   178
    Problem Six. Rewriting sentence fragments   181
    Problem Seven. Effective fragments?   181
Choosing Predication   184
    Problem Eight. Predication choices   184
Coordination   185
Subordination   186
IMPLICATIONS FOR THE WRITER   187
Choose Effective Subject-Verb Combinations   187
    Problem Nine. Improving subject-verb combinations   190
Chunk Sentences Effectively   190
    Problem Ten. Effective chunking   193
IMPLICATIONS FOR THE READER: CHUNKING   194
SUMMARY   196
FINAL WRITING ASSIGNMENTS
    I. Rechunking Sentences   197
    II. How Big Is a Chunk?   198
FOR FURTHER READING   198

7 Style in Description and Narration   199

YOU ARE AS MUCH AS YOU SEE   199
    Problem One. A journal assignment   202
TEXTURE IN DESCRIPTIVE AND NARRATIVE WRITING   202
RECOGNIZING BOUND AND FREE MODIFIERS   206

Problem Two. Recognizing free modifiers   208
Problem Three. Creating free modifiers   209
Clarifications   210
Problem Four. Identifying free modifiers   213
Problem Five. Beginning your novel   215
Levels of Generality in the Sentence   215
Problem Six. Annotating free modifiers   218
THE GRAMMAR OF FREE MODIFIERS   219
The Free Noun Phrase   219
Problem Seven. Mastering the free noun phrase   221
Problem Eight. Experimenting with free noun phrases   221
The Free Verb Phrase   222
Problem Nine. Mastering the free verb phrase   223
Problem Ten. Experimenting with the free verb phrase   223
The Free Absolute Phrase   224
Problem Eleven. Mastering the free absolute phrase   225
Problem Twelve. Experimenting with the free absolute
phrase   225
Other Free Modifiers   226
Problem Thirteen. Mastering free prepositions and
adjectives   227
IMPLICATIONS FOR WRITERS: THREE SUGGESTIONS   228
Problem Fourteen. Modifier placement   229
The Cumulative Sentence   230
Problem Fifteen. The cumulative sentence in transactional
writing   231
The "Cookbook Principle" of Narration   231
Problem Sixteen. A lesson from a cookbook   231
Showing and Telling   233
SUMMARY   234
Problem Seventeen. The master sentence   234
FINAL WRITING ASSIGNMENTS
I. Assignments in Narration   235
II. Assignments in Description   235
III. Assignments Mixing Narration and Description   236
FOR FURTHER READING   236

8 Style as Craft   237

Problem One. Peanuts   240
IMITATION AND STYLE   240
THE RHYTHMS OF WRITING   242
Parallelism   242
Problem Two. Parallelism   244
Problem Three. Problems in parallelism   245

The Balanced Sentence   245
   Problem Four. Balancing acts   246
Antithesis   246
   Problem Five. Antithesis   247
THE ELASTICITY OF THE SENTENCE   247
Deletion   248
   Problem Six. Deletion   249
Expansion   249
   Problem Seven. Expansion   251
THE EXPLOSIVENESS OF MEANING   251
The Periodic Sentence   251
   Problem Eight. The periodic sentence   252
The Inverted Sentence   252
   Problem Nine. Inversions   253
THE EXPLODING SENTENCE   253
   Problem Ten. The exploding sentence   255
AND WITH NO STYLE AT ALL   255
   Problem Eleven. And with no style at all   257
SUMMARY   257
IMPLICATIONS FOR THE WRITER   257
IMPLICATIONS FOR READERS: RECOGNIZING
PARODY   258
   Problem Twelve. Parody   258
FINAL WRITING ASSIGNMENTS
   I. The Display Piece   260
   II. The Extended Imitation   260
   III. Parody   260
   IV. A Public Statement   260
   V. A Private Statement   260
FOR FURTHER READING   261

9   **The Print Code: Punctuation   262**

   Problem One. The importance of the comma   262
SENTENCE CONNECTORS   264
   Problem Two. The Great Punctuation Game, first
   version   269
   Problem Three. Mastering sentence connectors   270
   Problem Four. Experiments with the comma splice   273
SEPARATORS   274
   Problem Five. The Great Punctuation Game, second
   version   276
SERIES CONNECTORS   278
   Problem Six. The Great Punctuation Game, championship
   version   280

SPECIAL PROBLEMS IN THE PRINT CODE   282
Special Uses of Italics and Quotes   282
  Problem Seven. Special uses of quotation marks   285
  Problem Eight. Scare quotes and italics   285
The Uses of the Hyphen   286
  Problem Nine. The hyphen   287
SUMMARY   288
IMPLICATIONS FOR THE WRITER   288
FINAL WRITING ASSIGNMENTS
  I. Repunctuating   289
  II. Earlier Punctuation   289
  III. Transcribing Speech   289
  IV. Repunctuating Speech   289
FOR FURTHER READING   290

UNIT IV   THE WORLD OF WORDS

10   Words, Words, Words   293
  Problem One. Problems in word choice   295
WORD LADDERS   296
General and Specific   297
  Problem Two. From levels of generality to levels of
  abstraction   299
Abstract and Concrete   300
DENOTATION AND CONNOTATION   301
  Problem Three. The I'm a/You're a/He's a Game   302
  Problem Four. Playing politician   303
LITERAL AND FIGURATIVE   303
A GRAMMAR OF METAPHOR   304
  Problem Five. Creating figurative language   306
Dying, Dead, and Fossilized Metaphor   307
  Problem Six. Revitalizing dead metaphors   309
  Problem Seven. Analyzing figurative language   309
REGISTER: THE COMPANY WORDS KEEP   310
  Problem Eight. The social register of words   312
Levels of Language   313
  Problem Nine. "Webster's New Word Book"   316
Euphemisms and Weasel Words: Telling It Like It
Isn't   316
  Problem Ten. Captain Euphemism   318
Shoptalk and Jargon: Words At Work   319
  Problem Eleven. Jargon   319

Regional and Social Dialects: Words We Live In   320
Slang: Words with Their Shoes Off   323
Sex: Words that Wear the Pants   323
SUMMARY   325
IMPLICATIONS FOR THE WRITER   325
FINAL WRITING ASSIGNMENTS
    I. Word Maps   325
    II. Denotation and Connotation   325
    III. Figurative Language   326
    IV. Register   326
FOR FURTHER READING   327

11   **Diction and the Dictionary   328**

    Problem One. *Decisions, Decisions!*   329
VOCABULARY BUILDING   331
THE DICTIONARY AS WORD-HOARD   334
The Fallacy of "THE" Dictionary   335
    Problem Two. The standard college dictionary   335
    Problem Three. The dictionary as a source of
    knowledge   338
Beyond the College Dictionary   340
ENGLISH AS LANGUAGE   341
Old English   346
Middle English   348
    Problem Four. Explaining language change   350
Modern English   351
    Problem Five. Reading Shakespeare   352
    Problem Six. Native words and borrowed words   352
World English   353
    Problem Seven. A class project   354
WORDS CHANGE MEANING WITH TIME   355
SUMMARY   359
FINAL WRITING ASSIGNMENTS
    I. A Dictionary Assignment   359
    II. Group Reports or Class Projects   362
    III. Word-Hoard, Incorporated   363
FOR FURTHER READING   365

12   **The Print Code: Spelling   368**

THE PROBLEM OF SPELLING   369
    Problem One. Two discovery problems   370

THE SYSTEM OF ENGLISH SPELLING   373
  Problem Two. Spelling and meaning   375
IMPROVING SPELLING   376
The Etymological Basis of English Spelling   376
  Problem Three. Spelling and meaning   378
The Schwa Vowel   379
  Problem Four. The schwa vowel   379
  Problem Five. Finding the schwa vowel   381
Homonyms   382
  Problem Six. Homonyms   383
Word Forms   383
  The -ed System   384
  Problem Seven. The missing -ed hunt   385
  The -s Systems   386
  Problem Eight. A special problem in subject-verb
  agreement   388
  Problem Nine. The possessive -'s   390
  Problem Ten. The -s systems   390
  Adjective and Adverb Form   391
  The Rule Systems of Spelling   392
  Problem Eleven. The rule systems of spelling   393
SUMMARY   394
FINAL WRITING ASSIGNMENTS
  I. The Print Code   394
  II. Playing with the Print Code   396
  III. Investigating the Print Code   396
  IV. The Changing Print Code   396
  V. Alphabets   397
FOR FURTHER READING   397

UNIT V LARGER ELEMENTS OF ARRANGEMENT

13 The Formative Principle   401

  Problem One. A found poem   403
FORM AS SCAFFOLDING FOR IDEAS   403
Grasping Form in Reading   405
  Problem Two. The importance of plan   405
  Problem Three. Finding a plan   407
  Problem Four. A reading quiz   408
  Problem Five. Building form and meaning   409
Creating Scaffolds of Meaning as Writer   411
  Problem Six. "Never fall for the same trick twice"   420

OPEN FORM IN WRITING: THE FORMATIVE IDEA   421
    Problem Seven. Identifying top-level structures   426
Opening and Closing   427
    Problem Eight. What did the farmer say to the hen?   428
SUMMARY   430
IMPLICATIONS FOR THE READER   430
    Problem Nine. A problem in reading   430
IMPLICATIONS FOR THE WRITER   432
FINAL WRITING ASSIGNMENTS
    I. Finding Fixed Forms in Reading   432
    II. How to Read a Newspaper   432
    III. Fixed Forms in Your Profession   433
    IV. Writing to a Fixed Form   433
    V. Discovering a Poem   434
FOR FURTHER READING   435

14 Two Writing Tasks: The Essay Answer and the
    Investigative Paper   436

THE ESSAY EXAMINATION   436
    Problem One. A magic secret   437
    Problem Two. A true/false test on essay tests   439
Why Do Instructors Give Essay Examinations?   439
How To Study for Essay Exams   440
A Deceptively Simple Suggestion: Read the Exam   441
Another Deceptively Simple Suggestion: Answer the
Question   442
    Problem Three. Analyzing essay questions   443
Organize Your Answer Like a Newspaper Story   443
    Problem Four. Answering the question in the terms of the
    question   445
    Problem Five. Learning from reading   446
THE INVESTIGATIVE PAPER   446
The Goals of the Investigative Assignment   446
Steps in Writing the Investigative Paper   448
    Problem Six. The research journal   448
Focusing a Preliminary Topic   448
Surveying Resources   451
    Problem Seven. Mapping your library   451
    Problem Eight. Thinking like a librarian   454
    Problem Nine. Creating reference works   458
    Problem Ten. Investigative problems   460
Reading and Notetaking: Summary, Paraphrase, and
Quotation   460

Drafting the Paper   464
  Problem Eleven. Working with summary, paraphrase, and the stylish and purposeful use of quotation   465
Footnote and Bibliography Form   467
  Features Common to All References   468
  Bibliography Form   469
  Footnote Form—First Entries   477
  Special Problems   478
  Second Footnote References   482
  Final Typing: Manuscript Form   483
SUMMARY   485
FINAL WRITING ASSIGNMENTS
  I. A Recommendation   485
  II. The Making of . . .   487
  III. A Trial   487
  IV. The Controversy over . . .   488
FOR FURTHER READING
  I. Reference Guides   488
  II. Indexes   488
  III. Abstracts   488
  IV. Other Investigative Tools   489

UNIT VI INVENTION

15 Analysis: Thinking with Concepts   493

YOU ARE AN "INVENTION MACHINE"   493
ON READING THIS UNIT   494
PRINT EXPLICITNESS   495
  Problem One. An exercise in explicitness   497
ARGUMENT: STATING THE CASE AND FINDING GOOD REASONS   499
  Problem Two. The freshman essay examination   499
Stating the Case   500
  Problem Three. Stating the case   501
  Problem Four. Being "Dear Abby"   501
The Scope of Argument: Good Reasons   502
  Problem Five. Good reasons   503
ANALYZING ARGUMENTS   505
  Problem Six. Where's the Warrant? first series   507
  Problem Seven. Where's the Warrant? second series   509
  Problem Eight. Analyzing an argument   514
  Problem Nine. The process of arguing in your field   515

A NOTE ON FALLACIES   515
The Appeal to Authority   516
Against the Person   516
The Appeal to Pity   517
The Bandwagon Appeal   517
Begging the Question   518
False Cause   518
SUMMARY   519
FINAL WRITING ASSIGNMENTS
   I. Ways of Arguing   519
   II. Stating the Case   519
   III. Print Explicitness   520
   IV. An Argument for Analysis   525
FOR FURTHER READING   530

16   The Common Places of Invention   532

DEFINITION   533
Positive Uses of Definition   534
A Heuristic for Definition   536
   Problem One. Definition as discovery   537
CLASSIFICATION   539
   Problem Two. Experiments in classification   539
   Problem Three. Classification as discovery   541
   Problem Four. An exercise in classification   542
ILLUSTRATION   543
   Problem Five. Illustration as discovery   544
COMPARISON AND CONTRAST   545
SUMMARY   548
IMPLICATIONS FOR THE WRITER   548
FINAL WRITING ASSIGNMENTS
   I. Inventing Arguments   550
   II. Two Experiments in Definition   550
FOR FURTHER READING   553

17   The Special Places of Invention   554

ASSUMPTIONS ABOUT DISCOVERY   554
   Problem One. A confidence-destroying quiz   555
   Problem Two. "Four straight lines"   556
   Problem Three. Lost on the moon: Thinking in a
   new context   558

THE MODEL OF THE WORLD IN THE MIND   559
Seeing the World   560
   Problem Four. Knowing baseball   564
A HEURISTIC FOR DISCOVERY THINKING   566
"Cross-Breeding" Ideas   566
   Problem Five. Exercises in cross-breeding   568
Think Paradigmatically   569
   Problem Six. Paradigms for spelling research   570
   Problem Seven. Paradigms for writing   572
Think Analogically   572
   Problem Eight. Forcing Analogies   574
Think Visually   575
SUMMARY   576
IMPLICATIONS FOR THE WRITER   576
   Problem Nine. Problems for a rhetorician   576
FINAL WRITING APPLICATIONS
   I. Discovery Thinking   578
   II. The Martian Perspective   578
   III. Paradigms for Belief   578
   IV. Discoveries   579
FOR FURTHER READING   579

18   Revising: From First Draft to Final Product   581

A DYNAMIC MODEL OF REVISION   582
Free Write a First Draft as Soon as Possible   584
Read All Drafts Aloud   585
Revise Structurally, from the Top Down   585
Find Ways To "Re-see" Your Drafts   586
Save Surface Detail for Final Revision   587
Treat the Final Draft as Printed Copy   588
AN EXAMPLE OF THE REVISION PROCESS   589
Major Changes in Structure   590
Revising Central Claims   590
Elaborating Paragraphs   591
Shortening Paragraphs   592
Revising Sentences and Word Choices   593
Two Check-lists for Revision   593
Four Student Papers for Revision   595
PUTTING IT ALL TOGETHER: A COMPLETE WRITING
SITUATION   600
   Problem One. An advanced placement question   600
Problems Presented by the Question   602

Standards for Grading   604
Examples for Evaluation   605
    Problem Two. Grading student responses   605
Comments on the Sample Essays   608
    Problem Three. Ranking your essay   609
FINAL WRITING ASSIGNMENTS
    I. The Interview   609
    II. The Self-Analysis   610
    III. The Writing Process of a Professional   610
FOR FURTHER READING   610

Appendix A   A Brief Glossary of Usage   611

Appendix B   Answers to Selected Problems   615

Index   631

UNIT I

STARTING-POINTS

1

Writing Fluently

I think that one is constantly startled by the things that appear before you on the page when you're writing.

SHIRLEY HAZZARD

I don't see writing as a communication of something already discovered, as "truths" already known. Rather, I see writing as a job of experiment. It's like any discovery job; you don't know what's going to happen until you try it.

WILLIAM STAFFORD

The first problem the writer faces is the blank page. Most of us have trouble getting started, many of us find ways to avoid writing, and some of us find it hard to dream up five hundred words for a five-hundred-word theme.

But have you noticed that you don't have the same problem with thinking? No one complains about not thinking enough; our heads are naturally full of thoughts. And talking isn't normally a problem either. Words are there when we need them. We usually don't need to worry about what to say next, because it comes right out—we say what we want to say.

Why is writing so much harder?

A comparison may help to explain. There are times when talking is difficult: in a job interview, for example, where people may be so intent on making the right impression that they choose words carefully, and sometimes trip over them, or in a foreign language class, where people have to think what they want to say and then translate it into the foreign language. Writing is like this sort of talking. Writing is a "foreign language," in the sense that the squiggles on the page that make up writing seem far removed from the ease of speaking. And writing is like a job interview, in that the writer is intent on making the right impression on the reader.

Here's a good hint about job interviews: relax. And here's a good hint about foreign language classes: practice. This chapter applies those two hints to writing: relax and practice.

Writing and speaking are very different; writing is not merely written-down speech. But writing doesn't have to be that much harder than speaking. As a matter of fact, you can train yourself, much as an athlete trains, to help your words flow smoothly onto a blank sheet of paper. This chapter is about getting started, about writing *fluently.* (The word *fluent* is related to *flow* and *fluid;* writers who write *fluently* have gained *fluency.*)

Our goals in this chapter are:

■ to convince you that the blank page needn't be the problem it perhaps has been;

■ to explore methods to help you get words down on a page almost as swiftly as you fill your head with thoughts or the air around you with words; and,

■ to explore a view about writing—we want to make writing natural instead of artificial, to make it what William Stafford, in the headnote to this chapter, calls a "discovery job."

A STARTING-POINT

To help us explore writing as a "discovery job," we've punctuated this text with problems, aimed at connecting our discussions with your own writing. The first problem is an experiment: You might think of yourself as a scientist in a laboratory who is about to test someone else's theory. The theory is this: Forcing yourself to write as fast as you can will make writing easier.

Problem One. A minute of writing   Write as many words as you can in one minute. Write about "turtles" or "what happened today." There are only two rules: 1. Do not stop writing—if you can't think of what to write, write "can't write" over and over until new words come to mind; 2. don't worry about spelling or grammar—the goal is to put as many words on paper as you can in one minute. Proceed when ready.

When you've completed one minute of writing, count the number of words you wrote, then multiply that number by fifty.   ■

Here is an example of one student's accomplishment in a minute of writing. (Examples in this text are numbered so we can refer back to them later.)

1.1　Happens happens can't write. Things happen throughout the day that can make a person depressed or very happy. Can't write. Being late for a class and everyone in the room staring at you until you sit down, or the teacher making a snide remark can ruin the day.　　　　　　　　　　　　　　　　　　　[48 words]

We can make two comments about this example (and, we suspect, about your experiment as well). The first comment is that there are a lot of words in a minute of writing—2400 words in a normal 50-minute class, if the writer could keep up this speed, six times the 400 words or so that most students produce in an hour of writing. The second comment is that there are some possibilities here. The student wouldn't turn in 1.1 as a finished piece of writing, but, as we'll see, there's a strong personal experience buried in that rough beginning.

Free Writing

Just one experiment in *free writing,* as we'll call it, isn't a fair test of our theory that it will make writing easier, because you'll have to try free writing several times before you'll feel comfortable with it. But regular experiments of this sort can do several things for the writer.

They can build up writing muscles, just as regular exercise builds up other muscles. They can make writing a natural thing to do, like talking, instead of a painful task to be avoided. You'll find fewer and fewer *can't write*s as you practice. Filling a page with words will become easier and easier, and you'll find that you will become more confident about your own abilities.

More importantly, you'll find that you are able to bypass some of the mental blocks that used to get in your way. We often find ourselves, as writers, being worried about something other than the words we're writing, something that might range from, "I wonder if this is what she wants" to "I never get these commas right." These worries have to pull our minds away from the hard struggle with words, the fight to form them into meaning. Free writing can cut through such worries; it forces us to put our mind to the task at hand. That's a crucial first step.

Such writing is likely to be "grubby prose," as one writer put it; certainly free writing doesn't give us the polished sort of writing we connect with published novels or even with successful writing in college. But consider how much some writers rely on speed:

- When French mystery writer Georges Simenon gets an idea for a novel, he checks his health with a doctor and moves into an empty apartment. He writes continuously for eleven days and finishes a novel. He does this several times a year. He's written over two hundred and fifty novels.
- Many businessmen dictate their letters and memos into a tape recorder, to be transcribed later by a secretary. Essentially, they can write as fast as they speak.
- Journalist Hunter S. Thompson has said that he spends any amount of money to buy the best typewriter he can. He wants to remove all possible blocks between his mind and the page.

There's no reason why your writing shouldn't be fluent and easy, at least most of the time. After all, you bring with you all the equipment a fluent writer needs:

- You can think. As a matter of fact, you're thinking all the time— perhaps not about things that are tied to school, but you are thinking nevertheless. And that means that you've got opinions, beliefs, ideas, facts, details, questions, answers, fears, responsibilities, likes, dislikes, arguments, loves, hates—all the thoughts that make you you. To paraphrase a philosopher, you think, and therefore you exist. You have the one thing all writers need: something to write about.
- You can speak and understand at least one language, English. You've probably been talking English since you were three or four years old, and you could probably understand some English even before you could speak it.
- You know the mechanics of reading and writing. You know how to make marks on paper, and you know how to interpret the marks that other people make. You not only know how to speak and understand English, you also know something about reading it and writing it. You may not know as much about reading and writing as you'd like to, but you must know something about it (or you wouldn't be understanding a word we're saying).

You can think, you can speak and understand a language, and you know how that language is translated into written form. That doesn't make you very special—as far as we know, every normal human being thinks, and every normal human being over the age of six or so knows how to speak and understand at least one language. A hundred years ago, perhaps only four or five people out of a hundred knew anything about reading and writing, but that's changing very fast, and it looks as if, by the end of this century, most people in the world will be able to read and write their language. You begin with all the native equipment you need to succeed in a college-level writing course.

Problem Two. Experiments in fluency   Over the next week or so, try daily exercises in free writing. Time yourself. Write for five minutes each day about any topic that comes into your head. Each time, count the number of words you've written in five minutes. We'll bet that you'll increase your fluency—and even find it easier to come up with ideas for writing.   ■

The Journal

Many professional writers keep *journals,* "notebooks for ideas," in which they regularly enter their observations, descriptions, random thoughts. Centuries ago, writers would keep "commonplace books." They would copy passages they liked in their reading or enter thoughts of their own. Today, such journals can be records of a trip of adventure, such as the *Journals of the Lewis and Clark Expedition;* they can be raw material for writing, such as the journals kept by novelists and poets; they can be diaries, written with no thought of a reader, such as the diary written by thirteen-year-old Anne Frank as she was hiding from Nazi soldiers in World War II (it became a best-seller, *The Diary of Anne Frank,* and was made into a popular film).

Try keeping a journal, writing something in it each day. A journal serves as another way of opening up the mind to words and experiences; it can be as fascinating a process of discovery as the free writing we've suggested. In fact, you may want to use a journal to experiment with free writing.

A journal, then, is more than an exercise in fluency. It can be a way of capturing experiences more vividly by writing them down, a way of fixing with words events that otherwise fly past us. The account below, written by James Agee from a journal entry, captures a meal with a family of poor tenant farmers with an immediacy that forms precisely an experience of fifty years ago. You'll note that Agee is concerned both with the details of the experience and with his own place in it, his own stance as a writer.

1.2   The biscuits are large and shapeless, not cut round, and are pale, not tanned, and are dusty with flour. They taste of flour and soda and damp salt and fill the mouth stickily. They are better with butter, and still better with butter and jam. The butter is pallid, soft, and unsalted, about the texture of cloth-cream; it seems to taste delicately of wood and wet cloth; and it tastes "weak." The jam is loose, of little berries, full of light raspings of the tongue; it tastes a deep sweet purple tepidly watered, with a very faint sheen of a sourness as of iron. Field peas are olive-brown, the shape of lentils, about twice the size. Their taste is a cross between lentils and boiled beans; their broth is bright with seasoning of pork, and of this also they taste. The broth is soaked up in bread. The meat is a bacon, granular with salt, soaked in the grease of its frying: there is very little lean meat in it. What there is is nearly as tough as rind; the rest is pure salted stringy fat. The eggs taste of pork too. They are fried in it on both sides until none of the broken yolk runs, are heavily salted and peppered while they fry, so that they come to table nearly black, very heavy, rinded with crispness, nearly as dense as steaks. Of milk I hardly know how to say; it is skimmed, blue-lighted; to a city palate its warmth and odor are somehow dirty and at the same time vital, a little as if one were drinking blood. There is even in so clean a household as this an odor of pork, of sweat, so subtle it seems to get into the very metal of the cooking-pans beyond any removal of scrubbing . . . and it seems to be this odor, and a sort of wateriness and discouraged tepidity, which combine to make the food seem unclean, sticky, and sallow with some invisible sort of disease.

Let Us Now Praise Famous Men

Thus daily journal-writing works two ways: It works inside, exercising your ability to put words on paper, just as a runner practices wind sprints for training, and it works outside, forming your experiences and your place in them. For novelist Joan Didion, the journal is, in a metaphor, a bankbook for the mind, "paid passage to the world out there."

1.3   How it felt to me: that is getting closer to the truth about a notebook. I sometimes delude myself about why I keep a notebook, imagine that some thrifty virtue derives from preserving everything observed. See enough and write it down, I tell myself, and then some morning when the world seems drained of wonder, some day when I am only going through the motions of doing what I am supposed to do, which is write—on that bankrupt morning I will simply open my notebook and there it will all be, a forgotten account with accumulated interest, paid passage back to the world out there: dialogue overheard in hotels and elevators and at the hat-check counter in Pavillon (one middle-aged man shows his hat check to another and says, "That's my old football number") . . .

"On Keeping a Notebook,"
from *Slouching Towards Bethlehem*

Brainstorming

Businesses use a different technique to create ideas. It's called "brainstorming." When a problem arises, executives gather in a conference room and brainstorm: Each person tosses ideas out just as they come to mind, and no one is allowed to criticize individual ideas. As a matter of fact, far-fetched ideas are encouraged, and the whole point is to think as rapidly and as broadly as possible. Brainstorming sessions often come up with or invent better, more imaginative solutions to problems than businesses do through the normal process of memos and meetings and messages. There aren't really "rules" to brainstorming: Ideas appear naturally, bumping off another idea perhaps, or growing out of a fantastic idea that turns out not to be as impractical as it seemed, or sneaking through a kind of rambling "what if we did so and so" conversation.

Brainstorming, as a business technique, has many similarities to the free writing that we've been suggesting as a writing technique, and both techniques have a lot to do with language, with thinking, and with the discovery of ideas and arguments. Both brainstorming and free writing are designed to break down the normal social and psychological barriers that get in the way of thought. Both pay no attention, at first, to how good an idea or piece of writing is: The whole point of both techniques is to get out on the table as many ideas, or as much writing, as possible. And both techniques insist that ideas don't have to mean anything—a totally unreasonable suggestion at a brainstorming meeting is as valuable as a reasonable one (since it might turn out to have the kernel of an ingenious idea inside it). Both techniques seem to work: Businesses come up with imaginative solutions to problems, and you may have found yourself coming up with some bits of inventive and intelligent writing.

Problem Three. Brainstorming, Incorporated   Brainstorming, Incorporated, is an independent consulting firm for businesses, large and small. You find it an interesting place to work, fresh out of college, for each day is different from the last. Here, for example, is a list of tasks that you might find on your desk one Monday morning.

a. General Motors has called, asking us to find a new way to clean the rear windows of hatchback automobiles. Please offer several suggestions.

b. Acme Business Supply has hired us. They want to find new uses for paper clips. Please suggest some.

c. A few years ago, the Temporary Toy Company made tons of money selling "pet rocks" as Christmas presents. They want us to suggest some possible gimmicks for the coming Christmas season. We need to find some way to sell people a totally worthless item. Suggestions?

d. A large salvage company has a problem. They've purchased five thousand used police cars. There's no difficulty in selling the cars, but they want to know what to do with five thousand police sirens. Any ideas?

Choose one of these tasks and brainstorm for ideas. Your boss doesn't want a finished, perfect solution; in fact, she encourages wild ideas, as many as possible. ■

Part of the success of brainstorming and free writing, as ways of coming up with ideas, is that both rely on the naturally creative use we make of language. Another part of their success, though, is that they refuse to be trapped by a rigid system. We are, quite simply, not sure what happens when people come up with good ideas or good pieces of writing.

THE WRITING PROCESS

We have very little evidence, really, about how people write—a few important studies of the writing process, some personal accounts, and some theories of how people create and communicate—and that evidence is contradictory, confused, and uncertain. That confusion might be expected, though, for each writer must work out his or her own method of writing. Moreover, writing can be used for several purposes, from jotting down a shopping list to writing a television script, from copying a recipe to creating a poem that may last as long as the language, and we shouldn't expect to boil down all kinds of writing to a few steps.

Most authorities, however, agree that it's useful to think of the writing process as involving three steps: prewriting, writing, and revising. *Prewriting* includes such mechanical behaviors as getting hold of pen and paper and sitting down at a desk; it includes such mental behaviors as thinking about what you're going to say or talking over your ideas with a friend. For some authorities, prewriting should be a very structured affair, with a series of increasingly detailed outlines and increasingly detailed plans; for others, prewriting should be as loosely structured as a brainstorming session. Prewriting for a shopping list may be as simple as realizing you need to go shopping; prewriting for a research paper may involve hours of reading and planning. In free writing, prewriting may be said not to exist at all, just as it doesn't exist for a poet who starts a poem out without thinking of where it might go.

Writing covers the composition of the first complete draft. It may be done at a single sitting, or it may stretch over days, or weeks, or months. Writing may come as swiftly as the free writing we've been working with, or it may be a slow, agonizing process.

Revising covers the steps between the first draft and the final version. For some writers, revising may be built into the writing stage: The novelist Ernest Hemingway used to write a paragraph a day—a slow rate of composition—but when a paragraph was finished, he usually never touched it again. For other writers, revising may be a lifetime project, as it was for the poet W. H. Auden, who returned to rewrite poems he had published fifteen or twenty years before. Revising may be a simple process of editing the first draft, or it may involve major changes in the original. The student whose free writing we looked at above saw a potential in the hurried sentence that began "being late for a class and everyone in the room staring at you," and, after several rewrites, turned in the finished work of 1.4.

1.4 I stared at the door for what seemed like minutes, knowing I was late, and knowing what to expect. I took a deep breath and opened the door slowly—it only made the squeaking worse. All eyes turned toward me, and the professor stopped lecturing. The class watched me as I pushed my way to a seat in the second row. I heard the professor say something as I sat down, then he started back into the lecture. I didn't take a single note the whole hour.

In many professional writing situations, rewriting can involve several different people—editors, copyreaders, colleagues, and friends may all make suggestions for revising a first or a second or a third draft.

So far, though, we've stressed the middle step in that three-step process. That's because it seems to us that the three steps interact with each other, so that the process of writing from a general plan may cause that plan to change, the process of revising may cause the writer to recreate or reorder what had been thought to be complete, as in our student's rewrite. The important thing for a writer is to be open to ideas as they come.

Our conclusion is supported by a recent look at the writing processes of students and professionals. One researcher, Janet Emig, questioned sixteen professional writers about their process of writing. Only four of them started by making outlines or other formal prewriting; the rest simply "took off" on a first draft. She also studied twelfth-grade writers: Most of them worked without formal outlines, though they usually began writing with a good sense, in their minds, of what they wanted to say.[1]

Problem Four. How students write   How do students go about writing? What parts of the writing process seem hard for them, and what parts are easy? Can you develop, as a class, any "rules about writing" that seem to work, or do you have any "tricks of the trade" that you might want to share? Try free writing on this topic for ten minutes. (Some of our students, given this free writing task, have written several hundred words about how hard it is for them to write.) You may want to discuss your results as a class.   ■

If we're not sure how to break the process of writing into a series of mechanical steps, how then can we go about teaching it? And more important, how can you go about learning it?

We need to start by separating the kind of learning that goes on in a writing (and reading) course from the kind of learning that goes on in other courses. On one hand, we've already insisted that improving your reading and writing is not a mechanical matter, so it's not like learning how to type or how to keypunch for a computer—that is, it's not a matter that can be taught step by step, each step leading naturally to the next, for all aspects of writing are active at all times. We may make arbitrary divisions of this process, but you should realize, as a writer yourself, how arbitrary such divisions are.

On the other hand, improving your writing and reading isn't like learning American history or psychology or botany. Learning, in such classes, is a matter of mastering a given set of facts and theories and of being able to apply them. Such learning is hardly mechanical learning, for the knowledges that such courses deal with are complex and difficult. But those knowledges are different from learning to write or learning to read. For one thing, they in part can be tested objectively, and by and large writing ability can't: It has to be done, to be acted out.

That view suggests that learning writing is more like learning a sport, like learning how to play basketball. Basketball players may spend hours of practice working on a particular shot—say a jump shot; they'll practice shot after shot, they'll think about how they move their feet, how they hold the ball, how they make their moves to get free for the shot. But when they are in a game, if things are going well, they won't have to worry about all those details; their feet will move the way they're supposed to, their fakes will work, their hands will cradle the ball as they should—and all this will happen without having to think consciously, in the way that you have to think about American history in order to learn it.

We might explain what basketball players are able to do by saying that their practice has internalized their movements, put them inside their head so that they become natural ways of moving and shooting, ways that don't have to be thought about consciously. In fact players become too self-conscious; they begin to worry too much about the details of what they're doing—how they move their feet, for example—and when that happens, we say they've "tightened up" or "lost their touch." Perhaps the same expressions could be used about the position that we put you in at the beginning of this chapter when we worried you about the blank page.

Writing, then, is not mechanical, at least when it's working well. It seems certain that writers do not start with the smallest units—words and sentences—and build them up like blocks. Rather, writers seem to have "internalized their movements"—put them inside their head in the same way that basketball players have—so that they can start out with some overall concept, or idea, or purpose for writing, and work out words and sentences in the process of putting it down on paper. As a result, most writers don't quite know what they're going to say until they start saying it, and much of the excitement of writing is watching the ideas and words discover themselves. In other words, most writers don't seem to begin with detailed advance outlines and then mechanically shade in the details. Textbooks have to have chapters, and writing courses have to have regular classroom hours, but the whole purpose of taking the writing process apart is to let students put it back together, to let them internalize it.

Internalizing the ability to write and to read effectively, however, is only one small part of a range of skills you've already internalized—the ability to use language.

THE LANGUAGE YOU USE

We find human language a fascinating topic in itself, for language seems to be the feature that sets us off from the rest of the animal kingdom. And language, of course, is the means by which the writer communicates. The connection between language and writing is, in fact, a very complicated one, as the problem below may show.

Problem Five. Writing nonsense   Free write one minute of nonsense. The rules of free writing still apply, and we'll add one more rule: Do not make sense. That is, what you write must be utter nonsense. Your first three words are, "The blue is . . ."   ■

Here's a sample of what one student wrote in a minute of writing nonsense:

1.5 The blue is sky is can't think blue is sky my pie and own row can can't think is now how cow up down over can't think think of the now is blue green and red and yellow but I can't . . .

The interesting thing about such an experiment is that the writer can't help but make sense. Meaning creeps into the writing, no matter how hard the writer tries to avoid it. Passage 1.5 is riddled with patterns that make sense—patterns of meaning ("The blue is sky," "blue green and red and yellow"), patterns of sound ("is sky my pie and own row"), and patterns of language ("the now is blue," "but I can't"). We find that fact fascinating: The writer can't push pen across paper without becoming enmeshed in sound, meaning, and language. Language is the water we swim in, the air we breathe, the clothes our mind wears, and writing fluently is an open door for those natural abilities.

As a start, we will discuss two features of your language ability:

- the difference between knowing a language and knowing about a language: the difference between *knowing how* and *knowing about;*
- what it means to be "competent" in a language: the concept of *language competence.*

Knowing How and Knowing About

Consider the two passages below, the first an imaginary conversation, the second an imaginary announcement at a banquet.

1.6 "So there we were, stuck out on the freeway at three in the morning, trying to flag down somebody to help. Finally this guy from Trinidad stopped. He took us into an all-night gas station, waited while we got somebody to tow the car in, then ran us out to a motel and made sure we could get a room before he went on."

"From Trinidad, huh."

"Yeah. He was a history professor. I don't know what we would have done if he hadn't stopped."

"Did he speak English?"

"Yeah. They speak it down there. It's a little different from the way we speak English, but it's still English. We could understand him perfectly. He knew English."

1.7 "Welcome, ladies and gentlemen, to the meeting of the Linguistic Scientists of America. This meeting has been dedicated to the memory of Professor Inga Diagraff, the Swedish linguist who, before her sudden death last week, was to have been our main speaker this evening. Professor Diagraff spent her life in the study of English. She published two hundred and ninety-seven books on English grammar, and was considered to be a world authority on English. If anyone can be said to have known the English language, it was Professor Diagraff. She knew English."

Both passages end with the same claim: The person "knew English." And both times the claim is true: The man from Trinidad knew English because he grew up speaking it, and the woman from Sweden knew English because she spent her life studying it.

Yet the two claims may mean entirely different things. The person from Trinidad *knew how* to speak English; the person from Sweden *knew about* English. There's a difference between *knowing about* something and *knowing how* to do something. All speakers of English know *how* the language works, even if they know nothing *about* the language, about its grammar, for example. That means you know something you didn't know you knew, as problem seven will show.

Problem Six. Knowing how and knowing about   Write down the rule for ordering adjectives of age, number, and nationality in English. If you don't know the rule. write "don't know."

(You probably wrote "don't know." At least we've never found a student who did know the rule for ordering adjectives of age, number, and nationality in English. There's one sense, then, in which you don't know many of the rules of English. You don't *know about* them.)

Now examine the word sets below. Arrange each group of words in what sounds like a natural order:

girls	young	the	French	four
lechers	aged	those	Scottish	six
ducks	elderly	the	Canadian	many

We've never found a student who knew the rule we asked for, but we've never had a student who knew English and understood our instructions who didn't arrange the sets like this:

the	four	young	French	girls
those	six	aged	Scottish	lechers
the	many	elderly	Canadian	ducks
	(number)	(age)	(nationality)	

Notice the pattern: first a word like *the* or *those*, then an adjective showing number (*four, six,* and *many*), one showing age (*young, aged,* and *elderly*), one showing nationality (*French, Scottish, Canadian*), and finally a noun (*girls, lechers, ducks*).[2] You've now organized three phrases with adjectives of number, age, and nationality, and you could make up more phrases with the same pattern.

You've proven to yourself that you do know the rule for ordering adjectives of number, age, and nationality: You couldn't have put "the four young French girls" in the right order unless you knew the rule. Yet you probably claimed, at the beginning of the problem, that you didn't know the rule. The fact is, you *knew how* to use the rule even though you didn't *know about* the rule.   ■

Problem six shows that there are two different ways we use the word *know:* 1. We use it to indicate *knowing how* to do something, as you knew how to arrange the words, and 2. we use it to indicate *knowing about* something, as a linguist, a scientist of language, can be said to know about this rule.

In other words, "knowing how" to do something is the kind of internalized skill that we talked about in the last section. It is something that's in your head, a potential, even though (as we saw in the last problem) you may not know that it's there. It's *a tacit or implicit kind of knowledge,* an ability to perform a task.

"Knowing about," on the other hand, is *a formal and explicit kind of knowledge.* It's something you have instead of something you can do. It's the kind of knowledge that you master in a course like Biology or History or Psychology. You know you have it.

This distinction is rather important when it comes to "knowing" language, for it may help us to work out more precisely what is involved in developing one's reading and writing ability. Notice, first off, that there's no necessary connection between knowing about something and knowing how to do something. An automobile engineer may know all about cars, but that doesn't necessarily make him a good driver. A mathematician may be able to predict all the angles that govern the motion of billiard balls, but that knowledge doesn't necessarily make her a good pool player. Linguists may know all about English grammar, but that doesn't necessarily make them good writers.

Of course, there are some things that you must "know about" in order to "know how" to do something. A driver, for example, has to *know about* traffic signs, speed limits, and so on—the things that are tested in a driver's test. But both good drivers and bad drivers know these matters. Similarly, a reader or writer has to *know about* some things—for example, that a written sentence begins with a capital letter and ends, generally, with a period. But these are basic matters, essentially preconditions to writing.

Problem Seven. Exercising competence . Here is another problem exploring your language competence, your "knowing how" knowledge of English. This problem looks at word groups like "call up," "fall down," "look at," and "think over."

Sometimes these word groups can't be separated. The first sentence in the group below sounds fine, but the second one doesn't: No one who knew the language would say it.

■ Several people fell down the slippery stairs.
■ *Several people fell the slippery stairs down.

The sentence that doesn't "sound right" is marked with an asterisk (*).

Other word groups that look the same as this word group can be separated, with the second word closer to the end of the sentence. Thus, both sentences below sound fine:

■ I called up my taxidermist.
■ I called my taxidermist up.

In the list below, mark the sentences that "don't sound right" with an asterisk. Read the sentence aloud if you're not sure.

a. I'll think over your offer.

b. I'll think your offer over.

c. He walked on the sidewalk.

d. He walked the sidewalk on.

e. Reading starts with knowing language.

f. Reading starts knowing language with.

g. Eat up all your supper!

h. Eat all your supper up!

i. He looked at the unhappy duck.

j. He looked the unhappy duck at.   ■

Problem seven is not a problem for most native speakers of English. (If you wish, check your answers in the answer section at the end of the book—there we provide answers for many, but not all, problems in the text.) But it's hard to explain this skill in a formal way; it relies on your language competence.

Language Competence

Your knowing-how ability to use the English language is your *language competence*. That competence is what lets you talk with your friends and with strangers, even those who may not talk exactly the way you do. It allows you to say more or less anything you want to say and to understand more or less everything that's said to you. Your language competence underlies your ability to write and to understand sentences that others write (this sentence, for example).

This competence is inherently, basically, *creative*. In your everyday speaking, as well as your writing, you use sentences that are brand-new, made up for the occasion. Even reading, we'll notice shortly, is in a way creative. Your competence, then, is not merely a matter of knowing the words of a language. In fact, speaking only about competence, the number of words you know is not that important. In fact, that competence is what lets you learn new words, like *competence*, to fit them into your language sense. So competence is more abstract, more general, than just words alone; it's an internalized or underlying sense of how the language works. It even works with nonsense.

Problem Eight. Kinds of nonsense   None of the following sentences make any sense at all. But they don't make sense in three different ways; they illustrate three different kinds of nonsense. The first kind of nonsense we'll call *Nonsense 1;* here's an example:

■ *Nonsense 1:* Proozlies pixilate froobally on the craydidle.

The second kind of nonsense we'll call *Nonsense 2:*

■ *Nonsense 2:* Hortense drank the typewriter after she baked it.

A third kind of nonsense is *Nonsense 3:*

■ *Nonsense 3:* Deftly onions the slices he.

Identify the sentences that follow as *Nonsense 1, Nonsense 2,* and *Nonsense 3.*

   a. Wringdraddles fribble the antickled trunt.

   b. I stubbed my stomach.

   c. Town in of tool-and-die is a convention manufacturers.

   d. Swashless grinted eadles sloap fruminously.

   e. Sincerity sunbathes in the index.

   f. Spring in, to turned conversation romance.

   g. I think I just ate Oklahoma.

   h. Few pahrumps can be asphibbled by quizologistic marstickulators.

   i. Sentences backward read to difficult it's.

j. The prinkled glork spooshed on the ibidimous crankle.

k. Colorless green ideas sleep furiously.

l. Language apparently human beings a have all machine built-in.   ■

Problem Eight shows you three basic parts of your language competence. You have a *word sense* that lets you know whether a word is an English word—or likely to be an English word—or not. You have a *grammar sense* that tells you whether sets of words are put together right—notice that this grammar sense lets you read "proozlies pixilate froobally on the craydidle" as if it were an English sentence, even though your word sense tells you it's not. Finally, your *meaning sense* is alert to problems: You can't stub your stomach, much less eat Oklahoma.

You developed this complex language sense as a child, quite naturally. Nobody taught you how to speak English—you simply learned it. All children do.

All human beings learn language. There are some exceptions to this claim—some people who cannot speak or whose mental development does not allow them to learn language—but they make up a small part of any group. And there is a precondition: Humans have to be exposed to a language to learn it. But, given those qualifications, every human being will learn at least one language. Interestingly enough, if a child is exposed to two languages, he or she will normally learn them both. Many Spanish-surnamed American children learn both English and Spanish; many French Canadians learn both English and French; many children in Belgium grow up learning three languages, French, German, and Flemish.

All languages are learned in the same way. Individual children will learn the language they are exposed to at faster or slower rates, just as they learn to walk at different times. But the way babies learn to walk is the same for virtually all babies: They sit up, they crawl, and they walk. And the way children learn a language seems to be the same for all children and all languages. For example, all children seem to learn the sound system of their language before they learn the words, so you'll hear a baby who is learning English babble away in sound patterns that resemble English—statements, questions, and so on—while a Japanese baby will begin to babble in Japanese. One scientist surveyed studies, from all over the world, of children learning their mother tongue (encompassing many different language families) and concluded that there is a "universal developmental sequence": Each child learns to speak the language he or she is exposed to in the same way, in the same general time sequence.[3]

The same generalization, by the way, seems to hold true for all dialects of language. The child of a Park Avenue matron will learn English at the same rate as the child of a welfare mother in Harlem, or the child of a sugar cane worker in Trinidad, or the child of a farmer in New Zealand. Each child will learn the variety of English to which he or she is exposed.

All languages are equally complex. We may feel, when we hear a foreign language, as if we're hearing the babbling of a child. But, if all children learn all languages at the same rate, then all languages would seem to present the same learning task. They must be equally complex. We're speaking of their system, their grammar, not their vocabulary. In terms of their system, all languages appear equally complex. (Speakers of English do find it easier to learn French as adults than to learn Mandarin Chinese, but that's because the system of French is more like that of English than that of Mandarin Chinese.)

Again, this generalization also seems to hold true for all dialects of a language. The variety of English spoken in Scotland is different from the English spoken in Kenya, but Kenyan children seem to learn their variety at the same rate that Scottish children learn their variety, so the dialects would appear to be equally complex.

Reading Competence

This language competence informs your reading and writing as well as your speaking and listening. We'd like to end this discussion by showing you how even reading can be a creative exercise. We're going to give you a passage to read, one that uses several words you haven't seen before. We're betting that you can read the passage and, by the end of it, understand a new word, the word *t'ief,* even though you've probably never seen it written down or heard it spoken. Read the passage that follows, trying to make sense out of what's happening rather than trying to understand every word. If in doubt, keep reading.

1.8   Was the rain what cause him to t'ief a pair of shoes from by a shoemaker shop in Park Street. Is the first time he ever t'ief, and it take him a long time to make up his mind. He stand up there on the pavement by this shoemaker shop, and he thinking things like, Oh God when I tell you I hungry, and all the shoes around the table, on the ground, some capsize, some old and some new, some getting halfsole and some getting new heel.

It have a pair just like the one he have on.

The table cut up for so, as if the shoemaker blind and cutting the wood instead of the leather, and it have a broken calabash shell with some boil starch in it. The starch look like pap; he so hungry he feel he could eat it.

Well, the shoemaker in the back of the shop, and it only have a few people sheltering rain on the pavement. It look so easy for him to put down the old pair and take up another pair—this time so, he done have his eye fix on a pair that look like Technic, and just his size, too, besides.

. . .

And it look to him as if t'iefing could be easy, because plenty time people does leave things alone and go away, like how now the shoemaker in the back of the shop, and all he have to do is take up a pair of shoes and walk off in cool blood.

Well, it don't take plenty to make a t'ief. All you have to do is have a fellar catching his royal, and can't get a work noway, and bam! By the time he bounce something somewhere, an orange from a tray, or snatch a bread in a parlor, or something.

Like how he bounce the shoes.

Samuel Selven, "Calypsonian"

Example 1.8 is from a short story that takes place on the Caribbean island of Trinidad; it's about an unemployed calypso singer named Razor Blade, who's out of money and has holes in his shoes. Here, Razor Blade t'iefs a pair of Technics from by a shoemaker shop, and he decides that bouncing the shoes is okay—"it don't take plenty to make a t'ief."

We suspect you've learned the meaning of the word *t'ief*. In "to t'ief a pair of shoes," it means "to steal or shoplift." In "it look to him as if t'iefing could be easy," it means "stealing or theft." The word has four meanings: "to steal," "stole," "theft," and "a thief."

How were you able to understand a word you'd never seen before? Because you are a competent user of language. Your *word sense* suggests a link between sound and spelling, connecting the new word *t'ief* with the familiar word *thief*. Your *meaning sense* reacts to context. "To t'ief a pair of shoes" might mean "to shine a pair of shoes," but that meaning doesn't fit the whole context, "to shine a pair of shoes from by a shoemaker shop." Your *grammar sense* adjusts to the extended range of meaning of your sense of thief, as in "is the first time he ever t'ief."

Reading, in this sense, is a kind of guessing game. You participate actively in reading; a printed page doesn't unfold its meaning passively, word by word. You discover that meaning, by predicting, guessing, even making false starts, all the while using your language competence to fit the printed page into your sense of the world. Example 1.8 didn't tell you that bouncing a pair of shoes is about the same as t'iefing a pair of shoes, and that both expressions mean "to steal or shoplift."

You figured out that meaning, and you were able to do so because you know something about how written and spoken language go together.

Problem Nine. A proverb from Trinidad   Now that you have a sense of how the word *t'ief* works in the English of Trinidad, you may be able to figure out the meaning of the following proverb:

■ T'ief t'ief t'ief; God laugh.

The proverb is translated in the answer section at the end of the book, but don't look it up too quickly. Think about it.   ■

SUMMARY

We have explored three ways of putting ideas on paper, three ways of improving fluency: free writing, journal-keeping, and brainstorming. We have reviewed the writing process—prewriting, writing, and revising—noting that many writers "write themselves into" a topic, without formal prewriting. We explained this creative ability by analogy with the skills of a basketball player, who has internalized the movements that make up the game.

Finally, we explained those "internalized movements" by reference to your *language competence,* your "knowing how" sense of language. We have seen that these "knowing how" skills help both reader and writer discover meaning.

IMPLICATIONS FOR THE WRITER

This chapter—indeed, this textbook—may ask for a new way of thinking about writing and about learning to write. In part, our advice is straightforward and very positive: relax and practice. But our advice is also rather complex, for our discussion of your language competence suggests that you may be able to master, to internalize, skills that you gain by doing, by "learning how," rather than by study, by "learning about." It's a continuing process, a "discovery job." Basketball players never stop practicing, and ballet dancers take lessons throughout their career.

FINAL WRITING ASSIGNMENTS

I. Starting Your Journal   Your instructor may have specific suggestions, even requirements, about your journal, and your daily writing may be a requirement of the course. If not, we'd suggest that you begin your own journal. Find a time to write, a place to write, and a journal to write in. The time may be early morning or late evening or even a few minutes sandwiched between classes—but you should have a regular time set aside each day for your journal. The place may be a writing desk at home or a regular seat in the library. Some writers collect journal entries on loose sheets of paper; most prefer some kind of bound booklet, like a standard spiral notebook or even the bound blank diaries available in most bookstores. Look on this journal as a savings account, as an investment in written language.

II. From Free Writing to a Finished Paper This assignment asks you to move from free writing to a finished paper. You'll need pen, paper, and a friend. Begin with a ten-minute spurt of free writing, and give it to a friend to read. Ask the friend to put a line in the margin to mark passages that he or she likes. Look at your friend's marks, but don't revise the draft. Instead, begin a new free writing, and again ask your friend to read it. Repeat the process three or four times.

Then collect your drafts and revise them as a finished paper of about 500 words. Be prepared to discuss the differences you found in this way of approaching the writing process, as opposed to normal textbook advice.

III. The Writing Process Below are three discussions of the writing process—by a philosopher, a journalist, and an English teacher. You may wish to use the passages as models for a theme describing your own process of writing. You may wish to supplement them by transcribing taped interviews with other writers—students, professionals, business people. Or you may simply wish to react to the three accounts, noting the features they share and discussing their effect on your own writing.

> **A** Very gradually I have discovered ways of writing with a minimum of worry and anxiety. When I was young each fresh piece of serious work used to seem to me for a time—perhaps a long time—to be beyond my powers. I would fret myself into a nervous state from fear that it was never going to come right. I would make one unsatisfying attempt after another, and in the end have to discard them all. At last I found that such fumbling attempts were a waste of time. It appeared that after first contemplating a book on some subject, and after giving serious preliminary attention to it, I needed a period of subconscious incubation which could not be hurried and was if anything impeded by deliberate thinking. Sometimes I would find, after a time, that I had made a mistake, and that I could not write the book I had had in mind. But often I was more fortunate. Having, by a time of very intense concentration, planted the problem in my subconscious, it would germinate underground until, suddenly, the solution emerged with blinding clarity, so that it only remained to write down what had appeared as if in a revelation.

The most curious example of this process, and the one which led me subsequently to rely upon it, occurred at the beginning of 1914. I had undertaken to give the Lowell Lectures at Boston, and had chosen as my subject "Our Knowledge of the External World." Throughout 1913 I thought about this topic. In term time in my rooms at Cambridge, in vacations in a quiet inn on the upper reaches of the Thames, I concentrated with such intensity that I sometimes forgot to breathe and emerged panting as from a trance. But all to no avail. To every theory that I could think of I could perceive fatal objections. At last, in despair, I went off to Rome for Christmas, hoping that a holiday would revive my flagging energy. I got back to Cambridge on the last day of 1913, and although my difficulties were still completely unresolved I arranged, because the remaining time was short, to dictate as best I could to a stenographer. Next morning, as she came in at the door, I suddenly saw exactly what I had to say, and proceeded to dictate the whole book without a moment's hesitation.

Bertrand Russell, "How I Write"

B So I went over to *Esquire* magazine after a while and talked to them about this phenomenon, and they sent me out to California to take a look at the custom car world. Dale Alexander was from Detroit or some place, but the real center of the thing was in California, around Los Angeles. I started talking to a lot of these people, like George Barris and Ed Roth, and seeing what they were doing, and—well, eventually it became the story from which the title of this book was taken, "The Kandy-Kolored Tangerine-Flake Streamline Baby." But at first I couldn't even write the story. I came back to New York and just sat around worrying over the thing. I had a lot of trouble analyzing exactly what I had on my hands. By this time *Esquire* practically had a gun at my head because they had a two-page-wide color picture for the story locked into the printing presses and no story. Finally, I told Byron Dobell, the managing editor at *Esquire,* that I couldn't pull the thing together. O.K., he tells me, just type out my notes and send them over and he will get somebody else to write it. So about 8 o'clock that night I started typing the notes in the form of a memorandum that began, "Dear Byron." I started typing away, starting right with the first time I saw any custom cars in California. I just started recording it all, and inside of a couple of hours, typing away like a madman, I could tell that something was beginning to happen. By midnight this memorandum to Byron was twenty pages long and I was still typing like a maniac. About 2 A.M. or something like that I turned on WABC, a radio station that plays rock and roll music all night long, and got a little more manic. I wrapped up the memorandum about 6:15 A.M., and by this time it was 49 pages long. I took it over to *Esquire* as soon as they opened up, about 9:30 A.M. About 4 P.M. I got a call from Byron Dobell. He told me they were striking out the "Dear Byron" at the top of the memorandum and running the rest of it in the magazine. That was the story, "The Kandy-Kolored Tangerine-Flake Streamline Baby."

Tom Wolfe, *The Kandy-Kolored Tangerine-Flake Streamline Baby*

C In high school I wrote relatively easily and—according to those standards—satisfactorily. In college I began to have difficulty writing. Sometimes I wrote badly, sometimes I wrote easily and sometimes with excruciating difficulty. Starting early and planning carefully didn't seem to be the answer: sometimes it seemed to help, sometimes it seemed to make things worse.

Whether or not I succeeded in getting something written seemed related only to whether I screwed myself up into some state of frantic emotional intensity: sometimes about the subject I was writing about; occasionally about some extraneous matter in my life; usually about how overdue the paper was and how frightened I was of turning in nothing at all. There was one term in my junior year when by mistake I signed up for a combination of courses requiring me to write two substantial papers a week. After the first two weeks' crisis, I found I wrote fluently and with relatively little difficulty for the rest of the term. But the next term, reality returned. The gods of writing turned their back again.

The saving factor in college was that I wasn't sure whether I cared more about skiing or about studies. But then I went to graduate school and committed myself to studies. This involved deciding to try *very hard* and plan my writing *very carefully*. Writing became more and more impossible. I finally reached the point where I could not write at all. I had to quit graduate school and go into a line of work that didn't require any writing. Teaching English in college wasn't what I had in mind, but it was the only job I could get so it had to do.

After five years I found myself thinking I knew some important things about teaching (not writing!) and wanting badly to get other people to know and believe them. I decided I wanted to write them down and get them published; and also to return to graduate school and get my degree. This time I managed to get myself to write things. I always wondered when the curtain might fall again. I hit on the technique of simply insisting on getting *something* written a week before the real deadline, so I could try to patch it up and make it readable. This worked. But as I watched myself trying to write, it became clear I was going through fantastically inefficient processes. The price I was having to pay for those words was all out of proportion to any real value.

Peter Elbow, Writing Without Teachers

FOR FURTHER READING

We recommend one book particularly, Peter Elbow's *Writing Without Teachers* (New York: Oxford University Press, 1973), a writing teacher's account of his own growth in writing, with helpful suggestions for student writers. We have reprinted a selection from the book in the final writing assignment of this chapter.

Students may also wish to investigate what professional writers say about their writing process. A regular series of interviews is *Writers at Work: The Paris*

Review Interviews, published by Viking Press, now in four volumes, edited by Malcolm Cowley (vols. 1 and 2) and by George Plimpton (vols. 3 and 4).

NOTES

1. *The Composing Process of Twelfth Graders* (Urbana, Ill.: National Council of Teachers of English, 1971).
2. It is possible to put the words in a different order, such as "the *French* four young girls," but native speakers of English would guess that such a speaker would not be a native speaker of English or would have a special context in mind.
3. Dan I. Slobin, "Developmental Psycholinguistics," in *A Survey of Linguistic Science,* ed. W. O. Dingwall (College Park: University of Maryland, 1971).

2

The Dimensions
of Rhetoric

To begin the inquiry, it will be necessary to say a few words about
rhetoric.

RICHARD M. WEAVER

The word *rhetoric* has a fishy smell about it nowadays. It's commonly
used to mean empty or inflated language, or to refer to a misleading
argument as opposed to a good one. Thus the campus politician urges
us to "cut the rhetoric and get down to the issues," and President
Nixon, quoted by one of his staff, offered the word to suggest that
language be used to deceive:

2.1   You can say this Administration will have the first far-reach-
ing attack on the problem of hunger in history. Use all the rhetoric, so long as it doesn't cost any money.

quoted in *Look Magazine*

We think of this sense of the word as "mere rhetoric."

But there must be another sense of the word *rhetoric*. After all, you
may be taking a course called "Introduction to Rhetoric," and this text
proudly bears the subtitle *A New College Rhetoric*.

A dictionary can help with a problem of this sort, where a word has
two different senses. Here is one dictionary entry for the word *rhetoric*.

2.2   **rhet|o|ric** (ret′ər ik), *n.* **1** the art of using words in speaking
or writing so as to persuade or influence others: *The communication*

of those thoughts to others falls under the consideration of rhetoric (John Stuart Mill). **2** the language used: *Blifil suffered himself to be overpowered by the forcible rhetoric of the squire* (Henry Fielding). **3** a book on rhetoric: *Aristotle himself has given it a place in his Rhetoric among the beauties of that art* (Joseph Addison). **4** mere display in language: *the exaggerated rhetoric of presidential campaigns (New York Times); the limp loquacity of long-winded rhetoric, so natural in men and soldiers in an hour of emergency* (Algernon Charles Swinburne). [<Latin *rhētorica*<Greek *rhētorikē* (*téchnē*) (*art*) of an orator<*rhētōr;* see etym. under **rhetor**]

The World Book Dictionary

This information clears up our problem with the word's meaning. We notice, in the brackets at the end of the entry, that *rhetoric* was first a Greek word (which we might have guessed from its spelling), and that it meant the art of an orator—a public speaker. It later broadened to include writing as well as speaking, and—although our dictionary entry doesn't show it—we can now use the word in a broader sense, as when we speak of "the rhetoric of film" or "body rhetoric." Our common meaning of "mere rhetoric" is given in definition four, with examples from the *New York Times* and a nineteenth-century writer, Swinburne. The first three definitions, however, offer more positive senses of the word. Rhetoric is "the art of using words . . . to persuade or influence others" (definition one), and thus one can be said to use rhetoric well (definition two) and refer to a book as a rhetoric (Aristotle's *Rhetoric*, cited in definition three, or our subtitle, *A New College Rhetoric*). These three senses might be called "true rhetoric," as opposed to the "mere rhetoric" of definition four.

Our aim, in this chapter, is to map the dimensions of this "true rhetoric," particularly as it helps us to explain the tasks of writer and reader. Thus, where chapter One started "inside," with your ability to put words on paper, this chapter looks "outside," at the persuasive purposes of writing. Of course, not all writing is persuasive. Notes to yourself may be simple helps for remembering—shopping lists, journal entries, lecture notes—and some printed materials are pure records of fact—telephone books, stock market listings, the box scores of baseball games.

But if we take the notion of seeking "to persuade or influence" in a very general sense, we can see how much of writing is rhetorical. Poems and short stories may dramatize the author's experience, but they seek to influence the reader by their form; they ask you to believe in or be convinced by the imaginative experience. A chemistry textbook attempts to influence, as well as inform, the reader. Even a mathematical formula attempts to persuade. Einstein's $E = mc^2$, for example, might be said to be "rhetorical": It uses the code of mathematics rather than the code of print, and that is, in itself, a kind of argument (compare the effect of $E = mc^2$ with the same statement in words, "Energy is equivalent to the mass times the square of a constant, c, which is the speed of light"); and it presents a definite order of emphasis (compare the equivalent equation $C^2 = \frac{e}{m}$). In this general sense, then, most of the writing we do is rhetorical—certainly all the writing we do in a writing class.

Problem One. The word rhetoric In each of the following quotations, decide whether the word *rhetoric* (or *rhetorical*) is used to mean "mere rhetoric" or "true rhetoric," using the context of the word as a clue.

a. [The emotional confrontation] showed that the real problems of the Police Division and the community are being aggravated by persistent, divisive rhetoric.

The Cincinnati Enquirer

b. The Urban League intends to translate the symbols into substance and the rhetoric into relevance.

Time Magazine

c. Rhetoric at its best tries to teach the pupil to exploit the possibilities the language gives him.

Joseph E. Grimes, *The Thread of Discourse*

d. The trial was only a few hours old, but I was already annoyed. Rothblatt [the defense attorney] took off on a rhetorical binge about "this temple of justice" and the "hysteria of overwhelming publicity" that brought an objection from the prosecutors.

John J. Sirica, *To Set the Record Straight*

e. As the clamor for basic skills continues to grow, it may be time for the fourth R—Rhetoric—to reenter the classroom.

Psychology Today

f. English teachers . . . have almost abandoned the very name of rhetoric, and the classical tradition is now completely in our hands.

W. M. Parrish, "The Tradition of Rhetoric"

g. Without rhetoric there is silence—and tyranny.

Sol Chaneles, *"The Pestilent Cosmetic, Rhetoric"*

h. For all the rhetorical smoke, the President and the Democrats are not that far apart on many other aspects of the program.

Time Magazine

i. In its best sense, rhetoric seeks to draw men together, attempts to establish agreement by willing consent, and tries to create an identity of purpose among them, to promote meaningful action.

In these terms, rhetoric remains one of man's best hopes for a better day.

The Holt Guide to English

THE USES OF RHETORIC

As the Greek origin of the word would suggest, "true rhetoric" has been around much longer than the "mere rhetoric" of today. True rhetoric began in Greece, in the fifth century B.C., as a conscious, *knowing-about* tradition[1] in response to two events in human culture. One was the beginning of democratic government. Citizens needed "to persuade or influence others" to gain their votes on political questions, and they had to plead their own cases in the new courts of law. The other event was the beginning of writing in our modern sense. Writing had been used, in one form or another, for thousands of years before this, but only for governmental or religious purposes: to keep tax lists or to convey religious laws in a secret code that only a few knew how to read. When the Greeks created an alphabet that let them "write down speech," they began a new use of writing, one that we'll explore shortly under the heading "The Code of Print."

We need to be quite clear about the value of this 2500-year-old tradition: Rhetoric matters. The word itself, as we've seen, has lost much of its prestige, and job advertisements for "junior executive," "senior architect," or "chief engineer" are much more likely to read "good writing skills essential" or "must be able to communicate effectively" than to read "rhetorical ability crucial" (or perhaps "rhetorician wanted"?). But the principle remains the same: communications skills (as we now loosely speak of rhetorical ability) are essential in any profession.

Moreover, college students are active rhetoricians in almost every course, using their writing ability to "persuade or influence" instructors in the most direct way possible: to earn a grade. "Mere rhetoric" won't help with this; instructors have had long experience in detecting empty or inflated language. And rhetoric alone won't guarantee an "A" in, say, American History. But at the moment the student begins to package her knowledge of American history in writing, she should be able to turn to rhetoric, the art of effective communication.

There's another value to the study of rhetoric, albeit a negative one. Conscious attention to "true rhetoric" is our only protection against the "mere rhetoric" around us. We're constantly assaulted by others who attempt to use the power of the written or spoken word to persuade or influence us—on television, in political campaigns, daily through signs, slogans, and salesmen. Without the ability to separate "true rhetoric" from "mere rhetoric," we can only be victims—as consumers, as citizens, and as business professionals. German industrialist Albert Speer explained Hitler's rise to power by saying, "few of us were inoculated against his message." Accordingly, we like to think of this attention to rhetoric as an "inoculation"—a sort of vaccination for the mind, against those who would use language to deceive us.

Put more strongly, rhetoric is power. It is personal power—that is, power to control one's own life—for the ability to deal with one's experiences on paper is a way to resee them and to understand them. In this sense, one writes to put things in shape, to order one's life. Eldridge Cleaver, writing from prison, is eloquent about this shaping power of language:

> **2.3** I lost my self-respect. My pride as a man dissolved and my whole moral structure seemed to collapse, completely shattered.
>   That is why I started to write. To save myself.
>
> *Soul on Ice*

True rhetoric, since the Greeks, has also been a form of public power, a means of controlling others by persuasion. The public power of rhetoric is not the power of a club, forcing others to obey against their will, but rather the power of rational discussion, of the free interplay of ideas, of reasoned choice. In this ideal sense, rhetoric is "good reasons"—and "good reasons" are the essence of democracy.

In chapter One, we compared writing to playing the game of basketball. That's a useful comparison. But this game is an important one. You can protect yourself against the "mere rhetoric" around you, expand your ability to come to grips with your own experience, and assume the public responsibilities of a citizen—by conscious attention to what has been, since the Greeks, "the art of rhetoric."

BUILDING A DYNAMIC MODEL OF WRITING

We'll use the concepts of rhetoric to build a particular model of writing, one that we like to think of as a *dynamic* model of writing (*dynamic:* "active, energetic, in motion"; compare *dynamo, dynamite*). We can contrast that model with a *static* model of writing, one that you might build in the problem below.

Problem Two. A static model of writing?   Below are statements about writing classes, each followed by an abbreviated code: SA = "strongly agree"; MA = "mildly agree"; N = "neutral"; MD = "mildly disagree"; SD = "strongly disagree." Read each statement, and then decide what *most students* would think about the statement as it applies to *most writing classes*. That is, respond to what most students think about most writing classes, not to what you think about the class you're taking now. Circle the appropriate abbreviation for each statement.

a. One learns nothing from writing; it's simply a matter of putting down what one already knows.

SA   MA   N   MD   SD

b. Students should think of the parts of writing as fixed and absolute. Thus one should think of THE correct spelling, THE proper grammar, THE varied sentence structure, THE paragraph, THE five-hundred-word theme, and so on.

SA   MA   N   MD   SD

c. Writing for English classes has very little to do with the real world; it's an artificial kind of thing.

SA   MA   N   MD   SD

d. Instructors never give students enough credit for all the work they put into a writing assignment.

SA   MA   N   MD   SD

e. One's grade on a writing assignment is always beyond one's conscious control. One's grade is determined by the prejudices of the instructor, the limits of one's background, and so on.

SA   MA   N   MD   SD

Our students, at the beginning of a writing class, tend to think that most students would agree with the statements of problem two. They build a *static model of writing*, one that we might restate as follows:

2.4   Writing for writing classes is artificial and mechanical. It has no relevance to the real world. One writes down what one already knows, with special attention to *the* correct way to express it. One is never rewarded for one's effort, and one's grade is always beyond one's conscious control. As a result, one learns nothing from writing; it's simply a matter of showing the instructor what you already know.

Developed this way, such a "model of writing" may seem artificial and coldly abstract. But here's a bit of a tape-recording of a thirteen-year-old British student talking about writing—what he says implies a "model of writing" very close to that of 2.4.

2.5 *Interviewer:* But don't you find that when you're writing you put things down in a different way than you could if you're talking?

David: I think that talking brings out more things in you than just writing it down on a piece of paper. I mean you write it down to show the teacher that you've done it but it doesn't bring out any more knowledge in you, I don't think. Well, just getting a piece of paper, saying, oh, I'll write this all down, you know, and just to show the teacher that you've done it and he just ticks it and you've done that bit of work.

London University Writing Across the Curriculum
Project, From Talking to Writing

For this teenager, talking is dynamic—"It brings out more things in you." Writing, on the other hand, is static, "just writing it down on a piece of paper." "It doesn't bring out any more knowledge in you": It's a mechanical act, done solely for the instructor.

Contrast a writer with a dynamic model of writing—this the opening monologue from Woody Allen's film *Manhattan:*

2.6 [The screen shows a series of black-and-white pictures of New York City. On the soundtrack we hear the sound of a typewriter and a writer reading to himself as he types, at times commenting on his work.]

He adored New York City. He idolized it all out of proportion. *(No, that's not it.)* He romanticized it all out of proportion. To him, no matter what the season was, this was still a town that existed in black and white and pulsated to the tunes of George Gershwin.

(Ah, no . . . let me start over.)

Chapter One. He was too romantic about Manhattan, as he was about everything else. He thrived on the hustle-bustle of the crowds and the traffic. To him, New York meant beautiful women and street-smart guys who seem to know all the angles.

(No, too corny for my taste . . . try to be more Malamud.)

Chapter One. He adored New York City. To him, it was a metaphor for the decay of contemporary culture. The same lack of individual integrity that caused so many people to take the easy way out was rapidly turning the town of his dreams . . .

(I'm turning into a creature . . .)

Chapter One. He adored New York City, although to him it was a metaphor for the decay of contemporary culture. How hard it was to exist in a society desensitized by drugs, loud music, television, crime, garbage . . .

(Too angry. I don't want to do that.)

Chapter One. He was as tough and romantic as the city he loved. Behind his black-rimmed glasses was the coiled sexual power of a jungle cat. (*I love this.*) New York was his town, and it always would be.

Woody Allen and Marshall Brickman,
screenplay for *Manhattan* (1978)

The quandaries of Allen's fictional speaker are humorous enough— he's not sure how he wants his speaker to sound, he's not sure what attitude he wants to take about New York City, and he's very concerned with what his readers will think. But we can say that he's thinking (and writing) dynamically, even rhetorically.

In fact, it's precisely the dynamic quality of this imagined writer's halting beginnings that make them *rhetorical*. As a result, we may be asking quite a bit from you as reader, and as developing writer: We may be asking for a new way of thinking about writing. We can't convince you of a new way of thinking in just one chapter; this chapter can only sketch out a general model, a dynamic model of rhetoric, that we'll return to over and over. The key terms of that model are: Rhetoric is *choice* in a *context* for a *purpose*.

Rhetorical Choice

Consider an everyday problem of persuading others: You want someone to close a window. Here are a few of the choices available to you (certainly not all of them):

2.7A   Please shut that window.

2.7B   Hey, buddy, shut that window, will you?

2.7C   You better shut that window.

2.7D   Could I impose by asking you to close that window?

2.7E   If you don't shut that window right now, I'll never speak to you again.

2.7F   If you're not too busy and wouldn't mind doing me a favor, I'd sure like to have that window closed.

2.7G   Shut the window right now.

2.7H   Must you always leave the window open like that?

2.7I   I hate to say this right now, but . . . but do you think it would affect our relationship . . . I mean really affect our relationship . . . if I were to ask you to get up, I mean, like right away, and shut the window?

Each of these choices changes our request somewhat, by adding qualifications, threats, terms of politeness, or what linguists delight in calling "whimperatives" ("Could I impose by asking . . ."). But, even in this simplest of requests, there's no single right way to say "Shut the window." Rather, there's a dynamic interplay of purpose and context; each choice tries to achieve the same purpose, having the window closed; the differences suggest something about the *context* of the request.

Rhetorical Contexts

We have a social sense of how language works, and so we have little difficulty making guesses about the contexts in which one chooses to say "Shut the window." Some choices seem overly polite; they "whimper," suggesting that the speaker feels apologetic, even less important than the listener:

2.7J   I hope you won't mind shutting the window.

2.7K   I know you're busy, but could you possibly take the time to shut that window?

Other choices are much less polite; they suggest the speaker outranks or has authority over the listener:

2.7L   Shut that window.

2.7M   From now on, I expect that window to be kept closed.

Other choices are still more indirect; they make the request without actually mentioning it.

2.7N   That window needs to be shut, doesn't it?

2.7O   You've been leaving the window open a little too much, don't you think?

(Are we correct in hearing a husband speaking to his wife, or a wife to her husband?)

We can further imagine a printed sign:

2.7P   Windows are to be kept closed.

And we can even imagine a context where the request might not be stated at all:

2.7Q "It's quite cold in here, Jeeves."
"I'll shut the window, madam."

This sort of exercise in choice should be enough to do away with a static sense of *the* single right and proper way to express a message. The best way to say "Shut the window" depends on context—on who your listener is, what your relationship with the listener is, where you are, how you want to present yourself. Rhetoric is choice in a context.

Problem Three. A first exercise in rhetorical choice Find at least ten ways to express one of the messages below. Be prepared to discuss what each choice suggests about the context of the message.

   a. Hey, buddy, can you spare a quarter?

   b. What a groovy pad!

   c. The repast was, quite simply, divine.

   d. These are the times that try men's souls.

   e. Don't you think it's a little too expensive?   ■

The Rhetorical Triangle as Context

At a basic level, the context of rhetoric can be captured with a model of any communication, from a poem of lasting value to a simple request: A speaker or writer presents a message to an audience or reader. This model is commonly called the *rhetorical triangle;* it's shown in Figure 2.1.

   The rhetorical triangle is a very simple model—one that we will eventually replace with a more complicated one. But it gives a first framework for thinking about writing and reading. It can explain our reading, and it can help us to generate ideas for writing. In more formal terms, the rhetorical triangle is both an *explanatory model* and a *generative model.*

   As an *explanatory model,* the rhetorical triangle clarifies what goes on as we communicate. We adapt our messages to our audiences: A lecture on Einstein's $E = mc^2$ would take one form as a college lecture, another form as a talk for twelve-year-olds, another form as a popular television talk show. We present ourselves differently for different audiences: We are one person in a college classroom, another person in front of twelve-year-olds, still another person on television. Similarly, as readers or audience, we adjust our expectations to what we're viewing or watching. We expect one sort of humor on *Happy Days* and another sort on *Three's Company.* We expect one kind of reading from the

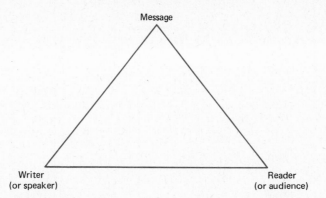

FIGURE 2.1   The Rhetorical Triangle

newspaper, a second from a college textbook, and a third from an adventure novel.

We can carry this explanatory model one step further, for we can picture each point of the triangle as serving as a source for persuading others—the *message* can be persuasive by offering *good reasons;* this is the area of *logical argument.* Be persuaded by this message because it's the best thing to do.

2.7R   Don't you think it would be more comfortable in here if we closed that window?

The *audience* can be persuaded by *popular appeal;* this is the area of *emotional argument.* Be persuaded by this message because everyone else is persuaded by it.

2.7S   Since our country is faced with an energy crisis, we should all pitch in and keep the windows closed to conserve heat.

The speaker can be persuasive by his or her authority or background. This is the area of *personal argument,* of what's generally called *ethical appeal,* from the Greek *ethos,* "character." Such an appeal can take the form of authority: Do this because I say so.

2.7T   Johnny, shut that window immediately, and then return to your seat.

(We should immediately recognize the context of this message: the context of *school.*) A personal argument can also be based on the speaker's wisdom or background.

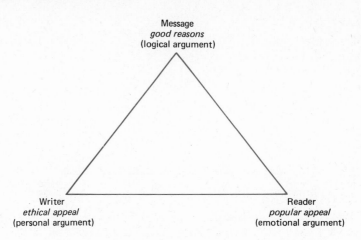

FIGURE 2.2 Arguments within the Rhetorical Triangle

2.7U I've been in the heating and cooling business for twenty-eight years, and my guess is that you will keep this house a lot cooler in the summer if you'd shut the windows in the daytime.

Thus we can refine our model by adding the arguments available to reader, message, and writer, as shown in Figure 2.2.

We can see these three forms of appeal at work in all writing—in the "mere rhetoric" of most advertising, for example. Some advertisements stress the popular appeal—often called "the bandwagon argument." "We're the Pepsi generation"; "I'm a Pepper, you're a Pepper, he's a Pepper too"; "You've come a long way, baby." All these slogans ask the audience to join a group of popular people, to jump on the bandwagon. A brandy advertisement from a 1979 issue of *Newsweek* similarly stresses the qualities of the reader:

2.8 Makes a rich man pour. E&J Brandy. Rich. Rare. Remarkably smooth.

Other advertisements stress personal appeal. Most obviously, a personal appeal offers a famous person who endorses a product—one thinks of quarterback Joe Namath in pantyhose a few years ago, or Catherine Deneuve endorsing a perfume. "We're number two, but we try harder," insists a car rental company. Another brandy advertisement in the same issue of *Newsweek* offers a statement by a speaker; it seeks to persuade you by stressing his integrity:

2.9 "Splash our brandy with soda. Its smooth, pleasing taste comes through sip after sip. And only we make the Christian Brothers Brandy. Our tradition of quality is your assurance that the taste is always good—light, mellow, and smooth—any way it's served." (signed) Brother Timothy F. S. C. Cellarmaster

Another advertisement in the same issue, by the NBC radio network, offers facts to persuade; it offers good reasons for advertising on radio.

2.10 Adults, 18 plus, spend almost as much time listening to radio (3 hours, 27 minutes per day) as they do watching the picture tube (4 hours, 9 minutes per day) and much much more time than they spend with other media such as newspapers (37 minutes daily) and magazines (20 minutes daily).

Thus the rhetorical triangle has a sort of "consumer affairs" value for the reader. It helps us ask "What kind of appeal am I being presented with, and why should I consider this message?"

Problem Four. Appeals in advertising Collect three advertisements— either newspaper or magazine advertisements that you can tear out or television advertisements that you can summarize in a few sentences. One of the three ads should center on personal appeal, another should center on popular appeal, and the third should center on logical appeal. (Of course, all three appeals will be present, in one way or another, in all ads; try to find ads that emphasize one appeal over the others.) For each, explain the appeal that you think it emphasizes and why—in no more than a sentence or two. ■

The rhetorical triangle is also a *generative model* for the writer. By the term "generative model" we mean that the rhetorical triangle forms questions for the writer that can lead to arguments, strategies, and appeals. It generates ideas. The rhetorical triangle generates three obvious questions:

- Who are my readers?
- How will I present myself?
- What is my message?

And, since our model is a dynamic model, it generates questions by playing the parts of the triangle against each other:

- Out of all the arguments available to support this message, which would be most effective for this audience?

■ What attitude should I adopt toward my message? Why would that attitude be effective for my audience? (A question of *tone.*)

■ What attitude should I adopt toward my audience? Why would that attitude be an effective way to carry this message? (A question of *voice.*)

Our last two questions, those of *tone* and *voice,* are important enough to deserve full treatment in the next chapter, "Voice, Tone, and the Writer's Stance." We'll concern ourselves here with message, audience, and their interaction.

The *message* of a piece of writing would seem to be quite simple: The message is what it says it is. But things aren't that simple. After all, we've seen twenty ways to convey the message "Shut the window" already in this chapter. In the next we'll explore, among other things, cases in which "He's a nice guy" can mean "No, he's not." And, as we saw in the screenplay of Woody Allen's *Manhattan,* professional writers seem remarkably willing to change courses in midstream, moving to create a new message from the one they began with.

The *audience* of a piece of writing is its reader (or readers). Much of the informal writing we do has very specific audiences in mind—a note to a roommate pinned on a door, a letter to a friend, an article in the student newspaper. Some formal writing assignments specify the readers, or imagined readers—as do our assignments at the end of this chapter. Classroom assignments often have a single reader—the instructor—who may be reading the paper in part to arrive at a grade for it. The artificiality of this last case—the instructor as reader—is discussed at the end of this chapter, under "implications for the writer." We might note, however, that the instructor reading a student theme acts as a "representative reader." That is, the instructor doesn't merely say "What do I personally think of this?" (although that's part of any reader's response), but rather "How good is this?" The instructor thus reads neutrally, as a member of what we call the "universal audience."

The *universal audience* is the implied reader of any writing that is not directed at a specific group of people. We can think of the universal audience as all intelligent, fair-minded people of good will. This universal audience of print is not quite the same as the "audience" implied, say, by television advertisements—the audience of print is more concerned with "good reasons" than with musical production numbers or endorsements by celebrities. The universal audience of print recognizes and rejects arguments that are false or incomplete, but it is persuaded by reasonable arguments. The universal audience is, of course, a convenient fiction, but it is a useful one for the developing writer, who may tend often to view his audience too narrowly—as this instructor or that instructor.

The relationship of message and audience is a dynamic one, for a shift in audience often leads to a corresponding shift in the way a message is presented, the strategies that are used to persuade. We might show this dynamic relationship by turning again to advertising, this time to two ads adjusting a message for two different audiences. The first advertisement, directed at a general audience, appeared in *Newsweek* as a quarter-page ad, with an illustration showing the front of a cassette tape recorder:

2.11 *Big Name Recording Star* AKAI cassette decks are known world-wide for quality sound and state-of-the-art features. Including AKAI's exclusive GX Heads—guaranteed for 150,000 hours, over 17 years of play. See our wide selection of cassette decks at your AKAI dealer. . . .

There are "good reasons" here, but the primary appeal is personal: Their products are "known world-wide"; the company is a "big name recording star."

But in a second ad, this one written for the more specialized reader of *Stereo Review* magazine, the company makes a more flattering appeal to the reader, and it expands the good reasons with more technical language. This ad takes up a full page; the illustration shows fingers holding a tape head.

2.12 *Good Sound Is in Your Head* AKAI's GX Head is guaranteed for over 17 years.

What you're looking at is AKAI's exclusive GX Head.

A technical departure from any other recording/playback head design on the market today. Its composition: glass and crystal ferrite.

Imagine, if you will, a virtually wear-free head with a smooth glass face that doesn't allow dust to collect. A head that AKAI guarantees to perform for over 150,000 hours. That's 17 years of continuous, superb play.

It's a head that many audiophiles feel has set the industry's performance and durability standards. And you'll find it exclusively in AKAI cassette and reel-to-reel decks.

All of which means that to get the clean, crisp sound your head deserves, use ours.

Here the company offers more good reasons—the glass and crystal heads are a technical innovation. But they now stress audience appeal rather than personal appeal. The reader is invited to join "many audiophiles" (that is, "lovers of good audio," of good sound), and the reader is invited to share the joke comparing his good head with their good head. The company assumes that this reader will not need to be reminded of the reputation of their products.

The sort of adjustment of message to audience illustrated in these advertisements, again, is a natural enough adjustment. It's one we do without thought in speaking situations, in large part because our audience is there in front of us, and we adapt our messages to them as part of our normal social behavior. In writing, though, our audience is unseen; our readers are not in front of us. Thus the writer must imagine, even create, the readers he wishes to communicate with; the writer creates his own audience. That's a particular problem for the developing writer. One rhetorician notes that developing writers tend to be *writer-centered*, that is, focused entirely on their efforts in constructing their written messages. She suggests that writers need to become *reader-centered* at some point in the revision process, that is, focused primarily on how their message will be received. The rhetorical triangle, by providing a model of such a shift in focus, helps us to think consciously about our reader's needs; it refines the questions we ask ourselves as writers. Thus it is a generative model for the writer.

Problem Five. The rhetorical triangle as a generative model The problems below are not writing problems as such, but they are problems in communication, and you may find the solutions by visualizing the problems in the terms of the rhetorical triangle. Write out answers if your instructor suggests.

a. An older man began to have difficulty in hearing. He found a large plastic button and placed it prominently in his ear, with a cord running down into his coat. He found his hearing improved, and concluded that the button made an excellent hearing aid. How can you explain this curious result?[2]

b. In 1904, all Europe became fascinated by the wonderful abilities of Clever Hans, an eight-year-old stallion that was able to communicate with people by tapping its hoof. Hans was able to solve mathematics problems by tapping out the answers, and he could also tap out answers in words, using a code in which the letter *a* was one tap, the letter *b* two taps, and so on. After exhaustive tests, a group of thirteen scientists and experts issued a report stating that Clever Hans was indeed responding in human language, that there was no trickery involved. Only later did another scientist find the true explanation for Clever Hans' abilities. What was it?[3]

c. Eskimos need to kill seals in the winter for food and clothing. Seals have to keep holes open in the ice, to breathe through, and the Eskimos try to spear them when they come up for air. The problem is that seals hear quite well through the water, and they go to another breathing hole when they hear a hunter approach one. How would you solve this problem?[4] (Note: Obvious solutions are ruled out—crawling up to the hole, for example, or trying to close all the holes but one—and your answer should make use only of the technology available to primitive Eskimos.) This is a particularly difficult problem—you may want to compare answers as a class. ■

The Larger Contexts of Rhetoric

Beyond the immediate interaction of writers, message, and reader are the larger contexts of rhetoric. It's easy enough to see, for example, that messages change form with time. In the 1930s, one cigarette company proudly claimed "More doctors smoke Camels than any other brand," and another used the slogan "Not a cough in a carload"—appeals that disappeared as evidence of the danger of cigarettes accumulated.

Similarly, a scientist might communicate with the same audience—fellow scientists—in one way at lunch and in a quite different way in a scientific paper. In fact, here's a rather clear example of that difference in context. One of the most famous written sentences of modern biology is given in 2.13; it's been called "one of the great understatements of all time."

2.13 It has not escaped our notice that the specific pairing we have postulated immediately suggests a possible copying mechanism for the genetic material.

James Watson and Francis Crick, "Molecular Structure of Nucleic Acids"

In private, in a Cambridge restaurant called the "Eagle," one of the authors of the paper spoke quite differently:

2.14 Thus I felt slightly queasy when at lunch Francis winged into the Eagle to tell everyone within hearing distance that we had found the secret of life.

James Watson, *The Double Helix*

In one context, a confident "We have found the secret of life"; in a written scientific paper, a carefully guarded "possible copying mechanism for genetic material."

A full list of these larger contexts would include location (a scientific

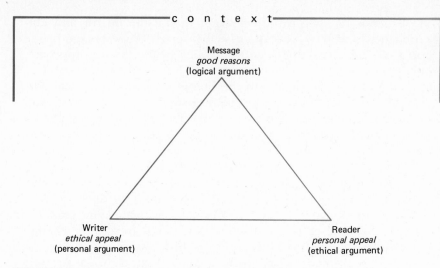

FIGURE 2.3 The Larger Contexts of the Rhetorical Triangle

paper or a restaurant), time (the 1930s or the 1980s), and occasion ("I love you too, Margaret," the TV hero says brusquely, "but there's no time to talk about that now," and he turns to fire another shot at the gangsters who surround them). We can expand our model by placing the rhetorical triangle under a general heading, "Contexts," as shown in Figure 2.3.

The contexts of communication account for the issues presented in problem four. The man with a button in his ear did indeed hear better—not because a button is a good hearing aid, but because his listeners, thinking he was wearing a hearing aid, naturally spoke louder. The man, neglecting the larger contexts of communication, came to a false conclusion.

Oskar Pfungst, the graduate student who solved the problem of Clever Hans, may not have had the rhetorical triangle in mind when he found the answer, but he himself was clever enough to think about the audience involved. It turned out that Clever Hans was not a very smart horse—he couldn't use language—but he was a very sympathetic horse, and he knew he would be rewarded when he stopped tapping at the right point. Clever Hans was very good at sensing the audience's subconscious reactions, and when they indicated, by slight body movements, that the right point was reached, the horse stopped tapping. When given a problem with an answer hidden from the audience, Clever Hans was unable to respond.

Similarly, the Eskimo people solved their seal-hunting problem by thinking about the seal's point of view. In our terms, they considered their audience. (We won't give away the solution, but we can give one more hint: The solution involves team-work.)

Communication Codes

Before writing was invented, a person wishing to communicate with another person had, at most, two choices: He could talk to the person, or he could ask a third party to take the message to the person. The development of writing added another *communication code,* the code of print, and the technological inventions of the last hundred years have dramatically multiplied the codes, or media, of communication. How do you say "I love you"?

- write a personal letter
- print it in a book or pamphlet
- announce it over the radio
- send a sound tape recording
- send a videotape recording
- announce it over television
- use the telephone
- send a telegram

- hire a skywriter
- rent a billboard
- put an ad in the personal columns of the newspaper
- carve it on a tree
- send a mailgram
- make a movie
- tell someone

Such a media explosion can still be approached through the rhetorical triangle: A person sends a message to an audience. But note that each communication code, each medium, has its own internal limits and its own strengths, even its own internal logic. Skywriters can't handle very long messages, for example, and messages carved on trees tend, for different reasons, also to be rather short. We add communication code to our developing model, in Figure 2.4, and we'll shortly turn our attention to the code that concerns us most, the code of print.

Purposes and Goals in Writing

Writers communicate for a purpose, to achieve a goal. We can clarify purpose in writing by turning back to the rhetorical triangle—is the writer primarily interested in message, reader, or writer? We can clarify the goals of the writer by turning to a traditional image—the open hand of harmony and the closed fist of truth.

Purpose in Writing

Writing may be directed toward the reader—it intends to move the readers to action, to convince them of something, to make them behave

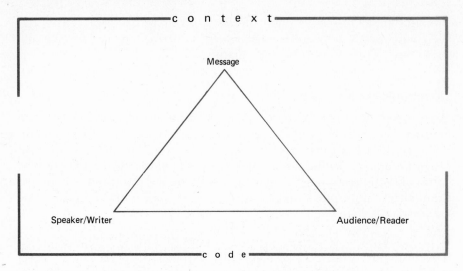

FIGURE 2.4 Communication Codes and the Rhetorical Triangle

in some way. Such writing does business in the world, and, accordingly, we call it *transactional writing,* since the purpose is to transact business. Transactional writing includes writing designed to convey information (traditionally called expository writing)—directions for putting a bicycle together, a college textbook, a student paper explaining or analyzing a subject—and writing designed to persuade (traditionally called argumentative writing)—a political speech, advertising in general, a student letter to a newspaper arguing for a point of view or suggesting a solution to a problem.

Other writing may focus on the message itself. It will be self-contained, without reference to what's happening in the world. We call such writing *poetic writing,* and it includes most of what we think of as imaginative literature—poems, plays, short stories, and novels.

Finally, the writer may look at her own experience, her own feelings and emotions. Such writing turns toward the speaker; we call it *expressive writing* because it expresses personal experiences and emotions.

This framework is also a dynamic one, for the purposes of writing may mix together. A poem may affect a reader, as well as have a pleasing form. It might be intricately tied to the writer's emotions. A piece of descriptive writing might turn toward the writer's feelings (expressive), toward the shape of the description itself (poetic), or toward the audience, to convince them of a particular view (transactional). We add these purposes to our developing model in Figure 2.5.

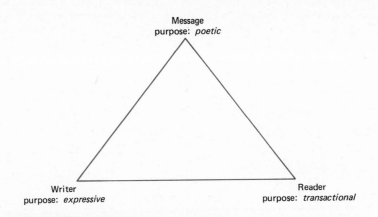

Message
purpose: *poetic*

Writer
purpose: *expressive*

Reader
purpose: *transactional*

FIGURE 2.5 Purpose and the Rhetorical Triangle

Truth and Harmony as the Writer's Goals

In classical Greece, rhetoricians pictured the speaker as approaching an audience with one of two gestures, an open hand or a closed fist. The "open hand" was a gesture of agreement, an invitation for the audience to join the speaker in a group decision; it signified the goal of *harmony*. The "closed fist" set the speaker apart from the audience; he promised to deliver unpleasant facts or views, truths which the audience would not want to hear. The closed fist signified the goal of *truth*. In the ideal world envisioned by true rhetoric, the goals of truth and harmony would merge, speaker and audience moving harmoniously toward truth.

In actual practice, in public speaking in ancient Greece and in writing today, speakers and writers must generally choose between the goals of truth and harmony. Politicians, for example, must balance the needs of the real world (truth) against the beliefs of their voters (harmony). Too often politicians choose harmony instead of truth, but John F. Kennedy's *Profiles of Courage* is a series of biographies of politicians who had the courage to choose truth as a goal. Similarly, the developing writer may choose to hide personal feelings (truth), in the hopes of giving the instructor what the instructor expects. As Linus says in the comic strip *Peanuts*, after being rewarded for a "Summer Vacation" theme, "As the years go by, you learn what sells."

Thus we must recognize false goals as well as true goals, just as we recognize a "mere rhetoric" paralleling a true rhetoric. Instead of the legitimate goal of harmony, the writer may sink to *flattery*, speaking to the worst feelings of the audience. The rhetoric of truth, in politics and

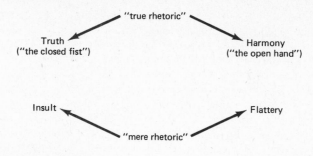

FIGURE 2.6 Rhetorical Goals

elsewhere, can sink to the rhetoric of *insult*. True rhetoric and "mere rhetoric" lead to quite different goals. These are shown in Figure 2.6.

SUMMARY

We began by isolating a "true rhetoric," distinct from the "mere rhetoric," as the term is commonly used. We explained the uses of that true rhetoric—as a protective device against the mere rhetoric around us, as a useful personal skill, and as an essential part of a democracy.

We then developed a "dynamic model of rhetoric," centered on the key terms of *choice* in a *context* for a *purpose*. This model begins with the *rhetorical triangle* of *writer, reader,* and *message.* The rhetorical triangle serves as an explanatory model for readers, isolating the appeals presented to them, and it serves as a generative model for writers, helping them to ask questions to produce arguments and strategies.

We noted the larger contexts and codes of communication, and we discussed the writer's purpose (*expressive, poetic,* and *transactional*) and goal (*truth* and *harmony,* each with its false counterpart, *insult* and *flattery*).

IMPLICATIONS FOR THE WRITER

The larger implications of the model of rhetoric sketched in this chapter will be explored through the rest of this text; this chapter is merely an introduction to the dynamics of communicating in print. But we do need to discuss three preliminary implications: the nature of print as code (since two of our chapters begin with the heading "The Print Code"); the nature of school as a context (since we want to identify an artificial kind of "writing for school"), and the classical "offices" of rhetoric (since they provide the formative principle of the organization of this text).

The Code of Print

In March of 1870, the elder brother of the American poet Walt Whitman, Jesse Whitman, died in an insane asylum, and the poet's mother wrote him the following letter:

> **2.15** o Walt aint it sad to think the poor soul hadent a friend near him in his last moments   and to think he had a paupers grave   i know it makes no difference but if he could have been buried decently. . . . i was thinking of him more lately than common   i wish Walter you would write to Jeff and hanna that he is dead   i will write to george   i feel very sad of course if he has done ever so wrong he was my first born   but gods will be done good bie Walter dear

This is a touching and effective letter: It establishes the sense of loss shared by mother and son; it lays plans for telling other relatives about the death; and it puts Jesse's death in the larger context of "God's will be done." Mrs. Whitman's simplicity, emotion, and sensitivity are clearly evident.

At the same time, though, that we as readers are touched by this letter of a hundred years ago, we are also, as readers, aware of other feelings about it, for it's clear that Mrs. Whitman is not used to communicating in print. The letter is written as an outflowing of emotion, without the formal salutation and closing of most letters. It stays entirely within the writer's verbal code (as in "aint it sad"). And it ignores most of what are usually called the conventions of print—spelling, punctuation, paragraphing. We can rewrite the letter to make it conform to the conventions of print, adding some clarifications in brackets. The result is both better, and worse, than the letter Mrs. Whitman actually wrote:

> **2.15A** Oh Walter,
> Isn't it sad to think that the poor soul hadn't a friend near him in his last moments. And isn't it sad to think that he had a pauper's grave. I know it makes no difference, but if he could have been buried decently. . . .
> I have been thinking of him more, lately, than [I did before].
> I wish, Walter, that you would write to Jeff and Hanna [and tell them] he is dead. I will write to George.
> I feel very sad, of course, Walt. [Even] if he had done ever so many wrong things, he was [still] my firstborn son. But God's Will be done.
> Good-by, Walter dear.

We've rewritten the letter to bring it closer to what we call the *print code*. The print code includes obvious features like punctuation, capitalization, and spelling; it also includes less obvious features like formal conventions (we arranged the letter to look like letters normally do), wording (we changed "aint it sad" to "isn't it sad"), and sentence idioms (notice our difficulty in translating "i was thinking of him more lately than common" into the print code).

In this case, the translation is unnecessary, even undesirable. It imposes the code of print on a private communication between two people very close to each other; it makes a private message into a public one, weakening the closeness and sorrow, the directness, of Mrs. Whitman's lament.

But most writing is aimed at a broader audience than a single person. Like a "Letter to the Editor" in a newspaper or magazine, many written messages pretend to be written to a single person, but are really more public, written for readers in general, for our "universal audience." Most of us, therefore, try to make our written messages conform to the conventions of print—we want our readers to concentrate on what we have to say, not to be distracted by surface features of our writing. We realize, of course, that these surface features, these conventions, are less important than what we have to say. We usually leave them until the last stage of writing, the proofreading stage, when we give our work a last run-through for surface detail, just as we often give ourselves a final look in the mirror before going out. Surface detail is important in the way that buttoning a shirt is important, or not eating peas with a knife. It's part of the *manners* of writing, not the matter of writing.

Indeed, we see the *print code,* as a term, encompassing far more than surface conventions. The print code includes ways of crafting sentences on paper that are different, to a degree, from our ways of crafting spoken sentences. (Though a well-written sentence will consistently identify itself as a sentence that reads well aloud.) The print code includes arrangements—paragraphs, structures of argument, patterns of organization—that don't match those of normal conversation. (Though, again, some people—good college lecturers, for example— have transferred arrangements from their writing to their formal speech. We might say they've learned to "talk in paragraphs.") The print code also includes its own methods of invention and argument; a writer we'll quote in the next chapter goes so far as to call it "a mode of thought itself." Moreover—and this is one of the major difficulties facing the developing reader/writer—the code of print has its own history, the history of the forms and structures of the written language itself. Seen in this way, the term *print code* becomes the very subject of this text.

School as a Context

Sociolinguists are people (*linguists*) who study language in its social set-ting (*socio-*). They find that people talk one way inside a school build-ing and another way outside. Schools, after all, have their own goals and responsibilities. It's not surprising that they develop their own ways of using language. Some shared language is necessary in schools, for communication involves people from widely different backgrounds. Language in school is also public language—you're "on stage," as it were, in the classroom. Moreover, many school subjects require very special vocabularies—particularly the sciences and professional schools. (A chemistry experiment, for example, wouldn't work too well if the instructions read, "Take a glass, man, and toss in some hydrochloric acid and maybe some, like, base or something . . .")

Writing classes, too, develop their own "language," partly because writing assignments are artificial: Real writing happens when writers have something they want to communicate, while school writing works by due dates and formal assignments. Too often, as a result, writing is a task rather than a process of self-discovery, and being "correct," whatever that means, becomes more important than saying something worthwhile and saying it effectively. At worst, instructors are inundated with writing that tries to say nothing at all, while saying it in the nicest way imaginable.

Ken Macrorie has coined a name for that kind of writing—the kind of writing you do for English classes when you have nothing to say. He calls it "Engfish" (because it's not really English at all, but a separate language used only for assigned papers). Consider, for example, the following first paragraph from a student theme—a made-up example, in this case, but not too far from some actual student papers we've seen:

> **2.16** Education is a major problem in our modern world of to-day. Many people are concerned about education and how to im-prove it. I am also concerned about education, and many times I have asked myself, "How can we improve education in America?" After much thought, I have decided that there are many solutions to the problem of education in our modern world of today.

Now reread the paragraph, but instead of the word "education," in-sert the word "politics." In fact, insert about any word you want in the paragraph—*unions,* or *foreign policy* or *democracy*—and it will work in about the same way. It doesn't have much to say, except how sincere the author is (and we always distrust the sincerity of people who tell us they're sincere—we suspect "flattery" rather than "harmony"), but it says it "correctly." (You can almost hear the writer counting up the words and saying, "Sixty-four words, only four hundred and thirty-six more to go.")

For Ken Macrorie, this kind of Engfish is "telling lies" in language, and he sees it as an outgrowth of the social lies we educate people to participate in:

> **2.17** Any person trying to write honestly and accurately soon finds he has already learned a hundred ways of writing falsely. As a child he spoke and wrote honestly most of the time, but when he reaches fifteen, honesty and truth come harder. The pressures of his ego are greater. He reaches for impressive language; often it is pretentious and phony.
>
> *Telling Writing*

The alternative to "telling lies" is "telling truths," and Macrorie suggests trying the "free writing" that we discussed in the last chapter as a first step toward becoming truthful with language. But, whether truthfulness is encouraged by free writing or not, the ideal of a writing course is that point where personal truth and honesty merge with the public responsibilities of the print code. At that point, the writer assumes the role assumed from a true rhetoric, a role expressed by a Roman writer as "the good man speaking well."

The "Offices" of Rhetoric: Invention, Arrangement, and Style

In chapter One, we developed one model of the writing process—prewriting, writing, and revision. The Greeks had a different model; they spoke of the "offices" of rhetoric—invention, arrangement, and style. These "offices" were like mental rooms for the Greeks, and they "saw" the speaker or writer walking from one office to the next. In the office of *invention* the speaker would find ideas—what we would now call "something to say." In the office of *arrangement*, the speaker would find an organization, a way of ordering ideas. In the office of *style*, the speaker would "dress" ideas in words.

We're aware, now, of the artificiality of this division. Dealing with style, as we saw in chapter One, can involve invention, and thinking of an idea may be inseparable from thinking of an organization to express it. But the division does provide us with a useful way of talking about writing. In fact, it provides the structure of this text. After this unit, "Starting-Points," we turn to smaller elements of arrangement, then to matters of style, then to larger elements of arrangement, and then to invention. We invert the traditional order of the Greek offices, for we began by noting that language is naturally creative; we are, all of us, "inventing" all the time.

FINAL WRITING ASSIGNMENTS

I. Programming Director You have just been appointed programming director of one of the three major television networks (choose one). You will want to redesign program offerings in prime time (8–11 P.M.; 7–10 P.M. in the midwest), creating new programs as necessary. Then you'll want to explain those decisions in three letters: a press release, explaining your changes to the public; a memo to the president of the network (one he can pass on to the Board of Directors); and a memo to your employees.

II. Political Campaign There's a reasonable chance that a political campaign is going on right now. If so, you have an excellent opportunity to watch rhetoric in action. Gather campaign literature from candidates for a particular election, and monitor speeches, television advertisements, and press conferences. Report to the class on the appeals you find, using the vocabulary presented in this chapter. You may wish to conclude your report by supporting one of the candidates, offering "good reasons" for your choice.

III. Direct Mail, Incorporated The result is always the same, a one-page letter touting a certain product to a specific list of people whose addresses your company has purchased. What keeps it interesting (for a budding rhetorician like yourself) is the variety of products and audiences, for each pairing demands a different approach. Choose one product and two audiences for direct mail letters; then compose two different letters, one directed at each of the two different audiences.

Products: an American Express card; a disposable shoe shine kit ("good for thousands of shines"); a record collection, "The History of Rock 'n' Roll" ("four records shipped to your home each month for the next seven years"); a battery-operated portable dishwasher ("the backpacker's dream"); a kit for building a tennis court in the backyard; a book series, *The Complete Home Medical Advisor.*

Audiences: members of the Alaskan Villages Regional Council; members of the PTA in Ossining, New York; members of the "Pachuko Kings" Motorcycle Club of East Los Angeles; members of the American Medical Association (all doctors); members of the faculty at Pahrump State College, Grand Forks Nebraska; members of the Jogging Club in Calgary, Canada; members of the Senior Citizens Society of Tampa, Florida; members of the Young Republicans Club of Indianapolis, Indiana; parolees from the Vermont Women's Correctional facility.

IV. The Facts of Life in Midville   It was the same answer, all the way up the line. "It's Board of Education policy, that's all. There's no need to discuss it further."

"Oh but there is need to discuss it further," you said to yourself, over and over again. Mr. Newcomb, the principal at Wheatley Elementary School, had called you into his office last month. It was Board of Education policy, he explained: Pregnant teachers had to take a leave of absence, starting at the beginning of their fifth month of pregnancy, and so you would have to give up your fourth-grade class to a substitute teacher three months before the school year ended.

"Why?" you asked incredulously. After all, you knew that class, and you knew how to work with them—a substitute couldn't do nearly as well. You could do anything any other teacher could do; a little thing like pregnancy wasn't going to slow you down. Besides, with a baby on the way, you needed the money.

It was the same answer all the way up the line—the principal, the director of the Midville school district, even the member of the Board of Education who was willing to talk to you. "It's Board of Education policy, that's all. There's no need to discuss it further."

When pushed, they would offer reasons, but not *good reasons*. The students would make jokes about a pregnant teacher, they said. Or parents would complain. Or other teachers would want to teach when they were pregnant. "It's better to keep the facts of life away from fourth-graders," Mr. Newcomb had said.

After thinking it over, you made the decision: to call for a public hearing by the Board of Education. Now it was time to put that decision into action. You started your list: 1. a letter to the Board of Education protesting the policy and asking for a public hearing. This would have to be a short letter, outlining the reasons for your request, and it would have to be a public letter, one that you could release to the newspapers and television stations; 2. a letter to the parents of your students, explaining what you were doing and why—a page at most; 3. a letter to your parents—they'd better hear the news from you, before the press picked it up, for they were a conservative couple and wouldn't normally approve of questioning authority. You thought another minute and added another item to the list: 4. you'd better write out a statement to read to your fourth-grade class, just so you got it right. They would need to understand what you were doing; otherwise they would pick up—and misunderstand—rumors on the playground. This statement should be short, very simple, and very supportive of them, the kids.

V. Working with Goals and Codes Review the AKAI magazine advertisements cited as examples 2.11 and 2.12; they are the raw material for this assignment, which asks you to recreate the message of those advertisements in a different code and context and with a conscious goal. Choose one of the "codes and contexts" and one of the "goals" from the lists below:

Codes and contexts: a 60-second radio commercial to be read by the disc jockey of a "top 40" AM radio station in New York City; a 60-second prerecorded radio commercial to be played over the FM classical music station in· Dallas, Texas; a 60-second prerecorded television commercial to be shown on prime-time national TV; a 60-second television commercial to be shown on a late-night rock program; a 60-second television commercial for a local hi-fi store to be shown on the late-night movie on a local channel in Wheeling, West Virginia; a half-page magazine advertisement to appear in the program notes for the Santa Fe Opera Company; a full-page magazine advertisement to appear in the rock magazine *Creem.*

Goals: truth ("the closed fist"); harmony ("the open hand"); insult; flattery. You may need to make up more information about the product, but do not indicate the code, context, or goal of your advertisement. Your audience, the class, may be asked to guess those from your presentation.

For a magazine advertisement, you may wish to create a complete ad, pasting in a photograph, or you may simply wish to indicate the photograph in brackets, and present the text of the ad; for the radio commercial to be read, you should provide a script; for the prerecorded radio and television commercials, you may either create your own (assuming you have access to an audio or video tape recorder), or provide a scenario plus a script (a scenario is a brief outline of sound effects, pictured action, and so on). (Note also that each context implies some limits on your imaginary budget: You might want to have a song composed, and played by the Saint Louis Symphony for the national TV commercial, but you could not afford such luxuries in the TV commercial for the local station.)

FOR FURTHER READING

Paul Watzlawick's *How Real is Real?* (New York: Random House, 1976) is a witty exploration of how people communicate, an unabashedly entertaining book by a psychiatrist/philosopher. Equally entertaining are two books on communications media, Edmund Carpenter's *Oh! What a Blow that Phantom Gave Me!* (New York: Bantam, 1974), an anthropologist's look at media in primitive and modern cultures, and Marshall McLuhan and Quentin Fiore's *The Medium*

Is the Message (New York: Bantam, 1967), a simplified version of McLuhan's thesis that "the medium is the message."

Robert Cirino's *Power to Persuade: Mass Media and the News* (New York: Bantam, 1974) offers a series of case studies of media decisions, with suggested activities.

NOTES

1. Of course, we all have a natural, "knowing-how," ability to use language to persuade. All peoples have "rhetorics," persuasive ways of speaking, and the four-year-old pleading to stay up an extra hour is using language to persuade as surely as the politician plying us for our vote. The "true rhetoric" of the Greek tradition assumes that this "art of rhetoric" can be transmitted by formal study, as a "knowing-about" skill. (For the difference between "knowing how" and "knowing about," see chapter One.)
2. Cited in James L. Kinneavy, *A Theory of Discourse* (Englewood Cliffs, N.J.: Prentice-Hall, 1971), p. 287.
3. Paul Watzlawick, *How Real Is Real?* (New York: Random House, 1976), pp. 30–33.
4. A. D. Moore, *Invention, Discovery, and Creativity* (New York: Doubleday, 1969), pp. 9–11.

3

Voice, Tone, and the Writer's Stance

It is probably no mere historical accident that the word *person*, in its first meaning, is a mask. It is rather a recognition of the fact that everyone is always and everywhere, more or less consciously, playing a role. . . . It is in these roles that we know each other; it is in these roles that we know ourselves.

ROBERT EZRA PARK

We introduced the rhetorical triangle of writer, reader, and message in the last chapter by asking you to take a simple message and restate it in six different ways. It's possible for you to do that because you have developed a *social sense* of language in action, a social sense that's active all the time. Certainly it's common to hear people use expressions like "I didn't like the way she said that," or "I didn't like his tone of voice." And consider the social skill you use as you tune across a radio dial, accurately identifying each station by the "voice" of the announcer—the formal voice of the announcer on a classical music station, the muted voice of an "easy listening" station, the down-home voice of a country music station, the frenetic patter of a rock disc jockey. In ordinary speech, then, we communicate by gesture, attitude, and tone of voice, as well as by what we say.

THE WRITER'S STANCE

This chapter asks you to transfer your social sense of language to the written page. Writers do present themselves to readers, for behind a

written page is someone choosing words and connecting them, someone deciding to be playful or serious, understated or enthusiastic. Thus
we can return to the rhetorical triangle of chapter Two, adding arrows
to identify *voice, tone,* and *stance,* as shown in Figure 3.1. By *voice,* we
mean the way a writer presents herself to her audience; by *tone,* we
mean the writer's attitude to her subject. Together, voice and tone make
up the writer's *stance,* her solution to the rhetorical problem of adapting a message to an audience.

We draw these terms, by analogy, from ordinary speaking into writing, and we might clarify them with further analogies. We might think
of the stance of a boxer or a ballet dancer, or the stance of a batter in
a baseball game. We might think of the "voices" adopted by comedians
like Lily Tomlin or Richard Pryor or Cheech and Chong, who create
new characters by shifting voice and mannerism. We might think of
the tone a parent uses to chastise a child for a prank, then think of the
parent using a different tone to laugh about the prank with a friend.

Of course, the task of a writer who reaches his audience through
print is much less natural than the task of a speaker, in part because
the writer has so little going for him—he can't wink or shrug his shoulders, he can't stretch out his syllables or chuckle over them or speak
loudly or softly. (He can try to SHOUT! by using punctuation, but
such attempts never quite work the way they do in speech.) All the
writer can do is manipulate words on the page.

On the other hand, the writer has advantages in being hidden behind the page. The audience has no clue to the writer's size, her color,
her accent, even how serious she is—no clues, that is, except what can
be inferred from the words on the page. As a result, writers can trick
audiences: They can sound confident, self-assured, and forceful, even
though they might be weak, unsure, and afraid. Writers can project the
voice they want to project. In the world of print, at least, you can be
anything you want to be.

TRYING ON SOME VOICES

One way to develop a sense of voice, tone, and stance in writing is to
try fitting into a number of different written voices, just as you might
try on several suits in a department store. You don't have to "buy" the
voices we'll present—some of them are unattractive, and we don't want
to force you into the straitjacket of an uncomfortable voice. But the
experience can be useful for the developing writer, for it can make you
more open to the choices you make as writer. Moreover, you should
become more aware of the many voices of print, as reader as well as
writer, and thus more alert to the voices you meet in the writing of

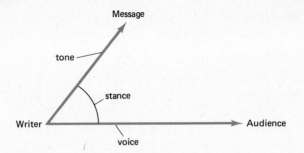

FIGURE 3.1   Voice, Tone, and the Writer's Stance

others. Above all, the experience should underscore our dynamic model of rhetoric, sketched in chapter Two, for the writer's search for a voice and a stance is an active interplay of message and audience.

The Bubblegum Voice

Rock music aimed at very young teenagers is often called "bubblegum music," and what we call the *bubblegum voice* is the voice of magazines that deal with this music, magazines with titles like *16, Tiger Beat, Flip,* and *Fave.* You'll probably remember seeing them clustered together at the magazine stand, even if you've never looked inside one. You'll hear that voice speaking clearly in the sentences that follow, picked almost at random from an outdated collection of such magazines.

3.1   HI! I'm Betsy Barton, FUNTIME's Editor. There are several changes in this issue of FUNTIME and I want so much to know what you think of them! So please, *please* tell me?

16 Funtime

3.2   Whenever Michael Gray's in a "quacky" mood, he heads for the pond at Knott's Berry Farm in Anaheim, Calif. for a "ducky" day with some feathered friends.

Flip Teen Magazine

3.3 And it will be a *new* David Cassidy you'll be seeing—confident, mature, nobody's tool and nobody's fool!

16

3.4 Wayne is still into Western style clothes and he's got some neat Levis with brass studs on the sides he wears around a lot.

Tiger Beat

3.5 But Hazel is a sweet and considerate girl, not a typical "spoiled brat" type of "poor little rich girl."

Spec and Loving Fashions

That's not a "hard" voice to understand, now is it? Gee, we could even write that way ourselves, couldn't we? Wouldn't that make a "fun" book to read? Please, *please* tell us! Golly, here's more:

3.6 BRR—baby, it's cold outside! But don't fret, pet, cos at your friendly neighborhood newsstand is a package of goodies so *red-hot* it's gonna *warm* you all over! All you gotta do is snuggle up to the *blazin'* new *April* issue of *16 Magazine*—on sale now—and you'll just melt with delicious delight. . . . Warm your *hands,* your *hearts,* every *inch* of you by picking up the new April issue of *16!*

16 Funtime

We sense, as readers, an intense voice in such passages, as if the writers were trying to be close, almost physically close, to their readers. It's a sweet voice, and it seems purposely feminine (although you might recognize a similarly sweet, but quite male, voice in the patter of a top forty radio disc jockey). We've picked passages from different magazines, but we sense a common writing stance, the same tone (excitement, awe, enthusiasm) and the same voice (sweet, sincere, intense). We can't tell, of course, whether these writers are all sweet young females who are very close to their readers—they simply manage to sound that way. (We imagine the author as a paunchy middle-aged man with a day's growth of beard, sitting behind a typewriter with a cigar in his mouth.)

These magazines are written for an audience of middle-class girls, perhaps nine to fourteen years old, essentially prepubescent girls. This audience wants to be informed of the goings-on of those people whose records they buy and whose TV shows they watch; they want to be into the "real" life of stardom and excitement and, golly, love! And that's essentially what the voice of the magazine gives them: It's close, it's chatty, it's playful; it brings with it an aura of excitement and intensity.

Of course, it's not an attractive voice. The intensity wears thin after a sentence or two, at least for adult readers. Moreover, we should recognize that the bubblegum voice, so consciously girlish in tone, is a sexist voice, a voice that exploits our sense that there's somehow a girl's way of approaching experience, implying that the "girl's way" is not as important or serious as the "man's way." Perhaps people reading the magazine need to be introduced to that stereotype as they enter a sexist society; perhaps, on the other hand, they are victimized by that stereotype. Fortunately, most writers, male and female, outgrow the bubblegum voice, and we return to it now as a way to exercise our response to voice in writing, with a conscious sense of play.

Problem One. The bubblegum voice   Here's the first half of a feature article from *16 Magazine*. Read it with special attention to the "voice" of the writer.

> **RICK—red-hot 'n X-rated!** Ouch! Better watch your step 'round racy Rick Springfield these days—cos he's gettin' so-o-o scorching red-hot that if you aren't careful, you just *may* get burned!
>
> Just what is happening to this seemingly sweet 'n sensitive dreamy-eyed musician that *may* be giving him an "X" rating? . . . Take a look at some of the "X-rated" facts of Rick's life—then decide if you can handle his kind of style!
>
> RICK IS . . .
>
> **X-travagant!** His clothes are one-of-a-kind originals, made especially for him. One hand-made sweater, for instance, cost him more than most people need to live on for a whole week! But he's also quite extravagant and generous with the *presents* he gives to others—he sends his parents, brother and friends gifts galore anytime something in a store window strikes his fancy! He's the flashy type—the girls he likes don't necessarily have to be that way. And if he likes a girl—you can *bet* she's going to be treated *X-travagantly!*
>
> **X-troverted!** Rick is *not* the shy type! He's not the kind to sit and analyze every little thing he says or that's said to him. He's not the least bit hesitant to "open up" to people with whatever's on his mind! He lets it all hang out—his mind, his opinions and most of all his heart!

The article continues with four more headings, "X-pressive!" "X-otic!" "X-perienced!" and "X-traordinary!" Write paragraphs to complete those headings, using the same voice as the rest of the article. Feel quite free to invent details about "racy Rick"—to elaborate, even lie, in order to focus solely on writing in an identifiable voice.   ■

Bubblegum writing looks different from ordinary writing, even as reprinted here, without the photographs and layout of the original. It uses several devices to make print look like or imitate speech:

- It uses lots of questions, doesn't it? These seem an attempt to talk to the reader, to make her feel part of the story.
- It uses funny spellings for words (*cos, so-o-o, gotta*) to make them closer to spoken words.

■ It's *just* "chock-full" of quotes, italics, and exclamation points. These devices help to bring into writing the sounds of spoken language; they also suggest that the bubblegum writer is a bit uneasy about words, thus calling attention to them.

3.7 Take a look at some of the "X-rated" facts of Rick's life. . . .

The bubblegum voice also plays with words:

■ It uses rhyme ("don't fret, pet").
■ It plays with the sounds of words ("delicious delight"; "sweet 'n sensitive").
■ It uses puns (a "ducky day" is a day with ducks).
■ It uses slang and clichés ("poor little rich girl").

Thus we might summarize our reaction to the bubblegum voice by saying that its controlling purpose is to move right off the page, literally to talk to the reader, as if reader and writer were sitting together, giggling, on the reader's bed. It doesn't work, for most adult readers; we're put off by the fake intensity and the saccharine sweetness. We sense a huckster, a manipulator, rather than a close friend.

Our negative reaction is instructive, for it echoes a point about speech and writing made in the last chapter. Writing is not simply, or only, speech written down. That's what the bubblegum voice tries to achieve, written-down speech, and its failure suggests that adult writing must aim at a more complex voice.

The Neutral Voice of Journalism

If the bubblegum voice is loud, subjective, and excited, the voice that speaks to us in the news columns of the daily paper is flat, unemotional, and objective. "Just the facts, ma'am," as a television detective used to say.

3.8 A fire of undetermined origin destroyed an apartment building on East First Street yesterday, Fire Chief Ed Davis reported. According to Chief Davis, the fifty-seven elderly residents of the building were evacuated safely, although most of their belongings were destroyed in the fire, which spread upward from the basement of the older building.

Damages were estimated at $3,000,000 by insurance claims adjusters at the scene of the fire.

Seven firemen and three residents were taken to General Hospital for smoke inhalation. A hospital spokesman said today that all patients were in good condition.

Chief Davis said that arson was "a distinct possibility" and that investigators will begin searching the debris for evidence today.

County documents listed the owner of the building as the Urban Management Corporation. Richard "Rippling" Waters, chief shareholder in the corporation, was unavailable for comment.

(Fire Department records indicate that seven inner-city apartments owned by Mr. Waters, through three separate holding companies, have been destroyed by fire within the last three years.)

Most of us are experienced newspaper readers, and we have no trouble making some guesses about this imaginary story. The building sounds like a slum tenement, and we have reason to suspect the owner, "Rippling" Waters, of setting fire to the tenement to collect the insurance. But we make those conclusions ourselves; they're not, strictly speaking, in the story. The story only gives the facts, and every fact has a source. Are the patients in good condition? —Well, a "hospital spokesman" said they were. Is arson a "distinct possibility"? —Well, those were Chief Davis's exact words. In part, this care with sources stems from legal reasons: Newspapers may report public information and may quote the opinions of others, but they cannot directly accuse the property owner of a crime, even though they may invite the reader to do so. A false or damaging accusation is libel, and the legal penalties are heavy.

But the understated factuality of newspaper reporting gives news stories a special voice, a voice that is often quite complex. We'll focus on one aspect of that voice, the opening sentence—what journalists call the "lead sentence." Here are some typical examples from wire service reports.

3.9 MANAGUA, NICARAGUA—President Anastasio Somoza, declaring again he is not resigning, called a meeting of Congress in his bomb-proof bunker Saturday here as his national guard reported advances against guerrilla forces in nearby Masaya.

Associated Press

3.10 WASHINGTON—Twenty years after being exposed to radiation at a 1957 Nevada nuclear weapons test nicknamed Smokey, nine of 22 rhesus monkeys developed cancer, according to an Atlanta, Ga., researcher.

Washington Post News Service

3.11 COLUMBUS, OHIO—Ohio's mental health director said Saturday that deficient methods of analysis have caused distortion in a report by the state's Legislative Budget Office on his department's personnel contract practices.

Associated Press

The choice of "fact" and the presentation color the report significantly: "Again" reminds us that President Somoza has been under pressure to resign, and "declaring" is weaker than, say, "promising"; the "bomb-proof bunker" adds a hint of danger, as does "nearby" added to Masaya. "Guerrilla forces" is a much stronger phrase than other choices— "dissident rabble," "rebel bands," "leftist revolutionaries."

Seen from this perspective, the neutrality of journalism becomes as powerfully rhetorical as any other writing. Choices are made to persuade, as well as to inform, the reader.

A second question to ask is, "Where's the reporter?" The mythical reporter in our fire story must have done a good bit of legwork. She must have visited the fire, and talked there with the Fire Chief, the survivors, and the insurance claims investigator. She must have called the hospital for a report. She obviously reviewed County and Fire Department records, she probably reviewed newspaper files, and she may have made return calls to the Fire Chief. Moreover, our reporter must have had feelings of her own as she wrote the story. That legwork and those feelings are consciously filtered out of the story—"just the facts, ma'am." This is a significant limitation—the writer is missing—and it has led to the appearance of a new voice for reporting the news, the voice of the "new journalism."

The Voice of the "New Journalism"

In 1971, homosexuals in New York City organized a protest march. The *New York Times'* lead sentence reported the event in the restrained, factual voice of traditional journalism:

> **3.13** About 5000 homosexual men and women marched in a happy parade from Greenwich Village to Central Park yesterday afternoon in a demonstration of gay pride and unity.
>
> Paul H. Montgomery, *New York Times*

Reporter Tom Burke from rock magazine *Rolling Stone* also filed a report; his "lead sentence," whatever else we may think of it, marks a new approach to journalism:

> **3.14** Don't misunderstand, they aren't your traditional Hilton rubes, this Pasadena burgher and the little woman, they have viewed with compassion the Louds and wouldn't be caught dead in New York in madras shorts or cameras on straps like talismans, but this, *this,* it does give them pause and they freeze at the curb like Lot's wives, hit full-face by the nightmare custard pie of it:

10,000 perverts advancing at high noon Sunday down Seventh Avenue in sumptuous mufti; cosmic males in lime platform wedgies,
aggressive males with volley-ball shoulders holding hands, bearded
boys in WAC uniforms, lesbians in waffle stompers, Sweet ORR
coveralls and baseball caps, all led triumphant through Manhattan
by a dozen gargantuan transvestites, brazen demonic Gorgons in
taxi-dancer Lurex gowns, big vinyl wigs like fuchsia or champagne
toadstools, and beaded bags which they twirl like batons, the self-
appointed majorettes of the Hieronymus Bosch homecoming.

It's hard to know where to begin, how to approach such a verbal
fireworks display, the voice of the "new journalism," as it's come to be
called. But we should share, as readers, a sense of novelty, and we
might begin to account for that response.

■ The reporter invents a dramatic situation, that of a tourist couple
facing the marchers. The faceless neutrality of traditional journalism is
replaced by a dramatic situation—we are, in a new sense, there.
■ The reporter speaks directly to us—"Don't misunderstand"—and
he tries every device available to him to make us feel the drama of the
event.
■ More than that, he doesn't talk down to us, and he doesn't pause
for the background detail of ordinary news. He imagines a reader who
knows that the Louds were a Santa Barbara couple undergoing a divorce in a TV documentary at the time, and about Lurex gowns and
waffle stompers and the grotesque paintings of Renaissance artist Hieronymus Bosch—a reader, in short, who knows everything.
■ He is metaphoric and allusive. (An *allusion* is a reference to some
object or event.) Here Burke *alludes to* a homecoming parade, in which
"gargantuan transvestites" are majorettes. He compares the tourists to
Lot's wife, and then switches to a different allusion to see them hit with
a "nightmare custard pie." Indeed, the allusions crowd in upon and
overlap with each other, and they come from every place—the Bible,
mythology (Gorgons), film (the custard pie, "high noon Sunday"), a
high school parade.
■ He is not afraid of words, not bound by the normal way we fence
words out of our writing. He slips into the language of the characters
he invents (one might imagine a Pasadena couple saying, "We wouldn't
be caught dead in New York in madras shorts, but this, *this*, it did give
us pause"), and slips as easily out of it.
■ Thus, he uses a chameleon voice, ready to shift colors and point of
view and vocabulary at every chance.

■ Finally, then, he uses a "show off" voice, one that purposely calls attention to itself ("Look, reader, what a colossal sentence!"). The voice of the new journalism is in part pure display, a chance to demonstrate the chances the writer is taking. In part also, however, the voice attempts to let us see events, through print, with a new immediacy.

"New journalism," as a term, has been applied to a wide range of personal approaches. It's not a single, tightly controlled voice like that of the bubblegum voice writer or the traditional journalist, but rather a loose collection of similar styles. What these voices share is a firm rejection of the voice of the news reporter—in fact, writer Tom Wolfe makes this rejection a central feature of his approach to the new journalism. Note how Wolfe slyly moves from a fairly neutral voice to the stylistic play of the new journalism.

3.15 The voice of the narrator, in fact, was one of the great problems in non-fiction writing. Most non-fiction writers, without knowing it, wrote in a century-old British tradition in which it was understood that the narrator shall assume a calm, cultivated, and, in fact, genteel voice. The idea was that the narrator's own voice should be like the off-white or putty-colored walls that Syrie Maugham popularized in interior decoration . . . a "neutral background" against which bits of color would stand out. Understatement was the thing. You can't imagine what a positive word "understatement" was among both journalists and literati ten years ago. There is something to be said for the notion, of course, but the trouble was that by the early 1960s understatement had become an absolute pall. Readers were bored to tears without understanding why. When they came upon that pale beige tone, it began to signal for them, unconsciously, that a well-known bore was here again, "the journalist," a pedestrian mind, a phlegmatic spirit, a faded personality, and there was no way to get rid of the pallid little troll, short of ceasing to read. This had nothing to do with objectivity and subjectivity or taking a stand or "commitment"—it was a matter of personality, energy, drive, bravura . . . style, in a word . . . The standard non-fiction writer's voice was like the standard announcer's voice . . . a drag, a droning . . .

To avoid this I would try anything.

"The New Journalism"

Problem Three. The new journalism Return to the reporter's notes of problem two, and rewrite one incident in the voice of the new journalism. You'll have to invent details and voices that a new journalist would include, and so you'll have to imagine yourself "inside" a news story in a new way. Do anything to avoid the "pallid little troll" of traditional journalism. ■

Of course, different readers have different reactions to this voice. To some, it's tasteless and crude, a threat to rational discussion and to shared values. To others, it's a vital and exciting voice, a way of opening up the page to the activity of the mind. We're of the latter opinion. Though in this text we keep our own voice closer to "the traditional voice of textbooks," we find that reading the new journalism makes us more conscious of stances writers choose, more conscious of the details of experience and the words that capture them.

The Bureaucratic Voice

Compare examples 3.16 and 3.17:

3.16 I see the duck.

3.17 The web-footed, flat-billed aquatic mammal is in the process of being perceived by the writer of this sentence.

Both 3.17 and 3.18 say the same thing, "I see the duck." Example 3.17 says it right out, in four plain words. Example 3.18 takes eighteen words to say the same thing.

Offhand, we might wonder why anybody would want to waste eighteen words to say what might be said in five. But apparently people do, for the worlds of business, government, and even education are filled with sentences that look more like 3.17 than 3.16. It's the corporate voice, the committee voice, the bureaucratic voice.

We read the bureaucratic voice as if it were a foreign language: First you read it, then you decide what it means. Here's a recent example from an Urban Studies journal:

3.18 There exists a high prevalence of rodent infestation in inner-city environmental areas.

Oh. "There are lots of rats in the ghetto." Here's a more complex example, from a sociology journal:

3.19 In effect, it was hypothesized, that certain physical data categories including housing types and densities, land use characteristics, and ecological location constitute a scalable content area.

This could be called a continuum of residential desirability. Likewise, it was hypothesized that several social data categories, describing the same census tracts, and referring generally to the social stratification system of the city, would also be scalable. This scale would be called a continuum of socio-economic status. Third, it was hypothesized that there would be a high positive correlation between the scale types on each continuum.

Ready to be tested on the passage? Here's a restatement in plain English.

3.19A Rich people live in big houses set farther apart than those of poor people. By looking at an aerial photograph of any large city, we can distinguish the richer from the poorer neighborhoods.

Malcolm Cowley, "Sociological Habit Patterns
in Linguistic Transformation"

Our first impulse is to take the bureaucratic voice as a joke, an elaborate hoax on the reader. We can tell funny stories about it—our favorite is told by Edgar Dale:

3.20 A plumber once wrote to a research bureau pointing out that he had used hydrochloric acid to clean out sewer pipes and inquired, "Was there any possible harm?" The first reply was as follows: "The efficacy of hydrochloric acid is indisputable, but the corrosive residue is incompatible with metallic permanence." The plumber then thanked them for the information approving his procedure. The dismayed research bureau tried again, saying, "We cannot assume responsibility for the production of toxic and noxious residue with hydrochloric acid and suggest you use an alternative procedure." Once again the plumber thanked them for their approval. Finally, the bureau, worried about the New York sewers, called in a third scientist who wrote: "Don't use hydrochloric acid. It eats the hell out of pipes."

Edgar Dale, "Clear Only If Known"

Or we might take powerful and effective statements and bloat them into the bureaucratic voice. Here are two examples:

3.21 I see one-third of a nation ill-housed, ill-clad, ill-nourished.

President Franklin D. Roosevelt

3.21A It is evident that a substantial number of persons within the Continental boundaries of the United States have inadequate financial resources with which to purchase the products of agricultural communities and industrial establishments. It would appear that for a considerable segment of the population, possibly as much as 33.3333 per cent of the total, there are inadequate housing facilities, and an equally significant proportion is deprived of the proper types of clothing and nutriment.

a restatement by Milton Hall,
cited in Stuart Chase, "Gobbledygook"

3.22   I returned and saw under the sun, that the race is not to the swift, nor the battle to the strong, neither yet bread to the wise, nor yet riches to men of understanding, nor yet favor to men of skill; but time and chance happeneth to them all.

Ecclesiastes

3.22A   Objective consideration of contemporary phenomena compels the conclusion that success or failure in competitive activities exhibits no tendency to be commensurate with innate capacity, but that a considerable element of the unpredictable must invariably be taken into account.

a restatement by George Orwell, "Politics
and the English Language"

Problem Four. Reading the bureaucratic voice Translate each of these bureaucratic passages back into plain English. All are well-known proverbs or sayings.

a. It is fruitless to attempt to indoctrinate a superannuated canine with innovative maneuvers.

b. Male cadavers are incapable of yielding any testimony. *Dead men tell no tales*

c. A revolving lithic conglomerate accumulates no congeries of a small, green bryophitic plant. *Rolling stone gathers no moss*

d. A vocable to the sapient is adequate. *word to wise is sufficient*

e. Missiles of ligneous or petrous consistency have the potential of fracturing my osseous structure, but the appellations will eternally remain innocuous. *Sticks & stones can break my bones but names will never hurt me.*

f. Neophyte's serendipity! *Beginners luck*

g. It is bootless to become lacrymose over precipitately decanted lacteal fluid. *It foolish to cry over spilled milk*

h. All articles that coruscate with resplendence are not truly auriferous. *All that glitters is not gold.*

i. Where there are visible vapors having their provenance in ignited carbonaceous materials there is conflagration. *where there's smoke there's fire*

j. Pulchritude possesses solely cutaneous profundity. *Beauty is only skin deep.* Maxwell Nurnberg, *Word Play*

■

Problem Five. Writing the bureaucratic voice   Here's a much harder problem: Rewrite each of the following sensible, every-day English expressions in the bureaucratic voice.

   a. You're fired.
   b. They fell in love and got married.
   c. Too many cooks spoil the broth.
   d. Double-space all your papers.
   e. Jack and Jill went up the hill
       To fetch a pail of water.
   f. A miss is as good as a mile.
   g. No man is an island.
   h. God loves a cheerful giver.
   i. No smoking.
   j. How do you like them apples?

     The jokes, the translations, the games—all at the expense of the bureaucratic style—are good clean linguistic fun. But the bureaucratic voice needs to be taken more seriously. For one thing, most of us are mildly infected with the disease, for, once learned, it's a remarkably easy voice to write in. The writer doesn't have to worry about making sense, about a reader, about being clear about what is meant, even about having a voice as a writer; the words may tumble out gracelessly, but for the most part they tumble out effortlessly. For another thing, we certainly have to come to grips with reading the bureaucratic voice, for it's all around us, in textbooks, contracts, forms, and college catalogs.
     The bureaucratic voice is designed to hide the writer under a protective cloak of words. The writer is, after all, trying to hide the writer, to speak in the voice of a corporation or a government. The president of the corporation may say, "I want everybody to come to work on time," but the writer who comes up with the memo for employees is more likely to write, "All personnel are expected to be at their work stations at the appointed time." In fact, the writer is apt to fatten the message into a couple of paragraphs, in the hopes that workers will swallow the message more easily. "Don't blame me," says the bureaucratic voice, "I'm not responsible." Thus, when we read, "Paychecks will be delayed," or even more likely, "There will be a delay in paycheck distribution," we're silently encouraged not to ask whose fault it is.
     We don't like the bureaucratic voice. In part, our objections are rhe-

torical: Writing should convince a reader, not mystify him. In part, they are moral or ethical: We feel that writing, as uniquely human, ought to be humane. And now those objections are supported by law: Many states now require that contracts be understandable to those who sign them, and the government—and many corporations—are finding that clear communications are much less costly than unclear communications. (If you suffer from the bureaucratic voice, we make suggestions toward a cure in chapter Six, Sentence Choices.)

Problem Six. Bureaucrat for a day   To show you how dreary the bureaucratic voice is, here's an actual working example. You're the maintenance manager at the Three Mile Island Nuclear Reactor in Harrisburg, Pennsylvania, and the following memo, one of hundreds you might receive each day, comes across your desk. Obviously, there's no problem with the reactor. Or is there? Be prepared to discuss how you would respond to the memo.

August 3, 1978

References 1 and 2 (attached) recommend a change in Babcock & Wilcox's philosophy for HPI system use during low-pressure transients. Basically, they recommend leaving the HPI pumps on, once HPI has been indicated, until it can be determined that the hot leg temperature is more than 50°F below T_{sat} for the RCS pressure.

Nuclear Service believes this mode can cause the RCS (including the pressurizer) to be solid. The pressurizer reliefs will lift, with a water surge through the discharge piping into the quench tank.

We believe the following incidents should be evaluated:

1. If the pressurizer goes solid with one or more HPI pumps continuing to operate, would there be a pressure spike before the reliefs open which would cause damage to the RCS?

2. What damage would the water surge through the relief valve discharge piping and quench tank cause?

To date, Nuclear Service has not notified our operating plants to change HPI policy consistent with References 1 and 2 because of our above-stated questions. Yet, the references suggest the possibility of uncovering the core if present HPI policy is continued. We request that Integration resolve the issue of how the HPI system should be used. We are available to help as needed.

Exhibit No. 5, *Transcript of Proceedings,*
President's Commission on the Accident at Three Mile Island,
Public Hearing, January 18–19, 1979   ■

VOICES TO AIM FOR

So far we've looked at voices that are easy to recognize and not too hard to imitate, but not at voices that are useful models for the developing college writer. The student may well wish to ask at this point, "What voice should *I* use? What's the right voice for college writing?"

Our dynamic model of rhetoric gives no simple answer to these questions. The "correct" stance, for a given audience, context, and message, is simply one that does the job, ideally with a certain grace or flair. There is no single "correct" stance; there are stances available, voices to adopt, and the choice, within limits, is up to you. Moreover, the many shades of voice in effective communication don't slot themselves into rigid types as easily as do the voices we've looked at.

But the student has a right to expect some sort of answer to "What voice should *I* use?" One range of voices is given in a final writing assignment in this chapter, where we print the views of three English instructors, and you have, before your eyes, our "voice," at least our "freshman textbook voice"—like most writers, we do many different voices. And in this section, we'll speak of two voices that are legitimate models, what we call "the committed personal voice" and "the detached discursive voice." We do so hesitantly and with qualifications: These are not the only "correct" voices, nor are they voices that can be mastered as easily as the voice of the bubblegum writer. They are ideals for the developing writer, voices to aim for.

The Detached Discursive Voice

The detached discursive voice is the public voice of ideas, "detached" because the writer, whatever his or her personal feelings, tries to persuade or inform by concentrating on ideas, and "discursive" because the writer is consciously creating a *discourse* with an audience that goes beyond an immediate, known group—with what we called the "universal audience" in chapter Two. You'll meet this voice in most books on serious topics, including the best of your textbooks, you'll meet it in magazines like *Harper's, Atlantic,* and the *New Republic,* and you'll hear a version of it on TV news shows like *Meet the Press* and *60 Minutes.*

We cite a complex example first—by British writer Raymond Williams—because its subject matter is itself what we call the detached discursive voice, specifically the movement of that voice from eighteenth-century philosophy and criticism to the nineteenth-century novel, to "fictional analysis" (and if you've read a novel from a nineteenth-century writer like George Eliot or Thomas Hardy, you'll recognize that much time is taken on "fictional analysis"):

3.23 It seems clear that the base from which fictional analysis was developed is the important eighteenth-century tradition of philosophical and critical analysis, itself often well evidenced in the essay. The strengths of this tradition are, in a special way, the strengths of literacy. It is easy to react against the formalities of diction and construction which of course occur in such prose, but these are only the surface marks of an essential stance between writer and reader, willingly and habitually accepted on both sides, in which rationality, precision and sustained argument become possible, in new ways, once the language has been learned. It is true that this method has been repeatedly imitated, as a kind of social manner: in sermons, correspondence columns, political speeches, we can hear the whirring sound of a merely polite mind putting pen to paper. But it is only in ignorance and prejudice that we would then disregard, for all the hated formality of the sound, the real reach of this prose: the composed page; the sense of time gained, time given; the mind working but also the mind prepared, in an exposition which assumes patience, reference, inspection, rereading. Such prose, indeed, is a kind of climax of print, and especially of the printed book: a uniformity of tone and address; an impersonality, assuming no immediate relation between writer and reader but only possession, in a social way, of this language; a durability, as in the object itself, beyond any temporary impulse or occasion.

The Pelican Book of English Prose

Remember, we say "a voice to aim for." Certainly this is difficult reading, in part because of the shortness of our quotation—Williams spends the next several pages clarifying this paragraph. But we ought to recognize the point of the passage, that this voice is part of a continuing tradition that represents, "in a special way, the strengths of literacy." Learning this "language," Williams implies, is not easy, and he is careful to note how much public writing falls short of it.

A second example may clarify the range of the detached discursive voice—it's that of an American writer, Robin Lakoff, working with more specific examples to support the argument that, in American society, men are seen in their roles in the world, while women are seen in sexual roles. To do this, she notes that we make quite different responses to sentences like 3.24A and 3.24B:

3.24A He's a professional.

3.24B She's a professional.

She then continues to note the larger problem behind such a response.

3.25 The sexual definition of woman, however, is but one facet of a much larger problem. In every aspect of life, a woman is identified in terms of the men she relates to. The opposite is not usually true of men; they act in the world as autonomous individuals, but women are only "John's wife," or "Harry's girl friend." Thus, meeting a woman at a party, a quite normal opening conversational gambit might be, "What does your husband do?" One very seldom hears, in a similar situation, a question addressed to a man, "What does your wife do?" The question would, to a majority of men, be tautological: "She's my wife—that's what she does." This is true even in cases where a woman is being discussed in a context utterly unrelated to her relationships with men, when she has attained sufficient stature to be considered for high public office. In fact, in a recent discussion of possible Supreme Court nominees, one woman was mentioned prominently. In discussing her general qualifications for the office, and her background, the *New York Times* saw fit to remark on her "bathing-beauty figure." Note that this is not only a judgment on a physical attribute totally removed from her qualifications for the Supreme Court, but that it is couched in terms of how a man would react to her figure.

"Language and Woman's Place"

This voice can reach from philosophical movements to party chatter, and with that range of reference comes an openness of vocabulary: Lakoff reaches from the plainness of "John's wife" to the formal precision of "autonomous individuals" and "tautological"; Williams ranges from the abstractions of "uniformity," "durability," and "impersonality" to the concrete "whirring sound" of the misuse of this voice.

Above all, the detached discursive voice is a composed voice, consciously *written language* in its formality, its care in argument, its contrived sentence patterns. Yet at the same time it leans on, and manipulates, the strengths of spoken language—in its words, its rhythms, its patterns of sound, emphasis, and repetition.

Thus the detached discursive voice finds a middle road between the extremes of the bureaucratic voice and the bubblegum voice. The bureaucratic voice, at one extreme, ignores spoken language and the reader's needs. The bubblegum voice, at the other extreme, moves too close to the reader in an attempt at written-down speech. The detached discursive voice is aware of the rhythms of speech and aware of a reader; it assumes a stance that's worth trying out.

The Committed Personal Voice

The committed personal voice expresses private feelings and experiences. It is "committed" because the writer takes those feelings and experiences seriously. It is "personal" because they are invested with the force of the writer's personality. The committed personal voice is thus an "I" voice—though many other "I" voices are possible, and the "I" pronoun is not the defining feature of this voice.

The committed personal voice is important enough for us to devote a chapter to it—chapter Seven, *Style in Description and Narration*—because the ability to deal with one's own experiences on paper is, to us, central to the development of writing ability—and it is also "a new way of knowing." Because of that attention, we won't discuss the voice here, but we will present you with a problem in responding to personal voices. It will allow you to formulate your own answer to the question of dealing with your experiences on paper, and it may help to clarify our final remarks in this chapter.

Problem Seven. Reading personal voices   A few years ago the magazine *Rolling Stone* opened its pages to its readers by requesting "autobiographic mass feedback." The magazine received 1067 narratives, 200 of which were printed. We print three below. They offer useful attempts at the "committed personal voice," and, because they were written by ordinary people, outside the walls of a classroom, for publication in a magazine that emphasizes rock music, they can be evaluated as voices, not as writing for an English class.

Read each passage, and be prepared to discuss them as a group in terms of the following questions:

■ How would you characterize the *stance* of each writer? More particularly, what *voice* does each writer present to her reader, and what *tone* does she adopt toward her message?

■ A rhetorical stance is both a means of discovery, a perspective on experience, and a self-imposed set of blinders, closing off other areas of experience. What perspectives are implied by each of these stances, and what limits does each imply?

■ Which writer do you find most effective *as a writer*? What standards do you use to make such a judgment, and how are they related to the concerns of this chapter?

Passage A

Me!

I had a lonely childhood; where I lived there were no other children my age that lived near—only a cousin or two, but they were quite a few years younger than me. The town I lived in was rather small and it always seemed to me that all possible playmates lived so far away. My parents were quite strict and it was only after much persuading that I obtained permission to go out of the yard. This staying home has its effects on me even now. I spend much time at home, reading, cooking and writing.

When I started school, I went to a very old school house not far from where I lived. It had three classrooms, two baths and a kitchen. I was a painfully shy little tyke with ankle socks and a permanent.

My teacher for the next three years was in a class all by herself. She was an old woman, say in her late 60s. The only reason they kept her was that no one else would teach three classes in the same classroom, for not much pay. She abused the children, the worst being eating cokes and doughnuts while teaching the class, or hitting them.

The principal was also different. She had a drinking habit and it wasn't an odd sight to see her sit in the car, get juiced, and come in to get all her students cokes so they wouldn't tell on her.

My childhood passed rather uneventfully, getting only pimples and a complex to remember it by. Sort of a keepsake.

Around this time I discovered religion. My parents got very religious all of a sudden, and started going to church. I hated it at first; we never went before, so why start now? I finally converted to the Baptist faith. I wasn't no zealous convert who went around preaching hell, fire, and brimstone.

My teen years weren't much different from my young years. I was still shy and found it so hard to talk to anyone. So my parents and a couple of helpful teachers took me to a psychiatrist. In my opinion I saw nothing wrong with me, but then, what I felt didn't count. Those teachers who didn't even know me convinced my parents that something was wrong with a person who didn't like to talk to people.

Analysis didn't help me; I was defensive and wouldn't respond to any of the questions or "games" they planned. The only thing that really happened to me at that time was when I was given some pills that had side effects on certain types of people. But the good doctors didn't tell my mother that. I went into convulsions and wasn't almost admitted to a hospital because it was the middle of the night.

In spite of my trip into analysis, I was still shy and spent much time at home reading a great deal. I read many religious books such as *Pilgrim's Progress* and the Bible. I took organ lessons on which I played classical and religious music. Even though I was a Beatle fan, I never played rock and roll on the organ.

School was one tiring ordeal. I hated school. Staying home became a favorite pastime of mine. I only felt safe within the confines of the house. I spaced the days I was absent so as to not arouse any suspicion.

I did have some tragic experiences. One which always stands out in my mind was when my brother was killed in Vietnam. His death is constantly before me as I look back at all the things I could have done for him but didn't. Only those who have went through that know how it really feels!

When you are a teenager you are supposed to date. I never did, and for a long time thought it was my looks. Now I am no beauty, but after seeing some of those who even wound up married I know now it wasn't my looks.

Graduation from high school finally came. The happiest time of my life. After a few months, I got a job typing at Spencer Gifts. It wasn't very exciting sitting there typing all day so I quit. My main ambition is to write. I used to write stories, and my seventh grade English teacher told me that I was college material and had real talent. Imagine!

Right now, however, I have went through so many personal changes. My religious life is nil. It left me with so many unanswered questions that it no longer seemed real—only a ritual you go through every Sunday.

I still stay at home. I read still, mainly books and magazines and newspapers. I cook but don't gain weight. Writing and politics take up most of my life. So here I be, a dateless 18-year-old who wonders if she will be doing the same thing when she is 30.

Passage B

My Life and Pleasures

Can you imagine a mother of five girls an avid rock lover? I believe I have all the loves and joys possible to a woman of 33. As of the present, I am a homemaker and Brownie Scout teacher, along with the role of motherhood and wife. I also, more or less, plan the songs and music to be used in a local Rock Band. I am literally tone-deaf, but occasionally play the tambourine with groups.

Music has been my whole life for as long as I can remember. At two years old, I used to sit by my record player for hours on end. All of my life I wanted to be a drummer. But, to my parents' belief, it wasn't ladylike! I took piano, accordion, and organ lessons, but wasn't satisfied. My girls are all musically inclined, and would rather listen to Alice Cooper than watch television. My nine- and 13-year-olds play the guitar, and my six-year-old has a four piece drum set. We also have bongos, a conga drum, tambourine, harmonica, bleach bottles, etc., and really "get it on" to the music with our own little rock session. I believe our whole life revolves around music, everything from Grand Funk and Janis Joplin to Neil Young.

Kids from all over come over to jam with us, or just to rap with us. My husband will be 40 years old next month. Kids find it so hard to believe that people our age can be so far-out! We never miss Rock Concerts or Rock Festivals, and really dig all the Hippies, Long-Hairs, and Heads. I think we have a very close-knit family and a very rich and meaningful life.

This sounds as if all my life revolves entirely in just listening to my records and tapes. True, to a certain sense. But, while music is on, I make good use of my time. I love arts and crafts of all kinds, and I am always making something. I have refinished furniture, reupholstered furniture, engaged in candlemaking, ceramics, plastic resin, macrame, embroidery, string art, batic, glass staining, flower arranging, felt and art foam projects, papier mache, collages, and tie-dyeing, among others. I even tried my hand at drawing. But, I found I'm not too artistic. Our whole family engages in making Christmas decorations and gifts for friends. You wouldn't believe our basement and garage—boxes and sacks galore! I would like to have a head shop and craft shop someday.

As for my other hobbies, I believe cooking is my main one. I have seven recipe boxes, plus 63 cookbooks, all of which I use avidly. I love to read, as you might surmise from our four bookcases full of books. My main interests are of the sinister, nightmarishly haunting type science fiction, "adult only" books, mysteries, the Black Arts, and Astrology.

We also like outdoor sports, such as swimming, water skiing, sledding, roller and ice skating, or a ride in the country on our 750 Norton. I believe this just about sums up my life: a busy one of motherhood, rock music, arts and crafts, cooking, reading, and outdoor sports with our five daughters. What more fulfillments in life could one woman ask for?

Passage C

1969 Abortion

I had full conscious realization the moment I conceived and I knew I didn't want a baby. New York City had ruined all aspects of my health. My friends got together $200 for me and I returned to D.C. to look for an abortion. I was staying at the Free Press house and there was a hip (?) doctor hanging out there. I asked him if he could find me a good abortion and he said, "sure—it costs $600." I told him I only had $200 and he said I had to have $600. So I found a funky one for $200. Michael drove me over to a ghetto development apartment and I went in alone as arranged. A young black woman met me and took my money. Then she inserted a rubber catheter into my uterus which would begin the labor-like expulsion of the tiny fetus.

I went home and waited. Mary stayed with me. The contractions began and they hurt a lot. In the middle of this, some friends from New York came in and tried to whisk me away to California. I tried to explain the situation. I went in the bathtub and out came, it seemed like, all my insides—and a tiny peanut-sized person. I was sad and glad—confused, I guess. Everyone fell asleep; I stayed awake all night with the most excruciating pains and feelings. The pain lifted me up to another place, it was so heavy.

In a couple of days I developed a bad fever and infection after being turned away from one hospital (there questioned by police whom I lied blatantly to), admitted to one and operated on. I ran away, to my friend's house in the country, and was glad to be alive, as spring awakened all life around me.

■

READING FOR TONE

We've neglected tone, the writer's attitude toward his or her subject matter, to concentrate on *voice*, the way writers present themselves to readers. That's because *voice* seems more central to the developing writer. *Tone*, after all, is built into many writing assignments. One is hardly going to attempt a satiric paper about abortion, and the writer who jokes about the Civil War in a history examination has chosen the wrong time to exercise a sense of humor.

But readers need to be sensitive to tone, for the tone of a piece of writing is the most important clue of sorting oneself out as reader—just how am I expected to take this?

Suppose, to take a fairly straightforward example, we read the first sentence of this short story by Max Shulman:

3.26 Cool was I and logical.

If we're careful readers, we ought to have a double response. On one hand, the character tells us how smart he is. On the other hand, the way the character tells us makes us doubt what he says—would anybody with any sense actually write, "Cool was I and logical"?

In other words, we begin to suspect that something's going on—the words may mean exactly the opposite of what they seem to mean. Our suspicions continue as we read further:

3.27 Cool was I and logical. Keen, calculating, perspicacious, acute and astute—I was all of these. My brain was as powerful as a dynamo, as precise as a chemist's scales, as penetrating as a scalpel. And—think of it!—I was only eighteen.

"Love Is a Fallacy"

By this point, the alert reader is mentally set for a satire. Quite rightly, we expect a story that will poke fun at this priggish young man. This sort of "reading through the surface" of writing is a common enough experience. With this story we cooperate with the author in laughing at this character. In other cases, we may reject the tone offered us by the author—as we rejected the adoring attitude that the bubblegum stance asks us to adopt toward its heroes.

But certain reading experiences may challenge our sense of tone more severely. Responding to tone is particularly complex in works of imaginative literature, for often writers ask us to respond in ways that differ from our stock responses in everyday life. A novelist may present an unpleasant character, yet ask us for sympathy; a poet may invest a scene with a feeling that we would not expect to give.

In part, our sense of tone in writing develops with more reading. Responding to the clues novelists give becomes easier as we read more novels, and the dry-as-dust medical textbook may have exactly the right tone for the medical student.

For the most part, our vocabulary for talking about tone in writing is a simple transfer of the words we use to talk about "tone of voice" in speaking: serious, understated, playful, formal, sarcastic, and so on. Several words, however, are used only to refer to tone in print, particularly to tone in works of literature:

■ *irony*. Irony is the literary equivalent of sarcasm in speech. An ironic work may say one thing, yet suggest another, as in passage 3.35 above.
■ *parody*. A parody imitates the style of a writer by making it seem distorted, by overemphasizing its features. (We offer examples of parody on pp. 258–260.)
■ *satire*. A satire mocks a point of view or position by adopting it ironically. Thus the Shulman story, 3.27 above, is both ironic and satiric.

Problem Eight. Recognizing parody Below are brief profiles of eight ballet dancers. Four are profiles of actual dancers; they are taken from the 1979–1980 program of the Pittsburgh Ballet Company. Four are parodies of such profiles; they are taken from the 1979–1980 program of "Les Ballets Trockadero de Monte Carlo," a comic ballet company in which men mock the pretensions of ballet by performing in female costumes, complete with tutus and toe shoes. (All profiles have been edited to remove mention of the ballet company.)

Identify the parodies, and be prepared to discuss the features common to both the actual profiles and the parodies.

a. LAUREN ROUSE received her early training at Chicago's Stone-Camryn School of Ballet. She also studied with Frederic Franklin, Ben Stevenson, Katherine Crafton, and Robert Joffrey. She danced with the Chicago Ballet, the Joffrey II, the National Ballet in Washington, D.C., before joining the company in 1977 as soloist. She danced the lead roles in numerous productions . . . including *Firebird, Frankie and Johnny,* and *Romeo and Juliet.*

b. MARGARET LOWIN-OCTEYN, D.B.E., was recently knighted by the Queen for her unstinting services to English ballet and good horsemanship. Long a pillar of the Stonehenge Ballet (which she founded in a year no living person has been able to ascertain), Dame Peggy has been a symbol of dignity and durability to at least four generations of balletomanes. She may be further venerated in the upcoming film biography, *The Endless Journey.*

c. DEIDRE SALYER was born in Oklahoma City, Oklahoma, and trained with Miguel Terekhov, Yvonne Chouteau, and Victoria Leigh. A dance major at Oklahoma University, she appeared with her college company and joined our company in 1973. She has danced in almost every ballet in the company repertoire. Ms. Salyer, a soloist, also teaches at the Ballet Theatre School and was recently appointed as Regisseur and Repetiteur.

d. FRANCESCA CORKLE has been dancing almost all her life. She trained at her mother's school in Seattle, Washington, until she was 15 when she joined the Robert Joffrey School in New York. She soon became a member of the Joffrey Ballet with whom she danced for 10 years. Known for her brilliant technique, speed, and vivacious wit, Ms. Corkle won critical acclaim for her roles in *Confetti, Kettentanz, Le Beau Danube, L'Air d'Esprit,* and *Pineapple Poll.* In 1974 Robert Joffrey choreographed *Remembrances* for her. Her performance prompted Patricia Barnes to write . . . "this ballet has made her a great dancer." Ms. Corkle joined the company as principal dancer in 1979.

e. IDA NEVERSAYNEVA, Socialist Real Ballerina of the Working Peoples Everywhere, has just returned from a great triumph at the Varna Dance Festival in Bulgaria, where she was awarded a specially created Plastic Medal for Bad Taste. Comrade Ida became known as a heroine of the revolution when, after effortlessly boureeing through a mine-field, she hurled a Molotov Toe-Shoe into a capitalist bank.

f. ZAMARINA ZAMARKOVA's frail, spiritual qualities have caused this elfin charmer to be linked to a lemon souffle poised delicately on the brink of total collapse. Her adorably over-stretched tendons exude a childlike sweetness that belies her actual age.

g. TATIANA YOUBETYABOOTSKAYA is one of those rare dancers who with one look at a ballet not only knows all the steps but can dance all the roles. As a former member of the Kiev Toe and Heel Club, she was awarded first prize at the Pan Siberian Czardash and Kazotski Festival for artistic mis-interpretation.

h. ELEANOR D'ANTUONO began her professional career at 14 in New York with Ballet Russe de Monte Carlo where she became soloist after 2 years. . . . Ms. D'Antuono, often mentioned as America's most versatile ballerina, has a vast repertoire including the principal roles in most of the classics as well as works created especially for her. In January 1979, Ms. D'Antuono toured the Soviet Union, the first American ballerina to be invited to appear with Soviet companies. . . .　■

SUMMARY

We have explored *voice*—the way in which a writer presents himself to reader—and *tone,* the attitude a writer adopts to a subject-matter. Tone and voice make up the writer's *stance.* We have examined four voices— the bubblegum voice, the neutral voice of conventional journalism, the exuberant voice of the "new journalist," and the stuffy voice of the bureaucrat. We have approached each of these voices by: 1. examining our immediate responses to that voice; 2. attempting to adopt that voice in our own writing; and 3. pointing to specific features of choice that create that voice.

We then offered "two voices to aim for" as models for the developing writer, voices we called "the neutral discursive voice" and "the committed personal voice." We concluded with a discussion of responding to tone as reader.

IMPLICATIONS FOR THE WRITER

This chapter has a moral, one that we might express this way: *The writer's stance is a way of seeing, and a way of not seeing.* By that we mean that a stance is an entry into a piece of writing. It opens some perspectives, but closes off others.

Consider, as an example, the voices we've examined and the entries they would have to the same writing topic—the same problem, event, or situation. Each voice would lead to a particular stance, and therefore to a particular mode of approaching the topic. The bubblegum voice would be, golly, just *so-o-o* excited by everything that the details would blur together, covered in marshmallow emotion. The bureaucratic voice would have its own stance, one far distant from topic and audience, clouded by its own convoluted language. The journalistic voice would see facts and only facts, and the voice of the new journalist, similarly, would stress what its own stance made available: details, activities, subjective impressions. Even the voices we've offered as voices to aim for would bring with them their own approach to the topic, the neutral discursive voice weighing alternatives and qualifications in a public, controlled stance, the committed personal voice centered on its own involvement with the topic.

Choosing a stance as a writer, then, is a way of choosing what you can learn from a writing assignment. It is a way of being human by means of the written word.

FINAL WRITING ASSIGNMENTS

I. An Identifiable Voice Find a single identifiable voice and report on it to the class. The voice need not be (and perhaps should not be) the voice of a single writer. Many magazines, for example, have consistent voices, and editors may rewrite articles to bring them into line with the shared voice of the magazine. (A list of such magazines would include *Time, Cosmopolitan,* and *New Yorker,* as well as many specialized magazines.)

Present your findings in a form that seems appropriate, or one suggested by your instructor. Our discussion of voice offers one alternative; and you might consider more adventurous rhetorical stances. You might, for instance, act as if you were the editor of a magazine and send a memo to your writers, explaining the voice you want them to adopt. Or you might wish to parody the voice you select (for parody, see pp. 258–260).

II. A First-Person Voice   Find a novel or short story written in the first person (the "I" voice)—perhaps from the new-book shelf in the library. Using only the first paragraph or two as evidence, explain the inferences that you, as reader, make about the character speaking to you. In other words, what is the written voice of this character, and what predictions can you make about the story that will follow?

III. Reading for Tone   The three passages below present problems in reading for tone, in sensing the writer's attitude to his or her subject— particularly as we've taken the passages out of context. Be prepared to discuss the tone of each passage, and, if your instructor directs, write a short paper assessing the tone of one of the passages. The first passage is a complete chapter from a biography: What are the writer's feelings about the family he describes, and how are they revealed? The second passage is written by an Amerindian writer: What stance does the writer adopt, and how does it illuminate the subject in a new way? The third passage is a complete chapter from a novel; here the question of tone and stance becomes particularly complicated, for you must assess both the character's (Maria's) attitude toward the scene and the author's attitude toward those characters (and toward Maria).

A   I must now attempt to say something about Virginia's mother's family. Here there is a good deal of uncertainty, of legend, and of scandal.

According to Virginia's cousin H.A.L. Fisher, the historian, there was at the Court of Versailles during the last years of the old regime a certain Chevalier Antoine de l'Etang; his person was pleasing, his manners courtly, his tastes extravagant and his horsemanship admirable. He was attached to the household of Marie Antoinette—too much attached it is said, and for this he was exiled to Pondicherry where, in 1788, he married a Mlle. Blin de Grincourt.

M. de l'Etang entered and died in the service of the Nawab of Oudh; he left three daughters. Adeline, the one with whom we are concerned, married a James Pattle who was, we are told, a quite extravagantly wicked man. He was known as the greatest liar in India; he drank himself to death; he was packed off home in a cask of spirits, which cask, exploding, ejected his unbottled corpse before his widow's eyes, drove her out of her wits, set the ship on fire, and left it stranded in the Hooghly.

The story has been told many times. Some parts of it may be true. It is certainly true that Mrs. Pattle came to London in 1840 with a bevy of daughters and that these ladies had a reputation for beauty. Four of them should be mentioned in these pages: Virginia, Sarah, Julia, and Maria.

Virginia Pattle, the most beautiful of the sisters, married Charles Somers-Cocks and became Countess Somers; she was a dashing, worldly woman, impulsive, rather eccentric, who lived in great style. Of her daughters, one became Duchess of Bedford; the other, Isabel, married Lord Henry Somerset. This alliance, though grand, was by no means happy. Lord Henry, a charming man it seems, delighted Victorian drawing rooms with his ballads. He was, I believe, the author of *One More Passionate Kiss;* this embrace was reserved, however, not for his beautiful wife but for the second footman. Lady Henry endured his infidelities for a time but presently she could stand no more. She confided in her mother who, allowing her indignation to master her prudence, made a public scandal. The sequel is interesting in as much as it gives a notion of the ethos of the Victorian age and of a system of morality which Virginia Woolf and her contemporaries were to encounter and oppose.

Lord Henry fled to Italy and there lived happily ever after. His wife discovered that she had been guilty of an unformulated, but very heinous, crime: her name was connected with a scandal. Good society would have nothing more to do with her. She was obliged to retire from the world and decided to devote herself to the reclamation of inebriate women, a task which she undertook with so much good sense and good humor that she won the affection and admiration, not only of men of charity and good will, but even of the women she assisted.

Quentin Bell,
Virginia Woolf: A Biography

B   Into each life, it is said, some rain must fall. Some people have bad horoscopes, others take tips on the stock market. McNamara created the TFX and the Edsel. Churches possess the real world. But Indians have anthropologists.

Every summer when school is out a veritable stream of immigrants heads into Indian country. Indeed the Oregon Trail was never so heavily populated as are Route 66 and Highway 18 in the summer time. From every rock and cranny in the East they emerge, as if responding to some primeval fertility rite, and flock to the reservations.

"They" are the anthropologists. Social anthropologists, historical anthropologists, all brands of the species, embark on the great summer adventure. For purposes of this discussion we shall refer only to the generic name, anthropologists. They are the most prominent members of the scholarly community that infests the land of the free, and in the summer time, the homes of the braves. . . .

Vine Deloria, Jr., *Custer Died for Your Sins*

C   She had watched them in supermarkets and she knew the signs. At seven o'clock on a Saturday evening they would be standing in the check-out line reading the horoscope in *Harper's Bazaar* and in their carts would be a single lamb chop and maybe two cans of cat food and the Sunday morning paper, the early edition with the comics wrapped outside. They would be very pretty some of the time, their skirts the right length and their sunglasses the right tint and maybe only a little vulnerable tightness around the mouth, but there they were, one lamb chop and some cat food and the morning paper. To avoid giving off the signs, Maria shopped always for a household, gallons of grapefruit juice, quarts of green chile salsa, dried lentils and alphabet noodles, rigatoni and canned yams, twenty-pound boxes of laundry detergent. She knew all the indices to the idle lonely, never bought a small tube of toothpaste, never dropped a magazine in her shopping cart. The house in Beverly Hills overflowed with sugar, corn-muffin mix, frozen roasts and Spanish onions. Maria ate cottage cheese.

Joan Didion, Play It as It Lays

IV. The Right Voice? The three passages that follow are taken from college writing texts; each discusses the voice (or *persona*) that the author sees as appropriate for the college writer. The differences among them are striking, and those differences alone may provide material for an answer to the question each passage considers: What sort of voice should the developing writer aim for? But other issues might be raised as well. Each writer, for example, presents his or her own voice to the reader: How well do the writers manage to meet their own criteria or expectations about voice in writing? What kind of evidence or argument does each passage present, and how does that affect the persuasiveness of the voice and the message?

Passage A concludes a discussion of modern writers' views of style; passage B is from a freshman textbook; passage C follows an anthology of remarks by scientists and artists about the subjectivity of the modern world.

A There must be no gap between expression and meaning, between real and declared aims. For some people, some of the time, this simply means *not* telling deliberate lies. For most people, it means learning when they are lying and when they are not. It means learning the real names of their feelings. It means not saying or thinking, "I didn't *mean* to hurt your feelings," where there really existed a desire to hurt. It means not saying "luncheon" or "home" for the purpose of appearing upper-class or well-educated. It means not using the passive mood to attribute to no one in particular opinions that one is unwilling to call one's own. It means not disguising banal thinking by polysyllabic writing or the lack of feeling by cliches that purport to display feeling.

The style is the man, and the man can change himself by changing his style. Prose style is the way you think and the way you understand what you feel. Frequently, we feel for one another a mixture of strong love and strong hate; if we call it love and disguise the hate to ourselves by sentimentalizing over love, we are thinking and feeling badly. Style is ethics and psychology; clarity is a psychological sort of ethic, since it involves not general moral laws, but truth to the individual self. . . . If the style is really the man, the style becomes an instrument for discovering and changing the man. Language is expression of self, but language is also the instrument by which to know that self.

Donald Hall, "An Ethic of Clarity"

B The open class asks for a different kind of writing. For the open class serves the human purpose of language, the primary purpose for which human speech evolved. That is, *sharing experience* and *responding to others*.

Here you write about whatever thoughts and feelings you want to share—for your teacher to read and respond to, and, if you wish, for your classmates to read and respond to.

Here you respond, in writing, to something somebody—teacher or classmate—says in class. Or what I say on the printed page to you.

Which means you simply *talk on paper*.

That may sound like a revolutionary idea. Students tell me that somewhere in somebody's English class they somehow got the notion that what they wrote was not supposed to sound like talking. They tell me that nobody *really* talks to English teachers. Not the way they talk at home. Or with friends. Even on perennial theme topics like tell-me-something-about-yourself or what-you-did-on-your-summer-vacation, you try to say what you think the teacher wants you to say, the way the teacher wants you to say it.

Before sitting down to that dead-end again, let a student who has used this book point you in the right direction:

The best thing that happened to me in this class was learning to respect my own writing.

That student had discovered that writing is not the mysterious thing he thought it was, that it's not an esoteric act limited only to English teachers and the gifted few, that it's not a painful, joyless academic grind.

Writing is human behavior. Like talking.

Talking to say whatever you are concerned about, whatever you feel strongly about, whatever you spend a lot of time thinking about—whatever you think is worth saying.

Even when your sense of failure is greater than your sense of self-worth, you are still the most important person in the world to you. Let that person speak in your writing. Turn on to your *own* unique voice, use your *own* everyday language—the language you use in the corridors and at parties, the language that is a part of *being yourself*.

Lou Kelly, *From Dialogue to Discourse*

C First, let's be logical about it. Given the kind of dilemma with respect to knowledge and language that this book defines, what sort of style might we *expect* in our time? What sort of speaking voice adopted by the writer, what mask, would be appropriate in a world where, as we have seen, the very nature of nature may be inexpressible? If we live in a pluralistic and fluxlike universe, what manner of word-man should we become in order to talk about it? Well, we might at least expect a man who knows his limits, who admits the inevitably subjective character of his wisdom. We might expect a man who knows that he has no right in a final sense to consider himself any wiser than the next fellow, including the one he is talking to. The appropriate tone, therefore, might be informal, a little tense and self-conscious perhaps, but genial as between equals. With our modern relativistic ideas about the impossibility of determining any "standard dialect" for expressing Truth in all its forms, we might expect the cautious writer to employ many dialects, to shift from formal to colloquial diction, to avoid the slightest hint of authoritarianism. The rhythm of his words will be an irregular, conversational rhythm—not the symmetrical periods of formal Victorian prose. Short sentences alternating erratically with longer sentences. Occasional sentence fragments. In sum we might expect a style rather like *this!*

> Walker Gibson, "A Note on Style and the Limits of Language"

FOR FURTHER READING

Walker Gibson has written two useful books on voice in writing: one, *Tough, Sweet and Stuffy* (Bloomington: Indiana University Press, 1967), is a study of modern American prose; the other, *Persona* (New York: Random House, 1969), is a short textbook with writing applications. Richard A. Lanham's *Revising Prose* (New York: Random House, 1979), another textbook, offers suggestions for avoiding the bureaucratic voices he calls "the official style" and "the school style."

We might also mention two short essays of interest. Wayne C. Booth's "The Rhetorical Stance," in his *Now Don't Try to Reason with Me* (Chicago: University of Chicago Press, 1972), though addressed to writing instructors, is often reprinted in anthologies for students; it argues that finding a rhetorical stance, a balance of message, audience, and voice, is the central task of the writer. Kenneth J. Gergen's "The Healthy, Happy Human Being Wears Many Masks," *Psychology Today* (May 1972), is a more general article on the "voices" we adopt in everyday life.

Two anthologies provide a sampling of the "new journalism": *The New Journalism*, ed. Tom Wolfe and E. W. Johnson (New York: Harper & Row, 1973), and *Reporting: The Rolling Stone Style*, ed. Paul Scanlon (Garden City, N.Y.: Anchor/Doubleday, 1977).

UNIT II

SMALLER
ELEMENTS
OF ARRANGEMENT

From Talk to
Written Discourse

Form . . . is an arousing and fulfillment of desire. A work has form
in so far as one part of it leads a reader to anticipate another part, to
be gratified by the sequence.

KENNETH BURKE

In chapter One, we explained the natural ability of speakers of a language like English to speak and understand sentences. We called that ability the *language competence* of speakers, and we noted that the same competence that explains how people talk and listen also explains how they read and write.

But speaking or understanding sentences by themselves is only a small part of what happens with ordinary language, for the sentences we speak don't appear one by one, separated from everything around them. Instead, they appear in streams of speech, in patterns of sentences. Sentences follow sentences—as you talk with friends, listen to a disc jockey or a college professor, or even read a paragraph like this one—and part of your language ability is the ability to sort out the meanings that accumulate as sentences follow upon sentences.

This business of the building-up of meaning sentence by sentence has traditionally been called *arrangement,* for it involves ordering ideas, that is, arranging them in some way. This two-chapter unit is concerned with the smaller elements of arrangement: In this chapter, we explore the elements of arrangement that are common to speaking and writing, and in the next chapter we explore the special feature of arrangement in writing, the paragraph.

Our key word in this chapter is coherence. We'll define and explain coherence, and we'll isolate three elements that give coherence to speaking and writing: repeating key words and sentence patterns, connecting ideas, and providing a framework of meaning for readers. The benefits promised by this chapter are small-scale, concerned only with the linking of sentence to sentence. But, as we'll see, attention to these small elements of writing can sometimes lead to clear-cut improvements in the way writers present themselves to readers.

THE COMPLEXITIES OF COHERENCE

The word *coherence* identifies a quality of speaking and writing that might loosely be restated as "hanging together." Coherent speech or writing "hangs together"; it makes sense. Most commonly, we use the negative form, *incoherence:*

4.1 "He was so upset by the accident that he was incoherent. He didn't make any sense at all."

That everyday use of the word suggests that mastering coherence in writing simply extends a skill you already have: recognizing and creating coherence in speaking.

Problem One. Creating coherence   Several words are removed from the passages below. The number of letters in each missing word is shown with blanks. Guess the missing word.

As you do (and the task is not simple), notice the patterns that you use to predict the correct answers. (Answers are given in the answer section at the end of the book.)

A   Richard Petty didn't want to _ _ a stock car driver when _ _ was growing up. He got into it because, as _ _ _ says, "When your old man is winning every _ _ _ _ in sight, people kind of expect you to _ _ _ _ _ _ in his footsteps."

Petty climbed into his first _ _ _ _ car when he was 21 years _ _ _. He finished sixth in that first _ _ _ _ _, in Columbia, S.C., in July 1958. Eight years _ _ _ _ _, he had _ _ _ 55 races, eclipsing his father's record of 54 _ _ _ _ _, the most ever won before _ _ a stock _ _ _ driver.

Time Magazine

B   Willie Sanders was taking a day off. In a waterfront bar called The Hatch, across the _ _ _ _ _ _ from the Todd Shipyards in San Pedro, Calif., Willie, a 37-_ _ _ _ _-old riveter, sipped _ _ _ beer. "You get to the point," he _ _ _ _ _, "where you stare at the rivets and to make _ _ _ _ mean something you start counting them like _ _ _ _ _ _ _ _ sheep.

When you _ _ that, you better watch _ _ _. Some guys tell you that means you're _ _ _ _ _ crazy. So when it happens to _ _, I just go home and watch _ _ _ _ _ _ _ _ _ _ until I can come back and face it _ _ _ _ _ _. My kid looks at me and says, 'dad, what're you doing _ _ _ _ again?' I tell him, 'Listen, kid, you're going to _ _ _ _ _ _ _ one day. You just won't understand _ _.' I can never explain _ _ him. You just can't get the feeling of _ _ _ _ it's like there until _ _ _ get behind a riveting gun and begin blasting away. Some _ _ _ _ like to think they're fighting a war. It makes _ _ _ _ feel good."

Newsweek

■

Coherence Is a Pattern of Meaning

Your ability to do reasonably well on problem one is in part explained by a sense of pattern alone—most obviously, the patterns of letters shown by the blanks. Thus, you probably recognized "didn't want to _ _ a stock car driver" as "didn't want to *be* a stock car driver" because the blanks rule out "didn't want to *see* a stock car driver" or "didn't want to *emulate* a stock car driver." But even here the most important patterns were those created by *meaning:* you rejected other two-letter words that didn't fit your "sentence sense"; we've never had a student guess "to *of* a stock car driver" or "to *is* a stock car driver."

Coherence, then, is a *pattern of meaning.* Patterns of meaning range from expected phrases, as in "21 years *old*," to more complex guesses about the way the world works: "I just go home and watch *television*"; "listen, kid, you're going to *college* one day." Patterns of meaning include repeated key words that chain sentences together:

4.2 Petty climbed into his first *race* car. . . . He finished sixth in that first *race*. . . . Eight years later, he had won 55 *races*, eclipsing his father's record of 54 *races*.

They even include complex responses to the "voice" of the speaker, perhaps allowing you to guess "some *guys* like to think they're fighting a war."

The complexities of coherence, then, are often easy to recognize, but hard to explain. We create coherence, as readers and listeners, because we need to make sense of the world. Put another way, readers and listeners actively build meaning within sentences and between them. Turn to a friend and say, "I believe in Laura Norder," and the friend will probably hear "law and order" instead of the woman's name, for the remark makes more sense that way. Few readers have more than a moment's difficulty with sentence 4.3:

4.3   She had tears in her dress and tears in her eyes.

But the different pronunciations of *tears* could not possibly have come from the letters on the page; they came from the reader's sense that eyes have "tears" (pronounced "tiers") and dresses have "tears" (pronounced "tares").

Readers and listeners are equally active in connecting sentence pairs to make them coherent.

4.4   I can't make it to class. My car broke down.
4.5   I won't be at the office today. I have jury duty.
4.6   I can come to your party. My car broke down.

We insert a mental *because* to connect each of these sentence pairs, almost without thinking about it. But each logical connection involves an active reader: one who assumes that the speaker of 4.4 needs a car to get to class, who understands 4.5 in terms of knowledge about the nature of jury duty in American society, and who creates the complex circumstances that give meaning to 4.6—perhaps creating a speaker who planned a long car trip, but can come to the party now that the trip is cancelled.

Problem Two. Logical connection   There's a pattern of meaning connecting each of the sentence pairs below. The pattern can be identified by one or more of these three words: *because, therefore,* and *then.* Select the appropriate word in each case.

a. I went to the store. I needed milk, chile salsa, and deodorant.

b. I went to the store. I went home.

c. John is intelligent, hard-working, and interested in improving himself. He should do well in the course.

d. Olivia's enchiladas lack the delicate flavor and subtle nuance of Priscilla's. We always go to Priscilla's for enchiladas.

e. Writers should try to make logical connections. We ought to discuss logical connections in this textbook.

f. Homer ate three and a half pounds of rice and beans, two quarts of Gatorade, and nine bagels. He was hungry.

g. The point to recognize about language is this: Although there are an infinite number of possible sentences in a language, the number of rules which produce these sentences must be limited or finite—after all, children are able to learn most of those rules by the age of six. Language can be called a finite set of rules capable of producing an infinite number of sentences.

h. Hepzibah ordered the combination plate—a taco, an enchilada, and a tamale, with beans and rice. She must have been hungry.

i. Timothy ate two potato chips and a raisin. He fell asleep.

j. The country purchased fifty-five jet planes. It was ready for war. (How many possible answers? Why?)

k. The ice melted. Mark was happy with his discovery. (How many possible answers? Why?)

l. It's hot in this room. The third baseman will be out of action for three weeks. (How many possible answers? Why?)

Our students come up with elaborate readings that connect totally unrelated sentences, such as the last one in problem two:

4.7 It's hot in this room. (Obviously, the third baseman is in the room, sick with the fever, and the thermostat has been turned up to make her comfortable. But, if she's got a fever, she's not going to be able to play for some time. *Therefore:*) The third baseman will be out of action for three weeks.

4.7A It's hot in this room. (Then the third baseman came in from the cold, and then he caught a chill, and then he became ill. *And then:*) The third baseman will be out of action for three weeks.

4.7B It's hot in this room. (That's because there are so many of us crowded in this hospital room. That's because we all like the third baseman and wanted to sympathize with her. *Because:*) The third baseman will be out of action for three weeks.

Such mental ingenuity only underscores the active nature of reading and of listening. This has its humorous side, when readers build up the wrong meaning from the words on the page. A student tells us about reading a difficult scientific essay, about this science and that science, and being suddenly stumped by a word that he first saw as *con-science*, a science that was new to him. Only when he read further did he discover the unexpected word *conscience*. We tested example 4.8 below as an exercise in reading incoherence.

4.8 There was a knock on the door, I opened the door, and the new gerbil walked in. The class cheered wildly.

Donald Barthelme

Many of our students, though, created coherence out of incoherence by assuming that we had made a typing error—they read the passage as, "the new girl walked in."

Such mistakes aside, this point about coherence—that readers actively build meaning—is a positive one. It means that writers can expect to have an active reader, one willing in part to build coherence. But it also suggests that writers must be conscious of their readers, that they need to give them a chance to build meaning. And it demands that writers, in most writing contexts, avoid incoherence.

Incoherence Measures Coherence

There's nothing particularly wrong with incoherence in some situations—as we'll see, it's a common device in poetry and in certain kinds of writing—but it demands a special set of strategies from the reader. Consider, for example, the writing of a mental patient suffering from schizophrenia:

> **4.9** Have just been to supper. Did not knowing what the woodchuck sent me here. How when the blue blue blue on the said anyone can do it that tries. Such is the presidential candidate.

The first sentence is clear enough, and there are bits of meaning here. But this disturbed individual has lost touch with the mind's need for coherence.

We sense a similar lack of connection in some poetry, where the poet asks the reader to supply or create connection.

> **4.10** The apparition of these faces in the crowd;
>   Petals on a wet, black bough.
>
>   Ezra Pound

In this example, the lack of coherence leads us to reconstruct or rebuild the meaning of the poem. The poem is titled "In a Station of the Metro" (the Metro is the Paris subway), and that bit of knowledge helps us to build a visual picture of a crowd of faces in a subway station. The poem offers us two images, faces and petals, and we hunt for a pattern of coherence—perhaps "the apparition of the faces in the crowd" is like (or reminds me of) "petals on a wet, black bough." Thus we make a logical connection and we build a framework for meaning:

> **4.10A** apparition
>   faces::petals
>   crowd::bough

Building such a simple framework does not give us the "meaning" of the poem, but it is a first step in creating that meaning. Thus some poetry challenges our sense of coherence by asking us to become more active readers.

We often meet similar kinds of incoherence in written prose. Passage 4.11 was written by anthropologist Edmund Carpenter: It provides a series of unconnected statements, linked only by repetition of the key word *telephone*:

4.11 "Hello, Central. Give me Dr. Jazz." *Jelly Roll Morton.* The telephone is said to be the only thing that can interrupt that most precious of all moments.

Aimee Semple McPherson was buried with a live telephone in her coffin.

I once observed a man walking alone past a public phone which rang just as he passed. He hesitated and then, after the second ring, answered it. It couldn't possibly have been for him.

I called various public phones on streets & in terminals and, when someone answered, as almost invariably someone did, I asked why he had answered. Most said, "Because it rang."

They Became What They Beheld

We sense a pattern here, but it's a pattern of association, not of meaning. The writer leaves it to the reader to build the meaning— something about the force of the telephone in modern society, we suspect.

Here's another example, taken from the opening paragraph of E. L. Doctorow's novel *Ragtime,* set in the early 1900s:

4.12 The best part of Father's income was derived from the manufacture of flags and buntings and other accoutrements of patriotism, including fireworks. Patriotism was a reliable sentiment in the early 1900's. Teddy Roosevelt was President. The population customarily gathered in great numbers either out of doors for parades, public concerts, fish fries, political picnics, social outings, or indoors in meeting halls, vaudeville theatres, operas, ballrooms. There seemed to be no entertainment that did not involve great swarms of people. Trains and steamers and trolleys moved them from one place to another. That was the style, that was the way people lived. Women were stouter then. They visited the fleet carrying white parasols. Everyone wore white in summer. Tennis racquets were hefty and the racquet faces elliptical. There was a lot of sexual fainting. There were no Negroes. There were no immigrants. On Sunday afternoon, after dinner, Father and Mother went upstairs and closed the bedroom door.

There are flashes of coherence here. We can find logical connections in some of the sentences: "Father's income was derived from . . . accoutrements of patriotism [*for*] Patriotism was a reliable sentiment . . . [*because*] Teddy Roosevelt [*a patriot*] was president. [*and*] The population customarily gathered in great numbers." We can recognize sentence patterns ("There were no Negroes. There were no immigrants."). But, for the most part, the passage strains our reading precisely because it is incoherent. We're constantly jumping to make connections— between tennis racquets and sexual fainting and Negroes; between true statements and false statements (women *were* stouter then, but there *were* Negroes and there *were* immigrants). Here the incoherence is functional: The early 1900s was a period of profound split, of discontinuity, and the opening paragraph of the novel dramatizes that discontinuity.

We measure incoherence, then, by our sense of coherence. Our sense of order in reading is never more active than when writers refuse to cooperate with it.

Problem Three. An exercise in incoherence   The eight passages below have been gathered from two sources: the spoken or written sentences of schizophrenic patients, and the writing of literary artists (poets or novelists). Identify those passages that you think are by mental patients with the letter *P,* those by artists with the letter *A.* (Not always an easy task, by the way, since we've removed the passages from their contexts.)

a. The bizarre excesses are right all tents of the itinerants. One afternoon the children are delighting and for entertain it in a roundabout of the horses-wood, the swings and arm-chairs of the chains turn of an axis.

b. I've known her from an ample nation choose one; then close the valves of her attention like stone.

c. He would never forget his first encounter with his stepmother. . . . [He] stepped forward with a gallant try at putting everyone at ease.

"And what," he said in his most courtly manner, "would you like us to call you?"

"I would like you to treat me as my own children do," Gussie Gold replied with a graciousness equal to his own. "I would like to think of you all as my very own children. Please call me Mother."

"Very well, Mother," Gold agreed. "Welcome to the family."

"I'm not your mother," she snapped.

d. Proliferate is a complete time about a word that is correct. There is under a horse a new sidesaddle. Went came in better than it did before.

e. Dance a clean dream and an extravagant turn up, secure the steady rights and translate more than translate the authority, show the choice and make no more mistakes than yesterday.

f. So, the battalion, the front. Well, how was it? And then it was a hospital, and so—oh dear, oh dear, oh dear—and then better, talking nothing at all. In the north there are bears, which I must bring to your attention.

g. She saw the hard, cutting edges of the new houses, which seemed to spread over the hillside in their insentient triumph, the triumph of horrible, amorphous angles and straight lines, the expression of corruption triumphant and unopposed, corruption so pure that it is hard and brittle.

h. There has been no rain since April. Every voice seems a scream. ■

COHERENCE IN SPEAKING AND WRITING

It's worth repeating two points. First, humans have a fundamental need to make connections, to create coherence. We are, in the simplest terms, compelled to make sense out of the world. Second, no one taught you the patterns and connections that work between sentences. They come along with living in a world and knowing a language. It would be silly to offer a course in talking—people already know how to do it. The specific patterns and connections of written language, however, do need to be taught in school courses—that's what you're reading about at this moment, as a matter of fact. But this part of language written down is a natural extension of the skills you use in everyday speech.

Everyday speech, when we think about it, falls neatly into two kinds: "just talking" and "talking about." "Just talking" is a conversation without pattern—speakers can hop from sex to politics to duck farming. If we ask such speakers about their conversation, a likely answer would be "Oh, we didn't talk about anything special, we just talked."

"Talking about," on the other hand, is focused conversation. A single topic is discussed at length. Imagine, for example, asking one friend about a conversation with another friend. One possible answer is the one above, "Nothing much, we just talked." But a real conversation, a "talking about," would be reported in a more coherent form: "Well, mostly we talked about her husband. . . . He's been. . . . Last week he. . . . She's worried about how . . . so she's decided. . . ." "Just talking," then, is unstructured; it's incoherent. Any topic may be raised at any time. "Talking about" is structured; it's coherent. Indeed, we

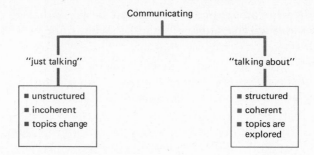

FIGURE 4.1 "Just Talking" and "Talking About"

have a formal way of recognizing "talking about": when people are talking about something it's impolite to change the topic without an apology ("I hate to change the subject, but . . ."). These differences are summarized in Figure 4.1.

"TALKING ABOUT" IS STRUCTURED

Obviously, we're concerned as writers with something much closer to "talking about" than "just talking." (When writers "just talk" on paper, as in free writing or journal keeping, the results are likely to be quite incoherent.) As an example of "talking about," one that takes us one step away from ordinary conversation, we'll overhear a business conversation on the telephone. The conversation was recorded in the 1940s; it illustrates the sort of "talking about" we use in business, in classrooms, and in conversation with someone who doesn't share our background. In this example, the topic is typewriters. The office has ordered typewriters with pica type (which prints somewhat larger letters, helpful for making stencils); the order has been delayed, but typewriters with elite type are available—it prints smaller letters, but may still be usable. Since it's a spoken discourse, it is printed without punctuation.

4.13 A: I wanted to tell you one more thing I've been talking with Mr. Davis in the purchasing department about our typewriters
B: yes
A: that order went in March seventh however it seems that we are about eighth on the list
B: I see

A: we were up about three but it seems for that type of typewriter we're about eighth that's for a fourteen-inch carriage with pica type
B: I see
A: now he told me that Royce's have in stock the fourteen-inch carriage typewriters with elite type
B: oh
A: and elite type varies sometimes it's quite small and sometimes it's almost as large as pica
B: yes I know
A: he suggested that we go down and get Mrs. Royce and tell her who we are and that he sent us and try the fourteen-inch typewriters and see if our stencils would work with such type
B: I see
A: and if we can use them to get them right away because they have those in stock and we won't have to wait
B: that's right
A: we're short one typewriter right now as far as having adequate facilities for the staff is concerned
B: yes
A: we're short and we want to get rid of those rentals
B: that's right
A: but they are expecting within two weeks or so to be receiving— ah—to start receiving their orders on eleven-inch machines with pica type
B: oh
A: and of course pica type has always been best for our stencils
B: yes
A: but I rather think there might be a chance that we can work with elite type
B: well you go over and try them and see what they're like and do that as soon as you can so that we'll not miss our chance at these.

Charles Carpenter Fries,
The Structure of English

This passage clearly hangs together: It's coherent talk rather than random talk. It has a clear beginning and ending: The first speaker raises the issue in the first sentence ("I want to tell you one more thing"), and the discussion ends when the second speaker approves a specific course of action. It would be impossible for the second speaker to change the topic of discussion—to hand towels in the ladies' rooms, for example—until the topic has been completed.

We can find two kinds of pattern in this conversation. There is a

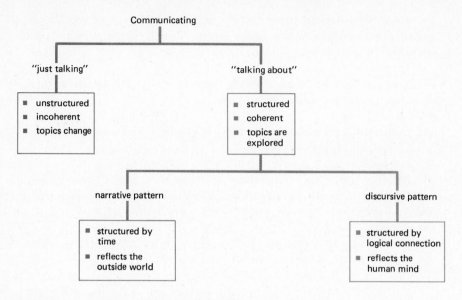

FIGURE 4.2　Narrative and Discursive Patterns

narrative pattern, in which the events are strung out in an "and then" pattern:

4.13A　he suggested that we go down *and* [*then*] get Mrs. Royce *and* [*then*] tell her who we are and that he sent us *and* [*then*] try the fourteen-inch typewriters *and* [*then*] see if our stencils would work with such types

And there is a more important pattern, one that provides a framework of logical connections. Statements are coherent because we connect them logically:

4.13B　*and if* we can use them [*then*] to get them right away *because* they have those in stock *and* [*so*] we won't have to wait

We'll call this kind of order a *discursive* pattern; it "discourses," or talks over, rather than narrates.

Both discursive patterns and narrative patterns achieve coherence. Narrative patterns link events in time—that happened *and then* this happened—in the natural order they occur in the real world. Discursive patterns link ideas and events by logical frameworks—this happened *because* that happened; *if* this happens *then* that will happen; *al-*

though that happened, *nevertheless* this happened. We're primarily concerned in this unit with discursive patterns: They come less naturally to the developing writer, and they are the most common pattern expected in college level writing assignments. Moreover—and this is a very big *moreover*—discursive patterns may well reflect the patterns the mind uses to store information, just as narrative patterns reflect the order of events in the world. The ability to see a narrative pattern (that happened *and then* this happened) and to create a discursive pattern (this happened *because* that happened) demands an active mind, a discursive mind. These distinctions are shown in Figure 4.2.

That sense of discursive patterns accounts for the overall coherence of this conversation. At the highest level the pattern is that of problem and solution. The statement of the problem involves old information and new information; the solution involves an argument and an approval. We've outlined this pattern in Figure 4.3.

PROBLEM:	"I wanted to tell you one more thing . . ."
Old Information:	"I've been talking with Mr. Davis . . ."
response:	"yes . . . I see . . ."
New Information:	"now he told me that Royce's . . ."
response:	"oh . . . oh . . ."
SOLUTION:	"he suggested that we go down . . ."
Argument:	"we're short one typewriter right now . . ."
response:	"that's right . . ."
Approval:	"well you go over and try them . . ."

FIGURE 4.3 Framework of Meaning in Passage 4.4

The same sense of discursive patterns is also reflected in the details of the conversation.

One feature is the *repetition* of key words. The topic word *typewriter* becomes the key word in the conversation: *typewriter* or *typewriters* appears five times, along with *machines* once; and it's referred to six times with pronouns ("if we can use *them* to get *them* right away because they have *those* in stock"). Moreover the topic word *typewriter* so dominates the conversation that it can be left out with no loss of meaning ("that order" means "that typewriter order"; "a fourteen-inch carriage" means "a typewriter with a fourteen-inch carriage"). The two subtopic words are *pica* and *elite;* they tend to be balanced off against each other:

4.13C of course pica type has always been best . . .
but I rather think that we can work with elite type . . .

Another feature is the use of logical connection. The passage relies, like most conversations, on *and* as the principle connective, a narrative pattern ("he suggested that we go down *and* get Mrs. Royce *and* explain . . ."), but it also uses other connectives, discursive ones—*but, of course, if, because,* and so on.

A third feature is the use of a logical framework. The conversation as a whole has a problem and solution framework, and the sense of connection is repeated over and over again in the details:

4.13D   elite type varies } general statement
   sometimes it's quite small
   and sometimes it's almost as large as pica } specific statements

Three basic features thus seem to separate discursive talk from plain talk. The first feature is repetition. Instead of moving randomly from topic to topic, discursive talk focuses upon a single topic, and hence the key words that identify topic and subtopic are naturally repeated. The second feature is the use of connectives to tie meanings together. And the third is the use of logical frameworks. These three features make up the stuff, the basis, of coherence in writing as well.

In writing, though, the situation changes—primarily because the reader is not physically present in front of the writer. As a result, some sentences that might be clearly understood in conversation are impossible (incoherent) when written down:

4.14   Meet us here tomorrow with a stick about so big.

The phrase "so big" has no meaning without a gesture to show how big; "tomorrow" has no reference in the timeless world of print, nor is there a "here" shared by reader and writer. Even "us" is not a real us, but a disembodied "voice" created by the reader. In writing, then, the need to chain meaning for the reader becomes much more important, and what we do naturally in speaking presents particular problems in writing.

SUMMARY

Organized speaking or writing, as opposed to mere talk, is *coherent*. Coherence, the sense that speaking or writing "hangs together," is a pattern of meaning the mind will accept. We measure coherence by its opposite, incoherence. Coherence can be achieved by a narrative pattern or by a discursive pattern. A discursive pattern, in speaking or writing, is marked by three features: repeating words and sentence patterns, connecting ideas, and using logical frameworks. These features become more important in writing, as opposed to speaking, because the listener is absent, unable to question what we say.

IMPLICATIONS FOR THE WRITER

Let's ask one final question about the telephone conversation discussed above: How does the speaker know what to say next? The speaker obviously has an overall plan, to present a problem and suggest a solution, but what controls how sentences follow sentences? The answer is simple enough—it's the basis of any conversation: The speaker listens to the listener. In our telephone conversation the listener responds to new information ("oh"), agrees ("that's right"), and shows that he (or she) understands ("yes . . . I see"). In a face-to-face conversation, those verbal responses would be supplemented by gestures, body movements, and facial expressions. Those responses are the speaker's best clue to what to say next.

In writing, those responses are absent, and writers must spin out what they want to say next only in terms of what they've already said. This difference leads to a simple but effective suggestion: When writing, pause often to reread what you've already written. In doing so, you shift from writer to reader; you become concerned—rightly concerned—with what your reader will create from the words on the page.

(And research suggests that better writers do indeed spend more time rereading than do weaker writers.)

More specifically, we'd like to explore how the features of coherence pay off in writing—by repeating key words and sentence patterns, by making logical connections, and by creating frameworks of meaning. To give this discussion a precise focus, we'll ask you to read the passages of problem four before continuing.

Problem Four. Evaluating coherence   Three pairs of passages are printed below, labeled Group A, Group B, and Group C. Read each pair, and decide which passage of the two is the better written. Your instructor may ask you to be able to defend your answer in class discussion, or he or she may ask you to explain each choice in a sentence or two. We'll refer back to these passages in the discussion that follows.

Group A

Passage One   Thomas's love of poetry began, not with ideas, but with words. In answering some questions about his writing, he reported that, as a child, he had been attracted by the sounds of the words in nursery rhymes, but had paid little attention to their meanings: "The words, 'Ride a cock-horse to Banbury Cross' were . . . haunting to me, who did not know then what a cock-horse was nor cared a damn where Banbury Cross might be. . . ." Language seemed not to refer to the real world but to generate through its sounds intimate new realities which the child could appropriate as his own: "And these words were to me, as the notes of bells, the sounds of musical instruments, the noises of the wind, sea, and rain, the rattle of milkcarts, the clopping of hooves on cobbles, the fingering of branches on a window pane, might be to someone deaf from birth, who had miraculously found his hearing."

When he decided to become a writer, Thomas's attitude toward words was "The first thing was to feel and know their sound and substance; what I was going to do with those words, what use I was going to make of them, what I was going to say through them, would come later." This emphasis on the reality of words themselves continued when he became aware of their magic capacity for referring to the qualities and sensations of life.

Passage Two   Much of the emphasis of twentieth century literature is placed on what is happening right now. Life is a moving process and, for most writers, the traditional concerns of the past are no longer meaningful to what is happening in the present. The poet tries to make some sense, or at least present a realistic view as he perceives it, of the natural world and human relationships and consciousness. There are various themes that he deals with in his literature, such as America is a junkyard, a place that didn't deliver its promise. Along with this is the individual's sense of not belonging, of having been told that he is close to God and captain of his fate. But he is not at home in his own world because there is a gap between what he thinks should be and what is. The poet is aware of this split between the real and the actual and he uses his perception of reality and his insight to organize his material into some kind of statement about his personal discontent with the world and/or deep concern with what the world is like. Allen Ginsberg's "Sunflower Sutra" and William Carlos Williams' "To Elsie" are concerned with the themes of America as a junkyard and America as a place that didn't deliver its promise.

Group B

Passage One   Frederick had decided to capture Saxony so that he could seize its resources, take advantage of additional manpower, and perhaps use the occupied lands as a bargaining point to achieve a quick peace. Within a few weeks he defeated the bulk of the Saxon troops and incorporated them into his own armies. In Saxon archives he found documents tending to prove the allied plans to partition Prussia, and these he published to justify his actions. He then invaded Bohemia, defeated a small Austrian force, and hoped that peace could be restored after these brief, lightning successes.

But Frederick had completely miscalculated the effect of his Blitzkrieg. It did not intimidate his opponents, but reaffirmed their aim to destroy Prussia. In the spring of 1757, his enemies increased in numbers and tightened their alliances. Russia dispatched an army; Sweden entered the field; the Empire, represented by most of the German states, collected troops against Frederick, who was accused of having breached the peace with his invasion of Saxony; and the Franco-Austrian alliance was turned into an offensive pact. Frederick for his part looked in vain for allies. Turkey could not be persuaded to attack Russia. England alone agreed to renew the Convention of Westminster, to pay a million pounds sterling in subsidies, and to assign some Hanoverian forces to fight France.

Passage Two   France had shown itself to be an unworthy ally by not aggressively attacking the Austrians. Frederick had also shown that he could "doublecross" his allies by his "secret" arrangements with Maria Theresa against France. Another important consequence was that Austrian aims were not satisfied, as she had lost Silesia without gaining other territories to counterbalance this. Frederick was not finished either. He began to adopt a policy of quick, decisive victories with a peace or truce following to build up his resources. (It was more his aim than a reality.)

In 1744, the Second Silesian War began. Again, France was allied with Prussia. Frederick hoped to secure his Silesian gains partly by acquiring certain mountain passes vital to its defense. France again appeared as an untrustworthy ally by not pushing the Austrians or pursuing them. Maria Theresa was determined to gain territory, either Silesian or Bavarian. Victories were won on both sides. However, Frederick feared a long engagement would again drain his resources. Realizing the futility of further war, he eventually was able to secure peace in 1745, after Maria Theresa's armies were defeated to a limited extent. As a result of this war, Frederick thought little of France as an ally. He had gained little from it in any territorial sense. However, Prussia had risen in European eyes to a significant degree of power. Her armies were to be respected. The polarity of Berlin and Vienna in German affairs had begun to develop.

Group C

Passage One   Each generation of young people is inclined to believe that their generation is the first to experience the problems encountered when maturing and finding out the essentials of life, yet the contrary is true. Each and every generation of youths, from the beginning of time on up into the twentieth century, run into the same difficulties and hardships as their fathers had discovered years before and as their fathers' fathers had done. The conflict of interests and ideas between parent and child creates a situation far more common than was believed to be so. Rebellion and disagreement on the part of the child to his parent in maturation is one step toward a sense of individualism for that child, and, although his values may not truly be what he believes in, the main goal of the child is to declare that he is finally able to judge for himself and make concrete decisions on his own mental level.

Passage Two   In some societies each generation is expected to rebel—to flout the expressed wishes of the old men and to take power from men older than themselves. Childhood may be experienced as agonizing, and small boys may live in fear of being seized by elderly uncles and aunts who perform terrifying ceremonies in their honor. But when the same small boys are grown, they expect their brothers and sisters to carry out on behalf of their children the same ceremonial behavior that had so terrified them. In fact, some of the most stable . . . cultures, such as those of the Australian aborigines or the Banaro of the Keram in New Guinea, are characteristic of societies in which the whole population is involved in a ritual of torture and initiation. . . .   ■

Repetition

Writers are often advised to avoid repetition, to "vary their sentence structure," and to "avoid repeating words." That's good advice, to some degree: Awkward repetition isn't useful, and monotonous sentence patterns are boring. But often the cure is worse than the disease, and the advice hides the real value of repetition as a help for the reader. Readers chain meanings together, as we've seen, and the more links the writer can provide for that chain the better. Good repetition is a help rather than a hindrance.

Repeat Key Words

The following passage is—how do we say it politely?—not untypical of a certain kind of student prose:

4.15 I ordered the lobster. The waiter brought the shellfish. I eagerly tasted the dainty morsel. The crustacean was delicious.

Readers can sort through such prose (if they know that a crustacean is a shellfish which is the lobster consisting of morsels). But what a lot of extra work it is, and how unnecessary. Such a habit—constantly looking for new words for old things—is sometimes called "elegant variation": In searching to avoid repetition, the writer becomes artificial, or "elegant." We can contrast elegant variation with useful repetition in the first group of passages in problem four. Passage one has a clear focus on a central idea, announced in the first sentence and repeated regularly.

4.16 Thomas's love of poetry began, not with ideas, but with words . . . words . . . sounds of the words . . . words . . . sounds . . . words . . . words . . . sound . . . words . . . words. . . .

Contrast the elegant variation of passage two, where the lack of focus may grow from the writer's desire to avoid repeating the words *poetry* and *poet:*

4.17 emphasis . . . literature . . . right now . . . life . . . writers . . . the present . . . the poet . . . themes . . . literature . . . the individual's . . . the poet . . . themes. . . .

The elegant variation of this passage misleads the reader, almost as if the writer wanted to hide the subject matter. (Passage two is by a student writer; passage one is by critic Jacob Korg.)

Repeat Sentence Patterns

Group B of problem five presented you with two passages about the Second Silesian War. You may now know more about the Second Silesian War than you wanted to know. But, subject matter aside, you probably found passage one easier to read than passage two, and students usually defend that answer by arguing that it is "better organized" or "easier to follow." They're right, of course. Passage one is from a history textbook, and passage two was written by a student. Passage one is "readable" because the basic subject-verb patterns stress the central focus of the passage—what Frederick did, why he did it, and what his enemies did in response. As a result, the sentence patterns created a framework of meaning. We've outlined those repeated sentence patterns in 4.18, italicizing the logical connections.

4.18 Frederick had decided . . . *so* he could seize . . . take advantage . . . *and* perhaps use. . . . He defeated . . . *and* incorporated. . . . He found documents . . . *and* these he published. . . . He *then* invaded . . . defeated . . . *and* hoped. . . .

But Frederick had miscalculated . . . his Blitzkrieg. It did not intimidate his opponents, *but* reaffirmed their aim. . . . His enemies increased . . . *and* tightened. . . . Russia dispatched . . . Sweden entered . . . the Empire . . . collected . . . *and* the Franco-Austrian alliance was turned. . . . Frederick . . . looked in vain for allies. Turkey could not be persuaded. . . . England alone agreed to renew . . . to pay . . . *and* to assign. . . .

Passage two, on the other hand, shifts its sentence patterns from sentence to sentence. The coherence of the action must be clear to the writer, but it's not clear for the reader. The passage sounds as if twenty wars were going on instead of one.

4.19 France had shown. . . . Frederick had *also* shown. . . . *Another* important consequence was. . . . Frederick was not finished. . . . He began. . . . (It was more. . . .)

The . . . war began. France was allied. . . . Frederick hoped. . . . France *again* appeared. . . . Maria Theresa was determined. . . . Victories were won. . . . However, Frederick feared. . . . He *eventually* was able. . . . Frederick thought. . . . He had gained. . . . *However*, Prussia had risen. . . . Her armies were to be. . . . The polarity . . . had begun to develop.

Problem Five. Repetition in word and sentence pattern This exercise dramatizes the importance of repeating key words and sentence patterns. You should be able to predict most of the omitted words, simply by relying on your sense of repetition. Some are tricky.

a. Nobody wants to be dull. But if the alternative to _ _ _ _ _ _ _ _ is dishonesty, it may be better to be _ _ _ _.

> Walker Gibson, *Tough, Sweet and Stuffy*

b. The prose of Huckleberry Finn established for written speech the virtues of American colloquial _ _ _ _ _ _. This has nothing to do with pronunciation or grammar. It _ _ _ something _ _ _ _ _ _ _ ease and freedom in the use of language. Most of all _ _ _ _ _ _ _ _ _ _ _ _ _ the structure of the sentence, which is simple, direct, and fluent, maintaining the rhythm of the word-groups of _ _ _ _ _ _ and the intonations of the _ _ _ _ _ _ _ _ voice.

> Lionell Trilling, "Introduction" to Mark Twain's *Huckleberry Finn*

c. "A Dollar don't do as much buying for me as _ _ used to _ _, so _ _ _ _ ' _ _ _ _ _ _ _ _ _ for a _ _ _ _ _ _."

> (Langston Hughes' character Jesse Simple, explaining to his boss why he'd slowed down his work.)

d. Words should count, they should make sense, and the great enemy of _ _ _ _ _ i n g _ _ _ _ i b l y is _ _ _ _ i n e s s.

> Sheridan Baker, "Scholarly Style, Or the Lack Thereof"

rep: Repetition   Avoid awkward repetition. Awkward repetition arises most commonly by using the same word in different senses:

First Draft	*Revision*
Many employers employ a special strategy with new employees. (Here the word employ is used— or employed—in three different senses.)	Many bosses use a special strategy with new employees. (This version shifts the tone slightly and avoids awkward repetition.)
After a while, after dinner, we decided to find out what he was after, after all. (four different meanings for *after*)	After a while, dinner being over, we decided to find out, at last, what he wanted. (awkward repetition removed)

Logical Connection: Transition

It's commonly believed that shorter sentences are easier to read and understand than longer sentences. But a simple experiment casts doubt on that belief. One group was given a series of two short sentences, as in 4.20:

4.20   He was late for work. His car broke down.

Another group was given the same idea, but now linked with a logical connection, a transition word:

4.20A   He was late for work because his car broke down.

When the two groups were tested for understanding, the second group remembered more of what they had read: They not only remembered the *because* connection, but they were also better at remembering the two basic sentences. That finding makes sense in the light of our discussion above: The longer sentences are better remembered because they ask the reader for less work; they come as logically related ideas.

Logical connection seems more important in reading than in speaking. Sentences 4.20, if spoken, would be accompanied perhaps with a shake of the head or an emphatic stress, suggesting the *because* connection. Readers don't have these oral cues, and logical connection becomes more important for the writer. Writers must chain meanings for readers, and transition words are the essential links in that chain.

One writer has grouped transition words under the meanings they can signal, calling this a "grammar of coherence." In our version, we use key words to show how meanings are chained within sentences and between sentences. The key word *but,* for example, signals a change of direction—here, within a single sentence:

4.21 A man who has never gone to school may steal from a freight car; but if he has a university education, he may steal the whole railroad.

Theodore Roosevelt

(We place linking words in boxes.) The same connection may link two sentences. In example 4.22 below, the author uses a related word, *yet.* Note that we read this word as logically the same as the word *but.*

4.22 Language, like the body, is so comfortable and familiar that we hardly notice its presence or its complexity. Yet once examined closely, the accomplishment of any ordinary speaker is rather astonishing.

Richard Ohmann, "Grammar and Meaning"

(Other words signal the linking of the key word *but—however, in contrast, nevertheless, on the other hand, in spite of, instead, on the contrary, still.*)

Of course, the writer may leave the linkage unstated, asking the reader to link the sentences:

4.23 I have understood the population explosion intellectually for a long time. I came to understand it emotionally one stinking hot night in Delhi a couple of years ago.

Paul Ehrlich, *The Population Bomb*

To understand these sentences, the reader must create coherence by seeing the contrast between "intellectually" and "emotionally" as a *but* linkage:

4.23A I have understood the population explosion intellectually for a long time. [but] I came to understand it emotionally one stinking hot night in Delhi a couple of years ago.

A different linkage can be signaled by the key word *so:*

4.24 Another well-known word which might be defined etymologically [that is, by its origin] is *republic,* derived from the Latin *res*
meaning *thing* and *publicus* meaning *public* or *people,* so that a republic is in literal terms a thing of the people.

Douglas Ehninger, Influence, Belief, and Argument

A *so* linkage between sentences can be signaled by more formal words—
thus, therefore, as a result, consequently.

4.25 The word *anthropology,* for example, comes to us from the
Greek words *anthropo,* a combining form meaning *human being* or
man, and *logy,* another combining form meaning *science of.* Thus ,
we have anthropology, the science of man.

Douglas Ehninger, Influence, Belief, and Argument

A third linkage may be signaled by the word *because,* in meaning the
logical opposite of *so.* Thus we may invert our *so* examples to create
because examples:

4.26 A republic is in literal terms a thing of the people, because
it is derived from the Latin *res* meaning *thing* and *publicus* meaning
public or *people.*

Within sentences, a *because* linkage may be signaled by other words
(*since, for, due to*), but there seems to be no single transition word to
link a sentence with a sentence with the meaning of *because.* It seems
clear, however, that readers can create this linkage:

4.27 Anthropology can be defined etymologically as the science
of man. [because] It comes to us from the Greek words *anthropo,*
meaning *human being,* and *logy,* meaning *science of.*

A fourth linkage introduces an example. We like to think of it as a
"colon" linkage, from the use of the colon as a punctuation mark: to
introduce an example within a sentence.

4.28 Similar widenings of meaning can be seen in the popular use of words from other fields⌈:⌋ *allergic* from medicine, *complex* from psychology, *alibi* from the law courts, and so on.

Charles Barber, The Story of Language

Examples may be introduced by linking words (*for example, to illustrate, specifically, for instance*) or, again, the reader may be asked to create coherence:

4.29 Some parents cannot resist the temptation of saddling their child with a running-joke first name. ⌈"colon"⌋ The Federal Bureau of Statistics issued a list in 1973 that included Cherry Pye, Etta Apple, Mery C. Christmas, Mac Aroni, and Cigar Stubbs.

Christopher Anderson, The Name Game

A fifth linkage marks a restatement or clarification; we mark it with the key words *that is to say*. Linking words that signal the same linkage include *to repeat, in other words, to clarify,* and within sentences, the word *or*. This linkage can be expressed in some form or it can be left for the reader to create:

4.30 Writing then is not easy. ⌈[that is to say]⌋ Putting it more systematically⌋ it imposes demands on the performer which do not characterize in the same way either our other *active* use of language (talking) or our *receptive* ones (reading and listening).

Carol Burgess et al.,
Understanding Children Writing

4.31 I took the container from the shelf and examined it more closely. ⌈"colon"⌋ The label read *P. Broca.* ⌈[that is to say]⌋ In my hands was Broca's brain.

Carl Sagan, Broca's Brain

The linking word *and* is particularly rich in meaning. An example will isolate that richness:

4.32 I studied hard, ⌈and⌋ I earned a good grade.

Example 4.32 most naturally means, "I earned a good grade *because* I studied hard"; this would be the meaning that we signal with the key word *so:*

4.32A I studied hard, | and [so] | I earned a good grade.

The linking word *and*, however, can also mean *and then,* suggesting only that two events are connected in time.

4.33 I got up, | and [then] | I brushed my teeth.

We call this connection a *narrative and,* and we mark it with the key words *and then* (related words are all time words: *next, later, after that, then*).

There is a third linkage signaled by *and;* this linkage simply means that items are joined in a list:

4.34 Betty had a hot dog, | and | Timothy had a hamburger.

We wouldn't normally read sentence 4.34 as an *and so* or as an *and then* connection.

4.34A Betty had a hot dog, | and [so] | Timothy had a hamburger. (?)

4.34B Betty had a hot dog, | and [then] | Timothy had a hamburger. (?)

Moreover, sentence 4.34 can be reordered, where our *and so* and *and then* sentences sound extremely odd when they are reordered:

4.34C Timothy had a hamburger, | and | Betty had a hot dog.

4.33A I brushed my teeth, | and [then] | I got up. (?)

4.32B I earned a good grade, | and [so] | I studied hard. (?)

We call this *and* a *discursive and;* it is the linkage signaled by words such as *furthermore, moreover, in addition,* and by a simple listing—*first, second, third,* and so on.

We list these possible linkages in Figure 4.4, labeling it a "grammar of coherence." The chart lists six *discursive* linkages, signaled by the key words *but, so, because, "colon," that is to say,* and *and,* and one narrative linkage, signaled by the key words *and then.* These linkages are labeled *coherent* linkages. But writers, we've noted, may also be purposefully incoherent, and we recognize such planned incoherence with the label "jump."

KEY WORD	RELATED WORDS
(Coherent Linkages)	
(Discursive Order)	
but	however, in contrast, nevertheless, on the other hand, instead, in spite of, still, yet, on the contrary
so	thus, as a result, consequently, therefore
because	since, for, due to
"colon"	for example, to illustrate, for instance, specifically
that is to say	to repeat, in other words, to clarify, to restate, or
and	furthermore, in addition, moreover, first, second, third . . .
(Narrative Order)	
and then	next, later, after that, then, subsequently
(Incoherent Linkages)	
"jump"	

FIGURE 4.4   A Grammar of Coherence

The notion of a "jump" makes sense of such associative leaps as a Joan Didion passage presented earlier:

4.35   There has been no rain since April. [*jump*] Every voice seems a scream.

Even discursive writers may "jump," at least for a few sentences, leaping from one idea to another. Most often such "jumps" create what might be called "local incoherence"—the connection is explained as the reader continues. For example, here is a scientist explaining the difficulty of thinking of the human brain as if it were a person—and in the process introducing you to the delightful word *homunculus* ("little man"). He "jumps" from a statement to the beginning of a story:

4.36   I think there is at least one [idea we should avoid]: the fallacy of the homunculus. [jump] Recently I was trying to explain

to an intelligent woman the problem of understanding how it is we
perceive anything at all, and I was not having any success.

F. H. C. Crick

The jump here is from a discursive framework to a narrative framework, but the story makes coherent sense as a whole:

4.36A I think there is at least one [idea we should avoid]: the
fallacy of the homunculus. [*jump*] Recently I was trying to explain
to an intelligent woman the problem of understanding how it is we
perceive anything at all, and I was not having any success. [*for*]
She could not see why there was a problem. [*and then*] *Finally*
in despair I asked her how she herself thought she saw the world.
[*and then*] She replied that she probably had somewhere in her
head something like a little television set. "*So* who," I asked, "is
looking at it?" [*and then*] She *now* saw the problem immediately.

This framework, or "grammar," of coherence is a useful device, for
it allows us, as readers, to "track" the coherence of discursive writing,
and it helps us, as writers, with the difficult question of what to say
next. In "tracking" discursive writing, we become aware of different
possible readings—how often one reader's "that is to say" is another's
"colon" or "thus"; we learn how often writers mark such logical relationships by using transitions to link sentences; and we sense something
of the complexities of coherence in actual writing. ["jump"] If our
minds contain a homunculus watching some mental television set, the
little man (or little woman, as the case may be) is an active and agile
one.

Problem Six. Sentence-to-sentence connections Use the "grammar of
coherence" of Figure 4.4 to provide a logical transition word to link
each sentence group below. That is, label each connection using the
words *and then, and, but, because, so, or, "that is to say," "colon,"* and
"jump." Differences of opinion are to be expected; often the lack of
larger framework does not allow a single correct answer. (You may also
wish to test this grammar of coherence by "tracking" through a continuous passage of discursive prose.)

a. My premise, which is not amenable to statistics, is that we are all, as a whole, as a nation, dumb. We simply don't know very much.

Roger Price

b. We conclude that in the field of public education the doctrine of "separate but equal" has no place. Separate educational facilities are inherently unequal.

Chief Justice Earl Warren

c. Once when former President Taft prepared to make a speech, he discovered his spectacles were missing. He asked if someone in the audience would lend him a pair.

Lloyd Chessman

d. There is only one trait that marks the writer. He is always watching.

Morley Callaghan

e. I have a problem. I *see* language.

Roland Barthes

f. "You know, a gar don't eat no dead bait. He don't eat no chicken liver like a catfish."

Junior Cook

g. "Winter time in Harlem sure is a blip," Simple complained. "I have already drunk four beers and one whiskey and I am not warm yet."

Langston Hughes

h. "I had never been behind a library desk in my life. At library school there is no practice teaching. It was another world. There was no pressure, nothing. There were books."

"Librarian," Studs Terkel

i. "Most of the time I'm sitting down here reading, a paper or a book. I got a locker full of one thing or another. The day goes. I have a shine man in the back. At least you have someone to talk to. That takes a little of your monotony off it. Deadly sometimes."

"Washroom Attendant"

j. "Aw no, I don't feel tense. I've been around this stuff ever since I was a kid. I started working a coal mine when I was in high school during the war. I started in the laboratory and went to survey. These are company jobs. A miner is a UMW man. I don't think there's a union man that wants to see the ground torn up."

"Strip Miner" ■

Problem Seven. Creating coherence Each of the frameworks below offers eight logical connections, picked randomly from the framework of Figure 4.4. Choose two patterns and fill out the pattern by creating a nine-sentence passage. You'll find your writing somewhat awkward, since we normally work the other way in writing—from meaning to pattern rather than, as here, from pattern to meaning. But the exercise should underscore the dynamics of coherence, the active nature of reading and of writing. Some suggested starting sentences: "Starve a cold and feed a fever"; "Logical connections are important in writing"; "I seldom think about Peru."

a. . . . and . . . because . . . so . . . so . . . colon . . . and . . . but . . . that is to say.

b. . . . so . . . colon . . . but . . . so . . . that is to say . . . and . . . and . . . colon.

c. . . . that is to say . . . so . . . that is to say . . . and . . . so . . . because . . . colon . . . so.

d. . . . jump . . . but . . . because . . . so . . . colon . . . and so . . . that is to say . . . because.

---

trans: Transition   Whenever possible, mark logical connections by adding transitional words or phrases.

First Draft	*Revision*
Most football injuries are the results of illegal hits. Some injuries cause permanent damage. Players should be fined, even banished from the game, for repeated illegal tackles.	Most football injuries are the result of illegal tackles. Such injuries can cause permanent damage. Therefore, players should be fined, even banished from the game, for repeated illegal tackles. (The transition words clarify the logic of the author—and repeating the key words "illegal tackles" avoids elegant variation.)
Readers may interpret words in different ways. They may come up with different meanings. The meaning is in the reader's mind.	Because readers may interpret words in different ways, they may, as a result, arrive at different meanings. Meaning, in other words, is in the reader's mind. (The transition words are helps for the reader—and, as an indirect result, they avoid the monotonous sentence patterns of the first draft.)

Frameworks of Meaning

If you tried the writing exercise of problem seven, you probably came out with what has to be called "coherent writing," since there's a logical connection between each sentence, but writing that may have seemed somehow to lack an overall pattern or development, to lack a *framework of meaning*. Here, for example, is a student attempt to write in one of the patterns of problem seven:

4.37 I seldom think about Peru. [And] I seldom think about Argentina. [[for]] [After all], I am not basically concerned about South America. [[so]] [As a result], I seldom think about those countries. [[so]] [Thus], I don't consider what's going on, politically and economically, in those countries. [["colon"]] [For example], I don't know the main industry of Peru. [[and]] [Furthermore], I don't know the leader of the government in Argentina. [[but]] [However], I should be more concerned with those countries. [[but]] [On the other hand], what does it matter?

The achievement of this student is obvious enough—he's mastered a "grammar of coherence." But it's equally obvious that there's a degree of failure here, for the passage reads like what it is, an artificial exercise. Analyzing that failure takes us beyond the connecting of sentence with sentence; it takes us close to the paragraph, the topic of the next chapter, and it takes us close to the "larger elements of arrangement" discussed later in the text. In other words, it takes us to the level of *framework*.

We like to call this lack of framework "spinning one's mental wheels," on a crude analogy with a car stuck in the snow—the motor is running and the wheels are going around, but nothing is moving. It's a common enough experience for developing writers—we sense it, for example, in the student passage from page 109. The student writer is spinning her mental wheels about the generation gap: She's quite sure there is one, but she's not sure what to do with it:

4.38 Each generation of young people is inclined to believe that their generation is the first to experience the problems encountered when maturing and finding out the essentials of life, yet the contrary is true. Each and every generation of youths, from the beginning of time on up into the twentieth century, run into the same difficulties and hardships as their father's had discovered years before and as their fathers' fathers had done. The conflict of interests and ideas between parent and child creates a situation far more common than was believed to be so. Rebellion and disagreement on the part of the child to his parent in maturation is one step toward a sense of individualism for that child, and, although his values may not truly be what he believes in, the main goal of the child is to declare that he is finally able to judge for himself and make concrete decisions on his own mental level.

Note that this problem in arrangement seeps through to affect word choice ("in maturation" for "when growing up"), sentence structure ("Rebellion and disagreement on the part of the child . . ." for "Children develop individuality by rebelling against their parents . . ."), and even the central claims (can the writer reasonably promise to survey the generation gap "from the beginning of time"?).

In contrast, what's most evident when one turns to a comparable piece of professional writing (page 109), from Margaret Mead's *Culture and Commitment,* is the sense of framework. The passage is carefully qualified ("in some societies"), and, by the last sentence, Mead has been able to shift to specific cultures ("the Banaro of the Keram in New Guinea"). The reader senses an idea being developed, not a writer spinning mental wheels.

Problem Eight. Frameworks of meaning   As experiments in working with frameworks of meaning, fill in details of meaning to flesh out two of the following frameworks of meaning into paragraph-length compositions, adding material from any subject area you wish. You may wish to consider, as a class, whether your paragraph-length compositions could be extended to a 500-word theme.

Framework A. Most people seem to believe that. . . . They act like. . . . But I don't agree that. . . . Instead, I think that. . . . After all, . . . Moreover, . . . Thus, . . .

Framework B.   There are lots of reasons why. . . . But the most important one is that. . . . That's important because it means that. . . . Furthermore, it means that. . . . And, finally, it means that. . . .

Framework C.   Few American families these days really. . . . They just don't. . . . In fact, they don't even. . . . As a result, fathers are . . . , and mothers are. . . . Similarly, children are . . . , especially teenagers, who find themselves. . . .

Framework D.   The problem, finally, is that we don't. . . . Obviously, there are only two workable solutions to this problem: either we . . . or we. . . . But if we attempt to try the first solution, we will find. . . . Therefore, our only alternative is to try the second solution, to. . . .   ■

---

coh : Coherence   The reader does not see, at this point, any coherent framework of meaning. Often, such a framework needs to be stated directly, so the reader can understand the developing plan.

First Draft

There are many opinions on abortion. One group believes . . . (This version provides no framework, no plan—the reader expects only a list of opinions.)

Revision

There are many opinions on abortion, but they can, for clarity, be separated into two groups— those who emphasize the rights of the mother, and those who emphasize the rights of what they call "the unborn child." (This version stresses the framework, the plan of division.)

This chapter will begin by making you more conscious of the features of discourse that are common to both speech and writing; let's begin by. . . . (An early version of the first part of this chapter. It gives the reader little sense of plan or framework.)

Our key word in this chapter is *coherence*. We'll define and explain coherence, and we'll isolate three elements that give coherence to speaking and writing: repeating key words and sentence patterns, connecting ideas, and providing a framework of meaning. (Here, we attempt to practice what we preach: Identifying a key word and providing a framework for the reader.)

IMPLICATIONS FOR READERS: SQRRM

Readers and writers have a curious kind of relationship: They're often unknown to each other, generally separated in time and space, and they share only the most general of assumptions—writers assume that readers will read, and readers assume that writers will make sense. Think, for example, about our curious relationship with you: We share only these pages and some vague notion of making sense.

This curious relationship presents a problem for readers—consider reading a textbook chapter, for example. The reader plods through the text, sentence by sentence, but is expected to come out of the experience, not with a copy of the chapter inscribed in his or her head, sentence by sentence, but with an understanding of the chapter, of ideas and their relationship. In this section, we'll present one approach to textbook reading, an approach that asks you to become aware of ideas and relationships as you read. The approach has a name, formed from the letters that outline its steps, SQRRM: *S*urvey, *Q*uestion, *R*ead, *R*eview, *M*ap. We'll examine each of these steps below.

Survey

A chapter survey is much like the topographical survey that map-makers conduct. Map-makers take a quick overview of the territory to be mapped, and then return later for details. Survey a textbook chapter by turning through the pages quickly, noting the chapter title, the subheadings in the text, the charts, graphs, illustrations. Often textbooks offer preliminary overviews at the beginnings of chapters or summaries at the end as a way of helping the reader to survey and review.

Use your survey to make a rough map of the chapter by arranging the key words you find in a quick survey of the chapter. A survey of this chapter might lead to a beginning map that uses the key words of the chapter title, "Coherence: From Talking to Writing," to create a first map like that of Figure 4.5.

Question

Your preliminary survey should be enough for you to ask some questions about what you're going to read: What am I expected to get from this chapter? Why was it assigned? The key words in the chapter will give you a start on questioning: In surveying this chapter, for example, you'll recognize the importance of words like *repetition, connection, logical frameworks,* and *SQRRM.* Often textbook chapters end with questions for discussion; they provide the readers with a good sense of what they are expected to master. Our problems and final writing assignments serve much the same purpose.

Read

Now that you've surveyed the chapter, sketched a preliminary map, and questioned what you're going to read, you're ready to begin reading. We've made a number of suggestions about reading through this text, and we needn't repeat them here, except to suggest that you read

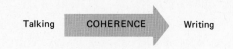

Talking   COHERENCE   Writing

FIGURE 4.5   A "Survey" Map of this Chapter

steadily, without getting bogged down by words or details, and that you read with pencil in hand, marking difficult words, questioning, and underlining. By surveying and questioning before beginning to read, you should have made the reading task much easier. There will be no sudden surprises—a driver glances at a roadmap before a trip for the same reason.

Review

Having read the whole chapter, you should find that difficult sections make better sense than they did at first, and that you can review the chapter to clear up any difficulties in the first reading. The review may take only a minute or two, but it should be enough to fix the ideas firmly in your memory.

Map

You're now ready to return to your first map of the chapter and expand it into a full map. A full map is an attempt to space out the ideas in a chapter on a single page. You'll notice, glancing through this text, how often we've attempted to map ideas visually, through charts and figures, at the same time that we present them in words. Your map is for your own use, and many of our students develop different visual signals to remind themselves of logical relationships. One student's visual map of this chapter is shown in Figure 4.6; it is simply one of many different ways of mapping our meaning.

Problem Nine. Experiments in mapping   You won't be able to evaluate our suggestions about reading textbook chapters—Survey, Question, Read, Review, Map—unless you try them out. Here are several suggestions.

- try mapping other chapters of this textbook, and compare your attempts as a class;
- as a class, survey other textbooks you might share, and in small groups compare "maps" of different chapters;

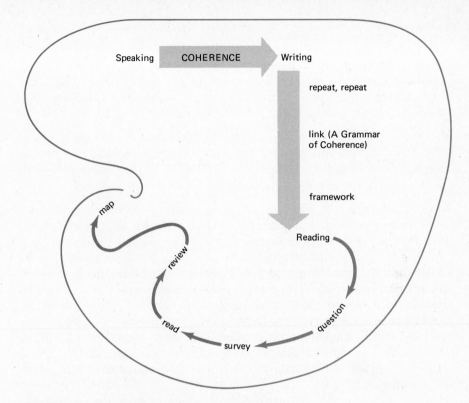

FIGURE 4.6 One Reader's "Map" of this Chapter

■ attempt to map the flow of meanings in something that does not use a purely logical framework—a poem or a short story, a television drama, the evening news on television, a football or basketball game.

FINAL WRITING ASSIGNMENTS

I. Try this experiment several times and report your findings in a short paper: Break all the rules of coherent speaking—interrupt speakers, give irrelevant replies, go out of the way to break all the patterns of ordinary talk (say "good-bye" instead of "hello," "hello" instead of "good-bye"). What are the reactions of your audiences, and what do those reactions tell you about the coherence of ordinary conversation?

II. Examine any presidential conversation in one of the many available transcripts that were a side-effect of the Watergate affair (check the library card catalog under "Watergate" and "Richard M. Nixon"). Write a brief report on the coherence of the conversation and your reaction to it.

III. Examine a poem that appears "incoherent" on the surface, and explain how you are able to create a coherent reading of it. (The focus of this assignment is not on interpreting the poem, but rather on your process of making sense of it.)

IV. You may have found yourself in a situation, at one time or another, that seemed incoherent, that didn't make sense (the first day of college, for example, or beginning a new job). Explain how you were able to create coherence or understanding from that situation.

V. The coherence of film is of a different order, a different kind, than coherence in writing. For example, a movie might begin with a long shot of New York City, then cut, without any logical transition, to a pan shot up the side of an apartment building (perhaps filmed months earlier than the first shot), and then cut to a shot of some modern Doris Day in a bathtub (filmed on a Hollywood sound stage). Yet the viewer creates a coherence from those shots—the star in a bathtub in an apartment in New York City. Examine the "coherence" of film by discussing a single television commercial or a short scene from a movie, trying to define the "smaller elements of arrangement" in film. (The rhetorical vocabulary of chapter Two may be helpful in dealing with this assignment.)

FOR FURTHER READING

Most treatments of coherence in writing are rather technical and not particularly helpful for the developing writer. Chapters One and Two of Peter Farb's *Word Play: What Happens When People Talk* (New York: Bantam, 1974) do offer, however, a popular introduction to the complexities of conversation, and David G. Hays' "Language and Interpersonal Relationships," in *Language as a Human Problem,* ed. Einar Haugen and Morton Bloomfield (New York: Norton, 1974), is a more technical discussion of the subject.

The study hint we call "mapping" is discussed, for reading teachers, in Marilyn B. Hanf's "Mapping: A Technique for Translating Reading into Thinking," *Journal of Reading,* 14 (1971), 225, and, for general readers, in Tony Buzan's *Use Both Sides of Your Brain* (New York: Dutton, 1974).

The Discursive Paragraph

Shaped by the writer's individual style and by the reader's expectations as well as by the logic of the subject-matter, the paragraph is a flexible, expressive rhetorical instrument.

ARTHUR A. STERN

In the last chapter, we were concerned with the features of coherence present in both speech and writing. In this chapter, we'll explore a feature of writing that has no equivalent in speaking: the paragraph. Paragraphs are possible only when language is written. There's no possible way for a speaker to mark off a paragraph, as the sign of the paragraph is a visual sign and not a spoken one—the indentation of a few spaces at the beginning of the first line.

Nevertheless, the written paragraph builds upon skills that you've already developed in speaking and listening—even if you can't fully explain those skills. Our first problem in paragraphing, then, is designed to convince you that you have a good working sense of *when* to paragraph, even if you can't explain the *why* of paragraphing.

Problem One. When Is a paragraph?   Each of the two passages printed below was originally printed as three separate paragraphs. Using the editing symbol ¶, meaning "begin a new paragraph here," indicate the two points at which you think the author began new paragraphs. The first passage is from a popular introduction to jazz; the second is from a highly technical discussion in *Science* magazine. (In this problem, and at other points in this chapter, we place a letter after each sentence—a, b, c, and so on—to simplify class discussion.)

Passage A

If we look at jazz history without reference to maps, but with only the concrete musical evidence of recordings, the first firm artistic fact we encounter is that from the mid-Twenties through the late Thirties Louis Armstrong's genius as an intuitive improviser affected the work of every jazz musician.(a) Certainly as a soloist, Armstrong inevitably had his imitators.(b) But more important, he had his legitimate followers who worked out some of the implications of his style for themselves without doing imitations.(c) That Louis Armstrong was a powerful and compelling player should go without saying.(d) He also had a more sophisticated sense of harmony and melody than any who had gone before him, and he gave the music a new stylistic language.(e) Further, he had a rhythmic sense that was not only surer than what had gone before him but different, and, as André Hodeir pointed out . . . his rhythmic message was the essence of his contribution to jazz.(f) It is no coincidence that the word *swing* came into use among musicians while the music was under Armstrong's tutelage, for it is their word to describe his idea of jazz rhythm.(g) He could play a phrase that had been around long before his time, but he would inflect it, accent it, pronounce it in such a way that it had a very different impetus and momentum, and this basic rhythmic impetus opened up the music to twenty years of development in melody and harmony as well.(h) In short, his influence was profound, and from 1923 to 1943 most jazz, big band or small, is significantly "Louis Armstrong Style."(i)

Martin Williams, *Where's the Melody?*

Passage B

Cellulose fibers make up only a part of the primary cell wall.(a) They are embedded in a matrix of other molecules, most of which are also polysaccharides.(b) In the cell walls my colleagues and I have examined most closely there are three (in addition to cellulose): xyloglucan, arabinogalactan and rhamnogalacturonan.(c) They are named for their principal monosaccharide constituents.(d) Xyloglucan consists mainly of xylose and glucose, although it contains small amounts of other sugars as well.(e) Arabinogalactan is made up of arabinose and galactose, and rhamnogalacturonan contains rhamnose and galacturonic acid.(f) The chemistry of these polysaccharides is considerably more complex than that of cellulose.(g) In cellulose all the sugar units are identical, and they are all bonded to one another in the same way.(h) In the other polysaccharides there are two or more kinds of sugar unit, connected by several kinds of glycosidic linkage.(i) Just two molecules of a six-carbon sugar, such as glucose, can be joined in 11 distinct ways, and three different sugar molecules can be arranged in more than 1,000 ways.(j) Since a single polysaccharide molecule can consist of hundreds of sugar units, the potential complexity is enormous.(k) Fortunately for us, in the actual molecules of the cell wall we have encountered only about two dozen kinds of glycosidic bond.(l) Moreover, all the polysaccharides in the primary wall have been found to consist of relatively small repeating substructures.(m) The largest of these substructures has 10 sugar units.(n) If it can be determined how the substructures are put together, the entire molecule can be described.(o)

Peter Albersheim, "The Walls of Growing Plant Cells"

■

Passage B of problem one is especially interesting in regard to the "when" of paragraphing, for it deals with a complicated subject and is hard reading for nonspecialists (like us). Yet, in a metaphorical sense, scientist Albersheim's concern with the arrangement of cells has a curious likeness to our topic, the arrangement of sentences into paragraphs. Indeed, our goal is much the same as his:

5.1 If it can be determined how the substructures are put together, the entire molecule can be described.

Some awareness of "substructures" seems to explain how students solve problems in "when to paragraph." Certainly students are remarkably successful at such problems. For example, the guesses of one freshman class about the paragraphing of passage two in problem one are given in Figure 5.1. The students' guesses are over 70 percent accurate (the actual paragraph breaks are crosshatched). But even more interesting is the limited range of choices: Students chose only seven of the fourteen possibilities, and all their choices are reasonable ones. The narrow range of choices suggests that students are reading this difficult passage with a sense of "substructures." They recognize the paragraph as a basic unit of print, and they know a great deal about the "when" of paragraphing. What about the "why" of paragraphing?

To find out, we asked the same freshman class to write for five minutes, without stopping, on the topic of this chapter, "the paragraph." Here's a typical response:

5.2 Every paragraph has a topic sentence topic sentence topic sentence. The topic sentence is the first sentence and then you give examples. Every paragraph starts a new topic. But the topic sentence isn't always the first sentence but every paragraph has a topic sentence and examples. Paragraphs have several sentences can't

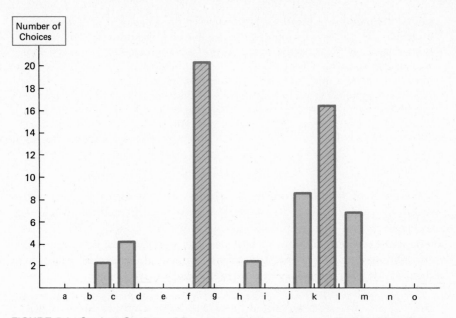

FIGURE 5.1 Student Choices of Paragraph Breaks in Passage B of Problem One

write they give examples. Topic sentences can't write can't write can't write.

This student took a good shot at a hard target, but he doesn't have much mental ammunition—only "topic sentences" and "examples." His comments seem inconsistent, for he's not sure whether the topic sentence is always the first sentence or not. His own paragraph (insofar as he was trying to write a paragraph) doesn't follow his own description—there are, for example, no examples. Finally, his description doesn't explain the skills he used (and you used) in working with problem one, where questions of meaning and "substructure" were more important than topic sentences or examples as such.

There's a big gap, then, between the paragraphing skills of this student and his ability to articulate those skills in writing. In this chapter we try to close that gap, and we do so in three steps:

■ first, we provide a new vocabulary for talking about the paragraph—*commitment and response* instead of "topic sentence and examples";

■ second, we use *levels of generality* to explain the "substructures" of the paragraph;

■ third, we explain what we call "breaking the paragraph barrier," for the student author of example 5.2 won't move toward the suppleness and agility of the printed paragraph until he discards the idea that "every paragraph starts a new topic."

First, however, note the limits of our discussion. We begin with an *ideal* kind of paragraph, one that the chapter title identifies as "the discursive paragraph." We won't list all the exceptions and qualifications to our simplified discussion. (Paragraphs that don't meet our ideal framework will be called *anomalous* paragraphs, using the scientific word for "not commonly expected.")

A NEW VOCABULARY: COMMITMENT AND RESPONSE

A vocabulary for writing is a way of thinking about writing, and our feeling is that paragraphing skills can be improved by finding better words to talk about paragraphs, the words *commitment* and *response*.

A *commitment* is a promise. We offer promises all the time in speaking, so commonly that we don't even need to identify them as promises:

5.3 *Speaker A:* "I'll meet you at the library at 6:30."
Speaker B (at the library at 6:45): "Where is he? He *promised* he'd be here."

Speaker B is correct in understanding Speaker A's statement as a promise; that's simply built into the speech situation.

Similarly, some statements in ordinary conversation are *commitments:* promises to talk about something in more detail.

5.4 *Speaker A:* "The food in the cafeteria is lousy."
Speaker B: "It's not so bad."
Speaker A: "Oh, come on. You know how bad the hamburgers are. And the drinks are watery. And the french fries taste like soggy cardboard."

Here Speaker A makes a commitment and, when Speaker B disagrees, responds to that commitment by supporting the claim. In speaking, however, commitments may be ignored or sidestepped; we can always talk about something else:

5.5 *Speaker A:* "The food in the cafeteria is lousy."
Speaker B: "That picture's crooked. Biology is a snap course. There's a new monster movie at the Palace."

In writing, however, such commitments can't be ignored; they *are* promises. Thus the paragraph, as a basic unit of writing, generally follows a commitment-response framework. The first sentence, the commitment sentence, makes a promise, and the response sentences fill out, expand, elaborate, or fulfill that promise. The commitment sentence announces the limits of the paragraph; the response sentences work within those limits, defining, clarifying, even offering examples.

A Commitment Is a Topic Plus a Comment

Why is it better to think of "commitment sentences" instead of "topic sentences"? For one thing, topic sentences, as normally described, can appear at the beginning of paragraphs, toward the middle, or at the end—and some textbooks speak of "implied" topic sentences, hovering over a paragraph like a benign ghost, a sort of discursive ectoplasm, as it were. Commitment sentences, on the other hand, are guiding sentences. They lead readers into the paragraph by telling them what it is about; they draw a line around the subject-matter.

More importantly, writers who think of making commitments will remember their promise to the reader. A commitment sentence is a promise about a topic, not simply a "topic." That's a significant difference, a better way of thinking about the paragraph. Here, for example, are some "topics":

5.6 I'm writing about Louis Armstrong.

5.7 I'm writing about polysaccharides in cell walls.

5.8 I'm writing about commitment sentences.

5.9 I'm writing about food in the cafeteria.

Here are the same topics reconsidered as commitments: promises about topics.

5.6A I'm writing about Louis Armstrong, and I promise to show how his genius influenced others from the mid-twenties through the thirties.

5.7A I'm writing about polysaccharides in cell walls, and I promise to explain their glycosidic linkage.

5.8A I'm writing about commitment sentences, and I promise to show the value of thinking about topics plus promises.

5.9A I'm writing about the food in the cafeteria, and I promise to show that it's lousy.

In other words, thinking about "topic sentences" limits writers to "topics," and the result is often a series of random shots at a topic, shots that ignore the lines drawn by the commitment.

Commitments Guide Paragraphs

Thinking of "commitment sentences" also helps us to see that promises have to be general enough to allow us to respond to them, yet specific enough to be sketched in fully. Thus, on one hand, there's the danger of "dead-level fact," a sentence that cannot be developed:

> **5.10** Ophelia, a Leghorn hen owned by an Ottumwa, Iowa, farmer, laid seven eggs on October 19, 1956.

On the other hand, there's the danger of promising too much, drawing too big a frame by making too general a promise.

> **5.11** Every paragraph ever written has a commitment-response framework.

Besides being false, as we'll see, example 5.11 would seem to commit the writer to examining "every paragraph ever written," or at least a reasonable sample, showing that each has a commitment-response structure.

Finally, commitment sentences may not only draw a line around a topic, but also establish the framework of the discussion. That is, they may make a promise about the "shape" of the discussion as well as its subject. Thus *reading for commitments* has as much value, for the reader, as writing with commitments has for the writer. Readers need to see, critically, whether promises are fulfilled.

---

com : Commitment The commitment sentence of the paragraph seems too general; it doesn't offer a precise promise; or it makes a commitment that can't be developed.

First Draft	*Revision*
Next, there's the question of television advertising. (Offers a topic, not a commitment.)	Children are also disillusioned by television advertising. (Makes a specific promise.)
Pirsig's novel, *Zen and the Art of Motorcycle Maintenance,* considers everything. ("A neat trick," the curious reader might respond.)	Pirsig's novel, *Zen and the Art of Motorcycle Maintenance,* covers subjects from the philosophical to the ordinary, yet manages to combine them in a unified whole. (Offers a commitment that can be developed.)

Problem Two. Commitment sentences   Be prepared to discuss the following commitment sentences written by professional writers. What is the topic, and what promise is made about it? Is the commitment at a reasonable "level," so that it can be fulfilled in a paragraph? What can you predict about the form of the response sentences?

a. In our culture, it is a woman's body which is considered important while it is a man's mind or his activities which are valued.

Aileen Pace Nilsen

b. The language of the film is a language composed of dialects, each clearly identifying the region inhabited by the user.

Ronald Harwood

c. There were two ancient Greek philosophers, long before even Socrates haunted the streets of Athens, who had diametrically opposed views of reality.

Emmanuel Mesethne

d. Apart from teaching him Latin, Stratford Grammar School taught Shakespeare nothing at all.

Marchette Chute

e. The film director's desire for a more flexible and mobile instrument that would enable the camera to move freely about the set led to more sophisticated machinery.

Lee R. Bobker

f. The process of learning is essential to our lives.

g. The crucial point I wish to make here is that language is the basic instrument of the social reality.

Geneva Smitherman

■

LEVELS OF GENERALITY IN THE PARAGRAPH

A typical business firm or government organization delegates responsibility by *levels of generality*, with the president, at the top, with the most general responsibility, the vice-presidents a step below, down the levels of management to department heads to specific workers at specific machines. Figure 5.2 shows a partial organization chart for the National Endowment for the Humanities. Each step down the chart narrows the responsibilities; the chart moves from general to more specific.[1] If we examine the chart from the top down, we can describe positions as *coordinate* or *subordinate*. The Director of the Division of Fellowships has a responsibility coordinate with that of the Director of State Programs; both are subordinate to the Chairman.

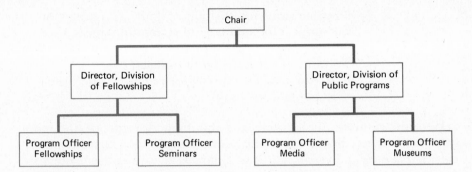

FIGURE 5.2 A Partial Organization Chart for the National Endowment for the Humanities

We can present the same information in outline form, and we can number the levels of responsibility, calling the Chairman "1" and the Division Directors "2" and so on; thus we would create an outline like this:

5.12   1] Chairman of the National Endowment for the Humanities
      2] Director, Division of Fellowships
        3] Program Officer, Fellowships for the Professions
        3] Program Officer, Summer Seminars and Summer Stipends
      2] Director, Division of Public Programs
        3] Program Officer, Media Programs
        3] Program Officer, Museums and Historical Programs

The same notion of levels of generality can explain the "substructures" of a paragraph as well as of an organization. In fact, we can turn the organization chart of 5.12 into a paragraph, again numbering the levels of generality, now sentence by sentence:

5.13   1] The National Endowment for the Humanities is an independent Federal agency founded to serve all areas and levels of humanistic study in the United States.(a)
      2] The Endowment's Division of Fellowships offers support for humanistic study.(b)
        3] This support includes a fellowship program for those in nonacademic professions.(c)
        3] It also includes summer programs and stipends for those in academic professions.(d)

2] The Endowment's Division of Public Programs offers support for a number of community agencies.(e)
3] This support includes funding for media programs to reach the adult public.(f)
3] It also includes support for museums and historical organizations.(g)

Here the number "1" identifies the commitment sentence, the most
general sentence. Sentences b and e are coordinate with each other,
each explaining a division and each followed by two subordinate sentences explaining specific programs. The notion of levels of generality,
then, can describe paragraphs as well as organizations. It gives us a way
of picturing the substructures of the response to a commitment, a way
of describing the "why" of paragraphing—and thus a way into the
"how to" of paragraphing.

The Three-Sentence Paragraph

We can most easily present levels of generality in the paragraph by
starting with the "three-sentence paragraph," and then moving to more
complex paragraphs. We offered transition words to explain how one
sentence is linked to another in the last chapter, and we can now rein-
troduce those words, listing them as words that mark coordinate relationships (*and, but, or*) and as words that mark subordinate relationships
(*for, so, that is to say,* and the "colon" introducing an example). With
these words in mind, we can explain a three-sentence paragraph like
that of 5.14:

5.14 In our culture, it is a woman's body which is considered im-

portant while it is a man's mind or his activities which are valued.

[*colon*] A woman is sexy. [but] A man is successful.

Aileen Pace Nilsen

We can further explain the "why" of this passage by numbering the
levels of generality, as in 5.14A. (Note that the numbers in 5.14A show
levels of generality; we are not numbering the sentences.)

5.14A   1] In our culture, it is a woman's body which is considered important while it is a man's mind or his activities
which are valued.(a)
colon   2] A woman is sexy.(b)
but   2] A man is successful.(c)

The two response sentences (b and c) are at the same level of generality, coordinate with each other. Thus we will call this a *simple coordinate framework*. We can explain the "why" of this framework with five tests:

■ The two response sentences are at the *same level of generality*, about "a man" and "a woman."
■ The two response sentences use the *same pattern*, "a man is" and "a woman is," suggesting that they are coordinate with each other.
■ The two sentences *can be linked* with the coordinate marker *but*.
■ The two response sentences *can be switched* without changing the meaning or the framework of the paragraph.
■ Each sentence *develops one claim* made in the commitment sentence; thus we can add arrows to map the sentence further:

5.14B   1] In our culture,

> → it is a woman's body which is considered important
>
> → while it is a man's mind or his activities which are valued.
>
> └─ 2] A woman is sexy.
> └─ 2] A man is successful.

The other expected three-sentence framework is a *simple subordinate framework*, each sentence moving further down the levels of generality, as in 5.15.

5.15   1] The language of the film is a language composed of dialects, each clearly identifying the region inhabited by the user.(a)
  2] Producers, directors, technicians all have their own jargon; the screenwriter is no exception.(b)
    3] The screenplay dialect is individual and capable of infinite variety.(c)

> Ronald Harwood,
> "The Language of Screenwriting"

We can explain the "why" of this paragraph using the same five tests as above:

■ *Level of generality.* Each sentence is more specific than the preceding one, from "dialects" in general to specific "dialects" to one specific "dialect."

- *Sentence pattern.* Here each sentence uses a different pattern.
- *Transition words.* The transition words we "read into" the paragraph are subordinate words. Indeed, we can use the subordinate markers "colon" and *for* to rewrite the paragraph as a sentence:

5.15A The language of the film is a language composed of different dialects, each clearly identifying the region inhabited by the user[:] producers, directors, technicians all have their own jargon; the screenwriter is no exception, [*for*] the screenplay dialect is individual and capable of infinite variety.

- *Order.* The order of the response sentences cannot be switched, as they can in most coordinate frameworks. Here the reader must work down through levels of generality.
- *Develops a claim.* Direction arrows show that each sentence responds to the sentence before. Sentence c responds to the commitment of sentence a, but it does so by means of (or perhaps by way of) sentence b:

5.15B

1] The language of the film is a language composed of dialects, each clearly identifying the region inhabited by the user.(a)

2] Producers, directors, technicians all have their own jargon; the screenwriter is no exception.(b)

3] The screenplay dialect is individual and capable of infinite variety.(c)

Not all tests will work with all paragraphs, of course, and, as we'll see, there is room for legitimate disagreement about levels of generality. Moreover, not all three-sentence paragraphs are simple coordinate frameworks or simple subordinate frameworks. But for our purposes, other frameworks are *anomalous;* they are not what we're looking for.

Problem Three. The three-sentence paragraph   Label each of the three-sentence paragraphs below as *simple coordinate frameworks* (that is, assign a level of 1] 2] 2]), as *simple subordinate frameworks* (1] 2] 3]), or as *anomalous frameworks.* Be prepared to defend your choices using the five tests above: level of generality, sentence pattern, transition words, order, and development of claim.

a. Do not fear to repeat what has been said.(a) Men need truth dinned into their ears many times and from all sides.(b) The first rumor makes them prick up their ears, the second registers, and the third enters.(c)

René Laennec

b. Methods of learning animal languages vary widely.(a) You can do it by wearing a magic ring, like King Solomon, or by taking a cocktail of dragon's blood, like Siegfried.(b) But there are much simpler ways, such as having your ears cleaned out, or carrying churchyard mould in your hat.(c)

Claire and W.M.S. Russell

c. There was never any such thing as witchcraft.(a) Nobody can do magic.(b) Nobody can fly through the air on a broomstick or conjure up the devil or cast spells on a neighbour.(c)

Gilbert Highet

d. I have sought love, first, because it brings ecstasy—ecstasy so great that I would often have sacrificed all the rest of life for a few hours of this joy.(a) I have sought it, next, because it relieves loneliness—that terrible loneliness in which one shivering consciousness looks over the rim of the world into the cold unfathomable lifeless abyss.(b) I have sought it, finally, because in the union of love I have seen, in mystic miniature, the prefiguring vision of the heaven that saints and poets have imagined.(c)

Bertrand Russell

e. Not all tests will work with all paragraphs, of course, and, as we'll see, there is room for legitimate disagreement about levels of generality.(a) Moreover, not all three-sentence paragraphs are simple coordinate frameworks or simple subordinate frameworks.(b) But for our purposes other frameworks are *anomalous;* they are not what we're looking for.(c)

f. At the Ancient Astronauts Conference there was talk of the wonderful ball.(a) It was said to be eight inches in diameter, 22 pounds in weight, made of stainless steel and capable of performing odd feats.(b) Set in motion by a twist of the hand, it would wander around drunkenly for up to ten minutes, giving off little rattling noises.(c)

Timothy Ferris

g. The paragraph, like many other good things, was wrecked by mass production.(a) When newspapers, and then magazines, began to be published for the millions, writers soon found their readers short-winded.(b) They would hold their brains together for three or four sentences, no more.(c)

Henry Seidel Canby

Expanding Coordinate Frameworks

Let's look again at a simple coordinate framework:

5.16 1] There were two ancient Greek philosophers.(a)
2] There was Parmenides.(b)
2] And later there was Heraclitus.(c)

The framework remains the same regardless of the amount of information the writer puts in the framework. In fact, example 5.16 is a simplified version of an actual paragraph, which adds a more precise commitment, stressing the differing opinions of the philosophers.

5.17 1] There were two ancient Greek philosophers, long before even Socrates haunted the streets of Athens, who had diametrically opposed views of reality.(a)

"colon" 2] There was Parmenides, who argued that all change is illusory, transitory, imperfect, unreal.

and 2] And later there was Heraclitus, who saw reality as a flowing river, apparently the same but never the same, to whom all was constant flux and change, and who dismissed the permanent as unreal, as evidence of human imperfection, as a distortion of reality.

Emmanuel Mesethne

The simple framework, then, is not limited to simple meanings. The designs of meaning complicate and embroider the framework, and the framework can be expanded as needed. Example 5.18 offers a simple coordinate framework carried to five sentences:

5.18 1] Stratford Grammar School taught Shakespeare nothing at all.
2] It did not teach him mathematics or any of the natural sciences.
2] It did not teach him history.
2] It did not teach him geography.
2] It did not teach him modern languages.

Again, we note that the writer has used sentence patterns to support the meaning, repeating the same sentence pattern in each coordinate response. If we "vary the sentence structure," without thinking of the framework of meaning, we hide the coordinate framework, and we turn a clear paragraph into a verbal puzzle:

5.18A Stratford Grammar School taught Shakespeare nothing at all. Mathematics was not a part of the school curriculum, and there also were not any of the natural sciences in the list of courses. Shakespeare was not able to take a history course. Geography was not presented to him. The school that Shakespeare attended also did not have a department of modern foreign languages.

Instead, the writer, Marchette Chute, builds a "varied sentence structure" by adding detail, keeping the coordinate framework in front of the reader and weaving specifics into that framework.

5.18B   1] Apart from teaching him Latin, Stratford Grammar School taught Shakespeare nothing at all.(a)
2] It did not teach him mathematics or any of the natural sciences.(b)
2] It did not teach him history, unless a few pieces of information about ancient events strayed in through Latin quotations.(c)
2] It did not teach him geography, for the first (and most inadequate) textbook on geography did not appear until the end of the century, and maps and atlases were rare even in university circles.(d)
2] It did not teach him modern languages, for when a second language was taught at a grammar school it was inevitably Greek.(e)

The simple coordinate framework, then, supports the commitment sentence by stringing items in a coordinate series, often by numbering them ("first . . . second . . . third . . ."), and usually by signaling the coordinate framework by using the same sentence pattern. Each sentence develops the commitment at the same level of generality.

Problem Four. The simple coordinate framework   The paragraph below uses the now familiar simple coordinate framework. We print it as a normal paragraph, without separating the sentences or numbering the levels of generality, but you'll notice, in reading, that your mind adjusts to the framework as well as to the meaning. You've moved from the *when* to the *why*. (Notice also that the paragraph, which comes near the end of a civil rights discussion by Martin Luther King in the early 1960's, lists his disappointments in an emphatic series.)

All of this reflects disappointment lifted to astronomical proportions. It is disappointment with timid white moderates who feel that they can set the timetable for the Negro's feelings. It is disappointment with a federal administration that seems to be more concerned about winning an ill-conceived war in Vietnam than about winning the war against poverty here at home. It is disappointment with white legislators who pass laws in behalf of Negro rights that they never intended to implement. It is disappointment with the Christian church that appears to be more white than Christian, and with many white clergymen who prefer to remain silent behind the security of stained-glass windows. It is disappointment with some Negro clergymen who are more concerned about the size of the wheel base on their automobiles than about the quality of their service to the Negro community. It is disappointment with the Negro middle class that has struggled out of the muddy ponds into the relatively fresh-flowing waters of the mainstream, and in the process has forgotten the stench of the backwaters where their brothers are still drowning.

> Martin Luther King, Jr., "Where Do
> We Go from Here: Chaos or Community?"

■

Now write two paragraphs of your own that follow the same simple coordinate framework.

Some sample topics:

■ kinds of students at your school
■ food in the cafeteria
■ why a course is easy (or hard)
■ why you are happy
■ problems facing the country (or can you narrow that general topic?)

Simple Subordinate Frameworks

The other simple framework is the simple subordinate framework. In such a framework, each sentence responds specifically to the sentence that preceeds it. Such a response can take several forms: a restatement ("that is to say"), a conclusion ("therefore"), a reason ("for"), and, most commonly, an example (*"colon"*). An example of a simple subordinate framework is the paragraph you're reading right now. That is, the second sentence explains the first, the third clarifies the second, the fourth offers an example, and this sentence, the fifth, is a "that is to say" sentence. Therefore this paragraph both explains and illustrates the subordinate framework.

Subordinate frameworks will occur naturally as writers seek to chain ideas, to deal with effects and results, as in 5.19.

5.19   1] The film director's desire for a more flexible and mobile instrument that would enable the camera to move

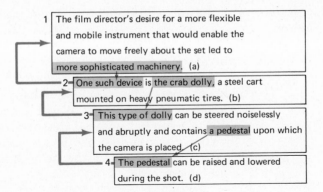

FIGURE 5.3   A Simple Subordinate Framework

freely about the set led to more sophisticated machinery.(a)
2] One such device is the crab dolly, a steel cart
mounted on heavy pneumatic tires.(b)
3] This type of dolly can be steered noiselessly and
abruptly and contains a pedestal upon which the
camera is placed.(c)
4] The pedestal can be raised and lowered during the shot.(d)

Lee R. Bobker, *Elements of Film*

A simple subordinate framework, then, is a kind of chain, each sentence linked to the one before. We can picture this framework with a
diagram, showing how each sentence is linked to the one before, as we
have diagrammed example 5.19 in Figure 5.3. Or we can see the subordinate framework as a process of anticipating reader's questions, sentence by sentence, each sentence providing a more specific response.
Thus we can offer a rather silly dialogue of promise, question, and
response:

5.20 "I really liked that movie."
"What did you like about it?"
"The way it kept you in suspense."
"How did it keep you in suspense?"
"You never knew what was going to happen."
"What do you mean by that?"
"That scene where John Wayne went into the castle, for instance:
you didn't know whether he was going to find the dwarf again, or
the belly dancer, or the monster."

Adapted to written form, the silly conversation becomes a silly subordinate paragraph:

5.20A   1] I enjoyed the movie.(a)
        2] The best thing about it was the suspense.(b)
           3] You never knew what was going to happen.(c)
               4] The scene in which John Wayne entered the castle is a good example of this suspense.(d)
                  5] You didn't know whether he would find the dwarf again, or the belly dancer, or the monster.(e)

The subordinate framework, then, can be written out by inserting possible reader's questions, as in this example by Jacob Bronowski:

5.21   1] The process of learning is essential to our lives.(a)
      [What evidence supports this claim?]
      2] All higher animals seek it deliberately.(b)
      [How?]
        3] They are inquisitive, and they experiment.(c)
        [What's an experiment?]
          4] An experiment is a sort of harmless trial run of some action which we shall have to make in the real world; and this, whether it is made in the laboratory by scientists or by fox cubs outside their earth.(d)
          [So what?]
          5] Perhaps that is what gives them both their air of happiness and freedom in these activities.(e)

Problem Five. Simple subordinate frameworks Below is a paragraph by Claude Brown, lamenting what he saw as the breakdown of the language of urban black ghettoes, places he calls "Soulville" in the paragraph.

As increasingly more Negroes desert Soulville for honorable membership in the Establishment clique, they experience a metamorphosis, the repercussions of which have a marked influence on the young and impressionable citizens of Soulville.(a) The expatriates of Soulville are often greatly admired by the youth of Soulville, who emulate the behavior of such expatriates as Nancy Wilson, Ella Fitzgerald, Eartha Kitt, Lena Horne, Diane Carroll, Billy Daniels or Leslie Uggams.(b) The result—more often than not—is a trend away from spoken soul among the young soul folks.(c) This abandonment of the Soul language is facilitated by the fact that more Negro youngsters than ever are acquiring college educations (which, incidentally, is not the best treatment for the continued good health and growth of soul); integration and television, too, are contributing to the gradual demise of the spoken soul.(d)

"The Language of Soul"

■

As you read the paragraph, you should have recognized the subordinate framework, even though we did not indent and number the levels of generality. Thus you should be ready to attempt a few such paragraphs of your own. Write two paragraphs in subordinate frameworks. Possible topics:

- the food in the cafeteria
- why a course is easy (or hard)
- what makes you angry
- a good job or a good movie

Mixed Paragraph Frameworks

We've now examined two paragraph frameworks. First we examined the coordinate framework, in which each response sentence is at the same level of generality:

5.22   1] The food in the cafeteria is lousy.(a)
        2] The drinks are watery.(b)
        2] The french fries are soggy.(c)
        2] And the hamburgers are stale.(d)

And then we examined the subordinate framework, in which each sentence developed more specifically the preceding one:

5.23   1] The food in the cafeteria is lousy.(a)
        2] The hamburgers are stale.(b)
            3] Yesterday I had one that was so bad I couldn't eat it.(c)
                4] It looked like a fried inner tube, and it tasted like it had been cooked last Tuesday.(d)

Two steps will take us from these simple frameworks to the dynamic nature of the normal discursive paragraph. The first step is to mix the two frameworks, continuing to indent and to number level of generality:

5.24 1] The food in the cafeteria is lousy.(a)
2] The drinks are watery.(b)
2] The french fries are soggy.(c)
2] And the hamburgers are stale.(d)
    3] Yesterday I had one that was so bad I couldn't eat it.(e)
        4] It looked like a fried inner tube, and it tasted like it had been cooked last Tuesday.(f)

This gives us a mixed paragraph framework, the most common type. We'll examine a mixed framework sentence by sentence, noting the options available to the writer at each point. The paragraph we'll examine is the final paragraph of a speech by Geneva Smitherman about the adequacy and importance of the language behavior of the black community. She begins with a general statement about the importance of language:

5.25A 1] The crucial point I wish to make here is that language is the basic instrument of the social reality.(a)

The next sentence explains more specifically how language is the basic instrument of social reality:

5.25B 2] Created in the human environment, adaptable and subject to change, it is a tool that man manipulates to a desired end.(b)

Language is, generally, an "instrument"; it is, more specifically, a "tool." At this point, the writer has three choices: end the paragraph; write a subordinate sentence, explaining how language is a "tool"; or write a coordinate sentence:

5.25C 2] It is power.(c)

Here again the writer has three choices: end the paragraph; write a coordinate sentence (we would expect the same sentence pattern, "it is . . ."); or write a subordinate sentence, explaining more specifically how language is "power":

5.25D 3] Black language, though often superciliously termed "nonstandard English," contains as much power, complexity and usefulness as other varieties of American English, including the so-called "Standard" idioms.(d)

Notice here the chaining of meaning: If language is an instrument, it is a tool and it is power, and if language is power, then black language has as much power (and complexity and usefulness) as other varieties. At this point, the writer's options expand: end the paragraph; write a coordinate sentence (perhaps beginning, "Appalachian English . . ."); work back, however awkwardly, to the second level (possibly, "Moreover, language is fun"); and, of course, develop more specifically the claim about the social reality of black language:

5.25E 4] A quick glance at the street environment of Black America reveals an oral culture where one's social survival is exactly proportionate to his ability to *rap* and *cap*.(e)

5] *Rapping* is language facility directed toward making a point in a powerful manner.(f)

At this point, the reader might predict the beginning of the next sentence, for one senses a pattern:

5.25F 4] . . . his ability to *rap* and *cap*.

5] *Rapping* is language facility directed toward . . .

5] *Capping* is language facility directed toward . . .

The writer does fulfill that expectation, but first chooses to extend her claim about the social use of *rapping*:

5.25G 5] *Rapping* is language facility directed toward making a point in a powerful manner.(f)

6] The skillful *rapper* wins the adulation of his peers and becomes a culture hero.(g)

7] (Unknown to many, Rap Brown's given name is not Rap but Hubert; he was dubbed "Rap" because of his ability to deliver a message, that is, his ability to *rap*.)(h)

5] *Capping* is language facility directed toward conquest of one's opponent through verbal attack.(i)

6] In the ghetto jungle of Claude Brown's "promised land," even physical survival may depend on *capping* ability: many a black cat *has capped his way out of a rumble,* i.e., averted a fight by employing his verbal repartee and linguistic wit to shame an opponent into leaving the scene.(j)

At this point, the mixed framework is essentially complete. The commitment of the paragraph is important enough, however, to be restated in a concluding sentence (labeled "C"), so that the paragraph moves from general statement to restatement to specific examples, then back to the general statement:

5.26   1] The crucial point I wish to make here is that language is the basic instrument of the social reality.(a)

2] Created in the human environment, adaptable and subject to change, it is a tool that man manipulates to a desired end.(b)

2] It is power.(c)

3] Black language, though often superciliously termed "nonstandard English," contains as much power, complexity and usefulness as other varieties of English, including the so-called "Standard" idioms.(d)

4] A quick glance at the street environment of Black America reveals an oral culture where one's social survival is exactly proportionate to his ability to *rap* and *cap.*(e)

5] *Rapping* is language facility directed toward making a point in a powerful manner.(f)

6] The skillful *rapper* wins the adulation of his peers and becomes a culture hero.(g)

7] (Unknown to many, Rap Brown's given name is not "Rap" but Hubert; he was dubbed "Rap" because of his ability to deliver a message, that is, his ability to *rap.*)(h)

5] *Capping* is language facility directed toward conquest of one's opponent through verbal attack.(i)

6] In the ghetto jungle of Claude Brown's "promised land," even physical survival may depend on *capping* ability: many a black cat has *capped his way out of a rumble,* i.e., averted a fight by employing his verbal repartee and linguistic wit to shame an opponent into leaving the scene.(j)

C] As Ralph Ellison has said, "One uses the language which helps to preserve one's life, which helps to make one feel at peace in the world, and which screens out the greatest amount of chaos."(k)

The *content* of such a paragraph is clearly beyond the reach of the developing writer; it's a product of Professor Smitherman's study of, and participation in, the black community. But the *form* of such a paragraph is within reach: As one works out substructures of meaning, one creates ideas to fill out a commitment.

Problem Six. The master paragraph The paragraph challenges in this problem are only representative of the challenges you can create for yourself or for other members of the class. You may wish to expand paragraph topics you've attempted before, or to find new topics.

a. Write a paragraph that uses the levels of generality used by the Geneva Smitherman paragraph above:

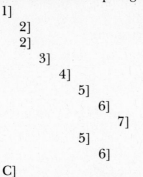

    1]
       2]
       2]
          3]
             4]
                5]
                    6]
                        7]
                5]
                  6]
  C]

b. Write a paragraph with a commitment, a restatement, and three examples, with each example developed in two sentences. Your paragraph will have this form:

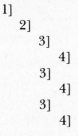

    1]
       2]
          3]
             4]
          3]
             4]
          3]
             4]

c. Write a ten-sentence paragraph, beginning, "There are two solutions to the problem of. . . ." End with a concluding sentence explaining why one solution is better than the other. Your paragraph may have the following framework:

    1] There are two solutions to the problem of. . . .
        2] The first solution is. . . .
           3]
              4]
                5]
        2] The second solution is. . . .
           3]
              4]
                5]
    C]

                                            ■

Fudge Factors

Scientists and mechanics talk of "fudge factors," informal ways of fitting the unruly world into some framework—explaining away a slight error in an experiment or improvising a part if a replacement isn't available. Explaining the why of paragraphing is at least as complicated as doing a science experiment or fixing a car, and we feel justified in adding a few fudge factors to our discussion.

Introductory and Concluding Sentences

Although example 5.25 above has just a single concluding sentence, it's possible to extend concluding remarks to two or more sentences, labeled C1, C2, and so on.

5.26   1] The food in the cafeteria is lousy.
        . . .
        C_1] Obviously, something must be done.
        C_2] Perhaps we need a new manager.

Similarly, writers may write introductory sentences, such as the first sentence after the last heading; these can be labelled I_1, I_2, and so on.

5.27   I] Scientists and mechanics talk of "fudge factors" . . .
        1] . . . we feel justified in adding a few fudge factors of our own.

5.28 I_1] The cafeteria is clean, friendly, and inviting.

I₂] The staff is courteous, considerate, and conscien-
tious.

1] But the food, sadly enough, is lousy. . . .

Sometimes You Can't Tell

Consider a short paragraph like 5.29.

5.29   I had a terrible day. I was late for work. My car broke down.

It's possible to read this paragraph in two ways, as a simple coordinate
framework or as a simple subordinate framework—that is, as in 5.29A
or 5.29B:

5.29A   1] I had a terrible day.
"colon"   2] I was late for work.
and   2] My car broke down.

5.29B   1] I had a terrible day.
"colon"   2] I was late for work.
for   3] My car broke down.

Thus you'll find a certain legitimate range of differing opinions as you
move from contrived textbook examples to real paragraphs. There's a
clear difference, though, between legitimate alternatives ("sometimes
you can't tell") and readings that are simply wrong, as in 5.29C, because they violate our sense of how the world works.

5.29C   I] I had a terrible day.
but   1] I was late for work.
so   C] My car broke down. [a "wrong reading"]

Stress the Rhetoric of a Paragraph, Not Its Logic

We've treated "for" and "so" sentences as subordinate sentences, as in
5.29B above, even though the logic of levels of abstraction might suggest otherwise, since "I was late for work" and "My car broke down"
are at the same level of generality. What we lose logically, though, we
gain rhetorically, for we clarify the substructures of, say, commitment
and restatement:

5.30   1] Do not fear to repeat what has been said.
for   2] Men need truth dinned into their ears many times
            and from all sides.

René Laennec

Some Paragraphs Are Anomalous

Most discursive paragraphs seem to move within the commitment-response framework we've discussed in this chapter. But the paragraph, as our headnote on page 129 reminds us, is "a flexible, expresssive rhetorical instrument," and we can expect to meet anomalous paragraphs in many contexts. Transition paragraphs are common, concluding one topic and beginning another; thus

> **5.31**   C] We've explained levels of generality in the paragraph.
> I] We'll now explain what we mean by "breaking the paragraph barrier."

One can construct "backward paragraphs," turning a normal discursive structure inside out:

> **5.32A**   1] Banana skins can be dangerous.
> 2] People shouldn't drop them carelessly.
> 3] Today I slipped on one and fractured my tibia.
>
> **5.32B**   3] Today I slipped on a banana skin and fractured my tibia.
> 2] People shouldn't be so careless with banana skins.
> 1] After all, they can be dangerous.

Finally, we can find anomalous paragraphs with no commitment sentence as such:

> **5.33**   1] I have sought love, first, because it brings ecstasy—ecstasy so great that I would often have sacrificed all the rest of my life for a few hours of this joy.
> 1] I have sought it, next, because it relieves loneliness—that terrible loneliness in which one shivering consciousness looks over the rim of the world into the cold unfathomable lifeless abyss.
> 1] I have sought it, finally, because in the union of love I have seen, in mystic miniature, the prefiguring vision of the heaven that saints and poets have imagined.
>
> Bertrand Russell

Such anomalies needn't disturb us unduly. Indeed, we'll find, as we go on to "break the paragraph barrier," that such anomalies may be so only at the level of the paragraph—they may be explained by the larger movement of commitment and response.

SUMMARY

Instead of a summary, we offer a paragraph—a student paragraph written by the same student who wrote the free writing we cited at the beginning of this chapter ("Every paragraph has a topic sentence topic sentence topic sentence."). This is a more considered effort, developed from a commitment sentence supplied by the instructor; nevertheless, it marks, for this writer, a solid growth in the "how to" of paragraphing. The student has indented and numbered levels of generality.

5.34   1] Most discursive paragraphs have a commitment-response structure.(a)
> 2] The commitment sentence offers a promise to the reader.(b)
>> 3] Thus it limits the development of the paragraph.(c)
>> 3] Moreover, it often suggests something about the structure of the response sentences.(d)
> 2] The response sentences develop the commitment; they are structured by level of generality.(e)
>> 3] Coordinate sentences are at the same level of generality.(f)
>> 3] Subordinate sentences move down the level of generality. (g)
> C₁] Of course, not all paragraphs follow this pattern rigidly.
> C₂] Writers may choose, for example, to write introductory or concluding sentences.

IMPLICATIONS FOR WRITERS

This view of the paragraph has obvious implications for writers, as the problems we've presented have suggested. We'll explore two further implications of this view of the paragraph, one taking us back into the substructures of the paragraph ("punctuate by the paragraph, not by the sentence") and one taking us beyond the artificial limits of the paragraph ("breaking the paragraph barrier").

Punctuate by the Paragraph

Let's return to a few sentences from the middle of a paragraph we examined before:

5.25G

    5] *Rapping* is language facility directed toward making a point in a powerful manner.(f)

    6] The skillful *rapper* wins the adulation of his peers and becomes a culture hero.(g)

    7] (Unknown to many, Rap Brown's given name is not "Rap" but Hubert; he was dubbed "Rap" because of his ability to deliver a message, that is, his ability to *rap*.)(h)

    5] *Capping* is language facility directed toward conquest of one's opponent through verbal attack.(i)

We're interested in the punctuation of sentence (h): How can we explain the parentheses that surround the sentence, and the semicolon that joins what might have been separate sentences? We can't explain that punctuation at the sentence level; it makes sense only at the paragraph level: The parentheses set off the example, keeping the reader's attention on the more general claims about rapping and capping, and the semicolon links two base clauses to stress again the subordinate nature of the sentences. In other words, the paragraph framework explains the punctuation of the sentence.

That example leads to an important piece of advice for writers: Punctuate by the paragraph, not by the sentence. We can clarify this point by mispunctuating another paragraph examined before:

5.14A In our culture, it is a woman's body which is considered important. [But] it is a man's mind or his activities which are valued. A woman is sexy. A man is successful.

This mispunctuated version is hard to read: We're offered one commitment, then another, then a response to the first, and then a response to the second:

5.14B 1] In our culture, it is a woman's body which is considered important.

    1] But it is a man's mind or his activities which are valued.

    2] A woman is sexy.

    2] A man is successful.

For a final example, note the semicolon forced on the student writer of 5.34:

5.34A　　2] The commitment sentence offers a promise to the reader.(b)

. . .

2] The response sentences develop the commitment; they are structured by level of generality.

(The question of punctuation as part of the print code is explored in more detail in chapter Nine.)

Breaking the Paragraph Barrier

Problem Seven. Topic sentences in magazines　A writer took a standard textbook definition of *topic sentence* and tested it against discursive articles in recent issues of magazines like *Harper's, Atlantic,* and *The New Yorker.* What percentage of paragraphs would you predict had conventional topic sentences at the beginning of the paragraph? To make your choice easier, here are five predictions. Choose one: a) 99 percent; b) 84 percent; c) 56 percent; d) 37 percent; e) 11 percent.　■

In aviation in the late 1940s, pilots of the new jet planes probed with terror what they called the "sound barrier"—the speed of sound, roughly 700 miles an hour, identified as Mach 1. As pilots reached speeds of .7 Mach, .8 Mach, and .9 Mach, they lost elevator, aileron, and rudder control, and they were subject to severe buffeting. Many engineers predicted that a plane reaching Mach 1 would disintegrate in midair. "Breaking the sound barrier," it was predicted, was impossible.

On October 14, 1947, Army pilot Chuck Yeager, flying the experimental X-1 rocket, broke the sound barrier; he became, in effect, the first human in space.

5.35　The X-1 had gone through "the sonic wall" without so much as a bump. As the speed topped out at Mach 1.05, Yeager had the sensation of shooting straight through the top of the sky. The sky turned a deep purple and all at once the stars and the moon came out—and the sun shone at the same time. He had reached a layer of the upper atmosphere where the air was too thin to contain reflecting dust particles. He was simply looking out into space. As the X-1 nosed over the top of the climb, Yeager now had seven minutes of . . . Pilot Heaven . . . ahead of him. He was going faster than any man in history, and it was almost silent up here, since he had exhausted his rocket fuel, and he was so high in such a vast space that there was no sensation of motion. He was master of the sky. His was a king's solitude, unique and inviolate, above the dome of the world. It would take him seven minutes to glide back and land. . . .

Tom Wolfe, *The Right Stuff*

We find that developing writers face a "paragraph barrier" as forbidding as the "sound barrier" was to pilots in the 1940s. "Every paragraph has a topic sentence," they recite, and "every paragraph starts a new topic," as if, say, using two paragraphs to explore the same topic or even (gasp!) not having a topic sentence would subject them to the writerly equivalent of losing elevator, aileron, and rudder control and being subjected to severe buffeting. The "paragraph barrier" is an absolute.

But it's easy to break the paragraph barrier. Here are three writing experiences of our own where we "broke the paragraph barrier"; perhaps they will help you to do the same. One of us wrote a short textbook on writing, some years back. He drafted the manuscript on the typewriter, breaking the barrier by shaping his paragraphs to the shape of the typed page. Unfortunately, his editor hadn't told him that the text would appear in narrow columns, a couple of inches wide, and in that context his paragraphs looked endless, even forbidding, dragging down one column and then down the next without a breathing space for the reader.

In an opposite experience, one of us wrote an article for a technical journal that used small type and wide margins. Here his paragraphs, again shaped on the typewriter, seemed much too short, giving the article the look of popular journalism rather than serious scholarly research. To break the paragraph barrier effectively, then, it is useful to know what final form the writing will be in.

One of us can remember consciously breaking the paragraph barrier for the first time. He had begun what we now recognize as a coordinate framework, "There are four reasons for . . ." and had worked through "first," "second," and "third," explaining each reason in a couple of sentences—thus the framework of 5.36:

5.36 1 There are four reasons for. . . .
        2] First . . .
          3]
        2] Second . . .
          3]
        2] Third . . .
          3]

He confidently wrote, "fourth, and most importantly," still within that paragraph, when he stopped, suddenly aware of the paragraph barrier. Logically, his "fourth, and most importantly," belonged in the same paragraph. But rhetorically his "fourth" needed a new paragraph: He had written a long paragraph already, and his concluding reason was more important than the other three. Quite consciously, he broke the paragraph barrier: He started a new paragraph. It may have been illogical, but it was rhetorically effective.

In fact, like skillful magicians, we have broken the paragraph barrier even as we discuss it. These three paragraphs might have been shaped as two paragraphs, as one, as three, even as six—as suggested in the outline of 5.37:

5.37	1] But it's easy to break the paragraph barrier.	[commitment sentence for 3-paragraph sequence]
	2] Here are three writing experiences . . .	
	3] One of us wrote . . .	[optional paragraph]
	3] In an opposite experience, one of us wrote . . .	[actual paragraph]
	3] Indeed, one of us can remember . . .	[optional paragraph]
	2] In fact, like skillful magicians, we have broken the paragraph barrier. . . .	[actual paragraph]
	C] The paragraph, in short, is a supple and agile unit.	[actual paragraph]

The paragraph, in short, is a supple and agile unit. It adapts to physical shape, as in the short paragraphs of newspapers. It adapts to expectations about paragraph length—British writers, for example, tend to use longer paragraphs than do American writers. And it adapts to rhetorical contexts—the writer who looked for conventional topic sentences in magazines found them in only 11 percent of the paragraphs he examined;[2] we would expect a much higher percentage in textbooks. From this view, we can see how limiting the paragraph barrier can be, and when we look beyond the paragraph, we can see larger frameworks of commitment and response:

5.38	1] Three passions, simple but overwhelmingly strong, have governed my life: the longing for love, the search for

knowledge, and unbearable pity for the suffering of mankind.(a)

2] These passions, like great winds, have blown me hither and thither, in a wayward course, over a deep ocean of anguish, reaching to the very verge of despair.(b)

¶   3] I have sought love, first, because it brings ecstasy— ecstasy so great that I would often have sacrificed all the rest of life for a few hours of this joy.(c)

3] I have sought it, next, because it relieves loneli- ness—that terrible loneliness in which one shivering consciousness looks over the rim of the world into the cold unfathomable lifeless abyss.(d)

3] I have sought it, finally, because in the union of love I have seen, in mystic miniature, the prefigur- ing vision of the heaven that saints and poets have imagined.(e)

4] This is what I sought, and though it might seem too good for human life, this is what—at last—I have found.(f)

Bertrand Russell, *Autobiography*

By itself, Russell's second paragraph is anomalous; seen within the larger movement of commitment and response, it becomes an effective way of breaking the paragraph barrier.

Problem Eight. Breaking the paragraph barrier   Experiment with sev- eral ways of breaking the paragraph barrier. Here are some sugges- tions:

■ Write the longest single paragraph you've ever written—250 words, even 350 words—on a subject that might be discussed in a college textbook. Then discuss how you would reparagraph the sentences for the student newspaper or for a popular magazine.

■ Write a two-paragraph sequence, in which the second paragraph de- velops a commitment in the first paragraph. Your second paragraph might offer an extended example of a claim made in the first para- graph, or the first paragraph might offer a commitment like "There are two reasons for . . . ," with the second reason becoming a sec- ond paragraph.

■ Write an anomalous paragraph, and then place it within a larger pattern of commitment and response.

■ Return to one of the paragraphs written in response to earlier prob- lems in this chapter, and expand it by adding more sentences to it, until you force yourself to break the paragraph barrier.

■ Passage 5.35, page 157 above (on Chuck Yeager breaking the sound barrier), suggests a last possibility: Begin by writing, "I went through the paragraph barrier without so much as a bump," and continue writing for two paragraphs. ■

IMPLICATIONS FOR READERS: THE OUTLINE

The outline is a formal way of marking levels of generality in an extended piece of writing. The outline is thus an organized summary. As such, it provides a useful way of picturing a textbook chapter and of planning an essay.

Informal Outlines

Informal outlines—often called "scratch" outlines—are shortened notations of the order in which topics might be considered, using one or two levels of indentation to show a framework:

5.39 Civil Service
    pay
    fringe benefits
      job security
      retirement
    locations
      Washington
      elsewhere

Scratch outlines are a necessity in planning answers to essay examinations, and many writers use such outlines as a way of beginning any writing assignment. But notice that such an outline presumes that the writer knows what those topics mean; the headings are simply reminders. For outlines that are useful to readers, we need to turn to more formal frameworks.

Formal Outlines

Formal outlines are usually divided into *topic outlines* and *sentence outlines*. A topic outline expands a scratch outline by lettering and numbering the headings. A topic outline submitted with a written paper normally begins with a thesis sentence. Example 5.39A offers a topic outline developed from the scratch outline above.

5.39A *Thesis:* Working conditions in the United States Civil Service are, in general, excellent.

    I. Pay
   II. Fringe benefits
      A. Job security
      B. Retirement
  III. Assignments
      A. United States
        1. Washington, D.C.
        2. Other United States locations
      B. Foreign.

Such outlines provide a reader with a helpful overview of a paper. But note that the topic outline is limited as a study aide—the outline above, for example, doesn't tell us that civil service salaries are high because they are regularly adjusted to be comparable with jobs outside government. Thus the most helpful outline for students is the sentence outline. The sentence outline expands topics to complete sentences, to commitments.

5.39B *Thesis:* Working conditions in the United States Civil Service are, in general, excellent.
    I. Salaries tend to be relatively good.
      A. They are equated with comparable salaries outside government.
      B. They are regularly adjusted with cost-of-living increases.
   II. There are also many fringe benefits.
      A. Job security is quite high.
      B. Retirement benefits are good.

The sentence outline is a good study aide. For example, a student might supplement an informal "map" of a textbook chapter (discussed in chapter Four) with a formal sentence outline of the chapter.

The formal outline differs from the levels of generality used to discuss the paragraph in that it is a logical framework. Thus a convention is that "every 1 must have a 2, every A must have a B." That is, every level of indentation must have at least two entries—otherwise, so the argument runs, you wouldn't need the division.

Problem Nine. The sentence outline We offer below a sentence outline of this chapter, with some sentences left out. Enter the missing headings, remembering to use full sentences.

    I. The normal discursive paragraph uses a commitment-response framework.

    A. The commitment sentence is a topic plus a comment.
    B.
  II. Paragraph development can be explained by level of generality.
    A. A coordinate framework is a series of responses at the same level of generality.
    B.
    C. Most commonly these frameworks are mixed together.
    D. There are some exceptions to these frameworks.
      1. Sometimes writers add introductory or concluding sentences.
      2.
      3. Some paragraphs are anomalous.
III.
    A. Writers should punctuate by the paragraph.
    B.
  IV. This view of the paragraph is related to outlining.
    A. Informal or "scratch" outlines are helpful in taking essay tests.
    B.
      1. A topic outline lists topics.
      2. A sentence outline uses complete sentences.   ■

FINAL WRITING ASSIGNMENTS

I. From Paragraph to Theme You have probably written several paragraphs in response to problems in this chapter, and you may have found that you have written yourself into a topic that is worth exploring beyond the level of a paragraph. Take one of the paragraphs written in response to problems, and expand it from a paragraph to a 400- to 600-word theme. For example, the sentences in a simple 1-2-2-3 paragraph might become commitment sentences of paragraphs in a longer theme—although, of course, the structure might change as the paper develops.

II. Reparagraphing As a final assignment in chapter Fifteen we reprint two articles from the *New York Times*. As might be expected in a newspaper, both articles use rather short paragraphs. Reparagraph the articles for publication in textbook form. Write a short paper explaining your decisions.

FOR FURTHER READING

Our approach to the paragraph draws, in part, on two sources you may wish to consult: the discussion of commitment and response in Robert M. Gorrell and Charlton Laird's *Modern English Handbook,* 6th ed. (Englewood Cliffs, N.J.: Prentice-Hall, 1977), and Francis Christensen's "Generative Rhetoric of the Paragraph," in his *Notes Toward a New Rhetoric,* rev. ed., with Bonniejean Christensen (New York: Harper & Row, 1978).

NOTES

1. We discuss *general* and *specific* in more detail in chapter Seven, dealing with the sentence, pp. 215–218, and in chapter Nine, dealing with words, pp. 296–299.
2. Richard Braddock, "The Frequency and Placement of Topic Sentences in Expository Prose," *Research in the Teaching of English,* 8 (1974), 287–304.

UNIT III

STYLE

6

Sentence Choices:
Clarity and Directness

> It is possible to communicate fairly complex ideas in a style that is, from the point of view of the reader, easy to read, but which from the point of view of the writer is, I can assure you, extremely complex to write.
>
> JOSEPH WILLIAMS

The Romans used the word *stylus* to refer to the quill or point that scribes used to write on papyrus or clay. (The word *stylus*, in English, is used to refer to the needle of a stereo set.) The stylus of a scribe would be gradually shaped by the pressure of his handwriting, and each scribe came to prefer his own stylus, the one shaped to his own hand. The word *stylus*, even in the original Latin, broadened in meaning to refer to habits of expression as well as handwriting. Thus our word *style*.

But the word *style* has continued to broaden in English, so that we can now speak of the "style" of a dress or the "style" of a third baseman. Our topic in this unit, then, needs to be narrowed to sentence style, or, more precisely, *prose style*. (Prose is ordinary writing, as opposed to poetry.)

The prose style of a writer consists of two parts: the words chosen and the way they are arranged into sentences—or, more technically, *diction* and *syntax*. The two sentences below mean about the same thing; they differ in diction:

6.1 The dog wagged its tail.

6.2 The canine oscillated its caudal appendage.

This aspect of style—word choice—is discussed in the next unit. In this unit we consider syntax—the arrangement of words into sentences. Examples 6.3 and 6.4 differ in syntax, though they mean about the same thing.

6.3 The boy threw the ball.

6.4 The ball was thrown by the boy.

In this chapter, we'll look at ways of achieving two goals of style that most writers (and most readers) would consider to be highly desirable qualities: clarity and directness. Writers ought to be clear and direct. But as our headnote suggests, being clear and direct may be much more difficult than it first appears; an easy-to-read style can be very hard to write. Nevertheless, we can offer some straightforward hints about being clear and direct, and we can build your confidence in your control of the written sentence. We'll do so in three steps:

- First, we'll ask you to become more conscious about the role of choice in crafting sentences. We'll look at sentence choice by experimenting with the technique called *sentence combining*.
- Second, we'll ask you to think about writing in a new way, not as "What do I want to write?" but as "What will my reader understand?" One writer refers to this shift as becoming "reader-centered" rather than "writer-centered," and we'll work toward this shift by introducing two elegant, if rough-hewn, concepts, those of the *meaning chunk* and the *dumb reader*.
- Finally, we'll ask you to master a bit of the grammar of the English sentence. Our discussion will be relatively painless, and you may find it useful.

SENTENCE COMBINING

There is no inevitably correct or right choice in sentence style; there's no one style for every occasion. There are only styles—choices of expression. Each style—each set of choices—has to be judged on how well it works in a rhetorical context: on its appropriateness to the stance of the writer, the meaning to be conveyed, and the audience addressed. "Please pass the salt" may be appropriate for a formal dinner, but "Toss me the salt, will you?" might be a better choice at a picnic. "I do believe that the smell of smoke and the sight of flames engulfing the curtains is indicative of a situation of potential conflagration" gets its message across, if slowly, but in most situations you'd be smarter to shout "FIRE!" at the top of your voice.

The best way to get a feel for sentence choices is the exercise called *sentence combining.* There are no hidden correct answers to these first exercises; we simply want to start you on the business of this chapter, making choices about sentences.

Problem One. Sentence combining   The two passages below are written in short sentences. They seem choppy and disconnected, like the writing of "Dick and Jane" books for first graders. Rewrite the passages to make them clear and direct for adult readers.

You'll need to add or subtract words and to change the forms of words. But try not to change the basic meaning of the passages.

A   The cattle tick is small. The cattle tick has a body. The body is flat. The cattle tick is an insect. It sucks blood. It has a curious life history. It emerges from the egg. It lacks legs. It lacks sex organs. It attacks animals that have cold blood. Then it sheds its skin several times. It acquires its missing organs. It mates. It is ready to attack animals. These animals have warm blood. The female cattle tick is eyeless. Her skin is photosensitive. It directs her to the tip of a twig. She waits. Her metabolism slows. It is almost suspended entirely. Ticks have waited for eighteen years. They wait for a signal. The signal is butyric acid. Butyric acid is present in sweat. The sweat is that of animals that have warm blood. She smells the scent. She throws herself toward the scent. She lands on an object. She senses if the object is warm. If it is, she buries her head into the skin. She drinks the blood. Only then do the sperm release. Only then are the eggs fertilized. The tick drops from the animal. The tick lays its eggs. The tick has lived for years. The tick has lived for one moment. The moment is fulfillment.[1]

B   There was a big change. The change was in the English language. The change came after 1066. The Normans came from France in 1066. They conquered England. They stayed in England. They spoke French. They made French the language of government. The English still spoke English. The two languages interacted. English changed in many ways. English borrowed words from French. Often the French word replaced an English word. But often both words stayed in English. An example is interesting. The example is about words. The words are for animals and meat. The English were servants. They worked on the farms. They used English words for animals. The words were *pig* and *cattle* and *sheep* and *deer*. The French sat at the table. They were served the meats. The meats were *porc* and *boeuf* and *mouton* and *venaison*. These became English words. The English words are *pork* and *beef* and *mutton* and *venison*. Thus English developed one word for the animal. And it developed another word for the meat.   ■

Here are several student versions of an opening sentence or two from the first sentence combining problem. How do we decide which version is the best?

6.5   The cattle tick is a small insect that has a flat body and sucks blood. It has a curious life history.

6.6   The cattle tick, a small, flat-bodied, blood-sucking insect, has a curious life history.

6.7   The cattle tick is an insect which is small, with a flat body. It sucks blood and has a curious life history.

Each of these versions is "correct English," and there are many other versions possible, all equally correct. Which version is the best? It depends—on message, reader, writer, and context.

- It depends on *the reader*. Example 6.5 might be better for a sixth-grade textbook; example 6.6 might be better for an adult reader.
- It depends on how *the writer* wishes to present herself. The passage implies a fairly formal tone and a knowledgeable writer (perhaps 6.6 again?).
- It depends on *the message*. Example 6.7 makes sucking blood as important as having a curious life history, and example 6.8, below, distorts the meaning and would be unacceptable.

6.8   The small cattle tick is a curious insect with a body that is flat and a life history that sucks blood.

- It depends on *the context*. In this case, the sentences lead to a discussion of the "curious life history" of the cattle tick and thus we might prefer 6.6, which places more emphasis on that life history.

We use that example to make an important point: Being clear and direct does not mean being short and simple. Indeed, the most complex of the three seems best, more clear and more direct because it "chunks" the information more effectively. Readers read in "chunks" of meaning.

MEANING CHUNKS

Suppose we were to ask you to memorize the letters in example 6.9.

6.9   xmetnrepie

You'd find it hard to do, and if we showed you the letters for only a second or so, you'd probably remember only four or five of them. Here is the same memory task, the same ten letters, only now "chunked" in a different way:

6.9A experiment

These letters aren't hard to remember; readers of English can produce them even when they see them flashed on a screen for as little as a fiftieth of a second. This result isn't surprising: The first arrangement gave you ten letters to remember, ten chunks, and the second gave you only one chunk, the word *experiment*. Thus we'll speak of "chunking" meaning for the reader.

Psychologists explored this kind of chunking in an ingenious set of experiments. They asked subjects to listen to tape-recorded sentences, interrupted with a short burst of noise, called a "click," as in 6.10:

6.10 Jack was in the boat that had a leak.
↑
"click"

Subjects were then asked where the click occurred. They tended to hear the click at the beginning or ending of a chunk of meaning, not where it actually occurred. They would respond, for example, as in 6.10A:

6.10A Jack was in the boat that had a leak.
reported ⌐↑   ↑⌐ *actual*
"click"

In fact, the psychologists were able to make the click jump, in the minds of listeners, by changing the chunks of meaning in the sentence.[2] Notice how the click shifts, for listeners, in the following pair of sentences:

6.11 Your eagerness to win the horse is quite immature.
actual ⌐↑   ↑⌐ *reported*
"click"

6.12 In its eagerness to win the horse is quite immature.
reported ⌐ ↑ ↑⌐ *actual*
"click"

What's happening? Listeners and readers understand language in chunks, not word by word, and being clear and direct in writing means chunking meaning effectively.

Ambiguity: Mischunking

Ambiguous sentences are sentences with two or more possible meanings. They are interesting, for they illustrate how readers chunk meaning. Examples 6.13 and 6.14 are ambiguous sentences:

6.13   They are eating apples.

6.14   The chicken was too hot to eat.

We can show the ambiguity by putting the sentences into two contexts, forcing them to assume two different meanings.

6.13A   The campers are enjoying themselves. They are eating apples.

6.13B   Those apples are expensive, but they are worth it. They are eating apples.

6.14A   We fried the chicken. The chicken was too hot to eat.

6.14B   The chicken walked listlessly around the barnyard. The chicken was too hot to eat.

Notice how each possible reading creates different chunks of meaning:

6.13A   They [are eating] apples.

6.13B   They are [eating apples].

6.14A   The chicken was too hot [for us] to eat [the chicken].

6.14B   The chicken was too hot [for the chicken] to eat.

Ambiguous sentences point out the difficulty of communicating in writing, where we're not present to explain our meaning to the reader. They point out, in fact, how dumb our readers are. (Read on.)

Problem Two. Ambiguity   Each of the sentences below is ambiguous. Rewrite each sentence in two ways, forcing one or another of the possible meanings. For example, one might remove the ambiguity from "they are eating apples" by offering two versions:

■ Those apples are eating apples.
■ Those children are eating apples.

Similarly, one might remove the ambiguity from "the chicken is too hot to eat" by offering the following versions:

■ The chicken we fried is too hot for us to eat.
■ That chicken in the barnyard feels too hot to eat.

The first examples are contrived examples, some humorous; the last examples, some equally humorous, are from student papers.

a. John likes entertaining women.

b. Use more colorful language.

c. SCHOOL SEEKS RETARDED TEACHERS [newspaper headline]

d. The Xerox machine reproduces anything on white bond-weight paper.

e. The student newspaper took pictures of the university cooking students.

f. She's an oriental art expert.

g. He finished the race last Friday.

h. Use indelible ink and varnish over it.

i. She worked as a disturbed girl's counselor.

j. I have always been an outdoor lover.   ■

The Dumb Reader

In speaking of "the dumb reader," we don't mean to isolate some readers and call them dumb. Rather, we say that *all* readers are dumb, dumb in the sense that they don't have access, as writers do, to what writers want them to read. Given a chance, any reader, because he is dumb, will misread.[3] In fact, with a little ingenuity, we can turn you into a dumb reader. We can almost guarantee that you'll misread sentence 6.15, at least until you get to the end.

> **6.15** I was afraid of Ali's powerful punch, especially since it had already laid out many tougher men who had bragged they could handle that much alcohol.

Most readers interpret *punch* as a blow, until the last word forces them to see it as a drink. A more complex challenge is presented by 6.16:

> **6.16** The freight trains carried weighed more than the freight airplanes carried.

It works every time. The dumb reader chunks "freight trains" together until he or she comes to the impossible sequence "carried weighed," at which point the sentence must be solved again:

6.16A THE FREIGHT trains carried WEIGHED MORE THAN THE FREIGHT airplanes carried.

Because all readers are dumb readers, in the special sense of that phrase, all writers have trouble with the dumb reader, particularly writers, such as journalists and students, who have to write under tight deadlines, with little time to think of the reader. So even professional writers have trouble with the dumb reader. A reporter for the Rochester (Mich.) *Clarion,* hurrying to meet a deadline, confidently writes a lead sentence:

6.17 Although he's been dead for 19 years, thanks to the dedication and determination of one Rochester woman, Edgar Guest has not been forgotten.

The reporter wants the reader to make the Rochester woman responsible for keeping alive the memory of poet Edgar Guest; the dumb reader, chunking the sentence as it's written on the page, makes the Rochester woman responsible for the death of the poet. Rechunking the sentence eliminates the problem.

6.18 Although he's been dead for 19 years, Edgar Guest has not been forgotten, thanks to the dedication and determination of one Rochester woman.

Similarly, another reporter dashes off a short sentence, utterly clear to the writer:

6.19 The warranty aids home owners with defects.

Knoxville (Tenn.) Sentinel

The writer sees one chunk of meaning:

6.19A The warranty aids . . . with defects.

The dumb reader sees another chunk:

6.19B . . . home owners with defects.

Here there are several possible solutions. The writer might eliminate the confusing words:

6.19C The warranty aids with defects.

Or the writer might add more information to prevent the dumb reader from misreading:

6.19D The warranty aids home owners who find defects in their home.

Such mistakes by professional writers ought to give some confidence to the developing writer, for they suggest that all writers at all levels have trouble with the dumb reader. The next two problems ask you to rewrite mistakes by professional journalists; the examples are drawn from a regular column in the *Columbia Journalism Review*. We turn then to types of mischunking more common in the developing writer, the *fused sentence,* in which the reader is offered two competing ways of chunking, and to problems of pronoun *reference.*

Problem Three. Chunking headlines "You're hired," Lou Grant says, in his typically blunt voice. "You're on the rewrite desk, and your first job is to check our headlines. Make sure they are clear and direct for the reader."

a. Boycott snowballs in Pontiac.

b. Talks to bear on Seattle future.

c. City to add 12 foot cops.

d. Building needs to be aired.

e. Village burning said illegal.

f. FBI plans to handle future assassinations.

g. Chains popular as bridal gifts.

h. Smoking riskier than thought.

i. Wives kill most spouses in Chicago.

j. Suspect held in killing of reporter for Variety. (A special problem.) ■

Problem Four. The rewrite desk "You're promoted," says Grant. "You're in charge of the rewrite desk. Make sure our readers will read what our reporters want them to read. That will mean rechunking sentences, adding clarifications, and taking out confusing words."

a. After years of being lost under a pile of dust, Walter P. Stanley, III, found all the old records of the Bangor Lions Club at the Bangor House.

b. Mrs. Consigny was living alone in her home in Nakoma after her husband died in 1954 when the telephone rang.

fus : Fused Sentence   A fused sentence begins one way and ends another way; thus it "fuses" two sentence patterns, offering the reader two possible ways of reading the sentence.

First Draft	*Revision*
This was the view of the expert about which she told us about. (This "fuses" two patterns, "about which she told us" and "which she told us about.")	This was the view of the expert about which she told us. *OR* This was the view of the expert she told us about. *OR* She told us about the expert's views. (The first two choices "unfuse" the sentence, the first more formally, the second more informally. But, as the last option suggests, the best revision is often to back out of the sentence and start over.)
Therefore, the most difficult decision I have had to make about is which college I wish to attend. (A fused sentence, moving in several directions at once.)	Therefore, the most difficult decision was choosing a college to attend. (This revision moves the sentence in one single direction. Most often, though, the best answer is to back out of the sentence and start again:) I had a hard time picking a college.

c. State police charged Craft with firing several gunshots into a Plumcreek Township mobile home occupied by four persons and a pickup truck last November.

d. For the second time in 13 months, a man who has been supplying authorities with information on cigarette smuggling in Pennsylvania has been slain.

e. Greeson pulled out the knives that Goode said he killed his wife with and stabbed himself. He laid them before the jury along with pictures of the victim's body.

f. Two men—one carrying a dynamite bomb and the other an officer of the New Jewish Defense League—were arrested today on charges of plotting to bomb the Egyptian government Tourist Office in Rockefeller Center, the FBI announced.

g. After the blast, Cooper said, his company marched to within 100 to 200 yards of the tower, then reduced to a 20-foot pile of molten steel.

h. Newman, author of two Book-of-the-Month Club books on the abuse of language, hinted in a speech to nearly 1,300 persons in the Memorial Union Theater that efforts to improve language may be the result of attacks on pompous, inane, verbose language such as his.

i. I found no serious scholar in the field who fully agreed with him, and indeed his own dean and two fellow professors rebuked him publicly for using his position to attack the Delaney Amendment, which bans carcinogens in a campus publication.

j. The Mormon Church has no doctrinal position on when life begins but takes a hard line against abortion performed for reasons other than to save the life of the mother or in cases of rape or incest after counseling with a bishop.   ■

---

ref : Reference   Keep pronoun references clear for the reader. The writer always knows who is doing what; sometimes the reader can't tell.

First Draft

Rich skated down the right wing, watching the goalie come out to meet him. He skated directly at him. ("Who," asks the reader politely, "skated directly at whom?")

Student government has ignored the needs of commuter students, by refusing to install lockers. They have ignored the interests of minority students by scheduling only white entertainment. This shows their lack of concern for the students as a whole. (This is coherent prose, but the reader has trouble seeing what student government has done in general— the problem is in the unclear reference, *this*.)

Revision

Rich skated down the right wing, watching the goalie come out to meet him. The goalie skated directly at him, trying to cut off his view of the goal. ("Thank you," responds the reader politely.)

. . . This insensitivity to the needs of all students shows their lack of concern for the student body as a whole. (Here the writer explains the reference *this*, giving the reader a better sense of her argument.)

A DRAM OF GRAMMAR

At this point we need to introduce a more formal vocabulary for talking about the printed sentence. That means grammar, and we imagine the groans from our readers. But the grammar we'll present will be fairly brief, a dram of grammar—in fact, only six words:

■ recognizing that *sentence bases* have *subjects* and *predicates,* and that the *predicates* consist of a *verb* and completing words.

■ recognizing that meaning is added to sentence bases by *coordination* and *subordination,* terms that may be familiar from our discussion of the paragraph in chapter Five.

Moreover, when we combine this vocabulary with the notion of chunking for the dumb reader, already discussed, we'll develop some practical hints on being clear and direct. Finally—perhaps best of all—we can show you that you already know what we're asking you to learn.

The Sentence Base

We've spoken before about your underlying "language competence," which informs both your speaking and writing. We'd like now to isolate one part of that language competence, your knowledge of how sentences go together. We'll ask you to predict how sentences go together in another language, and your prediction will tell us an interesting fact about sentences in English.

Problem Five. Asking questions in German   Below, in the first column, are statements in German, with English translations. In the second column, we have changed the first of those sentences from statements into questions. Guess the German form of the question for the next two statements, either writing your answer in the space provided or writing it on a separate sheet, as your instructor directs.

Er singt.   Singt er?
("He sings.")   ("Does he sing?")

Maria singt gut.
("Maria sings well.")   _____

Der Mann singt gut.
("The man sings well."   _____

There are many *logical* ways to answer problem five—most of the possibilities deal with *word order.* For example, German speakers might

quite logically turn statements into questions by saying them back-
wards. This guess would give us 6.20:

6.20 Er singt. ⇒ Singt er?
Maria singt gut. ⇒ Gut singt Maria?
Der Mann singt gut. ⇒ Gut singt Mann der?

Similarly, it's logically possible to guess that German speakers form
questions by exchanging the first and last word of a statement. This
guess would give us 6.21:

6.21 Er singt. ⇒ Singt er?
Maria singt gut. ⇒ Gut singt Maria?
Der Mann singt gut. ⇒ Gut Mann singt der?

What's interesting is that these and other logical possibilities never
show up when we give the problem to students. Students respond to
the *grammar* of the sentence, not to the *logic* of word order. They guess
that German forms questions by inverting the order of *subject* and *predicate*. This guess gives them 6.22:

6.22 Er Singt. ⇒ Singt er?
Maria singt gut. ⇒ Singt gut Maria?
Der Mann singt gut. ⇒ Singt gut der Mann?

That's not a correct guess, but it's a good one—it's exactly how questions are formed in modern Greek. The only other choice students
make is to guess that German forms questions by inverting the *verb* and
the *subject,* leaving the other part of the *predicate* where it is. This guess
gives us 6.23, which happens to be the correct form for questions in
German.

6.23 Er singt. ⇒ Singt er?
Maria singt gut. ⇒ Singt Maria gut?
Der Mann singt gut. ⇒ Singt der Mann gut?

In other words, students approach this problem by using their un-
conscious awareness of the terms we want to introduce: A *sentence base*
consists of a *subject* and a *predicate,* and a predicate consists of a verb
and other words that may be used to complete the sentence. The subject and predicate may each be a single word, as in "he sang," or both
may be quite long. This awareness of sentence bases is so strong that,
in doing sentence combining problems, you may be quite aware of

picking one sentence as the "base" and chunking into it the meaning of the other sentences. We will emphasize the importance of sentence bases, in this chapter and the next, by printing the words that make up the sentence base in capital letters.

6.6A THE cattle TICK, a small, flat-bodied, blood-sucking insect, HAS A curious life HISTORY.

Figure 6.1 lists a number of sentence bases.

Not all written or spoken sentences have full subjects and predicates. In ordinary speech we can leave out parts of the sentence base, say in answering questions.

6.24 "Where's the cauliflower?"
"In the refrigerator."

Commands, like "Help!" or "Cogitate!" lack a subject, the understood *you,* and we recognize patterns like "easy come, easy go" and "the more, the merrier" as sentences, even though they lack the normal subject-predicate order.

But in most writing situations, sentences must be punctuated as full subject-predicate units. A sentence punctuated without a sentence base is called a *fragment* or *incomplete sentence,* and most writers, in most contexts, avoid them entirely. Some professional writers, though, do slip in a fragment, now and then, in informal writing. Like this. For em-

Subject	Predicate	
	Verb	Completor
The general	slept.	
The admiral	ate.	
The bureaucrat	ate	his dinner.
The rabble rouser	gave	the police a hard time.
She	seems	comfortable.
What she tried to do	was	keep the kitten quiet.
They	became	friends.
It	is	Jack.
The professor	ought to have been about to be giving	the students the test.

FIGURE 6.1 Typical Sentence Bases

phasis. And some kinds of writing—magazine advertisements, for example—rely heavily on the fragment. But the developing writer, aiming at a college audience, is best off punctuating sentences to include complete sentence bases.

Problem Six. Rewriting sentence fragments Below are two magazine advertisements. They use sentence fragments for emphasis. Rewrite the ads, removing the sentence fragments. You may find that several fragments can be chunked into a single sentence.

A. "21 million Americans over 16 can't read a Want Ad."
You'll find them all over America. Doing nothing. Going nowhere.
Twenty-one million Americans who never had a chance. Because no one ever helped them want to read.
Reading is FUN-damental (RIF) has a simple, incredibly successful way to keep today's youngsters from winding up in the same boat.
A way to make them want to read. To make them grow up to be the kind of bright, ambitious adults you want working for your company.
Books they pick out themselves. For keeps. Because once you give a kid a book he can call his own—a kid who never had much of anything that really belonged to him—he'll want to read it.

RIF, Inc.

B. "Switzerland is good for you."
To the Swiss hospitality is a fine art. Practiced, and perfected, in every hotel and restaurant.
To your host in a mountain resort it can mean airing the bed linens in the Alpine sunshine. To his counterpart in Basel, leaving a morsel of chocolate on your bedside table. . . .
But beyond these matters, Swiss hospitality has unique, more personal interpretations. Such as sharing with guests a precious, private collection of fine art.
In Zurich, for example, you can dine in the presence of Picassos and Chagalls. With the roses on your table seemingly keyed to the colors of the Vuillard painting by your side. You sip your wine and choose a roll from a silver basket. You smile because you feel pampered. And welcome.

Swiss National Tourist Office

■

Problem Seven. Effective fragments? The passages below all contain sentence fragments, used for specific effects by the authors. Repunctuate or rewrite the passages to remove the fragments, and be prepared to discuss the contexts in which fragments might be appropriate.

a. That is why I started to write. To save myself.

Eldridge Cleaver

: Sentence Fragment   The sentence fragment, or incomplete sentence, is a group of words without a sentence base, set off as a complete sentence. Thus sentence fragments are punctuation mistakes. Notice the problem they give the reader:

■ Though sentence fragments are often used. For special purposes. By many writers. They are rightly. Treated as mistakes. When they slow. Or mislead the reader.

With normal punctuation, the passage is much easier to read:

■ Though sentence fragments are often used for special purposes by many writers, THEY ARE rightly TREATED AS MISTAKES when they slow or mislead the reader.

Sentence fragments fall into three groups:

■ fragments in which the subject-predicate unit is understood;
■ fragments that are afterthoughts;
■ fragments that are sentences, but sentences headed with a word that does not introduce a complete sentence.

First Draft

TIMOTHY IS 6 feet 9 inches TALL AND WEIGHS 300 POUNDS. A body that a grizzly bear could be proud of. (The second sentence has no sentence base.)

Revision

TIMOTHY IS 6 feet 9 inches TALL AND WEIGHS 300 POUNDS. HE HAS A BODY that a grizzly bear could be proud of. *OR:* TIMOTHY IS 6 feet 9 inches TALL AND WEIGHS 300 pounds—a body that a grizzly bear could be proud of. (The first revision adds a complete sentence base; the second revision ties the fragment to the previous sentence.)

b. Our life being so episodic we are always wanting to hitch our wagons to stars. Which cannot be done.

Louis MacNiece

c. There is, rather suddenly, a resurgence of interest in the legal field that goes by the name "obscenity." Not that it ever lacked for interest.

Charles Rember

WE USE FRAGMENTS in speaking. Which would be incorrect in writing. (*Which* cannot introduce a sentence base.)

WE USE FRAGMENTS in speaking. THEY WOULD BE INCORRECT in writing. *OR:* WE USE FRAGMENTS in speaking which would be incorrect in writing. (Again, the first revision adds a complete sentence base, while the second tacks the fragment to the previous sentence.)

INFLATION WILL undoubtedly CONTINUE. Although we may be able to learn to live with it. (*Although* cannot introduce a sentence base.)

INFLATION WILL undoubtedly CONTINUE, although we may be able to learn to live with it. *OR:* INFLATION WILL undoubtedly CONTINUE. However, WE MAY BE ABLE TO LEARN to live with it. (The first revision tacks the fragment to the previous sentence; the second shifts from a subordinating word, to *although,* to a coordinating word, *however.*

The question of words that can introduce sentence bases is in part absolute: Sentence bases introduced with *which, although, because,* and similar words are always considered fragments. In part, however, it is a question of formality: We've avoided using the word *so* to introduce sentence bases, for the most part, although it is common in informal writing, and some instructors even advise students to avoid the words *and* and *but* to introduce sentence bases, although we do so in this text. When in doubt, shift to a more formal sentence connector—*therefore* for *so, moreover* for *and, however* for *but,* and so on.

---

d. How does one turn students on? By being genuinely, enthusiastically interested in them. By preparing lessons that excite their imagination. By making the class format flexible. By being honest and fair. By showing how your course will help them cope with today.

Walter Hogan

e. An attractive thought. Detail in writing is great. Focus is essential. Unsupported abstractions are frustrating.

Jeffrey Youdelman

f. To write fully, you must use all your senses. Remember how places and objects smell, the taste of the back of your hand, the touch of concrete, the sound of a laugh—an American's laugh, a Southerner's laugh, a Northerner's. Such variety.

Ken Macrorie

g. We hold these truths to be self-evident, that all men are created equal, that they are endowed by their Creator with certain inalienable Rights, that among these are Life, Liberty and the pursuit of Happiness. That to secure these Rights, Governments are instituted among Men, deriving their just Powers from the consent of the governed.

Declaration of Independence

h. To write by fragments: the fragments are so many stones on the perimeter of a circle: I spread myself around: my whole little universe in crumbs; at the center, what?

Roland Barthes

■

Choosing Predication

Writers compose in a line, from right to left, and the sentence normally moves the same way, from subject to verb to completing words. Each step in that movement narrows the choice available to the writer. Choosing a subject limits the verbs that can be chosen: A subject like "the book" limits the writer to verbs like "costs," "is," and "looks"; it rules out other verbs, those such as "dreams," "thinks," and "harvests." Choosing a verb limits the completing words: "The book costs" forces the choice of words like "plenty" or "ten dollars"; "the book was" forces the choice of different words—"expensive" or "about three hundred pages long."

Our term for the choice of subject-verb combinations is *predication*. Predication is an essential part of being clear and direct, for it provides the base on which the meaning of a sentence is built. You may have been conscious of choosing sentence bases in sentence combining, and the problem that follows is designed to make you more aware of how predication affects sentence choices.

Problem Eight. Predication choices   Rewrite each of the sentences below by changing the predication, following the instructions given. Be prepared to discuss the effect of your revision. The first two have been done as examples.

a. Cuernavaca, the capital of Morelos State, is connected by rail-
(subject) (verb)
road to Mexico City. Begin "A railroad . . ." ⇒ "A railroad
(subject)

connects Mexico City to Cuernavaca, the capital of Morelos State."
(verb)
(Note that there are other possible choices.)

b. The deepest point in the world is in the Pacific Ocean, the Mar-
(subject)   (verb)
iana Trench near Guam, where the bathyscaphe Trieste reached a
depth of 34,884 feet in 1960. Begin "The bathyscaphe
. . ." ⇒ "The bathyscaphe Trieste reached a depth of 34,884
(subject) (verb)
feet in 1960, at the Mariana Trench in the Pacific Ocean near
Guam, the deepest point in the world." (Again, other choices are
possible.)

c. Several methods are used by accountants to calculate periodic
depreciation. Begin "Accountants . . ."

d. The foundations of modern American dance were built by
Ruth St. Denis, a mystic who was interested in the dances of the
Orient. Begin "Ruth St. Denis built . . ." Then begin "Ruth St.
Denis was . . ."

e. Michael DeBakey successfully implanted the first artificial
heart in 1966, achieving a major breakthrough in heart surgery.
Begin "Michael DeBakey achieved . . ."

f. The darter, a small, freshwater fish, takes its name from its
swift, darting movements while swimming. Begin "The darter is a
small . . ."

g. Metabolic reactions are of two kinds, anabolism and catabolism.
Begin "There are two . . ."

h. Monorails are vehicles suspended from a single rail, usually
powered by electric motors. Begin "Monorails, vehicles . . ."

i. Minority groups may persist because of their desire to retain
their particular traditions. Begin "The persistence of . . ."

■

Coordination

Sentence bases can be tied together, as a "compound sentence," with
the use of a simple connective:

6.25 IT WAS A long STORY ⃞AND⃞ IT WAS A sad STORY.

Grace Paley

6.26 HE THOUGHT he had been patient, ⃞BUT⃞ PATIENCE
HAD MADE HIM TIRED.

Eudora Welty

You'll note that the connecting words, *and* and *but,* are boxed, to show that they don't belong to either sentence base. We'll continue to box sentence connectors in the examples that follow.

Sentence bases can be tied together in other ways. A single subject can have several predicates:

6.27 HE READ over what he had written, CHEWED HIS PEN-CIL, AND CONTINUED.

Cyprian Ekwensi

We can combine several subjects with a single predicate:

6.28 RALPH AND HIS DUCK PLAYED together.

Indeed, for special emphasis, we can place a series of subject-verb combinations around a single set of completing words, exploiting your natural "sentence sense" to the fullest.

6.29 BUT in a larger sense, WE CANNOT DEDICATE—WE CANNOT CONSECRATE—WE CANNOT HALLOW—THIS GROUND.

Abraham Lincoln, "Gettysburg Address"

Subordination

Words that are added to the bare sentence base are *subordinated.* They modify the meaning of the sentence base:

6.30 IT WAS A sad STORY.

The sentence base, capitalized, carries the grammar of the sentence; the modifier *sad* gives it meaning. Thus, modifiers are essential to meaning, and one secret to sentence style is to achieve control over how one handles modifiers. That topic—handling modifiers—is in essence the subject matter of the next chapter, but we'll begin in this chapter to mark a difference in two kinds of modifiers. We'll mark one kind of modifier with lower case letters:

6.31 AN ancient MAN CAME WALKING down the canyon toward him.

And we'll mark another kind of modifier with italic letters; notice that you can hear the difference as the sentence is read aloud:

6.31A AN ancient MAN, *leaning every step on a twisted staff,* CAME WALKING down the canyon toward him.

This difference is important in chunking sentences; it suggests that effective sentences, clear and direct sentences, chunk meanings for the reader:

6.31B AN ancient MAN CAME WALKING down the canyon toward him, *leaning every step on a twisted staff, clad in a blanket and deerskin moccasins, a blue headband round his long, ice-white hair.*

Rob Schultheis

IMPLICATIONS FOR THE WRITER

We've looked at how readers respond to sentences, noting that all readers are "dumb readers" and that readers "chunk" meaning as they read. We've looked briefly at the grammar of the English sentence, identifying the *sentence base* of *subject* and *predicate*.

That background allows us to suggest some ways to be more clear and direct in your own writing. You can be more clear and direct by:

■ choosing effective subject-verb combinations; and
■ chunking meaning effectively.

Choose Effective Subject-Verb Combinations

Very young children will often misinterpret sentences like 6.32:

6.32 THE COW WAS KISSED by the duck.

They will say the sentence means "the cow kissed the duck," rather than giving its actual meaning, "the duck kissed the cow." We can explain this mistake by saying that these children assume that the subject always does what the verb says. In other words, they assume that English sentences present an actor (in the subject) and an act (in the verb). We will call this an *actor/act pattern.*

You're too sophisticated a language user to be fooled by "the cow was kissed by the duck." But we fooled you earlier in this chapter, when we presented example 6.16, beginning "the freight trains carried," and we fooled you because you expected the subject to present an actor ("the freight trains") and the verb to present an act ("carried"). The sentence was hard to read because it violated a natural strategy readers use—to expect an actor/act pattern in the subject and verb.

Therefore, you can help your readers by using the subject-verb combinations they expect, the actor/act pattern. You can be more clear and direct if you use actors as subjects and actions as verbs:

6.33 CHEMISTRY IS A difficult COURSE, especially for someone like me, who is ill at ease in a science course.

6.33A I FIND CHEMISTRY DIFFICULT, because I feel ill at ease in a science course.

Of course, 6.33 makes a somewhat more general claim than 6.33A, and it emphasizes chemistry instead of the writer. But 6.33A is more clear and direct, because it is easier to read.

6.34 Metabolic REACTIONS WERE MEASURED by the doctors.

6.34A THE DOCTORS MEASURED how the metabolism reacted.

Here again the second version is easier to read. In 6.33A the subject, "reactions," is being measured, not doing the measuring; in 6.34A "the doctors measured" and "the metabolism reacted" are actor/act patterns—the subject does what the verb says.

The most common way to regain actor/act patterns is to change a passive sentence to an active sentence, as in 6.34A above and the examples below.

6.35 THE TELEPHONE WAS INVENTED by Thomas Alva Edison. ⇒ THOMAS ALVA EDISON INVENTED THE TELEPHONE.

6.36 THE SUGGESTION that California might be taken from Mexico WAS MADE by Richard Henry Dana. ⇒ RICHARD HENRY DANA SUGGESTED that we might take California from Mexico.

Passive sentences do have uses. They can be used when we're not interested in, or don't know, who did the action. The actor can be moved to the end of the sentence, and then omitted.

6.37 THE POSTMAN DELIVERED THE MAIL. ⇒ THE MAIL WAS DELIVERED by the postman. ⇒ THE MAIL WAS DELIVERED.

6.38 SOMEONE ROBBED MY APARTMENT. ⇒ MY APARTMENT WAS ROBBED by someone. ⇒ MY APARTMENT WAS ROBBED.

pass: Passive Sentences   Passive sentences, discussed above, are often indirect or unemphatic. Certainly they are harder for the reader to read than their active equivalents.

First Draft	*Revision*
Submission of abstracts of current research is invited by the committee. (Passive sentence.)	The committee invites submissions of abstracts of current research. (Active sentence is preferable.)
This mark is called the *firn line* by glaciologists. (Passive sentence.)	Glaciologists call this mark the *firn line*.

Some writers, however, fall into the habit of overusing the passive, perhaps because they feel it is more formal. In general, prefer the actor/act pattern, as shown in 6.35 and 6.36.

More generally, you can find actor/act patterns by finding the verbs buried in nouns.

6.39   THE group's PERFORMANCE WAS WITHOUT ENTHUSIASM.

6.40   PARENTS ARE normally PROTECTIVE of their children.

Example 6.39 has a verb, "performed," hidden in the noun "performance"; example 6.40 has a verb, "protect," hidden in the noun "protectiveness."

6.39A   THE GROUP PERFORMED without enthusiasm.

6.40A   PARENTS normally PROTECT THEIR CHILDREN.

Similarly, you can reestablish actor/act patterns by questioning the use of the subject-verb combinations *it is, there is,* and *there are:*

6.41   THERE ARE various negative THEMES that the modern poet uses to portray America, such as seeing America as a junkyard, a place that didn't fulfill its promise.

6.42   IT IS IN GARDEN GROVE, a city near Disneyland, that they live.

These combinations are often called "dummy subjects," for they have no real meaning (what's raining in "it is raining"?). Writers who have the habit of overusing dummy subjects can develop the skill of finding actor/act patterns, and make it a basic part of rewriting:

6.41A THE MODERN POET USES various THEMES to portray America, such as seeing America as a junkyard, a place that didn't fulfill its promise.
6.42A THEY LIVE in Garden Grove, a city near Disneyland.

Problem Nine. Improving subject-verb combinations Revise the following student sentences to make them more clear and direct for the reader. Try to find actor/act patterns to use as subject and verb. The first are fairly straightforward; the last somewhat more difficult.

a. There are a number of explanations for the Civil War that are offered by historians.

b. His remembrance of the event was clear.

c. It is the origin of language that I wish to explore.

d. The implementation of the program was the accomplishment of the Fine Arts Committee.

e. Hamlet is another example of characterization by soliloquy.

f. Before her death, Antigone encounters Creon face to face, and it is here that her character is most forcefully asserted.

g. Before a person or possessions can be searched, probable cause must be established by the official.

h. However, Prussia had risen in the eyes of the rest of Europe to a position of power. Prussia had risen because her armies were respected.

i. Margaret Mead's view of other cultures can be seen to have more problems than it resolves. It has these problems because American culture is not viewed with the same neutrality.

j. Another writing aid I would like to develop is that of better flexibility and variety in expression. ■

Chunk Sentences Effectively

We want you to recognize a particular kind of sentence, one we will call the "stylistically dead" sentence, and we offer two examples, one a student sentence, the other a rewritten version of a previous example. Notice what happens as you read them.

6.43 The fact that I have worked for several years in the drug store in my home town is an important and central factor and aspect in my decision to consider undertaking the five years of study which will be required for me to earn a degree in pharmacy.

6.44 An old, ancient man who was leaning every step on a twisted staff and who wore a blanket, deerskin mocccasins, and a blue headband around his long hair, which was ice-white, came walking down the road to the bus stop which stood at the end of the long straight highway which ran through the center of town.

Note first that there's nothing *grammatically wrong* with these sentences; both are correct English sentences. But, read aloud, they reveal a dull rhythm, a monotone; they are *stylistically dead* sentences. Both share a general problem in chunking: They give the reader no pause, no emphasis, no sense of movement. They paste their meanings into long noun clauses, supported by a single verb, clauses through which the reader must plod as if on a forced march. (Note also, though we won't pursue the point, that they are remarkably easy sentences to write, once the trick has been mastered.)

The most general advice we can offer is that you become sensitive to the stylistically dead sentence, that you learn to "hear" the lack of rhythm and emphasis. More specifically, you can learn a few tricks that will help. One skill is to edit for deadwood—that is, more simply, remove all the words you can remove. Here's an example:

6.43A . . . is an important and central factor and aspect in my decision to consider undertaking the five years of study which will be required for me to earn a degree in pharmacy.

- "Is it an important factor or the central one?" "Well, the central one, I guess."
- "What's the difference between a factor and an aspect?" "I just mean factor."
- "Are you still considering?" "No, I'm enrolled."
- "Do all pharmacy students take five years of study?" "Yes."
- "What's the shortest way to, say, 'a degree in pharmacy'?" "A pharmacy degree."

6.43B . . . is the central factor in deciding to undertake the five years of study required to earn a pharmacy degree.

We've replaced thirty-one words with nineteen words, and made a solid gain in clarity and directness.

A second rewriting skill is the opposite one—learning when to put words in. Here you must think of your reader. The sentence below, written by a graduate student for a general audience, is an example of "overchunking," of writing that ignores its reader.

6.45 As the wind blows past the crest slope, its surface velocity decreases due to the air space increase and the vegetation surface roughness.

For a normal reader, even the phrase "crest slope" may be a problem, and the rest of the sentence becomes a clogged puzzle. The solution is to stretch out the meaning for the reader:

6.45A As the wind blows past the slope of the crest, it slows down, partly because it has more air space available and partly because the roughness of the vegetation impedes it.

A third skill is to listen for *paste predication*—the subject-verb combination that is present on the page only to get to the end of the sentence. Notice the second sentences in these student examples; you should be able to hear the paste predication.

6.46 I WORKED two SUMMERS at the saw mill. I WORKED two SUMMERS to develop my strength and agility.

6.47 GEORGE ELIOT ANALYZES THE intellectual STERIL-ITY of Victorian England. SHE ANALYZES THIS STERILITY by placing her imaginative central characters in the unimaginative land of Middlemarch.

The second sentence in these examples wastes the reader's time, for the reader must go back through information the reader already knows. The answer to this problem is to tighten the structure, to subordinate for clarity. The reader handles one longer sentence much more easily than two shorter ones; the meaning is chunked more effectively.

6.46A I WORKED two SUMMERS at the saw mill, *to develop my strength and agility.*

6.47A GEORGE ELIOT ANALYZES THE intellectual STERIL-ITY of Victorian England, *by placing her imaginative central characters in the unimaginative land of Middlemarch.*

Note again that clarity and directness, in these examples, have nothing—or nearly nothing—to do with sentence length as such, but a great deal to do with the kind of chunking that's used.

sub : Subordination   Connect related ideas for the reader by reducing base clauses.

First Draft	*Revision*
The conflict between parent and child is serious. It is so serious, in fact, that it cannot be resolved. (The short sentences slow down the reader.)	The conflict between parent and child is serious—so serious, in fact, that it cannot be resolved. (Here the combined sentences seem much tighter for the reader.)
George Meredith's *Modern Love* is a dramatic dialog between a husband and wife who have lost the love they once had for each other. The poem is a recounting of Meredith's marriage to Mary Peacock, the daughter of the English satirist, Thomas Love Peacock. (These sentences sound choppy, and they are also confusing to the reader, who can't sense a controlling purpose.)	George Meredith's *Modern Love* is a dramatic dialog between a husband and wife who have lost the love they once had for each other, based on Meredith's marriage to Mary Peacock, the daughter of the English satirist, Thomas Love Peacock. (The second sentence is subordinated to the first, providing a more readable sentence, and giving a clearer indication of the writer's purpose.)

Problem Ten. Effective chunking   The student passages that follow present various kinds of difficulties in chunking meaning for the reader. Most of the passages are taken from the writing of advanced composition students, so the problems are often complex. Rewrite the sentences, assuming a college-level audience.

a. Each generation of young people is inclined to believe that their generation is the first to experience the problems encountered when maturing and finding out the essentials of life, yet the contrary is true. Each and every generation of youths, from the beginning of time on up into the twentieth century, run into the same difficulties and hardships as their fathers had discovered years before and as their fathers' fathers had done.

b. The role of plea bargaining in the judicial prosecution of criminals is of primary importance to legal administrative agencies. The importance of it can readily be seen when we observe that, for the number of arrests and convictions, relatively few reach the jury trial stage.

c. Two models of perceptual sampling which purport to account for phenomenal simultaneity are examined by Allport. One is the Discrete Moment Hypothesis which proposes that sensory input is quantized into discrete periods. The other is the Travelling Moment Hypothesis in which the moment is considered to be a continuous running input sample.

d. Speculations can be made on why the American electorate votes as they do. It can be hypothesized that voting is a social activity rather than a political activity. The social characteristics of a person determine how that person thinks in political terms.

e. Advertising seems to be correlated with the trend of the times toward social and status needs with the emphasis on convenience and leisure. In a generation of pleasure-seekers, there are those who seek their pleasure through amassing, not fortunes, but symbols of status. Even though there may not be a conscious desire to procure a certain product, when someone else who perhaps does not have as much sales resistance is seen owning one, the advantages are quickly recalled from the drilling of commercials. ■

Many readers of this chapter may be taken aback by our suggestions about clarity and directness. "I've spent my whole life learning to write complexly, with big words and fancy sentences, and you're telling me to start over," one student responded to an early version of this chapter. Some matters *are* very complex, and some audiences—those for a technical journal, for example—*are* quite sophisticated. And, in chapters Seven and Eight, we'll suggest some powerful ways to achieve a complex style, ways which don't interfere with the reader's need to pull meaning from writing.

IMPLICATIONS FOR THE READER: CHUNKING

Normally,   we read for meaning.   After all,   the meaning, the sense,   is what we're after.   And,   since we've learned that we read in chunks,   we can see why reading for meaning   is a good idea.   If we rely too much on the words   of written sentences,   we may find ourselves reading too slowly   —a word at a time—   so the meaning gets lost   in the jumble of words.

It may be a paradox   but the faster we read   —within limits— the more we understand.   When we read rapidly, the mind helps   the eye to choose   chunks of meaning, groups of words,   and the mind reads   those groups as easily as   it reads single words   or groups of letters.

Fast readers don't remember   the words they read
—they don't do as well   as slower readers
in remembering word for word   what they read.
But fast readers do better   in remembering the meaning
of what they've read.
     In this section   (as if you haven't noticed)
we're trying to force you   to read in word groups
by separating sentences   into meaning chunks.
This way of laying out sentences   may slow you down,
forcing you to take in   smaller chunks of meaning
than you're used to.   But it doesn't hurt   to be forced
to reduce your reading speed.   It's a necessary shift
in reading some writing—   poetry, for example,
often forces readers to slow down,   to rely more
on the texture of sentences,   to hear the play of words.
"Some books,"   wrote Francis Bacon,
three hundred and fifty years ago,   "are to be tasted,
others to be swallowed,   and some few
to be chewed and digested."
     Other readers may find   this chunking of print
forces them to speed up,   to take in chunks of meaning,
instead of single words.   Slower readers may find
they're reading faster   and understanding more.
     Thus all readers   benefit by chunking.   At this reading speed,
controlled by chunking,   the reader is very close
to the speed of words   as they're spoken aloud.   And thus,
the reader is kept   close to the connections
of speaking and writing,   connections that good writers,
consciously or unconsciously,   keep in their writing.
Gertrude Stein,   an experimental writer,   insists on connecting
writing and speaking.   The passage below,
talking about punctuation marks,   is a particular challenge
to your reading of sentences,   and therefore a good way to end
a chapter on the sentence.

6.48 There are two different ways of thinking about colons and semi-colons you can think of them as commas and as such they are purely servile or you can think of them as periods and then using them can make you feel adventurous. I can see that one might feel about them as periods but I myself never have, I began unfortunately to feel them as a comma and commas are servile they have no life of their own they are dependent upon use and convenience and they are put there just for practical purposes. Semi-colons and colons had for me from the first completely this character the character that a comma has and not the character that a period has and therefore and definitely I have never used them. But now dimly and definitely I do see that they might well possibly they might have in them something of the character of the period and so it might have been an adventure to use them. I really do not think so. I think however lively they are or disguised they are they are definitely more comma than period and so really I cannot regret not having used them. They are more powerful more imposing more pretentious than a comma but they are a comma all the same. They really have within them deeply within them fundamentally within them the comma nature. And now what does a comma do and why do I feel as I do about them.

What does a comma do.

I have refused them so often and left them out so much and did without them so continually that I have come finally to be indifferent to them. I do not now care whether you put them in or not but for a long time I felt very definitely about them and would have nothing to do with them.

As I say commas are servile and they have no life of their own, and their use is not a use, it is a way of replacing one's own interest and I do decidedly like to like my own interest my own interest in what I'm doing. A comma by helping you along holding your coat for you and putting on your shoes keeps you from living your life as actively as you should lead it and to me for many years and I still do feel that way about it only now I do not pay as much attention to them, the use of them was positively degrading. Let me tell you what I feel and what I mean and what I felt and what I meant.

Gertrude Stein, "Poetry and Grammar"

SUMMARY

We've been concerned with how readers read sentences and with how writers write them. We've noted that readers—all readers—are "dumb readers" because they can only respond to the word on the page, not to what writers meant. We noticed that readers "chunk" words together in meaning, with particular reference to ambiguous sentences, sentences that can be chunked two ways. We then looked at the grammar of the English sentence, isolating the *sentence base* of *subject* and *predicate,* the predicate containing the verb and other words to complete the sentence.

From this discussion we developed implications for writers, that they should search for emphatic predication, and that they should chunk meaning effectively for the reader. We concluded with a discussion of how readers, in the process of reading, chunk words in groups.

FINAL WRITING ASSIGNMENTS

I. Rechunking Sentences   Below are two longer exercises in sentence choice. Passages A and B are taken from passages printed at the end of chapter One. We have rewritten Passage A to overchunk, combining as many sentences as possible. We have rewritten Passage B to under-chunk, into short primerlike sentences. Rewrite the two passages, try-ing to achieve a normal degree of chunking for the reader, and then compare your rewrites with the originals.

Passage A

Very gradually I have discovered ways of writing with a minimum of worry and anxiety, for when I was young each fresh piece of serious work used to seem to me for a time—perhaps a long time—to be beyond my powers and I would fret myself into a nervous state from fear that it was never going to come right, making one unsatisfying attempt after another, in the end discarding them all, until at last I found that such fumbling attempts were a waste of time, for it appeared that after first contemplating a book on some subject, and after giving serious preliminary attention to it, I needed a period of subconscious incubation which could not be hurried and was if anything impeded by deliberate thinking—a period of incuba-tion that sometimes let me find, after a time, that I had made a mistake, and that I could not write the book I had had in mind, but often I was more fortunate, for, having, by a time of very intense concentration, planted the problem in my subconscious, it would germinate underground until, suddenly, the solution emerged with blinding clarity, so that it only remained to write down what had appeared as if in a revelation.

Passage B

So I went over to Esquire after a while. I talked with them about this phenomenon. They sent me out to California. They sent me to take a look at the custom car world. Dale Alexander was from Detroit or some place. But the real center of the thing was in California. The real center was around Los Angeles. I started talking to a lot of these people. I talked to people like George Barris and Ed Roth. I saw what they were doing. Well, eventually it became the story from which the title of this book was taken. The story was, "The Kandy-Kolored Tangerine-Flake Streamline Baby." But at first I couldn't even write the story. I came back to New York. I just sat around. I worried over the thing. I had a lot of trouble analyzing ex-actly what I had on my hands. . . . So about 8 o'clock that night I started. I typed the notes out in the form of a memorandum. The memorandum began, "Dear Byron." I started typing away. I started right with the first time I saw any custom cars in California. I just started recording it all. Inside a couple of hours I was typing along like a madman. I could tell that something was beginning to happen. By midnight this memorandum to Byron was twenty pages long. I was still typing. I was typing like a maniac. About 2 a.m. or something like that I turned on WABC. WABC is a radio station. It plays rock and roll music all night long. I got a little more manic. I wrapped up the memorandum about 6:14 a.m. By this time it was 49 pages long. . . .

II. How Big Is a Chunk?   Take two or three pieces of writing from different sources—say from a textbook you find difficult, a newspaper, a popular magazine. Read a paragraph or two, using a slash mark (/) to divide the text into chunks that you find comfortable. Then investigate your process of chunking texts: Does simpler or easier writing allow you to mark longer chunks? Does punctuation always mark a chunk? Does the topic-comment separation mark chunks? How big, for you, is a chunk? (There are no right answers to this investigation—different readers will chunk differently, and it will depend, as well, on the complexity of the readings.)

FOR FURTHER READING

Additional exercises in sentence combining are available in Donald A. Daiker, Andrew Kerek, and Max Morenberg, *The Writer's Options* (New York: Random House, 1978), and William Strong, *Sentence Combining* (New York: Random House, 1973).

NOTES

1. Adapted from John Bleibtrau, *The Parable of the Beast* (New York: Macmillan, 1968).
2. K. Abrams and Thomas G. Bever, "Syntactic Structure Modifies Attention During Speech Perception and Recognition," *Quarterly Journal of Experimental Psychology,* 21 (1969), 280–90.
3. We borrow the notion of the dumb reader from Walker Gibson, "The Reader as Dumb Reader," *College Composition and Communication,* 31 (1980), 192–95.

Style in Description and Narration

We are as much as we see.

HENRY DAVID THOREAU

Narration tells a story—it's an active mode of writing. Description looks at a scene or a person or a situation—it's a static mode of writing. You might think of a picture or a painting, something fixed in time, as a kind of description, and you might think of a motion picture, moving through time, as a kind of narration. In most cases, description and narration work together: Think, for example, of the witness to a crime telling the police what happened (narration) and then telling the police what the criminal looked like (description).

Writing descriptions and narrations is like being a police witness: Detail is all-important. We'll focus on sentence style as a way to pull detail into descriptions and narrations, and the skills you'll master should feed into other writing tasks—explaining, arguing, analyzing. Our discussion, then, will focus on the potentials of sentence style. At the same time, though, our assignments will pull you in another direction—outside, toward the world of human experience, because what is described or narrated must be seen, seen in detail, before it can be articulated for the reader.

YOU ARE AS MUCH AS YOU SEE

Consider a brief section of a first draft of a narrative paper by a freshman student:

7.1 As I walk through the wooded forest, I can smell the pleasant scent of autumn in the air. The wind is brisk and bitter, blowing the marvelously colored leaves of red, orange, and yellow from the tall trees to the ground below. Hearing the crackling of dried leaves beneath my feet, I glance to the ground, only to notice the broken twigs, cracked earth, and dying grass that once was a crisp summer green. Looking around at the wonder of the forest, my attention is caught by the movement of a squirrel gathering nuts among the scattered leaves for the long winter cold that lies ahead.

This writer has a firm sense of the effect she wants to present to the reader, to capture the beauty of autumn and yet warn of "the long cold winter that lies ahead." And the writer is clear about her own feelings— the pleasant scents, the marvelously colored leaves, and so on. But the reader is unlikely to find the scene convincing. The writer's eye is not open; the writer is responding to the scene instead of seeing the scene. As a result, she turns to commonplace expressions, she writes herself away from the scene in front of her, and she appeals only to the reader's stock responses to a "wooded forest" (is there any other kind of forest?).

We can improve this passage slightly by attention to style. We might question the hackneyed language, as in "the long cold winter that lies ahead." We might point out that the last sentence, read by a "dumb reader," can mean "my attention is looking at the wonder of the forest" (and how, exactly, does one look at a wonder?).

The writer improved the passage in a different way, by beginning to look at the world closely, to see what she was describing, and to struggle with the hard task of shaping that observation into words. The final draft dispensed with the "wonder of the forest" and looked instead— really looked—at the squirrel mentioned in passing in the first draft.

7.2 The paws, rounded into the shape of a shovel, dug insistently in the twigs and dried grass, one paw pulling across the ground toward the body, then the other. Then, suddenly, the squirrel rocked backward and arched its head forward. It unclenched its paws, the black nails shining in the light, and it rocked forward and grasped a nut. The squirrel sat straight up, perpendicular to the ground, and began chewing rapidly, its crooked teeth flashing up and down, the muscles in its cheeks and jaw constricting and then pushing outward, revealing their shape beneath the gray fur.

The strain in this rewrite shows through. This is "hard writing," where the first draft was "easy writing." But it marks a clear-cut improvement in quality: We *see* this squirrel, as readers, where in the first draft we are only invited to share clichés. The improvement in writing grows out of the improvement in seeing: You can see the muscles of squirrels as they chew; this squirrel has irregular teeth and long nails. And with that effort—the effort required to see and the effort required to shape that seeing for a reader—comes a new discovery, which the student expressed in a final evaluation:

7.3 I never knew you could learn so much from writing.

The two skills of seeing and reporting are obvious essentials in narrative and descriptive writing, and they are skills essential in most professions. In fact, one of the most convincing descriptions of the power of "seeing" was written many years ago by a biologist who studied under the famous scientist Louis Agassiz.

7.4 When I sat me down before my tin pan, Agassiz brought me a small fish, placing it before me with the rather stern requirement that I should study it, but should on no account talk to anyone concerning it, nor read anything relating to fishes, until I had his permission to do so. To my inquiry, "What shall I do?" he said in effect: "Find out what you can without damaging the specimen; when I think that you have done the work I will question you." In the course of an hour I thought I had compassed that fish; it was rather an unsavory object, giving forth the stench of old alcohol, then loathsome to me, though in time I came to like it. Many of the scales were loosened so that they fell off. It appeared to me to be a case for a summary report, which I was anxious to make and get on to the next stage of the business. But Agassiz, though always within call, concerned himself no further with me that day, nor the next, nor for a week. At first, this neglect was distressing; but I saw that it was a game, for he was, as I discerned rather than saw, covertly watching me. So I set my wits to work upon the thing, and in the course of a hundred hours or so thought I had done much—a hundred times as much as seemed possible at the start. I got interested in finding how the scales went in series, their shape, the form and placement of the teeth, etc. Finally, I felt full of the subject, and probably expressed it in my bearing; as for words about it then, there were none from my master except his cheery "Good morning." At length, on the seventh day, came the question, "Well?" and my disgorge of learning to him as he sat on the edge of my table puffing his cigar. At the end of the hour's telling, he swung off and away, saying: "That is not right." Here I began to think that, after all, perhaps the rules for scanning Latin verse were not the worst infliction in the world. Moreover, it was clear that he was playing a game with me to find if I were capable of doing hard, continuous work without the support of a teacher, and this stimulated me to labor. I went at the task anew, discarded my first notes, and in another week of ten hours a day labor I had results which astonished myself and satisfied him. Still there was no trace of praise in words or manner. He signified that it would do by placing before me about a half a peck of bones, telling me to see what I could make of them, with no further directions to guide me. I soon found that they were the skeletons of half a dozen fishes of different species; the jaws told me so much at a first inspection. The task evidently was to fit the separate bones together in their proper order. Two months or more went to this task with no other help than an occasional looking over my grouping with the stereotyped remark: "That is not right." Finally, the task was done, and I was again set upon alcoholic specimens—this time a remarkable lot of specimens representing, perhaps, twenty species of the side-swimmers or Pleuronectidae.

I shall never forget the sense of power in dealing with things which I felt in beginning the more extended work on a group of animals.

Autobiography of Nathaniel Southgate Shaler (1907)

Our first assignment in description is similar to that given to Shaler; it asks you to develop "the sense of power in dealing with things" by closely observing an object change through time.

Problem One. A journal assignment Find a small object that will change over a period of one or two weeks. You might consider a natural object—a weed, a leaf, a flower—or you might consider a piece of food—a square of cheese, a bit of yogurt. Place the object on your writing desk in some sort of frame—on a sheet of paper or an envelope. Observe this object daily, at some regular time, and note your reactions in a journal. Concentrate on describing the object as it is, and set as your goal the development of a "sense of power in dealing with things" through written language. ■

TEXTURE IN DESCRIPTIVE AND NARRATIVE WRITING

We borrow the word *texture* from clothing. A piece of cloth can be described as "thick" or "thin" in texture, and we'll apply the same words to writing: A "thin" piece of writing has very little modification, little detail. We find a thin piece of writing at the end of Ernest Hemingway's novel *The Sun Also Rises*. (We print it here using a notational system we developed in the last chapter, with the *sentence bases* in capital letters, the *bound modifiers* in lower case letters, and the *free modifiers* in italics. The distinction between bound modifiers and free modifiers will be explained shortly.)

7.5 *In the morning* IT WAS all OVER. THE FIESTA WAS FINISHED. I WOKE about nine o'clock, HAD A BATH, DRESSED, AND WENT DOWN-STAIRS. THE SQUARE WAS EMPTY AND THERE WERE no PEOPLE on the streets. A few CHILDREN WERE PICKING UP ROCKET-STICKS in the square. THE CAFES WERE JUST OPENING AND THE WAITERS WERE CARRYING OUT THE comfortable white wicker CHAIRS AND ARRANGING THEM around the marble-topped tables in the shade of the arcade. THEY WERE SWEEPING THE STREETS AND SPRINKLING THEM with a hose.

I SAT in one of the wicker chairs AND LEANED BACK comfortably. THE WAITER WAS IN NO HURRY to come. THE white-paper ANNOUNCEMENTS of the unloading of the bulls and the big schedules of special trains WERE still UP on the pillars of the arcade. A WAITER wearing a blue apron CAME OUT with a bucket of water and a cloth, AND COMMENCED TO TEAR DOWN THE NOTICES, *pulling the paper off in strips and washing and rubbing away the paper that stuck to the stone.* THE FIESTA WAS OVER.

Ernest Hemingway, The Sun Also Rises

This way of printing the passage stresses its lack of texture. The passage is spare and lean, mostly simple sentence bases connected by *and* or by a series of coordinate actions. The first two sentences and the last repeat the same statement—"it was all over," "the fiesta was finished," "the fiesta was over."

The passage occurs near the end of the novel, a story of emotional loss, and we sense, as readers, that the speaker's refusal to elaborate or to deal with his feelings reflects a sense of desolation, of emptiness, and perhaps we sense also that the repeated statements, "the fiesta was over," create an echoing effect, so that they suggest that more than simply the fiesta was over, that "[everything] was all over."

This spare, lean prose has given Hemingway the reputation of being a tight-fisted, tough writer, and certainly he deserves it. Here the lack of texture, of sentence modification, is adapted to the emotional qualities the author wants to evoke. Elsewhere in the novel, though, we find a different degree of texture in style. Here is an earlier passage in the novel:

7.6 I LEANED way over the wall AND TRIED TO SEE into the cage. IT WAS DARK. SOMEONE RAPPED on the cage with an iron bar. *Inside* SOMETHING SEEMED TO EXPLODE. THE BULL, *striking into the wood from side to side with his horns,* MADE A great NOISE. *Then* I SAW A dark MUZZLE AND THE SHADOW of horns, AND *then* THE BULL CHARGED AND CAME into the corral, *skidding with his forefeet in the straw as he stopped, his head up, the great hump of muscle on his neck swollen tight, his body muscles quivering as he looked up at the crowd on the stone walls.* THE two STEERS BACKED AWAY against the wall, *their heads sunken, their eyes watching the bull.*

THE BULL SAW THEM AND CHARGED. A MAN SHOUTED from behind one of the boxes AND SLAPPED HIS HAT against the planks, AND THE BULL, *before he reached the steer,* GATHERED HIMSELF AND CHARGED where the man had been, *trying to reach him behind the planks with a half-dozen quick, searching drives with the right horn.*

There's a difference in texture here, a difference in descriptive detail. We put about a third of the words in italics, as free modifiers. This shift in texture goes along with a shift in mood, and the passage seems to explode into action as if keyed by the word *explode* in the fourth sentence. Our first sample seemed "thin" in texture; this passage is obviously "thicker," conveying the action with a fuller sense of felt detail. (Indeed, if we were to shift to literary criticism, we might note that these choices of texture serve the author's purposes, for this bull, trapped in a cage yet battling against its entrapment, is a mirror-image of the narrator, Jake Barnes, who submits too willingly to the forces that entrap him.)

We can find still heavier textures in the writing of Hemingway. The passage below, from a short story, "The Undefeated," is even thicker in descriptive detail—and it's no accident that here we see man and bull matched, human grace and intelligence, animal force and strength.

7.7 *Alone in the center of the ring* THE BULL STOOD, *still fixed.* FUENTES, *tall, flat-backed, walking toward him arrogantly, his arms spread out, the two slim, red sticks, one in each hand, held by the fingers, points straight forward.* FUENTES WALKED forward. BACK of him and to one side WAS A PEON with a cape. THE BULL LOOKED at him AND WAS no longer FIXED.

HIS EYES WATCHED FUENTES, *now standing still. Now* HE LEANED BACK, *calling to him.* FUENTES TWITCHED THE two BANDERILLOS AND THE LIGHT on the steel points CAUGHT THE bull's EYE.

HIS TAIL WENT UP AND HE CHARGED.

HE CAME STRAIGHT, *his eyes on the man.* FUENTES STOOD STILL, *leaning back, the banderillos pointing forward. As the bull lowered his head to look,* FUENTES LEANED BACKWARD, HIS ARMS CAME TOGETHER AND ROSE, *his two hands touching, the two banderillos descending red lines,* AND *leaning forward* DROVE THE POINTS into the bull's shoulder, *leaning far in over the horns and pivoting on the two upright sticks, his legs tight together, his body curving to one side to let the bull pass.*

Here the texture is fuller, with most of the words in free modification (in italics). Sentences become fragments or merge together as the writer presents a complex action in a complex way.

We can draw two conclusions from these examples. First, writers can vary the texture of their writing by the kind of modification they use. Second, free modifiers are an important part of heavily textured narrative and descriptive writing. If that's so, then we can suggest some ways—some very specific ways—to improve your narrative and descriptive writing by doing two things: locking in the notions of bound and free modifiers, and providing some structured exercises in using free modifiers.

RECOGNIZING BOUND AND FREE MODIFIERS

Bound modifiers are tied, or "bound," to their position in the sentence; as their name indicates, they can't be moved without changing the meaning of the sentence.

7.8 Only Thomas Mann wrote *Death in Venice.* (No one helped him write it.)

7.8A Thomas Mann only wrote *Death in Venice.* (Someone else directed the movie.)

7.8B Thomas Mann wrote only *Death in Venice.* (He wrote nothing else.)

Each time we shift the bound modifier, we change the meaning slightly. Moving a bound modifier changes the meaning of the sentence.

7.9 THE tall WOMAN wearing a red dress WELCOMED THE MAN.

7.10 THE WOMAN WELCOMED THE tall MAN wearing a red dress.

We can construct quite long sentences using bound modifiers. When we do, we recognize what we called the "stylistically dead" sentence in the last chapter. Using a lot of bound modifiers makes sentences difficult to read.

7.11 THE PAGES of the green Chemistry textbook that I paid twenty dollars and fifty cents for at the crowded bookstore that is at the end of the narrow street that runs from the new campus to the main road to the next town ARE BLANK because the careless printers who printed it forgot to put black ink in their busy printing presses.

The problem with sentence 7.11 is not its length; it simply places too much burden on the reader's memory. By the time the verb, "are blank," is reached, the reader may well have forgotten the subject, "the pages." In terms that we introduced in the last chapter, the sentence is hard for the reader to "chunk."

Free modifiers can normally be moved. They can appear in front of the sentence base, in what we'll call a *left-branched* position:

7.12 *Carrying a load of books,* THE INSTRUCTOR ENTERED THE CLASSROOM awkwardly.   [*left-branched free modifier*]

They can appear following the sentence base; that is, in a right-branched position:

7.12A THE INSTRUCTOR ENTERED THE CLASSROOM awkwardly, *carrying a load of books.*   [*right-branched free modifier*]

And they can be embedded into the sentence base, normally between the subject and predicate:

7.12B THE INSTRUCTOR, *carrying a load of books,* ENTERED THE CLASSROOM awkwardly.   [*embedded free modifier*]

This example suggests a second identifying feature of free modifiers: They are set off from the sentence base by punctuation, normally by commas. In embedded free modifiers, as in 7.12B, both marks of punctuation appear, at the beginning and ending of the modifier. In left-branched or right-branched position, only the final or initial mark appears:

7.13 TIME IS THE continuous LOOP, *the snakeskin with scales endlessly overlapping without beginning or end.*

We like to speak of the second punctuation mark as being "over-weighted" by the capital letter at the beginning and the period at the end, for the second mark reappears as we add a coordinate sentence:

7.13A TIME IS THE continuous LOOP, *the snakeskin with scales endlessly overlapping without beginning or end,* OR TIME IS AN ascending SPIRAL if you will, *like a child's toy Slinky.*

Bound modifiers are not set off with punctuation.
Two features, then, identify free modifiers:

■ They are set off by punctuation.
■ They can normally be moved.

These two features account for the usefulness of free modifiers. Because they can be moved, they increase the options available to writers. Because they are set off by punctuation, they are easier for readers to "chunk" than are bound modifiers, for the punctuation signals the meaning groups.

Problem Two. Recognizing free modifiers   Underline the free modifiers in the following sentences. Look for word groups that are set off by punctuation and that can be moved without changing the meaning. Identify the position of each free modifier: left-branched, embedded, or right-branched. Answers are given at the end of the book.

a. After the accident, his face had a long time healing.

Dorothy Canfield

b. But along with their scars, black people have a secret.

William Grier and Rice M. Cobbs

c. Jargon, the sublanguage peculiar to any trade, contributes to euphemism when its terms seep into general use.

Time Magazine

d. New Jersey has nearly a thousand people per square mile—the greatest population density of any state in the Union.

John McPhee

e. Moving beyond a first draft, McPhee generally picks up speed.

William L. Howarth

f. Now that it has more central heating and fewer mouldering gibbets, the countryside is more pleasant than it was.

Katherine Whitehorn

g. The babies were all under one year old, very funny and lovable.

Grace Paley

h. I remember sitting behind him, rubbing the shoulder and hoping he would always think it was rheumatism and remember only the autumn hunting days.

Lillian Hellman

i. He had grown up, one of the ten children of Russian Jewish immigrant parents, on tough Notre Dame Street in Montreal, where the major sports were craps, poker, and petty larceny.

Joseph Epstein

j. After the lions had returned to their cages, creeping angrily through the chutes, a little bunch of us drifted away and into an open doorway nearby, where we stood for a while in semidarkness, watching a big brown circus horse go harumphing around the practice ring.

E. B. White

■

Problem Three. Creating free modifiers   We can present free modifiers as problems in sentence combining, since most often what has been combined in one sentence might have been written in two. For each of the following sentence groups, use the first sentence as the sentence base, and add the information in the next sentences as *free modifiers.* (It's usually possible to use a bound modifier as well, but avoid that if possible.) Representative answers are given at the back of the text.

Study the models before proceeding.

■ **Model**   The dog ran down the hill. It barked loudly.   ⇒   The dog ran down the hill, *barking loudly.* OR *Barking loudly,* the dog ran down the hill. OR The dog, *barking loudly,* ran down the hill. (*Note:* Not all positions will be possible for all sentences.)

■ **Model**   It is a summer day. It is hot and humid. It is without a breeze.   ⇒   It is a summer day, hot and humid, without a breeze. OR Hot and humid, it is a summer day, without a breeze. (*Note:* Here one would probably reject, on stylistic grounds, "It, hot and humid, without a breeze, is a summer day.")

a. The children looked at the clown. Their eyes were wide with wonder.

b. The Chinese factotum grabbed the microfilm. He grabbed it with a quick movement of his hand.

c. I speak with authority. I am a student and the mother of four students. (Hint: Begin "As a . . .")

d. The winners celebrated. They formed a tight huddle. They gave a loud cheer. (Hint: "formed" ⇒ "forming"; "gave" ⇒ "giving.")

e. The duck waddled across the farmyard. It quacked loudly.

f. The hockey player raced down the sideline. The puck was cradled in his stick. His eyes were on the net.

g. The wheat fields spread out before them. The grains rustled softly in the breeze. It was as if they were brushed by a gentle hand.

h. The mackerel banged its head against the side of the tank. It banged its head again and again. It banged its head with quick, darting movements.

i. The woman looked at the elephant. The woman was tall and well dressed. The elephant was playing in the water.

j. We stood there quietly. We held hands. Our heads were together. We watched the sea gulls. ■

Clarifications

Our vocabulary is likely to be new to you—free modifiers and bound modifiers, branched to the left or right of the sentence base or embedded between subject and predicate. And the payoff isn't immediately obvious—few of you want to become novelists, like Ernest Hemingway. Some clarifications are in order, clarifications about our goals in this chapter and what they demand of the developing writer, and clarifications about the details of the English sentence.

We have set new stylistic goals in this chapter. In the last chapter, we were concerned with clarity and directness. In this chapter, as we look out to the complexity of objects and events in the world, we set goals of stylistic complexity, of putting *texture* into our writing. Thus we aim at a certain elegance or grace in style.

These goals place special demands on the student. They ask you to "take chances" rather than "play it safe," to experiment with the potentials of the written sentence. To achieve this goal, to become an "experimenter" with language, you need to be aware of the potentials of free modifiers.

Note first that commas serve several purposes in sentences. They mark off free modifiers, as in 7.14:

7.14 HE WAS FORTY, *a short man with a wealth of black hair.*

They connect sentence bases, as in 7.14A:

7.14A HE WAS FORTY, AND HE HAD A WEALTH of black hair.

And they connect items in series, as in 7.14B:

7.14B HE WAS A short, thickset MAN with a wealth of stiff, black hair.

These commas separate words; they don't mark free modifiers. Note that the commas in 7.14B have very little to do with the way the sentence sounds when read aloud. The comma in 7.14, however, is a "comma you can hear." Because the punctuation of free modifiers controls the reader's chunking of a sentence, those commas are "heard by the inner ear," while series commas are not:

7.14C HE WAS FORTY, *a short, thickset man with a wealth of stiff, black hair, combed straight back without a parting, like a Slav bicyclist.*

John Updike

Thus the author's punctuation determines whether a modifier is to be read as bound or free. Often the punctuation is optional, and the author indicates to the reader how the sentence is to be read.

7.15 HE ADVANCED along the shore with a creeping bow-legged hobble.

Truman Capote

7.15A HE ADVANCED along the shore, *with a creeping bowlegged hobble.* [alternate punctuation]

7.16 THE NIGHTMARE of the plague WAS COMPOUNDED for the fourteenth century BY THE awful MYSTERY of its cause.

7.16A THE NIGHTMARE of the plague WAS COMPOUNDED, *for the fourteenth century,* BY THE awful MYSTERY of its cause.

Barbara Tuchman

Truman Capote chose to treat the modifier as bound; Barbara Tuchman chose to treat a very similar modifier as free. (You should begin to try to develop the skill of "hearing free modifiers" as sentences are read aloud—note the difference the punctuation has on your reading of 7.16 and 7.16A.)

We'll make one exception to the general rule that "the author's punctuation determines whether modifiers are bound or free." We will treat all words in front of the subject as *free by position,* whether punctuated or not.

7.17 *Alone in the center of the ring,* THE BULL STOOD.

7.17A *Alone in the center of the ring* THE BULL STOOD.

Ernest Hemingway

Hemingway chooses to omit the optional comma, perhaps to tighten the action. But we clarify the sound and the logic of the sentence if we say that any words, pulled from their natural position and placed in front of the subject, are marked as free modifiers, whether punctuated or not. Again, this distinction is a "heard" distinction.

7.18 SOMETHING SEEMED TO EXPLODE inside.

[bound modifier]

7.18A *Inside,* SOMETHING SEEMED TO EXPLODE.

[free by punctuation]

7.18B *Inside* SOMETHING SEEMED TO EXPLODE.

[free by position]

Whether punctuated or not, the sentence is chunked by the reader as "inside, something," not as a single unit.

Finally, we need to note that there are restrictions on the movement of some free modifiers, restrictions of meaning and restrictions of style. The free modifiers in this James Baldwin sentence refer back to the sentence base; they can only be right-branched.

7.19 NEGROES WANT TO BE TREATED LIKE MEN: *a perfectly straightforward statement, containing only seven words.*

Similarly, most readers find the embedded structure in 7.20B to be stylistically "odd"; it simply doesn't sound right to our stylistic ear:

7.20 *Holding hands,* THEY STOOD there quietly.   [*left-branched*]

7.20A THEY STOOD there quietly, *holding hands.* [*right-branched*]

7.20B THEY, *holding hands,* STOOD there quietly.   [*embedded?*]

Our reaction seems to depend on the "weight" of the subject, for when we add more words, more "weight," the oddness disappears:

7.20C THE BOY AND THE GIRL, *holding hands, their heads together,* STOOD there quietly, *watching the sea gulls.*

These rather technical distinctions should become clear as you work with the sound of printed sentences. And, as you work to develop that "inner ear," you should be more conscious, as reader and as writer, of the movement of sentence style.

Problem Four. Identifying free modifiers   Underline the free modifiers in the following passages, and be prepared to identify them as left-branched, embedded, or right-branched. The first four have been analyzed for you; if you cover our answers with a sheet of paper and attempt your own answers, you'll get immediate feedback. Our answers to the next four are in the answer section at the end of the text. The last example presents a longer passage, the first paragraphs of a novel.

a. Brilliant rainbows melt across the ceiling, dissolving into dreamy puffs and hypnotic lassos of pure laser light.

Julia Orange

Analysis   The single comma separates the right-branched free modifier from the rest of the sentence. The modifier, "dissolving . . .", might be moved to the beginning of the sentence or even embedded ("rainbows, dissolving . . . , melt . . ."). The free modifier describes, in more detail, how the rainbows melt across the ceiling. The correct answer, then, is to underline the right-branched free modifier:

■ Brilliant rainbows melt across the ceiling, *dissolving into dreamy puffs and hypnotic lassos of pure laser light.*

b. The minister, a pale, feeble-looking man with white hair and blond chin-whiskers, took his seat beside the small table and placed his Bible upon it.

Willa Cather

Analysis   This is a more complicated example, for it asks you to hear (or see) the difference between the punctuation of a free modifier (the complete phrase, "a pale . . . man with . . . chin-whiskers") and of items in a series (the comma separating "pale" and "feeble-looking"). There are also, to our ears, more restrictions on the movement of this modifier; it sounds a bit odd—a bit too far from its reference—if placed at the end of the sentence. Note the importance of treating the embedded modifier as a single unit:

■ The minister, *a pale, feeble-looking man with white hair and blond chin-whiskers,* took his seat beside the small table and placed his Bible upon it.

c. The women wore beaded capes, silk or satin dresses with trains, and their most precious jewels.

Isaac Bashevis Singer

Analysis   There are no free modifiers in this sentence; the commas separate the three items the women wore: capes, dresses, and jewels. You might want to reread sentences *a, b,* and *c* aloud—or at least with your inner ear alert—to hear the difference in free modifiers and series constructions.

d. On the table a book lay, a Bible, an ordinary kind of Bible with worn, imitation leather covers.

Robert Penn Warren

Analysis There are three free modifiers in this sentence, all adding detail to the sentence base, "a book lay." We call the first three words, "on the table," *free by position* since they are left-branched, in front of the subject. The free modifier, "a Bible," is separated with commas; it describes the subject, "a book," more precisely. The final words of the sentence are another free modifier, a single unit (the commas between "worn" and "imitation" separate items in series) describing the Bible in more detail.

■ *On the table* a book lay, *a Bible, an ordinary kind of Bible with worn, imitation leather covers.*

e. He carries a briefcase, lobbies Congress for environmental causes, builds an empire in Utah, appears organized and on the move, but he's still a fogbound romantic, easily slipping into memories of the foreign ports, the diaries of his youth, in which he was just another Edgar Allan Poe.

Chris Hodenfield

[Two hints: box the word *but,* to sort out the sentence bases, and listen for the sound of the sentence "shifting gears," as it were.]

f. After that we rode on in silence, the traces creaking, the hoofs of the horses clumping steadily in the soft sand, the grasshoppers shrilling from the fields and the cicadas from the trees overhead.

E. W. Teale

g. Here beside me on the table as I write, occasionally running a tentative paw through the littered sheets of manuscript and notes, is Hobie Baker, a tawny yellow tomcat, named for the great hockey player.

Stuart Chase

[Hint: find the sentence base—"here is Hobie Baker"—and follow punctuation as a clue.]

h. Most of the time she simply rode in a standing position, well aft on the beast, her hands hanging easily at her sides, her head erect, her straw-colored ponytail lightly brushing her shoulders, the blood of exertion showing faintly through the tan of her skin.

E. B. White

i. The pain began to rise and I planted my feet against the floor-board and held, stiff-armed, onto the edges of the seat. But the pain grew fast, rose suddenly up with a wild willful surge, breaking my hold and bending my head against the windowpane, where I saw, before the great pain closed my eyes, the house of Uncle James passing among the pine trees.

The truck moved on, churning the gravel on Blackshear Road, and the pain began to fall. We came up to the railroad tracks, and Tommy pushed forward the gear; the truck bolted over the rise of the tracks and we turned onto the highway. On the open road Tommy drove with his hands clenched hard on the wheel, and in the back of the truck John David stood up behind the window, his tight scared face squashed against the pane, looking through the cab and onto the narrow straight black road, which streamed out ahead of us now as far as we could see, into the town and out of it and on to Booth County.

Martha Stephens, *Cast a Wistful Eye*

■

Problem Five. Beginning your novel Passage i in problem four, just above, is the beginning of a short novel. In problem four you read the passage as an exercise in identifying free modifiers; in this problem we ask you to consider it as a passage of narrative, as the beginning of a novel, and we'll then ask you to compose the first two paragraphs of your own novel. Like most modern novels, this passage begins precisely with the action, with no background, with no location, with no sum-mary. The central character uses an "I" voice, which allows the author to contrast the character's inner feelings (we later learn she is about to give birth to a child) with the world outside. The passage has no formal beginning or end; it is simply a "slice out of time." But it is unified by a *controlling tone,* a sense of the effect the writer wants to have upon a reader. The same factors—a choice of narrative stance, a lack of formal opening and closing, a sense of controlling tone—are evident in pas-sages cited earlier, from a novel by Ernest Hemingway (7.5, 7.6, 7.7) and a revised piece of student prose (7.2).

With these rhetorical problems in mind, compose the first few para-graphs of your own novel. Do not worry about "organizing" the pas-sage—indeed, the assignment asks that the passage be without a formal beginning or end. Rather, choose a "slice of time" and develop it fully for a reader. ■

Levels of Generality in the Sentence

In chapter Five we examined *levels of generality* in the paragraph. We noted that some paragraphs use a *coordinate* pattern, a general statement supported by a series of details or examples, and we visualized that pattern by indenting sentences and numbering them:

7.21   1] The food in the cafeteria is terrible.
             2] The hamburgers are lousy.
             2] The shakes are watery.
             2] The french fries are soggy.

7.22   1] We caught two bass.
             2] We hauled them in briskly as though they were mackerel.
             2] We pulled them over the side of the boat in a businesslike manner without any landing net.
             2] And we stunned them with a blow on the head.

In other paragraphs we saw a *subordinate* pattern, each sentence more specific than the one before.

7.23   1] The food in the cafeteria is terrible.
             2] The hamburgers are particularly lousy.
                3] They are stale, tough, and tasteless.
                    4] Yesterday I had one that tasted like a fried inner tube.

7.24   1] I was rather interested in my fellow prisoners.
             2] They were on the whole slightly below the usual level of intelligence.
                3] This lack of intelligence explains why they were caught.

Most commonly, we saw a *mixed* pattern, coordinate and subordinate relationships working together.

This way of laying out paragraphs works equally well with sentences. It provides a visual way of showing how sentences are heard and understood.

7.22A   1] We caught two bass,
             2] *hauling them in briskly as though they were mackerel,*
             2] *pulling them over the side of the boat in a businesslike manner without any landing net,*
             2] *and stunning them with a blow on the head.*

E. B. White

Here the three free modifiers are coordinate: Each is on the same level of generality, explaining in more detail the sentence base, "we caught two bass"; each uses the same structure, an -*ing* verb; and they are linked with the coordinate word *and*.

7.24A 1] I was rather interested in my fellow prisoners,
  2] *who seemed in no way morally inferior to the rest of the population,*
  2] *though they were on the whole slightly below the usual level of intelligence,*
  3] *as was shown by their having been caught.*

Bertrand Russell

This is a mixed pattern, the two free modifiers at the second level offering comments at the same level of generality (on morality and intelligence), the free modifier at the third level commenting more specifically on intelligence.

In this way of visualizing sentences, grammar and meaning work together in complex ways, and we can turn back to sentences presented earlier and lay out their meaning on the page:

7.25 2] *With a clattering on the wood in the hollow box,*
  1] the bull charged and came out into the corral,
  2] *skidding with his forefeet in the straw as he stopped,*
  3] *his head up,*
  3] *the great hump of muscle on his leg swollen tight,*
  3] *his body muscles quivering as he looked up at the crowd on the stone walls.*

Ernest Hemingway

7.26 2] *On the table*
  1] A book lay,
  2] *a Bible,*
  3] *an ordinary kind of Bible with worn, imitation leather covers.*

Robert Penn Warren

In a coordinate sentence, with more than one sentence base, we label each sentence base as a first level, and box the coordinating word to remove it from the sequence:

7.27 1] Time is the continuous loop,
  2] *the snakeskin with scales endlessly overlapping without beginning or end,*

OR 1] time is an ascending spiral if you will,
  2] *like a child's toy Slinky.*

Annie Dillard

For embedded modifiers, we need to adopt a special notational device. We place paired slashes (/ /) in the sentence base, to indicate the removed free modifier, and place slashes around the free modifier and its punctuation:

7.28 1] The minister / / took his seat beside the small table and placed his Bible upon it.

2] /, *a pale, feeble-looking man with white hair and blond chin-whiskers,/*

Willa Cather

This way of annotating sentences is worth mastering. It will lock in the connection between the sound of sentences and their shape. And it will develop a sense of the potentials for adding detail and texture to your own writing.

Problem Six. Annotating free modifiers Write out the sentences below, numbering and indenting the levels of generality. Our answers for the first four are given in the answer section at the end of the book.

a. It is a winter day, overcast and still, and the town is closed in itself, humming and muttering a little, like a winter beehive.

Wendell Berry

b. The planes dive soundlessly, like toys on strings, all but hitting the five-foot trees as they pull out of their dives and simultaneously drop their payloads in the target area, usually with a concerted accuracy—plane after plane after plane—that is almost unbelievable.

John McPhee

c. Crane sat up straight, smiling shyly, looking pleased, like a child who has just been given a present.

Irwin Shaw

d. Now she ran to the bundle, picked it up, and scuttled to the black mouth of the alley a few feet away—a rather tall woman, bent, and in dark clothes from head to feet.

Dashiell Hammett

e. There were no shops on this wide street that he was walking along, only a line of tall houses on each side, all of them identical.

Roald Dahl

f. Connie sat out back in a lawn chair and watched them drive away, her father quiet and bald, hunched around so that he could back the car out, her mother with a look that was still angry and not at all softened through the windshield, and in the back seat poor June all dressed up as if she didn't know what a barbecue was, with all the running yelling kids and the flies.

Joyce Carol Oates

g. The Grandmother, muffled down in the back seat in the corner of the old carryall, in her worn sealskin pelisse, showing coffee-brown at the edges, her eyes closed, her hands waving together, had been occupied once more in losing a son.

Katherine Anne Porter

h. To the right, the clustered lights of the village spread thinner, becoming a line along the valley floor and finally disappearing in the distance.

Timothy Houghton

i. He lumbered into the city room, a big guy in his middle twenties, wearing a suit too dark for the season, and the disconsolate frown of a hunter who has seen nothing but warblers all day.

James Thurber

j. He could bear to think of her only after she had overpassed the common life of everything and lay in her bed, on her back, her narrow heels close together in a painful precision, her face calm, eyes closed, preferably with moonlight falling across her face, her right arm flung back on the pillow, crooked over her head, her left arm laid across the mound of her breasts.

Robert Penn Warren

■

THE GRAMMAR OF FREE MODIFIERS

The problems that follow are structured exercises in sentence combining. You don't have to worry particularly about mastering the vocabulary that introduces these problems—the vocabulary is simply a handy way of providing labels—but you should work carefully through the problems, listening with your inner ear to the sound of sentences, with the hope of increasing the potentials of your own style.

The Free Noun Phrase

The free noun phrase is a reduced sentence headed by a noun. Example 7.29 gains focus and emphasis by reducing predication, packing the meaning of three sentences into one:

7.29 The Marx Brothers starred in film comedies noted for their zany sight gags and verbal wit. The Marx Brothers were Chico,

Groucho, Harpo, and Zeppo. Such films included *Animal Crackers, Horse Feathers,* and *Duck Soup.* ⇒ The Marx Brothers, *Chico, Groucho, Harpo, and Zeppo,* starred in film comedies noted for their zany sight gags and verbal wit—*Animal Crackers, Horse Feathers, and Duck Soup.*

(Note again, as this example is read aloud, that the commas separating the free modifiers are "heard commas," while those separating the items in series are not heard.)

Most commonly, the free noun phrase develops a word in the base clause, thus establishing a strong connection between the phrase and the clause:

7.30   1] Of course it was a hell of a nerve for an instructor with so little experience in a college / / to ask them to elect *him* head of department.
2] */, an Easterner not long in the West,*
2] *until recently a stranger to most of his colleagues,/*
Bernard Malamud

Often the writer may enforce such a connection by repeating a key word or by breaking a word into subparts or by adding what might be called a "generalizing word"—all devices appropriate for transactional writing as well:

7.31   2] *On nearly every page of this paper*
1] I have had to resort to syntactic devices to keep the noun phrases within bounds—
2] *devices / / that are practically unknown to our textbook writers.*
3] */, such as this appositive,/*
Francis Christensen

7.32   1] The medieval abbey was a self-contained community—
2] *the abbey church,*
2] *the dormitory,*
2] *the dining hall,*
2] *the guest house for travelers,*
2] *and a large courtyard surrounded by a cloister,*
3] *a sheltered area.*

7.33   1] The discovery that germs pass diseases led to the isolation of the causes of such diseases as anthrax, diphtheria, tuberculosis, and leprosy—
2] *an achievement unmatched in previous medical history.*

Problem Seven. Mastering the free noun phrase   For each example below, use the first sentence as the sentence base and add to it, as free noun phrases, the information in the sentences that follow. Begin by noting the model sentences. Possible answers for the first six examples are given in the answer section at the end of the book.

■ **Model**   We walked into the milking-shed. The milking-shed was a long room with perhaps thirty rusted stanchions.   ⇒   We walked into the milking-shed, a long room with perhaps thirty rusted stanchions.[1]

■ **Model**   The village of Holcomb stands on the high wheat plains of western Kansas. The plains are a lonesome area that other Kansans call "out there."   ⇒   The village of Holcomb stands on the high wheat plains of western Kansas, a lonesome area that other Kansans call "out there."
Truman Capote

a. They had a child. The child was a little girl.

b. The obvious leader of the party was an old man. The old man was Loren Pierce.

c. I was born in 1927. I was the only child of middle-class parents.

d. The moderator stepped in occasionally. The moderator was an "award-winning aerospace journalist" for *Chicago Today*.

e. Tina had given a fishing line to the American. Tina was the Jamaican girl. The American was Kennedy.

f. He is the child and product of the disrupted times. He is a perfect specimen of his generation.

g. He was my sister Mim's crazy husband. Her husband was a mystical child of darkness. Her husband was a bright, talented, sheepish, tricky, curly-haired man-child of darkness.

h. By the end of the week they all knew him. They knew the hungry mouth. They knew the insufferable humorless eyes. They knew the intense ugly blue-shaved face.

Problem Eight. Experimenting with free noun phrases   Add free noun phrases to the following sentences. Consider the assignment as an experiment, and feel free to take chances, to go beyond mechanical answers.

a. The children met Mr. Fox at the newly opened zoo.

b. The hunter sharpened the knife on the stone.

c. The class watched anxiously as the two faced each other.

d. Amy was more surprised at the event than her brother.

e. It was a typical Friday afternoon at the office.

f. He held out his hand, and the doctor looked at it carefully.   ■

The Free Verb Phrase

The free verb phrase has a verb as its headword. Most commonly the verb is an *-ing* verb.

7.34   The woman walked up the library stairs. She was carrying a large stack of books.   ⇒   The woman walked up the library stairs, *carrying a large stack of books.*

Of course, there are other ways to combine the sentence bases of 7.34—we might, for example, use a bound modifier:

7.34A   The woman who was carrying a large stack of books walked up the library stairs.

The advantage of the free modifier is that it allows us to expand the sentence without "overweighting" it, as happened in example 7.11, for the details fall naturally into place after the sentence base.

7.34B   1] The woman // walked up the library stairs,
2] /, *carrying a large stack of books,/*
2] *bent forward at the waist,*
2] *lifting her feet haltingly,*
2] *and pausing to look up every few steps.*

A professional example captures these potentials precisely—a simple sentence base expanded, after the adverb *really,* with a series of *-ing* verbs, detailing the process:

7.35   1] She had left him,
2] *really,*
2] *packing up suddenly in a cold quiet fury,*
2] *stabbing him with her elbows when he tried to get his arms around her,*
2] *now and again cutting him to the bone with a short sentence expelled through her clenched teeth.*

Katherine Anne Porter

The free verb phrase can go beyond the *-ing* verb (the present participle) to include past participles, as the headword *caught* in 7.36:

7.36   1] He lay barely breathing and stared at the point where it had disappeared,
2] *caught in a spell of loathing and admiration.*

Ralph Ellison

Problem Nine. Mastering the free verb phrase   Use the first sentence in each set as the sentence base, using a free verb phrase. Many times, as in the model sentence, you'll need to reduce the verb that serves as the headword of the free modifier.

■ **Model**   The barbeque cook stood in the doorway. He wore a dirty white apron. He watched them. ⇒ The barbeque cook, *wearing a dirty white apron,* stood in the doorway, *watching them.*[2]

a. They were coming for him. They walked in step like a tap-dance team returning for a third encore.

b. Father was stepping out like a boy. Father was pleased with himself. (Hint: left-branch or embed?)

c. He mounted the steps and went through the screen door. He heard it bang behind him.

d. Next to the child's mother was a red-headed youngish woman. The woman read one of the magazines. The woman was working on a piece of chewing gum.

e. Annie came to the door. Annie tried to smile and curtsy. Annie tidied her hair. Annie wiped her hands on her pinafore.

f. A bicyclist was riding near him on gleaming wheels. The bicyclist cupped his fist to his mouth like a megaphone. The bicyclist cheered him along as they do at races.   ■

Problem Ten. Experimenting with the free verb phrase   Add free verb phrases to the following sentences. Experiment—go beyond the single free modifier to try a coordinate series, listing several details.

a. He gave the elephant the peanut gingerly.

b. The bees swarmed over the beekeeper.

c. Kate and Ralph drove slowly through downtown.

d. "You're not going to keep that microfilm!" Rebecca said quietly.

e. Mark started into his serve.

f. Beth walked through the paintshop and into the assembly line.   ■

The Free Absolute Phrase

What we call the *absolute phrase* is the most complex of free modifiers, easier shown than explained.

7.37 1] The two steers backed away against the wall,
         2] *their heads sunken,*
         2] *their eyes watching the bull.*

Ernest Hemingway

7.38 1] She was asleep,
         2] *her head dropping forward,*
         2] *the chin lazily closeted in the sink of the neck,*
         2] *and her lips hanging loose and slack.*

George Lamming

The absolute combines the features of a verb phrase and a noun phrase. It can be presented, as a sentence-combining problem, as a deletion of a form of the main verb *to be* (*is, are, was, were,* and so on):

7.37A The two steers backed away against the wall. Their heads WERE sunken. Their eyes WERE watching the bull. ⇒ The two steers backed away against the wall, *their heads sunken, their eyes watching the bull.*

7.38A She was asleep. Her head WAS dropping forward. The chin WAS lazily closeted in the sink of the neck. And her lips WERE hanging loose and slack. ⇒ She was asleep, *her head dropping forward, the chin lazily closeted in the sink of the neck, and her lips hanging loose and slack.*

In meaning, the absolute divides an action into parts: the general action in the sentence base, the details in the free modifiers. It asks for a certain "leap" from the reader, but here grammar and meaning and reader (and writer) cooperate by making connections that can only be approximated in other ways:

7.39 I followed and came out on high ground. The high ground was a slope covered with pine needles. ⇒ I followed and came out on high ground WHICH WAS a slope WHICH WAS covered with pine needles. ⇒
         1] I followed and came out on high ground,
         2] *a slope covered with pine needles.*

Caroline Gordon

Problem Eleven. Mastering the free absolute phrase   Use the first sentence in each set below as the sentence base, and add the meaning of the following sentences as free absolute phrases. Answers are given in the answer section.

■ **Model**   Now he faced the raging crowd with defiance. Its screams were penetrating his eardrums like trumpets shrieking from a juke-box.   ⇒   Now he faced the raging crowd with defiance, *its screams penetrating his eardrums like trumpets shrieking from a juke-box.*

Ralph Ellison

■ **Model**   The weasel backed up against the far wall of the box. Its yellow body was tense as a spring. Its teeth were showing in a tiny soundless snarl.   ⇒   The weasel backed up against the far wall of the box, *its yellow body tense as a spring, its teeth showing in a tiny soundless snarl.*

a. She's flushed and silent. Her mouth is half open.

b. The priest stood transfixed. His jaw was slack.

c. And then the duck skidded across the surface of the lake. Its wings were flapping nervously. Its legs were breaking the water into a series of silvery arcs.

d. The boys split up. Some of them were taking the subway down to Greenwich Village. Others were heading for the Empire State Building.

e. Then these melodies turn to ice as real night music takes over. The pianos and vibes are erecting clusters in the high brittle octaves. A clarinet is wandering across like a crack on a pond.

f. He watched the stage-coach go by. The four horses were spanking along as the driver flicked them. The polished metal was gleaming in the sun. The body was swaying as the wheels rose and fell in the rough trail.   ■

Problem Twelve. Experimenting with the free absolute phrase   Add one or more free absolutes to the sentences below. Try to visualize the action or statement, and then break it into parts. Experiment—try to go beyond the minimum requirements of the assignment.

a. She looked idly at his shoes.

b. Timothy stood patiently at the corner.

c. Hepzibah took the microfilm and ran to the waiting helicopter.

d. He skated faster.

e. We watched them walk up the stairs slowly.

f. Both men and women are harmed by sexism. (A special challenge.) ■

Other Free Modifiers

Free modifiers can take many other forms, most of which come naturally to the developing writer, and thus needn't be discussed in much detail. Two additional patterns should be mentioned, however: the free modifier headed with an adjective or cluster of adjectives, and the free modifier headed with a prepositional phrase. Both are illustrated by a John Updike sentence:

7.40   1] He was a young farmer,
            2] *in his late twenties or early thirties,*   [prepositional phrase]
            2] *thin as a grasshopper.*   [adjective phrase]

There are stylistic restraints on the positioning of adjectives. Our ear won't accept a single adjective as a free modifier; it doesn't have enough "weight":

7.40A   He was a young farmer, *thin.*

Adjectives must come as a phrase (a group of words), as in 7.40, or as a set of adjectives (a cluster), as in 7.40B:

7.40B   1] He was a young farmer,
            2] *thin, curly-haired, and handsome.*   [adjective cluster]

Prepositional phrases, in their normal position in the sentence, can be free or bound, depending on the author's choice:

7.41   1] Prepositional phrases / / can be free or bound,
            2] /, *in their normal position in the sentence,/*
               [prepositional phrase punctuated as free modifier]
            2] depending on the author's choice.   [verb phrase]

7.41A   1] Prepositional phrases in their normal position in the sentence can be free or bound,
            2] *depending on the author's choice.*

The most useful prepositions are *like* and *as,* prepositions that introduce a metaphor to sharpen an image:

dangl: Dangling Modifiers A "dangling" modifier is not clearly attached to the sentence base. It forces a reading from the reader that is not intended by the author.

First Draft

After eating our dinner, the boat took us home. (Here the "dumb reader" invents a very hungry boat.)

On one hand, he's got good balance; on the other hand, he's too short to play center. (The "dumb reader" confuses literal and figurative and balances the poor player in a handstand.)

Revision

After we ate our dinner, the boat took us home. (The revision clarifies who did the eating.)

He has good balance, but he's too short to play center. (The revision loses something of the formality of the original, but it saves the reader from rereading.)

As writers begin to take chances with free modifiers, they will, almost inevitably, dangle one now and then. The answer is not to avoid taking chances (how else can one learn?), but to develop the habit of rereading drafts, one last time, remembering the dumb reader.

7.42   1] Joad's lips stretched tight over his long teeth for a moment, and
    1] he licked his lips,
      2] *like a dog,*   [prepositional phrase]
        3] *two licks,*   [noun phrase]
           4] *one in each direction*
            from the middle.   [noun phrase]

John Steinbeck

Problem Thirteen. Mastering free prepositions and adjectives Use the first sentence in each group below as the sentence base, and add the meanings in the following sentences to it as free modifiers. Possible answers are given in the answer section.

■ **Model** There was Madame behind the counter. Madame was round. Madame was fat. Madame was white. ⇒ There was Madame behind the counter, *round, fat, and white.*[3]

■ **Model** Small, separate clouds swam slowly in the west over the Sierra. The clouds were like fish with bright edges. ⇒ Small, separate clouds, *like fish with bright edges,* swam slowly in the west over the Sierra.

Walter Van Tilburg Clark

a. He went to speak to Mrs. Bean. Mrs. Bean was tiny among the pillows.

b. She was by the bedside now. She was very deliberate. She was very calm.

c. My fingers were well adapted to this kind of work. My fingers were strong and sensitive from their long training.

d. She stood before him. She stood with a relaxed dignity. She stood like a priestess at the top of some immensely long stone staircase.

e. Rose was different today. Rose was more tense. Rose was more careful.

f. The students finished the sentences. The students were confident. The students were alert. The students were like dutiful apprentices.   ■

IMPLICATIONS FOR WRITERS: THREE SUGGESTIONS

We'll offer a somewhat longer narrative to examine how free modifiers work in contexts beyond the sentence. The passage in 7.43, from a short story by Irwin Shaw, will serve as a model for a final writing assignment; it will also allow us to develop three suggestions about narrative and descriptive writing:

■ as a general rule, right-branch free modifiers (*the cumulative sentence*);
■ in narrations, lay out the narrative line in sentence bases, adding detail in free modifiers (we'll call this the "cookbook principle");
■ "show the reader" rather than "tell the reader" by using detail and comparison instead of evaluation.

You'll want to read the passage at least twice, first to get the meaning of the passage (a touchdown run in a football game), then to analyze more carefully how the author achieves the texture of the passage (perhaps by underlining the free modifiers). You might need to be warned about one device: Irwin Shaw tightens the action by occasionally leaving out expected connectives.

7.43 Darling tucked the ball in *and* spurted at him . . . ⇒ Darling tucked the ball in, spurted at him.

Here, as elsewhere, the lesson is a positive one: Note what writers achieve by taking chances.

7.44 The pass was high and wide and he jumped for it, feeling it slap flatly against his hands, as he shook his hips to throw off the halfback who was diving at him. The center floated by, his hands desperately brushing Darling's knee as Darling picked his feet up high and delicately ran over a blocker and an opposing linesman in a jumble on the ground near the scrimmage line. He had ten yards in the clear and picked up speed, breathing easily, feeling his thigh pads rising and falling against his legs, listening to the sound of cleats behind him, pulling away from them, watching the other backs heading him off toward the sidelines, the whole picture, the men closing in on him, the blockers fighting for position, the ground he had to cross, all suddenly clear in his head, for the first time in his life not a meaningless confusion of men, sounds, speed. He smiled a little to himself as he ran, holding the ball lightly in front of him with his two hands, his knees pumping high, his hips twisting in the almost girlish run of a back in a broken field. The first halfback came at him and he fed him his leg, then swung at the last moment, took the shock of the man's shoulder without breaking stride, ran right through him, his cleats biting securely into the turf. There was only the safety man now, coming warily at him, his arms crooked, hands spread. Darling tucked the ball in, spurted at him, driving hard, hurling himself along, his legs pounding, knees high, all two hundred pounds bunched into controlled attack. He was sure he was going to get past the safety man. Without thought, his arms and legs working beautifully together, he headed right for the safety man, stiff-armed him, feeling the blood spurt instantaneously from the man's nose onto his hand, seeing his face go awry, head turned, mouth pulled to one side. He pivoted away, keeping the arm locked, dropping the safety man as he ran easily toward the goal line, with the drumming of cleats diminishing behind him.

Irwin Shaw, "The Eighty Yard Run"

Problem Fourteen. Modifier placement Here are two word-counts. The first presents the number of words in the sentence bases and in the three free modifier positions, left-branched, embedded, and right-branched, in passage 7.44 above. The second count is based on an extensive sample of student and professional writing—transactional writing as well as narrative and descriptive writing.[4] Examine these two counts, perhaps performing a similar count of a sample of your own writing, and develop generalizations about using and positioning free modifiers.   ■

	Count 1	Count 2	
	Passage 7.44	freshmen	professionals
Percentage of words in free modifiers	70.3	16.1	30.3
Percentage of words left-branched	2.6	11.8	8.8
Percentage of words embedded	0	0.8	4.2
Percentage of words right-branched	67.7	3.5	17.3

The Cumulative Sentence

Francis Christensen, a writing teacher, identified what he called the *cumulative sentence,* a sentence that, like this one, adds detail to the sentence base by using right-branched free modifiers.

> **7.45** The main clause, which may or may not have a sentence modifier before it, advances the discussion; but the additions move backward, as in this clause, to modify the statement of the main clause or more often to explicate it or exemplify it, so that the sentence has a flowing and ebbing movement, advancing to a new position and then pausing to consolidate it, leaping and lingering as the popular ballad does.
>
> "A Generative Rhetoric of the Sentence"

Thus, the cumulative sentence "accumulates" meaning, and Christensen called his approach to sentence style a "generative rhetoric" because it generates detail to support the sentence base, much as you generated detail in the problems above.

Cumulative sentences make sense psychologically as well. Left-branched modifiers have to be held in the mind until the sentence base clarifies them—the word counts in problem fourteen suggest that professionals keep their left-branching as short as possible. Embedded modifiers interrupt subject and predicate; professionals, though they do embed, keep embeddings short, about 4 words (which we matched in this sentence). You can test this by speaking aloud, trying to use free modifiers. You'll find it easy to speak in right-branched free modifiers, simply adding an afterthought. You'll find it much harder to embed, and almost impossible to left-branch for more than a sentence or two.

Of course, the Irwin Shaw passage above, with over two-thirds of the words in free modification, is typical only of highly textured narrative and descriptive writing, and, even in that passage, not every sentence is a cumulative sentence. But the more general word-counts support Christensen's view, showing that professionals right-branch about one sentence in four, and they suggest that experimenting with cumulative sentences in narrative and descriptive writing may pay off as well in transactional writing.

Problem Fifteen. The cumulative sentence in transactional writing This textbook is transactional writing; it does business in the world. Examine our prose for cumulative sentences, and be prepared to identify the grammatical structures that we, at least, find useful in transactional writing. Choose a chapter other than this one, and, if your instructor directs, write up your findings in a short paper.   ■

The "Cookbook Principle" of Narration

We begin with a problem taken from the simplest of narrations—cookbook recipes, telling someone how to go about cooking something.

Problem Sixteen. A lesson from a cookbook   The sentences below are taken from *The Joy of Cooking,* by Irma S. Rombauer and Marion Rombauer Becker. As is typical in recipes, each sentence base has an understood subject, *you.* Read the sentences carefully, noting sentence bases and free modifiers, and consider the following question: Where does *time* go in narrations, and where does *detail* go?

a. Roll out the dough in a thin sheet, ⅛ inch for pastry, ¼ inch for biscuit dough. Cut it into four squares, large enough to enclose the apple entirely.

b. Wring out a cloth and suspend it, like a jelly bag, above a large pan. Again push the scummy crust to one side and ladle the soup carefully, straining it through a cloth.

c. Add the gelatin to the egg whites in a slow stream, whipping the pudding constantly.

d. With a wooden mallet, lightly crack the crab shells, being careful not to pound any shell bits into the meat.

e. Spread the mayonnaise as you would frosting, with firm strokes of a spatula, working quickly, for it tends to congeal even at room temperature.   ■

Cookbook writers seem to follow naturally a rule for writing narrations that we might state as "Stretch out the action in time in the sentence base, and add detail in free modifiers":

7.46 1] Spread the mayonnaise as you would frosting, [time]
2] *with firm strokes of a spatula,* [detail]
2] *working quickly,* [detail]
3] *for it tends to congeal even at room temper-* [detail]
ature.

You can see the same principle at work in Irwin Shaw's "The Eighty Yard Run": the narrative line in the sentence base, the details in free modifiers:

7.44A 1] Darling tucked the ball in, [and] spurted at him, [time]
2] *driving hard,* [detail]
2] *hurling himself along,* [detail]
3] *his legs pounding,* [detail]
3] *knees high,* [detail]
2] *all two hundred pounds bunched into controlled attack.* [detail]

We formalize this principle, the "cookbook principle of narration," in Figure 7.1.

Developing writers, we find, tend to conflate time, to interpret narrative time for the reader, and thus they miss opportunities for detail and texture in writing. Compare, for example, the first draft and revision of the student sentences below.

7.47 2] *Having entered the library,*
1] she went directly to the reference book,
2] *pulling it out quickly.* [first draft]

7.47A 1] She entered the library,
2] *pulling the door open with one hand,*
2] *stepping through,*
2] *and wincing as it slammed behind her,*
1] and she went directly to the reference book,
2] *her heels punctuating her way with a staccato rhythm,*
3] *like drumbeats.*
1] She knelt down,
1] and she pulled it out quickly,
2] *lifting with the left hand,*

FIGURE 7.1   The Cookbook Principle of Narration

> 3] *one finger inside the book's spine,*
> 2] *and cradling the book with the right hand.*

Showing and Telling

Here's a student sentence that "tells" the reader:

7.48   It was a lovely cat, eagerly eating its delicious dinner.

The key words here tell the reader that the cat was *lovely,* that it ate *eagerly,* and that its dinner was *delicious.* That is, they are evaluative words, for they tell the reader how to respond. We find only four evaluative words in the long passage from Irwin Shaw's "The Eighty Yard Run" (example 7.44); Shaw "shows" the reader by providing detail.

The general principle, "show rather than tell," seems to develop from the particular nature of communicating in print. We can't trust writers to tell us what to think, the way we can trust people we speak with; writers need detail to let us make our own judgments. It also has to do with the principle we began this chapter with, "You are what you see," for evaluating the lovely cat may mean not seeing it, rushing to a judgment as it were.

7.48A   The orange and white cat, *its long fur rippling,* stood over the dish, *bobbing its head down for a bite, and then raising it as it chewed, occasionally wiping its mouth with a broad lick.*

There's no "lovely, eager" cat eating a "delicious" dinner in this revision, but there is an attempt to see the action, and let the reader see it as well. In writing, that's more effective.

Of course, the evaluation and the detail mix together in most good writing, and we might end, as we began, with a sentence by Ernest Hemingway, where the evaluative word *insultingly* is pinned down by a comparison and validated by the supporting detail.

7.49 The gypsy was walking out toward the bull again, *walking heel-and-toe, insultingly, like a ballroom dancer, the red shafts of the banderillos twitching with his walk.*

Ernest Hemingway

SUMMARY

We defined description and narration, and we stressed, in both, the need for close observation of the world. We defined *free modifiers,* word groups that are movable and are separated from the sentence base by commas. We noted that free modifiers can be *left-branched, embedded,* and *right-branched,* and we developed a system for annotating *levels of generality* in the sentence. We looked at several kinds of free modifiers—noun phrases, verb phrases, absolute phrases, and adjective and participle groups. We concluded by discussing the importance of the *cumulative sentence,* by noting the "cookbook principle" of narration, and by stressing the importance of *showing* the reader rather than *telling* the reader.

Problem Seventeen. The master sentence   The sentences below are all "master sentences," effective precisely because of their control over the movement of free modifiers. If your instructor directs, use one of the sentences as the basis for a controlled sentence imitation, as discussed in the next chapter. Or, without direct imitation, construct your own "master sentence." As a minimun requirement, let it be at least fifty words in length.

A   One of the images we have before us now is that of Tom Seaver pitching: the motionless assessing pause on the hill while the sign is delivered, the easy, rocking shift of the weight onto the back leg, the upraised arms, and then the left shoulder coming forward as the whole body drives forward and drops suddenly down—down so low that the right knee scrapes the sloping dirt of the mound—in an immense thrusting stride, and the right arm coming over blurrily and still flailing, even as the ball, the famous fastball, flashes across the plate, chest-high on the batter and already past his low, late swing.

"Talk of the Town," *New Yorker*

B   [Of the dancer Pavlova] As her little bird body revealed itself on the scene, either immoble in trembling mystery or tense in the incredible arc which was her lift, her instep stretched ahead in an arch never before seen, the tiny bones of her hand in ceaseless vibration, her face radiant, diamonds glittering under her dark hair, her little waist encased in silk, the great tutu balancing, quickening and flashing over her beating, flashing, quivering legs, every man and woman sat forward, every pulse quickened.

Agnes de Mille, "Pavlova"

C I was born in a large Welsh town at the beginning of the Great War— an ugly, lovely town (or so it was and is to me), crawling, sprawling by a long and splendid curving shore where truant boys and sandfield boys and old men from nowhere beachcombed, idled and paddled, watched the dockbound ships or the ships steaming away on to wonder and India, magic and China, countries bright with oranges and loud with lions; threw stones into the sea for the barking outcast dogs; made castles and forts and harbours and race tracks in the sand; and on Saturday afternoons listened to the brass band, watched the Punch and Judy, or hung about on the fringes of the crowd to hear the fierce religious speakers who shouted at the sea, as though it were wicked and wrong to roll in and out like that, white-horsed and full of fishes.

Dylan Thomas, *Quite Early One Morning*

■

FINAL WRITING ASSIGNMENTS

I. Assignments in Narration

A. The selection from Irwin Shaw's "The Eighty Yard Run" (7.44) provides a model for a narrative assignment involving some kind of physical activity. Take an event with some clear-cut beginning and end— a free throw, a lap across a pool, even a walk to class—and present the event in a textured description of about 400 words.

B. Think of an event in your life—a small event, essentially an incident that was significant to you—and try to capture it in words. Don't *tell* the reader why the event was significant; find a way to present detail that *shows* its significance.

C. Write two narrations of the same event, using the perspectives of two different people. You might, for example, write of a conference with an instructor from your perspective and from the instructor's perspective, or you might write of an incident in a family or in a courting situation. Indeed, you might take several perspectives on the same event, perhaps aiming first at an absolutely neutral, nonevaluative perspective.

II. Assignments in Description

A. Write a description of an object that might appear to be ugly—a junkyard, an unkempt house, a crowded beach. But try to be nonjudgmental, simply describing the object or scene as it is—indeed, you may find a kind of beauty in ugliness.

B. Describe an object you feel strongly attached to—a house, a room, a piece of furniture. Do not explain to your reader why you feel the way you do about the object; provide the detail to support that feeling.

III. Assignments Mixing Narration and Description

A. The *Reader's Digest* prints a regular feature, "The Most Unforgettable Character I've Ever Met." Write such a feature, but aim—rather than at the sentimentality of many *Reader's Digest* articles—at a clear and detailed "fixing" of that person in space and time.

B. Write a letter to your best friend, describing the campus and explaining a typical day in classes and outside them. Set yourself a special goal: the best letter I've ever written.

FOR FURTHER READING

Francis Christensen explains his "Generative Rhetoric of the Sentence" in a text, *The New Rhetoric* (New York: Harper & Row, 1977), and in a collection of essays for teachers, *Toward a New Rhetoric* (New York: Harper & Row, 1978), both with Bonniejean Christensen.

But perhaps the best advice we can give is that you read widely in modern narration and description. Anthologies of short stories are widely available, and they will give you a taste of narrative writing. And we will mention the names of a few modern descriptive writers whose work appeals to us—most have one or more books available in the bookstore or college library: Roger Angell and Roger Kahn, writing on sports; Annie Dillard, Loren Eiseley, and Rachel Carson, essays on nature and ecology; John McPhee and Peter Matthiessen, travel essays; E. B. White and Joan Didion, more speculative essays; Nora Ephron, essays on feminism and other topics; Berton Roueché, a series of books on medical problem-solving; and Robert Coles, a series of studies of "children in crisis."

NOTES

1. Adapted from a sentence by Stephen Diamond: "We walked into the milking shed, a long room with perhaps thirty rusted stanchions, only three of which were in service, soon to be reduced to two."
2. Adapted from a sentence by James Baldwin: "The barbeque cook, wearing a dirty white apron, his conked hair reddish and metallic in the pale sun, and a cigarette between his lips, stood in the doorway, watching them."
3. Adapted from a Katherine Mansfield sentence: "There was Madame behind the counter, round, fat, white, her head like a powderpuff rolling on a black satin pin-cushion."
4. The statistics are taken from Lester Faigley, "Another Look at Sentences," *Freshman English News,* 7, no. 3 (Winter 1979), 18–21.

8

Style as Craft

> . . . a writer, like an acrobat, must occasionally try a stunt that is too much for him.
>
> E. B. WHITE

The word *craft* has two senses. It has the sense of a skilled trade, of *craftsmanship,* as a potter or a welder or a mechanic might be said to practice a craft. It also has the sense of aiming for an effect, of *craftiness.* Both senses of the word are somewhat suspect nowadays. We distrust people who are "crafty," for we value naturalness and honesty as opposed to what we see as artificiality or pretense. And even the positive sense of "craftsmanship" has been debased by advertising, for machine-stamped plastic chairs are sold by inviting us to admire "the craftsmanship of their heirloom designs."

This chapter tries to revitalize both senses of craft as they apply to writing. Our dynamic model of rhetoric builds a picture of a writer who is "crafty," in the sense of seeking to persuade by manipulating the written word. And that model posits a writer who is a *craftsman,* who takes conscious pride in the making of sentences.

Craftsmanship in style is a constant in all good writing, once we move beyond the bare-bones level of cookbook recipes and lists of ingredients on food packages. We sense this conscious pleasure in the play of language in the example below, where N. Scott Momaday uses a simple vocabulary and loose sentence structure to explain the memories of a native American boy:

8.1 It didn't snow much out there, but when it did the whole land as far as you could see was covered with it. It went on sometimes all night, and you could see it outside through the smoke hole, swirling around in the black sky. And sometimes the flakes came in and melted on the floor around the fire, and you were glad there was a fire. You could hear the wind, and you were little and you could get way down under the blankets and see the firelight moving around on the logs of the roof and the walls, and the floor was yellow and warm and you could put your hand in the dust and feel how warm it was. And you knew that your grandfather was there, looking out for you. You woke up sometimes, and he was there stirring the fire to keep it going, and you knew everything was all right. And the next morning you got up and went out and it was cold and there was snow all around. Maybe the sun was out and the snow was so bright it hurt your eyes. It drifted up against the hogan and covered the top of it, and the hogan looked like a little hill all covered with snow and you could see the smoke coming out of it and smell the coffee and the mutton. You put your hands in the snow and rubbed your face with it and it made you come alive and feel good and your hands were red and wet with the snow. You were little and you looked all around at the snow; it was piled up on the brush and you could see the dark branches under it, and the sheep were bleating in the corral and the poles of the fence were heaped high with snow, and underneath you could see the wood, how it was almost black with water. There was a gully a little way off, and inside of it, where the snow had fallen off, the earth was a deep red and there were bits of brush growing out of it and covered with snow. They looked like handfuls of cotton or wool. Everything was changed. . . . And it was getting late and you rode home in the sunset and the whole land was cold and bright. And that night your grandfather hammered the strips of silver and told you stories in the firelight. And you were little and right there in the center of everything, the sacred mountains, the snow-covered mountains and hills, the gullies and the flat, the sundown and the night—everything—where you were little, where you were and had to be.

House Made of Dawn

Another writer, John F. Kennedy, uses a complex series of patterns, formal and balanced, to make a public statement on assuming the Presidency of the United States:

8.2 Now the trumpet summons us again—not as a call to bear arms, though arms we need—not as a call to battle, though embattled we are—but a call to bear the burden of a long twilight struggle year in and year out, "rejoicing in hope, patient in tribulation"—a struggle against the common enemies of man: tyranny, poverty, disease, and war itself. . . .

In the long history of the world, only a few generations have been granted the role of defending freedom in its hour of maximum danger. I do not shrink from this responsibility—I welcome it. I do not believe that any of us would exchange places with any other people or any other generation. The energy, the faith, the devotion which we bring to this endeavor will light our country and all who serve it—and the glow from the fire can truly light the world.

And so, my fellow Americans: Ask not what your country can do for you—ask what you can do for your country.

My fellow citizens of the world: Ask not what America will do for you, but what together we can do for the freedom of man.

"Inaugural Address"

The two styles are poles apart: one public, the other private; one stressing an individual experience, the other a public dedication; one loose and accumulative in structure, the other rigid, emphatic, and oratorical. Both writers, though, despite their differences, are craftsmen: using the resources of language available to them to sway the reader by the process of communicating, by the texture of their styles, as well as by what they say. Both writers merge what they say into the process of saying it: The remarkable final sentence of the Momaday passage grows naturally out of the slow piling up of details; the famous conclusion that ends the Kennedy speech seems to follow inevitably from the similar sentences that precede it. Both writers use the natural rhythms of speech—Kennedy's passage was delivered as a speech, and Momaday's uses the oral patterns of a child's talk. Yet both writers also lean upon our sense of style in the world of print, our sense of "speech written down": Kennedy consciously echoing the images of public leadership ("the trumpet summons us," "bear the burden," "truly light the world"); Momaday expanding mere talk into a written vision of a world that, to the child, is a quiet picture of harmony, "where you were and had to be."

This chapter will explore, in some detail, the potentials of "speech written down," of style as a part of the complex *code* of print. In doing so, we'll turn back to an old-fashioned way of learning style, that of mastering the sentences of skilled writers by imitating them. Our first problem, though not completely serious, may help to justify that old-fashioned way of learning.

Problem One. Peanuts What's funny about the character Schroeder in the comic strip "Peanuts"? Look at the comic strip again if you don't remember what Schroeder does. ■

IMITATION AND STYLE

Everybody imitates. The tennis player watches the coach slice a backhand and then tries to copy the flow of her stroke; the beginning carpenter learns from the movements of the more skilled worker next to him; the teacher, just starting out, may quite unconsciously adopt the mannerisms of teachers that have influenced her.

Thus imitation is a basic way of learning any performance skill. You learn baseball or sewing or automotive repair by imitating—by watching the professionals and consciously or unconsciously modeling your practice on theirs. Rock bands usually begin by imitating successful rock bands, and poets and novelists, as well as cooks and business executives, do the same.

Stylistic imitation, of one kind or another, has been part of the rhetorical tradition for most of its history. More recently, we've learned, from studies of how we develop our language abilities, to speak of "early-blooming" and "late-blooming" language skills. "Early-blooming" skills are the basic patterns of language, spoken or written. "Late-blooming" skills are for the most part patterns that are frozen in the traditions of print; mastery of these skills continues through—and beyond—one's college years.

Thus there's always a gap, for developing writers, between the complexity of the ideas and images in their heads and their ability to form that complexity in writing. In this regard, we think of Schroeder, in the comic strip *Peanuts,* in his typical pose: seated on the floor in front of a toy piano with a bust of Beethoven on it, the score of a Beethoven sonata in front of him. Schroeder has four keys on his toy piano; the musical score in front of him would be complex even on an eighty-eight-key concert grand. Schroeder needs to "expand his keyboard." In much the same way, developing writers need to expand their "stylistic keyboard," to develop more options for choice. Imitating the written sentence is one way to develop those options.

Our model of sentence imitation involves three steps:

■ *copy* the model
■ compose a *close imitation* of it
■ then compose a *free imitation* of it.

We can explain that model with an example, a short passage by the nineteenth-century British author, Lewis Carroll:

8.3 "Now! Now!" said the Queen. "Faster! Faster!" and they went so fast that at last they seemed to skim through the air, hardly touching the ground with their feet, till suddenly, just as Alice was getting quite exhausted, they stopped, and she found herself sitting on the ground, breathless and giddy.

Through the Looking-Glass

The first step is to *copy* the passage word for word. Copying is a way of making a passage your own, of actively recreating the movements of words that you sense only passively in reading. (At times, as we present models for imitation, we'll indent or spread out sentence parts to stress their relationship, much as we indented levels of generality in the last chapter; you may find it worthwhile to experiment with this device in your own copying.)

The next step in mastering the sentence is to write a *close imitation* of the passage. A close imitation sticks tightly to the original, following the sentence as closely as possible while changing the words. The sentence, of course, may be shifted slightly to keep new meanings clear; the purpose is to translate the original into a new form. Here is a student's close imitation of this model—he adapted the sentence to describe a class engaged in the speed writing discussed in chapter One:

8.4 "Write! Write!" shouted the instructor. "Faster! Faster!" And the class wrote so fast that it seemed like their pens had grown wings, scarcely touching the surface of the paper, till suddenly, just as Ralph was running out of ideas, the instructor shouted "Stop!" and he found himself slumped in his seat, drained but satisfied.

The last step is to write a *free imitation* of the model. A free imitation tried to capture the spirit of the model; it's not limited to the specific patterns. A close imitation is done with the model in front of the writer; with a free imitation the model is put away, and the writer takes off on his own. You can expand your free imitations as far as your own creativity will allow. As an example, here is a student's free imitation of the Carroll passage.

8.5 The ride started slowly, picking up speed as the cars revolved faster and faster, so that they found themselves pushed back against the cushions, as if they were being whirled at the end of a string, till finally, just as Susan was beginning to give in to the paranoia creeping over her, they slowed and stopped, and she found herself climbing out, her body moving stiffly while her mind continued to whirl at the end of the string.

These student sentences are "mere" imitations, yet they provided, for those students, a chance to come to grips with, and to master, a highly complex structure. Thus you should find, as you experiment with sentence imitation, that what begins as mechanical copying can become a creative act. As you follow our model—copying, close imitation, free imitation—you learn from written sentences. You expand your stylistic keyboard.

THE RHYTHMS OF WRITING

Writing is, in some complex way, a kind of music. The patterning of pauses with punctuation, the sounds of sentences as they spread across the page, the movement of meaning—all this contributes to the craftsmanship of style, to the music of sentences. But sentence rhythm, unlike musical rhythm, is intricately tied to meaning: The rhythm of sentences grows out of the meaning of sentences. "How do you tell the dancer from the dance?" William Butler Yeats asked, referring to this harmony of form and content in art, and that same identity of dance and dancer, meaning and form, is built into the rhythm of sentences.

Parallelism

Parallelism in sentences repeats a pattern, sometimes varying it as a jazz musician will vary the melody of a song. Here is a fine example of parallelism in writing, from a speech given by Prime Minister Winston Churchill to the British people at the darkest moment of World War II, after the withdrawal of British troops from Dunkirk in Belgium— we spread the sentence across the page to show the elements of parallelism:

8.6 We shall fight on the beaches,
  we shall fight on the landing grounds,
  we shall fight in the fields and in the streets,
  we shall fight in the hills;
  we shall never surrender,
and even if, which I do not for a moment believe,
  this island or a large part of it were subjugated
       and starving,
then our Empire beyond the seas,
   armed and guarded by the British fleet,
  would carry on the struggle,
until, in God's good time,
  the new world, with all its power and might,
   steps forward to the rescue
      and liberation of the old.

Parallelism can be set up between sentences ("we shall fight . . . we shall fight") or between parts of sentences ("subjugated and starving" . . . "rescue and liberation"). It can be an effective, if formal, device for emphasis; it can also be overused or intrusive. One sixteenth-century writer, John Lily, used parallelism so extravagantly that one of his books, *Euphues and His England,* gave its name to an overelaborate style—a *euphuistic* style.[1] The answer to such affectation was wittily phrased by Francis Bacon, who mocked the empty use of parallelism with his own careful use of the same device:

8.7 So that these four causes concurring,
           the admiration   of ancient authors,
           the hate   of the school-men,
           the exact study   of languages,
     and the efficacy   of preaching,
  did bring in an affectionate study
           of eloquence and *copie* of speech,
                which then began to flourish.
This came speedily to an excess,
  for men began to hunt
    more after words than matter;
and more after the choiceness of the phrase,
           and the round and clean composition of the sentence,
           and the sweet falling of the clauses,
           and the varying and illustration of their words
                with tropes and figures,
  than after the weight of the matter,
           worth of subject,
           soundness of argument,
           life of invention,
           or depth of judgment.

The Advancement of Learning (1605)

Obviously, this elaborate parallelism is the style of 1605, not of today, and the modern reader may benefit from a partial "translation" of the sentence:

8.7A Then the study of eloquence and copiousness (or elaboration) began to flourish, for four reasons: Writers admired the ancient authors of Greece and Rome; they hated the dry "school-men" of the medieval period; they began to study language more carefully; and they were impressed by the efficacy (the success) of the elaborate styles of preaching. Such eloquence, however, was soon overstressed. Men began to look for words instead of subject matter, for choice phrases and "round" (or full) sentences, and rhythmic clauses, and words that were varied by figures of speech ("tropes and figures"), instead of. . . .

Such parallelism goes beyond our natural facility with spoken language, and it suggests that written style may have more "piano keys" than we might at first recognize. Playing with these new keys expands our awareness of language written down.

Problem Two. Parallelism   Choose either example 8.6 or 8.7 as the basis for your own experiment in parallelism. First, copy the sentence. Then write a *close imitation* of it. You might choose, for example, to translate Winston Churchill's stirring message to the British people into a promise to yourself ("I shall study in the library . . ."), or you might translate Francis Bacon's complaint about writers into a complaint about television programs ("So these four reasons coming together, the interests of advertisers . . ."). Then write a *free imitation* of the passage you choose, turning away from the model itself to try to capture the possibilities of parallelism in style.   ■

---

par : Parallelism   Keep like items in like form. A pattern at one point in a sentence should, normally at least, be continued at the next point. Once a pattern is set up it ought to be followed.

First Draft	*Revision*
I like hunting, hiking, and to fish. (The first two examples are in *-ing* form, but the last shifts to a *to* form.)	I like hunting, hiking, and fishing. OR I like to hunt, to hike, and to fish. (Both versions keep parallel elements in parallel form.)
Businesses use letters to communicate outside the company, and memos are used within the company. (Here the writer shifts the expected pattern.)	Businessmen use letters to communicate outside the company, and they use memos within the company. (The revision shifts to a "people word" as subject, and keeps the same sentence pattern. A more formal version might keep all parts of the parallelism: "and they use memos to communicate within the company.")

Problem Three. Problems in parallelism   The first four sentences below are by student writers who neglect parallel structure. Rewrite them
to establish parallelism. The last four sentences are written by professional writers, who break down the reader's sense of parallelism. Rewrite these sentences to set up a parallel pattern, and be prepared to
discuss the effect of your rewrite.

a. I've always been concerned with "good English," and writing
logically is another area I worry about.

b. This shortage will either force us to deal with wastefulness or
people will find life much more difficult.

c. We looked forward to commencement, and, although it was
found to be dull, it pleased us to have it over.

d. Urban planners are constantly faced with problems, and poli-
cies and plans are developed to solve them.

e. Winter brings blizzards, hot tornadic winds arise in the spring,
and in summer the prairie is an anvil's edge.

N. Scott Momaday

f. Good writers are those who keep the language efficient. That is
to say, keep it accurate, keep it clear.

Ezra Pound

g. He [Thoreau] had little active imagination; of the receptive he
had much.

James Russell Lowell

h. But his figures were neat and his margins straight/And his cuffs
were always clean.

W. H. Auden

■

The Balanced Sentence

The balanced sentence is parallelism stretched to the extreme, a subtle
echo made into a fixed refrain:

8.8   The love of liberty is the love of others; the love of power is
the love of ourselves.

William Hazlitt

The key to the balanced sentence is the semicolon; the pattern of the
first half is repeated in the pattern of the second half. The example
from Hazlitt is an extreme form of balance—we can provide an analysis
by aligning the balanced parts:

8.8A The love of liberty   is   the love of others;
　　　　the love of power   is   the love of ourselves.

The great age of balance in style was the eighteenth century; it's almost as if writers of that period thought in terms of balance. The balanced sentence can accumulate levels of balance, degrees of parallelism:

8.9 We are all prompted   by the same motives,
　　　　　　　all deceived   by the same fallacies,
　　　　　　　all animated   by hope
　　　　　　　obstructed   by danger,
　　　　　　　entangled   by desire,
　　　　and seduced   by pleasure.

Samuel Johnson

There's a certain attractiveness or neatness to the balanced sentence; it gives us a sense that things do fall into place—or perhaps we should say, they balance out. Certainly the mind with a sense of balance is never at a loss; one statement leads inevitably leads to the next. We're perhaps more cautious about balance in sentences today, and many beginning writers must learn the lesson that Brendan Gill learned when he joined the staff of *New Yorker* magazine and began to write for their informal "Talk of the Town" section:

8.10 I cultivated at that period (shades of my Victorian father!) a style too fancy for its own good and certainly too fancy for "Talk" and other pieces. I remember on one occasion happening to catch a glimpse of a characteristic comment by Whitaker; circling a long and elaborately balanced sentence of mine, he had scribbled in the margin of the galley, "If you tapped this sentence at one end, it would never stop rocking."

Here at the New Yorker

Problem Four. Balancing acts   Choose example 8.8 or 8.9 as the basis for sentence imitations (copy, close imitation, free imitation). Aim for sentences that will never "stop rocking." You might wish to choose a subject from college life ("We students are all hemmed in by the same requirements . . .") or from your ordinary experience ("The dislike of liver is . . ."). ■

Antithesis

The opposite of balance is antithesis (*anti* + *thesis*). Where balance looks for likeness, antithesis looks for difference; not what something is, but what it is not. The pattern of antithesis appears in Kennedy's Inaugural Address: not only in formal antithesis ("Ask not what your country can do for you—ask what you can do for your country"), but also as an implicit pattern of qualification ("Not as a call to battle, though embattled we are"). Antithesis is perhaps the most distinctively human use of style, for language, and only language, can say what is *not* as well as what is. Antithesis as a feature of style reflects, perhaps even develops, a critical and questioning habit of mind:

8.11   Meanwhile, such spelling reforms as *thru* for *through, nite* for *night,* and *enuf* for *enough,* although they do no particular harm, do no particular good.

Harold Whitehall

8.12   In spite of going to only a third rate college, he had, on his own initiative, come out with a first-rate education; in spite of growing up dominated by a small mind, he had ended up with a large one; in spite of all her foolish views, he was free of prejudice and unafraid to face facts.

Flannery O'Connor

8.13   Wars on nations change maps. Wars on poverty map changes.

Muhammad Ali

Antithesis and balance are not the common sentence types that they were two hundred years ago. They seem somewhat too formal, too literary for the modern ear. But they can be used, occasionally, with effect. And more important, experimenting with these sentence types has to develop habits of mind—the search for likenesses and differences, the search for what is and what is not—that are basic to the process of communicating in print.

Problem Five. Antithesis   Choose one of the examples above and construct your own antithetical sentence. You might wish to choose a topic from another course: "Of course, such teaching reforms as televised lectures . . ."; "When I start a class at this school . . ."   ■

THE ELASTICITY OF THE SENTENCE

The rhythm of sentences awakens us to the music of balance, parallelism, and antithesis. We can also think of sentences as if they were rubber bands, expanding and contracting, elaborating meaning or restricting it, going on and on, only to, abruptly, like Alice on her ride, stop short. The elasticity of the written sentence seems more modern, closer to speech, than the formality of balance and antithesis.

Deletion

The extreme of deletion, of leaving out, is Alfred Jingles, a character invented by Charles Dickens:

8.14 "Heads, heads—take care of your heads!" cried the loquacious stranger, as they came out under the low archway, which in those days formed the entrance to the coach-yard. "Terrible place—dangerous work—other day—five children—mother—tall body, eating sandwiches—forgot the arch—crash—knock—children look round—mother's head off—sandwich in her hand—no mouth to put it in—head of a family off—shocking, shocking!"

Pickwick Papers

A more common kind of deletion leaves out the sentence parts that the reader can predict, so that instead of a balanced sentence we find an unbalanced one:

8.15 At twenty years of age, the will reigns; at thirty, the wit; and at forty, the judgment.

Benjamin Franklin

8.16 Books are the best of things, well-used; abused, among the worst.

Ralph Waldo Emerson

The writer who deletes sentence elements often sounds curt or shortwinded; often a degree of deletion is used to set up the reader for a rush of fullness, of elaboration:

8.17 We are mistaken. The know-it-all state of mind is just the result of being outside the mucous-paper wrapping of civilization. Underneath is every thing we don't know and are afraid of knowing.

I realized this with shattering force when I went to New Mexico.

New Mexico, one of the United States, part of the U.S.A. New Mexico, the picturesque reservation and playground of the eastern states, very romantic, old Spanish, Red Indian, desert mesas, pueblos, cowboys, penitentes, all that film-stuff. Very nice, the great South-West, put on a sombrero and knot a red kerchief round your neck, to go out in the great free spaces!

That is New Mexico wrapped in the absolutely hygienic and shiny mucous-paper of our trite civilization. That is the New Mexico known to most Americans who know it at all. But break through the shiny sterilized wrapping, and actually *touch* the country, and you will never be the same again.

D. H. Lawrence

Problem Six. Deletion   Example 8.17 offers a longer passage for imitation. Copy the passage. Write a close imitation—here you might wish to stick close to the subject matter of the model ("We are right . . . When we first went to Dubuque . . ."). Then write a free imitation—perhaps about taking a new course or learning a new sport.   ■

Expansion

We can delete, cut short, lop off, curtail, stop. Similarly, we can say again, expand, repeat, elaborate, add on, continue. Sixteenth-century rhetorician George Puttenham introduces the "figures"—the devices of style—in a long sentence that captures the possibilities of expansion:

8.18 Figurative speech is novelty of language evidently (and yet not absurdly) estranged from the ordinary habit and manner of our daily talk and writing and figure itself is a certain lively or good grace set upon words, speeches, and sentences to some purpose and not in vain, giving them ornament and efficacy by many manner of alterations in shape, in sound, and also in sense, sometime by a surplusage, sometime by defect, sometime by disorder, or mutilation, and also putting into our speeches more pith and substance, subtlety, quickness, efficacy or moderation, in this or that sort turning and tempering them, by amplification, abridgement, opening, closing, enforcing, meekening or otherwise disposing them to the best purpose.

The Arte of English Poesie (1589)

Our modern elaborations are, frankly, less elaborate. But the potential for "a certain lively or good grace" remains in the English sentence, the potential, for example, of doubling back to pick up and expand a word:

8.19 All his books [Samuel Johnson's] are written in a learned language—in a language which nobody hears from his mother or his nurse—in a language in which nobody quarrels, or drives bargains, or makes love—in a language in which nobody ever thinks.

Thomas Babington Macaulay,
"Boswell's Life of Johnson" (1831)

8.20   They are not talking much, and the talk is quiet, of nothing in particular, of nothing at all in particular, of nothing at all.

James Agee

Another device of expansion is a simple redefinition, a saying again, a going back over the same idea. The effect may be witty, as in the examples cited by Lewis Thomas below. But it also marks a habit of mind, a way of proceeding, that shows some care and concern for the reader, for the need to restate in order to clarify, to make clear:

8.21   Disease usually results from inconclusive negotiations for symbiosis, an overstepping of the line by one side or the other, a biologic misinterpretation of borders.

8.22   The ants were, together with the New Yorkers, an abstraction, a live mobile, an action painting, a piece of found art, a happening, a parody, depending on the light.

both by Lewis Thomas

The expansion of these sentences seems natural, inevitable. Other effects can be achieved by expanding different parts of the sentence:

8.23   All those clauses, appositions, amplifications, qualifications, asides, God knows what else, hanging inside the poor old skeleton of one sentence like some Spanish moss.

Tom Wolfe

8.24   He took us to the headwaters of the Beaverkill and taught us how to cast and how to strike a trout and how to play him and land him without a net and how to kill him clean and fast if he was definitely a keeper—something special—and how to unhook him and let him go if he wasn't.

Philip B. Kunhardt, Jr.

Expansion of sentence parts can move to expansions of sentences themselves, and when that process begins, a passage can almost take off by itself, as if characters in a novel could control their own stories. In example 8.25, Gordon Lish embeds a long series of observations and afterthoughts into a simple narrative sentence, ending with a sudden movement, from the specific to the general.

8.25   It's a gorgeous day, just right, and we go in—into a small living room with about nine people in it, all staring at that square of light: they're watching a game show, three generations of them, the grandparents (American Gothics, blooded, stolid) down to the near infants, wired, a funny show, I guess it's supposed to be, at least "joyous," but no one is laughing, no one is smiling, even; they're just fixed there in their places, staring (not looking, mind you, in the way that Sontag separates looking and staring: by God, this is "silent" art for the populace).

Gordon Lish

Problem Seven. Expansion Choose two of the examples above, 8.18 through 8.25, as models for your own imitations. Examples 8.19 through 8.24 offer shorter models; you might experiment with expansions that you might use in essay tests in other courses. Examples 8.18 and 8.25 are more complex—clearly master sentences—and they present great challenges for the developing writer. But as master stylist E. B. White reminds us in the chapter headnote, "a writer, like an acrobat, must occasionally try a stunt that is too much for him." ■

THE EXPLOSIVENESS OF MEANING

We turn now to sentences that manipulate the reader's sense of meaning. We'll look at the *periodic sentence,* the *inverted sentence,* and then at a particular achievement, the *exploding sentence.*

The Periodic Sentence

The periodic sentence is one in which the meaning of the sentence is not complete until the very end of the sentence. The periodic sentence is simply a drastic extension of a natural tendency—nothing, but nothing, until the very end, through all the interruptions, is clear:

8.26 That he was not altogether free from literary hypocrisy, and that he sometimes spoke one thing and wrote another, cannot be denied.

8.27 With the aid of colloquialisms, malapropisms, battered and fractured grammar, and a considerable amount of creativity, Colored English, the sound of soul, evolved.

Claude Brown

8.28 What we saw there was a scene that would remain fixed in our memories and our dreams from that day forward, as long as life pulsed inside us, as long as we mortal Yazoo boys carried the mandate of the Lord to live on this earth, and we would tell of it as long as people would wish to hear of it, and as toothless old men lying in bed all day we would describe it to our grandchildren and our great-grandchildren, and it would strike such terror in their hearts that they would repeat it and amplify it to their own progeny; so that moment of fear would live on and on, but exist never so vividly as in that exact instant that our senses allowed us not merely to look, but to endure the looking: because there, in the center of the big living room, were *seven giant Indians.*

Willie Morris

Problem Eight. The periodic sentence   Examples 8.26 and 8.27 are difficult to imitate in English because they end with the verb. (Compare, "Examples 41 and 42 to imitate, because they end with the verb, difficult are.") But such imitations, with care and analysis and sensitivity, can be achieved. Example 8.28 is more straightforward, because the basic topic plus comment pattern is maintained, with the conclusion established by fairly obvious devices. Take a sentence from this group, copy it, and write close and free imitations.   ■

The Inverted Sentence

An easier matter is the inverted sentence. Backward is the meaning constructed. Comment-topic the pattern is; not the topic-comment that normal is. Twisted the syntax is; complicated the grammar. Not a habit, hope we: "Backward ran the sentences," wrote Walcott Gibbs, in a celebrated parody of the early style of *Time Magazine,* "until reeled the mind." Effective, though, in small doses, they can be.

8.29   In a hole in the ground there lived a hobbit.

J.R.R. Tolkien

"A hobbit lived in a hole in the ground." Fair enough, given that we know what hobbits are and whether or not they normally live in holes in the ground. Inverted, the emphasis changes: "In a hole in the ground there lived a . . . snake, groundhog, gopher, ant." Tolkien's sentence, the opening sentence of the *Lord of the Rings* series, inverts our expectations about "in a hole in the ground." Another, similar opening sentence, equally suggestive:

8.30   On the pleasant shore of the French Riviera, about half way between Marseilles and the Italian border, stands a large, proud, rose-colored hotel.

F. Scott Fitzgerald

Inversion can be used to parody the inversions of an author:

8.31 Than Thomas Carlyle, the dyspeptic Craigenputtock sage, no man—not even you, Prince Albert!—has written English awkwardlier.

Robert Cluett

An inverted phrase can be stylishly linked with a phrase in natural order (technically, *chiasmus*, a Greek word for "crossing"):

8.32 Fat as a pig he was, and his face was the color of cottage cheese.

Brian Moore

Problem Nine. Inversions Copy and write close imitations of example 8.29 or 8.30, then, as a free imitation, write the first sentence of your novel. Or try imitations of examples 8.31 or 8.32, creating a parody of inversion or a neat chiasmus. ■

The Exploding Sentence

The most complicated sentence pattern that we'll ask you to experiment with is the exploding sentence. The exploding sentence is like the monster in the Beatles' cartoon film, the *Yellow Submarine*. The monster eats everything in sight, including the background, and then, alone on the screen, begins to swallow himself, leaving nothing. The exploding sentence is therefore a "self-consuming" sentence. Here's a witty example, the very first sentence of an essay.

8.33 A long, long time ago, in another century—1951, in fact— when you, dear younger readers, were most likely still in your nuclear-family playpen (where, if female, you cuddled a rag-baby to your potential titties, or, if male, let down virile drool over your plastic bulldozer), the famous critic told me never, never to use a parenthesis in the very first sentence.

Cynthia Ozick

The sentence is a masterpiece of misdirections, of jokes on the reader: "another century" turns out to be "1951," which leads the author to a long parenthesis on sex roles, itself marked with the misdirections that are technically called *oxymorons*, mismatches like "virile drool" and "plastic bulldozer." When we finally arrive at the sentence base, it re-

jects emphatically exactly what the writer has done. The end of the
sentence denies the middle.

The self-consuming passage is a characteristic of the style of some
writers of the seventeenth century—Francis Bacon, for example:

> **8.34** You may observe, that amongst all the great and worthy
> persons (whereof the memory remaineth, either ancient or recent)
> there is not one that hath been transported to the mad degree of
> love: which shews that great spirits and great business do keep out
> this weak passion. You must except nevertheless Marcus Antonius,
> the half partner of the empire of Rome, and Appius Claudius, the
> decemvir and lawgiver; whereof the former was indeed a volup-
> tuous man, and inordinate; the latter was an austere and wise man:
> and therefore it seems (though rarely) that love can find entrance
> not only into an open heart, but also into a heart well fortified, if
> watch be not kept.
>
> *Essays* (1625)

The elaborate joke of the passage might be set out as a simplified argument:

> **8.34A** 1. No great men fall in love. *Because:*
> 2. Great work keeps out love. *But:*
> 3. Great men have fallen in love. *So:*
> 4. Great men can fall in love. *So:*
> 5. Great men must keep watch against love.

The second half of the passage denies, by example, the proposition of
the first half; it "consumes" it in the sense that it leads us, as readers,
to an entirely different conclusion than it began with.

This feature of seventeenth-century style is connected with a "way of
knowing" in that period—with a belief that truth did not come neatly
packaged and arranged, but instead often came through a process of
rejecting truths for better truths, a process not of writing down truth,
but of writing into truth. That idea of process is, of course, central to
our own view of style.

Indeed, in many ways, modern style is moving back to the sense of
looseness and process of seventeenth-century style, back to a sense that
eloquence can be natural, that writers can convey the process of discovering truths rather than packaging them for their readers. Here is a
final example, by the master of the modern exploding sentence, Norman Mailer. You may need, to follow the explosion, some awareness of
the religious vocabulary: *Limbo* is the place of souls kept from Heaven;
and *expiation* can mean atonement for sins.

8.35 The telling monotonies of Limbo—those stupors that drifted like bad weather, apathies piling on apathies like old newspapers, the cackle of static, the playback of cocktail gabble, and the stations of the cross of feeling empty while waiting for subway trains and airline shuttles and waitresses in busy lunchrooms—having been the only items so far experienced, Mailer began to believe that this enforced immersion in every repellent experience (his vision filled with nothing but the faces of digital watches, the smell of pharmacies, the touch of polyester shirts, the wet wax paper of McDonald's hamburgers, the air of summer traffic jams, and shrieks of stereo as the volume is mislaid, even the little nausea that plastic highball glasses will give to the resonance of booze) was not necessarily going to scourge him around one eternity before dispatching him to another, but might instead be his expiation.

Problem Ten. The exploding sentence   Copy an exploding sentence, and write a close imitation. Then write your own exploding sentence. Exploding sentences are very hard to write, and you'll find the assignment a very hard one to accomplish, but as you work out, on paper, the process of shifting meaning and undercutting the expectations of the reader, you may find, strangely enough, that exploding sentences are very easy to write.   ■

AND WITH NO STYLE AT ALL

As we've noted, we're no longer completely at home with the elaborateness of earlier writers, and some writers, in revolt against such elaboration, have explored the possibility of writing "with no style at all." We no longer trust writing that has a conscious design upon us; we want to supply our own exclamations as readers, our own questions; we even find ourselves self-conscious about sentences that sound suspiciously like politician's talk. Ernest Hemingway's spare prose (see chapter Seven) is one attempt to write "with no style at all," and Hemingway issued a classic statement, in the voice of a soldier, of his preference for pared-down, direct writing.

8.36   I was always embarrassed by the words sacred, glorious, and sacrifice, and the expression in vain. We had heard them, sometimes standing in the rain almost out of earshot, so that only the shouted words came through, and had read them, on proclamations, now for a long time, and I had seen nothing sacred, and the things that were glorious had no glory and the sacrifices were like the stockyards at Chicago if nothing was done with the meat except to bury it. There were many words that you could not stand to hear and finally only the names of places had dignity. . . .

Abstract words such as glory, honor, courage, or hallow were obscene beside the concrete names of villages, and the numbers of roads, the names of rivers, the numbers of regiments and the dates.

The extreme of this movement was reached by the French "new novelists" of the 1960's. Their goal was "no style at all," no prettiness, no stylishness, not even a speaker, a narrative voice. Nothing, in theory, would separate the reader from the bare words on the page. Though, as this example suggests, new novelists were able to sneak in indirect comments by their control of tone:

8.37 Retracing his steps, Wallas notices, on the other side of the Rue Janeck, an automat of modest size but equipped with the most recent machinery. The chromium-plated dispensers are lined up along the walls; at the rear sits the cashier from whom the diners obtain special tokens. The entire length of the room is occupied by two rows of small round plastic tables attached to the floor. Standing in front of these tables, some fifteen people—continually changing—are eating with quick, precise gestures. Girls in white laboratory smocks clear the tables and wipe them off once the diners leave. On the white walls, a sign reproduced many times: "Please Hurry. Thank you."

Wallas examines all the machines. Each of them contains—placed on a series of glass trays, equidistant and superposed—a column of earthenware plates with precisely the same culinary preparation on each one reproduced down to the last lettuce leaf. When a column is emptied, anonymous hands fill up the blanks from behind.

Having reached the last dispenser, Wallas has not yet made up his mind. Besides, his selection is of slight importance, for the various dishes differ only by the arrangement of articles on the plate; the basic element is marinated herring.

Behind this last pane of glass, Wallas glimpses, one on top of the other, six replicas of the following composition: on a bed of toast, spread with margarine, is arranged a broad filet of herring with silvery-blue skin; to the right, five quarters of tomato, to the left, three slices of hard-boiled egg; set on top, at specific points, three black olives. Each tray also contains a fork and a knife. The circular slices of toast are certainly made for this purpose.

Wallas drops his token into the slot and presses a button. With a pleasant hum of its electric motor, the entire column of plates begins to descend; in the empty compartment at the bottom appears, then halts, the plate whose owner he has become. He removes it and the napkin that accompanies it and sets them both down on a free table. After having performed the same operation to obtain a slice of the same toast, accompanied this time by cheese, and once again for a glass of beer, he begins to cut up his meal into little cubes.

A quarter of tomato that is quite faultless, cut up by the machine into a perfectly symmetrical fruit.

The peripheral flesh, compact, homogeneous, and a splendid chemical red, is of an even thickness between a strip of gleaming skin and the hollow where the yellow, graduated seeds appear in a row, kept in place by a thin layer of greenish jelly along a swelling of the heart. This heart, of a slightly grainy, faint pink, begins—toward the inner hollow—with a cluster of white veins, one of which extends toward the seeds—somewhat uncertainly.

Above, a scarcely perceptible accident has occurred: a corner of the skin, stripped back from the flesh for a fraction of an inch, is slightly raised.

Alain Robbe-Grillet, The Erasers

Problem Eleven. And with no style at all Copy example 8.36 or the last part of 8.37 (the description of the tomato), and write a close imitation (words instructors use that make you suspicious? a description of a pineapple?). Your free imitation should be a conscious attempt to explore the potentials of writing "with no style at all." ■

SUMMARY

We have presented a method of mastering style as a craft: copying a sentence model, writing a close imitation of it, and then writing a free imitation of it. We applied that model to various kinds of sentences:

- the rhythmic potential of the sentence—parallelism; balance, and antithesis;
- the elasticity of the sentence—deletion and expansion;
- the explosiveness of the sentence—inverted, periodic, and "exploding" sentences;
- and finally, the possibility of writing "with no style at all."

IMPLICATIONS FOR THE WRITER

No pianist uses all eighty-eight keys on a concert grand piano in every performance. The keys are potentials, and the pianist may not evoke all the potentials of the instrument for a particular piece of music.

The potentials of written language stretch back through history, and they go beyond any attempt to list them. The sentence types we've examined don't begin to exhaust the potentials of speech written down, and we certainly don't mean to offer a mechanical set of "patterns," ready-made for the writer to stuff meaning into.

Rather, we have two more abstract goals in this chapter. One is to establish the notion of writing as craftsmanship. By asking you to work in detail with the crafting of sentences, we hope to instill a sense of respect for the written sentence. The other goal is to establish the notion of "speech written down" as something more complex than "writing like one talks." The sentences we've examined lean on the movement of ordinary speech, its rhythms and its patterns, but they often go beyond the "early-blooming" structures of ordinary writing—not to stuffiness or mere wordiness, but to a quality of considered writing, of style as choice and discovery, that we have a hard time fixing on a modern name for. Earlier writers, such as those we've examined, had many such names: "copiousness," "a certain lively or good grace set upon words," a "turning and tempering" of sentences—above all, the word *eloquence* as a goal of the writer. Those terms, we feel, set enduring values for writers who aim at craftsmanship.

IMPLICATIONS FOR READERS: RECOGNIZING PARODY

Building up your skills as a craftsman of sentences can't help but build up your ability to appreciate sentences crafted by others. We spoke of your *language competence* in chapter One, referring to your natural ability to speak and understand sentences; we might at this point speak of your *stylistic competence,* your "late-blooming" ability to appreciate style as a craft.

We'll explore this stylistic competence by turning to *parody.* A parody is an exaggeration of a style rather than an imitation. Parodies take habits of style and extend them absurdly, so that the result pokes fun at the original style. Parodies, then, are a good test of how your stylistic competence works in reading. The final problem of this chapter should demonstrate this competence.

Problem Twelve. Parody Passages A and B below are taken from modern novels. Passages C and D are parodies of those novels. Identify the novel (A or B) that is parodied by each passage (C and D). Be prepared to discuss how the writers of C and D move from imitation to parody, noting specific features of the original that they poke fun at.

A They rushed down the street together, digging everything in the early way they had, which later became so much sadder and perceptive and blank. But then they danced down the streets like dingle-dodies, and I shambled after as I've been doing all my life after people who interest me, because the only people for me are the mad ones, the ones who are mad to live, mad to talk, mad to be saved, desirous of everything at the same time, the ones who never yawn or say a commonplace thing, but burn, burn, burn like fabulous yellow roman candles exploding like spiders across the stars and in the middle you see the blue centerlight pop and everybody goes "awww." What did they call such young people in Goethe's Germany? Wanting dearly to learn how to write like Carlo, the first thing you know. Dean was attacking him with a great amorous soul such as only a con-man can have. "Now, Carlo, let me speak—here's what I'm saying . . ." I didn't see them for about two weeks, during which time they cemented their relationship to fiendish allday-allnight-talk proportions.

Jack Kerouac, On the Road

B Where I want to start telling is the day I left Pencey Prep. Pencey Prep is this school that's in Agerstown, Pennsylvania. You probably heard of it. You've probably seen the ads, anyway. They advertise in about a thousand magazines, always showing some hot-shot guy on a horse jumping over a fence. Like as if all you ever did at Pencey was play polo all the time. I never even once saw a horse anywhere *near* the place. And underneath the guy on the horse's picture, it always says: "Since 1888 we have been molding boys into splendid, clear-thinking young men." Strictly for the birds. They don't do any damn more *molding* at Pencey than they do at any other school. And I didn't know anybody there that was splendid and clear-thinking and all. Maybe two guys. If that many. And they probably *came* to Pencey that way.

J. D. Salinger, Catcher in the Rye

C So, like I was saying, I always seem to be getting into these very stupid situations. Like this time I was telling you about. Anyway, I was walking through the forest and all when I see this very interesting house. *A house.* You wouldn't think anybody would be living way the hell out in the goddam *forest,* but they were. No one was home or anything and the door was open, so I walked in. I figured what I'd do is I'd probably horse around until the guys that lived there came home and maybe asked me to stay to dinner or something. Some people think they *have* to ask you to stay for dinner even if they *hate* you. Also I didn't exactly feel like going home and getting asked a lot of lousy questions. I mean that's *all* I ever do.

Dan Greenburg, "Catch Her in the Oatmeal"

D I was just thinking around in my sad backyard, looking at those little drab careless starshape clumps of crabgrass and beautiful chunks of some old bicycle crying out without words of the American Noon and half a newspaper with an ad about a lotion for people with dry skins and dry souls, when my mother opened our frantic banging screendoor and shouted, "Gogi Himmelman's here." She might have shouted the Archangel Gabriel was here, or Captain Easy or Baron Charlus in Proust's great book: Gogi Himmelman of the tattered old greenasgrass knickers and wild teeth and the vastiest, most vortical, most insatiable wonderfilled eyes I have ever known. "Let's go Lee," he sang out, and I could see he looked sadder than ever, his nose rubbed raw by a cheap handkerchief and a dreary Bandaid unravelling off his thumb. "I know the WAY!" That was Gogi's inimitable unintellectual method of putting it that he was on fire with the esoteric paradoxical mood. I said, "I'm going Mom," and she said "O.K.," and when I looked back at her hesitant in the pearly mystical UnitedStateshome light I felt absolutely sad, thinking of all the times she had vacuumed the same carpets.

John Updike, "On the Sidewalk"

■

FINAL WRITING ASSIGNMENTS

I. The Display Piece   Prove to your instructor that you are a craftsman of the written word by constructing a "display piece" to show off your skill in crafting sentences. Such a display piece, of course, is in part artificial, a product of a writing course rather than a product of an actual writing need. But you should be able to go beyond the limits of that artificial situation—perhaps by specifying an audience and a context for your paper.

II. The Extended Imitation   Our imitations in this chapter have been short, usually no more than a sentence or two. Developing writers can also profit from longer imitations, say of passages of 600 to 800 words. Such an imitation is best done as a "free imitation," trying to capture the basic overall movement of style. An extended imitation asks that you become conscious of how specific features of style contribute to tone and "voice" in writing, and it also asks you to be aware of the arrangement of sentences into larger patterns.

III. Parody   Imitation edges imperceptibly to parody, and our examples of parody may serve as models for your own attempt at parodying the style of a writer.

IV. A Public Statement   Prepare a "public statement" of 500 to 700 words, offered as a newspaper editorial, a letter to the editor of a newspaper, a "public letter" to a public official, or some similar form.

V. A Private Statement   There are always important things that a parent wants to say to his or her children—things that there's too often no chance to say in the bustle of everyday life. Here's your chance to write them down. (If you don't have children, imagine that you do.) Write a statement of 500 to 700 words to be given to your children.

There are several contexts for such a statement—to be given to each child as it reaches the age of eighteen, for example, or as a private letter appended to your last will and testament.

FOR FURTHER READING

Three studies of style can be recommended. Virginia Tufte's *Grammar as Style* (New York: Holt, Rinehart & Winston, 1971) is a careful taxonomy of sentence types with fascinating examples. Richard M. Eastman's *Style: Writing and Reading as the Discovery of Outlook,* 2nd ed. (New York: Oxford University Press, 1978), focuses, as its subtitle suggests, on style as a reflection of a writer's way of looking at the world. Chapter Four of Edward P. J. Corbett's *Classical Rhetoric for the Modern Student,* 2nd ed. (New York: Oxford University Press, 1971), explains the classical practice of imitation and offers additional models.

Two more advanced books deal with the history of English prose style, James R. Bennett's *Prose Style: A Historical Approach through Studies* (San Francisco: Chandler, 1971) and Louis T. Milic's *Stylists on Style* (New York: Scribner's, 1969).

Finally, we can recommend two anthologies of parody, Burling Lowrey's *Twentieth Century Parody* (New York: Harcourt, Brace, 1960), and Dwight MacDonald's *Parody* (New York: Random House, 1960).

NOTES

1. A *euphuistic* style, defined above, needs to be distinguished from a *euphemistic* style, a style using many euphemisms, discussed in chapter Ten, pp. 316–318.

The Print Code: Punctuation

9

> Punctuation, to most people, is a set of arbitrary and rather silly rules.
> . . . Few people realize that it is the most important single device for
> making things easier to read.
>
> RUDOLF FLESCH

Nothing in speaking quite corresponds to punctuation in writing. We don't punctuate our talk—unless perhaps when dictating to an untrained secretary ("In response to your letter comma I want to insist comma right from the start comma . . .").

Of course, there are some connections between punctuation in writing and the pauses and stresses of speaking. We end spoken sentences with a falling voice, which corresponds roughly to the period at the end of a written sentence. We show spoken questions by raising our voices at the end, roughly corresponding to the written question mark. And reading aloud any piece of writing will remind us how much we lean on punctuation, as in this sentence, to signal, for the reader, the chunks of meaning.

But, for the most part, punctuation is a separate system, a part of the print code—and not a trivial part, as the following problem will suggest.

Problem One. The importance of the comma The questions that follow are humorous—or intended to be so—and some are surprisingly difficult (and important). They should establish the central point of this chapter—that punctuation controls meaning for the reader. Choose an answer for each question, and be prepared to defend it.

a. Which would you rather be?
I am a pretty intelligent student.
I am a pretty, intelligent student.

b. Which speaker has a job?
The position I assume will involve hard work.
The position, I assume, will involve hard work.

c. Which sentence violates laws against child labor?
There will be a big parade with children carrying flags and horses.
There will be a big parade with children, carrying flags, and horses.

d. Both are bad table manners, but which is harder to do?
Don't break your bread or roll in your soup.
Don't break your bread, or roll in your soup.

e. Which is the neurotic personality?
She too eagerly seeks compliments.
She, too, eagerly seeks compliments.

f. Both instructors, in the following headlines, have problems—which one certainly has lost a job?
INSTRUCTOR QUITS CRITICIZING STUDENT WRITING.
INSTRUCTOR QUITS, CRITICIZING STUDENT WRITING.

g. Which speaker makes the bigger claim?
Everyone I know likes duck feathers for breakfast.
Everyone, I know, likes duck feathers for breakfast.

h. Things get more serious. Who has the bigger problem?
When she got back from the beach, she discovered that all her clothes which she had left in the car had been stolen.
When she got back from the beach, she discovered that all her clothes, which she had left in the car, had been stolen.

i. And now the championship question, worth a solid "A" grade. Which grading policy do you prefer?
All students who work hard will receive A's.
All students, who work hard, will receive A's.

adapted from Maxwell Nurnberg,
Word Play   ■

The question is, how does one go about learning punctuation? Here are three possible answers.

■ *Answer one.* Don't bother learning it. After all, the basic rule has been drummed into your head since the second grade: Always start a sentence with a capital letter and end it with a period. And, as we overheard one student advise another, "If you keep the sentences short, you don't have to worry about commas."

■ *Answer two.* Memorize all the do's and don't's of punctuation, and worry constantly about making mistakes. (Most of the do's and don't's, as we remember them, are don't's.) This solution isn't impossible, for there aren't that many rules—most dictionaries manage comprehensive guides to punctuation in three or four pages.

Answers one and two are safe answers. You're not likely to make many errors in punctuation if you limit yourself to an occasional, if hesitant, comma, and it is possible, if distracting, to punctuate by the rules. The rules, though, sometimes seem to cancel each other out (Is it rule seventeen, "Avoid needless commas," or rule thirty-four, "Never omit necessary commas"?). Thus we favor a riskier answer:

■ *Answer three.* Set out to become an active master of the punctuation system. Let your pages crawl with dashes, colons, parentheses . . . (even ellipses), until they become ready weapons in your writing arsenal.

That third option—mastering the system actively—is risky. You'll make mistakes as you learn. But those risks might be worth taking. For one thing, most of the effective sentences we've examined in the last chapters depend on punctuation, in part, for their effectiveness. Moreover, as Rudolf Flesch remarks in our headnote, punctuation is "the most important single device for making things easier to read."

This chapter aims to make you an active master of the punctuation system of the print code. It has a central argument, one that you discovered in problem one: *Punctation controls the meaning presented to a reader.* And it has three major divisions—the three major uses of punctuation:

■ Punctuation connects sentences.
■ Punctuation separates free modifiers.
■ Punctuation connects items in a series.

SENTENCE CONNECTORS

Let's begin with a draft paragraph from a student paper:

9.1 I thought I'd found an ingenious way to gather data for my study of regional dialects. I called two dozen toll-free numbers across the country, planning to study the dialects of the telephone operators. These are numbers for buying car parts or hairpieces, for joining the Army, or for reserving motel rooms. Unfortunately, my idea didn't work out as well as I had hoped. I knew where the operators were located. But, unless I told them the real reason for the call, I couldn't ask where they were born. Moreover, operators didn't cooperate when I tried to mumble, in order to see whether they said, "pardon me?" or "say what?" or "huh?" Somehow they understood everything I said, even when I wasn't sure myself. My only conclusion, after an hour of dialing, was that motel clerks in Kansas City aren't very friendly to college students who call long-distance to do a dialect survey. That conclusion doesn't tell me much about regional dialects. But I do have reservations for seven motel rooms in Kansas City.

That's a witty, informal paragraph. Certainly it's correct in its punctuation. But compare, as a reader, a rewritten version, done as an experiment to connect as many sentences as possible, using punctuation signals. Note the difference in readability.

9.1A   I thought I'd found an ingenious way to gather data for my study of regional dialects: I called two dozen toll-free numbers across the country (these are numbers for buying car parts or hairpieces, for joining the Army, or for reserving motel rooms), planning to study the dialects of the operators; unfortunately, my idea didn't work out as well as I had hoped. I knew where the operators were located, but, unless I told them the real reason for the call, I couldn't ask where they were born. Moreover, the operators didn't cooperate when I tried to mumble, in order to see whether they said, "Pardon me?" or "Say what?" or "Huh?"—somehow they understood everything I said (even when I wasn't sure myself). My only conclusion, after an hour of dialing—that motel clerks in Kansas City aren't very friendly to college students who call long-distance to do a dialect survey—doesn't tell me much about regional dialects. (But I do have reservations for seven motel rooms in Kansas City.)

The second version, done as an experiment, may be overpunctuated, and a final version might be a compromise of 9.1 and 9.1A. But the second version—with five long sentences instead of eleven short ones—seems somehow easier to read, and the sophistication of the tone seems closer to the tone the writer seeks to achieve.

Connecting two sentences into one is obvious enough, but it's a potent tool for the writer intent on leading her reader to connect ideas.

Notice, in the sentence you've just read, that two sentences are connected with what we call a *comma plus* connector: It connects two sentences with a *comma plus* another word—in this case, the word *but*. These sentences are closely related in meaning; they need to be closely related by punctuation. Essentially, that's all there is to connecting sentences with punctuation—sentences that are related in meaning need to be related in punctuation.

Four signals connect sentences: the semicolon (;), the colon (:), the dash (—), and the *comma plus*. They are all used in the last paragraph, which was written to show the different meanings they suggest.

The *comma* can also connect sentences, but only if the comma is followed by a connecting word. Thus we call it the *comma plus:* the *comma plus* a connecting word, as in the following examples:

9.2 Connecting two sentences into one is obvious enough , but it's a potent tool for the writer intent on leading her reader to connect ideas.

9.3 I thought of Chonita in heaven , and I saw her in her torn and dirty dress, with a pair of bright wings attached, flying round and round like a butterfly shouting, "Give me the hammon and the beans."

Americo Paredes

These examples show the two most common *comma plus* signals, the *comma plus* an *and,* and the *comma plus* a *but.*

The *semicolon* can also connect sentences. The semicolon, in modern writing, always signals a balanced pair; the first half is balanced by the second half. Thus the semicolon is like the pivot point of a teeter-totter or see-saw; one side is balanced by the other, like the words *teeter-totter* and *see-saw* themselves.

9.4 These sentences are closely related in meaning ; they need to be closely related by punctuation.

9.5 A sentence that sounds like a record with a deep scratch across its surface (click, click, click) is disagreeable ; but one whose larger elements recognizably match, like the three arches in the facade of a cathedral, gives pleasure.

Richard D. Altick

9.6   The period tells you that that is that ⟨;⟩ if you didn't get all the meaning you wanted or expected, anyway you got all the writer intended to parcel out and now you have to move along. But with a semi-colon there you get a pleasant little feeling of expectancy ⟨;⟩ there is more to come ⟨;⟩ read on ⟨;⟩ it will get clearer.

Lewis Thomas

Notice the rocking-horse rhythm of the semicolon; each second part balances the first part. It's not hard to use semicolons; you always know what to write next.

The colon works like an arrow: It shoots the reader forward: It clues him to expect more. Thus the colon points: It points to a second sentence that fills out the meaning of the first.

9.7   Thus the colon points ⟨:⟩ It points to a second sentence that fills out the meaning of the first.

9.8   The vision behind this book is simple and horrifying ⟨:⟩ it is the vision of the humanely educated Nazi.

Eliot Fremont-Smith

9.9   Colons are a lot less attractive than semi-colons, for several reasons ⟨:⟩ firstly, they give you the feeling of being rather ordered around, or at least having your nose pointed in a direction you might not be inclined to take if left to yourself, and, secondly, you suspect you're in for one of those sentences that will be labeling the points to be made ⟨:⟩ firstly, secondly, and so forth, with the implication that you haven't sense enough to keep track of a sequence of notions without having them numbered.[1]

Lewis Thomas

The *dash* may also connect sentences—usually when the second part marks a slight shift in direction, as here. Dashes are handy—the reader can expect a slight shift.

9.10   Dashes are handy ⟨ — ⟩ the reader can expect a slight shift.

9.11   "You know right dog-gone well that Roy don't never ask *no-*

body if he can do *nothing* ⎡—⎤ he just go right ahead and do like he pleases."

James Baldwin

9.12 The dash is a handy device, informal and essentially playful, telling you that you're about to take off on a different track but still in some way connected with the present course ⎡—⎤ only you have to remember that the dash is there, and either put in a second dash at the end of the notion to let the reader know that he's back on course, or else end the sentence, as here, with a period.

Lewis Thomas

Of course, these signals overlap in meaning, and it's possible to invent sentence pairs that might be linked with all of the connectors. In fact, we have just invented such a sentence pair:

9.13 Of course, these signals overlap in meaning ⎡, and⎤ it's possible to invent sentence pairs that might be linked with all of the connectors.   [the *comma plus* connector]

9.13A Of course, these signals overlap in meaning ⎡;⎤ it's possible to invent sentence pairs that might be linked with all of the connectors.   [the semicolon as connector]

9.13B Of course, these signals overlap in meaning ⎡:⎤ It's possible to invent sentence pairs that might be linked with all of the connectors.   [the colon as connector]

9.13C Of course, these signals overlap in meaning ⎡—⎤ it's possible to invent sentence pairs that might be linked with all of the connectors.   [the dash as connector]

One might even imagine a fifth possibility:

9.13D Of course, these signals overlap in meaning ⎡(⎤it's possible to invent sentence pairs that might be linked with all of the connectors⎡)⎤.   [parentheses to enclose an afterthought]

Thus we like to speak, in a metaphor, of the "weight" of punctuation. All of the examples above are "correct" in punctuation; they differ slightly in what they tell the reader. We choose the *comma plus* (9.13) for the sentence, for it seemed to be the "lightest" mark, appropriate for our informal tone. The semicolon seems the most formal; we might use it, say, for an article in a research journal. The colon (9.13B) seems more insistent: It badgers the reader. Seen this way, the "rules" of punctuation disappear, replaced by a rhetorical sense of punctuation— of how you want to present yourself to readers, of how you want them to respond.

Problem Two. The Great Punctuation Game, first version   The sentence groups below are taken from the February 1976 issue of *Esquire* magazine. The punctuation marks used to combine sentences have been removed and replaced with numbered blanks. In each blank, insert the punctuation mark that you think best signals the meaning relationship—colon, semicolon, or dash (and there's even one sentence connected with parentheses; it will need to be closed off at the other end as well).

a. But a photograph *is* daily life. To look at it is not to escape reality $\underset{1}{\underline{\quad}}$ it is to create—in a very complex way—reality.

Douglas Davis

b. The Cousins quickly learned that it was irrelevant whether or not one loved Grandfather $\underset{2}{\underline{\quad}}$ he must be respected.

Peter Collier and David Horowitz

c. The gold sparks wove themselves $\underset{3}{\underline{\quad}}$ they would not form anything solid.

James Dickey

d. Now the bridge is officially named for him, an action inspired by an "outsider" $\underset{4}{\underline{\quad}}$ no one who has lived in Chepachet less than thirty-five years is considered a native.

Harrison E. Salisbury

e. But his research [into heart disease] had provided him with the answer $\underset{5}{\underline{\quad}}$ he elected to undergo bypass surgery.

editor

f. On one level I know this to be hallucinatory and on another I believe it to be true, and in the long run it makes no difference which it is $\underset{6}{\underline{\quad}}$ we act on our hallucinations as surely as we act on anything else.

Joan Didion

g. Mr. Riley's operation, by the old standards, was almost boring.

It began at nine A.M. and ended at one-thirty-five P.M. $\frac{}{7}$ much of this time was spent opening and closing the chest.

William A. Nolen

h. Last year, after working a spell as a private investigator, Aynesworth joined *The Times Herald* and began working with Dudney. They make an interesting pair $\frac{}{8}$ Aynesworth is stocky and square, Dudney is lean and long-haired $\frac{}{9}$ Aynesworth is disorganized, Dudney is a compulsive file-keeper $\frac{}{10}$ Aynesworth works with the phone, Dudney writes.

Nora Ephron

i. The drink to order here is called the Mystery Drink $\frac{}{11}$ it is served with great fanfare $\frac{}{12}$ a beautiful minisaronged Polynesian girl comes forth with a slow, sensuous walk $\frac{}{13}$ she carries a flower-wrapped bowl and everything is quiet until she reaches a table, whereupon a gong strikes and the whole bar watches while she puts a lei around the neck of the one who ordered the drink, kisses him upon the cheek and glides away.

Catherine H. McBride

Problem Three. Mastering sentence connectors   Complete each of the sentence sets below, responding to the different meanings signaled by the dash, the colon, the semicolon, and the *comma plus*. For example, consider the following sentence:

■ Suzanne worked diligently on the law case.

One might use each of the four connectors to take the addition in different directions:

■ Suzanne worked diligently on the law case—she knew she didn't have a chance.
■ Suzanne worked diligently on the law case; Ralph lazily watched TV.
■ Suzanne worked diligently on the law case, but she didn't expect to win.
■ Suzanne worked dilligently on the law case: She knew how important it was.

We have listed the four possibilities in the first example; use them as a model for the other sentences.

a. Douglas was smart, hard-working, and anxious to please;
Douglas was smart, hard-working, and anxious to please—
Douglas was smart, hard-working, and anxious to please:
Douglas was smart, hard-working, and anxious to please, but

b. The duchess turned angrily to the physicist.

c. Don't tell me about Gauguin.

d. The student will be surprised at the information given about zebras.

e. There's a big difference between education and intelligence. (Suggested by a Charles F. Kettering sentence, "The difference between intelligence and education is this: intelligence will make you a good living.")   ■

The comma splice and the run-on sentence, defined in the box on page 272, rank high on the hit parade of errors in the print code; they are golden oldies of grammar—and understandably so, for the comma splice is widely used by professional writers in informal writing. In fact, the difference between an acceptable *comma plus* sentence and an unacceptable comma splice is quite technical—conjunctions can be used in comma plus sentences (words like *and, but, for, so, although, after*), while conjunctive adverbs cannot (words like *also, hence, moreover, then, thus*).

Moreover—to make things more complicated—students can solve the problem of comma splices by inventing a false rule, one that inserts errors elsewhere in their writing. One student created this (correct) revision:

9.14 It's cloudy, it looks like rain. ⇒ It's cloudy; it looks like rain.

But he understood the revision to mean, not "avoid comma splices by using the semicolon to link related sentences," but rather, incorrectly, "use semicolons instead of commas wherever possible," thus inserting errors elsewhere in other sentences:

9.15 She held the butterfly carefully, her hands together. ⇒ She held the butterfly; her hands together. (?)

(The semicolon is not a "heavy comma," except in special cases.)

The problem, then, is fairly complex, and it marks a special case in which writing for a college audience demands a different practice than writing for a general audience of a popular magazine. The editor of a popular magazine would not object to a comma used to join closely related sentences:

cs, ro : Comma Splice/Run-on Sentence Do not link two base clauses with a comma alone (a "comma splice" or "comma fault"), and do not link two base clauses with no punctuation (a "run-on sentence"). See the discussion that follows the examples and the exercises in problems four and five.

First Draft	*Revision*
I applied to several art schools, none could provide a scholarship.	I applied to several art schools; none could provide a scholarship. (The first version is a comma splice; the semicolon is better in formal writing. The writer has other choices as well, including the "comma plus" and—always a safe answer—separating the sentences.) I applied to several art schools, but none could provide a scholarship. I applied to several art schools. None could provide a scholarship.
The death penalty is claimed to deter crime, however it doesn't.	The death penalty is claimed to deter crime; however, it doesn't. (Note the improvement in emphasis. The first draft is a comma splice because *however* and similar words—*moreover, furthermore*—do not normally fit in the "plus" slot of the "comma plus." Again, the writer has other choices, including separating the two sentences with a period.)
He applied for the vacancy it was already taken.	He applied for the vacancy; it was already taken. (The first draft is a run-on sentence, with no signal to connect the two sentence bases.)

9.16 We arrived late, they were already eating.

But in college writing, the ban against such informality is absolute, and the developing writer needs to master the alternatives. The easiest alternative, of course, is to separate the sentences, as in 9.16A:

9.16A We arrived late, they were already eating. ⇒ We arrived late. They were already eating.

But we'd suggest that the developing writer experiment with the semicolon to connect sentences; it suggests what the writer wants to suggest to the reader—that the sentences are related in meaning:

9.16B We arrived late, they were already eating. ⇒ We arrived late; they were already eating.

Problem Four. Experiments with the comma splice   Some of the sentences below are comma splices—even run-on sentences—used by professional writers; others are not comma splices, but sentences that are appropriate for both formal and informal writing. Identify sentences that would be inappropriate for college writing, and rewrite them to remove the "error."

a. We think in generalities, we live in detail.

Albert North Whitehead

b. Life is a series of experiences, each one of which makes us bigger, even though sometimes it is hard to realize this.

Henry Ford

c. Actresses don't have husbands, they have attendants.

Margaret Anglin

d. The successful revolutionary is a statesman, the unsuccessful one a criminal.

Erich Fromm

e. Science is a flickering light in our darkness, it is but the only one we have and woe to him who would put it out.

Morris Cohen

f. He that is without sin among you, let him first cast a stone.

King James Bible

g. Bethe asked me what I wanted to eat, I shook my head, she ordered in Italian from a thin old lady who seemed to know her.

Lillian Hellman

h. About the only thing you can say about old age is, it's better than being dead!

Stephen Leacock

i. And then he looked directly at Tanner and grinned, or grimaced, Tanner could not tell which, but he had an instant's sensation of seeing before him a negative image of himself, as if clownishness and captivity had been their common lot.

Flannery O'Connor

j. I came, I saw, I conquered.

Julius Caesar

■

SEPARATORS

This discussion repeats principles from chapters Six and Seven, but that repetition is useful, for a basic principle in mastering the code of print needs to be repeated often: *Free modifiers are separated from the base clause by punctuation.* To review this principle, consider various ways one might combine the following sentence bases:

9.17   A small dog pranced across the puddles. Its nose was in the air.

One choice would be to connect the sentence bases by using a connecting signal, as discussed above:

9.17A   A small dog pranced across the puddles; its nose was in the air.

A second choice is to use a *bound modifier;* bound modifiers are not marked with punctuation.

9.17B   A small dog whose nose was in the air pranced across the puddles.

A third choice—the one we're concerned with here—is to use a *free modifier. Free modifiers are separated from the base clause with punctuation.*

9.17C   A small dog, its nose in the air, pranced across the puddles.   [embedded free modifier]

Example 9.17C illustrates a further principle: It's useful to think of this separating punctuation as always coming in pairs, one mark at the beginning of the free modifier and the other at the end. That may seem confusing, for, when we place the free modifier at the beginning of the sentence (left-branched) or at the end (right-branched), only one of the separators appears:

9.17D   Its nose in the air, a small dog pranced across the puddles.   [left-branched free modifier]

9.17E   A small dog pranced across the puddles, its nose in the air.   [right-branched free modifier]

We like to use our metaphor of the "weight" of punctuation, and speak of the other comma being "outweighed" by the capital letter at the beginning of 9.17D and by the period in 9.17E. This notion of weight becomes clear when we connect our example sentence with another sentence, for both punctuation marks then reappear:

9.17F A small dog pranced across the puddles, its nose in the air, and the children watched it happily.

Three punctuation marks are commonly used to separate free modifiers from the sentence base, the one used depending on the "weight" of separation the writer wants to suggest.

■ *Commas* (, . . . ,) are the most common mark, as in 9.17F.
■ *Dashes* (— . . . —) are heavier marks—separating asides, afterthoughts, details, or additions. Dashes come in pairs with embedded free modifiers.

9.18 Obviously the experiences of Negroes ⬚—⬚ slavery, the grueling and continuing fight for full citizenship since emancipation, the stigma of color, the enforced alienation which constantly knifes into our national identification with our country ⬚—⬚ have not been those of white Americans.

Ralph Ellison

Although, again, only a single mark may appear:

9.19 Bangs manes bouffants beehives Beatle caps butter faces brush-on lashes decal eyes puffy sweaters French thrust bras flailing leather blue jeans stretch pants stretch jeans honey-dew bottoms eclair shanks elf boots ballerina knight slippers, hundreds of them, these flaming little buds, bobbing and screaming, rocketing around inside the Academy of Music Theater underneath the vast old mouldering cherub dome up there ⬚—⬚ aren't they supermarvelous!

Tom Wolfe

Note the difference between the dash (—) and the hyphen (-), to be discussed later. A dash is typed as two hyphens.

■ *Parentheses* ((. . .)) may also be used (if the free modifier is an aside, as here). Parentheses may mark details or explanations:

9.20 Other words that have come into English from back-formation are *edit* (from *editor*), *burgle* (from *burglar*), *enthuse* (from *enthusiasm*), *televise* (from *television,* by analogy with pairs like *super-*

vise: supervision), *automate* (from *automation*), *laze* (from *lazy*), and many more.

W. Nelson Francis

And they may be used to enclose whole sentences, as asides, often as if the author were slipping in to talk with the reader, as in this sentence describing the prose style of President Harding:

9.21 It drags itself out of the dark abysm (I was about to write abscess!) of pish, and crawls insanely up to the topmost pinnacle of posh.

H. L. Mencken

Problem Five. The Great Punctuation Game, second version Use punctuation to separate the free modifiers in the sentences below, using commas, dashes, and parentheses as they seem appropriate. To remind you that some punctuation marks come in pairs, we have given the same number to the pairs, as in sentence *a*. The sentences are taken from the March 1976 issue of *Scientific American*.

a. The current model $\underset{1}{\rule{1cm}{0.4pt}}$ FACS-II $\underset{1}{\rule{1cm}{0.4pt}}$ detects cells with as few as 3,000 molecules of fluorescein $\underset{2}{\rule{1cm}{0.4pt}}$ a common fluorescent dye $\underset{2}{\rule{1cm}{0.4pt}}$ on each cell.

b. An essential step in the process is "doping" $\underset{3}{\rule{1cm}{0.4pt}}$ introducing a precisely controlled impurity into the semi-conductor material to alter its electrical characteristics.

advertisement

c. Among insects $\underset{4}{\rule{1cm}{0.4pt}}$ notably bees, ants, and termites $\underset{4}{\rule{1cm}{0.4pt}}$ social behavior is rare.

d. Although it is hazardous to forecast what might happen in such a rapidly changing industry $\underset{5}{\rule{1cm}{0.4pt}}$ one can predict that the price of the cheapest basic calculators $\underset{6}{\rule{1cm}{0.4pt}}$ already under $10 $\underset{6}{\rule{1cm}{0.4pt}}$ will be lower still.

e. For all the attention being directed toward heroin, cocaine and marijuana $\underset{7}{\rule{1cm}{0.4pt}}$ the favorite mood-altering drug in the U.S. $\underset{8}{\rule{1cm}{0.4pt}}$ as it is in almost every human society $\underset{8}{\rule{1cm}{0.4pt}}$ is alcohol.

p -in: Punctuate Introductory Modifiers   Separate introductory modifiers from the sentence base with a comma. This is often a matter of choice, particularly with short introductory modifiers.

First Draft

After a few weeks the project was completed. (Acceptable in most contexts.)

Having arrived at this decision point yourself in the right direction. (Here the lack of signal causes the reader to misread "decision point" as a chunk of meaning.)

Revision

After a few weeks, the project was completed. (More formal.)

Having arrived at this decision, point yourself in the right direction. (Allows the reader to follow the sentence more clearly.)

p -mod: Punctuate Free Modifiers   Free modifiers are "nonrestrictive"; they must be set off with commas.

First Draft

All students, who work hard, will receive "A's." (This sentence means that all students will receive "A's", a policy popular with students, but not with administrators.)

My mother who had a loud voice called down the block. (Implies that the writer has two mothers, one with a loud voice and one without.)

Revision

All students who work hard will receive "A's." (This sentence "restricts," or limits, the claim: Only students who work hard will receive A's.)

My mother, who had a loud voice, called down the block. (This version makes the modifier "nonrestrictive," properly limiting the writer to a single mother.)

f. For example $\frac{}{9}$ an FMC process $\frac{}{10}$ incorporating use of hydrogen peroxide $\frac{}{10}$ is ridding communities all over America of their most troublesome odor problems $\frac{}{11}$ those caused by sewage.

advertisement

g. Yet despite its relatively modest displacement $\frac{}{12}$ 5.3 litres or 326 cubic inches $\frac{}{12}$ $\frac{}{13}$ this engine develops an astonishing SAE net horsepower of 244 at 4,500 rpm $\frac{}{14}$ making it one of the most powerful engines offered by any manufacturer $\frac{}{15}$ regardless of displacement.

advertisement

h. This let-the-chips-fall-where-they-may attitude . . . has won [*Wall Street*] *Journal* writers and editors five Pulitzer Prizes for reporting $\frac{}{16}$ and two Pulitzer Prizes for editorial writing $\frac{}{17}$ which proves that the *Journal* isn't afraid to take a stand where a stand should be taken $\frac{}{16}$.

advertisement

■

SERIES CONNECTORS

Students often worry most about the conventions for punctuating items in series constructions. (A series construction is two or more words or phrases serving the same role in the sentence, such as the adjectives in "the tired, quizzical, happy, funky duck.") Such worry is understandable. There's a subtle difference in meaning, to use an example from rock music, between examples 9.22 and 9.22A:

9.22 The Average White Band
9.22A The Average, White Band

Example 9.22—the actual name of the group—asks us to see "a band which is average for a white band," while example 9.22A asks us to see "a band which is both white and average." We might best diagram these differences:

9.22 The Average White Band

9.22A The Average, White Band

There's another problem when we turn to series of three or more, which usually demand a connecting word, such as *and* or *or*.

9.23 He had a nose [,] eyes [,] hair [,] and a chin.
9.24 They served her eggs with ham [,] bacon [,] or sausage.

These examples illustrate one convention, separating each unit with a comma. This is a more traditional convention. But there's another convention, a more recent one, assuming that the connecting word by itself is enough to separate the last parts:

9.23A   He had a nose ⌊,⌋ eyes ⌊,⌋ hair and a chin.

9.24A   They served her eggs with ham ⌊,⌋ bacon or sausage.

This last convention is supported by newspapers and magazines, as a way to save space and ink. But some more conservative magazines, such as the *New Yorker,* still use the older convention, as does our publisher, and the college writer may choose it as well, especially in the few cases where the final comma is necessary to preserve the meaning for the reader.

A final problem is a special question of the weight of punctuation— when commas crowd in upon one another, and the writer must turn to the special use of the semicolon as a "heavy comma" in series constructions. Consider, for example, the choices of a *New Yorker* "Talk of the Town" writer listing first a series of items that can be linked with commas (boxed):

9.25   He showed us an elaborate silver glass holder covered with a flower design of different-colored enamels ("Twelve enamels, and you have to fire the piece separately for each one") ⌊,⌋ a blue enamelled Fabergé frame that held portraits of Nicholas and Alexandra ⌊,⌋ and a group of tiny enamelled eggs—the sort that used to be given as Easter presents.

The next sentence contains a very similar list, but with even more information, and the writer turns to the semicolon to separate the series construction from the other uses of the comma:

9.26   Then we had a chat with Elliott Sherman, a cheerful, bearded man who showed us a gigantic poster advertising "Carter the Great," a turbanned magician ("I found this a year too late") ⌊;⌋ two volumes of beautifully engraved German currency from the inflationary days of the nineteen-twenties ⌊;⌋ and a remarkable collection of movie-star snapshots. . . .

p̶ ̶s̶: Punctuate Series Constructions   Punctuate items in series to clarify the meaning for the reader.

First Draft

The room was cluttered with books, records and snapshots. (Acceptable in informal writing, and required by many newspapers and magazines.)

The United States has only a tired outworn unimaginative foreign policy. (This version asks the reader to read it as if it meant "unimaginative *because* outworn," and "outworn *because* tired.")

Attending the meeting were Dr. Gloria Cook, a member of the student review board, Professor Johnson, the librarian, and the Dean for Student Affairs. (The reader can read a meeting with five people or a meeting with three.)

Revision

The room was cluttered with books, records, and snapshots. (More formal, and more generally required by college audiences.)

The United States has only a tired, outworn, and unimaginative foreign policy. (This version sorts out the series construction.)

Attending the meeting were Dr. Gloria Cook, a member of the student review board; Professor Johnson, the librarian; and the Dean for Student Affairs. (A special use of the semicolon as "heavy comma.")

This pattern is common in business, law, and the sciences. (Note, however, that the semicolon as a "heavy comma" is limited to this single case; the semicolon is *not* merely a "heavy comma.")

Problem Six. The Great Punctuation Game, championship version
The sentences below show all three uses of punctuation: to connect sentences, to separate free modifiers, and to mark series constructions. Again, we repeat numbers to show paired marks of punctuation. Insert the punctuation that best signals the meaning to the reader. The sentences are taken from the March 29, 1976, issue of the *New Yorker,* and we noted that this magazine prefers the conservative way of marking series constructions.

a. Modern hotels offer the latest American Comforts without the agonies of ownership $\underset{1}{\_\_}$ a swimming pool for those who don't have one at home $\underset{2}{\_\_}$ a swimming pool without an eternally clogging drain for those who do.

Calvin Trillin

b. True $\underset{3}{\rule{1em}{0.4pt}}$ no new major masterpiece was unveiled $\underset{4}{\rule{1em}{0.4pt}}$ in fact $\underset{5}{\rule{1em}{0.4pt}}$ there were no first performances $\underset{6}{\rule{1em}{0.4pt}}$ though there were some American or New York premieres.

Andrew Porter

c. But at Dance Umbrella and at Dance Marathon there was the same clubby atmosphere $\underset{7}{\rule{1em}{0.4pt}}$ the audience seem to be composed of other dancers $\underset{8}{\rule{1em}{0.4pt}}$ students $\underset{9}{\rule{1em}{0.4pt}}$ and believers.

Arlene Croce

d. Mr. Richardson finds in the play a dramatic coherence that I've never detected in the reading of it $\underset{10}{\rule{1em}{0.4pt}}$ his masterly balancing of the various roles $\underset{11}{\rule{1em}{0.4pt}}$ granting each its just value even as the heroine increasingly dominated the action $\underset{12}{\rule{1em}{0.4pt}}$ is a welcome lesson in the art of direction.

Brendan Gill

e. With the help of a handsome catalogue $\underset{13}{\rule{1em}{0.4pt}}$ we learned that Mr. Schimmel owns twenty-five of the famous Amarna incised reliefs $\underset{14}{\rule{1em}{0.4pt}}$ Egyptian stone carvings from the Akhenaten period $\underset{14}{\rule{1em}{0.4pt}}$ $\underset{15}{\rule{1em}{0.4pt}}$ six pieces of archaic Cretan bronze armor $\underset{16}{\rule{1em}{0.4pt}}$ seven silver and gold objects found in a Royal Hittite tomb $\underset{17}{\rule{1em}{0.4pt}}$ four silver and electrum vessels from a site near Troy $\underset{18}{\rule{1em}{0.4pt}}$ a gold stalk of wheat from third-century Sicily $\underset{19}{\rule{1em}{0.4pt}}$ two Cycladic idols $\underset{20}{\rule{1em}{0.4pt}}$ some magnificent Roman portraits in marble and bronze $\underset{21}{\rule{1em}{0.4pt}}$ and a vast array of domestic and religious objects $\underset{22}{\rule{1em}{0.4pt}}$ statues $\underset{23}{\rule{1em}{0.4pt}}$ protomes $\underset{24}{\rule{1em}{0.4pt}}$ the forepart of an animal used decoratively $\underset{24}{\rule{1em}{0.4pt}}$ $\underset{25}{\rule{1em}{0.4pt}}$ toilet articles $\underset{26}{\rule{1em}{0.4pt}}$ jewelry $\underset{27}{\rule{1em}{0.4pt}}$ plates $\underset{28}{\rule{1em}{0.4pt}}$ ladles $\underset{29}{\rule{1em}{0.4pt}}$ and drinking cups.

"Talk of the Town"

f. A cousin to "Lord Love a Duck" $\underset{30}{\rule{1em}{0.4pt}}$ the film is an affectionate satirical salute to the square $\underset{31}{\rule{1em}{0.4pt}}$ though we laugh at the gaffes of the rawboned teen-age girls $\underset{32}{\rule{1em}{0.4pt}}$ the laughter isn't cruel.

film summary

g. Miss Tyler's mind is sharp and up-to-date. In a note following the text $\frac{}{33}$ her biography sounds cosmopolitan $\frac{}{34}$ born in Minneapolis $\frac{}{35}$ married to an Iranian psychiatrist $\frac{}{36}$ herself once a graduate student of Russian $\frac{}{34}$ $\frac{}{37}$ but she says she "considers herself a Southerner" $\frac{}{38}$ and she does apparently accept the belief $\frac{}{39}$ extinct save in the South $\frac{}{39}$ that families are absolutely $\frac{}{40}$ intrinsically interesting.

John Updike ■

SPECIAL PROBLEMS IN THE PRINT CODE

The three principles discussed above—connecting, separating, and marking series constructions—explain most punctuation in most sentences we write (or read). There are minor rules about dates, abbreviations, and so on—these are covered in the punctuation section of your college dictionary. There are also special signals in the research paper—for footnotes and quotations—and these are discussed in chapter Fourteen. We'll mention two special problems here: the special uses of italics and quotes, and the special uses of the hyphen.

Special Uses of Italics and Quotes

Italic type and quotation marks have special uses in the print code. (Italic type is type *like this,* and it's signaled in handwriting or typing by underlining.) Italic type—or underlining—is used to set off titles of books and magazines, to mark key words in textbooks, and to separate words from their meanings. The importance of separating words from their meanings can be shown by a children's rhyme:

9.27 New York is full of people, and Boston is full of lies; Houston is full of money, and Cincinnati is full of I's.

This little rhyme loses much of its humor when written down. It loses its ambiguity, for in print we have to use "I's" rather than "eyes," and thus give away the joke. The joke is that the first three statements refer to the real world—the city of New York is full of people—but the last statement refers to the word itself. It's the word *Cincinnati* that's full of I's, not the city of Cincinnati. We mark this, as in the last sentence, with italics, and thus a print form of the riddle would give away the solution:

9.27A New York is full of people, and Boston is full of lies; Houston is full of money, and *Cincinnati* is full of I's.

Or, for another example, consider two possible versions of the title of a song written by folksinger Joan Baez:

9.28 *Love* is just a four-letter word.

9.28A Love is just a four-letter word.

The first version makes a true—if trivial—statement: The word *love* has four letters. The second version is the actual title of the song: It makes a statement about the concept of love.

Quotation marks have three special uses, beyond signaling quotes. They are used to set off definitions—and thus you'll notice both italics and quotes in the example:

9.29 *To nitpick* means both "to remove lice eggs" and "to worry about small details."

They are also used as *scare quotes,* to "scare" the reader into special attention—as we try to "scare" you in this sentence. Notice that the scare quotes in 9.30 give the sentence a quite different meaning than it would have without them:

9.30 Following the lead of early "prescriptive" grammarians, some "scholars" and teachers conclude that it is illogical to say *he don't know nothing* because two negatives make a positive . . . it has been concluded by some "educators" that speakers . . . are deficient because they use language "illogically."

Victoria Fromkin and Robert Rodman,
An Introduction to Language

The scare quotes force a special reading: The "scholars" are not scholars, the "educators" are not real educators, and the "illogic" is not illogical.

Finally, quotes can be used as "cute quotes," calling attention to the writer's worry about words. Cute quotes are a feature of what we called the "bubblegum voice" in chapter Three, and we can find examples by turning at random to a teenage magazine:

9.31 John Travolta fully realizes that these times (when he's as "hot" as actors get) are the ones to be cherished. Though John has all the qualities of someone with "staying power" and will most

: Quotes and Italics   Use quotation marks for definitions and as scare quotes, but avoid quotation marks to call attention to words. Use italics for words as words.

First Draft

The "generation gap" is widening, and tomorrow's youth face an "uncertain" world. (Notice the peculiar tone the cute quotes give the passage.)

The concert was "simply divine."

Sandwich was originally the name of a person. ("What sandwich?" the reader might ask.)

Revision

The generation gap is widening, and tomorrow's youth face an uncertain world.

The concert was strong, even fascinating, but hardly overwhelming. (Here the writer's uncertainty about "simply divine" is a sign that the response is not fully formed, and the solution is to search for more precise words.)

Sandwich was originally the name of a person. (The revision indicates the word *sandwich* by underlining for italics.)

likely remain successful in show business all his life, you can never second guess "fate."

Tiger Beat

These aren't scare quotes: The writer *means* "staying power and "hot" and "fate." Rather, the writer is being "cute," as we are with this sentence with the word *cute,* by calling attention to words. Cute quotes seem to us rather affected, a sign that the writer doesn't trust his or her own words, and we'd suggest avoiding them. If you have the urge to use cute quotes, consider finding another word, one that is—dare we put cute quotes around the word?—less "cute." A good rule of thumb is to be scrupulous in the use of italics to mark words as words and in the use of definition quotes and scare quotes, but to avoid cute quotes entirely. Or, to repunctuate that sentence to show precisely what we don't mean: A *good* "rule of thumb" is to be *scrupulous* in the use of "definition quotes" and "scare quotes," but to avoid "cute quotes" *absolutely.*

Problem Seven. Special uses of quotation marks   Identify the quotation marks in the following examples as definition quotes, scare quotes, or cute quotes. Be prepared to discuss the appropriateness of each use.

a. It was a "perfect" tomato: thick-skinned, machine-ripened, bland, tasteless, and expensive.

b. The company took its . . . dessert as an example, citing the addition of anti-caking agents, sealed packages and the like to justify relabeling the product from time to time as "new" or "improved."

Consumer Reports

c. I "really" loved your "fascinating" party. It was "groovy."

d. At no stage are we able to prove that what we now "know" is true, and it is always possible that it will turn out to be false.

Bryan Magee, *Karl Popper*

e. I've changed many of my attitudes about food since we "went natural."

Jean Frazier, *Seventeen*

f. Do not "exercise" your dog on the lawn outside the building. Should an "accident" occur in the building, clean it with the sawdust, broom and scoop available.

manual of a dog training club

g. During the first 100,000 miles, or 5 years (whichever comes first), International Scout will repair or replace any vehicle body component which suffers "perforation" due to corrosion without charge for parts and labor.

1980 auto warranty

Problem Eight. Scare quotes and italics   Place italics (underlining) or scare quotes as needed in the sentences below. Some may have two or more possible versions—if so, give all possible versions, and be prepared to discuss their meanings. Some are tricky.

a. This sentence contains two words.

b. Railroad crossing without any cars; how do you spell it without any R's?

c. Psychology begins with Wundt's experiments in Germany. Psychology begins with the Greek word Psyche, meaning breath or soul.

d. They offered him an economy fare—that was $57.00 more than the luxury fare.

e. Physiology is awkward to write, but sex is pleasurable.

f. It was labeled a 100% natural fruit bar. The contents included sodium benzoate, BHA, BHT, and monocalcium phosphate, which, the label said in small print, were added as preservatives.

g. The final bill had Legal Notice printed on it.

h. Short is short, but long isn't long. San Francisco is longer than New York, but San Francisco isn't bigger than New York.

i. Droopy had had had had. Grumpy had had had. Had had was right. (A special problem.)   ■

The Uses of the Hyphen

The hyphen is half the length of a dash. The hyphen has its own key on a typewriter (-), while the dash is typed as two hyphens (- -). The hyphen is always used within words, for three purposes: 1. to break words at the end of a line (called hyphenation, naturally enough); 2. to join compound words (such as *co-operate* or *part-time*); and 3. to join some words as a single unit. A dictionary will help with the first two uses. It will lead you to natural line breaks, ones that help readers, like *diction-ary* and *hy-phen,* rather than unnatural ones, like *dicti-onary* and *hyp-hen,* which confuse readers. And the dictionary will tell you the current state of compound words as they move on a natural path from separation (*life time, half time*) to hyphenation (*life-time, half-time*) to joining (*lifetime, halftime*).

A dictionary, though, won't tell you much about using the hyphen to join words into a single unit, and that use can be an important part of precision in writing. Note, for example, that the following sentence can have two meanings.

9.32   The educators studied seven year old children.

The principle is that words to be taken as a single unit are joined with hyphens. Thus, if the delinquents are sixteen years old, they are *sixteen-year-old* delinquents. If the philosophers lived in the eighteenth century, they are *eighteenth-century* philosophers. A camera advertisement captures this use of the hyphen exactly:

9.33   Make sure your easy-to-use camera is really easy to use.

Thus we can return to our ambiguous sentence and use the hyphen to clarify the two possible meanings:

hy : Hyphen   Use the hyphen to break words at the end of a line, to join compound words, and to join words. Check a dictionary for the first two uses.

First Draft

First year winners of this scholarship may apply for a second year.

Revision

First-year winners of this scholarship may apply for a second year. (This revision tells the reader to read "first year" as a single unit.)

9.32A   The educators studied seven year-old children.

9.32B   The educators studied seven-year-old children.

Once mastered, this use of the hyphen can lead to a gain in writing maturity. In a test, high school and college students were asked to combine the sentences in 9.34:

9.34   Bauxite is an ore. Bauxite resembles clay.

The high school students tended to combine the two sentences in a longer form:

9.34A   Bauxite is an ore that resembles clay.

Only the college students produced, in significant numbers, a hyphenated form:

9.34B   Bauxite is a clay-like ore. (or even, "Bauxite, a clay-like ore, ...")

Problem Nine. The hyphen   Combine each of the following sentence pairs into a single sentence, using hyphens to join words in the second sentence as a single unit in the first sentence. The first example has been done for you.

a. Chaucer was a poet. He lived in the fifteenth century. ⇒   Chaucer was a fifteenth-century poet.

b. They studied gymnasts. The gymnasts were twelve years old.

c. Prudence is the only [such] basketball player in the league. Prudence is four feet tall.

d. I bought the car. It was newly painted.

e. Ralph has a mind. It resembles a machine. (Hint: Use *-like*.)

f. They served a strange green patty. It resembled a hamburger.

g. He did the problem reluctantly. The problem asked him to preposition with hyphens.

h. This attitude has won *Journal* writers many prizes. This attitude is let the chips fall where they may. (From problem four.)

i. She suggested a tax cut. It was for three years. It cut taxes ten percent a year. ■

SUMMARY

We have reviewed the three major uses of punctuation: 1. to connect sentences (with colons, dashes, semicolons, and the *comma plus*), 2. to separate free modifiers (with commas, dashes, or parentheses), and 3. to mark series constructions (usually with commas). We also discussed two special problems: the special uses of italics and quotation marks (italics—or underlining—to mark words as words, and quotes as "definition quotes," "scare quotes," and "cute quotes"), and the use of the hyphen.

IMPLICATIONS FOR THE WRITER

We use a classroom version of the Great Punctuation Game, asking students in teams to copy sentences from magazines without the punctuation, and then trying to guess the punctuation used. One team offered this sentence about John R. Silber, President of Boston College, taken from *Newsweek,* and here printed without punctuation:

9.35 Silber seemed to relish every moment in the spotlight until last week when a student newspaper accused his administration of selling admissions to its medical and law schools.

We tried several ways to punctuate this sentence, as a class, but we couldn't guess the original version. In fact, when we were given the punctuation used by the author, it didn't make sense—at least until we turned back to the sentence in its context. The sentence followed a general discussion of Silber, and it led to a discussion of the specific controversy. In that context, the author's punctuation seemed exactly right, in effect making the end of the sentence the commitment for the rest of the article:

9.35A Silber seemed to relish every moment in the spotlight— until last week, when a student newspaper accused his administration of selling admissions to its medical and law schools.

This experience underscored our belief that punctuation is best viewed, not as a question of dry-as-dust rules, but as an important part of the writer's control over the reader. In this sense, even punctuation is significantly rhetorical, for it contributes to the dynamic movement of effective writing.

FINAL WRITING ASSIGNMENTS

I. Repunctuating   Return to any completed piece of your own writing and rewrite it, connecting as many sentences as possible and in general using as many punctuation signals as you can. You may not prefer the rewritten version—though we suspect you'll find at least some of the changes helpful for the reader—but you should build up your command of punctuation signals.

II. Earlier Punctuation   The uses of punctuation we've discussed in this chapter reflect the practices of modern American writers. Things were not nearly so tidy a century or two ago, when punctuation was much freer (and, some may argue, much more expressive). Take a sample of writing from an earlier generation—the Declaration of Independence might be a good example—and edit it for a modern reader. Be prepared to discuss the changes you've made. (And check, by the way, to make sure that you have an original version of your example, not one that's already been edited.)

III. Transcribing Speech   The problem of transcribing spoken English into written English raises many of the issues discussed in this chapter. You might want to transcribe a taped conversation or speech, perhaps comparing your individual versions to arrive at a class consensus. It may be possible, using the journal *Vital Speeches,* to find an author's printed version of a speech you've been able to tape.

IV. Repunctuating Speech   As a related project, examine the samples we print from Studs Terkel's *Working* on pages 520–525. Terkel's transcription of speech is quite conservative; he seldom uses dashes, semicolons, or colons. Rewrite one of the passages, using as much punctuation as possible. Be prepared to discuss the differences between your version and Terkel's.

FOR FURTHER READING

Our treatment of punctuation is adopted from Harold Whitehall's *Structural Essentials of English* (New York: Harcourt Brace Jovanovich, 1951), a short, readable, and complete guide. We might also mention two much more informal discussions of punctuation, both of which we've quoted from in this chapter and elsewhere—Lewis Thomas's short essay "Notes on Punctuation" (in his *The Medusa and the Snail: More Notes of a Biology Watcher* [New York: Viking, 1979]) and Gertrude Stein's much more complicated "Poetry and Grammar" (in her *Selected Poetry and Prose*, ed. Patricia Meyer Spacks [Baltimore: Penguin, 1969]).

NOTE

1. Note that there are two conventions for punctuating a full sentence that follows a colon: One convention, used by our publisher (as in 9.7 and as in this sentence), allows a capital letter following the colon; the other convention does not use a capital letter, as in 9.8 and 9.9.

UNIT IV

THE WORLD
OF WORDS

10

Words, Words, Words

Polonius: What do you say, my lord?
Hamlet: Words, words, words . . .

SHAKESPEARE

We're seldom conscious of words as words. We're usually too busy using them. Every once in a while, though, we're brought up short by words themselves. It might be when we meet a word for the first time— the waiter saying, "The pizza will be ready in fifteen minutes . . . or maybe twenty, we're running a tad late." (*Tad,* apparently "a little bit," perhaps from *tadpole*?) It might be when we meet a bit of wordplay in an advertisement, as when the new check-cashing card, the "Owl Card," announces, "We're owl over town." It might be on a trip, when we learned that what we thought was a *soda* is to others *pop, tonic,* or a *soft drink.* More seriously, we might pause over a fresh and unexpected image in a line of poetry—Kenneth Patchen's "the sky is a handful of flung stars" springs to mind. We might even meet a word that calls attention to itself by its form, even its beauty or ugliness: *supercalifragilisticexpealidocious* or *veranda* or *phlegm.*

This three-chapter unit explores the world of words as words. In this chapter, we'll look at the dimensions of word choice (or *diction,* more technically). The next chapter will explore the history words carry with them, the history of language itself, and it will discuss that masterwork of words, the dictionary. Finally, we'll look at the spelling system of English, the "print code" of words. We suspect that you'll find these topics interesting in themselves, and we hope that our discussion helps you to become a more sensitive and more inventive wordsmith.

We will begin the discussion of word choice with an artificial device, simply for purposes of demonstration. We've taken the opening paragraph from an advertisement announcing a set of finely printed books, and we've put into it word choices that the copywriter might have considered. Each word choice in parentheses contains the word the writer used and other possible choices:

> **10.1** If you have ever (thought about, considered, dreamed of) owning (lovely, beautiful, good-looking) custom-bound books, but have hesitated to pay the (outrageous, very high, spiraling) prices asked for such (publications, tomes, books) . . . here is (exciting, earth-shaking, wonderful, super) news. The Easton Press is (pleased, happy, proud, proud as punch) to announce a (major, stupendous, groovy) publishing event: (*Great Works, Masterpieces, Classics*) *of American Literature.*
>
> adapted from an advertisement
> in *Psychology Today*

The copywriter who crafted this message may not have considered all these choices. But certainly the Easton Press must have discussed the title of their series. Perhaps they selected *"Masterpieces" of American Literature* knowing that the word *masterpiece* is usually applied to painting or sculpture, thus suggesting their books are works of art. And certainly the copywriter must have thought about her audience: a comfortably well-to-do audience, not specialists in literature, but instead people who would like to display a fine library, more for show than for reading. (Might we hunt for a word and call them *ostentatious* people?) Word choice, for the most part, would follow from that sense of audience. It would, for example, be a "major publishing event" rather than a "groovy publishing event" or a "stupendous publishing event." *Groovy* is too relaxed a word, too close to slang, and *stupendous* reeks of ads for second-rate movies. *Major* strikes the right note of confident sophistication.

We can outline some of the dimensions involved in such word choices; they make up the topics of this chapter.

- *general and specific.* Both *publications* and *books* refer to things that are printed, but *publications* is a more general term, covering magazines and brochures as well as books. *Proud, pleased,* and *happy* share a common positive meaning, but *proud* is more specific, suggesting justifiable happiness: "The Easton Press is proud to announce . . ." ("Proud as punch" is still more specific, but it seems trite and informal.)

- *connotative meaning,* the suggestiveness of words. The word *tomes* suggests large, even dull books; better use the more neutral *books.*
- *denotative meaning,* the "semantic sense" of a word (*semantics:* the study of meaning). Prices that are "spiraling" will continue to go up; prices that are "outrageous" are too high. Better to use the factual "very high prices," particularly since you will later argue that these books are relatively inexpensive.
- *literal and figurative.* The figurative "dreamed of" was chosen over the literal "thought about," but the warm word "wonderful" was chosen over the figurative—and perhaps too forceful—"earth-shaking."
- *the social standing of words,* what we'll call their *social register.* Books that are "good-looking" are perhaps too ordinary, like the word itself, and "lovely books" sounds too sweet; better to call them *"beautiful* custom-bound books."

These dimensions are at work, whether we think about them or not, in everything we write. In this case, the copywriter appeals to her audience by selecting rich, somewhat formal words.

10.1A If you have ever dreamed of owning beautiful custom-bound books, but have hesitated to pay the very high prices asked for such books . . . here is wonderful news. The Easton Press is proud to announce a major publishing event: *Masterpieces of American Literature.*

Problem One. Problems in word choice Here are three more problems in word choice, like those of example 10.1. The first sample continues the text of 10.1, and we've tried to make the choices quite obvious. The second is from the dust jacket of *the American Heritage Dictionary,* the third from *Seventeen* magazine. Choose one word from each set, and be prepared to discuss your choices.

a. This (classy, fancy, magnificent) heirloom library will (consist of, be made up of, total up to) 50 great books by the (superstars, giants, top dogs) of American literature. The books will be (neatly put together, impeccably crafted, impressively packaged). Sumptuously bound and decorated with (snazzy, out-of-sight, graceful) golden accents.

b. The American Heritage Dictionary of the English language is a (brand-new, completely new, spanking new) dictionary, new in content, new in format, new in the (wealth, abundance, profusion) of information it (purveys, accumulates, offers). It (presents, offers, displays) not only words and their meanings but also (extensive, exhaustive, detailed) notes on how to (employ, use, display)

them. These (illuminating, explanatory, profuse) notes are prepared with the (help, aid, assistance) of a (carefully chosen, select,
elite) panel of more than a hundred of America's most (notable,
popular, idiosyncratic) writers, editors, and public speakers.

c. [Photographs show a teenaged girl in bed in the top illustration,
and with her boyfriend in a smaller illustration at the bottom.]

"(Ugh! Yuck! Arggh!) Morning breath is the (worst, baddest,
most unpleasant) breath of the day.

"You know that (pasty, thick, floury) film that covers your
mouth, teeth, and gums while you're (asleep? sacked out? catching
forty winks?) And then, when you wake up, your breath is (unpleasant, yucky, really gross)? Well, Scope does a (great, super,
fantastic) job of (stopping, overcoming, fixing) all that. Use it first
thing, and your mouth will feel (clean and fresh, light and easy,
kissing sweet). . . . And (most importantly, of primary concern,
best of all), when you leave the house to meet your (buddies,
friends, comrades) your breath will be (okay, as fresh as spring,
minty-fresh), not (medicinal, mediciney, tinctured with the odor of
medicine)." ■

WORD LADDERS

In James Joyce's novel *A Portrait of the Artist as a Young Man* (1915), an
Irish schoolboy writes his name inside the cover of a geography textbook (for a class called "Elements" in Ireland) and then proceeds to
outline his place in the universe:

10.2   Stephen Dedalus
Class of Elements
Clongowes Wood College
Sallins
County Kildare
Ireland
Europe
The World
The Universe

We imagine many people have done something like that—it's a way of
sorting out how they fit into the world, how they belong. Joyce's character sees "himself, his name, and where he was." In doing so, he has
constructed a word ladder, a *ladder of generality,* moving from a specific
thing, Stephen Dedalus, to a general thing, the universe.

General and Specific

Words are labels, and they can be stuck to big (or general) things or to small (or specific) things. We might think of a department store, with a big sign for "hardware," an aisle labeled "electrical goods," a shelf for "light fixtures," and a slot for "adapter plugs." Words are like that. We can speak of "living things," a very general term that covers dandelions and real lions, buzzards and, in a way, brontosauruses (or is it brontosauri?); we can provide a more specific label "animals," and narrow the things we're speaking of. We can even be more specific and single out a particular animal—"cows." We might be more specific— "Hereford cows." And we can move to the limits of specificity in this example—there, out in that field, "Bessie the cow." In this case we've moved from the *general* to the *specific,* from labels that cover smaller and smaller groups to the label that tags one item only.

We can think of general and specific as a ladder, with the specific, "Bessie the Cow," at the bottom and the more general, "cows," at the top; or we can think of them as "levels of generality," as shown in Figure 10.1, with the general terms at the top encompassing the specific terms at the bottom.

We might note three things about the levels of generality in such a chart. First, the terms *general* and *specific* are *relative terms.* "Cows" is a fairly general term, but it's more specific than "animals," which is in turn more specific than "living things." Except for specifics, at the bottom of the levels, it's hard to label a word as more or less general or specific without another word for comparison. "Eagles" is . . . well, it's much more specific than "birds," but less specific than "American Bald Eagle" (and much less specific than "Bessie the Eagle"); it's at the same level of generality as "robins." In this sense, general and specific are

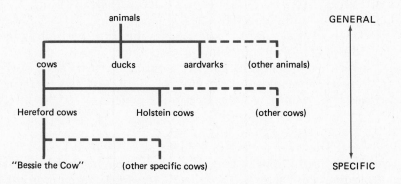

FIGURE 10.1 Levels of Generality

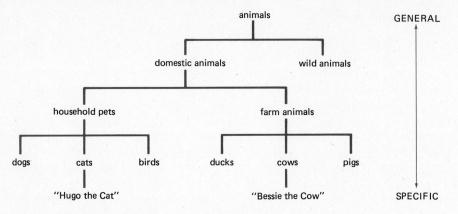

FIGURE 10.2 A Veterinarian's Levels of Generality

like all relational words. We can reasonably speak of a "small elephant" or a "large ant," even though ants are, relative to elephants, pretty small. From this follows a second point, that words have to be comparable. That is, they have to fit on the same ladder: "Is *eagle* a more general word than *Afghanistan?*" is perhaps an interesting question, but not one that can be answered.

Third, we might note that any general field can be classified in different ways, with different levels, depending on one's purpose. A veterinarian, we would imagine, might divide animals into "domestic animals" and "wild animals," with "domestic animals" further divided into "pets" and "farm animals," as in Figure 10.2. A zoologist, interested in the structure of animals, uses a different principle: Mammals are divided into two subclasses: One class includes the duckbilled playtypus and five species of spiny anteater (*Prototheria,* or "first beasts"); the other includes the other 4231 known species (*Theria,* "beasts"). This principle is shown in Figure 10.3.

The notion of levels or ladders of generality is a consistently useful tool for the writer. For one thing, the common advice "narrow your topic," which we restated in chapter Four as "restrict your commitment," can be restated again, as "find the right level of generality for your reader." Consider, as an example, the general statement of 10.3.

10.3 I exercised my pet.

A reader might pull several mental pictures from 10.3—walking your ocelot, putting your hamster on its exercise wheel, romping in the tub with your boa constrictor. A more specific sentence gives the reader a more precise picture, as in 10.4.

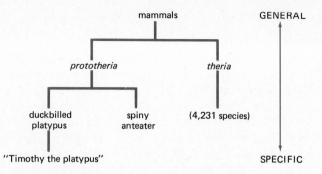

FIGURE 10.3 A Zoologist's Levels of Generality

10.4 I walked my dog.

Note, however, that the "right" level of generality depends on one's audience: One can be too specific for a given audience and purpose—

10.5 I walked Bessie. (Your dog? Or your cow?)

10.6 I walked my four-year-old golden retriever with the small scar on its left ear.

For another thing, writing coherent discourse, we've seen, is usually a matter of moving from general to specific, within the paragraph or even within the sentence, then moving partway back up. This paragraph, for example, continues to explain *general* and *specific*, one kind of word ladder, and we'll shortly move to another kind of word ladder, *abstract* and *concrete*. In fact, problem two below will help you to discover the need for this second word ladder.

Problem Two. From levels of generality to levels of abstraction   Arrange each of the lists below into levels of generality, building a chart like those of Figures 10.1 to 10.3. As you attempt this problem, you'll find the first two lists fairly easy, but the last two much more difficult, even impossible to handle as "levels of generality." Why?

a. department stores, men's clothing departments, places of business, restaurants, women's clothing departments.

b. athletes, infielders, baseball players, gymnasts, first basemen, football players, third basemen, soccer players.

c. fix, repair, mend, darn, overhaul, replace, amend, revise, edit.

d. barricade, dam, obstruct, block, hamper, impede, stop.   ■

Abstract and Concrete

As problem two suggests, we need a second distinction, matching that of general and specific, to deal with words that fall on a different word ladder, that of *concrete* and *abstract*. A *concrete* word or phrase points out something that is specific and real, something that can be picked up, as it were, and held in the hand. A concrete word has a precise referent in the real world; it points to something. "Bessie the cow" is therefore both concrete and specific, although picking her up might be a bit of a job. An *abstract* word or phrase, on the other hand, points out something vague, something that can't be touched or seen. *Love, miserliness,* and even *blueness* are abstract words. Thus the two distinctions, general/specific and abstract/concrete, come together at the bottom of the word ladder, for specific words are concrete words, but diverge at the top, for abstract words are quite different from general words (as suggested in Figure 10.4).

Abstract words are valuable and necessary. We need them, for they let us talk about more than we can see, about *graft* and *cleanliness* and *philosophy*.

The problem with abstract words, as many people have noted, is that we can confuse the abstract with the concrete, and feel that we have labeled something when in fact we have not. Political labels are an obvious example—we need to remember that words like "left-winger" or "conservative" or "un-American" may not have the same meaning for our audience that they have for us.

One way of making this point is to treat words as "maps of reality," and to insist that the "map" is a symbol of the territory, not the territory itself. We're guilty of confusing the map with the territory, already in this chapter, for poor "Bessie the cow," even with her cowbell tin-

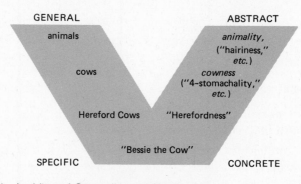

FIGURE 10.4 Ladders of Generality and Abstraction

abst : Abstract or General Diction   Use specific language; explain abstract claims concretely.

First Draft	*Revision*
She walked down the road.	She trudged down the alley. (More specific words sharpen the reader's picture.)
It was a good movie.	It was an exciting, even gripping, movie. (The claim is made more concrete for the reader.)

One solution to problems of abstract or general diction is to choose a more concrete or specific word, as above. There are other solutions:

■ The word can be sharpened by adding detail: "She walked down the alley slowly, her head down, her sliding feet raising the dust."

■ The precise meaning can be approximated in a series of attempts: "It was a good movie—an exciting, gripping, hold-you-terrified-in-your-seat movie."

kling in our minds, is not a real cow, but the map of a real cow—if you will, a verbal symbol of a real cow. Real cows have four legs, a tongue, and, we understand, four stomachs; *Bessie the cow* has only twelve letters.

For the writer, this suggests care in two directions: first, that one's words are adequate as "maps of reality"; second, that one's "map of reality" is shared with one's reader.

DENOTATION AND CONNOTATION

Some words and phrases sit around and point to things or relations, and that's about it: *pencil, poultry, file cabinet, below.* Other words and phrases pack punches—they point to things (their *denotation* or neutral meaning) and they also carry a suggestiveness, a *connotation: pig, Mother, virile,* and, in one sense, *behind.* The denotation of a word is its dictionary meaning, that is, what it *denotes;* the connotation of a word has to do with its overtones of meaning, that is, what it *connotes.* Such overtones may be good or bad, and thus we can speak of a "positive connotation" and a "negative connotation." *Famous,* meaning "well-known or widely recognized," has a positive connotation; *notorious* and *infamous* have the same denotation but quite negative connotations. *Policeman* is a fairly neutral word in its connotation, at least for most people. Other words map the same territory, but with different connotations: *guardian of the law* is more positive, *cop* more negative, and *pig* (for policeman) more negative yet.

Connotations are, to a large degree, shared by all speakers of a language—they're built into the language or the culture. A word like *love* seems inherently positive; a word like *snot* seems to have a built-in negative connotation. But our own experiences can color our reactions to words, so that we bring personal connotations to bear on language as well. Our reaction to *dogs* may be positive or negative, depending on whether we own them or are bitten by them. The words *cadaver* and *corpse* are obviously negative in connotation to most of us, but they are neutral terms to most doctors. *Dentist's office* has a negative connotation for most of us, but it has a positive connotation for dentists—and for interior decorators.

Subtle shifts in connotation can carry important loads of meaning and persuasion—a fact recognized most clearly in advertisements. The word "new" has a highly positive connotation in our society, and advertisers rush to add "new and improved" to a product even if they've only changed the packaging. In fact, the ads for many products—perfumes, for example—are pure connotation, entirely void of any denotative meaning.

The best way to show the importance of connotation is to play the "I'm a/You're a/He's a" game. I, for example, am *slender;* you, however, are *thin;* and she . . . well, she's obviously *skinny.* Or, if you prefer, I am *plump,* while you are *obese,* and he, sadly enough, is *fat.* In other words, the "I'm a" word has the most positive connotation, and the "he's a" word the most negative. I am *careful about money,* you are *miserly,* and she's a *skinflint.* I am *firm,* you are *stubborn,* and he's *pig-headed, obstinate, dogged, set in his ways.* Many female executives now take "assertiveness training," but their male colleagues complain they are "aggressive," even "pushy."

Problem Three. The I'm a/You're a/He's a Game   Find words with the same denotation as the words listed below, but with different connotations. List them in "I'm a," "you're a," and "he's a" columns, with the first containing the word with the most positive connotation, the last containing the word with the most negative connotation. We've given you three words in the first three examples, as a help in beginning.

   a. stomach, belly, abdomen
   b. odd, outlandish, kooky
   c. unclothed, naked, nude
   d. dilapidated

e. liberal

f. conservative

g. brave

h. automobile

i. stout-hearted

j. gregarious   ■

Problem Four. Playing politician   You are on the campaign staff of a candidate for the House of Representatives. She is trying to appeal to all voters, and she has become a master at using connotation to please everyone. Asked a question about taxes, she replies, "If you mean the unnecessary and unwarranted taxes that burden the homemakers of America, I'm against them; but if you mean the necessary support for vital social services and the arms that keep our country strong, I'm for them." Asked about pornography, she replies, "If you mean the disgraceful smut, the scurrilous, vile pandering that infects our cities, I'm against it; at the same time, of course, I must insist on our time-honored freedom of speech and caution against an over-emphasis on victimless crime."

At her next press conference, she expects to be questioned about 1. defense spending, 2. farm subsidies, 3. strikes by school teachers, 4. strip mining, and 5. whether church bingo ought to be prosecuted as gambling. She's asked you to write position statements for these issues. Use connotative language to take a firm stand on both sides of each issue.   ■

LITERAL AND FIGURATIVE

Some examples may clarify the difference between literal and figurative uses of words.

■ A college professor tells of talking with a foreign student in her office when a colleague stopped in to ask about a problem. "It's taken care of," she replied. "I chewed him out, and it won't happen again." "You mean," gasped the student incredulously, "that you bit him?" (There is, it appears, a literal *chewing* and a figurative *chewing*.)

■ A neighbor was having trouble starting his car. He returned to the house and told his wife, "I kicked it over, but nothing happened." His four-year-old daughter began crying. "Why did you kick our car over?" she said through her tears. (There is, it appears, a literal *kicking over* and a figurative *kicking over*.)

■ A psychologist tells of conducting a Seder (a ritual Jewish meal) and mentioning, while explaining the Exodus from Egypt to a group of children, that the Pharaoh's heart hardened to stone after one of the plagues. He noticed the bewilderment of some of the children, and asked a six-year-old what had happened. "God came down," said the child, "and turned the Pharaoh's heart into a stone." (There is, it appears, a literal *heart of stone* and a figurative *heart of stone*.)

As these examples suggest, the difference between the literal sense of a word, its basic meaning, and its figurative extensions is fairly clear-cut on an obvious level. A "heart of stone," at a literal level, is a serious medical problem; as a figurative expression it means "unsympathetic." To "kick over a car" can mean, literally, to turn it upside down and, figuratively, to operate a starter. To "chew out" someone can mean, figuratively, to chastise them; our foreign student, unfamiliar with that meaning, thought only of the literal meaning, to bite someone. Thus a literal use of a word is its primary or direct meaning: a "rainy day" is, literally, a day when it rains. As a figurative expression, in "saving for a rainy day," a "rainy day" means "hard times."

But things become a little more complex when we look closer. The *hard* in "hard times" is itself a figure of speech, transferring hardness as a quality from things to experiences. And even if we try replacing "hard times" with "difficult circumstances," a glance at the dictionary isolates the metaphors buried in those words (to use a metaphor): *Circumstances*, for example, literally "to stand around," is a combination of the Latin words for "stand" and "to go around" (as in *circumnavigate*). Thus many words seem metaphorical at the root—as common a word as *am* goes back to a source word *atmen*, which meant "to breathe" perhaps 10,000 years ago.

A Grammar of Metaphor

Some sorting-out, then, seems to be in order. A figurative expression— or, more loosely, metaphoric language—wrenches a word or phrase from its ordinary application and gives it a new one:

10.7 My love is like a red, red rose

Robert Burns (1794)

10.8 You don't miss your water till your well run dry.

traditional blues lyric

Example 10.7 is an explicit metaphor (technically a *simile*, a comparison introduced with *like* or *as*): It directly states the connection between the red, red rose and the poet's "love" (itself a figure of speech, a *personification* transferring his emotion, love, to his girl friend, his "love"). Example 10.8 is an implicit metaphor; we might restate its meaning awkwardly (and abstractly) as, "You don't realize how much you appreciate your beloved until she has left." Thus a first step in analyzing a figurative expression is to ask, What is being compared to what?

10.9 Certain people are like the bottom of a double boiler: they get all steamed up but don't know what's cooking.

anonymous

More importantly, the direct or implied comparison in metaphor or simile evokes a quality or emotion: That is, it serves a rhetorical purpose. Burns' "My love is like a red, red rose" transfers certain qualities of a rose to his beloved, but ignores others.

10.7A   My love is like a red, red rose
That's newly sprung in June;
My love is like a melody
That's sweetly played in tune

To read the simile correctly, we must ignore certain facts about spring roses—that they have thorns, are expensive and difficult to grow—and fix on other qualities—their beauty, freshness, youth. The next comparison, "my love is like a melody," enforces and expands certain of those qualities—that we might restate, inadequately, as harmony and beauty. Thus a full analysis of a metaphor or simile would explain both what is being compared to what—and, more importantly, why.

Notice also that figurative language varies in *complexity* and *elaboration.* The examples above are all *elaborated* figurative language: The comparison is extended beyond a single term. Most metaphors are single terms, tossed out so quickly we hardly notice them—the verb "tossed out" in this sentence, or the examples we began with, "chew out" and "kick over." Example 10.9, "certain people are like the bottom of a double boiler," is not a *complex* figure of speech—we might even call it trivial. It makes a witty point, but the point is obvious. The other examples are more complex; they're less easy to explain, less obvious—and therefore, despite our earlier remarks about precision in language, they are more effective. That's because figurative language is a way of discovery, and it demands a certain adaptation from the reader, a willingness to follow the writer's lead. Thus when seventeenth-century poet Thomas Campion begins a poem with "There is a garden in her face," we're asked, as readers, to suspend our immediate response (perhaps, "poor kid") and to follow the working out or elaboration of the comparison.

When a comparison is fully elaborated, it becomes an analogy: One thing is said to be *like* another (analogous to it), not simply to evoke a quality or emotion, but to convince or explain. Consider, as an example, an analogy used to explain, Alan Watts' attempt to visualize the Buddhist doctrine of *sunyata:*

10.10 The final Buddhist vision of the world . . . is symbolized as a vast network of jewels, like drops of dew upon a multidimensional spiderweb.

Psychotherapy East and West

Watts' "vast network of jewels" is strongly positive in connotation, but it is not, in itself, an argument. Compare an analogy that makes an argument, as in an advertisement—the handsome man by a mountain lake, a cigarette conspicuously in his hand:

10.11 Taste country fresh Salem. Light mountain breezes. Clear, rippling waters. And country fresh Salem menthol. That's satisfaction.

In this example, the analogies try to persuade—and instead of merely understanding, we'd better analyze how closely the analogy between springtime and Salem holds true.

Recognizing metaphors and analogies is thus a basic skill in reading. And we take metaphor and analogy quite seriously as writing skills as well: The problem that follows should convince you of the power of metaphor, and we'll pay special attention to analogy when we come to consider, in a later chapter, its importance as a device for discovering what one wants to write.

Problem Five. Creating figurative language   The sentences below are flat and mechanical. Enliven them by adding figurative language to clarify or explain. You may revise the sentences, perhaps adding a word to provide a "hook" for your comparison—one student, for example, rewrote sentence *a* as, "The two fighters circled each other warily, like two dogs meeting for the first time."

   a. The two fighters circled each other
   b. The chemical plant releases polluted air.
   c. The faint odor of gardenias filled the air.

d. I turned to the right, in a crouch, and held the ball out for the fullback.

e. Abstract words are hard to define, but easy to recognize.

f. Betty glanced quickly over her shoulder, then urgently shouted, "Duck!"   ■

Dying, Dead, and Fossilized Metaphor

The metaphors, similes, and analogies we've examined so far are *live* comparisons, newly coined for the occasion, fresh-minted (to elaborate the analogy) to define, explain, suggest, or persuade. But consider the following figurative language, picked out of the daily newspaper: The quarterback throws a "bomb," but on the next play he "eats the football"; a fire "roars through" a hotel and the death toll "climbs"; a letter-writer complains to a gossip columnist that her romance is "going up in smoke," and the columnist advises that "money talks"; politicians agree to meet at the "summit" to deal with "hardline" issues. Figurative language, of course, but shopworn and dull rather than fresh: *dying metaphors,* which are losing their force. Fires have been "roaring" so long that the lion behind the expression has been forgotten, and quarterbacks have eaten so many footballs that we no longer worry about their digestion. Dying metaphors are perhaps inevitable in newspaper writing—writers in a hurry can be excused for turning to the commonplace and expected. But the writer who wants a real response, a live response, from a reader will avoid them—and avoid more generally the trite, clichéd, or hackneyed expression (*cliché,* from the French: a commonplace expression).

One good argument for this advice—avoid trite expressions—is that they have little effect on the reader, for they don't carry the force they originally had. A better argument, though, is that they come ready-made, a substitute for thought rather than the product of thought. As George Orwell said on the subject, "an accumulation of stale phrases chokes [the mind] like tea leaves blocking a sink. . . . This invasion of one's mind by ready-made phrases . . . can only be prevented if one is constantly on guard against them" ("Politics and the English Language"). (And note the "live" quality of Orwell's language—"chokes," "invasion.")

Now consider another set of metaphors: the "hands" on a clock, the "arms" of a chair, the "legs" of a table, the "head" of a political party, the "leg" of a race. These aren't dying metaphors—they are *dead metaphors,* so dead in fact, that we don't often think of them as metaphors, and thus confidently speak of the *hands* on the *face* of a clock without

---

trite : Trite or Hackneyed Expressions   Avoid dying metaphors and clichés. Search out fresh, apt expressions, and, if all else fails, avoid figurative language.

First Draft	*Revision*
She was steaming as she entered the room.	She entered the room angrily, her eyes rock hard and her jaw set. ("Steaming" is a dying metaphor; the revision provides details to support the claim.)
Paul Revere's ride sounded the trumpet of freedom.	Paul Revere's ride marked the beginning of the Revolutionary War. (Literal and figurative clash awkwardly in the original version; better to avoid figurative language.)

---

noticing the grotesque personification that our words, if taken literally, might imply.

We can take one more step along the continuum of live, dying, and dead metaphors—to metaphors that are so dead they have become *fossilized*, so much a part of ordinary words that we do not think of them as originally metaphoric. Many of our borrowings from Greek and Latin are fossilized metaphors: *Educate* comes from a Latin word meaning "to lead out"; *inherent*, literally "to stick in"; *television*, literally "far-seeing." And many native English words have fossilized also: obviously so in *withstand, pigeontoed,* and *anchorman;* less obviously in *lord* (Old English *hlaf-weard,* "loaf-keeper"), *surly* (from Middle English *sir-ly,* "to act like a *sir,*" or knight), and *grasp* in the sense of "understand."

These fossilized metaphors can trip up the careless writer easily enough, for the result can be that curious beast, the *mixed metaphor.* Here again the best examples are from politics. "The president must put the ship of state back on its feet," insisted one politician. "I'm going to test the temperature of the political waters by throwing my hat in the ring as a trial balloon," announced a second. A third urged an anatomical impossibility upon a young backer, "To get ahead, young man, keep your nose to the grindstone, your shoulders to the wheel, your ear to the ground, and, young man, keep your eye on the ball."

More dangerous to our thinking are the fossilized analogies that are buried in our language long after the beliefs in which they originated have been discarded. For example, we still speak of *upper class, lower class,* and, especially, *middle class*—a spatial analogy developed in a period when people still viewed society as a pyramid, with some people naturally at the top and the king over all. Ossie Davis, a black writer, notices that blackness tends to have generally negative associations in American culture (*blackmail, blackball, smudge, murky, malignant, unclean, dirty*) while whiteness tends generally to have positive associations (*ivory, fair, chaste, clean, clear*). One might note that many African cultures have similar connotations for *black* and *white,* which may grow from our common ancestors' fear of night, but the "Black Is Beautiful" movement must be seen as a positive effort to rid our culture of the fossilized connotations of the word. It is useful to reflect that many of the key words we use in civilized discourse are fossilized metaphors—*culture, taste, liberal, conservative.*

Problem Six. Revitalizing dead metaphors For each of the dead or dying metaphors below, provide one context to force a literal meaning for the sentence, another to force a figurative meaning. For example, the dead metaphor, "she knows the score," might be given a figurative meaning:

■ She'll do all right in politics; she knows the score.

Or it might be given a literal meaning:

■ She'll do fine conducting the Mozart; she knows the score.

  a. He's a valuable member of the team.

  b. It's the dawn of a new day.

  c. It was just a pipe dream.

  d. He's all washed up.

  e. Keep your eye on the ball.   ■

Problem Seven. Analyzing figurative language You now have a method for analyzing figurative language (or, more loosely, metaphoric language) and a vocabulary for discussing its suggestiveness, its complexity and degree of elaboration, its status (live, dead, buried, fossilized), and its purpose (to explain or persuade). Use these terms to discuss and evaluate the examples below.

  a. . . . about the cool water
the wind sounds through sprays
of apple, and from the quivering leaves
slumber pours down.

> Sappho (c. 650 B.C.),
> trans. Kenneth Rexroth

b. Not till now had he seen, with eyes fully open, the rite of splashing solemnly about in a vocabulary, for splashing's sake, the preference for just jingling, for the sound they made, the bunch of keys that, rightly turned in the locks, were inlets to gardens by rivers in Bagdad.

C. E. Montague, A Mind Let Loose

c. Half a loaf is better than no vacation at all.

anonymous

d. An aged man is but a paltry thing,
   A tattered coat upon a stick, unless
   Soul clap its hands and sing, and louder sing
   For every tatter in its mortal dress.

W. B. Yeats,
from "Sailing to Byzantium"

e. If you can read this, you're keeping up with the Joneses.

bumper sticker

f. All things are full of deity: so also is the little edifice of a chicken, and all its actions and operations, the Finger of God or the God of Nature doth reveal himself.

Gabriel Harvey (1628)

g. If you've never realized how much we owe the medical profession, wait until you get your next doctor's bill.

anonymous

h. Like a rat-catcher, a word-catcher has worked hard to master the secrets of his trade. Not every man can catch a rat or define a noun, and if the grammarian has abandoned all foolish hopes of a place at the top of the totem pole, at its foot he wants no amateurs shouldering him aside.

James Sledd, "Who Is Subverting Whom?"

i. Don't change horses in the middle of a meal.

student sentence

j. I felt soiled and unclean, oily, like an old dishrag.

student sentence

■

REGISTER: THE COMPANY WORDS KEEP

Allow us, in a flight of fancy, to move from figurative to literal, and to imagine the world of words as if it were a real world. Words then become people, and we can conceive of a whole social world they might live in.

There, up at the university, would be the professors—*dean, syllabus, matriculate*—while down at the high school with the teachers—*values clarification, mini-course,* and *social studies*—would be the older students—*dude, bogue,* and *groovy*—and the younger ones—*giggle, date,* and *big whoop.* At the top floor of the corporate headquarters, sitting around the board room, would be the top-level management—*actuary, productivity,* and the head-person, *profit-and-loss.* In the law office below would be *litigation, countersuit,* and *pursuant,* while in the fabric shop on the ground floor we would find *mauve, cerise,* and *divine.* Out at the old folks' home, quietly rocking back and forth, would be *egad, land sakes,* and *vulgar.* In drab suburbia, the houses alike, row upon row, would be the colorless words that do most of society's work: *lathe, after, timeclock, carpet, cooking.* And, sadly enough, there on skid row, we would find the social outcasts sleeping it off in the doorways of dilapidated tenements—*guts, belly, fart,* and the infamous *ain't.*

As we said, a flight of fancy. But it underscores a basic fact about words: They cluster in social groups. A handy term for such social groups is *register,* from "social register," the perceived social standing of a word. We might, for example, speak of a "legal register" or a "race-track register," of a "cookbook register" or even (looking at ourselves using words like *register*) of an "English textbook register."

The writer adopts a stance toward audience and subject matter and, for the most part, the register of words follows naturally from that stance. You'll have little trouble, as reader, in picking the true version of the passages below, one by H. L. Mencken as a savage attack on the prose style of Thorstein Veblen, written in a tone of sophisticated contempt, technically a tone of invective, the other a class exercise in rewriting it.

10.12   And so it went, alas, alas, in all his [Thorstein Veblen's] other books. A penny's worth of news was packaged in a bunch of big words. In "The Higher Learning in America" the thing achieved its most damnable degree and its least valuable quality. It was as if the practice of that style were an unstoppable illness. The style was very hard to understand. It was very smelly. The illness was a sort of growing mental diabetes. It was a contagious illness of common knowledge. Words were piled upon words. Then all remembrance that there must be a semantic reference in them was misplaced. . . . One walked in a maze.

10.12A   And so it went, alas, alas, in all his other books. A cent's worth of information was wrapped in a bale of polysyllables. In "The Higher Learning in America" the thing perhaps reached its damndest and worst. It was as if the practice of that style were a relentless disease. The style was incredibly obscure. It was incredibly malodorous. The disease was a sort of progressive intellectual diabetes. It was a leprosy of the horse sense. Words were flung upon words. Then all recollection that there must be meaning in them was lost. . . . One wandered in a labyrinth.

Our class rewrite (the first version) loses the sophistication of Mencken's vocabulary. We turn to ordinary words for the elaborate register of the original ("mental" for *intellectual,* "maze" for *labyrinth*), and we substitute abstract or general words for the specificity of the original ("contagious illness" for *leprosy,* "least valuable quality" for *worst*). Even more seriously, we flatten the tone by blurring the figurative verbs ("packaged in" for *wrapped in,* "piled upon" for *flung upon*).

This sort of exercise suggests that we're very sensitive to the register of words. In fact, we carry around more information and sensitivity to the social world of words than any dictionary could ever include. A dictionary might tell us that *tomato,* used to refer to a young woman, is "slang," but our social sense of words can pin that down much more precisely—"like a Betty Grable movie," one of our students said, guessing correctly that it was current in the 1940s. Similarly, we can make a good guess at the age of someone who uses *ice box* for *refrigerator,* and Woody Allen, in the movie *Annie Hall,* is quick to point out to Diane Keaton that *neat* is no longer used in New York City, even though it may remain a neat word in the midwest.

This natural sense of register is part of our social sense of language; we seldom think about it consciously. But a quick tour of the social world of words may help to clarify some of the factors that go into word choice, and it should remind us of the complexities of the social world of words.

Problem Eight. The social register of words   As an investigative project in the social world of words, perhaps as a class or team project, find out what you can about the "social world" of one or more of the words or phrases below. You'll need to talk with several people, of different ages and social backgrounds, asking them questions like the following:

■ Would you use this word? Can you give me an example?
■ Have you ever heard anyone use this word? How did they use it?
■ Would you expect to hear this word on television? On what program?

   a. rod (meaning "gun")

   b. yeah (meaning "yes")

   c. chemist (meaning "pharmacist")

d. ice box (meaning "refrigerator")

e. record player (meaning "stereo")

f. to terminate someone (meaning either "to fire from a job" or "to kill")

g. to rap on someone (meaning "talk to someone")

h. dude (meaning "city person," as in *dude ranch*)

i. dude (meaning "person" or "man")

j. flaky (meaning "unmotivated")

k. point-of-sale terminal (meaning "computerized cash register")

l. contra-indicated (meaning "not a good idea")

m. a *soirée* (meaning "a party") ■

Levels of Language

The notion of *levels of language* was much simpler a generation or two ago. There were only three levels, and they were "formal," "informal," and "vulgar." Slang hardly existed, at least in the textbooks, and it was about as welcome as a social disease. "The unchecked and habitual use of slang (even polite slang) is deleterious to the mind," wrote George Kitteridge and James Greenough in 1901. "Vulgar language" did exist: It was dirty, low, commonplace, nasty, and unpleasant; it sat in the back of the room, slouched, and made ugly faces. "Formal language" also existed: It was nice, proper, prim, sweet, docile, and obedient; it sat in the front of the classroom, its knees together, and looked directly at the instructor. And "informal language"? Well, the textbooks had to admit that informal language might well exist. Usually they called it *colloquial* language—the Latinate word made it sound nicer. (Professor Kitteridge again: "I speak colloq. myself, and sometimes I write it.")

Words, in other words, came like chain store appliances: good, better, best. (And out behind the garage, probably sneaking a cigarette, was *bad*.) There were rigid levels of language, and the student had better choose the better, if not the best.

There's some justification for this rigid view. The student who writes "I ain't gonna go to no lecture" has violated some rather strong social norms, the linguistic equivalent of coming to class in a bathing suit. On the other hand, we've never had a student come to class in a bathing suit, and students seem to have learned the social standing of *ain't* and of double negatives—neither social error showed up in a recent national sample of writing of 240,000 9-, 13-, and 17-year-olds. A more common problem is illustrated by a student sentence like 10.13:

10.13 The meeting of the Finance Committee to discuss the proposed fund improvement plan was really zingy.

The problem, of course, is the sudden and awkward intrusion of the slang, "really zingy," into an otherwise formal sentence—"very successful" might have been a better choice.

But our dynamic sense of rhetoric forces us to question the "good, better, best" of earlier generations. For one thing, we have to ask questions about purpose, context, and stance: better for what goal, in what place, in what voice? "Really zingy" might be a really zingy phrase in another context, and the problem is not that it's bad, but that it's bad in that sentence. Moreover, we can see a professional writer, like H. L. Mencken in 10.12A above, reaching up and down the social register for the precise word he wants, reaching up for the technical words like *diabetes, leprosy, labyrinth* and down for *wrapped in, horse sense,* and *damndest.*

We also recognize that "vulgar" language—we'd now say the *vernacular*—has much more power and force than the textbooks admitted. In fact, one view of the history of the American novel treats that history as the triumph of the vernacular, for while the textbooks were timidly lifting their skirts to avoid the "vulgar," American novelists were gleefully wallowing in it. Witness, for a classic example, the vividness of Mark Twain's *Huckleberry Finn:*

10.14 All the stores was along one street. They had white domestic awnings in front, and the country-people hitched their horses to the awning-posts. There was empty dry-goods boxes under the awnings, and loafers roosting on them all day long, whittling with their Barlow knives; and chawing tobacco, and gaping and yawning and stretching—a mighty ornery lot. They generly had on yellow straw hats most as wide as an umbrella, but didn't wear no coats nor waistcoats; they called one another Bill, and Buck and Hank, and Joe, and Andy, and talked lazy and drawly, and used considerable many cuss-words.

We might clarify our dynamic view by offering a sample "informal" sentence:

10.15 I don't have any money.

Consider the vernacular alternatives available to a speaker. The speaker would have access to the "normal" version, but he or she might well have access to these alternatives, each providing its own emphasis:

10.15A   I don't got any money.

10.15B   I ain't got no money.

10.15C   I ain't got any money.

10.15D   I don't got no money.

10.15E   I don't got no money nohow.

These vernacular alternatives offer slight differences in meaning, and they are curiously more like the options available, for most of us, only in print, such as:

10.15F   I don't have any money.

10.15G   I have no money.

10.15H   No money have I.

10.15I   Money have I none.

Thus, rather than a "frozen" ideal of correctness and propriety, we can see an active interplay of purpose, voice, and audience. Most students of language now see a continuum of social scales of language use, not hard-and-fast "levels." And they find not one "scale" of good-better-best, but several scales: age, perceived correctness, occasion, mood, social class, purpose. Even the scale of "perceived correctness" is less absolute than most people think. The *American Heritage Dictionary* assembled a usage panel of about a hundred respected writers, teachers, and language scholars to judge the "correctness" of disputed usages: The panel only once reached perfect agreement, and they often split almost evenly between alternatives. There seems to be, from this evidence, at least a hundred different correctness scales. "Ain't I" for "am I not" is "bad" English in America; it remains standard today in upper-class spoken British English—and a hundred years ago "he don't" was equally standard in England.

This view of social levels of language certainly complicates the writer's choices. There's simply no single, firm external standard of correctness to base choices on. (Or should we, suddenly conscious of correctness, say "on which to base choices"? Or "upon which to ground decisions"? Or "upon which the selection of alternative lexical items can be established by means of extrinsic criteria"?) The lack of a single standard, however, can be liberating for the writer. It can return the primacy of voice, purpose, and audience to the writing act—in a phrase, writing can become rhetorical. The writer can become an active seeker of words instead of passively fencing them out.

Problem Nine. "Webster's New Word Book" The third edition of *Webster's New International Dictionary* (1961) dropped many of the usage labels that had been used in the second edition (1934)—among them *substandard, vulgar,* and *colloquial. The New York Times* responded in an editorial, the first paragraphs of which are printed below.

A passel of double-domes at the G & C Merriam Company joint in Springfield, Mass., have been confabbing and yakking for twenty-seven years—which is not intended to infer that they have not been doing plenty work—and now they have finalized Webster's Third New International Dictionary, Unabridged, a new edition of that swell and esteemed word book.

Those who regard the foregoing paragraph as acceptable English prose will find that the new Webster's is just the dictionary for them. The words in that paragraph all are listed in the new work with no suggestion that they are anything but standard.

Webster's has, it is apparent, surrendered to the permissive school that has been busily extending its beach head on English instruction in the schools. This development is disastrous because, intentionally or unintentionally, it serves to reinforce the notion that good English is whatever is popular.

Write a letter to the *Times,* protesting their judgment (or agreeing with it). One suggested approach: Would a student, even without usage labels in the dictionary, write a paragraph such as their first paragraph? ■

Euphemisms and Weasel Words: Telling It Like It Isn't

If you had to convey the news of a death in the family, you'd be likely to use an expression like "passed away" rather than "died" (or, more tastelessly, "kicked the bucket"). Of course, the person died rather than literally "passed away," but the softer term is more tactful, more polite. It is, however, a *euphemism,* the use of a mild or indirect phrase in place of a more direct or blunt word.

In this sense, euphemisms are a natural part of the social world of words—certainly harmless and occasionally humorous. We may laugh at the Victorians, who had to invent the euphemisms "light meat" and "dark meat" for chicken (because, of course, no proper young woman could publicly ask for a "breast" or a "thigh"), and who spoke of "limbs" rather than "legs" (carefully covering with skirts the "legs" of their pianos). And we can congratulate ourselves now that *syphilis* can be used in the news media (before the 1950s it was euphemistically "a social disease"), now that we can say *pregnant* rather than "expecting" or "in the family way," and now that dictionaries, since the 1960s, have been willing to admit that *fart* is a word (it had disappeared from dictionaries after Samuel Johnson listed it in his 1755 dictionary, with the elegant definition, "wind from behind"). Of course, we have to admit our own weaknesses: "Old people" have been euphemized to "senior citizens"; the "garbageman" has become a "sanitary engineer"; people are now "terminated," not "fired."

Euphemisms, in fact, tell us a good deal about the values of a culture, for words used in sensitive areas tend to pick up negative connotations and to be replaced by euphemisms. We're sensitive about death, and the old *gravedigger* has been replaced by *undertaker,* originally a general word for someone who undertook to do something, and that in turn has been replaced with the Latinate *mortician.* We're sensitive about alcohol, and so words for drinking-places need to be changed regularly: The old *saloon* (originally a euphemism itself, from French *salon,* a room) has been replaced by *tavern, bar,* and *cocktail lounge.* We're particularly sensitive about bodily functions, and so we could list hundreds of euphemisms for *bathroom* (itself a euphemism, replacing the earlier euphemism *toilet,* from the French *toilette,* originally a cloth used in shaving or hairdressing)—it has been a *Jakes* (in Elizabethan English), a *John,* a *convenience* (British), a *privy,* a *lavatory* (and British *lav*), *loo* (British, a pun on Waterloo, where Napoleon was defeated), a *latrine,* a *head,* a *washroom,* a *comfort station,* a *water closet* (and British *W.C.*), a *can,* a *potty,* and, of course, a *rest room.* We've even heard of a family that calls it "the euphemism," from a child's misunderstanding of the commas implied in a houseguest's remark, "I need, to use a euphemism, to 'wash up.' "

But euphemisms can be more serious. They can become "weasel words," designed to disguise rather than to be polite. Politics is a fertile area for the growth of euphemisms to disguise, and the political euphemism is not a laughing matter. The political euphemism is consciously used to hide and deceive. Government discussion of the Viet Nam war was saturated with euphemisms: Villages were burned and the inhabitants imprisoned—that was *pacification;* saturation bombing with B-52s was *ordnance delivery;* destroying crops was *defoliation;* the war itself was not a war but a *conflict.* These euphemisms form a framework to deceive, to hide the dirty business of the war, and one cuts through to the issues by first cutting through the fog of words. The Watergate affair was similarly clouded over with euphemism: Withholding information was *containment;* burglars were *plumbers;* the crime of breaking and entering became an *intelligence-gathering activity;* and clemency was offered "from the Oval office" or "from the highest levels of the White House." Many government employees served prison sentences for their involvement in Watergate; one cannot help but wonder how much the euphemistic language that framed the affair allowed otherwise ethical people to be involved.

Thus the process of euphemism, once started, has a tendency to run away with itself, deceiving even the deceivers. The euphemism, as a framework for viewing experience, is a distorting lens. Richard Ohmann, noting the euphemistic language of Pentagon memos about Viet Nam, makes the point clearly:

> **10.16** The rules of the *writing* game did not, of course, cause Vietnam. But they made it easier to think and do the unthinkable, because of the way they imposed mechanical analysis between the men of power and human and moral issues.
>
> *English in America*

At issue here are two questions, both for writers and for readers. Is writing used to communicate or to hide? And who, finally, is the master, the writer or the words? The euphemisms, the weasel words, the trite slogans, and the empty abstractions are happy to do our writing for us, our reading for us, and even our thinking for us. All we have to do is let them.

Problem Ten. Captain Euphemism   As you sit unnoticed at the back of the press conference, disguised as mild-mannered bespectacled reporter Clark Bent, you realize that the Mayor of Gotham City is in deep trouble. She badly needs to attract new industry to her decaying city, but she's stuck with a vocabulary that reeks with negative connotations—"city dump," "slums," "forced bussing," and so on. To complicate matters, angry feminists line the hallway, demanding an end to the sexism inherent in terms like *policeman, councilman,* and *seamstress.* Something must be done, and fast.

You leave your seat quietly and slip into the cloakroom, where you quickly change into the jeweled costume of . . . (organ music, please) CAPTAIN EUPHEMISM! Your mission is to euphemize (and incidentally to desex) the vocabulary of Gotham City. You'll want to report your results to the Mayor in a confidential memo. We give you below a list of words to work with, and we might start you off with a sample— wouldn't *city dump* be more appetizing as a *metropolitan sanitary landfill facility*?

a. traffic jam	**f.** urban sprawl
b. fireman	**g.** cheap labor
c. high property taxes	**h.** garbageman
d. police brutality	**i.** smog and pollution
e. crime in the streets	**j.** political corruption

■

Shoptalk and Jargon: Words at Work

A student reported the confusion of the first day on the job: "Take the 509 down to the dispatcher in the cube and pass the copyform over to the doubler," the boss said, and he could only stand there, bewildered by the shoptalk that he hadn't yet learned. *Shoptalk* is the vocabulary used in a specific company. As shoptalk moves out of a single shop to become common to a field, it becomes *jargon,* the specialized vocabulary of a trade or profession.

The word *jargon* has picked up a strongly negative connotation, and rightly so, for professional talk can solidify into a thoughtless use of stock phrases to mystify or disguise; jargon can become gibberish.

There's an obvious moral here for the writer: Remember your audience. A doctor does this naturally when he says to a patient, "That's a nasty bruise you've got there," then turns to a colleague and says, "The patient has a severe contusion," and finally, writing up his findings for a medical journal, states, "The patient had a serious subcutaneous hemorrhage." When we do not write for a specialized audience, though, we're best off using the shared vocabulary of everyday life rather than jargon—a bruise is a bruise. The student who wrote the passage below, for example, has trapped himself in a combination of jargon and slang, and his message is clear only to those who share all his in-group knowledge.

> **10.17** The snow job that UC veep Winkler gave us at the Withrow avoids the issue that the AAUP's been trying to get on the table, that is, the issue of contracts.

Stopping to spell out some of the jargon here would take more words (is UC the University of Connecticut? of Colorado, of California?), but the extra words might help gain a reader.

There's an even more important moral for the student, however, for "doing" chemistry or sociology or even English is, to a large degree, mastering the specialized vocabulary of the field. A doctor learns to "talk doctor," and a lawyer learns to "talk lawyer." The student might be wise to make "talking" the subject matter of a course a conscious part of learning. (It's wise, for example, to write out the terms of a field as preparation for an examination, particularly since you acquire most of the "talk" of a field passively, at a distance, through lectures or reading, while examinations require that you participate directly.) We discuss these matters further in chapter Fourteen.

The passages below are written in language appropriate for a specialized audience, but you may find some—or all—to be difficult or even impossible to read. Try to translate at least two of the passages into something approximating everyday English, using a dictionary for help. (This assignment may be much easier as a class or small-group project. Why?)

a. The sensitivity and signal-to-noise ratio (S/N) were not affected significantly by band-width. The IHF usable sensitivity was 13 to 14 dBf (2.4 to 2.7 microvolts, or μV) in mono and 17 dBf (4 μV) in stereo. The 50-dBf quieting sensitivity in mono was 14 or 15 dBf (2.7 to 3 μV) and in stereo it was 37 dBf (38 μV). The S/N at a 65-dBf (1,000 μV) input was 73.5 to 74.5 dB in mono and 68 to 70 dB in stereo.

test review of an FM tuner
in Stereo Review

b. The Proudest Roman filly, conditioned by Jimmy Picou, broke her maiden at first asking, topping Daisy Miller by slightly more than a length.

Sun Valley Sally also scored her first time out, beating Tuvalu, but wound up fourth against Heavenly Lass in her most recent.

Jack Wilson, The Daily Racing Form

c. The recurrent partials, including zero-elements, are the MOR-PHEMES of a language. They are determined by processes parallel to those used in phonology: inspection, commutation within a frame, complementary distribution. There is, however, no criterion parallel to that of phonetic similarity, for phonemic similarity is not a necessary basis for classifying morphemes; different morphemes may be homonymous, or the variants of one morpheme may have very different phonemic shapes, or some variants may be zero phonemically. . . .

George L. Trager and Henry Lee Smith, Jr.,
An Outline of English Structure

d. The ground decoration on this *écuelle,* simulating the effect of marble chips, is often referred to as *rose marbre en bleu.* Other examples . . . bear the same date letter, I for 1761, as in this example. Jean-Baptiste . . . was not the only artist to decorate the reserves of pieces with the *rose marbre en bleu* ground, for Guillaume Noël's mark is found on examples with flower painting very similar to that of Tandart's.

The Campbell Museum Collection

■

Regional and Social Dialects: Words We Live In

Television and radio have established, to a degree, a sort of national language. But we still learn our language from those close to us, and we still speak in ways that mark our part of the United States—and our social background. One need only notice, for example, the differences of speech in recent presidents.

Linguists have been able to map the geography of words rather precisely, simply by asking people in different parts of the country what words they use. A northern *pail* is a southern *bucket;* a northern *bag* is a southern *sack* (or *poke* or *tote*). What we thought was a *submarine* sandwich is to others a *hoagy,* a *grinder,* or a *hero.* We may sit on the *porch, stoop,* or *veranda* while we *hull, pod, shell,* or *shuck* peas, then stand *in line* or *on line* to wash them under the *faucet, spigot, hydrant,* or *tap.*

We feel positive about such linguistic variety. Variety in language is an inherent good in the same way that variety in animal species is an inherent good: The varieties of language give us more chances at being human, more ways of knowing through language. There is a vitality in the differences in our dialects that would be missed if we all spoke in the same way.

But the social and regional differences in language can occasionally cause problems for writers. The first version of a sentence of ours, from chapter Nine, originally read:

10.18   A semicolon is like a teeter-totter; one side balances the other side.

Our editor sent back the manuscript with a large question mark by the sentence. When we were able to sit down with the manuscript, the editor, born in New York City, said, "I don't understand what that means." We both grew up on the West Coast, and we replied, "It's perfectly clear." After five more minutes of discussion, she said, "Oh, you mean a see-saw." The revised version of 10.18 recognizes what had not originally occurred to us—that *teeter-totter* is a regional expression:

10.18A   A semicolon is like a teeter-totter or see-saw; one side balances the other side.

That revision seems a reasonable compromise of what we want to say with what our readers might understand, but the richness of dialects in the United States almost escapes our ability to respond to it in print, for a more complete expansion of that sentence might destroy its stylistic purpose:

10.18B   A semicolon is like what those of you who grew up in the west would call a *teeter-totter* and those who grew up in the east would call a *see-saw* (except for some of you from New England, who might say *teeter board* or *teetering board,* or those from Rhode *ww* : Wrong Word Choice   Reexamine your word choice, consulting a dictionary if necessary. The corruption "wrong word" covers a number of distinct problems. A mistake in spelling may lead to a surprising word in context—

- He was the persecuting attorney.
  (Here the writer means "prosecuting.") Or the writer may aim for a somewhat fancy word and miss catastrophically—
- She fell down the stairs and lay prostitute at the bottom.
  (Here the writer means *prostrate.*) Or a writer may miss, more subtly, the connotation or range of meaning of a word—
- The present context is intolerable.
  (Here the writer means *situation.*) Or a writer may miss slightly the exact denotation of a word—
- We appointed her *ad hoc* chairperson, until we could elect a permanent one.
  (The term *ad hoc* means "for a special purpose"; the better word here would be *interim.*) And, finally, the writer can slip slightly out of an appropriate register—
- The Rachmaninoff concerto was swell.
  (Rock concerts can be "swell," we understand, but concertos, if performed well, demand a more formal word—perhaps *superb.*)

  Fortunately, a standard college dictionary should solve most of these problems for the student, and our next chapter will discuss how to get the most benefit from one.

Island, who say *dandle,* or from Cape Cod, who say *tile* or *tilting board,* or central West Virginia, who say *ridy-horse*); one side balances the other side.

Beneath that variety, social and regional, there is a deep unity—the unity of being human and sharing a language. Black writer Sandra Haggerty sums up the unity behind the surface differences in black and white speech nicely:

10.19   You kiss your children, and we give 'em some sugar . . . You cook a pan of spinach, and we burn a mess of greens. You wear clothes, and we wear threads . . . You call the police, and we drop a dime. You say wow! We say ain't that a blip. You care, love, and hurt, and we care, love, and hurt. The differences are but a shade.

"On Digging the Difference"
(*Los Angeles Times*)

Slang: Words with Their Shoes Off

Slang expressions are the linguistic equivalent of social climbers. They tend to come from the bottom of society—drug culture, pop music, and criminal's argot are common sources of slang (*argot:* the jargon of criminals). Sometimes slang expressions rise to respectability. *Jazz, okay,* and *A-bomb* were slang a generation or two ago, as were *goof, phone* (a clipped form of *telephone*), and even *hot dog. Pot, hippie,* and *hangup* are now in the stage of emerging from slang. *Sensible, volunteer, job, shabby,* and *gamble* were labeled "low," "ludicrous," or "cant" by Samuel Johnson in 1755. Other slang expressions quickly disappear from the language. We would hardly compliment someone by calling them "the cat's pajamas" or "the bee's knees"—slang from the 1920s—and most of us now would also find "a real cool cat" to be agonizingly dated.

The distinguishing mark of most slang, then, is that it is constantly shifting, either dying out or moving into accepted language. (Thus, we hesitate to try to offer current slang terms—they would probably not be slang to many of our readers.) That shifting is natural, of course— the purpose of slang is to define an "in-group" that shares the slang, and as soon as everyone recognizes a slang expression, it has lost its function, and a new expression is needed.

Sex: Words that Wear the Pants

There are far many more insulting terms for women than there are for men. The connotations of the male *bachelor* or *single man* are quite different from the connotations of the female *old maid* or *spinster,* and the male *master* doesn't match the range of the female *mistress.* Being *unladylike* is not the equivalent of being *unmanly.* There are no feminine equivalents of *macho, manhood, manly,* and *virile* (at least not yet). There are "loose women," but not "loose men."

Those are unpleasant facts, but understandable ones. Language reflects culture, and a sexist culture will fossilize sexism in its vocabulary. "Women's words" are seen by speakers, male and female alike, as obviously sex-marked, *divine,* and *mauve,* and *adorable,* for example. Male words, on the other hand, are seldom considered sex-marked—swear words, for example, or *business, pool table,* and *football.* Many female terms are defined by the male term—*woman, housewife, female.*

In part, sexism in language will disappear with the disappearance of sexism in our culture. "Lady doctor" and "lady lawyer" will disappear as more female professionals enter those fields, just as "lady novelist" disappeared in the nineteenth century. We can make a conscious effort, female and male alike, to secure the same fate for such consciously sexist distinctions as *actor/actress, waiter/waitress,* and *poet/poetess.* And we can make the neutral *Ms.* (pronounced, in good southern fashion, "miz") equal to the neutral *Mr.*

But certain fossilized sexist words cause problems for writers today. The use of *man* as a term for *human being* is so deeply embedded in our public language that it may be impossible to remove it ("All men are created equal," "Man is the measure of all things"). *Chairperson* has fairly commonly replaced *chairman,* but *businessperson* is not so easily going to replace *businessman,* and even more difficult would be *policeperson, fisherperson, mailperson,* and *garbageperson.* There's one case on record of a woman named something like *Stratman* changing her name to *Stratperson,* but that seems endless. The Scottish *Mac-,* as in MacDonald, means "son of": would that give us *PersonDonald*? An *egg personmuffin*?

A particular problem is raised by the use of the neutral *he* in sentences like, "If the student works hard, he will improve." Many feminists have objected to the assumption built into this construction, and they have gathered a convincing body of evidence to suggest that they are correct—for example, the chairperson (male) of a college department confidently asserting, "We're going to find the best man for the job, regardless of his sex." But the most commonly suggested way around the problem, the use of "he or she" or "she or he," often becomes an unwieldy circumlocution: "If the student works hard, he or she will find that his or her writing will improve as he or she progresses." And other suggestions seem equally impractical:

- inventing new neutral pronouns, such as *hir* and *hem* ("hem will find that hir writing will improve"?)
- using special print signs, such as *s/he* and *her/his* ("s/he will find that her/his writing will improve")
- alternating forms ("he will find that her writing will improve"!?)
- using the "mistake" of plural *they, them,* and *their* ("the student will find that their writing will improve")

Many publishing houses and professional organizations now insist on one form or another of these suggestions, and all manuscripts are edited to conform with the standards. But standards vary widely. Until a consensus emerges, here are two suggestions:

- *he or she* is not always stylistically barbaric, and with reasonable care for continuity *he* and *she* can be altered without difficulty for the reader.
- it's often surprisingly easy to sidestep the problem by using the plural form, which isn't marked for sex ("If students work hard, they will find that their writing will improve").

SUMMARY

We have, in essence, explored a vocabulary for talking about words: the word ladders of general and specific and abstract and concrete; the difference between a denotative meaning and a connotative meaning; the distinction between literal and figurative uses of words; and the many dimensions of *register,* the "social standing" of words—levels of language, euphemism, shoptalk and jargon, regional and social dialects, slang, and sex-marked words.

IMPLICATIONS FOR THE WRITER

Our goal in this chapter has been to break down a common student model of language, one which divides words into "proper vocabulary," appropriate for college composition, and "improper vocabulary," which needs to be rigidly fenced out of one's writing. Our model is quite different; it recognizes the many scales for weighing words, and it stresses the importance of connotation, audience, and purpose in word choice. The writer who accepts this model will be more open to word choice, more aware of options and potentials, and (we insert slyly) more open to language.

FINAL WRITING ASSIGNMENTS

I. Word Maps

A. Examine a political pamphlet or a political magazine for the vocabulary used. Discuss the implications of that vocabulary, as it creates a "word map" (and therefore a "world map") for that group.

B. With the help of reference sources (see chapter Fourteen), find two or three articles that discuss a group that you are a member of—a social, racial, or cultural group, for example. Compare the vocabulary that you, as an insider, use to talk about the group with the vocabulary used by outsiders.

C. Spend some time listening to the radio, notepad in hand, noting the words used in songs and by announcers on stations playing different kinds of music. Explore the differences you find, and their implications, in a short paper.

II. Denotation and Connotation

A. Collect labels applied to a particular product, such as the names of cars or soaps or perfumes. Classify the labels and analyze their connotations and the appeals they make. (Or, as a variant, you may open a new business, "Names, Incorporated," and serve as the consultant to a soap or perfume or automobile company, reporting on possible names for a new product.)

B. Select an event covered in a recent *Time* or *Newsweek* and find a comparable report in a different magazine or in a newspaper. Analyze the connotations of the words used, trying to isolate the attitudes of the two sources.

C. *U.S. News & World Report* often presents paired interviews that explore "both sides" of a political or social issue. Select one pair of interviews and contrast the connotative vocabulary used by the two sides. (You may wish to consider the degree to which it is possible to provide a purely neutral and objective treatment of the issue in question.)

D. Browse through the paperback book stand at the supermarket or drugstore, noting the connotative words used on the front and back covers. What classes of connotative words do you find? Do those classes differ for mysteries, romances, westerns, and so on? What do these words imply about the readers of these novels?

E. Rhetorician Richard Weaver, in the 1950s, wrote an essay on the "god-terms" of the 1950s. A "god-term" is a word or phrase with such positive connotations that it wins immediate assent from an audience. Weaver identified such god-terms as "science" (as in "science tells us" or "experiments prove"), "progress" (as in "progress is our most important product"), and, of course, "new" and "improved" ("Ultimate Terms in Contemporary Rhetoric," in *The Ethics of Rhetoric* [Chicago: Henry Regnery, 1965]). Examine the vocabulary of advertising in an issue of a popular magazine or from an evening of watching television, and use the evidence to explore the "god-terms" of the 1980s.

III. Figurative Language

A. An obvious assignment: Discuss the figurative language of a poem or short story, paying particular attention to the qualities evoked by such language and its contribution to your total response to the work.

B. Examine the buried or fossilized metaphors in a textbook on any subject, paying particular attention to the analogies that seem basic to the discipline.

IV. Register

A. At the end of the war in Viet Nam, the Air Force compiled a list of new slang words for returning prisoners of war. The list, beginning with *acid* and ending with *zonked*, was made up of words that had come into the language during the five or so years the men had been imprisoned. Compile a list of perhaps twenty words to serve the same purpose today, and write a preface for your list.

B. Coin a new word—to explain a feeling or object that doesn't now have a name—and explain the meaning and register you want the word to have in a short essay.

C. Louise Pound gathered a massive list of words in a classic essay, "American Euphemisms for Dying, Death, and Burial," *American Speech* (1936). Gather a set of euphemisms from another area—drunkenness, money, bodily functions, for example—and explore your findings in a short essay.

FOR FURTHER READING

There are many excellent guides to the world of words, and we will attempt little more here than to offer a few choices to start you off. Three anthologies might be mentioned as starting-points: *Language: Introductory Readings,* ed. Virginia P. Clark, Paul A. Eschholz, and Alfred P. Rosa, 3rd ed. (New York: St. Martin's, 1981); *Introductory Reading on Language,* ed. Wallace L. Anderson and Norman C. Stageberg, 4th ed. (New York: Holt, Rinehart and Winston, 1975), and a more popular collection, *The Writer and the World of Words,* ed. Robert Bain and Dennis G. Donovan (Englewood Cliffs, N.J.: Prentice-Hall, 1975).

The notion of words as maps of reality is discussed by S. I. Hayakawa in *Language in Thought and Action,* 4th ed. (New York: Harcourt, Brace, Jovanovich, 1979), and he has also edited *The Use and Misuse of Language* (Greenwich, Conn: Fawcett, 1962), a collection of essays on the cultural implications of language use. George Orwell's classic essay, "Politics and the English Language," is of particular interest to writers; it is available in his collected essays and is widely reprinted. Richard D. Altick's *A Preface to Critical Reading,* 5th ed. (New York: Holt, Rinehart and Winston, 1969) has a good discussion of denotation and connotation, along with helpful suggestions about becoming a critical reader.

Peter Farb's *Wordplay: What Happens When People Talk* (New York: Knopf, 1973), a fine popular introduction to sociolinguistics, is available as a Bantam paperback. Roger W. Shuy's *Discovering American Dialects* (Urbana, Ill.: National Council of Teachers of English, 1967) is a good introduction to regional dialects in America; it includes an extensive dialect questionnaire.

Martin Joos's *The Five Clocks* (New York: Harcourt, Brace and World, 1967) is a linguist's delightful discussion of social and functional levels of language, and articles on sexism and language are collected in *Language and Sex: Difference and Dominance,* ed. Barrie Thorne and Nancy Henley (Rowley, Mass.: Newbury House, 1975). One social dialect is discussed in Geneva Smitherman's *Talkin and Testifyin: The Language of Black America* (Boston: Houghton Mifflin, 1977).

11

Diction and the Dictionary

Zounds! I've never been so bethumped with words.

SHAKESPEARE

You'll find at least one of them in the paperback rack of the drugstore, perhaps even three or four. They bear promising titles: *Seven Days to a Better Vocabulary!*, *Instant Word Power!*, *Vocabulary-Building in Five Minutes a Day!* They sell well, for most Americans are sure that: 1. they don't have a good vocabulary, and 2. there must be some secret remedy, some instant word power.

These paperbacks list and define many words, but their advice usually boils down to five rules for building vocabulary. We follow each rule with a question mark and a brief discussion.

11.1 Memorize all Latin and Greek prefixes and suffixes. (?)

Thus, after you've memorized Greek *kalli-* and *-pygian*, you'll immediately recognize the meaning of *callipygian*.

11.2 Break unfamiliar words into parts. (?)

Thus *lexicographer* will break into *lexico-* plus *-grapher*, telling you that it means "maker of dictionaries," just as *photographer* is "maker of photos" and telegrapher is "maker of teles." *Psychology* is the study (*-ology*) of the mind (*psyche*), so *etymology* must be the study of etyms.

11.3   Always look up new words immediately. (?)

The short story begins, "He crossed the field and entered the copse, wandering through the pleasant woods until he came to a gently flowing rill." When you come to *copse,* you should put down the book, look the word up in the dictionary ("a small forest"), then do the same for *rill* ("a small stream").

11.4   Write down new words and memorize them. (?)

After looking up *copse,* you would write it twenty times; then you would do the same for *rill.*

11.5   Use new words daily in conversation. (?)

"Hello, Joan. Do you think a callipygian lexicographer might find any etyms by the rill in the copse?"

We've now saved you $3.50 by giving you the secret rules of *Mighty Word Potency Overnight!* But, as our comments suggest, we have some doubts about such rules. In fact, they seem wrong-headed or (to help build your vocabulary) counterproductive. By the time student X has looked up *copse,* copied it twenty times, and then done the same for *rill,* student Y has finished the story and started her chemistry homework. Moreover, student Y can talk like a normal person, while student X is compelled, by rule 11.5, to talk about rills and copses and lexicographers—hardly a good start for a social life.

We're considering our own book for the drugstore racks. It would be titled *Ninety Years to a More Powerful Vocabulary,* and it would offer only two rules:

11.6   Read a lot.

11.7   Master the use of a standard college dictionary.

Our secret rules are radically different from those of the drugstore books, and we will begin with a few words about your vocabulary and how to improve it. First, however, welcome to a television game show.

Problem One. *Decisions, Decisions!*   You're nervous, even apprehensive, behind the curtain, but your mind clears when the curtain swings open and you step in front of the cameras to be greeted by the host, Marty Musclebound. "Welcome to *Decisions, Decisions!*" he burbles.

"You'll be given a common shopping problem and asked to make a decision in an instant. If you answer correctly, you'll be given a second problem, and then . . . our championship problem, perhaps worth thousands!

"As you know, this is 'Lexicon Week' on the show, and our consumer questions deal with words and dictionaries. Here's the first question: Do you want to buy this copy of *Mighty Power Over Words in Minutes,* fresh from the drugstore paperback rack? It costs $3.50, and I'm allowed to tell you that it mentions the value of using *copse, rill, callipygian,* and *lexicographer* daily in conversation. Do you want to buy it?"

Firmly and confidently, you answer with a loud "No."

"Correct!" shouts Marty, and the audience cheers wildly. "Now question two, a problem of word choice. Our championship can be worth 'uncounted thousands' or it can be worth 'uncountable thousands.' Which do you prefer, 'uncounted' or 'uncountable'?

A bigger problem, worth uncounted thousands to you. Or should it be "uncountable"? Smiling to yourself, you think, "Always break words into parts." *Uncountable:* not able to be counted. That's okay. *Uncounted:* not counted. That's not so good. The word *uncounted* has a figurative sense that means "uncountable," but it has a literal meaning as well. They might give you a handful of bills, claiming, "We haven't counted them." Literal and figurative.

You step to the microphone and, speaking very carefully, answer, "Uncountable thousands."

"Eureka!" shouts Marty. "Correct again. You're ready for the final question, worth uncountable thousands. Here, from your college bookstore, is the *Scribner-Bantam English Dictionary* (New York: Charles Scribner's Sons, 1977). It's a new dictionary, not a reprint of an outdated edition, and it's clearly printed, on good paper, with adequate margins. It's a sturdy book, and it's on sale for half price. You are allowed to examine sample entries, from *anvil* through *anxious,* for two minutes."

Quickly, you scan the entries.

---

an·vil /an′vil/ [OE anfilt(e)] *n* 1 block, generally of iron faced with steel, on which metals are hammered and shaped; **2** one of the three small bones in the middle ear

anx·i·e·ty /aŋzī′itē/ *n* (**-ties**) **1** mental uneasiness or distress arising from fear of what may happen; **2** eager desire for some purpose or object ‖ SYN solicitude, concern, trouble (see *care*)

anx·ious /aŋk′shəs/ [L *anxius* troubled] *adj* **1** giving or accompanied by worry over an uncertainty; **2** deeply concerned or troubled; **3** solicitous; desirous ‖ **an′xious·ly** *adv*

Too soon, you hear Marty pose the question: "Do you want to buy this as a standard college dictionary?"

Do you?

■

VOCABULARY BUILDING

We agree that people are right in wanting to increase their vocabulary, and we joke only about the books that try to help them do so. But we do want to offer a few clarifications.

First off, you don't have a single vocabulary in your head, arranged in alphabetical order, like a dictionary. Instead, you have four overlapping but distinct vocabularies: a speaking vocabulary, a writing vocabulary, a reading vocabulary, and a vocabulary that you can guess in context. Your *speaking vocabulary* includes the words you use every day. This vocabulary is surprisingly small—a few hundred words made up most of the words used in telephone conversations, one study reported. Your *writing vocabulary* is larger—ten to fifty thousand words, by one guess. The two vocabularies mix together: The everyday words of your speaking vocabulary are the bedrock of your writing vocabulary, and in some situations—talking about a science course with a friend, for example—you can use your writing vocabulary in speaking. But often the two vocabularies are different: A spoken "betcha" is a written *bet you;* a spoken "gonna" is a written *going to.*

Your *reading vocabulary* includes all the words you understand in reading, even if you don't use them in your writing. Your reading vocabulary is quite large—a hundred and fifty thousand words for a college graduate, by one estimate—and it's constantly growing, as new words are used in front of your eyes. Thus you're learning words much faster than you think you are, and you're learning painlessly, without formal study.

Finally, you have *guess vocabulary,* words that you can guess from context, even if you couldn't define them otherwise. Notice how easy it is to guess the meaning of *copse* and *rill* from context alone:

11.8 He crossed the field and entered the copse, wandering through the pleasant woods until he came to a gently flowing rill.

And notice that you have no idea of the meaning of *callipygian,* unless you've looked it up, for we gave you the word out of context. Thus, we'd suggest that you think of your vocabulary as a sort of mental filtration system, words seeping down through guess vocabulary to reading vocabulary to writing and speaking vocabularies. The more you read, the more your vocabulary will grow.

Our feeling, then, is that the drugstore books go about it in the wrong way. They try to put words into your speaking vocabulary before they're in your reading vocabulary, and they present words out of context, ignoring the social sense of words (their linguistic register, from chapter Ten). *Copse* and *rill,* for example, should remain only in your reading vocabulary, since they've dropped out of the speaking and writing vocabularies of most Americans. (And who needs a word like *callipygian*?)

Even the common advice, "Break words into parts," is not as helpful as it could be. If you can break *bicycle* into *bi-* plus *-cycle*, and *unicorn* into *uni-* ("one") plus *-corn* (Latin *cornu*, "horn"), you'll be able to understand *unicycle*, a one-wheeled cycle. But you'll be confused by *epicycle* and *cyclamate*, which depend on a different sense of the Latin root *cycle*, "circle." Of course, you'll naturally break words into parts when you need to, as you did with *uncounted* and *uncountable*, or as you might with a scientific word like *psychophysiology*. Our criticism is with instructions that make the advice too mechanical, changing reading into puzzle-solving, and ignoring the mind's natural filtration system for words.

We find humorous support for our view in *Pullet Surprises*, a book by an instructor who taught a high school vocabulary course. (The title is from a student's misunderstanding of *Pulitzer Prize*; he wrote: "In 1957 Eugene O'Neill won a Pullet Surprise.") The instructor kept notes on the mistakes students made when they applied the advice "Break words into parts." *Phonology*, one student guessed, was "the study of telephone etiquette." *Gubernatorial*, guessed another, "had to do with peanuts." *Polyglot* was defined as "more than one glot," and *homogeneous* as "devoted to home life." [1] The students were applying the advice diligently enough, but some secret about words was eluding them.

The standard college dictionary lets us in on that secret—a "secret" because of a fascinating paradox. Every child who learns English can be said, in a very real sense, to create the language anew. We can hear that creativity in mistakes children make, like saying "I eated it" or "The duck bited me"—they are creating rules for their language. *Baby-sit*, for most children, even older ones, does not have a root sense of "sitting with a baby," and so they form the past tense as "babysitted" rather than "babysat." Such creativity helps to explain why language changes—the past tense "helped" has replaced Shakespeare's "holp" in print and in most spoken dialects, and you will differ, as a class, in your preference for "dived" or "dove."

Yet, paradoxically, the language that children create is centuries, even millennia, old, and we speakers of English carry with us, embedded in our language, the history of that language. Take a common word as an example: *breakfast*. Our pronunciation suggests that we've learned the word without sensing its root meaning, "breaking a fast," although that root sense is kept in its spelling, and it must have been quite apparent when the word first appeared in the language around the fifteenth century. The word *break* was *breccan* in English a thousand years ago, and another thousand years before that it was *brek-* in a language called West Germanic. We can even guess that it was something like *bhreg-* in the earliest ancestor of English, spoken some ten thousand years ago. This root, *bhreg-*, also comes into English through the related Latin *frangere*, "to break," to give us *fragment, fraction, fragile, fracture,* and *refract.* Thus, breakfast with your family is really "breakfast" with two families—your own family and the language family you carry in your head.²

How will the dictionary help with this second family, and how will it build your vocabulary? Let's look up *lexicographer,* "a compiler of dictionaries." In a small pocket dictionary, our information would essentially stop there, a definition of the word and its spelling. In a standard college dictionary, though, we find a bracketed note on the origin of the word—technically, its *etymology.* That note refers us to the word *lexicon.* We skim down the page, passing *lexicography,* "the science of dictionary-making," and *lexicology,* "the study of the lexical component of language," a definition which sends us up to *lexical,* "relating to the words of a language." At *lexicon,* "the words of a language or profession," we're given the etymology of these related words.

11.9 [<ML<MGk, Gk *lexikón*, n. use of neut. of *lexikós* of words = *lex(is)* speech, word (akin to *légein* to speak) + *ikos* − IC]

The Random House College Dictionary

This is puzzling information. We're tempted to say that it might be Gk to you (*Gk* is a common dictionary abbreviation for "Greek"). But writers who solve this puzzle find a net of related terms—not only the ones we passed on the page (*lexicon, lexicographer, lexical, lexicography, lexicology*)—but a rich and hidden design. The original form, lexicographers think, must have been something like *leg-,* meaning "to collect or to speak." Our old word for a doctor, *leech,* comes from that root word, through a Germanic form *likjaz,* "enchanter," and it's now transferred to the blood-sucking worms used by early doctors. We've borrowed words such as *lectern, lecture, legible, intelligent, elect,* and *neglect* from the Latin form *legere,* "to gather, to choose, to read." From Greek *legein* come the *lexico-* words noted before, and also *dialect, dialog, catalog, epilogue.* A related Greek word, *logos,* "speech, word, reason," gives us *logic, apology, logarithm, prologue.* Other Latin forms give us new patterns in the design: *legal, legislation, loyal, privilege* from *lex,* "law"; *legacy, delegate, colleague* from *legare,* "to charge or commission"; even *ligneous,* "having the texture or appearance of wood," from *lignum,* "wood," or more literally, "that which is collected."

We went to a standard college dictionary for one word, and we found a rich tapestry of related words. That tapestry will help us to remember the word—we're unlikely to forget the meaning of *lexicographer,* now that it's connected with several words we already know.

Even more importantly, as one becomes more conscious of this secret history of words, one becomes a quicker, more adept learner of words and a more careful user of them. Poet Charles Olson stressed the value of such a conscious mastery of word histories in an informal letter to a younger writer:

> **11.10** I couldn't stress enough on this speech rhythm question the pay-off in traction that a non-literate non-commercial and non-historical constant daily experience of tracking any word, practically, one finds oneself using, back along its lines of force to Anglo-Saxon, Latin, Greek, and out to Sanskrit. . . .
>
> Letter to Elaine Feinstein

A poet, of course, is naturally, even necessarily, interested in the "traction" of words. Less expected is the fact that Malcolm X, a powerful speaker and writer, developed his writing skills by copying a dictionary. In prison, limited in reading and writing ability, he began in frustration to copy the first page of a dictionary.

> **11.11** I woke up the next morning, thinking about those words— immensely proud to realize that not only had I written so much at one time, but I'd written words that I never knew were in the world. Moreover, with a little effort, I also could remember what many of these words meant. I reviewed the words whose meanings I didn't remember. Funny thing, from the dictionary first page right now, that "aardvark" springs to my mind. The dictionary had a picture of it, a long-tailed, long-eared burrowing African mammal, which lives off termites caught by sticking out its tongue as an anteater does for ants.
>
> *The Autobiography of Malcolm X*

He continued until he had copied the entire dictionary. His advice is our advice:

> **11.12** I saw that the best thing I could do was get hold of a dictionary—to study, to learn some words.

THE DICTIONARY AS WORD-HOARD

When you invest in a new car, the first thing you do is read the owner's manual, so that you're sure you know how to get the best from your investment. The rest of this chapter is an "owner's manual" for a standard college dictionary. We will explore the information that's in (and *not* in) a standard college dictionary; we'll present enough information about the history of English to make sense of etymological abbreviations; and we'll discuss the ways words change in meaning.

Figure 11.1 offers sample entries from one college dictionary, with notes on the information it presents. Examine the information carefully.

A close look at the entries and our annotations should convince you of three points. First, a standard college dictionary tells the reader much more than an inexpensive pocket dictionary. (Thus the correct answer to Marty's game show question is a firm "No.") Second, simply by opening the dictionary at random, we've added two new words to our own vocabulary, the *anvil* of the ear and the *anxious seat* of a revival meeting. Third, the dictionary reminds us of the richness and variety of English.

The Fallacy of "THE" Dictionary

We often speak of *the* dictionary, in the same way we speak of *the* Bible. "The dictionary tells us," we say, or "Webster says," as if some linguistic Jehovah had inscribed the truth of language on stone tablets. You should by now have developed a sense of the constantly changing nature of language, and you might want to be suspicious of such claims. Words are too active, too slithery, to be pinned down like butterfly specimens, and, difficult as it is to accept, there is no single authority. To demonstrate the variety in language, examine, in Figure 11.2, the same entries, from *anvil* to *anxious,* in another standard college dictionary. We've noted some of the differences. (Even the name *Webster's* is no guarantee of authority, by the way—the heirs of Noah Webster, who published his dictionary in 1828, have long since lost the copyright to the name, and any dictionary can label itself a "Webster's.")

The two dictionaries differ on the pronunciation of *anvil;* they differ on the precise psychiatric meaning of *anxiety;* and the *AHD* considers "anxious" for "eager" to be a usage problem while the *NWD* apparently does not. We can expand the comparison by printing, in Figure 11.3, the same entries from three other standard college dictionaries.

Problem Two. The standard college dictionary   Using our annotations in Figures 11.1 and 11.2 as models, provide annotations for the three dictionaries printed in Figure 11.3.   ■

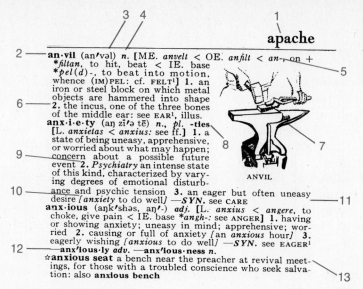

apache

an·vil (an′vəl) *n.* [ME. *anvelt* < OE. *anfilt* < *an*-ₜon + *filtan*, to hit, beat < IE. base *pel(d)*-, to beat into motion, whence (IM)PEL: cf. FELT¹] 1. an iron or steel block on which metal objects are hammered into shape 2. the incus, one of the three bones of the middle ear: see EAR¹, illus.

anx·i·e·ty (aŋ zī′ə tē) *n., pl.* -ties [L. *anxietas* < *anxius*: see ff.] 1. a state of being uneasy, apprehensive, or worried about what may happen; concern about a possible future event 2. *Psychiatry* an intense state of this kind, characterized by varying degrees of emotional disturbance and psychic tension 3. an eager but often uneasy desire [*anxiety* to do well] —*SYN.* see CARE

anx·ious (aŋk′shəs, aŋ′-) *adj.* [L. *anxius* < *angere*, to choke, give pain < IE. base *angh*-: see ANGER] 1. having or showing anxiety; uneasy in mind; apprehensive; worried 2. causing or full of anxiety [an *anxious* hour] 3. eagerly wishing [*anxious* to do well] —*SYN.* see EAGER¹ —anx′ious·ly *adv.* —anx′ious·ness *n.*

☆anxious seat a bench near the preacher at revival meetings, for those with a troubled conscience who seek salvation: also anxious bench

ANVIL

Webster's New World Dictionary of the American Language. Second College Edition. Ed. David B. Guralnik. New York: Collins World, 1976. Abbreviated *NWD.*

1 gives headwords showing first and last words on the page—a convenience offered by all dictionaries.
2 gives correct spelling; also indicates with symbol • how word is divided into syllables (letting you know how to hyphenate it at the end of a line).
3 indicates pronunciation; the symbol ′ marks stress. Note two pronunciations for *anxious*—the more common one is given first.
4 identifies part of speech (*n.* = noun).
5 summarizes etymology at beginning of entry. The etymology of *anvil* might be diagrammed as follows:

    Indo-European   *pel(d)* → (cross-reference to *felt*)
                                 ↓
    Old English   *anfilt* → (compound of *an* + *filtan*)
                                 ↓
    Middle English   *anvelt*
                                 ↓
    Modern English   *anvil*

6 numbers different meanings; this dictionary generally lists meanings in order of appearance chronologically.
7 provides an illustration for *anvil*—note also the reference at *anvil²* to the illustration at *ear¹*.
8 gives spelling of plural *anxieties* (but not for plural *anvil*, which has a regular form *anvils*).
9 labels technical sense of the word *anxiety*.
10 offers illustrative examples of use.
11 gives cross-references to lists of synonyms for *anxiety* and *anxious*.
12 gives spelling for related forms—but assumes their meanings will be understood.
13 lists compound *anxious seat* after main entry. Provides a special symbol ☆ to identify an Americanism; does not provide separate entry for less common *anxious bench*.

FIGURE 11.1 Information in a Standard College Dictionary

1   2

an·vil (ăn′vĭl) *n.* **1.** A heavy block of iron or steel, with a smooth, flat top on which metals are shaped by hammering. **2.** The fixed jaw in a set of calipers, against which the object to be measured is placed. **3.** *Anatomy.* A bone, the **incus** *(see).* [Middle English *anvil(t)*, *anvelt*, Old English *anfealt*, *anfilt* : *an*, ON + *-fealt*, "beaten" (see **pel-⁶** in Appendix*).]

3 ——

4 ——

5 ——

6 ——

anx·i·e·ty (ăng-zī′ə-tē) *n., pl.* **-ties. 1.** A state of uneasiness and distress about future uncertainties; apprehension; worry. **2.** A cause of such uneasiness; a worry. **3.** *Psychiatry.* Intense fear or dread lacking an unambiguous cause or a specific threat. **4.** Eagerness. [Latin *anxietās,* from *anxius,* ANXIOUS.]

7 ——

8 ——

     Synonyms: *anxiety, worry, care, concern, solicitude.* These nouns express troubled states of mind. *Anxiety* suggests feelings of fear and concern detached from objective sources, feeding themselves, as it were. *Worry* implies persistent doubt or fear that produces strong mental agitation. *Care,* often in the plural, implies mental oppression of varying degree arising from heavy responsibilities. *Concern* has more to do with serious thought than with emotion, and stresses personal involvement in the source of mental unrest. *Solicitude* is active concern for the well-being of another person or persons.

anx·ious (ăngk′shəs, ăng′shəs) *adj.* **1.** Worried and strained about some uncertain event or matter; uneasy. **2.** Attended with, showing, or causing such worry; full of anxieties. **3.** Eagerly or earnestly desirous. —See Synonyms at **eager.** [Latin *anxius,* from *angere,* to torment, choke. See **angh-** in Appendix.*] —**anx′ious·ly** *adv.* —**anx′ious·ness** *n.*

     Usage: *Anxious* is often followed by *for, about,* or an infinitive: *anxious for* (or *about*) *your safety; anxious to avoid danger.* The adjectives *anxious* and *eager* overlap to some extent, where *anxious* denotes "eagerly or earnestly desirous," but *anxious* is more appropriate in such contexts when there is some implication of apprehension or concern: *"Charlie had never fallen in love, but was anxious to do so on the first opportunity"* (Kipling). Where such implication is absent, *eager* is preferable: *eager to see your new car.* The example *anxious to see your new car* is unacceptable in writing to 72 per cent of the Usage Panel, but acceptable in speech to 63 per cent.

9 ——

10 ——

anvil

The American Heritage Dictionary of the English Language. Ed. William Morris. New York: American Heritage, 1969. [AHD]

1   gives a slightly different pronunciation for *anvil*

2   provides photograph.

3   offers an additional meaning for *anvil.*

4   labels *anvil* meaning *incus* as a special meaning in anatomy, but does not define *incus* nor reference illustration.

5   lists etymology at end of entry; provides a separate list of Indo-European bases in an Appendix.

6   definition uses nouns—"uneasiness," "apprehension," "worry"—where *NWD* uses verbs—"being uneasy, apprehensive, or worried about."

7   gives a slightly different psychiatric definition: Here *anxiety* must be without a specific cause or threat.

8   offers discrimination of synonyms after entry—in *NWD* this appears at *care.*

9   gives a separate usage note, citing the opinion of a panel of writers on *anxious* used to mean *eager.*

10   provides no entries for *anxious seat* and *anxious bench.*

FIGURE 11.2   A Second College Dictionary

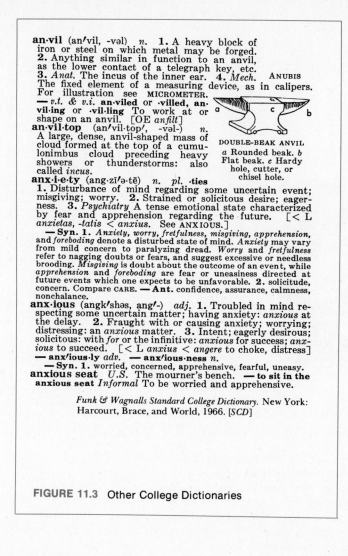

an·vil (an′vil, -vəl) *n.* **1.** A heavy block of iron or steel on which metal may be forged. **2.** Anything similar in function to an anvil, as the lower contact of a telegraph key, etc. **3.** *Anat.* The incus of the inner ear. **4.** *Mech.* The fixed element of a measuring device, as in calipers. For illustration see MICROMETER. — *v.t.* & *v.i.* **an·viled** or **·villed, an·vil·ing** or **·vil·ling** To work at or shape on an anvil. [OE *anfilt*]

ANUBIS

an·vil·top (an′vil·top′, -vəl-) *n.* A large, dense, anvil-shaped mass of cloud formed at the top of a cumulonimbus cloud preceding heavy showers or thunderstorms: also called *incus.*

DOUBLE-BEAK ANVIL
a Rounded beak. *b* Flat beak. *c* Hardy hole, cutter, or chisel hole.

anx·i·e·ty (ang·zī′ə·tē) *n.* *pl.* **·ties** **1.** Disturbance of mind regarding some uncertain event; misgiving; worry. **2.** Strained or solicitous desire; eagerness. **3.** *Psychiatry* A tense emotional state characterized by fear and apprehension regarding the future. [< L *anxietas, -tatis* < *anxius.* See ANXIOUS.]
— **Syn. 1.** *Anxiety, worry, fretfulness, misgiving, apprehension,* and *foreboding* denote a disturbed state of mind. *Anxiety* may vary from mild concern to paralyzing dread. *Worry* and *fretfulness* refer to nagging doubts or fears, and suggest excessive or needless brooding. *Misgiving* is doubt about the outcome of an event, while *apprehension* and *foreboding* are fear or uneasiness directed at future events which one expects to be unfavorable. **2.** solicitude, concern. Compare CARE. — **Ant.** confidence, assurance, calmness, nonchalance.

anx·ious (angk′shəs, ang′-) *adj.* **1.** Troubled in mind respecting some uncertain matter; having anxiety: *anxious* at the delay. **2.** Fraught with or causing anxiety; worrying; distressing: an *anxious* matter. **3.** Intent; eagerly desirous; solicitous: with *for* or the infinitive: *anxious* for success; *anxious* to succeed. [< L *anxius* < *angere* to choke, distress] — **anx′ious·ly** *adv.* — **anx′ious·ness** *n.*
— **Syn. 1.** worried, concerned, apprehensive, fearful, uneasy.

anxious seat *U.S.* The mourner's bench. — **to sit in the anxious seat** *Informal* To be worried and apprehensive.

Funk & Wagnalls Standard College Dictionary. New York: Harcourt, Brace, and World, 1966. [*SCD*]

FIGURE 11.3 Other College Dictionaries

Problem Three. The dictionary as a source of knowledge The answers to the questions below should be available in your standard college dictionary, with some thought and some hunting. With the hunting should come an increased sense of what's in your dictionary and how to get at it. Answer as many questions as you can—not all college dictionaries provide information to answer all questions.

a. What do the following words have in common: *pompadour, silhouette, quisling, leotard*? Add one more word to the list.

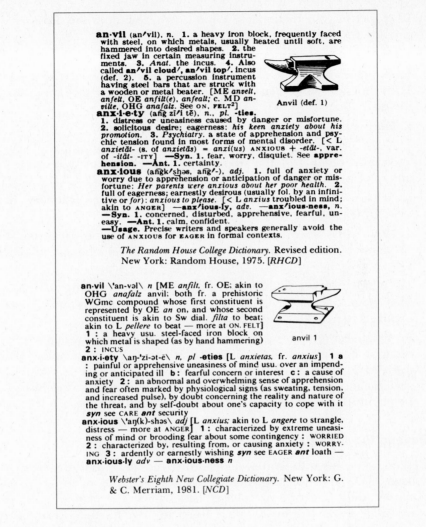

an·vil (an'vil), *n.* **1.** a heavy iron block, frequently faced with steel, on which metals, usually heated until soft, are hammered into desired shapes. **2.** the fixed jaw in certain measuring instruments. **3.** *Anat.* the incus. **4.** Also called **an'vil cloud'**, **an'vil top'**, incus (def. 2). **5.** a percussion instrument having steel bars that are struck with a wooden or metal beater. [ME *anvelt, anfelt,* OE *anfilt(e),* *anfealt; c.* MD *anvilte,* OHG *anafalz.* See ON, FELT²]

Anvil (def. 1)

anx·i·e·ty (ang zī'i tē), *n., pl.* **-ties.** **1.** distress or uneasiness caused by danger or misfortune. **2.** solicitous desire; eagerness: *his keen anxiety about his promotion.* **3.** *Psychiatry.* a state of apprehension and psychic tension found in most forms of mental disorder. [< L *anxietāt-* (s. of *anxietās*) = *anxi(us)* ANXIOUS + *-etāt-*, var. of *-itāt-* -ITY] **—Syn. 1.** fear, worry, disquiet. See **apprehension. —Ant. 1.** certainty.

anx·ious (angk'shəs, ang'-), *adj.* **1.** full of anxiety or worry due to apprehension or anticipation of danger or misfortune: *Her parents were anxious about her poor health.* **2.** full of eagerness; earnestly desirous (usually fol. by an infinitive or for): *anxious to please.* [< L *anxius* troubled in mind; akin to ANGER] **—anx'ious·ly,** *adv.* **—anx'ious·ness,** *n.* **—Syn. 1.** concerned, disturbed, apprehensive, fearful, uneasy. **—Ant. 1.** calm, confident.
—Usage. Precise writers and speakers generally avoid the use of ANXIOUS for EAGER in formal contexts.

The Random House College Dictionary. Revised edition. New York: Random House, 1975. [*RHCD*]

an·vil \'an-vəl\ *n* [ME *anfilt,* fr. OE; akin to OHG *anafalz* anvil; both fr. a prehistoric WGmc compound whose first constituent is represented by OE *an* on, and whose second constituent is akin to Sw dial. *filta* to beat; akin to L *pellere* to beat — more at ON. FELT] **1** : a heavy usu. steel-faced iron block on which metal is shaped (as by hand hammering) **2** : INCUS

anvil 1

anx·i·ety \aŋ-'zī-ət-ē\ *n, pl* **-eties** [L *anxietas,* fr. *anxius*] **1 a** : painful or apprehensive uneasiness of mind usu. over an impending or anticipated ill **b** : fearful concern or interest **c** : a cause of anxiety **2** : an abnormal and overwhelming sense of apprehension and fear often marked by physiological signs (as sweating, tension, and increased pulse), by doubt concerning the reality and nature of the threat, and by self-doubt about one's capacity to cope with it *syn* see CARE *ant* security

anx·ious \'aŋ(k)-shəs\ *adj* [L *anxius;* akin to L *angere* to strangle, distress — more at ANGER] **1** : characterized by extreme uneasiness of mind or brooding fear about some contingency : WORRIED **2** : characterized by, resulting from, or causing anxiety : WORRYING **3** : ardently or earnestly wishing *syn* see EAGER *ant* loath — **anx·ious·ly** *adv* — **anx·ious·ness** *n*

Webster's Eighth New Collegiate Dictionary. New York: G. & C. Merriam, 1981. [*NCD*]

b. Explain why the word *oxymoron* is itself an oxymoron. Is *sophomore* an oxymoron?

c. What three things do the following people have in common: George Sand, Isak Dinesen, George Eliot?

d. How are each of these word-pairs related: *map* and *apron, canary* and *canine, grammar* and *glamour*?

e. What is (or are) the plural (or plurals) of *agenda*? Of *fish*? Of *focus*? Of *syllabus*? Of *datum*?

f. Is *ain't* in your dictionary? What usage label does the dictionary provide for the word?

g. Why is *colonel* pronounced with an /r/?

h. Is there any historical basis for the pronunciation "axt" for *ask*? Is this metathesis or zeugma? Does your dictionary give an example of zeugma?

i. How is the word *bird* an example of metathesis?

j. Is the pronunciation "gotcha" for "got you" an example of palatalization or of a glottal stop? Does your dictionary give an example of palatalization?

k. What is the earliest meaning, recorded in your dictionary, of *nice*? Of *fond*?

l. How tall is an orangutan? While you're at it, be prepared to pronounce *queue, congeries,* and *arctic.* Is *congeries* singular or plural?

m. Which two words share essentially the same meaning: *abridged, bowdlerized, expurgated*? Is your dictionary abridged, bowdlerized, or expurgated? Or all three? Why, or why not?

n. What secret history connects the following words, which would seem at first glance to be unrelated? The *fetlock* of a horse, the *pawn* in a game of chess, a *trapeze* and a *trapezoid,* a *pedestrian,* a *podium,* an *octopus,* and a *cephalopod.* How does that secret history help with the meanings of *tripod, podiatrist,* and *impediment*? ■

Beyond the College Dictionary

Certain problems with words will lead the student beyond the standard college dictionary—to slang dictionaries, for example, or to larger dictionaries (only one or two college dictionaries, for example, list the word *callipygian*). These works are listed in "For Further Reading" at the end of the chapter. But we should take special note of the best historical dictionary in English, *The Oxford English Dictionary* (*OED*). This kind of dictionary traces how words change through time.

The *OED*, published in thirteen volumes between 1890 and 1933, remains a remarkable achievement. Some of the etymological information in the *OED* is outdated, and the dictionary is weak in covering Americanisms (ignored or shunted off to an appendix). Nevertheless, it remains an invaluable storehouse for students of literature (who'll find the meaning of Shakespeare's words), for lawyers (who'll find the meaning that interstate commerce had in 1776), for historians and political scientists, and for students of language in general (and we're all "students of language" in this sense). Figure 11.4 gives the *OED* entries for anvil and related words, and it comments on the information in the dictionary.

We add one final but important note: on the limits of dictionaries. No dictionary, regardless of its scope, can include everything about a word—its connotation, register, metaphoric transfers, slang uses, and so on. Even if a dictionary attempted such an impossible task, the information would be out-of-date by the time the dictionary appeared. The reader can expect a dictionary to define words clearly, with occasional examples, to provide distinctions among closely related words, to warn about some words, and to give clear and accurate pronunciations and etymologies. If the reader is unwise enough to accept such help as "laws writ in stone," the problem is not the dictionary's.

ENGLISH AS LANGUAGE

Our dictionary samples give us more of those pesky abbreviations: OE, ODu, OHG, Ger, MD, L, ME, and IE, among others. All dictionaries provide lists of abbreviations. But a mere list gives only the "what" of language change, and, to get command of the secret history of words, you need to understand the "why" of language change.

This section explains the "why" of word history with a brief history of English and its ancestors, focusing on changes in vocabulary. You should find that the common abbreviations like those above take on a fuller meaning, a logic of their own.

The moral of this brief history is straightforward: Much of the power and flexibility of English grows out of the successive enrichment of its vocabulary by borrowing and adapting. Moreover, much of the internal sense of words that you carry in your head—their register, level of abstraction, metaphoric extensions (the subject-matter of chapter Ten)—can be explained by the history of words within the language.

All languages change constantly (because each generation learns the language anew). When speakers of a single language separate into two groups—perhaps by one group migrating to a new territory—the dialect of each group changes in different ways. At some point, the two groups are no longer able to understand each other, and one language splits into two languages, different but clearly related. We have historical evidence of such a change in the case of Latin. After the fall of the Roman Empire in the fifth century A.D., the various Latin-speaking groups in Europe lost touch with each other, and Latin developed into the "Romance" languages, so named for their Roman source—Portuguese, Spanish, French, Italian, Romanian. These are distinct languages; a Romanian speaker will not understand a French speaker. But

ANVIL.

Anvil (æ·nvil), *sb.* Forms: 1 onfilti, onfilt(e, anfilte, 4 anfelt, -uylt, anefelt, -feld, 4–5 anfeld, -velt, 5 aneuelt, anuylde, anduell, 5–6 andfelde, 6 anvelde, anuilde, anuielde, (hanfeld), and(e)-vile, 6–7 anfeeld, anvild, anvile, anvill, 6– anvil. [Etymol. uncertain. OE. *onfilti*, is prob. cogn. w. ODu. dial. *aenvilte* (Verdam I. 184), and OHG. *anafalz*; f. *an, on,* prep. + a possible **filt-an* to weld, cf. *felt,* Ger. *filz,* and *falz* in *falz-ambosz.* The *f* has become *v* as in *silver,* and the final *t,* passing through *d,* is lost, as is frequent in dialects.

Onfilti, anafalz, can hardly be distinct from synonymous forms with *b*: OHG. *anaboɮ,* LG. *anebolt, anebelte, ambult,* ODu. *aenbilt,* usually derived from **aen-billen* = 'aankloppen', to strike upon' (Verdam 80); but more prob. an early variant of *aenvilte* above, due to some confusion. In OHG. *anaboɮ,* Sievers suggests a confusion of *anafalɮ* with the distinct *anabôɮ, anapôɮ,* MHG. *aneboɮ,* mod.G. *ambosz,* from *an + bôɮ-an,* Eng. BEAT. Mod.Du. *aanbeeld, ambeld,* seems assimilated to *beelden,* to form, fashion.]

1. The block (usually of iron) on which the smith hammers and shapes the metal which he is working.

a **800** *Corpus Gl.* (Sweet *O. E. T.*) 1071 *Incuda,* onfilti. *c* **1000** ÆLFRIC *Gram.* ix. § 33. 60 *Incus,* anfilt. *c* **1000** in Wright *Voc.* 286/2 *Cudo,* anfilte. *c* **1369** CHAUCER *Blaunche* 1165 As his brothers hamers ronge, Vpon his anuelt vp and downe [*v. r.* anuelet]. *c* **1380** *Sir Ferumb.* 1308 Anuylt, tange & slegge. **1388** WYCLIF *Ecclus.* xxxviii. 29 A smyth sittynge bisidis the anefelt. **1398** TREVISA *Barth. De P. R.* XVI. iv, Golde .. bitwene þe anfelde [**1495** andfelde] and þe hamoure .. streccheþ in- to golde foyle. **1413** LYDG. *Pylgr. Sowle* IV. xxx. (1483) 78 Harder than the hamour or the aneuelt. **1483** CAXTON *Gold. Leg* 358/1 They smyte on the stythye or anduell. ?*a* **1500** *Virgilius* in Thoms *E. E. Pr. Rom.* II. 44 They smyte vpon a anuilde. **1530** PALSGR. 740 To stryke with his hammer upon his anvelde. **1543** TRAHERON *Vigo's Chirurg.* IV. 14 d, A styth, or hanfeld. **1589** WARNER *Alb. Eng.* VI. xxx. (1612) 147 Vulcan .. limping from the Anfeeld. **1607** HIERON *Wks.* I. 439 Wee be like the smiths dog, who, the harder the anuile is beaten on, lieth by, and sleepes the sounder. **1611** BIBLE *Isa.* xli. 7 Him that smote the anuill. **1808** SCOTT *Marm.* v. vi, The armourer's anvil clashed and rang.

2. *fig.* (the whole expression being usually metaphorical).

1534 LD. BERNERS *Gold. Bk. M. Aurel.* (1546) E ij, My spyrite is betwene the harde anuielde and the importunate hammer. *c* **1593** SPENSER *Sonnet* xxxii, The playnts and prayers with which I Doe beat on th'anduyle of her stubberne wit. **1605** CAMDEN *Rem.* 200 Hammering me vpon the anvild. **1677** R. GILPIN *Dæmonol. Sacr.* (1867) 214 Our present posture doth furnish him [Satan] with arguments; he forgeth his javelins upon our anvil. **1845** FORD *Handbk. Spain* i. 59 They have yet to learn that the stomach is the anvil whereon health is forged. **1864** BURTON *Scot Abr.* I. i. 34 Hardened on the anvil of a war for national freedom. **1883** SIR H. BRAND in *Standard* 18 May 3/3 Matters that, so to speak, are on the anvil of the House of Commons.

b. *phr.* **On or upon the anvil**: in preparation, in hand.

1623 HOWELL *Lett.* (1650) II. 29 Matters while they are in agitation and upon the anvill. *a* **1674** CLARENDON *Hist. Reb.* I. II. 110 The Earl of Strafford .. whose destruction was then upon the anvil. **1755** *Mem. Capt. P. Drake* II. iii. 154 There was Rumours of a Peace being on the Anvil. **1785** BURKE *Nabob of Arcot Wks.* 1842 I. 319 He has now on the anvil another scheme.

3. *transf.* Anything resembling a smith's anvil in shape or use.

1678 BUTLER *Hud.* III. i. 340 When less Delinquents have been scourg'd, And Hemp on wooden Anvils forg'd. **1881** GREENER *Gun* 294 The anvil is shaped like an escutcheon, and is inserted in the cup of the cap, with the point against the detonating powder.

342

b. *esp.* in *Phys.* One of the bones of the ear; so called from its being struck by another bone called the 'hammer.' ————12

[**1594** T. B. *La Primaud. Fr. Acad.* II. To Reader, Who hath fashioned the instruments of hearing in the head like to a hammer and an anvile.] **1687** *Death's Vision* iii. 21 When the Perceptive Hammer shall not .. Consign Prescribed Blow Unto the Wonted Anvil. **1718** J. CHAMBERLAYNE *Relig. Philos.* I. xiii. § 5 The Auditory Bones are four in Number, the Hammer, the Anvil, etc. **1879** CALDERWOOD *Mind & Brain* 71 The head of the hammer rests on the central bone known as the anvil.

4. *Comb.* and *Attrib.*, as *anvil-block, -maker*, etc.; also **anvil-beater**, a smith; **anvil-headed** *a.*, having a head shaped like an anvil; **anvil-proof**, the standard of hardness of an anvil; **anvil rock** (see quot.); **anvil-smith**, a forger of anvils. ————13

1870 BRYANT *Homer* II. XVIII. 219 He spake, and from his anvil-block arose. **1677** *Cleveland's Poems* Ep. Ded. A iij b, Venus is again unequally yoaked with a sooty Anvile-beater. **1851** MELVILLE *Whale* xlvii. 303 The anvil-headed whale. **1616** BEAUM. & FL. *Faithf. Fr.* II. iii, Though their scullcaps be of anvil-proof, This blade shall hammer some of 'em. **1862** DANA *Man. Geol.* 330 Above the twelfth [coal bed in Kentucky] there is the massive Sandstone .. called the Anvil Rock, from the form of two masses of it in South-western Kentucky. **1831** J. HOLLAND *Manuf. Metal* I. 90 Some anvil-smiths .. forge the upper part .. out of one piece of iron.

Anvil (æ·nvil), *v.* [f. prec. sb.] ————14

1. *trans.* To fashion ɔn the anvil; chiefly *fig.*

1607 DEKKER *Wh. Babylon* F iij, Whilest our thunderbolts Are anuiling abroad. *c* **1700** *Gentl. Instr.* (1732) 303 You are now anvilling out some petty Revenge. **1748** RICHARDSON *Clarissa* (1811) VIII. 267 A roguery .. ready anvilled and hammered for execution.

2. *intr.* To work at an anvil.

1882 *Manch. Guard.* 7 June, Thomas anvilled away at burning horse-shoes. ————15

Anvilling (æ·nviliŋ), *vbl. sb. rare.* [f. ANVIL *v.* + -ING1.] Hammering out; chiefly *fig.*

1662 PHILLIPS *Dict.* Ded., What Siftings, Anvelings, Traversings, there ought to be of Authours.

Anwald, -weald, var. ONWALD, *Obs.*, power. ————16

1   does not divide word into syllables.

2   gives only modern British pronunciation (although spellings, given next, provide information about earlier pronunciations).

3   uses *sb.*, "substantive," in place of *noun*. (The key to abbreviations in the *OED* is given at the beginning of each volume.)

4   lists all recorded spelling forms, cited by century—*4–5* means 1400s and 1500s. (Spelling forms are of some interest: Note that they suggest the connection of *an-* and *on-* with *on;* note also that earlier writers used *u* and *v* interchangeably, so that 5 "aneuelt" should be read "anevelt.")

5   offers remarkably full etymology, with references to authorities (cited in full form in the final volume).

6   lists meanings in order of their appearance in the language.

7   gives brief but clear definition.

8   follows definitions with historical examples of the use of the word, beginning with the first recorded example. Examples give date, source (listed in full in the final volume), and original spelling—Chaucer's example, from 1369, might be translated, "As his brother's hammer rung, Upon his anvelt up and down." (Note also that such citations can give important information about the connotations and register of the word.)

9   includes metaphorical transfers.

10 includes phrases within entries.
11 includes full listing of transferred senses.
12 does not give technical definition of *incus* for the "anvil of the ear" (not current in 1890).
13 lists all compounds and attributive uses.
14 lists verb form separately.
15 lists "verbal substantive" form separately.
16 lists references to alternate spellings of obsolete words, here *onwald*, OE *on* + *weald* ("wealth or possessions"), replaced by French *power* (though it continues in *commonweal* and *commonwealth*).

FIGURE 11.4 Entries from the *Oxford English Dictionary* [*OED*]

the historical connection will be seen in their vocabularies. Figure 11.5 shows the connection between the words for "foot," "fish," "ten," and "tooth" in Latin, Italian, French, and Romanian, and the lack of connection with unrelated languages, Turkish, Japanese, and Swahili.[3]

Similarly, the English words *foot, fish, ten,* and *tooth* seem closely related to the German and Dutch words (Dutch *v* is pronounced "f"). These comparisons suggest that English is a Germanic language (not directly descended from Latin, as many believe). Further, there are regular connections between the Germanic languages and the Romance languages—the Latin *p* in *pedis* and *piscis* matches the Germanic *f* in *fuss* and *fisch;* Latin *d* in *decem* and *dentis* becomes English *t* in *ten* and *tooth.* This connection suggests that Romance and Germanic languages may share some more distant ancestor.

By examining hundreds of such examples, we can make some good guesses about how languages are related, and we can speculate about the nature of earlier forms of language families, forms for which we have no historical records (called "reconstruction"). English, German, Latin, and even Sanskrit and modern Hindi are part of the *Indo-European* language family. The ancestor of all Indo-European languages has been "reconstructed"; it is called *Indo-European* (IE in dictionary abbreviations) or Proto-Indo-European (PIE), since it is a "first" form (Greek *proto*, "first," as in *prototype* and *protoplasm*). Reconstructed IE forms are marked with asterisks, to show that they are "guessed-at" forms. We've already met IE **bhreg-*, "break," and **leg*, "to collect or speak"; and the IE form underlying both our *dentist* (a word obviously borrowed from Latin) and our *tooth* (native English) is **dent-*. Speakers of Indo-European, in the course of thousands of years, migrated across Europe, through the Near East, and into northern India. Figure 11.6 offers a simplified chart of the Indo-European language family. It includes all the languages spoken in central Europe (except Basque, a

INDO-EUROPEAN LANGUAGES				

Germanic Languages				
English:	**foot**	**fish**	**ten**	**tooth**
German:	fuss	fisch	zehn	zahn
Dutch:	voet	vis	tien	tant

Latin and the Romance Languages				
Latin:	pedis	pescis	decem	dentis
Italian:	piede	pesce	dieci	dente
French:	pied	poisson	dix	dent
Romanian:	piciov	peste	zece	dente

LANGUAGES NOT DEVELOPED FROM INDO-EUROPEAN				
Turkish:	ayak	balik	on	dis
Japanese:	ashi	sakana	jun	ha
Swahili:	mguu	samaki	kuma	jino

FIGURE 11.5 The Words *Foot, Fish, Ten,* and *Tooth* in Related and Unrelated Languages

language spoken in northern Spain), Russian and the Slavic languages, and, through Sanskrit, Modern Hindi.

English was not the first language spoken in England—that appears to be Celtic, a language that has now disappeared. Speakers of Celtic were conquered by three or perhaps four Germanic-speaking tribes—Angles, Saxons, Jutes, and Frisians—who invaded England in the middle of the fourth century A.D. These tribes spoke dialects of West Germanic, which merged to become the earliest form of English, called either Anglo-Saxon (abbreviated AS in dictionaries) or, as here, Old English (OE). By A.D. 600, speakers of Old English had been converted to Christianity, incidentally adopting the Roman alphabet, and written records begin to appear.

English is commonly divided into three periods, roughly dated as follows (with common dictionary abbreviations in parentheses):

- Old English (OE or AS): A.D. 400–1100
- Middle English (ME): 1100–1500
- Modern English (ModE or MnE): 1500–present

(The dictionary abbreviation *O* almost always means "old," and the abbreviation *M* almost always means "middle"—so OHG is Old High German and MF is Middle French, and so on.)

The dates attached to these labels are quite arbitrary. People did not make a group decision to stop speaking Middle English and start speaking Modern English on August 18, 1500. In fact, people alive at that time must have felt much as you do about language change: They were aware that speakers from different social backgrounds and from different areas spoke in different ways, and they were probably aware that some ways of speaking were old-fashioned while others were new-fangled (to use a good old-fashioned word that dates back at least to 1386). But they were not fully aware, any more than we are, that they were taking part in the gradual changing of language. Nevertheless, as Chaucer noted six hundred years ago, "in forme of speche is chaunge," and no language remains fixed or static.

Old English

We've been told that speakers of modern Icelandic have an easier time reading Old English than do speakers of Modern English. Certainly an Old English sentence looks rather foreign at first glance:

11.13 Bed him thet he scolde him given ealle that minstre tha haethen men haefden aer tobroccon.

We might pick out a word or two (*given, men*), and a closer look reveals the bedrock of vocabulary that continues from a thousand years ago. *Bed* is a shortened form of "he bade," meaning "he ordered" (modern *bid*); *scolde* is modern *should; minstre* means "monasteries" (related to ModE *minister* and *ministry*); and *tobroccon* is related to ModE *broke*, used here in the sense of "destroy":

11.13A [He] ordered him that he should give him all the monasteries the heathen men had destroyed.

As our example suggests, a remarkable amount of the vocabulary of OE remains in the language today. The ordinary words, the stuff of everyday life, tend to carry directly through from Old English: *home, life, heart, love*. One theory suggests that Old English words make up only ten to fifteen percent of the words in Modern English, but, be-

The chart emphasizes Western languages, especially those leading to English.

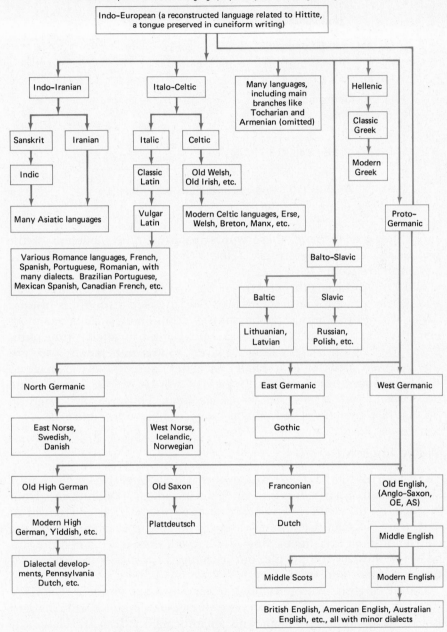

FIGURE 11.6 Simplified Chart of the Indo-European Language Family (from Robert M. Gorrell and Charlton Laird, *Modern English Handbook*, 6th ed. [Englewood Cliffs, N.J.: Prentice-Hall, 1976])

Normal Change	Primary Sources for Borrowing
Indo-European (IE)	
⇓	
Germanic (Gmc)	
⇓	
Old English (OE) ⇐	Latin (L) Danish (D, Dan)

FIGURE 11.7   Sources of Old English Vocabulary

cause they are so basic, these words make up ninety percent of the words we use in common talk. (How many of our words, in that last sentence, are from OE?)

Old English began the process of borrowing words from other languages, the process that has enriched the language through its history. Along with Christianity came borrowings from Latin, such as our modern *angel, candle, priest, church,* and *wine.* Danish invaders often plundered the English coast, sailing up rivers to loot settlements; they are the "heathen men" of example 11.13. They caused severe damage to the population, but they left a legacy of words—*sky, leg, scowl, thrust, spear, band, scab, slaughter, rape, crawl, die, crave.* Thus, we have a natural process of change enriched by borrowing, as shown in Figure 11.7.

Middle English

What spurred Old English to become Middle English? Quite simply, another raiding party, this time one that stayed. In 1066, invaders from Normandy, in northern France, conquered the English and stayed to rule (the Norman Conquest). French became the language of the courts and the government. English survived, since it remained the language of most of the people, but it changed drastically in pronunciation, grammar, and vocabulary.

Middle English is recognizably English. Here is a sample by Geoffrey Chaucer, writing in 1385 to compare changes in language with changes in courtship; we might begin with an informal modern translation of his remarks:

11.14A   You also know that the form of speech changes in a thousand years, and words that had value then now seem foolish and strange to us. Yet they spoke them that way, and succeeded as well in love as men do now. It's the same way with love: They have different customs in different ages and in different lands.

With that preview, Chaucer's original version shouldn't be impossible to understand:

11.14 Ye knowe ek that in forme of speche is chaunge
Withinne a thousand yeer, and wordes tho
That hadden pris, now wonder nyce and straunge
Us thinketh hem, and yet thei spake him so,
And spedde as wel in love as men now do;
Ek for to wynnen love in sondry ages,
In sondry londes, sondry be usages.

Troilus and Criseyde (1385)

Of course, the passage needs a few explanations. *Ek* is "also" (it remains buried in the language in "nickname," originally "an ek name"); *pris* (ModE *price*) is used in the sense of "value" (frozen in the phrase, "pearl of great price"); *spedde* meant "to go on, to succeed" (frozen in the old-fashioned "Godspeed"); *sondry* is ModE *sundry,* or "various" (as in the "sundries counter" of a drugstore).

Chaucer's words give us a sense of what happened to the vocabulary of Middle English: The stock of OE words remains (*know, in, of, love*), but layered on top of them is a set of words borrowed from French (*change, price, nice, strange, age, usage*). These words have been so "Englished" now that we're hardly aware of them as borrowed, but Chaucer shows the influence of French in his spelling of *chaunge* and *straunge.*

The fact that Chaucer, an educated court figure who knew French well, would choose to write in English in 1385 suggests that the English language was resurfacing as a socially acceptable language. As French noblemen remained in England over generations, English became more and more the proper medium of communication, not merely the common one.

When English resurfaces, it has become heavily "Frenchified" in its vocabulary. French words sometimes replaced English words, as F *ocean* replaced OE *wide-sea,* for example. More often, French words parallelled English words, taking on a slight difference in meaning, connotation, or register (F *people* and OE *folk;* F *adolescent* and OE *youth;* F *labor* and OE *work;* F *appellation* and OE *name;* F *story* and OE *tale*). As our examples suggest, the French borrowings seem generally more formal in register, often more neutral in connotation, and sometimes more restricted in meaning. Dictionaries indicate words borrowed from

Normal Change		Primary Sources for Borrowing
Indo-European (IE)		
⇓		
Germanic		
⇓		
Old English (OE)	⇐	{ Latin (L) { Danish (D, Dan)
⇓		
Middle English (ME)	⇐	French (F, also OF, MF)

FIGURE 11.8   Sources of Middle English Vocabulary

French with the abbreviation *F*, often *OF* (Old French) or *MF* (Middle French). And most French words, we'll recall, originate in Latin (*L*). These borrowings are summarized in Figure 11.8.

We'll mention one other fact of interest about Middle English: Our printed form of language develops at this time, basically between 1400 and 1500. It develops first as a means of government communication, as court documents begin to be written in English rather than French or Latin, and this government standard is still the basis of written English. Government clerks came from different parts of the country, with different dialects, but they seem to have worked together to form common habits of writing—to form an artificial standard, reflecting no single dialect. In spelling, the system in part reflected the pronunciation of Middle English (as in *knight* and *know* and *ghost*); more commonly, it tried to reflect the origin of Latin and French borrowings (so that the word commonly spelled *dette* became *debt*, and *faute* became *fault*). The matter was settled, as far as written English was concerned, when William Caxton, bringing the first printing press to England in 1476, chose to settle in Westminster, the seat of government, rather than in London, the center of business. Caxton used the artificial written standard to print books, creating what we call the print code, an artificial system, related to no single dialect.

Problem Four. Explaining language change   English words for fowl are the same for the animal and for the meat—the *duck* that quacks is the *duck* we eat, the *chicken* that pecks in the barnyard is the *chicken* we fry, and so on. The same is true of words for animals in most Indo-European languages. Thus, French *venaison* means both English *deer* and English *venison, porc* means both *pork* and *pig, boeuf* is both *beef* and *cattle.* English, however, has two sets of terms, one for the meat (*venison, beef, veal, pork, mutton*), and another for the animal (*deer, cow, calf, swine, sheep*). Try to explain this feature of English, checking the etymology of these words if necessary.

Similarly, note that the words for common occupations tend to come from Old English—*maker, baker, miller, blacksmith*—while those for skilled trades tend to be borrowed from French—*physician, attorney, judge, tailor, constable.* Can you explain this feature of English? How is your explanation related to the question of terms for animals and meat, above? And how do you explain apparent exceptions, such as *servant* and *butler,* borrowed from the French? ■

Modern English

By 1500, English approaches its modern form, and it turns to a new source for borrowing. In essence, English suffers another invasion, this time an invasion of words, Latin words. Education was conducted primarily in Latin, and the period itself is known as the Renaissance (French *re + naissance,* "rebirth"), for the renewed emphasis on classical learning. In fact, the original English meaning of *literate,* Latin "lettered," was "able to read and write Latin." Thus it was natural for English writers, schooled in Latin, to bring Latin words into the language. And they came into our reading and writing vocabularies as a flood: *abdomen, resuscitate, edition, decorum, paragraph, benefit, cadaver.* Some borrowings proved unnecessary, and quickly disappeared; others remained to enrich the language. We borrowed and quickly discarded *suppediate, illecebrous, exciccate,* and *aspectable;* we borrowed and kept *scientific, external,* and *obvious.*

The result of this borrowing was to give English example after example of word sets with roughly the same denotative meaning, but with subtle shifts in register. We can *start* (OE), *commence* (F), or *initiate* (L); we can *end* (OE), *finish* (F), or *terminate* (L). We can be OE *bad,* F *evil,* or L *malevolent;* we can OE *draw* or L *delineate,* be OE *old* or F *aged,* think with our OE *brain* or our L *cerebrum,* have an OE *belly* or an L *stomach.* Above all, as Shakespeare knew well, we can enjoy the range of words available to us:

11.15 Therefore, you clown, abandon—which is in the vulgar leave—the society—which in the boorish is company—of this female—which in the common is woman; which together is, abandon the society of this female, or clown, thou perishest; or, to thy better understanding, diest.

As You Like It (1592)

Problem Five. Reading Shakespeare   Many words have changed in meaning since Shakespeare wrote (roughly 1580 to 1603). You may be able to figure out the meanings by context; in some cases we've provided hints; and in other cases you'll need to consult a dictionary. Identify the meanings of the italicized words.

a. "Mice, rats, and such small *deer*." (*King Lear*)

b. "Thy head is as full of quarrels as an egg is full of *meat*." (*Romeo and Juliet*) Hints: the frozen "meat and drink"; the sentence cited in *c* below.

c. "I'll make a ghost of him who *lets* me." (*Hamlet*) Hints: a "let serve" in tennis; a sentence written in 1584: "Much meat eaten at night grieveth the stomach and letteth natural rest."

d. "I dreamt a dream *tonight*." (*Romeo and Juliet*)

e. "Doth she not count her blest . . . that we have wrought so worthy a gentleman to be her *bride*?" (*Romeo and Juliet*)

f. "My ships are safely come to *road*." (*Merchant of Venice*)

g. "Heaps of pearl, inestimable stones, *unvalued* jewels, all scattered in the bottom of the sea." (*Richard III*)

h. "O Captain! God's light, these villains will make the word as odious as the word *occupy*, which was an excellent word before it was ill-used." (*2 Henry IV*) A special challenge?   ■

Problem Six. Native words and borrowed words   The words in Group A are native English words; for each, find a borrowed French or Latin word. The words in Group B are borrowed from French or Latin; find a native English word for each. Which task proves to be harder? Why? Can you explain your findings in terms of our discussion of levels of vocabulary at the beginning of this chapter? Does your experience offer any suggestions for writers?[4]

Group A

chew	old	sell
walk	eat	believe
sad	friend	tell

Group B

repair	intense	terminate
prevaricate	desist	velocity
injure	decay	rotate

Most readers find that problem six gives solid backing to a common piece of advice: Prefer the native English word to the borrowed French or Latin word. Borrowed words tend, on the whole, to be only in reading vocabularies, while native English words are generally in our speaking vocabulary. Often it's surprisingly easy to replace a French or Latin word with a native English word, and we search for chances to do so in revising. Looking back through this manuscript, we find "converse" replaced by "talk," "utilize" by "use," "attempt" by "try," and in the last sentence (we almost wrote "the preceding sentence") "replace with" replaced "substitute for." Of course, it's not always possible to replace a Latinate word (we've used L *vocabulary* in this chapter, the OE *word-hoard* having disappeared). And, in some writing contexts, we may want to reach for the formality of voice that comes with a heavily Latinate vocabulary. But, if you think only of getting meaning across to the reader, prefer the native to the borrowed.

World English

We are tempted to add a fourth period of English to the conventional three—we would call it "World English." English in 1800 was a minor language, spoken by perhaps twenty million people in Britain and another million around the world. Today, English is spoken by at least three hundred million people. It is the first language learned by most citizens in North America, Great Britain, Jamaica, South Africa, New Zealand, and Australia, and it is the recognized language of government in Kenya, Pakistan, Uganda, Liberia, India, the Philippines, and elsewhere.

As a result, English has become a world language in its borrowings. We reach back to Greek for scientific words (*phonograph, television, chlorine, anthropoid*). Our Spanish heritage gives us *Chicano, adobe, tortilla, barbeque, potato* (originally from Nahuatl), and *tomato* (originally from Haitian). The list can be continued indefinitely: *sauerkraut* and *hamburger* from German; *kibitzer, phooey,* and *schlemiel* from Yiddish; *alcohol, algebra,* and *alcove* from Arabic; *bungalow, jungle,* and *pajamas* from Hindi; *tote, jazz, voodoo,* and *yam* from the west coast languages of Africa; *teak* from Dravidian; *coffee* from Turkish. And we in America have been taught to name our continent from Amerindian languages:

Normal Change		Primary Sources for Borrowing
Indo-European (IE)		
⇓		
Germanic (Gmc)		
⇓		
Old English (OE)	⇐	Latin (L) Danish (D, Dan)
⇓		
Middle English	⇐	French (F)
⇓		
Modern English (ModE, MnE)	⇐	Latin (L)
⇓		
"World English"	⇐	Greek (Gk)—in science World Languages

FIGURE 11.9   Sources of English Vocabulary

squash, skunk, possum, moose, Mississippi, Nantucket. The major sources of borrowing are summarized in Figure 11.9.

Problem Seven. A class project   This class project has two purposes: Individually, it asks you to become accustomed to using dictionary etymologies; as a class, it allows you to develop a sense of the dynamics of native and borrowed words as they are used in different contexts. Each member of the class should go to a different source, and look up the origin of the first twenty-five words in a randomly selected passage or speech. One student, for example, might pick twenty-five words by going down the page of a dictionary; another might copy down twenty-five words from an overheard conversation; another might select a passage from a college lecture. Try to gather a range of sources: the front page of a newspaper, a science text, a textbook that is hard to read and one that is easier to read, a good novel, and so on.

You might begin by discussing what you expect to find. One would expect, for example, to find more Latin words in print than in speech, and one might expect to find a high percentage of French words in legal writing or in cookbooks. (Why?)

Then look up the origin of your twenty-five words, classifying them as 1. native English (these words will go back to OE; often they will be traced back to a Germanic or IE root); 2. French (these words will come from French—F, OF, or MF—and often they will be traced back through Latin to IE); 3. Latin (these words will come directly from Latin, L); and 4. "other" (all other borrowings). Graph your results in a bar graph, working up from Native English to French to Latin to "other." Indicate the source of your passage at the top of the page. Compare your results as a class. ■

WORDS CHANGE MEANING WITH TIME

Our brief history of the language has suggested the importance of borrowing as a source of new words. But borrowing, important as it is, is not our major source of words.

By far the most common way of finding new words is to shift the meaning of an existing word. We can identify four primary shifts of meaning: *transfer, compounding, generalization,* and *specialization.*

Transfer involves moving a word from one meaning to another. Transfers can be small shifts in use, as when the noun *bank* (as in "Put your money in the bank") transfers to a verb ("Where do you bank?") and then to a figure of speech ("You can bank on it"). Often, however, transfers can involve complex figures of speech or analogies, as when breeze, "a small wind," becomes metaphorically "an easy course or examination" ("The math test was a breeze") or "an empty conversation" ("We were just shooting the breeze"). The *umbilical cord* of a spacecraft is an obvious transfer from anatomy to technology; *nose cone* and *abort* are similar transfers.

Compounding creates new words by putting words and word parts together. Compounds can be made up of two separate words: *double-date, babysit, splashdown,* and, of course, *breakfast.* Or, particularly in science, they can be created by combining parts of words—*trinitrotoluene, deoxyribonucleic acid. Rayon* was coined as a completely new word, but with the appearance of *dacron* and *orlon* we've created a new word part, *-on,* meaning something like "artificial fabric." *Hamburger* is the German city, *Hamburg,* plus the word part, *-er,* "from, or citizen of" (as in *Berliner* or *New Yorker*); words like *cheeseburger, doubleburger, fishburger,* and, sadly enough, *mamaburger,* imply that speakers break the word in a new way, *ham + burger.*

Indeed, we've lost our sense of the compounds that formed some words. *Breakfast, fulfill, oversee, forgive* still retain their original compounds, but other words have lost them—*daisy* was *daegeseage* in OE, "day's eye"; *garlic* was compounded of *gar* ("spear") and *leac* ("leek");

nostril from OE *nosu* ("nose") and *yrel* ("hole"). Some OE compounds have been lost, replaced by Latin or French equivalents—at times, we fear, not to the advantage of the language. OE *inwit* seems much more expressive than ModE *conscience; boc-craeft* ("book art") more to the point than *literature.*

The fascinating thing about compounding is the number of meanings that compounds can carry. A *lighthouse keeper* is not necessarily a *light housekeeper,* and, while a *blackboard* is black, a *surfboard* is hardly surf. A *maternity dress* is hardly comparable to a *paternity suit.* A *house dog* might possibly have a *doghouse,* but a *lapdog* does not have a lap, nor does a *house cat* have a *cathouse.*

Generalization is the spreading of a word from a narrow meaning to a larger one. *Barn* first meant a storehouse for barley (from a compound of OE *bere,* "barley," and *aern,* "house"); it has generalized to mean any building for storing grain (in England) or farm building generally (in American English). *Dreadfully* meant "full of dread, inspiring awe," yet we now speak of being "dreadfully bored." *Incredibly* meant "not to be believed," and *frightfully* meant "full of fright, terrifying"; stories can now be "incredibly true" and parties "frightfully dull." Similarly, we've generalized *immensely, mighty, perfectly,* and *pretty* so much that, in total disregard for earlier meanings, we can say "perfectly stupid," "immensely unimportant," "mighty weak," and "pretty ugly."

Often words generalize without our even being conscious of the process. The *New Century Dictionary* of 1927 defined *watch* as "a small timepiece operated by a coiled spring, for carrying on the person." Technology has carried us far beyond the coiled spring, and the word *watch* has quietly generalized to accommodate mechanisms with batteries, quartz crystals, LED readouts, and all the rest.[5]

Specialization is the opposite process, the narrowing of meaning. We saw this happening with euphemisms—*undertaker, pass away, drink. Starve* originally meant "to die" (as does German *sterben*); it's now so firmly specialized that we can talk about "starving to death." A *villain* was originally a servant or freeman; *vulgar* first meant simply "ordinary or common," as in the *Vulgate Bible; silly* once meant "innocent, simple." *Flour* and *flower* were the same word in ME: *Flour* was "the flower of wheat."

Examples like *villain, vulgar,* and *silly* show that specialization and generalization can involve shifts in connotation. Since we're concerned with increasing your vocabulary, we might offer the formal words for discussing changes in connotation. *Pejoration* is the process of going downhill in connotation. *Villain, vulgar,* and *silly* have added pejorative connotations. *Amelioration* is the opposite process, a word increasing in status; *knight* first meant "servant"; *earl* was originally OE *eorl,* "man";

enthusiasm was a pejorative word in the eighteenth century, suggesting fanaticism.

There are, of course, other ways to create words. Indeed, they can be invented from nothing, as were the trade names *Exxon* and *Kodak*. The following ways, however, are more common:

- *shortening.* We no sooner had television than we had *TV* in America and "the telly" in England. *Van* is a shortened form of *caravan; fan* is shortened from *fanatic,* and *cab* has replaced the longer *cabriolet,* a carriage.
- *acronyms.* Acronyms are words formed from initials. NASA and NATO now operate as words as well as abbreviations. *Radar* was coined from *RA*dio *D*etection *A*nd *R*anging system. The Goodyear company had no success with their first *limp,* or nonrigid, airship, the "A-limp"; the second, or "B-limp," was more successful—and a new acronym floated into the language: *blimp.*
- *blends.* Two or more words can be blended together to form a new word. Blends are common in advertising and journalism: *sexploitation, limon,* and, on television last night, *crunchewy* for a dog food and *stroft* for a toilet tissue. Other blends have escaped from their questionable origins: *smog* (a blend of *smoke* and *fog*), *brunch, motel.*
- *proper names.* Most of us have heard that the Earl of Sandwich, reluctant to leave the gambling tables, ordered his servants to slap a piece of meat between two slices of bread, entering his name into the language as he entered his invention into the kitchen. Fewer of us, however, are aware of the linguistic importance of Amelia Jenks *Bloomer,* or musician Adolphus *Sax,* or poor C. C. *Boycott,* the British soldier first victimized by his name. A *sadist* is not necessarily "sad"; the name (and the pronunciation) come from the infamous Marquis de Sade.

We can see these processes in more detail by tracing the development of a single word, *hackney. Hackeney* was a town in England, the origin of the word unknown. Around 1300, the name of the town transferred to a horse, particularly "a horse used for riding or driving," a *hackney horse* or a *hackney pony* in compounds. This first meaning carries down to modern English, particularly British English, in three overlapping senses. The most general is the original sense, an ordinary horse as opposed to a hunter or race horse, and thus, by transfer, a verb, *hacking,* and a clipped form, *hack.*

11.16 The hack is an outdoor horse, indeed all the best *hacking* used to be done in the country. . . . The hack was the horse on

which farmers rode round their farms, or which carried hunting
men to the meet while grooms walked their hunters.

C.E.G. Hope, The Horseman's Manual

More specific is British *hackney*, the equivalent of an American "trotter,"
a show horse pulling a light carriage (naturally enough, a *hackney carriage*). Most specific is *Hackney*, with a capital, a breed descended from
the Norfolk Trotter.

But an important specialization happened early in the history of the
word. By 1390 or so *hackney* was being used to mean "a horse let out
for hire, a rented horse." Rented horses aren't always the best, of
course, and by 1500 the word has picked up a pejorative meaning, "a
nag, a worn-out horse." It's possible that the tired nag may give us the
hacking in "a hacking cough." And by 1546 the word begins to generalize to other things. People available for hire are *hackneys*—and thus
hackney is a slang term for "thug" and then "prostitute" in Renaissance
English, along with *hackster*, "bully." By 1700 we hear of "hack writers," later of "hack politicians," and in 1851 of "hackwork." Thomas
Nashe writes of a "hackney proverb" in 1596, meaning "overused," and
this sense carries on to *hackneyed*, "trite or stale vocabulary," with much
of its original connotation still alive, as this usage note from the *Random
House College Dictionary* makes clear.

11.17   —Syn. 2. COMMONPLACE, BANAL, HACKNEYED, STEREO-
TYPED, TRITE describe words, remarks, and styles of expression that are lifeless and uninteresting. COMMONPLACE characterizes thought that is dull, ordinary, and platitudinous:
commonplace and boring. Something is BANAL that seems
inane, insipid, and pointless: *a heavy-handed and banal
affirmation of the obvious*. HACKNEYED characterizes that
which seems stale and worn out through overuse: *a hackneyed comparison*. STEREOTYPED emphasizes the fact that
situations felt to be similar invariably call for the same
thought in exactly the same form and the same words: *so
stereotyped as to seem automatic*. TRITE describes that which
was originally striking and apt, but which has become so
well known and been so commonly used that all interest has
been worn out of it: *true but trite*. 3. cliché, platitude.

The meaning "hired horse" undergoes another transfer, from horse
to carriage. This transfer gives us a number of compounds—*hackney
coach, hackney carriage, hackney-coachman,* and, by a further transfer,
even *hackney-boat*. Taxis are still commonly hackneys in British English,
and in America taxi-drivers (or "hackies") still speak of "hacking cabs."

That's a long word-road, from a "hackney horse" to a "hackneyed
phrase" to a "hack writer" to "hacking cabs." But *hackney* is a simple
word compared to *run* or *pipe* or *fly,* words that have transferred to
scores of meaning. You can run a business, run up bills, have a run of
luck, run your eyes down the page, or even, in the original sense, run
around the block. Counting compounds, the *Oxford English Dictionary*

devotes seventeen pages to the various meanings of *run*. And that dictionary, compiled in England generations ago, didn't have to worry about a *home run* or a stocking *run* or an airplane *runway*—and *runaway* referred to horses rather than teenagers.

The developing writer can draw several lessons from this vital process of change. It testifies to the power of language to adapt to new situations. It testifies to the creativity of language and of the human mind. It offers—at least to the writer with a good dictionary and the ability to use it—almost infinite possibilities of expression. The world of words is veined with rich ore; it's worth exploring.

SUMMARY

We distinguished four levels of vocabulary: speaking vocabulary, writing vocabulary, reading vocabulary, and "guess" vocabulary—words that the reader can guess from context. We made two suggestions for improving one's vocabulary: Read a lot, and master the use of a standard college dictionary. We examined several college dictionaries and one specialized dictionary, the *Oxford English Dictionary*.

We explained the etymologies given in dictionaries by a brief history of English, noting its development from Indo-European through Germanic, and summarizing its major divisions, Old English (with borrowings from Latin and Danish), Middle English (with borrowings from French), and Modern English (with borrowings from Latin). We noted that English is now a world language.

We identified four major ways in which words change meaning: compounding, transfer, generalization, and specialization. We mentioned also the processes of shortening, blending, adopting proper names, and using acronyms. We illustrated such changes by examining the history of the word *hackney*.

FINAL WRITING ASSIGNMENTS[6]

I. A Dictionary Assignment   This assignment is designed to give you a sense of the nature of words and their changes through history; perhaps more importantly, it will test your ability to organize complex data into a clear, coherent, and unified form.

A. Find at least three roughly synonymous words—words that have the same general denotation—and discriminate clearly among their meanings and functions. A list of suggested terms is given at the end of the assignment, but any three words will do—and some students may wish to deal with more words.

B. Begin by finding out as much as you can about the words. You should consider at least the topics mentioned below. Dictionaries will be of great help, but you will also have to rely heavily on your own intuitive sense of the words. Dictionaries are often out-of-date (language changes), incomplete (words change), and even inadequate (they can't capture everything the native speaker knows about the register of words).

Age. How long has the word been in the language? How long has it carried the particular meaning you're concerned with? (*Home* has been in the language since the beginning; it began to denote the plate in baseball only in the 1870s.)

Origin. Where did the words come from? (*Fat* is from Old English, *corpulent* is from French, and *obese* is from Latin—these origins do much to explain the registers of these terms.)

Development. Have the words changed meaning through time? How and why? (*Back* gained the general meaning of "opposite to the front," as in the *back* of a saw, through generalization; it has been specialized in words like *backstroke* and *backorder,* and transferred in words like *backlog* and *backup*—the latter examples all compounds.)

Denotative meaning. In the specific sense you're concerned with, what are the denotative meanings of the words? (*House* and *domicile* have the same denotative meaning, the word *building* has a more general meaning.)

Regional variation. Is the term limited to British or American English? Does it vary regionally in the United States? (The British buy *petrol,* and we buy *gas.* In Michigan you buy a *submarine* sandwich, in Philadelphia a *hoagie,* in Los Angeles a *hero.*)

Usage. Are any of the terms listed with usage labels? Are you sensitive about any of the terms? (One dictionary identifies *hopefully* as a word avoided by "precise writers"; another gives no such indication.)

Connotative meaning. What are the connotations of the terms? Have the connotations changed through time? (*Home* and *house* have the same denotations, but quite different connotations. *Tavern* seems to have been a neutral term until the nineteenth century, when it began to have a negative connotation.)

Age variation. Is the term more likely to be used by young people or old people? (Few people over fifty-five or so say *yeah;* few younger people use *ice box.*)

Social variation. Do the terms differ in social register? How? (*Ain't* is used primarily in working-class speech in the United States; in England, it's used by upper-class speakers in the phrase "Ain't I?")

Functional variation. What precisely are the functional differences among the terms? When and how would you use the words? Some words, for example, are more commonly written than spoken; others might be recognizably female words; while still others might be marked with other variations.

C. You now have a great deal of information about the words you've chosen—certainly more than you can use in a short paper, and perhaps more than you wanted to know. So you need, at this point, to think about the rhetoric of your paper: what you found interesting about the words, what you want to tell the reader about them, what connections you make among the bits of information, ways that the information might be presented. Then develop a single controlling commitment for the paper—the main idea that you want to present to the reader. This commitment should be formative—that is, it will make some information you've gathered important, other information less important, and some information irrelevant. The nature of your formative idea will determine what evidence you emphasize or omit. Do not try to put everything into the paper; above all, do not write a mechanical paragraph on each of the topics we've mentioned.

Put another way, it's your task as writer to put the data you've gathered to some use, to find a strategy for turning an apparently mechanical assignment into an interesting and persuasive piece of writing. Our final chapter offers two pieces of student writing based on this assignment.

D. A short list of terms is given below—they hardly exhaust the possibilities of the assignment. You'll also find the list of dictionaries in "For Further Reading" useful. We've identified each dictionary with an abbreviation. All information taken from sources should be identified, but you can use the abbreviations in parentheses. An example: "The prime meaning of *ready* is identified as 'ready for use or action' (*SCD*) or 'completely prepared' and 'in fit condition' (*RHD*)."

calculate, suppose, guess
colloquial, vulgar, common
bonnet, hood, lid
drunk, intoxicated, stoned
jive, shuck, snow
type of, kind of, variety
exhort, urge, influence
price, expense, cost
intelligent, brainy, egghead
power, potency, strength
land, ground, dirt

tummy, belly, stomach,
   abdomen
pharmacist, druggist, chemist
okay, sure, yeah, yup
fan, partisan, rooter
toilet, bathroom, can, john
pancake, hotcake, griddle cake
irrespective, regardless,
   irregardless
objective, neutral, detached
subjective, personal, biased

nice, good, pleasant
run, scamper, race
lie, falsehood, untruth, fib
dumb, stupid, idiot
finalize, finish, complete
college, university, school
famous, notorious, noted

red, commie, pinko, dupe
black, Negro, colored, Afro-
  American
Chicano, Mexican-American,
  la raza
crisis, affair, case
very, mighty, awfully

II. Group Reports or Class Projects These assignments are designed to supplement the topics we've considered in this chapter. Some—particularly the first—might be broken down as class projects; others might be usefully presented as reports to the class.

A. Evaluating standard college dictionaries. If a dictionary is indeed a lifetime investment, then the decision is worth considering in detail. Figures 11.1, 11.2, and 11.3 offer examples from five college dictionaries, along with some analysis; you might also wish to consider the following issues (perhaps as subcommittees reporting to an editorial committee that would compile a final evaluation): number of entries, specifically of new or scientific words, compounds, obsolete words and meanings; definitions—their clarity and completeness; etymologies—their fullness, adequacy, and clarity; treatment of usage; clarity and completeness of prefatory material; practical matters—availability, price, appearance, legibility. The product evaluations in *Consumer Reports* magazine offer a good model for the organization of such a report.

B. What do we know about the people who spoke Indo-European? And how do scientists go about answering such a question? (Read Paul Thieme's "The Indo-European Language," *Scientific American,* 199 [October 1958], 63–74, and the essays by Calvert Watkins on Indo-European in the *AHD.*)

C. What about language families other than Indo-European? More specifically, what about Amerindian language families? (Consult Charlton Laird's *Language in America* in "For Further Reading.")

D. Our discussion of the history of English almost completely ignores the development of a distinctively American English. What can you report about the development of American English as distinct from British English? (Start with Laird's *Language in America* and also examine Mencken's delightful *The American Language,* both cited in "For Further Reading.")

E. The publication of Webster's *Third New International Dictionary* in 1961 provoked a storm of controversy—about that dictionary and its predecessor, the *Second New International* (1934), and about the goals of an unabridged dictionary. That controversy is conveniently presented in the Sledd and Ebbitt anthology in "For Further Reading"; if that work isn't available, consult at least Wilson Follett's "Sabotage in Springfield," *Atlantic,* January 1962, pp. 73–77; Dwight MacDonald, "The String Untuned," *New Yorker,* March 10, 1962, pp. 130–34; James Sledd, "The Lexicographer's Uneasy Chair," *College English,* 1962, pp. 682–87; and Bergen Evans, "But What's a Dictionary For?" *Atlantic,* May 1962, pp. 57–62.

F. Samuel Johnson's 1755 *Dictionary* is the first important English dictionary. An interesting report might be written about Johnson's dictionary and his experiences in compiling it. The dictionary, with its important preface, ought to be available in some form; another starting-point is Charlton Laird's "Language and the Dictionary" (*NWD*).

G. How do modern lexicographers go about putting a dictionary together? How do they decide what words to include, what pronunciations to give, and what labels or illustrations to offer? Laird's *NWD* essay (cited in assignment F above) and the Grove anthology (cited in "For Further Reading") are starting-points, and the Merriam-Webster periodical *Word-Study,* if available, will provide a number of specific examples.

H. What is a "linguistic atlas"? How is a linguistic atlas compiled, and what information does it provide? Two starting-points are *Readings in American Dialectology,* ed. Harold B. Allen and Gary N. Underwood (New York: Appleton-Century-Crofts, 1971), and Carroll E. Reed's *Dialects of American English,* 2nd ed. (Amherst: The University of Massachusetts Press, 1973).

I. What sort of information does one find in the periodical *American Speech*? Examine the contents of several recent issues and report your findings.

J. Collect the vocabulary of a sport or specialized field—baseball, sewing, cooking, law, tennis, space science—and explain its origin and development.

K. Try poet Charles Olson's suggestion (in 11.10) by "tracking" the history of a word or word group. Our discussion of *hackney* provides one model for such an essay.

III. Word-Hoard, Incorporated It was a big risk, starting a brand-new sort of business, but Word-Hoard, Incorporated, is doing well, offering consulting services to businesses, governments, and private individuals. You're still running the business on a shoestring, though, doing most of your work in the reference room of your college library. Today you pick up the letters below at your post-office box and settle in to work.

A. A letter from the British government: "Dear Word-Hoard: We've just discovered that when Sir Christopher Wren was given a government contract to redesign the Houses of Parliament after the great fire of 1685 he was awarded the job for his 'aweful and artificial' designs. We're very happy with the work he did, but if his plans were awful and artificial, couldn't there have been some graft involved? Please advise."

B. A letter from the owner of Ye Olde Curio Shoppe: "Dear Word-Hoard: I'm very proud of the fancy title of my curio shop. But a customer yesterday said that *the* in English was never pronounced *Ye,* and that the name of my store was just silly and pretentious. Can you help me prove that he's wrong? By the way, he said that this was a thorny question."

C. A letter from the Women's Action Group (WAG): "Dear Word-Hoard: One of our members works in an office where she is not allowed any of the benefits given to male employees—no coffee breaks, no sick leave, no pay raises. When she complained, her boss (a man) responded, 'The Constitution says that all men are equal. It is obvious that no woman is a man. Therefore, no women are equal to men. So, logically, you have no right to the benefits given to our male employees.' Can you help us with this problem?"

D. A letter from a history professor at Pahrump University. "Dear Word-Hoard: I'm doing research on the origin of universities, and I wonder if you could help me by tracing the source of some common words used in higher education—words like *dean, matriculate, bachelor, college. . . .* Do these give us any hint about the nature of the first universities?"

E. A letter from a college student. "Dear Word-Hoard: My girlfriend is very stubborn. She insists on calling a *hoagy* sandwich a *hero* sandwich, and she even says that it's okay for her roommate to call it a *submarine* sandwich. Please help me with two things. First, explain to my girlfriend that the real name is *hoagy.* And second, since she's so stubborn, should I marry her?"

F. A letter from a high school student. "Dear Word-Hoard: Was a *nice* girl always a *good* girl? And what's so 'nice' about 'a nice distinction'? Thank you."

G. A letter from a college student. "Dear Word-Hoard: My boyfriend calls a *bag* a *sack,* a *pail* a *bucket,* a *faucet* a *spigot,* a *chipmunk* a *ground squirrel,* and *eaves gutters.* He even says *greasy* as if it were spelled with a 'z.' He says he grew up in Maine. Should I marry him?"

H. A letter from your new competitor, Lexicon Unlimited. "Dear Word-Hoard, you dummy. I've found the greatest book in the world on English etymology, and I'll be able to answer questions better than you can. It's Horne Tooke's *Diversions of Purley,* first published in 1803, and it's a gold-mine of information. Here's a sample:

'A *bar* in all its uses is a defence: that by which anything is fortified, strengthened or defended. A *barn* is a covered enclosure in which the grain, etc. is protected or defended from the weather, from depredations, etc. A *baron* is an armed, defenceful, or powerful man. A *barge* is a strong boat. A *bargain* is a confirmed, strengthened agreement. . . . A *bark* is a stout vessel. The *bark* of a tree is its defence. . . .'

Of course, the book is a little dated, but with a start like this, I can explain why *barbeque* sauce is so strong and why *bartenders* hide behind counters. Obviously, I've saved your business. Please send me a check for $942."

FOR FURTHER READING

Here is a brief list of dictionaries. You'll find some of these works helpful in solving the final assignments for this chapter. The introductory essays in standard college dictionaries will also supplement our discussion—the essay on "Usage, Dialects, and Functional Varieties" by Raven I. McDavid, Jr. (in the *RHD*), the essays, "Grammar and Meaning" by Richard Ohmann, and "The Spelling and Pronunciation of English" by Wayne O'Neil (both in the *AHD*), as well as the essays cited in the final assignments.

1. *Standard College Dictionaries.* Standard college dictionaries are referenced and illustrated in Figures 11.1, 11.2, and 11.3.
2. *Historical Dictionaries*
   The Oxford English Dictionary. Ed. James A. H. Murray, Henry Bradley, W. A. Cragie, and C. T. Onions. 13 vols. Oxford: Oxford University Press, 1933. [*OED*] Shown in Figure 11.4.
   A Dictionary of American English on Historical Principles. Ed. Sir William A. Bradley, et al. 2nd ed. 4 vols. Chicago: University of Chicago Press, 1960. [*DAE*]
3. *Unabridged Dictionaries.* (These dictionaries attempt to list every word in the language.)
   The Century Dictionary and Cyclopedia. 12 vols. New York: Century, 1911. Reissued in a shorter two-volume form as *The New Century Dictionary,* 1927. (Particularly valuable for long analytic entries for some key words.) [*NCD*]
   The Random House Dictionary of the English Language. Ed. Jess Stein. New York: Random House, 1966. (Shorter and less technical than the *New International* dictionaries below.) [*RHD*]
   Webster's Second New International Dictionary of the English Language Unabridged. Ed. William A. Meilson. Springfield, Mass.: Merriam, 1934. [*WSI*]

Webster's Third New International Dictionary of the English Language Unabridged.
Ed. Phillip Babcock Grove. Springfield, Mass.: Merriam, 1961. [*WTI*] (The
WSI made prescriptive usage distinctions and cited literary sources; the
WTI eliminated many usage labels and cited contemporary sources such
as newspapers, magazines, and political speeches. See the anthology ed-
ited by Sledd and Ebbitt, category 6 below.)

4. Etymological Dictionaries; Slang Dictionaries

A Comprehensive Etymological Dictionary of the English Language. Ed. Ernest
Klein. 2 vols. Amsterdam: Elsevier, 1966. [*CED*]

Dictionary of Word and Phrase Origins. Ed. William and Mary Morris. 3 vols.
New York: Harper & Row, 1962, 1969, 1971. [*DWPO*]

Origins: A Short Etymological Dictionary of Modern English. Ed. Eric Partridge.
London: Routledge & Kegan Paul, 1966. [*Origins*]

The Oxford Dictionary of English Etymology. Ed. C. T. Onions. Oxford: Oxford
University Press, 1966. [*ODEE*]

A Dictionary of Slang and Unconventional English. 7th ed. Ed. Eric Partridge.
New York: Macmillan, 1970. [*DSUE*]

5. Handbooks of Usage

(The *AHD,* in group 1 above, gives reports of a poll of professional writers
on usage issues, as does the *Harper Dictionary* below.)

Bryant, Margaret M. *Current American Usage.* New York: Funk & Wagnalls,
1962.

Ebbitt, Wilma R., and David R. Ebbitt. *Index to English.* 6th ed. Glenview, Ill.:
Scott, Foresman, 1977. (This book is a student guide rather than usage
handbook; it contains helpful discussions of grammar and punctuation as
well as usage.)

Evans, Bergen, and Cordelia Evans. *A Dictionary of Contemporary American
Usage.* New York: Random House, 1957.

Fowler, H. W. *A Dictionary of Modern British Usage.* 2nd ed. Rev. Sir Ernest
Gowers. Oxford: Oxford University Press, 1965.

Morris, William, and Mary Morris. *Harper Dictionary of Contemporary Usage.*
New York: Harper & Row, 1975.

Nicolson, Margaret. *A Dictionary of American English Usage.* New York: Signet
Books, 1958. (An adaption of Fowler's *Modern British Usage,* available in
an inexpensive paperback.)

6. Books on Language and Dictionaries.

Francis, W. Nelson. *The English Language: An Introduction.* New York: W. W.
Norton, 1965. Written for college freshmen.

Fromkin, Victoria, and Robert Rodman. *An Introduction to Language.* 2nd ed.
New York: Holt, 1974. A clear introduction to linguistic science.

Grove, Phillip B., ed. *The Role of the Dictionary.* Indianapolis: Bobbs-Merrill,
1967. A brief set of articles on the dictionary.

Laird, Charlton. *Language in America.* New York: Prentice-Hall, 1975. A
comprehensive account of Amerindian languages and English in America.

Lodwig, Richard R., and Eugene F. Barret. *The Dictionary and the Language.*
New York: Haydon, 1967. An introduction to words and their meanings.

Mencken, H. L. *The American Language.* The Fourth Edition and the Two Supplements. Abridged and ed. Raven I. McDavid. New York: Knopf, 1963. A revision of a classic, and still fascinating, work.

Pyles, Thomas. *The Origins and Development of the English Language.* New York: Harcourt, Brace & World, 1971. A fuller history of English.

Sledd, James, and Wilma R. Ebbitt, eds. *Dictionaries and THAT Dictionary.* Glenview, Ill.: Scott, Foresman, 1962. A casebook of reviews of *Webster's Third New International,* exploring what a dictionary is or should be.

NOTES

1. Amsel Green, *Pullet Surprises* (Glenview, Ill.: Scott, Foresman, 1969).
2. Of course, many of us are not ourselves descended from those early speakers of English. Many of us can trace our family back to a non-English language, and English may have been adopted by our ancestors by choice (by immigration, for example) or even by force (by slavery or colonization). Even then, however, the paradox remains true, for to adopt a language means to adopt its history.
3. We simplify foreign words and earlier versions of English, using a modern alphabet and omitting accent marks and other symbols.
4. Adapted from Joseph M. Williams, *Origins of English* (New York: The Free Press, 1975).
5. The attempt by advertisers to apply the Greek word *chronometer* to newer timepieces has apparently failed. Why might this be so?
6. Before attempting these assignments, you'll want to review the use of underlining, for italics, to mark words as words—in chapter Nine, pages 282–286.

12

The Print Code: Spelling

Errare humanum est—"To err is human"

This chapter is not for all readers. It's for readers who like puzzles, because the spelling of the print code is a particularly interesting puzzle. And it's for writers who are convinced that they'll never learn to spell, and who therefore approach each writing task fearfully, certain that the exact form of words will elude them.

Our goal is to uncover the systems at work in English spelling. As a result, we won't offer lists of "commonly misspelled words," and we won't list the "rules of spelling"—"*i* before *e* except after *c*," and so on. Instead, we'll take a broad view of spelling, including word forms like the -*s* and -*ed* markers, and we'll search for deeper, underlying patterns at work in the print code.

There's a good reason to search for such patterns in English spelling. Without some sense of pattern, writers would be forced to memorize the spelling of each separate word—an impossible learning task. Moreover, writers who find systematic patterns in their spelling errors can simplify their learning task. Consider, as an example, the student who has misspelled one hundred words in a writing class. Without a sense of spelling patterns, the student would be forced to memorize one hundred spellings. But if we could find two or three systematic patterns to explain those errors, the writer would have only two or three principles to learn: They would explain the one hundred misspelled words, and they would also carry over to the next word the writer puzzled about.

Error category	Explanation
"etym"	misspellings that do not reflect the etymological basis of English spelling—*thru* for *through, goverment* for *government.*
"schwa"	misspellings of the unstressed vowel schwa, such as *repatition* for *repetition, grammer* for *grammar.*
"hom"	misspellings of words that sound alike or nearly alike (*homonyms*)—*affect* for *effect, it's* for *its.*
"wf"	misspellings of word endings, specifically:
tense, *-ed*	wrong verb tense, usually a missing *-ed* ending, as in *suppose to* for *supposed to.*
plural, agr, poss	mistake in the *-s* system: plurals (*ten cent* for *ten cents*), subject-verb agreement (*she walk* for *she walks*), or possessive (*cities* for *city's*).
adj, adv	adjective and adverb form—compare *the dog smelled badly* with *the dog smelled bad.*
"sys"	mistake in the spelling system, such as the system for doubling letters (*hoping* for *hopping*) or for changing *-y* to *-i* (*citys* for *cities*).

FIGURE 12.1 A Classification of Spelling Problems

We find it useful to classify spelling errors under the four major headings shown in Figure 12.1, with the last category, "word forms," used for errors of tense and agreement as well as certain spelling errors. Your instructor may use these abbreviations in noting your spelling errors, or he or she may use the common abbreviation "sp" for all spelling errors. In either case, we suggest you use the headings to classify your own errors, for you'll be able to concentrate on kinds of errors that pose particular problems for you.

THE PROBLEM OF SPELLING

Why is spelling such a problem for writers? Centuries ago, it wasn't—because no one worried about spelling. People would spell words almost at random. They might spell *me* as *me* or *mee* (the seventeenth-century poet John Milton used both spellings in a single line of poetry); they might spell *some* as *some* or *som* or *sum*—and perhaps all three ways. The *Oxford English Dictionary,* you'll recall, lists all the different spellings of English words, and it lists, for example, the following different spellings for as simple a word as *book:*

12.1 bóc, booc, boc, bof, boke, booke, bock, boock, buk, buke, buick, buik.

That variety doesn't imply that earlier writers couldn't tell a Buick from a book; it simply means that they didn't worry about spelling—they were happy as long as they'd made a decent stab at the sound of the word. (And in Scotland, a few centuries ago, *buick* wasn't a bad stab at the sound of the word *book.*) Even now, though, the spelling system is not a single rigid pattern. In England, words like *color* and *honor* are spelled with a -*u* (as *colour* and *honour,* a pattern that we keep in *glamour*), and words that end in -*ize* in American spellings end in -*ise* in British spelling (such as *realise* and *idealise,* a pattern that we keep in such words as *exercise* and *surprise*). American dictionaries disagree about the spelling of certain words: Is it *part-time* or *parttime, aesthetic* or *esthetic*? Dictionaries differ.

Nevertheless, dictionaries agree on the spelling of most words, and correct spelling is an important part of the "manners" of writing. Indeed, in the modern age of computers, correct spelling is a necessity, for computers, unlike humans, cannot recognize a misspelled word. If you worry about your spelling, you may want to spend some time learning the systems. At the very least, building up your spelling skills will allow you to concentrate on more important matters. At best, having confidence in your mastery of spelling will give you more confidence in your writing skills in general, and this confidence should show through in the writing you produce.

Problem One. Two discovery problems Thinking over the two problems that follow may give you a start on our discussion of spelling.

The first problem asks you to predict the results of an experiment in reading performed a few years ago at the University of Toronto. Bilingual adults, fluent in both French and English, were asked to read aloud passages that mixed the two languages, sentences such as "There is a *cheval dans le* garden" ("There is a horse in the garden"). Can you predict what might have happened? A hint: The readers weren't slower at reading the mixture of two languages, but they made some interesting mistakes.

The second problem asks you to examine spelling mistakes made by a second-grade student and by a seventh-grade student.

- second-grade student: *capten* for *captain, choklet* for *chocolate, meny* for *many, minits* for *minutes.*
- seventh-grade student: *benefitiary* for *beneficiary, numberous* for *numerous, pronounciation* for *pronunciation, repeatition* for *repetition.*[1]

symbol	sound	symbol	sound
a	act, b<u>a</u>t, m<u>a</u>rry	ō	<u>o</u>ver, b<u>oa</u>t, n<u>o</u>
ā	<u>ai</u>d, c<u>a</u>pe, w<u>ay</u>	ô	<u>ou</u>ght, b<u>a</u>ll, r<u>aw</u>
â	<u>ai</u>r, d<u>a</u>re, M<u>a</u>ry	oi	<u>oi</u>l, j<u>oi</u>nt, j<u>oy</u>
ä	<u>a</u>lms, <u>a</u>rt, c<u>a</u>lm	o͝o	b<u>oo</u>k, p<u>oo</u>r
e	ebb, s<u>e</u>t, m<u>e</u>rry	oo	<u>oo</u>ze, f<u>oo</u>l, t<u>oo</u>
ē	<u>e</u>qual, s<u>ea</u>t, b<u>ee</u>, might<u>y</u>	ou	<u>ou</u>t, l<u>ou</u>d, pr<u>ow</u>
ēr	<u>ea</u>r, m<u>ere</u>	u	<u>u</u>p, l<u>o</u>ve
i	<u>i</u>f, b<u>i</u>g, m<u>i</u>rror, furn<u>i</u>ture	û	<u>u</u>rge, b<u>u</u>rn, c<u>u</u>r
ī	<u>i</u>ce, b<u>i</u>te, p<u>i</u>rate, den<u>y</u>	ə	unstressed sound of <u>a</u> in
o	<u>o</u>x, b<u>o</u>x, w<u>a</u>sp		alone, <u>e</u> in syst<u>e</u>m, <u>i</u> in easil<u>y</u>,
			<u>o</u> in gall<u>o</u>p, <u>u</u> in circ<u>u</u>s.

FIGURE 12.2 Vowel Symbols Used in Phonetic Transcriptions. From the *Random House Dictionary*.[2]

We might put the issue in these terms: The seventh-grade is a "better misspeller" than the second-grader. Can you explain what the seventh-grader has learned about the spelling system? ■

All developing writers struggle with spelling of English, and even mature writers complain about its artificiality. British playwright George Bernard Shaw once joked that we might reasonably spell the word *fish* with the letters *ghoti*. After all, Shaw argued, we use the letters *gh* to show the sound /f/ at the end of *enough*, we give the letter *o* the sound of /i/ in *women*, and we pronounce the letters *ti* as /sh/ in words like *nation* and *invention*.

(The slash marks—/ /—are used to enclose the sound rather than the spelling. Consonant sounds should be clear from context, as long as the reader will grant that the word *of* has the sound /v/ and that the beginning sound of *cat* is best marked as /k/. For vowel sounds, we use a simplified dictionary pronunciation key, as shown in Figure 12.2.)

Jokes aside, there's no one-to-one connection between letters and sounds. The vowel sound /oo/, for example, can be spelled with the letter *u* (as in *rUle*), with the letters *ui* (*frUIt*), with the letters *ou* (*grOUp*), with the letters *eu* (*rhEUmatism*), the letters *ue* (*flUE*), the letters *ew* (*grEW*), the letters *ooe* (*wOOEd*), and, of course, as in *tO*, *tOO*, and *tWO*.

This apparent confusion has led many people to suggest changes and "improvements" in the spelling system. A few minor changes have been made over the last two hundred years: We no longer spell words like *cynic* and *public* with a *-k* at the end, and Noah Webster, the dictionary Webster, convinced Americans to spell *cheque* and *theatre* and *catalogue* as *check* and *theater* and *catalog*. But by and large, our spelling system has been completely frozen; even such "logical" spellings as *nite* and *brite* and *thru*—also suggested by Webster—seldom show up in serious print.

Why might this be so? That is, why do we continue to use a system that seems to be so illogical and is obviously such a problem for learners to master? As a first step in answering that question, let's look at another system for spelling—in fact one that was proposed by the British Simplified Spelling Society in 1940. They proposed that English spelling be made completely *phonetic,* with every single sound represented by a single letter, so that readers could "sound out" each word they read, and each word could be spelled exactly as it sounded. (Since there are over forty-five sounds in the language, however, the proposed alphabet makes some compromises to keep the twenty-six letters of the alphabet.) Notice what happens as you read a phonetic code:

12.2   We instinktivly shrink from eny chaenj in whot iz familyar; and whot kan be more familyar dhan dhe form ov wurdz dhat we have seen and riten mor tiemz dhan we kan posibly estimaet? We taek up a book printed in Amerika, and *honor* and *center* jar upon us every tiem we kum akros dhem; nae, eeven to see *forever* in place of *for ever* atrakts our atenshon in an unplesant wae. But dheez are iesolaeted kaesez; think ov dhe meny wurdz dhat wood hav to be chaenjd if eny real improovment wer to rezult . . . But dhaer iz soe much misapprehenshon on dhis point, and such straenj statements ar maed, dhat it bekumz nesasary to deel widh dhis objekshon in sum deetael.[3]

There would be a big advantage to a phonetic code such as this one. Once students learned the letter-sound connections, they simply couldn't make a spelling mistake.

But consider the disadvantages. A phonetic system would work only if everybody spoke the same way, and we know that speakers of world English have many different dialects. We now spell *either* in one way, whether we pronounce it /ēthər/ or /īthər/. In a phonetic code, the two pronunciations would appear as different words. And would we really spell words the way we pronounce them? Most of us say "wanna" /wänə/ for *want to* in informal situations, saving the emphatic /wänt to/

for times when we're angry or very careful about our speech. On top of those problems, what about changes in the sounds of our language? If the spelling system were tied to pronunciation, we might find that we couldn't read books written long ago; we'd have to translate the writings of our great-grandfathers just as we translate foreign languages.

The advantage of a frozen spelling system, then, is that it is frozen. We can read the writing of authors who speak dialects of English quite different from our own, even though we might have trouble understanding their speech. And we can read the writings of any writer of the past (at least for the past four or five hundred years, since the language assumed its modern form). Our own writing, insofar as it keeps to the frozen spelling system, is similarly open to a wider audience than our own speech: We can write to people who couldn't understand the way we talk, and we can write to those who follow us, at least as long as the language remains reasonably close to its present form.

THE SYSTEM OF ENGLISH SPELLING

Think back to your process of reading 12.2, the passage in British Simplified Spelling. You probably found yourself sounding out each word, connecting the letters with the sounds, and then connecting the sounds with meanings. In other words, you'd be reading as shown in Figure 12.3, moving from spelling to sound to meaning. As a result, you may have found yourself reading much more slowly, sounding out each word as you came to it. (And you'll remember that mature readers don't normally sound out each word; they process meaning directly.) It might be possible to increase your speed as you became more accustomed to that kind of spelling, but the comparison does reveal a basic fact about the spelling system we do use: *Our spelling system is based primarily on meaning, not on sound.*

spelling	$\Rightarrow$	*sound*	$\Rightarrow$	*meaning*
rezult	$\Rightarrow$	/result/	$\Rightarrow$	"result"

FIGURE 12.3   Reading a Phonetic Code

Notice, for example, two words spelled by sound, along with their normal spelling:

12.3 riten [written]

riet [write]

Write and *written* are closely related in meaning, and our spelling system shows it, even though the pronunciation of the words doesn't. Moreover, *write* is different in meaning from *right* and *rite* and *wright*, yet they would all have the same spelling in the phonetic system.

Our spelling system is based on meaning rather than sound, and we can use that system, as mature readers, to short-circuit sound and move directly from print to meaning. That is, as shown in Figure 12.4, we don't have to "sound words out" in reading or spelling, for we can rely first on word shape and context—that's why good spellers learn to rely on whether the word "looks right" on paper. Of course, sound-spellings correspondences do exist, and we can "sound out" difficult words in our reading. But words that sound right can be remarkably hard to read if they don't connect with our meaning sense, as suggested by our problem, as readers, with 12.4:

12.4 The none tolled hymn she had scene bear fete in her rheum.

spelling	$\Rightarrow$	*meaning*	(sound)
result	$\Rightarrow$	"result"	/rezult/

FIGURE 12.4 From Print to Meaning

Our spelling system supports the transfer of print to the mind, because it shows how words are alike in meaning instead of showing their sound. English spelling, in the words of the authors of the most comprehensive treatment of sound-spelling patterns, is "a near optimal system for the lexical representation of English words."[4] In technical terms, our spelling system is based on the psychological reality of words (their meaning), rather than based on their physical reality (their sound). It gives *lexical* information, not *phonetic* information. In fact, the bilingual readers from problem one substituted French and English words for each other; so intent were they on meaning. They might read "There is a *cheval dans* the garden" as "There is a horse in *le jardin.*"[5]

A system like ours raises problems for the learner, as you're no doubt aware. The rest of this chapter will explore some of those problems. But, once learned, the system lets you read much faster than you could if you had to sound out each word.

Consider our spelling and pronunciation of the words *bomb* and *sign*. We pronounce these words as /bom/ and /sīn/, and we might spell them as they sound, as *bom* and *sine* (*sine*, of course, is a word for a math function). But notice what happens to the silent /b/ at the end of the *bomb* in words that are related in meaning:

12.5   bomb::bomBard::bomBardier

And notice the sense behind the silent *g* in *sign:*

12.6   sign::siGnal::siGnature

Our spelling of *sign* and *bomb*, then, reflects the meaning of the words rather than their sound. Thus we keep in spelling the connection in meaning of *divine* and *divinity*, of *serene* and *serenity*, even though our pronunciation changes. We keep in spelling the underlying form of *telegraph* even though the sounds change as the word changes form:

12.7   telegraph::telegraphic::telegraphy::telegrapher
          /teləgraf/ /teləgrafik/ /təlegrafi/ /təlegrəfər/

The pronunciation changes, but the spelling doesn't: It shows the underlying meaning shared by all four pronunciations. Thus much of the "illogic" of English spelling is illogical only from the point of view of sound; English spelling turns out to be remarkably efficient at preserving meaning.

Problem Two: Spelling and meaning   Each of the following words has a silent letter. Show how the spelling system preserves underlying meaning by finding a related word in which the letter is sounded for as many of the words as you can.[6] The first two are done for you.

  a. sign::siGnal
  b. bomb::bomBard
  c. muscle
  d. design
  e. condemn
  f. malign
  g. soften
  h. paradigm
  i. contempt

You may not have found related words for all the words in problem two, but you probably were able to connect *muscle* with *musCular* and *design* with *desiGnation*. Some of you may even have found a new word, *paradigm,* and connected it with another new word, *paradiGmatic.* In this way, mastering the spelling system becomes more than mere correctness in writing: It becomes a way of improving vocabulary (as you fit new words into a meaning system), and a way of improving your reading (as you respond to meaning rather than sound).

IMPROVING SPELLING

This analysis suggests that the spelling system we use presents readers with abstract information about meaning. Spelling is only incidentally connected with sound. One improves one's spelling, then, by breaking through the "sound barrier" of spelling to the underlying meaning of words.

The writer who looks only to sound as a clue for spelling will be constantly misled. The results are sometimes funny, as when one of our students created "for all intense porpoises" for "for all intents and purposes." More often, the results can seriously slow down the reader intent on meaning, as in the common "would of" for "would have" in sentences like 12.8:

12.8 I *would have* gone if she had asked me.

12.8A I *would of* gone if she had asked me. (?)

"Would of" captures the relaxed pronunciation of "would have," but it ignores the grammatical context. The writer has looked to sound instead of meaning. And you'll note, returning to problem one, that our second-grader's misspellings are very accurate renderings of sound—"capten," "choklet." But the seventh-grader's misspellings are better, in our terms, for they are related to meaning—"numberous," "pronounciation."

The best device for improving spelling, we find, is a spelling log. Such a log is shown in Figure 12.5—you'll notice that the form allows us to classify each mistake, thereby building an awareness of areas to work on. We'll demonstrate how to use such a log in the rest of this chapter.

The Etymological Basis of English Spelling

We've noted before the paradox that, while every speaker who learns English creates the language anew, every speaker also inherits the history of the language. Nowhere is that legacy more obvious than the

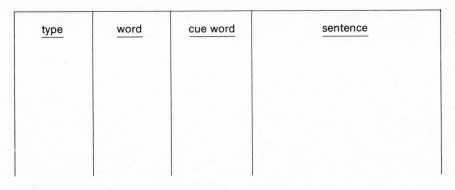

type	word	cue word	sentence

FIGURE 12.5 Format of a Spelling Log

spelling system, for that frozen system contains, insists on, the history of words—where we got them, how we used to pronounce them, what other words they are related to. The mature writer is alive to this historical nature of spelling and he spells words by relying on meaning and underlying relationships.

Consider, as an example of the etymology buried in spelling, the student error in "I had some *arons* to run." That's an intriguing spelling of the word *errands,* for it's very close to the relaxed pronunciation of the word. We tried the word on a freshman class, pronouncing it informally, as /erəns/. Using this pronunciation we collected four misspellings of the word:

12.9 arons   airuns   eruns   erands

The first three misspellings are closer to the sound of the word, but the final one is a better guess. It has the correct beginning, *er-,* even though that letter combination may be pronounced in many different ways (as in *Ernest* or *erotic,* for instance). And it has the *-d* at the end, even though the letter is not usually pronounced (and that's true of a number of words—*grand* is /gran/ in "we had a grand time" or "grandfather"). What's missing is the double *r,* and that's not a matter of sound, but of meaning: The word *errand* has become related to *ERRor* and *ERR* and *ERRatic,* and that relationship is captured in the spelling of the word.

In fact, the ability to sense the relationship of *err, error, erratic,* and *errand* that's frozen in their spelling is not a trivial matter. The meaning relationship between "make a mistake" and "wander" can be significant in building your vocabulary, for you now have at least a start on deciphering the meaning of other related words that you may not have met before:

12.10   Launcelot was a famous *knight-ERRant.*

12.11   The report of her death was *ERRoneous.*

12.12   There were so many mistakes in the book that the publisher had to print an *ERRata sheet.*

The spelling system, then, embodies the history of words. We spell *pneumonia* with a *pneu* rather than a *new* because the word retains in its spelling the sign of its Greek origin. That spelling has to be learned, of course, but once learned, and connected with the lungs (the root is the Greek word *pnein,* to breathe), the writer has a good start on spelling (and understanding) a whole set of related scientific words—from *pneumatic* and *pneumectomy* to *pneumobacillus* and even *pneumoconiosis.*

The influence of etymology is so strong that we've even changed the spellings of words to clarify their etymological origin. The word *crystal,* for example, was most often spelled *cristal* in the Middle English period; its spelling was changed to *crystal* in Modern English to show its relation to the Latin *crystallum,* crystal or ice. *Errand* was commonly spelled *erend* in Middle English.

As a result, the way words are pronounced sometimes gets in the way. We're stuck with "silent letters" at the beginning of *knapsack, knee, knight, knife, knob,* and *know* because they were all pronounced with an initial /k/ seven hundred years ago, and we still spell *answer* with a *w* centuries after we quit pronouncing it that way. Some writers develop silent "spelling pronunciations" for words such as *answer, February, salmon,* and *together*—for example, pronouncing the "w" in *answer* to remember that it's there.

Of course, etymology is not the answer to all misspellings, and some words, mostly borrowed ones, must be memorized:

12.13   pizza, sergeant, colonel, chaise longue, gestalt, *jeu d'esprit*

But if you find that your misspellings often neglect the etymology of words, you may want to make a conscious effort to connect spelling with meaning.

Problem Three. Spelling and meaning   Each of the misspellings below is a spelling based on sound rather than meaning. For each, find the correct spelling of the word, then give a related word to explain the spelling. The first two are completed for you. (You may find that you can't decipher some of the words.)

etym: Etymology   A misspelling that does not reflect the etymology of the word. Enter these words in your spelling log and find a related word to lock in the meaning of the word. Here are spelling log entries for the misspellings *recanize, exackly, straightlaced,* and *deepression:*

type	word	cue word	sentence
etym	recognize	cognition	I recognize that he is cognizant.
etym	exactly	exact	We will exact taxes exactly.
etym	straitlaced	strait	The straits of Gibraltar are strait-laced.
etym	depression	impression	His depression is impressive.

a. critter   creature::creation

b. ginral   general::generation

c. figger

d. reelly

e. playright

f. copywrite

g. birthwrite

h. penel code

i. eturnal

j. copyrighter

■

The Schwa Vowel

Does the word end in *-ance* or *-ence*, in *-ent* or *-ant*, in *-or* or *-er*? We've all been brought up short by spelling questions like these—in fact, almost all students have some trouble with the spelling questions like those of problem four below. But after reading the next few pages, you'll be able to identify all the correct spellings—and to explain why you know they are correct.

Problem Four. The schwa vowel   Circle the correct spelling in each of the following sets.

a. histry   history   histery   histary   histury

b. existence   existance   existunce

c. majer   major   majur   majar

d. demacratic   democratic   demucratic   demecratic

e. presdent   presadent   presedent   president

f. sentunce   sentance   sentence

g. repitition   repetition   repatition

h. precadent   precedent   precident   precdent

i. comparable   compairable   compearable   compirable

j. compastion   compsition   compesition   composition

k. janiter   janitar   janitur   janitor

l. manager   managor   managur   managir

m. illestrate   illustrate   illastrate   illistrate

n. indstry   indestry   indistry   industry

o. immigrate   immagrate   immegrate   immugrate

p. consalation   conselation   conslation   consolation

q. ablition   abalition   abolition   abelition

r. compatent   competent   comptent   compitent   ■

The word *schwa* (from the Hebrew word for "emptiness") identifies the most common sound in the English language. Technically, *schwa* is a "neutral untensed lax vowel," and it's written phonetically as an upsidedown *e:* /ə/. It's a sound that might be spelled *uh*, the sound that people make when they pause in speaking. Schwa is the most popular sound in the English language because every vowel sound that is not stressed is automatically spoken as a schwa. The word *vowel*, for instance, can be pronounced with only one vowel, /vouwl/, or with a schwa, /vouwəl/, or, more formally, as /vouwel/. You're almost sure to have a schwa in an unstressed *the*, /thə/, or at the end of *spoken*, /spokən/. There is a schwa at the end of sentence, /sentəns/, and there are four schwa sounds in the word *formidableness*.

Any vowel letter can be the sign of a schwa sound—the *a* in *human*, the *e* in *bullet*, the first *i* in *divide*, the *o* in *woman*, and the *u* in *particular*. There's nothing in the sound of the word that gives any hint at all about how the vowel might be spelled. All the words in problem four differ only in the spelling of the schwa sound, and many of them are common spelling problems.

But remember that we're discovering just how regular the spelling system is, particularly in revealing underlying forms. The sound /ə/ is *schwa*: Schwa Vowel Misspelling of the unstressed vowel, schwa, in a word. Find a related word to highlight the vowel. Here are spelling log entries for the misspellings *grammer, definate,* and *applicible.*

type	word	cue word	cue sentence
schwa	grammAr	grammAtical	We hope the grammar is grammatical.
schwa	definIte	finIte	We definitely must give a finite definition.
schwa	applicAble	applicAtion	The application is applicable.

an unstressed sound, but the spelling of the sound retains the stressed form of the vowel. And we can uncover or highlight the vowel sound of many syllables just as we popped up the *g* in *signal* or the *b* in *bomb*—by putting the word in a different form that will sound the full vowel. The sound of the final vowel of *formal,* for example, is a schwa, and the sound gives you no clue to the spelling. But the related word *formAl-ity* pops up the vowel spelling, and it's retained in the spelling of *formAl* as an underlying form. The word *history* is pronounced with the middle syllable dropped, as /histrē/, or with it reduced to a schwa, as /histərē/. But the related word *histOrical* highlights the sound of the middle vowel, and it's spelled the same way in both words. *Existence,* to take another example, ends with the sound /ənts/. This sound can be spelled *-ance* or *-ence* in English, depending on whether the word was borrowed from French or Latin. *Existence* was borrowed from Latin, and the word *ExistEntialists* can help you remember the *-ence* spelling.

There are times when this device won't work, for there are words that don't have a related word with the full vowel sound—there's no such word as *attendAncial* to pop up the spelling of *attendance,* for example, and the spelling of that word has to be memorized. (Or else you have to file it away in your mind as a word borrowed from French, and connect its spelling with other French words like *acceptance, assistance,* and *dominance.*) But the device of finding a related word will solve many spelling questions.

Problem Five. Finding the schwa vowel The words from problem four are listed again below, this time with the schwa vowel left blank. Enter the correct vowel, then prove your spelling correct by entering a related word that highlights the vowel sound. The first three are done for you.

a. histOry::histOrical
b. existEnce::ExistEntial
c. majOr::majOrity
d. dem_cratic
e. pres_dent
f. rep_tition
g. prec_dent
h. comp_rable
i. comp_sition

j. janit_r
k. manag_r
l. ill_strate
m. ind_stry
n. imm_grate

■

Homonyms

Few of us have problems with the spellings of *wood* and *would,* or *sine* and *sign,* or *vane, vein,* and *vain.* They sound alike—they're *homonyms*—but they are quite different in meaning and use, and we seldom mix them up. The problem comes with homonyms that are very close in meaning (*principal* and *principle, stationary* and *stationery, affect* and *effect*); with homonyms that may be new to us (*cite,* as distinct from *site* and *sight*); or with small spelling differences that mark important differences in meaning (*cloth* and *clothe, loose* and *lose, chose* and *choose, lead* and *led, casual* and *causal, weather* and *whether*).

Memory devices will work for some homonyms—"the princiPAL is your pal," for example—and others can be connected with related words (*site::situation, cite::citation, affect:affectation*). Most, however, need to be checked in a dictionary and memorized, again using your spelling log.

The homonyms *it's* and *its* pose a special problem—it's probably the most common single misspelling. *Its,* without the apostrophe, is the possessive: It needs to be connected with the following regular pattern:

12.14   her homonym
his homonym
its homonym
their homonym

Its homonym is a contracted form of *it is;* it's used when *it's* can be replaced by *it is.* *It's* can always be replaced by *it is.*

hom : Homonym   Misspelling of homonyms, words that sound alike or nearly alike. Connect the correct spelling with a related word, or contrast the homonyms.

type	word	cue word	sentence
hom	their, there, they're	our::their here::there they are	There's their house over there. They're home.
hom	affect effect	affection effective	Insults don't seem to affect my dog; they have no effect on him. (affect, "to influence"; effect, "to cause or bring about," "result")
hom	its it's = it is	his::its	Get the duck: It's time for its tranquilizer.

Problem Six. Homonyms   Enter the appropriate word in each blank.

a. The _____ is _____ because the _____ is _____. (hoarse, horse; coarse, course)

b. If you _____ the right _____, _____ the right law. (cite, site, sight)

c. _____ on _____ toes. (your, you're)

d. _____ going to drive _____ car? (who's, whose)

e. _____ _____ bad _____ _____ late _____ save the chicken from _____ inevitable fate. (its, it's; to, two, too)

f. Get your _____ from the _____. (council, counsel)

g. I'd _____ you to get some _____. (advise, advice)   ■

Word Forms

By "word form," we mean the different forms that a meaning unit can take. We can recognize, for example, that *form* is related to *formation, formative, formal, form's,* and *forming,* as well as *deform* and *inform. Write,* we noticed, can appear as *written, writing,* and *writer.* We would understand the coined words *writable, writerly* ("behave like a writer"), and *anti-writing* (a word created by our colleague Linda Bannister to describe ways to avoid a writing assignment); and we can connect the meaning (and spelling) of *write* with a legal *writ,* a tax *write-off,* or a *write-in* candidate.

Word forms—particularly word endings—are a spelling problem, in large part because we do not normally need to rely on them in reading—usually a glance at the beginning of a word, in context, is enough to remind us of the whole word. Moreover, some word forms are specific to print—we don't hear the apostrophe that separates *it's* from *its*, nor do we hear, directly, the double *p* that separates *moping* from *mopping*, or the missing *m* that turns a *comma* into a *coma*.

Fortunately, the word form systems are quite predictable, and they can be mastered with some conscious effort.

The -ed System

Here are three words, printed first as they would be spelled in British Simplified Spelling, then as they are normally spelled:

12.15 chaenjd   changed
           printed   printed
           wakt   walked

Notice the endings. In the system that copies sound, each word ends differently, reflecting the ending sounds /d/ (in *changED*), /əd/ (in *printED*), and /t/ (in *walkED*). And these ending sounds, the /t/ particularly, can be dropped off in speech: We all say *walked to* in "I walked to the store" with one /t/ sound, as /wäktoo/ rather than /wäkt too/, and some speakers will drop off ending sounds consistently in relaxed speech.

But in our spelling system, the three sounds are given the same spelling, *-ed*. The spelling doesn't copy the sound; it shows meaning—in this case, the meaning that can be expressed as "past tense." The reader of British Simplified Spelling has to connect each spelling with a sound, then connect the sound with the meaning as shown in Figure 12.6. In our system, the meaning "past tense" is separated from the sound and is shown directly by the abstract spelling *-ed* (which, after all, is no-

spelling		ending		sound	meaning
chaenjd	⇒	-d	⇒	/d/	
printed	⇒	-ed	⇒	/əd/	}"past tense"
wakt	⇒	-t	⇒	/t/	

FIGURE 12.6 Past Tense Endings in Phonetic Alphabet

spelling	ending		meaning	(sound)
changed				/d/
printed	-ed	$\Rightarrow$	"past tense"	/ed/
walked				/t/

FIGURE 12.7   Past Tense Endings Show Meaning

body's pronunciation). Thus reading or writing -*ed* reflects meaning directly, as shown in Figure 12.7.

Problem Seven. The missing -ed hunt   James Sledd of the University of Texas has remarked informally that the -*ed* marker of the past tense may be disappearing from the language. As we noted, that's now true of some spoken dialects all the time, and it's true of all spoken dialects some of the time. Although the -*ed* marker remains in formal print, we find increasing evidence in signs, menus, and advertisements that it is disappearing from relaxed print. *Iced tea* is increasingly seen as *ice tea*, shifting grammatically from a past participle plus a noun ("tea that is iced") to a noun-noun combination ("tea with ice"). What were "waxed beans" a generation ago have become "wax beans" today, and many colleges now speak of time off for faculty research or course preparation as "faculty release time" rather than "faculty released time." "Wax beans" is now common, and "release time" is growing, while "ice tea" remains a mistake.

We've jotted down several missing -*ed* endings from menus, supermarkets, and signs, and mixed them with several legitimate noun-noun

tense: Tense   An error in verb tense, usually a missing -*ed* ending. There are clear reasons why students often omit the -*ed* ending, particularly in contexts which lead to "suppose to" for "supposed to" or "prejudice" for "prejudiced," where the abstract written -*ed* is sounded as a /t/ sound. A good way to lock in the -*ed* system is to read drafts aloud, listening for the /t/, /d/, and /əd/ sounds that mark -*ed* endings.

type	word	cue word	sentence
wf: -ed	used to	—	I used to sleep late in the past.
wf: -ed	walked to	—	I walked to school, in the past tense.

combinations. Find the missing -*ed* endings (or possible -*ed* endings) in
the combinations below. Which of the missing -*ed* endings are acceptable to you; which are spelling errors?

business bribe	toss salad	creme rinse
shatterproof bottle	unfinish furniture	contact lenses
can goods	crochet stitch	bake potato
labor relations	corn beef	condition reflex
incline plane	home run	use car
wax paper	oversize load	skim milk

■

The -s Systems

It's no wonder that student writers sometimes have problems with the
-*s* systems of print, particularly with the -*'s* and -*s'*, which have no equivalent in speech. The -*s* systems are remarkably complicated. They have
three different sounds: /s/ in *spatS* and *markS;* /z/ in *shoeS* and *timeS;*
and /əz/ in *caseS* and *closeS.* They have four possible spellings: -*s* (*duckS,*
wordS), -*es* (*do::doES, princess::princessES*), and also the possessive -*'s* and
-*s'* ("the author'S book" and "the authorS' book"—the first written by
one author, the second by two or more). They have three quite separate uses. One -*s* ending marks the plural of most nouns:

12.16   one noun::two nounS; one cent::ten centS (but, "a ten cent
piece")

A different -*s* ending marks the "third person singular present tense
verb":

12.17   If she doES and he doES, it's likely they all do.

A third -*s* ending, with the apostrophe, marks possession:

12.18   It was Buddy Holly'S song, but it's the Rolling StoneS' now.

There are even more complications. The possessive marker on *Rolling Stones,* in 12.18 above, does not add an -*s*, since the word already
has one.[7] The contracted form of the verb *is* has a surface form very
like the *'s:*

12.19   The duck'S cooking. (Contraction of *the duck is.*)
12.20   The duck'S cooking was delayed. (Possessive—"the cooking
of the duck")

The -*s* plural and present tense markers change the spelling of -*y* to -*i*, but the possessive -*'s* does not:

12.21 The city'S struggle was deplored by other citIES.

By separating the three -*s* systems, we can clarify them and suggest ways to improve your mastery of them.

Plurals Most native English words add plurals by adding -*s* or -*es*. Some native English words, however, retain older forms (one fish::ten fish; one foot::ten feet; one child::six children). A particular problem comes with borrowed nouns that retain their Latin and Greek plurals: one *alumna*::*two alumnae;* one *medium*::two *media.* These words often live double lives, the English -*s* plural used in speech and the Greek or Latin plural used in print. The TV announcer who speaks of "the television media" would shift to "the television medium" if he became a newspaper reporter. Professors talk about their *syllabuses,* but they write articles about their *syllabi;* scientists say "the *data* is collected," but write "the *data* are collected" (one *datum*::two *data*); camera owners have three focuses, but lens grinders make three *foci;* nurseries sell *cactuses,* but botanists buy *cacti.* Most of these words are gradually shifting to standard -*s* plurals: Few now remember that *agenda* was originally a plural form, with a Latin singular *agendum.* But for the next hundred years or so, you will want to watch for Greek and Latin plurals in the print code.

Third-person singular present tense -s You may be familiar, from studying a foreign language, with the task of "conjugating" a verb. Here is the conjugation of the present tense of the verb *keep* in two forms, as it was in Old English, a thousand years ago, and as it is in the print code of today.

12.22

Old English	*Modern English*
ic cepE	I keep
thu cepEST	you keep
he ⎫	he ⎫
heo ⎬ cepETH	she ⎬ keepS
hit ⎭	it ⎭
we capATH	we keep
ge cepATH	you keep
hi cepATH	they keep

The -*s* ending on "she keepS" is a vestigial survivor of a much more complicated earlier system of English. (You'll recognize the earlier form, -*eth*, from Shakespeare and from the Bible—"He giveth us.") The -*s* ending on the verb appears with a singular third-person subject (he, she, it), and it disappears with a plural subject. Thus, we can create the "fabulous jumping -*s*" by switching between singular and plural subjects:

> **12.23A**   The dogS fight.
>
> **12.23B**   The dog fightS.

We can make the fabulous jumping -*s* hop again, this time by adding another verb, such as the helping verb *do:*

> **12.23C**   The dog doES fight.

And we can—magically—make the -*s* disappear by adding a different helping verb or by placing the verb in a subordinate clause:

> **12.23D**   The dog may fight.
>
> **12.23E**   I see that the dog fightS.
>
> **12.23F**   I see the dog fight.

Problem Eight. A special problem in subject-verb agreement   The sentences below are adapted from a variety of textbook sources. They suggest how far some writers are willing to separate subject and verb, and, as a result, how tenuous the question of subject-verb agreement can become. Choose the correct verb for each example, and be prepared to defend your answer.[8]

a. The idea that producers will place more on the market when price is high and less when price is low also _____ intuitively appealing. (*is* or *are?*)

> Willis L. Peterson,
> *Principles of Economics*

b. The way in which Athens came to be placed in the circumstances under which her power grew was this. (In the present tense, would the next to the last word be *is* or *are?*)

> Donald Kagan,
> *Problems in Ancient History*

c. The total minor scale pattern in Example 22, including the descending natural pattern and the ascending altered pattern, _____ called the melodic minor scale. (*is* or *are?*)

> Allen Forte, *Tonal Harmony*
> *in Concept and Practice*

---

agr : Agreement Agreement of subject and verb, usually an *-s* ending wrongly placed on, or not placed on, the verb. Reading a draft aloud, listening for the three sounds, /s/, /z/, and /əs/, that signal the *-s* verb ending, is a good method of watching for most *-s* verb endings. Two conventions, however, can cause problems:

■ the *-s* verb marker agrees with the headword in a phrase, not with the nearest word: It's "One of the ducks biteS people often" (the pattern is "one . . . biteS," not "duckS bite").
■ titles and some *-s* words are considered singular in some contexts: It's "The jaws of a shark seem dangerous" (plural), but "*Jaws* seemS to be a best-seller" (singular); it's "His ethics seem questionable," but "Ethics seemS to be an interesting subject."

---

d. Research with the semantic differential—applying it to wide varieties of concepts and dimensions and to different groups of people—consistently ___ to three or more less independent factors or basic dimensions. (*point* or *points*?)

P. H. Mussen and R. Rosenzweig,
Psychology: An Introduction

e. Yet an interest in landscape as such, and our ordinary patience with mere description and observation (as with mere anecdote in conversation or the newspapers), ___ legitimate in their own way. (*is* or *are*?)

Warner Bertoff,
The Example of Melville

Possessive -'s The apostrophe (') signals that a letter or letters have been left out:

12.24 He's not coming, and she won't either.

12.25 a blot on the 'scutcheon

12.26 Wait 'til the sun shines, Nellie.

The possessive ending was marked with an *-es* in Middle English (*The Lord's Prayer*::*The Lordes Prayer*). Scribes began to write *-es* as *-'s*, thus starting a special print form.[9] The test of a possessive is simple enough: Possessives can be rewritten as *of the* constructions:

12.27 the water bottle of the duck ⇒ the duck's water bottle

12.28   the meeting of the group   ⇒   the group's meeting

If two ducks share a water bottle, the ending shows first the plural *-s* and then the possessive apostrophe:

12.29   the water bottle of the ducks   ⇒   the ducks' water bottle
12.30   the orders of the generals   ⇒   the generals' orders.

Words that end in *-s* may be marked in either of two ways:

12.31   the novels of Dickens   ⇒   Dickens's novels *or* Dickens' novels

Problem Nine. The possessive -'s   Translate the "of the" constructions into possessives, using *-'s* or *-s'* as required. In doing the last three, you'll discover an interesting fact that separates possessive *-'s* from plural *-s*.

a. the English of the King   ⇒   the King's English
b. the lineup of the Reds
c. the craters of the moon
d. the constituents of the politician
e. the parasites of the bacillus
f. the sixth son of the sick sheik
g. the problem of John and the problem of Mary
h. the problems of John and Mary
i. the feathers of the duck over there
j. the castle of the Queen of England
k. the castles of the Queens of England.

Problem Ten. The -s systems   This problem is designed to lock in the various meanings of *-s* endings. Read the phrases below and then answer the questions that follow.

a. The duck bites
b. The duck's bite
c. The duck bite
d. The ducks bite
e. The ducks' bites
f. A duck bite

---

poss : Possession   Possessive *-s's* marker is omitted. Add *-'s* or *-s'* to show possession. Possession can be tested by rewording the phrase as an "of the" construction:

First Draft	*Revision*
the cities problems	the city's problems (the construction can be reworded as "the problems of the city")
the readers questions	the reader's questions OR the readers' questions (the construction can be reworded as either "the questions of the reader" or "the questions of the readers")

- Which of the word groups are complete sentences?
- Which can be completed by the words "can be annoying"?
- Which can be completed by the words "is annoying"?
- Which can be completed by the words "are annoying"?
- Which can be completed by the word "annoying"?   ■

Adjective and Adverb Form

Some modifiers shift in form to add an *-ly* as adverbs; others do not:

12.32 It was *hard* work. The man worked *hard*.

12.33 It was a *sudden* stop. She stopped *suddenly*.

The distinction can be humorously shown with the following pair of sentences.

12.34 The bloodhound smelled bad.

12.35 The bloodhound smelled badly.

The dog of 12.34 needs a bath; it has a bad smell. The dog of 12.35 has a more serious problem: It's poor at smelling.

The adjective *good* and its adverb form *well* pose several problems, for they have several overlapping meanings, as in these ambiguous sentences:

adj / adv : Use the appropriate adjective and adverb form.

First Draft	Revision
I washed the car good.	I washed the car well. (*Well* is more formal.)
The ambulance came quick.	The ambulance came quickly. (The more formal adverb form is preferred in print.)

12.36 She looked good. (Was she good-looking, or looking for something?)

12.37 She looked well. (*Well* as opposed to *ill*? *Well* meaning thoroughly?)

The choice of *good* and *well* is often a matter of social context. A used car salesman would probably say "runs good" rather than the more formal "runs well," but in most print contexts the adverb *well* would be more appropriate: "She sang well in the concert" instead of "She sang good in the concert."

The Rule Systems of Spelling

Consider the rule of spelling which tells writers whether or not to double a final letter when adding an ending, as in *run::running* or *write:: writing::written.*

12.38 The final consonant of one-syllable words is doubled if an ending beginning with a vowel (or y) is added, and if the word ends in a single consonant (except x) and is preceded by a single vowel.

The rule will give us the right spelling:

12.39 cup + ed ⇒ cupped
       cup + ful ⇒ cupful
       peel + ed ⇒ peeled
       tax + ed ⇒ taxed
       clam + y ⇒ clammy

sys : System Misspelling of the rule systems of English. Check
the correct spelling in a dictionary, then find a related example to lock in the rule. Here are spelling log entries for *mis-
pell, dispensible,* and *copyed:*

type	word	cue word	sentence
sys	copied	cry::cried	The copyist was being copied.
sys	dispensable	disability	He was able to be dispensable.
sys	misspell	missent	The letter was missent because the address was misspelled.

And it may be a useful one to memorize if you have repeated problems
with doubled letters. Frankly, however, we doubt that most writers
memorize and use such rules. Instead, they develop a "feel" for spelling, and that "feel" gives them the answer. Dictionaries, again, will help
with such problems, since they give the spellings of such word forms.

We might only note that there are principles behind such systematic
changes. Some doubled letters carry information about vowel sounds:
There's a big difference between a *liter* and a *litter,* or between *hoping*
and *hopping.* Other doubled letters maintain the logic of word formation:

12.40 il + logic $\Rightarrow$ illogic

  mis + spell $\Rightarrow$ misspell

Some Latin prefixes tend to assimilate—that is, to change their spelling
to fit with the beginning of the stem:

12.41 ad + cuse $\Rightarrow$ accuse

  ob + pose $\Rightarrow$ oppose

  com + rect $\Rightarrow$ correct

  sub + ceed $\Rightarrow$ succeed

Problem Eleven. The rule systems of spelling Complete the following
word form changes, doubling letters or removing final *-e* as needed.
The last four are issues about which dictionaries differ—you might
want to check the form you chose against the preference of your dictionary.

    a. ad + nounce

    b. ad + vise

    c. of + fend

    d. con + lision

    e. com + bat

    f. sub + ficient

    g. ad + mit

    h. benefit + ed

    i. judge + ment

    j. commit + ed

    k. knowledge + able ■

SUMMARY

We have offered an analysis of the patterns of English spelling, suggesting that our spelling system conveys more information about meaning than about sound. This analysis has led us to offer several facts to help improve spelling:

- spelling reflects etymology ("etym");
- related words can highlight vowel spellings ("schwa");
- homonyms can be contrasted ("hom");
- word-form spellings are systematic ("sys").

Here are two final suggestions for improving spelling. First, do crossword puzzles. Magazines with graded crosswords (easy, medium, hard, expert) are available at all newsstands, and they are a pleasant way of improving your command of the print code. Crossword puzzles automatically correct your spelling, and they also make you more conscious of word endings. (But *don't* do "word search" puzzles—they stress recognizing letter shapes instead of meaning.)

Second, start a spelling log. Buy a small notebook and rule it into four columns: Enter type of error (so you can begin to diagnose your error patterns), the word you've misspelled (spelled correctly), a cue word to remind you of the spelling, and a short sentence to lock in the spelling.

FINAL WRITING ASSIGNMENTS

I. The Print Code Transcribe the passages below into standard written English—at least as much of them as you can. The first is a *jeu d'esprit* by Howard Chace (so, after you finish it, you'll know what a *jeu d'esprit* is); the second a letter written in 1566. (Both are easier as group efforts.)

A

Ladle Rat Rotten Hut

(Heresy ladle furry starry toiling udder warts—warts welcher altar girdle deferent firmer once inner regional verging.)

Wants pawn term dare worsted ladle gull hoe lift wetter murder inner ladle cordage honor itch offer lodge, dock, florist. Disk ladle gull orphan worry putty ladle rat cluck wetter ladle rat hut, an fur disk raisin pimple colder Ladle Rat Rotten Hut.

Wan moaning Ladle Rat Rotten Hut's murder colder inset, "Ladle Rat Rotten Hut, heresy ladle basking winsome burden barter an shirker cockles. Tick disk ladle basking tutor cordage offer groin-murder hoe lifts honor udder site offer florist. Shaker lake! Dun stopper laundry wrote! Dun stopper peck floors! Dun daily-doily inner florist, an yonder nor sorghum stenches, dun stopper torque wet strainers!"

"Hoe-cake, murder," resplendent Ladle Rat Rotten Hut, an tickle ladle basking an stuttered oft.

Honor wrote tutor cordage offer groin-murder, Ladle Rat Rotten Hut mitten anomalous woof.

"Wail, wail, wail!" set disk wicket woof, "Evanescent Ladle Rat Rotten Hut! Wares are putty ladle gull goring wizard ladle basking?"

"Armor goring tumor groin-murder's," reprisal ladle gull. "Grammar's seeking bet. Armor ticking arson burden barter an shirker cockles."

"O hoe! Heifer gnats woke," setter wicket woof, butter taught tomb shelf, "Oil tickle shirt court tutor cordage offer groin-murder. Oil ketchup wetter letter, an den—O bore!"

Soda wicket woof tucker shirt court, an whinny retched a cordage offer groin-murder, picked inner windrow, an sore debtor pore oil worming worse lion inner bet. Inner flesh, disk abdominal woof lipped honor bet, paunched honor pore oil worming, an garbled erupt. Den disk ratchet ammonol pot honor groin-murder's nut cup an gnat-gun, any curdled ope inner bet.

Inner ladle wile, Ladle Rat Rotten Hut a raft attar cordage, an ranker dough ball. "Comb ink, sweat hard," setter wicket woof, disgracing is verse.

Ladle Rat Rotten Hut entity bet rum, an stud buyer groin-murder's bet.

"O Grammar!" crater ladle gull historically, "Water bag icer gut! A nervous sausage bag ice!"

"Battered lucky chew whiff, sweat hard," setter bloat-Thursday woof, wetter wicket small honors phase.

"O, Grammar, water bag noise! A nervous sore suture anomalous prognosis!"

"Battered small your whiff, doling," whiskered dole woof, ants mouse worse waddling.

"O Grammar, water bag mouser gut! A nervous sore suture bag mouse!"
Daze worry on-forger-nut ladle gull's lest warts. Oil offer sodden, caking
offer carvers an sprinkling otter bet, disk hoard-hoarded woof lipped own
pore Ladle Rat Rotten Hut an garbled erupt.

MURAL: Yonder nor sorghum stenches shut ladle gulls stopper torque wet
strainers.

B

A letter from Mary Queen of Scots to her cousin,
the Earl of Lennox, about a dispute between herself
and her recent husband, the King of France.

Richt traist cousing and counsalour we greit zow weill. We ressauit zour
lettre, and be the same persavis other newes nor we lukit for, quhilk at the
first, as thair is gude reasoun, we fand verie strange, and wald hane bene
contentit to keip thame to our selff, gif the wecht of the mater tweching
ws sa neir, as alsua oure haill realme, had not compellit ws to oppin the
same to our counsell, to have thair advyse, and to knaw vpoun quhat
ground sa sodayne ane interpryss is takin in hand. Thay this day, in the
audience of Monsieur le Croicq, the King of France's ambassadour, hes
spokin with the King being heir, requiring of him to knaw quhat is the
mater that he findis himself grevit in and mislykis, and gif the samyn stude
in our awin hand, we war content to do thairin quhat become us; as the
counsell likuiss offerit for thair parities that in reasoun he suld have al-
sweill to our self, as to our counsell, in Monsieur le Crocques prescence,
he mysknawis that he has ony sic purpos in hede, or ony caus of miscon-
tentacioun. Bot his spiking is conditionall, sua that we can vunderstand
gude to gif yow aduertisement heirof, that ze may weill persave in quhat
devoir [respects] we haue putt ourself to satisfie him in all thingis as accor-
dis vpoun reasoun. Like as he sall neuir by ws haue occasioun to the contrary. Subscriuit with our hand at Edinburgh, the last day of September
1566.

Zour guddochter

II. Playing with the Print Code Ewe shrub now bee reddy two come
pose ewer own mess age, a Judas pree. Jest right a long, boat bee shore
that your men tell lee awn coarse, sew ewer reed erse can fall, Oh.

III. Investigating the Print Code Examine some writing from the 1600s
or 1700s—in the original form if possible. Summarize the changes in
spelling and punctuation in a short report.

IV. The Changing Print Code CB radios began as "citizen's band radios" (the band of the citizen), became "citizens band radios" as they
became more popular (the band for citizens), and have now become
"citizen band radios" (the band of the citizen); "trade unions" began a

hundred years ago as "trades unions"; at one motel, half the signs read "Howard Johnson's," the other half "Howard Johnsons." Using whatever evidence you can find—in the yellow pages, want ads, student newspaper, your own observation—compile a brief report on "the changing print code." What does your evidence suggest about the direction of language change?

Interesting class reports might be written about several topics relating to this chapter—about the development of the alphabet, about spelling reformers (such as Noah Webster and George Bernard Shaw), about the difference between American spelling and British spelling, or about the systems of Chinese or Japanese writing.

FOR FURTHER READING

A short essay elaborating our view of the systems of spelling is Wayne O'Neil's "The Spelling and Pronunciation of English," in the *American Heritage Dictionary* (Boston: Houghton Mifflin, 1978), xxxv–xxxvii. There are also several spelling workbooks that will give you systematic practice—our favorite among them is Patricia M. Fergus' *Spelling Improvement,* 2nd ed. (New York: McGraw-Hill, 1973).

Much more complex, but consistently interesting, are related readings: I. J. Gelb's study of the alphabet, *A Study of Writing* (Chicago: University of Chicago Press, 1963); Charles Read's study of preschool children who develop their own writing systems, "Pre-School Children's Knowledge of English Phonology," *Harvard Educational Review,* 41 (1971); Takahiko Sakamoto's explanation of Japanese writing systems, "Writing Systems in Japan," in *New Horizons in Reading,* ed. John E. Merritt (Newark, Del.: International Reading Association, 1976), pp. 244–54; and Paul A. Kolers' "Experiments in Reading," *Scientific American,* 227 (July 1972), 84–91.

NOTES

1. Examples are from Julia S. Falk, *Linguistics and Language,* 2nd ed. (New York: John Wiley, 1978), p. 400.
2. Dictionary pronunciation keys, such as this one, rely on common Northern pronunciations, and many readers will find that their own pronunciation may depart from the samples given. Many speakers, for example, pronounce *Mary* and *marry* alike, and others have the same vowel sound in *ought* and *ox.*
3. Azel Wijk, *Regularized English* (Stockholm: Alquist & Wiksell, 1959), pp. 324–25.
4. Noam Chomsky and Morris Halle, *The Sound Pattern of English* (New York: Harper & Row, 1968), p. 49.
5. Paul A. Kolers, "Experiments in Reading," *Scientific American,* 227 (July 1972), 84–91.

6. Data in problems two, four, and five are adapted from Carol Chomsky, "Reading, Writing, and Phonology," *Harvard Educational Review*, 40 (1970), 287–309.

7. Style manuals and publishing houses differ in their preference for keeping the -*s's* (Keats's poems; Dickens's novels) or deleting it (Keats' poems, Dickens' novels).

8. The sentences are from Sandra Schor, "Writing to Read—Reversing the Order for Inexperienced Readers," *Composition and Teaching*, 1 (1978), 7–16.

9. The apostrophe is also used as a special marker for the plurals of signs and letters (watch your p's and q's; no if's, and's, or but's). Some style manuals and publishers use the apostrophe for numbers as well (the early 1900's; bet 8's and 12's); our publisher uses a more modern style (the early 1900s; bet 8s and 12s).

UNIT V

LARGER ELEMENTS OF ARRANGEMENT

13

The Formative Principle

The worker in wood needs to know the grain of the wood. . . . It is the grain of the living wood we are after, the character of the language by which we live and compose.

JOSEPHINE MILES

In unit Two, we discussed the "smaller units of arrangement," how sentences relate to each other (*coherence*—in chapter Four), and how they grow into paragraphs (chapter Five). In this unit, we discuss larger units of arrangement, the "shaping" of an essay (in this chapter) and the building up of an answer to an in-class essay examination and the writing of a longer research paper (in the next chapter).

We can't see the "shape" of "larger units of arrangement" in the same way that we can see the markings of sentences and paragraphs. Textbooks, like this one, mark larger units by chapters and subheadings, but such marks are seldom needed in shorter pieces. Perhaps, then, we might pin down the notion of these larger units by taking a message and changing its *form*—beginning, for example, with a note taped to a refrigerator and a sentence from an old physics textbook.

13.1 This is just to say I have eaten the plums that were in the icebox and which you were probably saving for breakfast. Forgive me—they were delicious, so sweet and so cold.

13.2 And so no force, however great, can stretch a cord, however fine, into a horizontal line which shall be absolutely straight.

William Whewell, Elementary Treatise on Mechanics (1819)

Both examples are unremarkable enough. But notice what happens when we keep the *message* the same and vary the *form* it assumes. Example 13.1, for example, is only incidentally a "note taped to a refrigerator"; its actual form was that of a poem, and when we re-examine it with the notion of "poem" in our minds, we change our sense of purpose and meaning:

13.1A   *This Is Just To Say*

> I have eaten
> the plums
> that were in
> the icebox
> and which
> you were probably
> saving
> for breakfast
>
> Forgive me
> they were delicious
> so sweet
> and so cold.

William Carlos Williams

As a poem, the statement becomes something else. "This is just to say" now takes on the role of "title"; and the two units separated on the page become "verse paragraphs." The word *saving*, given a line to itself, takes on a new resonance. The last two lines, "so sweet/and so cold," stretch themselves out in sound and in sense; they now become "conclusion to a poem" rather than "end of note on a refrigerator."

The poem suddenly becomes suggestive in a way that the same message, as a note, does not. It might suggest . . . perhaps something about enjoying the world now instead of saving it for later? That guess might be supported by the understatement of the title, and we might note that, with this guess in mind, the word *icebox* becomes more than "an old-fashioned word for refrigerator"; it reinforces our sense of a "poetic" meaning.

Our purpose, though, is not to analyze the poem, but to show how changing the "form" of a message changes our reactions as readers to it. In a similar way, we can change William Whewell's textbook rule into a carefully structured stanza, complete with rhyme, and when we do, we change our reaction to it.

13.2A   And so no force, however great,
      Can stretch a cord, however fine,
      Into a horizontal line
   Which shall be absolutely straight.[1]

Indeed, several modern poets have tried to awaken our sense of this dynamic power of form by creating poetry from ordinary sentences—"found poetry" it's called, and found poetry can be crafted from traffic signs, newspaper reports, TV programs. Elements may be repeated and rearranged, but nothing can be added. Here is a "found poem," found in the most common of objects, traffic signs:

13.3   *Yield*

Yield.
No Parking.
Unlawful to Pass.
Wait for Green Light.
Yield.

Stop.
Narrow Bridge.
Merging Traffic Ahead
Yield.

Yield.

Ronald Gross

Problem One. A found poem   Construct a "found poem." Find a sentence or passage—from a newspaper, textbook, advertisement—that shows promise of being "shaped" as a piece of poetry. You may rearrange, repeat, delete, but not add new material.   ■

FORM AS SCAFFOLDING FOR IDEAS

Here is an interesting discussion of an experiment; it allows us to ask, "Where does this sense of 'shape' come from?"

13.4   Nothing else on the face of the earth has the same effect as conversation between people. The nature of this situation is illuminated somewhat by a small experiment that I conducted in 1956. . . .
   The experiment strips conversation down to its barest essentials

by depriving the subject of all language except for two pushbuttons and two lights, and by suggesting to him that he is attempting to reach an accord with a mere machine. We brought two students into our building through different doors and led them separately to adjoining rooms. We told each that he was working with a machine, and showed him lights and pushbuttons. Over and over again, at a signal, he would press one or the other of the two buttons, and then one of the two lights would come on. If the light that appeared corresponded to the button he pressed, he was right; otherwise, wrong. The students faced identical displays, but their feedback was reversed: If student *A* pressed the *red* button, then a moment later student *B* would see the *red* light. On any trial, therefore, if the two students pressed matching buttons they would both be wrong.

We used a few pairs of RAND mathematicians; but they would quickly settle on one color, say *red*, and choose it every time. Always correct, they grew bored. The students began with difficulty, but after experience they would generally hit on something. Some, like the mathematicians, chose one color and stuck with it. Some chose simple alternations (*red-green-red-green*). Some chose double alternations (*red-red-green-green*). Some adopted more complex patterns (four *red*, four *green*, four *red*, four *green*, sixteen mixed and mostly incorrect, then repeat). The students, although they were sometimes wrong, were rarely bored. They were busy figuring out the complex patterns of the machine.

David G. Hays, "Language and Interpersonal Relationships"

The patterns, of course, came from the minds of the subjects themselves. The RAND mathematicians settled on comfortable, predictable shapes—a series of *red* lights. The students, more adventurous as they "talked" with each other, created more complex shapes—even though each thought he was dealing with a machine, and even though he was limited to pressing one of two buttons—shapes as complex as sixteen-stage, four-unit recursive combinations.

The experimenter offers this as a metaphor for human conversation. We might take it, more broadly, as a metaphor for the contract between writer and reader. Thus we speak, in our subheading, of form "as scaffolding for ideas," picturing a piece of writing as "constructed" or "built" much as a house is built up, brick by brick, in accordance with a master plan, the architect's drawing, which serves as what we call "the formative principle." We'll consider this first from the point of view of the reader, and then draw implications for the writer.

Grasping Form in Reading

People who study how we gain ideas from reading have begun to talk about the importance of two things: first, the importance of the reader's *plan* for reading, the expectations with which a reader begins to read; and second, the importance, for learning from reading, of grasping the overall *shape* of a piece of writing.

Problem Two. The importance of plan   This problem presents you with an experiment in reading and asks you to predict the result. Researchers selected eighteen common items of food—lettuce, chicken, ice cream, and so on. They put the names of these items of food in two stories, both of equal length. The first story was titled "John and Mary Go to the Supermarket," and it told how John and Mary bought each of the eighteen items. The second story was titled "John and Mary Go to the Restaurant," and it told how John and Mary had dinner at a restaurant, in the process mentioning each of the eighteen items. College students were asked to read one story or the other, and then, later, they were asked to remember as many items of food as they could. Readers of one story were far more successful in remembering than were readers of the other story.[2]

Which story do you think allowed the readers to remember more? Circle the letter identifying your answer below.

a. "John and Mary Go to the Supermarket."

b. "John and Mary Go to the Restaurant."   ■

When we go to the supermarket, we go up and down the aisles with a very general plan. We want to buy lettuce and ice cream and chicken, but we will pick these items off the shelf as they appear. If we shop at a supermarket that we know well, we may be able to order our list, knowing that the lettuce will appear first, in the "fresh fruits and vegetables" aisle that comes right after we pick up our shopping cart, then the chicken, in the meat counter at the back of the store, then the ice cream, up by the checkout counter. But if we go to an unfamiliar store, we might expect the items to be arranged differently. As a result, we might make a shopping list as a mere list, without trying to sort out the items, to arrange them.

But when we go to a restaurant, we have a much more detailed plan. If the restaurant is a fairly formal (and expensive) one, we might expect to be seated by a host, who would give us menus. Then the waiter would appear and ask if we wished to order cocktails. When we were ready, the waiter would take our orders, and then, after a time, bring our food. We might expect to begin with a salad—a lettuce salad in this case—and proceed through the main course (chicken) to the dessert (ice cream). Then we would pay the bill and, after leaving a tip for the waiter, depart.

Students who were given the "John and Mary Go to the Restaurant" story remembered far more items of food than did the students given the "John and Mary Go to the Supermarket" story. They did so because they were better able to connect the new information with what they already knew; the items ordered themselves instead of being a mere list: first the lettuce (as salad), then the chicken (as main course), then the ice cream (as dessert). Indeed, it's quite easy to read a "restaurant story" that matches what we expect "restaurant stories" to be:

13.5 John and Mary decided to go out to eat, and so they went to their favorite restaurant. After they were seated, the waiter came, and they decided to order cocktails. John ordered Chicken Kiev, with a salad and Brussels sprouts, and Mary ordered Beef Wellington, also with a salad. As usual, the food was excellent, and they didn't mind the delay in the service—after all, it was Friday night, and the restaurant was packed. So John left the waiter a good tip.

But it's very hard to read a restaurant story that departs from our expectations about "restaurants":

13.6 Ralph and Beth decided to go out to eat, and so they went to a restaurant they hated. After they were seated, the waiter came and brought their desserts. Ralph stood up and ordered Brussels sprouts, with a side order of Chicken Kiev. Beth ordered Beef Wellington, also with a salad. The waiter brought the food immediately. Ralph paid the bill and gave the waiter a good tip, and then they ate the food. After they finished their salad, they washed the dishes, said goodby to everyone in the restaurant, and left.

Your problem in reading 13.6 is not exactly with the words on the page; the problem is that the words on the page don't match the plan you began with as reader.

These plans become refined through experience. Investigators have found that younger children do not have as detailed a "restaurant plan" as do adults—they seldom mention paying the bill or leaving a tip, for example.

Problem Three. Finding a plan   Ask at least ten people one of the questions below, and tape record their answers. Transcribe the answers, and notice the similarities and differences. Then, in a short paper, create a general "plan" for doing this activity. You may find, of course, that some people have more detailed "plans" than other people, and you may find that we share firmer plans about some things ("going to a restaurant") than we do about other things ("getting an 'A' in an art history course"). If you select the first question, you may want to compare your results with those of two psychologists who decided to teach a computer to "go to a restaurant"—R. C. Schank and R. P. Abelson, *Scripts, Plans, Goals, and Understanding* (Hillsdale, N.J.: Lawrence Erlbaum, 1977).

   a. "What do people do when they go to a restaurant?"

   b. "How do you wash dishes?"

   c. "How do you buy a used car?"

   d. "How do you take an airplane trip?"

   e. "How do you study for a history test?"

   f. "How do you get an 'A' in an art history course?"

   g. "How do you get a job teaching in a high school?"   ■

We might clarify the notion of "plan" for reading by imagining sixth-grade students all reading the same passage in a textbook, say a passage about Brazil. One student might have a well-developed plan for "reading about a nation": She would expect to be given information on geography, history, form of government, principal exports—and as this information appeared, it would be stored in the expected slot. The other student might not have a well-developed plan for "reading about a nation." If so, she would be much less likely to learn as much from her reading, for she would not have a plan for storing the information.

Many of you might have taken a course in reading Shakespeare's plays in high school and college. If so, you probably found the first play to be very difficult to read, for you had little sense of what to expect. The second play was probably much easier: You expected things like characters and scenes, and you expected a certain kind of language. Our discussion of reading a textbook, in chapter Five, began with two pieces of advice—"survey" the chapter and "question" what you're going to read—that aimed at sharpening your "plan" for reading.

The reader's plan has a great deal to do with the writer's shaping of a piece of writing. The best advice, obviously enough, is "Give the reader the shape he expects to find." Or, at the very least, the advice is, "Tell the reader the shape you're going to use, so she can plan ahead." The passage below gives you no sense of its shape, and it provides you with no "plan" for reading it. It was rated "difficult to read" by the students who read it, and they remembered very little of what they read.

13.7 The procedure is actually quite simple. First you arrange things into different groups depending on their makeup. Of course, one pile may be sufficient depending on how much there is to do. If you have to go somewhere else due to lack of facilities that is the next step; otherwise you are pretty well set. It is important not to overdo any particular endeavor. That is, it is better to do too few things at once than too many. In the short run this may not seem important, but complications from doing too many can easily arise. A mistake can be expensive as well. The manipulation of the appropriate mechanisms should be self-explanatory, and we need not dwell on it here. At first the whole procedure will seem complicated. Soon, however, it will become just another facet of life. It is difficult to foresee any end to the necessity for this task in the immediate future, but then one can never tell.

> John D. Bransford and Marcia K. Johnson,
> "Consideration of Some Problems of Comprehension"

Problem Four. A reading quiz   Earlier in this chapter, you read a story about John and Mary going to the restaurant—it was, you'll recall, a "good" restaurant story, one that followed the "plan" that readers expect for restaurant stories. Here's a brief true/false quiz on your reading. Circle the correct word "true" or "false" for each question, and then turn back to the passage, 13.5, and correct your answers.

a. John and Mary went to their favorite restaurant. True or false?

b. Mary ordered Beef Wellington. True or false?

c. The restaurant was packed. True or false?

d. John paid the bill. True or false?   ■

We might sum up this discussion of how people get meaning from a piece of writing by saying that good readers read from the "top down"—they connect what's in the text with what they know of the world, and they respond to the broad outlines or "shape" of a piece of writing. Beginning readers have to read from the "bottom up": to break the word *cat* into its letters, "cee aye tee," to connect those letters with sounds and the sound of the word "cat," and only then connect the sound with the meaning of the word *cat*. Skilled readers do it faster: They get the meaning *cat* directly. You can see the importance of "top down" reading if you return to our last example, 13.7, and read it again, supplying the missing title, "Washing Clothes." The passage will make much more sense because you are reading from the top down.

As a result, skilled readers will often be less successful at remembering the details of what they read than will be less skilled readers. Skilled readers will remember fewer facts, but they will be better at making inferences (connecting what they read with what they know about the world) and at grasping the "top-level" meaning. Most of you, in taking the quiz of problem four, probably answered "true" to question *d*, "Did John pay the bill?" Yet when you returned to the passage, you found that the text did not *say* that John paid the bill. But it's quite positive to give a wrong answer: It shows that you're participating actively as reader; you're getting at the "formative principle" of the story.

Problem Five. Building form and meaning   The passage below is a "My Turn" column from *Newsweek* magazine. In that column, the magazine prints contributions from the public at large. The author, Jim Quinn, is identified as the author of a book, *American Tongue in Cheek*. We'll use this essay for two purposes: to investigate how readers grasp meaning from their reading, and to investigate how writers create a "scaffolding for meaning." *Newsweek* "My Turn" columns are particularly relevant for student writing, for they are written by the general public and, since they are always one page in length, they generally take the shape of a long student essay, about six hundred words.

Read the essay, underlining important sentences as you proceed. Then, without looking back at the essay, write a two-sentence summary of what you've read.

Hopefully, They Will Shut Up

Almost everybody in America has an illiteracy they love to hate because it makes them feel superior to other Americans: "Anyone can do what they like," "between you and I," "input," "different than," "hopefully." Sometimes the list seems endless. We are in the middle of a great national crusade to protect the language from the people who speak it.

The crusaders certainly seem to be having fun. Though they claim to see the Death of English approaching at any moment, there's a kind of rosy romantic glow to their despair. You get a picture of this gallant little band of the last literates going down to defeat with "Warriner's Grade Four Grammar" in one hand and "Best-Loved Poems of College English Departments" in the other. There are only two things wrong with this great conservative crusade of correctors: it is not conservative, and it is not correct. Though our popularizers of good grammar (let's call them pop grammarians for short) think they are defending standards and traditions, they keep attacking idioms that are centuries old. Here are a few examples:

Anyone Can Do What They Like. We must never combine any*one* with *they*, says John Simon in his new book *Paradigms Lost:* "that way madness lies." Simon seems to think this madness is brand-new, produced in part at least by feminists who want to overturn the old male grammar of "anyone can do what *he* wants" (and *she* better shut up about it). In fact, a wholesale confusion of number and case in pronouns has been a feature of standard English since Elizabethan times. This never hurt the writing of Shakespeare, Marlowe, Ben Jonson, Defoe, Swift, Jane Austen, Dickens, George Bernard Shaw and Oscar Wilde ("Experience is the name that everyone gives to their mistakes"). The use of *they* instead of *he*, in cases where both men and women are meant, is defended by such conservative, pre-liberation authorities as the *Oxford English Dictionary* (OED), our greatest historical dictionary, and Otto Jespersen, the distinguished scholarly grammarian of our language. If that be madness, as Simon says, it is a venerable and literary lunacy.

Between You and I. "Horrible!" wrote poet W. H. Auden, giving his expert opinion in *The Harper Dictionary of Contemporary Usage*. "All debts are cleared between you and I," wrote poet William Shakespeare (*Merchant of Venice*, Act III, Scene 2). Whom are we to trust? D. H. Lawrence points the way for us here. Never trust the artist, said Lawrence; always trust the art. A poet's idea of how language works is as likely to be correct as his idea of how a typewriter works. "You and I" in the accusative is an ancient (and indestructible) idiom. See the opening line of T. S. Eliot's "The Love Song of J. Alfred Prufrock": "Let us go then, you and I."

Input. "Computer cant," said Theodore Bernstein in *Dos, Don'ts & Maybes of English Usage;* "laymen sometimes take it over to sound impressive." In fact, "input" has been around since the eighteenth century. Sir Walter Scott used it to mean "contribution" in *The Heart of Midlothian* (1818). The Supplement to the OED shows noncant uses in such fields as economics long before the first computer use (1948). Input is not a computer word— it's an old word borrowed by computer scientists. No harm in borrowing it back.

Different Than. *"Different than* rather than *different from* is wrong," wrote Edwin Newman in *Strictly Speaking*. Short, simple, to the point and utterly without foundation. H. W. Fowler, in *Modern English Usage* (the bible of most pop grammarians), classes insistence on "different from" as a superstition. The OED notes that "different than" is considered by many to be incorrect, but that "different than" can be found in writers of all ages. Among them: Addison, Steele, Defoe, DeQuincey, Coleridge, Carlyle and Thackeray. Use "different from" if you want—but criticize "different than" and you're messing with the big guys.

Rhetoric. "Not so long ago," says William Safire, in *his* new book, *On Language,* "the predominant meaning of rhetoric was *the science of persuasion.*" Now we tend to use rhetoric to mean empty talk. Safire would like to rescue this good old word from our abuse and has a cure: use "bloviation," an old slang word dating back before 1851, for empty talk. The abuse of "rhetoric" dates back before 1851, too—to the sixteenth century. Among users cited in the OED: Spenser, Milton, Swift and Swinburne, who warns against "the limp loquacity of long-winded rhetoric, so natural to men and soldiers in an hour of emergency." And so natural, also, to pop grammarians when they invent cures for which there is no disease.

Hopefully, Better-Coordinated Programs Will Result. To John Simon, that use of "hopefully" is an infallible sign of illiteracy. " 'Hopefully' so used is an abomination, its adherents should be lynched," says poet Phyllis McGinley. Adherents include Theodore Bernstein, William Safire and the editors of the Concise Oxford, Random House, Merriam-Webster, Webster's New World and Standard College dictionaries. Did Phyllis McGinley really want all of them lynched? The author of the sentence that begins this paragraph was Dr. Nathan Pusey, the former president of Harvard. Does John Simon really believe that Dr. Pusey cannot read or write? Of course not. Both Simon and McGinley were merely using the limp and fuzzy rhetoric of pop grammar, where "illiterate" means only "hasn't read my stylebook."

A New Non-Worry: The Danger From the Right. Should we all worry that pop grammarians will succeed and that someday soon we'll have to talk what they call Good English? Not at all. Wrongheaded objections to idioms are as much a part of the history of English as the idioms themselves—and probably always will be. There will always be gallant little bands to fling themselves, and their violent rhetoric, in front of some age-old word they have made a fad of trying to stop. And there will always be the rest of us to run right over them. That's why English is still alive.

Jim Quinn

■

Creating Scaffolds of Meaning as Writer

Let us turn to a homely analogy, and compare the "shaping" of an essay with the packaging of a food product in the supermarket. Consider, to be more specific, the packaging of canned soups and frozen turkeys. Soup cans are all alike—the tomato soup, the chicken soup, and the beef barley soup all go into the 10¾-ounce cans that sit on the shelf, row on row, distinguished only by the name on the label and the recipe on the back. Frozen turkeys, on the other hand, are packaged individually, each in a tight plastic wrapper that assumes the shape of that particular turkey.

Soup cans explain what we call *fixed form:* A particular content, onion soup or minestrone, is packaged in the fixed form, "soup can." Turkey packaging, on the other hand, explains what we mean by *open form:* The form is elastic, shaping itself to the size of the particular turkey. Or, put another way, some writing is shaped by the expectations of the audience; it's written to a *fixed form.* Other writing is shaped by what the writer wants to say; it's shaped by a *formative idea.*

Indeed, the clearest example of a fixed form is a business form itself—an application for a driver's license or a job application. Here the writer need simply "fill out the form," entering his name in the blank labeled "name," and so on. (Although even here, in filling out a form, one needs to bring in outside knowledge about the world—we recall the unfortunate job applicant who, in the blank labeled *sex,* wrote "yes.")

Developing writers are perhaps most familiar with the fixed form called by one writer "the fifty-star theme" (because it's rewarded in high schools in all of the fifty states): the five-paragraph theme—an introductory paragraph, with a "thesis sentence" at the end (we would say *formative idea*), followed by three paragraphs, each with a "topic sentence" at the beginning (we would say *commitment sentence*), then concluding with a final paragraph summarizing the paper. We diagram the form of the fifty-star theme in Figure 13.1.

The fifty-star theme has some advantages as a fixed form. It's widely expected by readers, and many teachers note that readers of writing examinations, in particular, look for the form of the fifty-star theme to show that the writer can organize her writing. Because it is such a rigid fixed form, it's also a help to the writer—it provides a pre-existing form, a 10¾-ounce soup can. And many would argue that only after mastering this form can students move to more complex forms.

But there are some disadvantages to the fifty-star theme. Its rigidity can work against the writer—what if the writer discovers four things to say about his topic, instead of three? And, however valuable it is as a fixed form for "writing in school," it is not too valuable for writing in the world. There are "fixed forms" for technical reports in aerospace science, for police reports, for business letters, for job recommendations—but these have little to do with the form of the fifty-star theme.

Therefore, the developing writer may wish to go beyond the fifty-star theme, to broaden her sense of the potentials of shaping writing. We'll therefore examine some representative fixed forms and then proceed to the question of open form.

As a first example, here's a joking comment on the fixed form of a professional article in literary criticism a generation ago.

13.8 Now I suggest that if we analyze almost any piece of research which seems to us thoroughly workmanlike and satisfactory

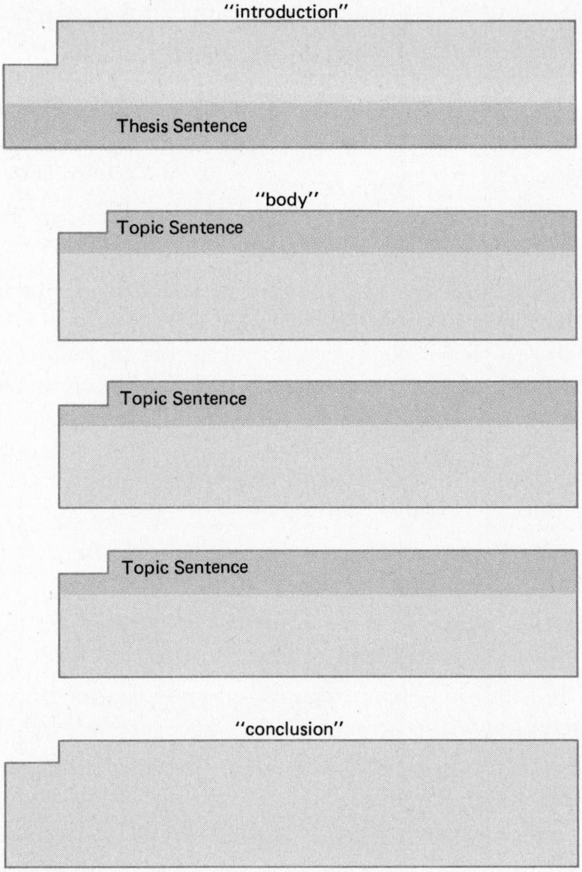

"introduction"

Thesis Sentence

"body"

Topic Sentence

Topic Sentence

Topic Sentence

"conclusion"

FIGURE 13.1   The Form of the "Fifty-Star Theme"

from all points of view, we shall almost always find that it falls into five parts in the following order.

1. The *introduction,* in which the author briefly states the present position of research on his subject and the views currently held on it.

2. The *proposal,* in which he describes in outline what he hopes to prove.

3. The *boost,* in which he proceeds to magnify the importance of his discovery or argument and to explain what a revolution it will create in the views generally held on the whole period with which he is dealing. This is, as it were, a taste of sauce to stimulate the reader's appetite.

4. The *demonstration,* in which he sets forth his discovery or argument in an orderly fashion.
5. The *conclusion,* or *crow,* in which he summarizes what he claims to have shown, and points out how complete and unshakable is his proof.

> R. B. McKerrow, "Form and Matter
> in the Publication of Research"

Interestingly enough, the sense of "shaping" articles in literary criticism has changed since this was written (in 1940), and editors and readers no longer expect to find it.

A quite different form is expected by readers of journals in psychology. Here, summarized from the *Publication Manual* of the *American Psychological Association,* is the fixed form of a psychological report:

13.9 *Title.* The title should summarize the main idea of the paper simply and, if possible, with style.

Abstract. An abstract is a brief summary of the content and purpose of the article.

Introduction. Its purpose is to inform the reader of the specific problem under study and the research strategy.

Method. The method section should tell your reader how the study was conducted.

Results. The results should summarize the collected data and your statistical treatment of them.

Discussion. After presenting the results, you are in a position to evaluate and interpret their implications, especially with respect to your original hypothesis. [The *Publication Manual* doesn't note it, but the typical psychological article will end with a mild disclaimer ("Our work is only beginning," they write, "and the results are inconclusive"), followed by a stirring call for further research ("This appears to be a particularly promising area for future research").]

References. Every article concludes with a list of all references cited in the text.

Still another fixed form is the legal brief, a short report on a court case. Here is the fixed form of a legal brief:

13.10 *Identification:* Give the name of the case, the court, and the date.

Facts: Characterize the plaintiff and defendant, and describe the facts of the case.

Issue. Identify the narrow question of law at issue in the case.

Decision. Explain what the court decided.

Reasoning. Explain the court's reasoning in coming to its decision. (This is the longest part of a legal brief, and often separate arguments are numbered.)

In Figures 13.2 and 13.3 we give annotated examples of two common fixed forms, the business letter and the job résumé.

There are two problems with fixed forms. First, readers, editors, and instructors giving writing assignments—even bosses on the job—may have a very fixed sense of form in mind, but—and this is a large *but*—. . . they don't tell you what it is. Here we think of a friend of ours, proudly taking on a new job as a reporter for a metropolitan newspaper, turning in his first story to his editor. He was proud of it.

13.11 As smoke billowed from the factory, valiant firemen fought, bravely but in vain, to control the destructive fire. . . .

His editor ripped his copy in half. "Go find out how this newspaper reports fires," he said. Our friend, going back to the newspaper files, found that every fire was reported with the same fixed form.

13.12 A fire of undetermined origin today (choose a verb: *damaged* or *destroyed* are the only choices) a (describe building or area) at (give address), fire officials reported. Damage was estimated at (give estimate).

The answer to this problem is that our friend should have checked the files *before* he wrote the report. That is, he should have developed his sense of shaping by reading and let that sense inform his writing. That's good advice in general: If you're new on the job, read several company memos before writing one (some companies prefer a very informal organization and style; others prefer more formal organization and style). In a school situation, it's perfectly legitimate to ask the instructor about preferred forms of organization; often the biology instructor is simply so familiar with the fixed form of a lab report in biology that she forgets her students are not.

The second problem with fixed form is that the developing writer may have too rigid a model of fixed form. We would argue that the newspaper's model for reporting fires is too rigid a model; it doesn't allow readers to sort out major fires from minor fires. In chapter Five, we argued against a rigid view of *the* paragraph, noting that it worked

119 Greenbriar Street
Glicksberg, IA 57588   1
June 21, 1981   2

3

Beverly Johnson
Customer Relations
The Newcomb Corporation   4
1111 Squirrel Drive
Bakersfield, CA 97321

5   Dear Ms. Johnson:

6   I was glad to receive your reply to my letter of
     May 12. You announced that my complaint had been
7   given a file number, F66378B, and you suggested that
     I again try to return the defective lawn mower to
     Glicksberg Hardware.

     However, Glicksberg Hardware refuses to let me
     exchange my defective mower for a new one. They
8   insist that they must have a formal authorization—
     they refer to a "factory recommittal form"—before
     allowing me to exchange my mower.

9   Please have the factory sales representative serving
     Glicksberg Hardware issue the "factory recommittal
     form."

     Thank you. Your prompt response and your company's
     concern are commendable.

                         Sincerely,   10

                         Alfred Otero

                         Alfred Otero   11

12   ao/mao

13   cc: Glicksberg Hardware

                  14

1 Your address should appear on all letters. It may be given, as here, above
   the date, or it may be given at the end, following your name.
2 Current date. (In some letter formats, all information—date, terminal remark, and signature—are given at the left margin; here we center the date
   and the closing information.)
3 One line separates date and person addressed.

4   Give complete address. (Here, giving the person's job title may speed delivery.)

5   A colon ends the salutation of a formal business letter; a dash or a comma may be used in informal letters. (And note that the neutral *Ms.* is now used in place of *Miss* and *Mrs.* in most businesses.)

6   In this format, the so-called "block paragraph," the beginning of the paragraph is not indented. Even if indentation is used, each paragraph should be set off by a blank line at the beginning and end.

7   The opening paragraph should give necessary background information—in our sample, the writer gives a company file number and mentions a past letter.

8   A clear "statement of the case."

9   A clear "request for action."

10 The closing remark.

11 Signature—usually four lines are left blank for a hand-written signature.

12 Initials of author and typist (unnecessary if typed by the author).

13 Indicates that a copy has been sent to a party involved. ("cc," meaning "carbon copy," persists, even though electronic copiers are now more commonly used.)

14 Letter is centered on the page.

FIGURE 13.2   The Fixed Form of a Business Letter

against one's ability to develop ideas. The writer who takes our model business letter and our model résumé as rigid models, unchangeable in all fields, has made a mistake. Letters and résumés vary from field to field. Even the spelling of the word *résumé* varies from one discipline to another: We use the older form, retaining the accents the word has in French; a different form, *resume,* is common in business and engineering.

We saw the negative effects of a rigid sense of form when we gave a class the assignment of problem five—to read Jim Quinn's *Newsweek* "My Turn" column, underline the important sentences, and write a two-sentence summary. Most of our students did well at the assignment; here's a particularly effective student version:

13.13   Many "pop grammarians" lament our declining usage standards, citing "illiteracies" such as "anyone can do what they like," "between you and I," "input," "different than," "hopefully," and the negative sense of "rhetoric." But they are wrong, for these forms have been widely used in the past, and they are accepted by many authorities.

personal experience   1

Carol N. Cranshaw
1616 W. Keno Street   2
Pahrump, Utah 78442
(616) 349-9006

3   Experience

4   June 1978–present. Secretary, Seven Wonders Finance
       Corporation, Pahrump, Utah. In addition to general
       secretarial duties, I serve as receptionist and do
5   some bookkeeping.

    September 1976–June 1978. Secretary registered with
       Personpower Temporary Help, Inc., Holt, Utah. Served
       as temporary secretary in a variety of offices,
       giving me wide experience in business procedures and
       practices.

    September 1975–June 1976. Part–time secretary
       (college work–study program), Department of
       Business, Pahrump Community College.

6   Education

    August 1981. Certificate of Completion, Legal
       Secretary Program, Pahrump Community College.

    September 1974–June 1976. Associate of Arts degree,
       Pahrump Community College. Major: Secretarial
       Studies.

7   Personal

    Age: 28   Married, two children
    Health: excellent Hobbies: family camping, reading

8   References

    Mr. J. Donald Jerome, Manager   Dr. Alice McMatters
    Seven Wonders Finance Co.   Chairperson,
    1899 School Street   Department of Business
    Pahrump, Utah 78441   Pahrump Community College
    (616) 802-0303   Pahrump, Utah 78440
                                     (616) 802-0404

9   Mr. Fred Summers, District Manager
    Personpower Temporary Services, Inc.
    2144 Driveway Blvd.
    Holt, Utah 78446
    (616) 733-7846

1 Various headings are used for résumés in various fields: "personal experience" (as here), "personal background," "resume," "résumé."
2 One might also choose to list a business address or a temporary address.
3 Headings may be centered or, as here, made flush with the left margins. Other relevant headings may be used: "Awards," "Career Objectives," "Organizations" (to which one belongs).
4 Work experience and education are listed in "backward order," beginning with most recent experience and working back through time.
5 This writer chooses to make a "argumentative" résumé, explaining the experience on the job. Other writers prefer a "neutral" résumé, simply giving job title.
6 In general, give years attended, degree, college, and major.
7 Optional—some writers prefer not to give personal background.
8 Often formal references are available through a college placement office.
9 It is expected that one has secured permission to use the names of references.

FIGURE 13.3 The Fixed Form of a Résumé

But a significant number of students read the passage, underlining it heavily, and wrote summaries that suggested they didn't understand the article—in fact, that suggested they completely misunderstood it.

13.14 We must protect the language from illiteracies like "between you and I." We need a great national crusade to protect us from these dangers.

Note that, while this writer is closer to Quinn's words, he is much farther from what Quinn actually argued.

We can explain the failure of these students to gain information from this task, in part, by their prior assumptions about usage issues. They seemed to think, particularly in an English class, that any discussion of usage would deal with the "single correct and proper" usage. The force of this assumption was so strong that they did not see that the author was taking a different position.

Moreover, they seemed to have read with a very rigid sense of form. The author of 13.14 pulls a phrase from the last sentence of paragraph one, right where the "thesis statement" would be in the fifty-star theme. But what we call the formative idea is not there; instead it's buried in the second paragraph:

13.15 There are only two things wrong with this great conservative crusade of correctors: it is not conservative and it is not correct.

Similarly, this reader must have read each paragraph as if the first sentence were the topic sentence:

13.16 *"Different than* rather than *different from* is wrong," wrote Edwin Newman in *Strictly Speaking.*

The problem is, of course, that Jim Quinn is not using a fixed form. He is developing his ideas with the scaffolding of an open form, a form that we might label "not this::but this," and diagram as in Figure 13.4. That form gives structure to each of Quinn's paragraphs.

13.17 *"Different than* rather than *different from* is wrong," wrote Edwin Newman in *Strictly Speaking.* Short, simple, to the point and utterly without foundation.

This rigid sense of form, in this reading task, made readers insensitive to tone (the "great conservative crusade of correctors," one suspects, from the sound of those repeated initial letters, is meant to be taken ironically), and it made them insensitive to the basic, "top down" thrust of Quinn's argument.

(Of course, many readers, whether instructors or students, may find "pop grammarians" more convincing in their arguments than Quinn is in his arguments, but we think all would agree that those arguments ought to be grasped fully.)

Could we argue that this rigid sense of form constrains such readers in similar ways when they shift to become writers? We suspect so. We argued as much in our treatment of the paragraph in chapter Five, and we suspect that a writer's control of "top down" structure of writing is very close to a reader's control of the same structure. If we are correct, then perhaps developing writers ought to test themselves beyond fixed forms of organization, to explore the poorly mapped waters of open form in writing.

Problem Six. "Never fall for the same trick twice" Write a one-sentence summary of the paragraph below. (Hint: Never fall for the same trick twice.)

There are undoubtedly many verbal skills which children from ghetto areas must learn in order to do well in the school situation, and some of these are indeed characteristic of middle-class verbal behavior. Precision in spelling, practice in handling abstract symbols, the ability to state explicitly the meaning of words, and a richer knowledge of the Latinate vocabulary, may all be useful acquisitions. But is it true that *all* of the middle-class

FIGURE 13.4 Diagram of a "Not This::But This" Argument, such as that of Problem Five

habits are functional and desirable in the school situation? Before we impose middle-class verbal style upon children from other cultural groups, we should find out how much of this is useful for the main work of analyzing and generalizing, and how much is merely stylistic—or even dysfunctional. In high school and college, middle-class children spontaneously complicate their syntax to the point that instructors despair of getting them to make their language simpler and clearer. In every learned journal one can find examples of jargon and empty elaboration—and complaints about it. Is the "elaborate code" of Bernstein really so "flexible, detailed and subtle" as some psychologists believe? Isn't it also turgid, redundant, and empty? Is it not simply an elaborated *style*, rather than a superior code or system?

William Labov, "The Logic of Nonstandard English"

■

OPEN FORM IN WRITING: THE FORMATIVE IDEA

Our term, the *formative idea*, corresponds somewhat to the traditional "thesis sentence." A thesis sentence is usually defined as "the sentence that states the main idea of the piece of writing." Our definition of the formative idea is a bit vaguer, but it is far more powerful. A *formative idea* is "an idea, or set of ideas, stated or implied, that offers the main idea of the paper *AND* serves as the shaping principle of the paper."

Jim Quinn's "Hopefully, They Will Shut Up" has a traditional thesis sentence, though not where a thesis sentence is normally expected:

13.18 There are only two things wrong with this great conservative crusade of correctors: it is not conservative, and it is not correct.

Considered as a thesis sentence, about all we can say is that it "states the main idea of the paper." But if we deal with more sentences in those first two paragraphs, we can see how that "thesis sentence" becomes *formative*—it controls the shape of the paper. Below, we print the formative idea of that essay in the first column, with our comments in the second.

13.19 Sometimes the list [of "illiteracies"] seems endless. . . .

This establishes the author's basic pattern of development—he offers a *list* of typical problems (we'll later call this open form *enumeration*).

We are in the middle of a great national crusade to protect the language from the people who speak it.

This establishes the tone of the essay—heavy-handed irony; it sets up the first half of the "not this::but this" paragraphs in the *list* development; and it suggests the basic form of the concluding paragraph.

[this crusade] is not conservative,

This sets up the first kind of argument: The argument that, because respected authors have used the disputed usage, the "pop grammarians" cannot pretend to be preserving tradition.

and it is not correct.

This sets up the second kind of argument: That many authorities accept the usage issue in doubt.

The formative idea, then, gives the writer both "something to say" *and* a way to say it. The structure of Quinn's paragraphs does not come from rigid notions of "topic sentence" and development; it comes from following the "shaping" power of his formative idea, as in the paragraph below, again set in two columns for analysis.

13.20 Different Than.

The heading of the paragraph continues the "list" organization.

"Different than rather than *different from* is wrong," wrote Edwin Newman in *Strictly Speaking.*

This sentence shows the "great national crusade"; it completes the "not this" section of the "not this::but this" argument.

Short, simple, to the point and utterly without foundation.

Turns the corner on the "not this::but this" argument.

H. W. Fowler, in *Modern English Usage* . . . classes insistence on "different from" as a superstition.	Offers an "it is not correct" argument by citing a recognized authority who accepts the usage.
The OED notes that "different than" is considered by many to be incorrect, but that "different than" can be found in writers of all ages.	Offers an "it is not conservative" argument by citing an authority that says the usage was common in the past.
Among them: Addison, Steele, Defoe, DeQuincey, Coleridge, Carlyle and Thackeray.	Cites specific names of major writers of the past who have used "different than."
Use "different from" if you want—but criticize "different than" and you're messing with the big guys.	Comes back to a charge in the first sentence of the essay—that we worry about usage in order to feel superior to others.

As the Quinn example shows, a formative idea may have several dimensions. Here, the basic list of usage questions provides the organizing principle of the essay; the "not this::but this" rhetorical appeal provides the principle of development for each paragraph; and the arguments from tradition and authority provide the source of evidence. The better summary, 13.13 above, caught all of these dimensions in the two sentences. She was reading from the "top down," grasping the "formative idea."

The formative idea may not necessarily be announced to the reader, and it may not necessarily have much to do with paragraph structure. In chapter One, "Writing Fluently," we offered one formative idea to the reader at the beginning of the chapter—announcing that we were going to explore several ways of putting words on paper more easily. But we kept another formative idea from the reader until the end of the chapter—you can use these ways of writing fluently *because* language is naturally creative.

Indeed, often the formative idea is "shaped through writing," rather than appearing, preconceived, before one begins the first draft. Where the "thesis sentence" of a piece of writing, in traditional terms, must be fully formed before the writer begins to write, a formative idea may grow out of dissatisfaction with another formative idea. In the final chapter, "Revision as Discovery," we discuss a revision of a chapter of this text, where we discovered a useful formative idea only after drafting a first version and submitting it to several readers.

The notion of a formative idea places no constraints of the shape of a piece of writing, but common shapes do emerge, as natural ways of organizing writing. These shapes are important for readers, for, as we've seen, they are essential for "top down" reading, and they are equally important for writers—not as fixed forms, but as forms that grow from a controlling idea. Here are four common "top down" structures.

Enumeration is a simple listing of specific instances of the general claim in the formative idea. The Quinn essay uses the word *list,* and it is structured as a list of specific usage issues. We use the more formal *enumeration* because it's related to the word *number,* and numbering such a list is often a courtesy to the reader: "first," "second," "third." We show the the "enumeration" shape of the Quinn essay in Figure 13.5.

Adversative structure is a common form of argument: "not this::but this," as in the diagram of Figure 13.6. Quinn's essay combines the adversative structure with enumeration.

Question/answer and *problem/solution* structures grow from formative

FIGURE 13.5 Enumeration as a Shaping Device in the Essay from Problem Five

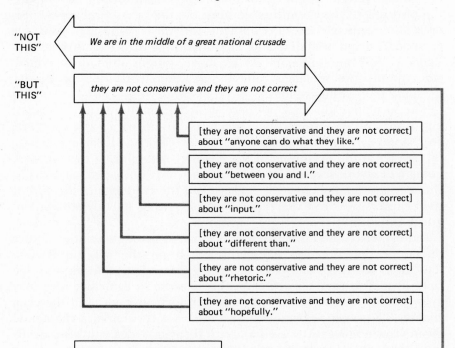

"NOT THIS"

We are in the middle of a great national crusade

"BUT THIS"

they are not conservative and they are not correct

[they are not conservative and they are not correct] about "anyone can do what they like."

[they are not conservative and they are not correct] about "between you and I."

[they are not conservative and they are not correct] about "input."

[they are not conservative and they are not correct] about "different than."

[they are not conservative and they are not correct] about "rhetoric."

[they are not conservative and they are not correct] about "hopefully."

That's why English is still alive.

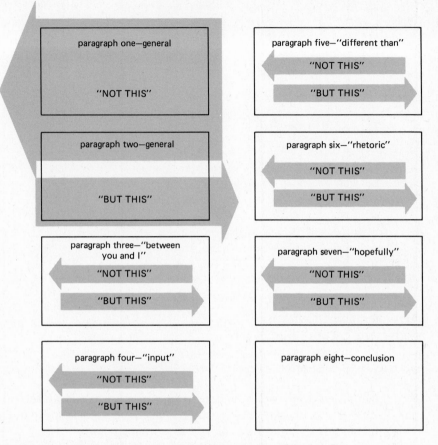

FIGURE 13.6 The Adversative Structure of the Essay in Problem Five

ideas offered, respectively, as questions and problems. This structure may take the simple form outlined in Figure 13.7, or it may combine with enumeration to produce the more complicated structure of Figure 13.8.

Cause/effect and *effect/cause* offer two possible ways of ordering pieces of writing built from a formative idea stressing how things relate. One might begin with traffic problems in New York City, and then one might suggest that they are caused by the freeway construction of the 1950s, which allowed more cars into the city without exploring other alternatives, such as limiting automobiles and improving mass transit (*effect/cause*). Or one might begin with the freeway construction and

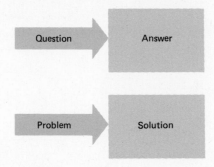

FIGURE 13.7 The Simple Shape of Question/Answer and
Problem/Solution Structures

then deal with its effects (*cause/effect*). Either way, this structure emphasizes the chaining of ideas, as the diagrams of Figure 13.9 suggest.

Problem Seven. Identifying top-level structures.   On a separate sheet,
list (enumerate) the four top-level structures discussed above:

- enumeration ("listing")
- adversative ("not this::but this")
- question/answer and problem/solution
- cause/effect and effect/cause   ■

Recognizing these top-level structures is an important reading skill, one
that filters back to inform one's writing. This exercise asks you to develop that skill as a skimming skill, not as a reading skill.

Skim through any chapter of this text—except this one—trying to
identify these top-level structures.

a. Begin at the paragraph level. Find one paragraph using each of
the four "shaping" principles above, and list the page number and
the first word of the paragraph (find either a question/answer or a
problem/solution structure; either a cause/effect or an effect/cause
structure).

b. Now shift to larger structural units. Find an example of each of
the "shaping" principles working at the level of several paragraphs,
even a chapter subheading. (For example, what "shaping principle" is
announced in the first subheading of chapter One?)

c. Now look for these "shaping" principles at the chapter level. Of
course, not all chapters use these "shaping" principles, but you should
be able to identify the principles used in the following chapters: Eight,
Nine, Ten, Eleven, Twelve, Sixteen, Seventeen.

Opening and Closing

The fixed form of the "fifty-star theme" offers a rigid model of beginning and ending an essay. One begins by offering a very general statement, then working down the "ladder of generality" to the "thesis sentence" at the end of the paragraph. One ends by offering a sum-

FIGURE 13.8 More Complex Shapes for Question/Answer and Problem/Solution Structures

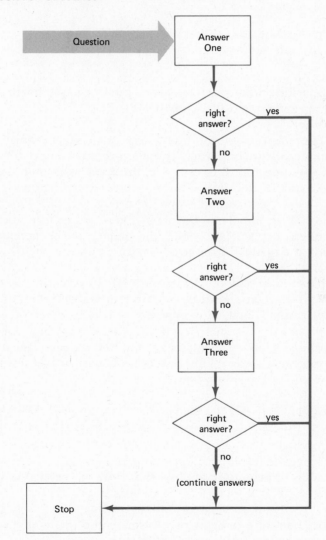

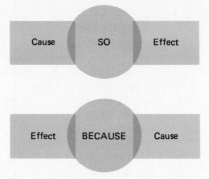

FIGURE 13.9 Shapes for Cause/Effect and Effect/Cause Structures

mary, by repeating what one has said. Thus, a sample beginning and ending paragraph from a fifty-star theme.

13.21 There are many important decisions that one must make in our modern, contemporary, twentieth-century world of today. Many of these decisions, once made, are hard to change, such as choosing a spouse, deciding to have a child, or settling on a career. Choosing a college to attend is one important decision. This paper will explore three important factors in choosing a college: the quality of student life at the college, the quality of the faculty as a whole, and the quality of the program in one's major field.

. . .

This paper has explored the important decision of choosing a college at which to attend. It has shown that this decision has three important factors. First, it is important to look at the quality of student life on the campus. Second, it is important that one have good teachers. Third, it is important that the college offer a good program in one's major. This last factor is particularly important when one enters the job market.

Problem Eight. What did the farmer say to the hen? What did the farmer say to the hen? (It's a joke—to be answered later.)   ■

These are legitimate ways of beginning and ending. There are other legitimate ways of beginning and ending. Here are several ways of beginning:

■ Suppose one were to begin at a lower level of generality than that of the formative idea—perhaps to begin with an example?

13.22 "We don't have a Criminology major right now," the admissions officer said, leaning toward me, "but we're sure to have one by the time you're a junior." I was immediately suspicious.

■ Suppose one were to begin with a comparison—an analogy—that would provide a formative idea for the shaping of the essay?

13.23 Choosing a college is like getting married—you're going to be together for a long time, and a divorce can be very painful.

■ Suppose—and we find this suggestion to be threatening to many developing writers, drilled in the "introduction" of the fifty-star theme—but just suppose that one were to follow the advice that the farmer gave the hen: "Cut the cackle and get to the egg." In other words, simply begin with what you want to say.

13.24 The three most important factors in choosing a college are the quality of life on the campus, the general quality of the faculty, and the quality of the program in one's major.

Similarly, here are several other choices for closing off an essay, beyond a simple summary:

■ Suppose one were to consider the limits of one's arguments?

13.25 Of course, other factors may be important for some students. The student who is undecided about a major, for example, may wish to choose a college offering a wide variety of programs. . . .

■ Suppose one were to evaluate one's argument?

13.26 The general quality of the faculty, however, is the most important of these three factors. After all . . .

■ Suppose (dare we suggest it?)—suppose one were to stand one's argument on its head?

13.27 Of course, few of us think this reasonably about attending college. Most of us choose a college blindly, pretty much at random, and . . .

■ Suppose one were to ask about the implications of one's argument? That is, to ask the question, "So what?" (This seems to us the most common way that professional writers close their essays.)

13.28   If this analysis is true, then admissions officers are going to have to start providing applicants with more information, and more honest information. More precisely, applicants have a right to know . . .

SUMMARY

We discussed the importance of "larger units of arrangement" by changing the *form* of a message, for example, changing a "note taped to a refrigerator" into a "poem." We approached form, as scaffolding for ideas, from a reader's perspective, noting the importance of the reader's expectations, or "plan," and its relation to the author's top-level organization. We separated *fixed form,* writing to an external shape, from *open form,* writing that responds to the *formative idea,* the idea, or set of ideas, stated or implied, that offers the main idea *and* serves as the shaping principle of the paper. We looked at the fixed form of the introduction and conclusion of the "fifty-star theme," and we suggested other possible ways of opening and closing essays.

IMPLICATIONS FOR THE READER

This discussion has several implications for readers. It suggests something about how one naturally improves one's reading ability—by refining one's "plan" for approaching a piece of reading, and by responding to "top level" structures rather than by being trapped in word-by-word reading. In fact, our advice is on the order of—when you have a problem understanding something, keep reading; don't stop to try to understand the specific words. That is, if a specific sentence in a textbook throws you—perhaps because you don't know a specific word—you're usually better off not stopping to look up the word. Mark the sentence, and continue reading. You may see the word used again and again, so that it becomes clear. At the very least, you will have grasped the top-level structure of the text, so that you can return to that problem sentence with a sense of how it fits in.

We can model that advice with a reading problem, taken from a recent text that teachers reading skills by showing the mental steps taken by successful readers. Begin by solving the reading problem below.

Problem Nine. A problem in reading   If deleting the letters R, I, and E from the word surmise leaves a meaningful three-letter word, circle the first S in this word surmise. Otherwise circle the U in the word surmise where it appears for the third time in the problem.   ■

Here is a transcript of a highly successful medical student, asked to think aloud as she solved the problem. As you read the transcript, note the point at which she follows our advice to keep reading.

13.29 [Subject began reading aloud.] "If deleting the letters R, I, and E from the word surmise . . ."
[Subject repeated the letters aloud.] "R, I, E."
[Subject crossed out the letters R, I, and E with her pencil. She then read the remaining letters aloud and pronounced the word they formed.] "S, U, M. S . . . Sums"
[Subject resumed reading.] "leaves a meaningful three-letter word, circle . . ."
[Subject stopped reading and thought aloud.] I'm getting to the section where I have to do something if the first part is true. I'm a little confused though, maybe I should start reading the sentence from the beginning. No, I'll read the rest of it.
"Circle the first S in this word surmise."
I am confused, let me start again.
"If deleting the letters R, I, and E from the word surmise leaves a meaningful three-letter word . . ."
No, *sums* is a four-letter word.
"Circle the first S in this word surmise."
So I won't do this.
"Otherwise circle the U in the word surmise where it appears for the third time in the problem."
So this is the direction I'm supposed to follow. Let's see, the word surmise appears once . . . twice in the first sentence. Then in the second sentence it appears—three and that's it. So that's the U I should circle. Now I'll reread the last sentence to make sure I followed the directions carefully.
"Otherwise circle the U in the word surmise where it appears for the third time in the problem."
I'll scan the sentence again to be sure that the word surmise doesn't occur anywhere except the three places I found it. Yes, I circled the right one.

adapted from A. Whimby and J. Lochhead,
Comprehension and Problem Solving

The reading problem asks for a great deal of close attention to the surface of the writing, the letters of the word *surmise.* But the medical student solves the problem by backing out of that detail to look at the top-level structure of the problem, either do this or do this.

IMPLICATIONS FOR THE WRITER

The question of the "larger units of arrangement" looms large in the minds of many developing writers. When we question a writing class about their goals for improving their writing, "improving my ability to organize my writing" is generally the most popular choice, far outranking the other choices we offer a class, choices like "developing a sophisticated style," "improving my control over the way I present myself in writing," "improving my ability to analyze the needs of my audience," or "improving my ability to invent ideas and arguments."

If the discussion in this chapter is correct, then that view of "organization" as a fixed form, removed from the expectations of an audience, the dynamic presentation of a self, and the artful crafting of a message, may be slightly misplaced. Even the Campbell's Soup company now offers alternatives to the 10¾-ounce soup can—the 19-ounce "chunky" soups and smaller individual cans. Can a developing writer aim at less?

FINAL WRITING ASSIGNMENTS

I. Finding Fixed Forms in Reading   Each of the following is—or may be—a *fixed form,* a standard pattern of organization. Choose one—or find a fixed form of your own—and explain what the fixed form is. Be as complete as possible.

We list first some fairly obvious fixed forms, and then suggest some more complicated ones.

a. An interview in *Playboy* magazine.

b. The "Cosmo tells all" column in *Cosmopolitan.*

c. A recipe article in *Good Housekeeping.*

d. An episode in any regular television comedy.

e. A chapter in a biology textbook.

f. A sonnet by John Donne (you'll find several in an anthology of English poetry).

g. A tragedy by William Shakespeare.

II. How to Read a Newspaper   Explain the fixed forms in a local newspaper. That is, we expect that experienced readers approach different parts of a newspaper—sports pages, news reports, editorial pages, entertainment sections, classified ads—with quite different expectations about how information in those different sections will be presented. Choose a single issue of the paper for analysis.

III. Fixed Form in Your Profession   Examine several issues of a journal in your profession, exploring the degree to which there are—or are not—fixed forms available to writers.

IV. Writing to a Fixed Form   Federal and state governments award billions of dollars a year for research and for activities in the community. These funds are generally awarded to individuals or groups who submit what are called "proposals" for specific projects. Below is an imaginary proposal request; think up a good way to spend some money and submit a proposal. Follow the fixed form exactly.

"Lady Chatterley Foundation: College and Community Grant Program"

The Lady Chatterley Foundation will award a number of "College and Community Grants" of $5,000 to $20,000 per year for periods of from one to three years. "College grants" will be awarded to groups or individuals who submit worthwhile proposals for projects to improve the quality of life at a college or university. "Community grants" will be awarded to groups or individuals who submit worthwhile proposals for projects to improve the quality of life in any American or Canadian community.

Proposals should consist of three parts.

Title Page. The title page should contain: 1. the words, "College Grant Proposal" or "Community Grant Proposal," as appropriate: 2. a short title for the project—no more than fifty typed characters, including the spaces between words; 3. the name of the project director (that's you); and 4. a summary of the project, in fifty words or less.

Proposal Narrative. The proposal narrative should be no more than 800 words in length. Your narrative may be organized in any form, but it will be evaluated on the following criteria. 1. *Problem.* Is there a precise statement of the problem to be addressed? Does the proposal show awareness of the history or background of the problem and of other attempts to deal with it? Is the problem important? 2. *Objectives.* What are the goals of the project? Is the proposal specific about what is to be accomplished? Is there a clear relation between the objectives of the project and the problem itself? 3. *Plan.* In very specific terms, what will be done to achieve the objectives of the project? (The most common reason for rejecting a proposal is that reviewers cannot discover precisely what is going to be done with the funds.) 4. *Evaluation.* How will the project be evaluated? How will the results or accomplishments of the project be made available to the interested public?

Budget Summary. The budget summary—no more than one page in length—should outline the expected costs of the project under the following headings: a. salaries and wages; b. consultants' fees; c. travel; d. facilities and equipment rental; e. equipment purchase; f. materials and supplies; g. other. Conclude by indicating the total funding requested.

V. Discovering a Poem   We have printed two poems below, but we have rearranged the lines to destroy their original order. The sentences have been scrambled, and they have been printed as prose rather than as poetry, destroying the line endings of the original poem.

Try to "discover" or "shape" a poem from one of these disordered lists. You can, of course, recover the original poem by going to the library, but it might be more interesting to compare your versions in class, discussing the effect of various orders and "shapes," each of which creates a new poem.

If the instructor directs, discuss, in a short paper, your decisions about shaping a poem.

Both poems present quite difficult problems in shaping, but our students find the second more difficult than the first. (We have, by the way, repunctuated the first, separating each sentence base into a separate sentence.)

A. Gerard Manley Hopkins, "God's Grandeur"

1. Generations have trod, have trod, have trod.

2. The world is charged with the grandeur of God.

3. The soil is bare now, nor can foot feel, being shod.

4. And for all this, Nature is never spent.

5. It will flame out, like shining from shook foil.

6. And all is seared with trade; bleared, smeared with toil; and wears man's smudge and shares man's smell.

7. Why do men then now not reck [heed] his rod?

8. And through the last lights off the black West went, oh morning, at the brown brink eastward, springs—because the Holy Ghost over the bent world broods with warm breast and with ah! bright wings.

9. It gathers to a greatness, like the ooze of oil crushed.

10. There lives the dearest freshness deep down things.

B. Sylvia Plath, "The Colossus"

1. I shall never get you put together entirely, pieced, glued, and properly jointed.

2. Your fluted bones and acanthine hair are littered in their old anarchy to the horizon-line.

3. It's worse than a barnyard.

4. My hours are married to shadow.

5. Nights, I squat in the cornucopia of your left ear, out of the wind, counting the red stars and those of plum-color.

6. Thirty years now I have laboured to dredge the silt from your throat.

7. Scaling little ladders with gluepots and pails of lysol I crawl like an ant in mourning over the weedy acres of your brow to mend the immense skull-plates and clear the bald, white tumuli of your eyes.

8. It would take more than a lightning-stroke to create such a ruin.

9. No longer do I listen for the scrape of a keel on the blank stones of the landing.

10. The sun rises under the pillar of your tongue.

11. I am none the wiser.

FOR FURTHER READING

The student may wish to supplement our discussion by turning to two textbooks that use quite different approaches. Frank D'Angelo's *Process and Thought in Composition,* rev. ed. (Cambridge, Mass.: Winthrop, 1979), offers a suggestive approach to "methods of development," and *Writing in the Arts and Sciences,* by Elaine P. Maimon et al. (Cambridge, Mass.: Winthrop, 1981), examines the fixed forms of various college writing assignments.

NOTES

1. X. J. Kennedy, *An Introduction to Poetry,* 4th ed. (Boston: Little, Brown, 1978), p. 163.
2. R. C. Anderson et al., "Frameworks for Comprehending Discourse," *American Educational Research Journal,* 14 (1977), 367–81.

14

Two Writing Tasks:
The Essay Answer and
the Investigative Paper

> To put the whole thing into a single sentence: you will never succeed
> in getting at the truth if you think you know, ahead of time, what the
> truth ought to be.
>
> MARCHETTE CHUTE

This chapter offers practical advice on the two writing assignments
you're most likely to encounter in college—writing an in-class answer
to an essay question and writing an out-of-class investigative paper,
usually involving library research.

THE ESSAY EXAMINATION

We take up the question of how to write an effective in-class essay answer because we find that students often feel that their performance in
in-class examinations doesn't reflect what they know about the subject-
matter and the effort they've put into studying. "I studied that book
for two hours every night, and all so-and-so did was party," runs a
typical complaint, "but she got a B+ on the exam, and I got a C−."

Behind such complaints is the feeling, on the part of many students,
that the game is rigged against them, that there's some magic secret no
one has told them. It may be surprising, but we feel there's some truth
in that feeling. There are indeed "magic secrets" to taking essay exams,
and we're going to let you in on them.

The most important "magic secret" is hidden in the problem below;
it's worth thinking about before reading further.

Problem One. A magic secret   Consider the conversation below.

Speaker A: "What time is it?"
Speaker B: "Ten minutes after three."
Speaker A: "Thank you."

Is there any situation where Speaker A might reasonably give a response other than "Thank you"? We're not thinking of other possible responses in general, such as "Oh, I'm late for work." Rather, try to think of a different social context, one that gives the question a new meaning. ■

Let's put the conversation of problem one on paper again, and note some of its features.

14.1   *Speaker A:* "What time is it?"
    Speaker B: "Ten minutes after three."
    Speaker A: "Thank you."

- The first speaker doesn't know what time it is.
- The first speaker wants to know what time it is, and she has reason to believe the second speaker knows.
- The second speaker understands that the first speaker doesn't know what time it is.
- The second speaker has performed a service for the first speaker—thus the polite response, "Thank you."
- Note, moreover, that speaker B might reasonably offer other responses—"I'm not sure—a little after three, I think"; "It must be after three"; and even, "Well, the big hand is pointing at the two and the little hand is pointing at the three." In each case, the polite response is "Thank you."

Now consider another possible conversation; it's our magic secret:

14.2   *Speaker A:* "What time is it?"
    Speaker B: "Ten minutes after three."
    Speaker A: "That's correct, Johnny."

We recognize the difference immediately. These speakers are in *SCHOOL:* Speaker A is a teacher, and speaker B is a student. Notice how this context changes the rules of the game:

- Speaker A knows what time it is.
- Speaker A doesn't want to know what time it is; she wants to know whether speaker B knows what time it is.

■ More precisely, speaker A is not interested exactly in whether speaker B knows what time it is; the question is designed to test something that the first speaker is, so to speak, hiding behind her back: Can speaker B "tell time"?

■ Speaker B *must* reply; it's not a matter of politeness, but of duty. Failure to reply means—you guessed it, a trip to the principal's office.

■ There is only one correct answer. Speaker B does not answer the hidden question if he says, "Well, it's a little after three." And "The big hand is pointing at the two . . ." is definitely wrong. It answers the question, of course, but it doesn't answer the hidden request, "Display your ability to 'tell time.' "

We might sum up these differences by calling the question in 14.1 a *real question*. The question in 14.2 has exactly the same form, but it has a quite different purpose. It is a *display question:* It asks speaker B to "display" his ability to "tell time" in terms of the specific question. (And, in a school context, the question might be posed, at 9:30 in the morning, with reference to a cardboard clock designed to test ability to "tell time.")

There are several years of study between Johnny displaying his ability to "tell time" and John taking an essay examination in Biology 200 or writing a paper for Psychology 150:

14.3 Discuss the importance of the adrenal glands in the human life system (15 minutes).

14.4 Paper assignment (due in one week): Compare and contrast the theories of personality of Freud and Jung. How do the differences in theory help to explain the differences in psychoanalysis practiced by followers of Freud and Jung?

But the similarities are greater than the differences: *Most school questions are display questions.* Your biology instructor already knows what the adrenal glands do in the human life system; in fact, he probably devoted a lecture to the subject. He may not know everything, but he certainly doesn't expect you to tell him anything new. Moreover, he's not particularly interested in what you know about the adrenal glands—he wants to "read through" that answer to estimate your ability to "do biology."

There are exceptions to the "display question" rule, of course. The graduate student doing doctoral research on the adrenal glands is expected to provide "real" answers. And in fields like philosophy or English, even freshman students may be given questions that ask for personal opinion or—surprisingly often—students may be given speculative questions that have no correct answer. Nevertheless, such questions are still aimed at letting the student display her ability to "do English" or to "do philosophy."

Problem Two. A true/false test on essay tests Answer the following true/false quiz on taking essay exams. After each statement, write the letter *T* if you think the statement is true, the letter *F* if you think it's false.

a. The night before an essay exam, you should try to cram.

b. The night before an essay exam, you should make sure you know how to spell the key terms of the unit, and that you have a good sense of their meaning.

c. The night before an exam, you should memorize as many examples as possible.

d. The more specific an answer is, the better it is.

e. Always begin writing answers immediately; don't waste time.

f. Always try to repeat back exactly what the instructor said, precisely in his own words.

g. Think through your answer to each question before you begin writing it.

h. Never put your own ideas in an essay answer.

i. Try to have a transitional phrase or connecting word at the beginning of every paragraph.

j. You should always write an introductory paragraph for essay exams.

k. Don't waste time trying to read the whole exam; start in at once on the first question.   ■

Why Do Instructors Give Essay Examinations?

A first answer to this question is obvious enough, given our discussion above: Instructors ask essay questions to let you display your knowledge. But why essay examinations, as opposed to out-of-class papers, true/false or multiple-choice questions, definitions, or any of the other testing devices available? Not to see what you "know" about the subject-matter in factual terms—multiple-choice questions are much better at testing that. Rather, to test your ability to see *relations* among facts, to *select* relevant facts from irrelevant facts, to *analyze* concepts, to *support* opinions, to *apply* information to new situations.

Instructors often don't stop to explain these purposes to students—

they're naturally too busy teaching the subject-matter—but recognizing the purpose of an essay examination is an important first step in finding strategies for studying for and taking essay examinations. The fullest instructions for taking essay examinations that we know of are printed in 14.5 below; they are the instructions for the 1975 California Bar Examination. We'd suggest that the student take any essay examination as if these instructions were given:

> **14.5** An answer should demonstrate your ability to analyze the facts presented by the question, to select the material from the immaterial facts, and to discern the points upon which the case turns. It should show your knowledge and understanding of the pertinent principles and theories of law, their relationship to each other, and their qualifications and limitations. It should evidence your ability to apply the law to the facts given, and to reason logically in a lawyer-like manner to a sound conclusion from the premises adopted. Try to demonstrate your proficiency in using and applying legal principles rather than a mere memory of them.
>
> An answer containing only a statement of your conclusions will receive little credit. State fully the reasons that support them. All points should be thoroughly discussed. Although your answer should be complete, you should not volunteer information or discuss legal doctrines that are not necessary or pertinent to the solution of the problem.
>
> Norman Brand and John O. White,
> *Legal Writing: The Strategy of Persuasion*

Legal exams, of course, differ from undergraduate essay exams in that they begin with a factual case. But the other general principles here apply to any essay examination: Mere memory for facts is not very important, and an answer that answers the question and only that "will receive little credit."

How To Study for Essay Exams

Don't cram! Essay exams test your ability to display *relations* among facts; not to display facts alone. Cramming the night before an examination is an excellent way of studying for an examination that tests your mastery of facts, such as a multiple-choice or true/false examination. Stuff the facts in your head, and they'll stay there long enough to get you through the exam.

The same strategy is disastrous for an essay exam. Your head is so stuffed with facts that you can't select relevant facts from irrelevant facts. The result is often an answer that "talks about" the subject instead of answering the question. It's as if the student had aimed a shotgun at a target, closed his eyes, and blasted away. Some of the shot hits the target, but most of it scatters elsewhere.

Instead, think of taking an essay exam as being like firing a high-powered rifle. You take careful aim at the bull's-eye, squeeze the trigger with a steady pressure, and put a single bullet in the center of the target.

That analogy demands quite different preparation. You should stretch out studying for an essay examination over several weeks. The textbook chapters have to be read well in advance of the exam, in order to let the information sink in. Notes have to be reviewed in advance, and you have to translate the lecture notes and reading material into your own words; rote memory won't help with an essay examination.

The night before an exam is a good time for a group study session. It allows you to talk about questions that might be asked—not that you want to guess about specific questions and try to zero in on one or two, but rather that you want to gain a general sense of what might be expected. More importantly, a group study session for a history exam lets you "talk history" as a preparation for "writing history." Reading a textbook or listening to a lecture are passive learning; an examination asks that you become an active learner.

And a final suggestion about being an active learner—make sure you can spell the words you'll be asked to write in the exam. It's worth a few minutes to write out the names of authors and characters before taking a literature exam, or to write out concepts and related words—*behaviorism, behavioristic, behavioristically.*

A Deceptively Simple Suggestion: Read the Exam

Let's assume you've arrived at the examination on time, and the questions have been distributed. Take ten seconds, look around the room, and say to yourself, "Twenty percent of these students won't read the exam." (Ten seconds into the exam, you haven't written a word, and you're already in the top eighty percent of the class.)

We're much more conscious of this problem as readers of exams than we were as writers of exams. The most obvious problem is *not paying attention to time.* The instructions on an examination make a contract between the instructor and the class as a whole; the instructor can't make an exception for one student without being unfair to the other students. Suppose the instructions for a 50-minute essay examination read, "Answer *three* of the *five* questions below." It's almost predictable, given a class of a hundred students, that twenty will not fulfill the implied contract: They will answer four or five questions, or, more commonly, they will spend so long answering one or two that they can only scratch out a sentence or two on the last. There may be good reason for spending a little more time on one answer than on another, but it's the student's responsibility to budget time. We'd suggest wearing a watch and dividing one's time before beginning, noting the time constraints on the examination. ("Let's see, I'll allow five minutes for proofreading, that'll mean fifteen minutes for each question. . . .")

We'd suggest that you read every question in an essay examination before beginning to answer the first one, even if you're not asked to choose among questions. Multiple-choice examinations, of course, are different: There you should begin working question by question, leaving the harder ones to return to. With an essay exam, however, you'll budget your time better if you read the whole exam.

Another Deceptively Simple Suggestion: Answer the Question

Of course one should answer the question. But that's harder than it might first appear. Consider question 14.3 again.

> **14.3** Discuss the importance of the adrenal glands in the human life system (15 minutes).

We would predict, in a given biology class, perhaps twenty percent of the students will leap off into an answer about *adrenal glands* without pausing to think about the specific demands of the question. Adrenal glands will be defined, explored in their evolutionary development, compared with other glands—everything, in short, except *discussed* in terms of *their importance in the human life system.*

We suggest a very specific way of marking up a question to make sure that you focus on its demands: Underline the topic word (what the question asks you to deal with); place the question word in a box (what you're asked to do), and place dashes under any restrictions or hints. Thus,

> **14.3A** | Discuss | the importance of the adrenal glands in the
>
> human life system.

The question word is particularly important, for it tells what you are expected to do. *Define* asks for the meaning of a concept or thing ("briefly define the adrenal glands"). *Describe* asks for an explanation of what something is or was ("describe the function of the adrenal glands"). *Compare* asks for one thing to be related to another in terms of likenesses and differences ("compare the importance of the adrenal gland with that of the pituitary gland"). *Discuss,* the most general of question words, may be restricted by the question ("discuss the importance of . . ."); if not, the word asks you to provide your own limits to the discussion. Other question words—*what, why, when, how*—imply similar limitations on the topic. Do what the question word asks you to do.

Problem Three. Analyzing essay questions   Analyze each of the following essay questions by underlining the topic words, placing the question word in a box, and placing dashed lines under restrictions or hints (see example 14.3A above).

a. How did the Reformation affect the political structure of Western Europe? Pay particular attention to the economic and educational results of the Reformation.

b. Compare and contrast the wet tropics and the wet-dry tropics. Give examples of each.

c. Briefly identify the major movements in child psychology from 1940 to the present.

d. Analyze the basic difficulties in using intelligence tests to predict student performance. In what way is social class particularly important?

e. Discuss the images of spiritual loss in Coleridge's "Dejection: An Ode" and lines 150–160 of "The Ancient Mariner." Does this comparison reveal a fundamental unity in Coleridge's work, or does it suggest a fundamental split between these modes?

f. Analyze the causes of the American Civil War.   ■

Organize Your Answer Like a Newspaper Story

A journalist may write ten columns of material on a story—a duck escaped from the San Diego Zoo. The ten columns will be sent out over wire services to newspapers across the country. The San Diego paper will want to print all ten columns; it's a hot local story. But other newspapers will want to print less—five columns, two columns, down to a paragraph in the *Latonia Daily Eagle.* Thus the story has to be written so that it can be cut at any point: the most important items first, less important items later.

A student writing an essay answer has a problem with time that's very much like the journalist's problem with space. An "introduction" is a waste of time in an essay exam, and building up to a dramatic

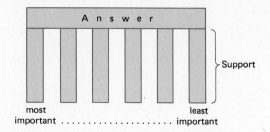

FIGURE 14.1 The Structure of the Essay Answer

conclusion—an effective device in an out-of-class paper—is ineffective if you run out of time before you can state that conclusion. Thus a journalist's strategy is a good strategy for the test-taker: most important things first. Answer the question, and then support your answer in the time available. We picture this strategy in Figure 14.1—note that taking a "support" column away, by the pressure of time, still leaves the essential structure intact.

That organization suggests that *planning* is very important in essay exams. You have to think your answer through as a whole before beginning to write. What one leaves out of an answer is as important as what one puts in, and one displays one's knowledge by organizing it carefully. We feel that students should spend one-fourth to one-half of the time in an exam planning their answer, using a scratch outline. (Once the material has been organized, it can be written at top speed; you won't have to stop to think.)

Your first sentence should *answer the question in the terms of the question*—that is, it should provide a brief answer to the question using the exact words of the question.

14.6 The adrenal glands play a very important role in the human life system.

(Notice that you can answer question 14.3, given above, even though you may know little about the adrenal glands.) This advice may seem mechanical, but consider your reader, intent on finding how you display your ability to "do biology" by answering the question, "Discuss the importance of the adrenal glands in the human life system," responding to 14.3 above and to other possible beginnings.

14.7 The adrenal glands are located above the kidneys.

14.8 The adrenal glands consist of two parts, the cortex, which secretes hormones, and the medulla, which secretes epinephrine, commonly called adrenalin.

14.9   The adrenal glands are very important in our modern, twentieth-century, contemporary world of today.

Problem Four. Answering the question in the terms of the question
Return to the essay questions of problem three, and answer as many questions using the terms of the question, as discussed above, as you can. If you cannot answer the question, explain why. (You should be surprised to find that you can answer questions you know nothing about—questions on wet and dry topics and plant mitosis, for example.)   ■

The second sentence is the perfect place to offer your own *formative idea* (this notion is discussed in chapter Thirteen), startling your reader with your intelligence, and giving him a good sense of the support you plan to develop. After all, all students will answer the question in the first sentence (if they've learned to answer the question in the terms of the question); the second sentence is precisely the place to offer your contribution. The instructor who asks on the exam, "Discuss the causes of the American Civil War," has probably spent three weeks discussing the causes of the Civil War; all students will "get the answer right." Weaker answers will move quickly to facts; better answers will show the ability "to reason logically in a historian-like manner to a sound conclusion," to paraphrase the California Bar Exams. Compare the following two beginnings:

14.10   The three causes of the Civil War are slavery, the political differences of the North and South, and their economic differences. Slavery was very important. The South was . . .

14.11   The American Civil War was caused by irreparable differences between the North and South—primarily slavery, political differences, and economic differences. But it was the economic differences—the South's cotton economy and the North's growing industrialism—that explain the other causes, for the cotton economy was used to justify slavery, and the political differences grew out of economic differences. Thus I shall begin by analyzing the economic differences separating North and South, then show how the other causes are explained by those differences.

Answer 14.11 is well on its way to a solid "A" grade, for it has established a formative idea. Answer 14.10, we fear, has slipped to "mere fact," and that often means, at best, a "C."

Finally, transitions are particularly important in essay exams. Your reader will be reading quickly, often under time pressure to turn in grades. And the reader has the further handicaps of having to read a series of other answers to the same question and of having to struggle with handwritten script. Any help along the way—transitions, a clear organization, a precise focus on the question—will be appreciated and, quite properly, rewarded.

Problem Five. Learning from reading   Return to problem two on page 439 and retake the test on essay examinations, changing any answers that you wish. Then check your answers against our answers, given in the answer section at the end of the book. You may, of course, disagree with our answers: Studying for exams is a very individual business, and each student must work out his or her own approach. And you may not accept our advice in this section. But you will have, as a crude measure, a rough sense of your "ability to learn from reading," by comparing your first answers to your second answers.   ■

THE INVESTIGATIVE PAPER

Almost any writing assignment is "investigative" in one sense or another, even if it only asks that you investigate your feelings about a subject. But the formal "investigative paper"—or often, the "research paper"—is a special writing task: You're commonly asked to compose a paper longer than the conventional 500-word theme; you're expected to examine different sources, usually by means of library research; and you're expected to give references to those sources in some standardized way.

The last of these tasks—standardized references—usually looms so large in the minds of students that the other reasons for assigning an investigative paper aren't emphasized enough. Perhaps a good place to begin, then, is with an obvious question: Why do instructors assign an investigative paper?

The Goals of the Investigative Assignment

Instructors have fairly precise goals in mind when they assign longer investigative papers. Most importantly, they want students to participate in the world of print: to write for the "universal audience" of thoughtful readers; to recognize that legitimate differences of opinion exist in the world of print; and to make thoughtful judgments about issues of importance.

These are not trivial goals, and the college investigative assignment is likely to be rather different from the "research papers" you may have half-heartedly completed in high school, spreading out a few reference works and hopping from one to the next, copying, but "changing the words" to avoid plagiarism, whatever that meant.

More specifically, the investigative assignment has the following goals:

- the student will be able to use the full range of information available in a college library;
- the student will be able to separate fact and opinion, and to judge the reliability of different interpretations of fact;
- the student will be able to integrate evidence and analysis of his or her own with that provided by other sources;
- the student will master the techniques of summary, paraphrase, and quotations;
- the student will carry out an extended discourse for the "universal audience," using more complex patterns of development than those of shorter pieces of writing;
- the student will accept the responsibility for using the words and ideas of others, including the mastery of a standardized form of reference.

Thus—though no one assigns "research papers" in the real world—the investigative assignment imparts useful skills. In choosing a car, for example, you might gather several opinions, judging the authority of each (rating a mechanic's opinion higher than that of a teen-ager); you might compare public information on prices, warranties, gas mileage, and resale value; you might do library research, checking reviews in automobile and consumer magazines; and you would evaluate this information critically, in the light of your own experience in a test drive. Similarly, many writing tasks in your professional career will be, in essence, investigative assignments. An engineer recommending a design, a lawyer citing precedents to support an appeal, a personnel manager deciding to purchase one brand of typewriter rather than another, a criminologist arguing for a prison educational program—all these professionals are doing "research papers," though they are unlikely to think of them as such.

Such goals suggest that the student should approach the investigative assignment as an intellectual challenge as well as a writing assignment. The last unit of this text, "Invention," will be of help in dealing with the mental challenges of the investigative assignment; in this chapter we'll focus on the investigative process and the documentation of sources.

Steps in Writing the Investigative Paper

A short investigative paper of a few pages might involve a minimum of fuss and bother—perhaps a look through the card catalog of the college library, a check of a couple of books, and a few notes in a notebook. Longer investigative assignments, however, require thinking ahead. Thinking ahead means having a plan. A plan gives you a sense of the steps you're going to take in your investigation; a method is a way of putting your plan into action. We offer in Figure 14.2 a rigid model of a plan for an investigative paper.

In Figure 14.2 the steps in investigation are separate and unrelated. Sometimes it works that way. Most often it doesn't. Surveying resources may change your sense of a topic, and note-taking may call for more surveys. Forming the paper may cause you to seek more resources, even to rethink your initial topic. The investigative paper needs a plan, but the plan should not be too rigid; the writer should not be trapped at the end by what she expected at the beginning (a warning echoed in our chapter headnote). A student who began his investigative paper on the possible Central Intelligence Agency involvement in the overthrow of President Salvador Allende of Chile found that the role of American business in that overthrow proved more interesting. A student who began her investigative paper on Food and Drug Administration rulings on cosmetics found she became more interested in the decision-making process in that federal agency. Thus we prefer that students think more loosely about a plan for investigation, more in terms of a model like that of Figure 14.3, and we ask that students keep a *research journal* in which they log their problems, shifts, and progress.

Problem Six. The research journal   Begin a research journal, keeping regular entries of your steps in writing an investigative paper. Date each entry. Keep the journal informal, but be open about problems and achievements. Begin your journal now with a first entry—"focusing a preliminary topic."   ■

Focusing a Preliminary Topic

A general topic for a research paper may be assigned ("write a ten-page investigative paper on Charles Dickens' novel *Hard Times*"), or it may grow out of your own interests and experiences. In either case, you'll need to narrow the topic to some reasonable dimensions at the start, or you'll be overwhelmed by the resources available even in a small library. Moreover, by focusing your preliminary topic, you'll have a sense of what you're looking for, so that initial reading won't have to

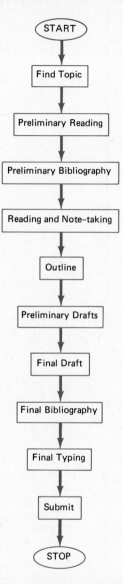

FIGURE 14.2   A Rigid Model of the Investigative Process

be repeated. In the two research journal entries below, students begin to focus on a preliminary topic.

14.12   April 4. Ten pages on *Hard Times*. That's not impossible; I'm an urban studies major, so Dickens' treatment of 19th century

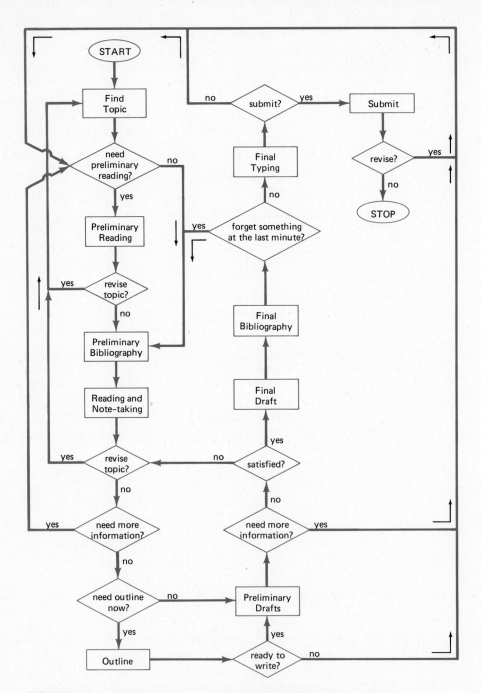

FIGURE 14.3 A Realistic Model of the Investigative Process (simplified)

urbanization interested me. Dickens' view of cities . . . maybe I'll reread the introduction . . . it mentions that Dickens was influenced by Carlyle, and I've heard of him. I start out with a title already: "The Influence of Thomas Carlyle on Dickens' *Hard Times.*"

14.13   May 2. I've been interested in the Hopi ever since I visited the reservation with my family a few years ago. The Hopi and the Spanish explorers . . . The land quarrel between the Hopi and the Navaho . . . Hopi religion . . . I don't know where to start. [instructor comment: "try an encyclopedia article; it might do some preliminary sorting-out"]

  May 4. I looked at two encyclopedias, but didn't make any notes. They helped though. I think I'll do the Hopi and the Spanish explorers (invaders?)—that will let me read some of the diaries of the explorers.

With a focused preliminary topic, you should find your sense of direction progressively narrowing, centering in on the commitment that you will develop in your final paper.

Surveying Resources

The college library is the writer's laboratory, and the writer ought to be as aware of how the library works as the scientist is aware of the workings of bunsen burners and filtration techniques. Fortunately, most college libraries have printed guides available, and many offer regular tours and instructions on using reference material.

Problem Seven. Mapping your library   Draw a physical map of your library, or use a printed map if one is available. Mark the following locations on your map.

- card catalog
- check-out desk
- periodicals room
- reference room
- microfilm room
- reserve book room or desk
- the "stacks," or book collection
- other special areas—record and tape collection; reading rooms, special collections

Now annotate your map by entering the following information:

a. How long may books be checked out for, and what is the fine for late payment? (Enter by check-out desk.)

b. Does the library use the Library of Congress system or the Dewey Decimal System for cataloging books? (The Library of Congress system begins with a letter/number combination, such as "PN204.2"; the Dewey Decimal System begins with a number, such as "615.412.") (Enter this information by the card catalog.)

c. Does the library post a subject guide for the cataloging system it uses? If so, mark it on the map.

d. Where can you find unabridged dictionaries? (Mark several locations, if possible.)

e. Mark the location of coin-operated copying machines, and list the price of a single copy. Mark the location of coin-operated typewriters, if available.

f. Can 8⅛ x 11-inch copies be made from material on microfilm and microfiche? (List this information by the microfilm room.)

g. How are reserve books catalogued? (List this information by the reserve book room or desk.)

h. Can students check out records or tapes? (List this information by the record and tape collection.)

i. Where does one go to ask questions about the reference collection? (List this information by the reference room.)

j. How are abstracts and indexes filed in the reference room? Is there a posted guide to the reference room? (List this information by the reference room.)

k. Where does one go to order a book on inter-library loan, if the book is not in your library's collection? (Mark this information in the appropriate place.) ■

A *bibliography* is a list of books and magazines (from Greek *biblio-*, book, plus *graphein,* to write). Your investigative paper, in its final form, will end with a formal bibliography, a list of the sources you've used. To start, you'll want to compile a "working bibliography"—a list of the items you want to examine.

At this point, you'll be gathering information in small chunks, in bits and pieces, without worrying particularly about where it will be used in your final draft. Thus you'll turn naturally to note cards—3″ x 5″ or 4″ x 6″—allowing you to sort items to hunt them down, and you'll also use note cards to make notes on your reading.

Your working bibliography will come from two sources: the card catalog for books, and indexes and abstracts for articles. The card catalog will list all books in the library under three headings—the author's last name, the title of the book, and the subject matter of the book. Most

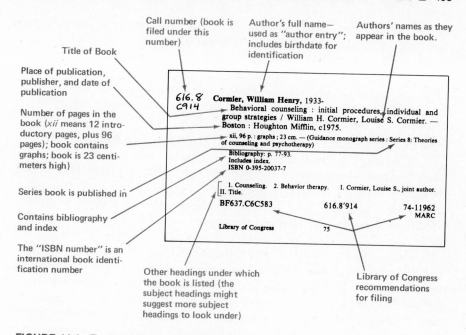

FIGURE 14.4   Typical Library Catalog Card

libraries use standard Library of Congress cards; we illustrate a typical card in Figure 14.4.

Note, first of all, that the card is used by librarians as well as by investigators. Thus it contains a great deal of information that you may not be interested in—the size of the book, Library of Congress recommendations about cataloging numbers (which may not match those used by your library), the ISBN number (an international book code). (But some of such information may be of help—you'd be interested in a book with a bibliography, since that might point to additional sources, and the various subject-headings might lead you to more books.)

Secondly, note that librarians are very fussy people. The small © by the publication date, 1975, shows that the publication date is taken from the copyright page, behind the title page, rather than the title page itself, and the author's full name is listed as a catalog heading, not the name he used on the title page (that's given in the main entry, following the title and the word *by*).

The card catalog—and the indexes you'll use—present you with your first problem in getting along with librarians: how to find the subject heading they use to list the information you're after. Our first two research paper topics don't present particular problems, as long as one develops the skill of "thinking like a librarian":

14.14 May 5. I tried the card catalog, looking first under "Hopi." Fifteen cards. I picked the four that looked best. I also tried "American Indian—History"—nothing. And "American History—Southwest"—three promising books.

14.15 April 6. I didn't expect much from the card catalog. I tried the obvious, "Dickens, Charles—*Hard Times*," and found a promising "casebook" anthology and then plodded through the "Dickens, Charles" entries until I realized they almost always had the call number "PR6018." So I went up to the stacks and looked. Found four good books and checked them out.

"Thinking like a librarian" is a special skill, but you're lost without it. And it's hard to explain, except in general terms. People's names get turned around: Dickens, Charles; they even undergo strange transformations: Librarians are the only group who think that Mark Twain was named Samuel Clemens. Some subject headings are from front to back: "United States Government"; other subject headings work back to front: "College Attendance—United States." To use card catalogs and indexes, begin to "think like a librarian": Generate as many topic headings as possible, and work from the most likely to the least likely.

Problem Eight. Thinking like a librarian   For each of the research topics below, generate as many topic headings as possible that might be used to locate information in card catalogs and indexes. If your instructor directs, find one book reference and one magazine reference, if possible. The first has been done for you.

a. I'm researching the career of Jane Fonda, particularly the connection between her political views and her acting career. Possible answer: I'll start with "Fonda, Jane," and then I'll figure out how the catalog and indexes list the movies—I'll try "film," "moving pictures," "motion pictures," "cinema" (and probably not "flicks"). Then I'll try several "politics and . . ." headings—"politics and the arts," "politics and film," and so on.

b. I want to write a paper on the uproar, a few years ago, when women reporters wanted to visit baseball locker rooms.

c. I want to research the "saccharin scare" of a few years ago, when the federal Food and Drug Agency (FDA) tried to ban saccharin as a carcinogen.

Basic Information	Supplemental Information
Author or Editor	And Additional Authors?
Title	And Subtitle: After Colon? Translator? Edition ("2nd ed.")?
Place Published ("New York")	Need State? (For "New York" or "Chicago," no; but "Hillsdale, N.J.")
Publisher (short form)	
Date of Publication	
	Series? ("Center for the Study of Reading Technical Report, No. 89")
Call Number (to find in stacks)	
	Other Information for Your Own Purpose? (such as "bibliography")

FIGURE 14.5   Information for a Bibliography Card

d. I want to investigate the discovery of DNA.

e. I want to investigate President Truman's decision to drop the atomic bombs on Japan at the end of World War II.   ■

Here's a useful hint as you begin to compile a working bibliography: Master the final bibliography form (discussed below) as you begin research, and translate all entries into that form as you begin research. It will save the step of having to do such translation later. For books, you'll want to gather the information listed in Figure 14.5. Information essential for all books is listed in the first column; special information relevant for some books is listed in the second column.

Figure 14.6 shows the information from the catalog card of Figure 14.4 typed on a student's notecard. The student has used the author's name as it appears in the book (not as the library listed it), and he has transcribed the entry into the form of the final bibliography. He's also headed the card with the author's name and date, as a help to alphabetizing and for reference.

Indexes (or more technically *indices*) point you to magazine articles, reviews, articles in books (and some indexes include books). They are more complicated than the card catalog, for there are many different kinds of indexes, with different formats and different coverage. You're probably most familiar with the *Reader's Guide to Periodical Literature*, which indexes popular magazines, such as *Time, Redbook, Sports Illustrated, Harper's,* and the *New Republic*. We analyze a column of the

Cormier 1975

Cormier, William H., and Louise S. Cormier.
    Behavioral Counseling: Initial Procedures,
    Individual and Group Strategies. Boston:
    Houghton Mifflin, 1975. bibl.

616.8
C914

FIGURE 14.6   Information from Library Card Typed on Student Bibliography Card

Reader's Guide in Figure 14.7. The index uses many abbreviations and shortcuts, so it's often impossible to translate it to a full bibliographical entry. In a bibliography card (Figure 14.8) taken from the entries above, the student has written out the full name of the journal and the date of the article, but she has been forced to leave space for the author's first name.

The serious investigator will want to go beyond the *Reader's Guide,* which lists only popular and nonscholarly journals. There are many other specialized indexes, which cover areas from engineering to education to nursing, and there are specialized guides to such things as book reviews, editorials, and essays in books. Some reference works give you not only the title of a reference, but also a brief summary of its contents, an *abstract.* Abstracts are particularly valuable, for they can often save a trip to the periodicals room, since you may decide that, despite the article's title, it's not really as interesting as you had thought. We print a sample abstract, regarding the Athabascans of central Alaska, in Figure 14.9; it's available in the ERIC educational file available in the microfilm room.

In general, indexes and volumes of abstracts will explain, in a "preface" or "introduction," what's in their work (and what's not in it) and how to read the entries. If in doubt, check the front of the book.

A glance around the reference room of a college library will convince you of the riches available there. The problem is, how does the beginning investigator find these sources? Here's a suggestion, a surprisingly helpful one: Invent the reference work you want. That is, decide the ideal work for your purposes, think of several names for it, and look for it under those names. Quite often it works. Even if it doesn't, you will have refined the question that you take to the reference librarian. The problem below asks you to create reference works to solve specific investigative tasks. By working out the answers to the problems and checking your answer against ours (given in the answer section at the end of the book), you should be ready to take on some investigative problems of your own.

FIGURE 14.7 Sample Entries in the *Reader's Guide to Periodical Literature*. Copyright © 1981 by the H. W. Wilson Company. Material reproduced by permission of the publisher.

Main subject entry

Entries alphabetical by title

Author entry

Some bracketed explanations

Entries give volume, page, month (day), and year of publication

"See also"—suggestions on other headings

Subheadings—centered

Abbreviated journal title

Cross-references

Gives additional information on contents (bibl—bibliography; f—footnote; il—illustrations; also pors—portraits)

Menu for a moveable feast. il House & Gard 152: 30-1 N '80
Small-scale holiday dinners. P. Wartels. Mademoiselle 86:72 D '80
DINOSAURS
Asteroid theory of extinctions strengthened. R. A. Kerr. il Science 210:514-17 O 31 '80
Dinosaur Jim, Sherlock of bones. F. Warshofsky. il por Read Digest 117:33-4+ O '80
DINWIDDIE, Richard D.
Creating the sounds of Christmas. por Chr Today 24:36-7 D 12 '80
—See Dinwiddle, R. it auth
DINWIDDIE, Ruth, and Dinwiddle, R. D.
Ten best Christmas records. pors Chr Today 24:22-3 D 12 '80
DIONNE, E. J.
New York. New Repub 183:20-2 O 25 '80
DIPERNA, Paula
Women engineers. il Work Wom 5:60-3+ N '80
DIPHENYL compounds
Not fit for man nor beast [PCB present in fish oil (feed ingredient)] il FDA Consumer 14:28 N '80
PCBs: the poison that won't go away. J. Culhane. Read Digest 117:112-16 D '80
Portable system for PCB disposal. il BioScience 30:853-4 D '80
Toxic waste still pollutes roadways [PCB spill in North Carolina] S. Begley. il Newsweek 96:25+ O 27 '80
DIPLOMAS
Differentiated high school diplomas. J. W. Keefe. Educ Digest 46:10-13 O '80
DIPLOMATE (dessert) See Desserts
DIPLOMATIC and consular service
Not-so-clean sweepers [broomball played by Moscow's diplomatic corps] W. E. Schmidt. il Newsweek 97:57 Ja 26 '81
DIRECT selling
See also
Mail order business
Party line. S. Kupferberg. New Repub 183:10-13 D 13 '80
DIRECTION, Theatrical. See Theater—Production and direction
DISABILITY Insurance. See Insurance, Disability
DISARMAMENT
See also
Independent Commission on Disarmament and Security Issues
Arms control and international security [address. October 24, 1980] P. A. R. Carrington. Vital Speeches 47:114-17 D 1 '80
Sin of silence. B. V. A. Röling. bibl f il Bull Atom Sci 36:10-13 N '80
Conferences
Disarmament education: a farewell to arms? [World Congress on Disarmament Education; symposium] UNESCO Courier 33:3-34 S '80
Study and teaching
See Peace studies

```
Warshofsky 1980

Warshofsky, F        . "Dinosaur Jim, Sherlock of
    Bones." Reader's Digest, October 1980, pp.
    33-34.
```

FIGURE 14.8 Bibliography Card Typed from *Reader's Guide* Entry (note blank spaces left for author's first name)

Problem Nine. Creating reference works For each of the investigative problems below, create the ideal reference work, invent two or three names for it, and then check your library reference room to see if such a work exists. The first problem has been answered for you; specimen answers to other problems are given in the answer section at the end of the text.

a. I'm investigating Arthur Jensen's theory of intelligence, outlined in his two books. The *Book Review Index* gives me references to reviews of those books, but hunting down each individual review will be time-consuming. Is there a shortcut that will let me get a quick sense of the opinion of each reviewer? *Possible answer:* I invented a reference work that would print a brief summary of each book review. I guessed it might be entitled *Abstracts of Book Reviews, Book Review Abstracts, Book Review Summaries,* or *Book Review Digest.* It existed under the last title, *Book Review Digest,* and it proved even more helpful than I'd expected. It gave brief excerpts from the reviews—though not all of those listed in the *Book Review Index*—and it also gave me the length of each review, so that I could go to the longer, more thoughtful reviews.

b. I'm researching U.S. involvement in the overthrow of President Salvator Allende in Chile, and I need a research guide that will give me a quick overview—the dates, a summary of events, and so on.

c. I'm investigating the trial of Dan White, who shot San Francisco Mayor George Moscone and Board of Supervisors member Harvey

Milk in 1978. White was convicted of manslaughter rather than murder, apparently because the jury believed the defense claim that he could not be held responsible for his actions, having consumed Twinkies, Coke, and other "junk food" before the shooting. What I need is a quick survey of how newspapers, particularly San Francisco newspapers, reacted to this verdict.

d. I'm investigating the origin of language, and I'm completely stuck. I found one book by inventing its title, *The Origin of Language,* but the *Reader's Guide* gives me nothing, nothing at all.

e. I'm a nursing major, and I'm stuck for a topic. (My instructor says

FIGURE 14.9 A Sample Abstract (This abstract appeared in *Research in Education.*)

Important Information

Less Important Information

Identification number—you would use this number to obtain the document in microfilm room

Authors' names

Title of article

Publisher

"Publication Date"

Cross-reference number (for librarians)

Series in which document is published

"Sponsoring Agency"—this work was supported with federal funds

Notes where one can obtain the document

"Publication Type"—with a code number for librarians

Coded information on price of a copy—the code is explained in *Resources in Education*

"Descriptors"—subject headings under which the document is listed in *Resources in Education*

"Identifiers"—major subject headings

Abstract—a brief summary of the document

Initials of the person who prepared the abstract

ED 175 276   FL 010 573
Scollon, Ron Scollon, Suzanne B. K.
Literacy as Interethnic Communication: An Athabaskan Case. Working Papers in Sociolinguistics, No. 59.
Southwest Educational Development Lab., Austin, Tex.
Spons Agency—National Inst. of Education (DHEW), Washington, D.C.
Pub Date—Apr 79
Note—30p.
Available from—Southwest Educational Development Laboratory, 211 East 7th Street, Austin, Texas 78701
Pub Type— Opinion Papers (120)
EDRS Price - MF01/PC02 Plus Postage.
Descriptors—Alaska Natives, Athapascan Languages, Cognitive Style, Contrastive Linguistics, *Cross Cultural Studies, *Cultural Differences, Cultural Factors, Culture Conflict, *Discourse Analysis, Ethnicity, *Ethnic Stereotypes, Language Skills, *Literacy, Second Language Learning, Socialization, Writing, *Written Language
Identifiers—*Athapaskan (Tribe), Kutchin (Tribe)
  English essayist literacy shares many features with the discourse patterns of English speakers. Where these patterns are different from those of another ethnic group, literacy will be experienced as interethnic communication. Athabaskan discourse differs from that of English in (1) presentation of self (an Athabaskan is silent with new acquaintances); (2) dominance and display (in Athabaskan culture silence is submissive, talk dominant); (3) projection of self-image (Athabaskan courtesy prohibits speaking well of one's self); and (4) closing formulas (Athabaskan has none). These differences result in mutual ethnic stereotyping. To an Athabaskan, to acquire English essayist literacy is to become smug, boastful, talkative, and arrogant. It is suggested that non-Western forms of literacy may be useful in approaching the problem of Athabaskan literacy. For instance, the Kutchin Athabaskans once developed a native literacy on the model of some African peoples, by reading and memorizing scripture (an authoritatively presented text) and spontaneously adopting therefrom forms of writing for practical use. (JB)

it has to be a controversial topic.) I'd like to find some nursing journals and skim through them, hoping they will give me some ideas toward a topic. ■

Problem Ten. Investigative problems   The investigative problems below ask you to "think like a librarian" and to "invent reference works." (So, if you happen to be a reference librarian reading this passage, please don't help students with these problems—they'll understand.)

When you solve a problem, state the answer, and then state briefly how you solved it—what worked and what false steps you took. If you don't find the answer to a problem, explain where you looked before you gave up.

a. What does the library think Studs Terkel's name is? What address can you use to write to him?

b. What word describes what Wayne Morse did at times during the "Telstar Debates" of the early 1960s?

c. What is the *Old Yellow Book*? What poet was interested in it?

d. In the spring of 1965, St. John's University was blacklisted by the AAUP. Why? (What's a "blacklist"? What's the AAUP?)

e. The word *nice* has had several meanings in the past that it does not have now. Give two of those meanings.

f. What is Hatha Yoga? How does it differ from other Yogas?

g. Who are the "hairy Ainu"? (Optional: What's happening to them now?)

h. When did scholar Alfred L. Kroeber die? What field did he specialize in before he died? (Optional: How does a little curiosity in the card catalog lead you to find the name of the "last wild Indian in North America"? Second optional problem: Alfred Kroeber's daughter is a noted science fiction writer; how might you find out her name?)

i. (An optional problem.) In 1941, the *New York Times,* along with other newspapers, reported on the undefeated season of Plainfield Teachers College, led by their star quarterback, Johnny Chung. Can you learn anything of interest about Johnny Chung and his team's undefeated season? ■

Reading and Notetaking: Summary, Paraphrase, and Quotation

As you begin reading, you begin the serious part of the investigative assignment—digesting, summarizing, comparing, criticizing, judging.

You will use combinations of three methods for notetaking:

- quotation: that is, recording the actual words of the author, in quotation marks, with a reference;
- summary: writing down a short version of the ideas of the author, with a reference;
- paraphrase: restating the ideas of an author in your own words, at about the same length, with an appropriate reference.

We find an "appropriate reference," at this stage of research, can be simply the author's name and a page reference. Thus, "Cormier, p. 42" would be enough to identify the book cited in figures 14.4 and 14.6 above—it would lead us back to the bibliography card with the full information about the book. The same shorthand reference can be carried into early drafts, so that numbering footnotes and providing full information about the sources can be left until your paper is ready to be put in final form. You may, of course, find two articles by the same person on your topic, or two authors with the same name—if so refine your referencing system to include dates ("Cormier and Cormier, 1975, p. 42") or initials ("W. Cormier, p. 42").

Summary, paraphrase, and quotation work together in any longer investigative assignment. We find that beginning investigators overuse quotation, so that much of their time is spent copying from books or articles. There are several advantages, at the notetaking stage, to using summary and paraphrase as alternatives. Most obviously, you have to understand a passage in order to summarize or paraphrase it, but not to copy it, so that summary and paraphrase work toward the more general goals of the investigative assignment, analyzing and synthesizing. And, when you are writing your first draft, a long quotation, simply copied down, forces you to stop again, at the drafting stage, to consider possibilities for summary and paraphrase.

An example may clarify our emphasis on summary and paraphrase. A journalism major, investigating American reporters in the Vietnam war, found the following book in the card catalog and copied down the following reference to it (in an appropriate form for a final bibliography entry):

14.16 Knightley, Phillip. *The First Casualty: From the Crimea to Vietnam; The War Correspondent as Hero, Propagandist, and Myth Maker.* New York: Harcourt Brace Jovanovich, 1975.

(He could have omitted the long subtitle, following the colon, but he felt that it was important in describing the content of the book.) He found the book in the stacks and took several useful notes from it. He liked one of Knightley's concluding paragraphs, and he copied most of the paragraph, placing it in quotation marks and briefly identifying the source.

14.17 "So in the reporting of Vietnam each day's news was swiftly consumed by the next day's. Too few correspondents looked back and tried to see what it added up to, too few probed beyond the official version of events to see what it added up to, too few probed beyond the official version of events to expose the lies and half-truths, too few tried to analyse what it all meant. There were language problems: few correspondents spoke French, much less Vietnamese. There were time problems: Kevin Buckley's investigation into 'Operation Speedy Express' took two men two and a half months. And there were cultural problems: apart from Bernard Fall's and Frances FitzGerald's, there were no serious attempts to explain to Americans something about the people they were fighting. On the whole, writers for non-daily publications came out better than most of their colleagues, because, free from the tyranny of pressing deadlines, they could look at the war in greater depth. . . ." (Knightley, p. 424)

(The ellipses [. . .] indicate that he did not copy the rest of the sentences in the paragraph.)

Consider other alternatives available to the writer. He could have summarized the paragraph:

14.18 Knightley criticizes American correspondents for their lack of analysis, for not learning the languages, for not conducting in-depth studies, and for not dealing with Vietnamese culture. He does, however, cite exceptions to his criticism, and he does note that magazines were generally better than newspapers in their coverage. (Knightley, p. 424)

Such a summary would be particularly appropriate for an investigative paper that turned toward the work of the exceptions Knightley cites.

Alternatively, the writer might have paraphrased the author.

14.19 Knightley concludes his survey of the reporting of the war on a critical note. The correspondents, he suggests, overwhelmed by the raw events of each day, did not question the news they were given, nor see the larger patterns of the war, nor take the time for sustained investigation—although here he does note, as an exception, Kevin Buckley's 1969 *Newsweek* special on the pacification scandal. Knightley notes that most correspondents spoke neither

Vietnamese nor French, and that, except for Fall and Fitzgerald, they did not try to understand the culture of the Vietnamese. Thus, while he finds magazine and book coverage superior to that of the newspapers, he feels that, on the whole, our coverage was poor. (Knightley, p. 424)

The paraphrase, restating the author's ideas at about the same length, might be particularly appropriate for a paper centering on different evaluations of press coverage. Note that this version makes it quite clear that the opinions are those of Knightley, not those of the author of the paraphrase. Note also that the paraphrase forces the writer to understand, while copying doesn't. Here, the writer offers a general interpretation of the judgment Knightley makes, and he uses his outside knowledge to clarify Knightley's reference to Kevin Buckley.

In the final version the student decided to mix paraphrase and quotation, using enough quotation to give the flavor of the original, but retaining his own control over the paraphrase:

14.20 Knightley sees the correspondents as "consumed" by each day's news: "too few correspondents looked back and tried to see what it added up to, too few probed beyond the official version of events to expose the lies and half-truths, too few tried to analyse what it all meant." Knightley mentions exceptions—Kevin Buckley, Bernard Fall, Frances Fitzgerald—and he admits that non-daily reporters, "freed from the tyranny of pressing deadlines," did better in reporting the war. But, for the most part, he presents a negative view: correspondents, caught up in the day's news as officially reported, were unable to see beyond the lies, unwilling to conduct detailed investigations, unmotivated to study French or Vietnamese, and not serious about probing the culture of the country. (Knightley, p. 424)

Summary, paraphrase, and quotation, then, can be mixed together in a number of ways, to support various purposes, and you'll find that making these decisions at the notetaking stage will later make drafting the first draft easier.

Summary, paraphrase, and quotation are all legitimate methods of notetaking. They need to be separated from an illegitimate form of notetaking: *plagiarism*. Plagiarism is presenting, as one's own work, the words or ideas of another writer. College instructors, who live by words and ideas, take plagiarism seriously. They view it as the academic equivalent of theft, and the penalties are often heavy. (These heavy penalties seem justified, by the way, since the equivalent of plagiarism in the real world is a violation of the copyright law, and there also the penalties are serious.)

It's important, to avoid plagiarism, that you develop the habit, at the notetaking stage, of *always* putting the author's words in quotation marks. Otherwise, when drafting the paper, removed from the source, you may find a note that looks like summary or paraphrase, and thus inadvertently offer the author's words as your own.

Our definition of plagiarism includes using "the ideas of another writer" as well as using the words of another writer. You do not avoid plagiarism by copying the passage and "just changing the words," as we've heard our children advised early in their schooling. Paraphrasing the ideas of another is perfectly legitimate—as long as you show, with a footnote reference, that you are using the ideas of someone else. If you offer them as your own, you are still guilty of plagiarism.

There are two obvious limits to this definition of plagiarism. You do not have to footnote ordinary fact and widely accepted ideas and beliefs. The reader does not expect a footnote to support the claim that the world is round. Charles Dickens' birthdate, the general outline of his life, the novels that he published—these are generally accepted facts, regardless of where you obtained them.[1] What are "widely accepted ideas and beliefs" change with time. Someone publishing an essay on the "theory of evolution" in 1859, without a reference to Charles Darwin, whose book on the theory of evolution was published that year, would have been obviously guilty of plagiarism (unless he discovered it independently, as did A. E. Wallace). Today, the theory of evolution is a widely accepted idea, and would not need a footnote. These distinctions, however, are clear-cut, and the plagiarized paper almost always announces itself in obvious ways to an experienced reader.

Drafting the Paper

Except for its length, the investigative assignment is written like any other paper. The investigative paper does present two specific problems, however: that of purposeful and stylish use of quotation and that of consistency of verb tense.

Consider, in terms of the purposeful and stylish use of quotation, the following student first draft.

14.21 In his preface to *The Complete Sherlock Holmes,* Christopher Morley says, "The whole Sherlock Holmes saga is a triumphant illustration of art's supremacy over life. Perhaps no fiction character ever created has become so charmingly real to his readers. It is not that we take our blessed Sherlock too seriously; if we really want the painful oddities of criminology let us go to Bataille or Roughead prisons. But Holmes is pure anesthesia." (Morley, p. 5)

Is this a stylish quotation? The quotation itself is certainly stylish, but the student's introduction is rather awkward. Consider a better—because more stylish—beginning:

14.22 "The whole Sherlock Holmes saga," Christopher Morley claims, "is a triumphant illustration. . . ."

Is 14.21 a purposeful quotation? The writer may be trying to suggest, in citing the title of the book, that Christopher Morley's views deserve special attention because he was chosen to introduce *The Complete Sherlock Holmes,* but that argument is better made explicitly. The first sentence of the quotation makes a general point about art, irrelevant to an investigative paper on Sherlock Holmes. The student writer of 14.19, in a rewrite, was able to work with the central thrust of the quotation in a stylish and purposeful manner:

14.23 For Christopher Morley, Sherlock Holmes is "so charmingly real" that he becomes "pure anesthesia."

Problem Eleven. Working with summary, paraphrase, and the stylish and purposeful use of quotation This text provides a number of opportunities to experiment with the writing skills just discussed: summary, paraphrase, and the stylish and effective use of quotes. The following are merely suggestions.

a. Provide a stylish and purposeful sentence quoting our advice about the stylish and purposeful use of quotes.

b. Integrate quotation and summary by creating a four- to eight-sentence summary of the Jim Quinn *Newsweek* column reprinted on pages 409–411.

c. Turn to the end of chapter One, pages 23–25, where we cite three writers on their writing processes. Use summary, paraphrase, and quotation to create an extended paragraph on the writing processes of professional writers.   ■

A second problem, that of shifting of tense patterns, comes about precisely because the investigative paper must fit together, into an ideally seamless argument, information compiled at different times. At some points the seams begin to show, as in this graduate paper:

shift : Shift of Tense   Keep verb tense consistent. This advice
does not mean that all verbs must be in the same tense (see
examples 14.16–14.18 above, for a logical shifting of verb
tense). Rather it means that verbs indicating the same
range should be kept in the same verb tense.

First Draft	*Revision*
Roosevelt naturally, in the last years of his presidency, concentrated on foreign affairs, particularly the war. Truman, caught up in the cold war, also stresses our world role. Eisenhower, himself a soldier, largely ignored developing social needs at home. Thus the time is ripe, when Kennedy assumes the presidency, for a massive attack on the social inequalities of our society.	Roosevelt naturally, in the last years of his presidency, concentrated on foreign affairs, particularly the war. Truman, caught up in the cold war, also stressed our world role. Eisenhower, himself a soldier, largely ignored developing social needs at home. Thus the time was ripe, when Kennedy assumed the presidency, for a massive attack on the social inequalities of our society.
(This version alternates past and present tense for events all occurring in the past.)	(This version shifts to the consistent use of the past tense.)
The woman stopped, before getting into her car, and walked back to us. She reaches into her wallet, and pulls out a twenty-dollar bill. . . .	The woman stopped, before getting into her car, and walked back to us. She reached into her wallet, and pulled out a twenty-dollar bill. . . .
(This version may reflect relaxed speech, where it's common, in telling a story, to shift from the past tense to the present tense: "This guy came up to me, and he says . . .")	(This version provides the consistency of the print code.)

14.24 In 1933 Bloomfield argues for essentially a taxonomic science of linguistics,[1] but Chomsky, writing in 1957, offered a more
generative goal.[2] More recently, the issue has been sharpened by
critics of Chomsky, who suggest . . .

The seam that's showing, of course, is inconsistency of tense. The
1933 argument is cited in the present tense and the 1957 article in the
past tense, giving the reader a curious sense of time warp. Similarly,

after the "issue has been sharpened" of sentence two, the reader expects "critics . . . who have suggested. . . ."

In general, a consistent past tense is most appropriate for an investigative paper, but the important point is consistency of tense.

Footnote and Bibliography Form

Footnote and bibliography form are as powerfully rhetorical as any other part of writing: The form of a reference responds to the context of communication and to the needs of the audience. In this text, for example, we use at least six different levels of reference:

■ We cite examples from professional writers in the text, generally with a minimal reference, the author's name and the title of the work. This is an informal reference, appropriate to the context (we don't expect you to look up these references).

■ We cite formal references in footnotes, and here we follow the footnote form that we will outline shortly. These references document claims made in the text; they provide you with the chance to check our claims by looking up the reference.

■ We make recommendations for further reading at the end of each chapter. We give full information for these books, since we encourage you to look at them, but we do so, generally, in the informal way that we'll discuss as "citing references in the text." Here, again, our reference form is determined by our readers' needs. For example, at the end of this chapter, we list a number of reference works, such as the *Art Index* and the *Book Review Digest,* but without a formal reference, since those works are found, arranged alphabetically or by subject, in the reference room of the library.

■ We make formal references to copyrighted works for which we need legal permission to reprint. Those references, on the back of the title page, use a still different form, that controlled by the context, "legal form for a copyright notice."

■ We make references that are "totally useless," in the sense that you don't know who we're talking about. "One writer has developed a 'grammar of coherence,' " we write, without telling you who that writer is, or elsewhere, "one writer speaks of being 'reader-centered' rather than 'writer-centered.' " We make such references to acknowledge a colleague, but to avoid cluttering our text with names that are, from your point of view, uninteresting.

■ On the other hand, in the Instructor's Manual that accompanies this text, we give formal references to those colleagues, because instructors need that information. In the Instructor's Manual, we use the bibliography form we recommend here, but we use a quite different footnote form, again to best respond to the needs of our readers.

Thus, though we'll present a formal system for footnotes and bibliographies, that of the Modern Language Association (MLA), you should be aware that there are a number of other systems, appropriate for different writing contexts.

Features Common to All References

The most important features of references are those shared by footnote entries and bibliographical entries. They are the following.

■ Titles of books and journals are underlined. The underlining, in a formal manuscript, is a signal to the printer to use italic type, and we suggest that you think consciously of underlining as "using italics." That way your sense of what you do, as writer, will match more closely with what you see in print. The practice of underlining titles of books and journals has spread across to titles of movies and television shows, which are now generally underlined rather than placed in quotation marks.

■ The titles of articles in journals and of chapters of books are placed in quotation marks.

■ The volume number of a journal is translated to arabic numerals (that is, regular numbers), even if it is printed in Roman numerals in the journal. Thus, "LXXXI" would be translated to "81." (Unabridged dictionaries will give you the full Roman numeral system.) Volume numbers, in our system, come in an identifiable place in footnote and bibliography entries, so the word "volume" and the abbreviation "vol" are unnecessary.

■ The names of authors are always printed first name first, as "Charles Dickens" rather than "Dickens, Charles," *with the exception of* the first name in a bibliography entry (which makes it easier to organize the bibliography entries alphabetically).

■ Single quotation marks('/') and double quotation marks ("/") shift rank with each other in a way that's easier to show than explain. Suppose one writer writes an article that appears in a journal, naturally without quotation marks:

14.25 Compensatory Education

Another writer, wishing to cite that article in her own title, shifts the rank of the original title in her own title, putting the original title in quotation marks:

14.25A   A Critique of "Compensatory Education"

The next writer, in his response to this article, shifts rank again, placing double quotes around the title of 14.22A and then moving the double quotes to single quotes:

14.25B   The Mistakes in "A Critique of 'Compensatory Education' "

The student, entering at the end of this sequence, must put the title of 14.25B in quotation marks, thereby again shifting the whole series— note that the single quotes alternate with the double quotes:

14.25C   "The Mistakes in 'A Critique of "Compensatory Education" ' "

Bibliography Form

We begin with the form for bibliography entries, even though the final bibliography can be prepared only from the final footnotes, because we suggest above that you master this form first, so that your working bibliography can be written out in the form you'll use when you complete the final version.

Bibliography and footnote references make a distinction between *books* and *journals.* Books are issued once, though they may be revised and reissued some years later in a "second edition" or "revised edition." *Journals* range from what we think of as magazines to the more formidable "scholarly journals," some of which appear only four times a year. Our footnote form for journals will also work for newspapers and weekly newsmagazines.

We find it useful to present bibliography and footnote form by means of a *flow chart,* of the kind used by computer programmers. A flow chart for making book entries in a bibliography is given in Figure 14.10. A flow chart may look quite intimidating at first, but, as you work through it, you should find it elegantly simple. You work through this flow chart by beginning at the oval START and moving through the chart to the oval STOP. The diamonds present *decision points,* which must be answered *yes* or *no,* leading you to rectangles with information to be entered. The "double boxes" give you information on punctuation and on the form of the entry. The "double-boxed" *ic,* for example, means "type in initial capital letters for the first word of the title and for all other words except for function words like *the, of,* and *with";* the double-boxed *it* by BOOK TITLE and SUBTITLE means "underline to indicate italics." The flow chart of Figure 14.10 gives us the biblio-

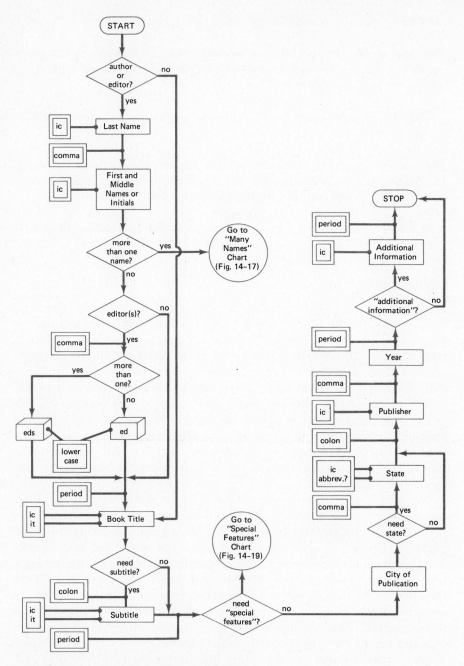

FIGURE 14.10 Bibliography Form for Books

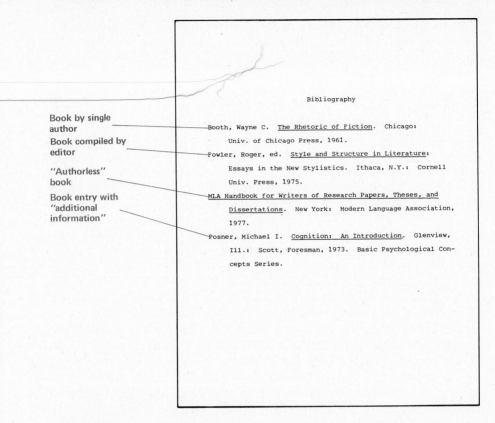

Book by single author

Book compiled by editor

"Authorless" book

Book entry with "additional information"

Note general form: Bibliography is titled, initial caps, and the page has margins of at least 1″ on all sides. Second and subsequent lines are indented 5 spaces.

FIGURE 14.11 Sample Bibliography Entries—Books

graphical entries of Figure 14.11, typed as they would be in a final bibliography.

As the first bibliography entry shows, a book entry normally cites: 1. the author or editor, with first and last names reversed; 2. the book title; and 3. which is treated as one unit, the place of publication, publisher, and date of publication. We would derive that bibliography entry from the flow by answering "yes" to the first decision point, "Author or editor?" (Decision point questions should be answered "yes" or "no". This question is to be read, "Is there an author or editor, or not?" Do not read "Is there an author or is there an editor?") Our "yes" answer leads us to enter the author's name: first the last name, followed by a comma (as marked in the double box), then the first name and middle initial. At the next decision point, "More than one name?" we would answer "no." A "yes" answer sends us to a separate flow chart which handles all multiple authors and editors.

The next decision point is "Editor(s)?" Some books are not *written by an author* but *compiled by an editor*—these are called anthologies, and you may be familiar, for example, with such anthologies in literature courses.[2] The first entry has an author, so our "no" answer takes us down to the period signaled by the double box, and then to the title of the book, which, the double boxes remind us, is to be typed in initial caps and to be underlined to signal italic type. The first entry answers "no" to the "Need subtitle?" decision point. The subtitle of a book should be included if it is useful to the reader. The subtitle of this text, *A New College Rhetoric,* would probably be included, since it helps describe what the book is about.

The next decision point, "Need 'special features'?" leads to another circled flow chart, dealing with translators, second and later editions, and multivolumed works. This flow chart will be discussed later.

Our "no" answer takes us to the publication data. After entering the city of publication, we are asked, "Need state?" Answer this question on a common sense basis. In Figure 14.11, we have answered "no" for New York and Chicago, but "yes" for Glenview, Ill., and Ithaca, N.Y. (Note that a double box allows you to abbreviate the state, and that another double box inserts the colon to introduce the name of the publisher.)

The publisher's name should be filled with an appropriately shortened form of the publisher's name on the title page. In our examples, we abbreviate "University," and we shorten "Scott, Foresman, and Company" to "Scott, Foresman." The following are appropriately shortened versions:

14.26 Lawrence Erlbaum and Associates, distributed by the Wiley Press ⟹ Lawrence Erlbaum

14.27 Pantheon Books, a Division of Random House, Inc. ⟹ Pantheon Books

The year rectangle asks for year of publication, as shown on the title page. If no date is given, the last date given on the copyright page following the title page may be used.

The last decision point, "All done?" allows us to enter any additional information that may be of interest to the reader. The last entry of Figure 14.11 includes information on the series of which the book is a part.

The second entry of Figure 14.11 answers "yes" to the "Editor(s)?" decision point. The flow chart then tells us to insert a comma and takes us to our first *perspective box*. A perspective box instructs us, "Enter the letters in this box," so we enter the letters *ed* (an abbreviation for *editor*). This entry answers "yes" to decision points, "Need subtitle?" and "Need state?"

The next entry, the *MLA Handbook,* is an "authorless book," that is, a book issued by a corporation or organization, with no author listed on the title page. In this case, we answer "no" to the first decision point, "Author?" and the flow chart takes us directly to the title.

The flow chart of Figure 14.10 predicts the entries of Figure 14.11, and it should do the same for any bibliographical entries you need to make. The basic principles for making each decision are 1. common sense and 2. the question, "Which answer would be best for my reader?"

Bibliography entries for journals follow the same three-section form that book entries do, marking each section with a period: 1. the author's name; 2. the title of the article, in quotation marks; and 3. the name of the journal, underlined to indicate italic type, with relevant publishing information. Figure 14.12 gives a flow chart for bibliographical entries for journal articles, and Figure 14.13 analyzes several citations from journals. You might want to spend a minute examining how the flow chart predicts the typewritten entries before continuing.

The only serious decision points, now that you are an experienced flow chart reader, are those labeled "Scholarly journal?" following the *title of journal* box and, following the "yes" arrow of that decision point to the next decision point, "Paged consecutively?"

Most magazines that you buy at a typical newsstand are "paged individually"—that is, the February issue begins on page 1 and the March issue again begins on page 1. Many of us find it difficult to conceive of putting a journal together in any other way. But some scholarly journals see themselves in a different way: They see themselves not as individual issues, kicking around someone's house, but as bound volumes on the library shelves, as volume 41 (1978). Thus they are "paged consecutively": The first issue might run from pages 1 to 120, and the second issue will begin with page 121. These journals provide a convenience for the scholars who read them: The scholar picks up the bound volume, opens to the page number, and begins reading. If the same scholar goes to, say, *Sports Illustrated,* issued weekly and paged individually, he must find the year, search for the month, locate the issue, hunt down the page, and then he can begin reading.

Thus we can find a first answer to "Scholarly journal?" Journals that are paged consecutively are "scholarly journals." You can discover this by inspecting the bound journal, seeing if a new issue begins with page

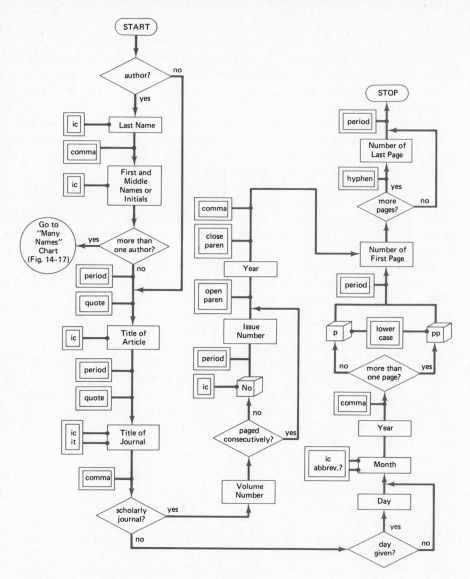

FIGURE 14.12 Bibliography Form for Journals

1, or by examining loose copies of unbound issues, asking the same question. You can even make a good guess from the information in an index: If the index cites an article in the March issue beginning on page 447, you can probably conclude that the journal is "paged consecutively," and thus is a scholarly journal.

A second answer is to mark off the "no" dimension. What is not a "scholarly journal"? Anything that you're likely to find at a typical magazine stand. The one exception, at this writing, is *Consumer Reports*, which is widely available on newsstands, but which, as a convenience to its readers—consumers, not scholars—is paged consecutively. But note that either way of referencing *Consumer Reports*—a "yes" answer or a "no" answer to "Scholarly journal?"—will accomplish your main purpose, giving the reader a chance to check your source.

Now let's explore the gray area of journals which are not paged consecutively but which might be described as scholarly journals. We might define by pointing to one: *Freshman English News. Freshman English News* is a small pamphlet of about 24 pages, published four times a year, read by instructors interested in (you guessed it) news about Freshman English. It's not available at airport newsstands, but, on the other hand, it's not paged consecutively—so a reference to year and page number

FIGURE 14.13 Sample Bibliography Entries—Journals

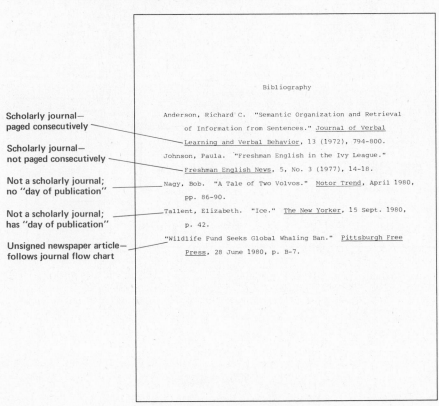

would give a reader four possible places to go—the pages of each of the four issues. Common sense tells us it's a "scholarly journal" that is not "paged consecutively," giving us the reference form of the second entry of Figure 14.13, specifying the number of the issue.

Journals that are not scholarly journals are referenced in a different way, with page numbers introduced by the abbreviations *p.* or *pp.*, and with a decision point separating magazines that "need date," like the weekly *The New Yorker*, from those that are issued monthly, like *Motor Trend*.

Note also, from the last entry on Figure 14.13, that the flow chart of 14.12 works with newspapers as well as with magazines, with obvious adjustments for page references.

FIGURE 14.14   Footnote Form—Books

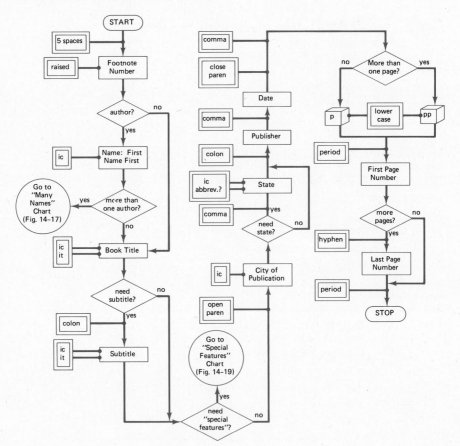

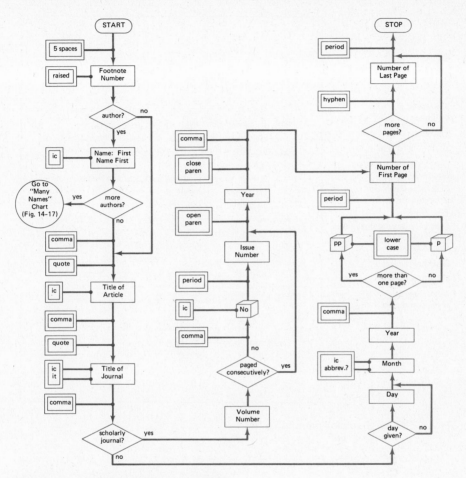

FIGURE 14.15 Footnote Form—Journals

Footnote Form—First Entries

Figures 14.14 and 14.15 give flow charts for footnotes to books and to journals, and Figure 14.16 lists representative examples as they would be typed on the footnote page of an investigative paper. Footnotes treat each book and journal as a single item, and thus they replace the periods of bibliographical entries with commas. And, since the entries are not alphabetized, all names are printed first name first.

These flow charts work in precisely the same way as the flow charts for bibliographical entries, so, with the help of the examples, they should be self-explanatory.

Title (centered)

Normal book reference

"Authorless book" reference

Book reference (includes subtitle)

Scholarly journal reference (no p. or pp. needed)

Scholarly journal not paged consecutively (includes issue no.)

Monthly magazine

Weekly magazine

Newspaper (note section and page)

Footnotes

[1] Wayne C. Booth, *The Rhetoric of Fiction* (Chicago: Univ. of Chicago Pr., 1961), pp. 63-65.

[2] *MLA Handbook for Writers of Research Papers, Theses, and Dissertations* (New York: Modern Language Association, 1977), p. 161.

[3] Michael I. Posner, *Cognition: An Introduction* (Glenview, Ill.: Scott, Foresman, 1973), pp. 87-88.

[4] Richard C. Anderson, "Semantic Organization and Retrieval of Information from Sentence" *Journal of Verbal Learning and Verbal Behavior*, 13 (1972), 799.

[5] Paula Johnson, "Freshman English in the Ivy League," *Freshman English News*, 5, no. 3 (1977), 14-18.

[6] Bob Nagy, "A Tale of Two Volvos," *Motor Trend*, April 1980, p. 90.

[7] Elizabeth Tallent, "Ice," *The New Yorker*, 15 Sept. 1980, p. 42.

[8] "Wildlife Fund Seeks Global Whaling Ban," *Pittsburgh Free Press*, 28 June 1980, p. B-7.

FIGURE 14.16 Sample Footnote Entries

Special Problems

Two special problems have been taken out of our flow charts for bibliography and footnote form and placed in separate flow charts—computer programmers call these subroutines. The first is identified as the "many names" flow chart; it explains what to do when a book or journal article has more than one name listed as author or editor. The flow chart for handling more than one author or editor is given in Figure 14.17, and in Figure 14.18 we give examples of footnote and bibliography entries written from the flow chart.

We have branched from the other flow charts at the point where the first author's or editor's name has been entered, but before the final punctuation. The first column takes us through the citing of two authors with a decision point, "Footnote?" that allows us to separate bibliography and footnote form, as shown in the first group of Figure 14.18.

If there are more than two authors, we answer "no" to "Two names?" which takes us to the next decision point, "Too many names?" The answer to this question is a matter of common sense—and the needs of one's audience. The author of a technical article in a psychology journal might wish to cite the four or five authors of another article, feeling that readers might need to have that information; an undergraduate student might legitimately prefer not to list them. A "yes" answer to "Too many names?" is always appropriate. The "yes" answer leads us to enter *et al.,* an abbreviation for the Latin *et alii,* meaning "and all the rest." This form is shown in the second group of Figure 14.18. ("Many names," of course, works with editors and translators as well as with authors.)

A "no" answer to "Too many names?" takes us to a column that loops us through the listing of the names until we are able to answer "yes" to

FIGURE 14.17 The "Many Names" Flow Chart

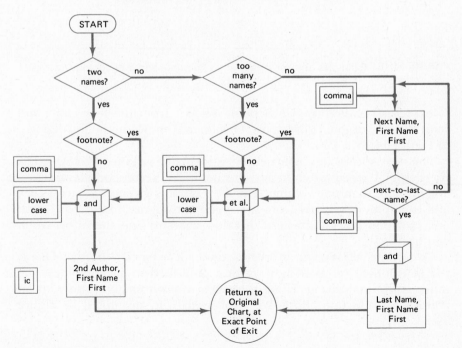

PRECONDITION: THE NAME OF THE FIRST AUTHOR OR EDITOR HAS BEEN WRITTEN, BUT WITHOUT ENDING PUNCTUATION. IF SO, START.

Two names

Book cited in
footnote

Scholarly article cited
in bibliography

Many names—et al. not chosen

Scholarly article cited
in footnote

Scholarly article cited
in bibliography

Many names—et al. chosen

Scholarly article cited
in footnote

Scholarly article cited
in bibliography

[9]Herbert H. Clark and Eve V. Clark, Psychology and
Language (New York: Harcourt Brace Jovanovich, 1977), p. 362.

Ervin-Tripp, Susan, and Dan Slobin. "Psycholinguistics."
    Annual Review of Psychology, 17 (1966), 435-474.

[10]Frederick Ball, Christine Wood, and Edward E. Smith,
"Semantic Targets Are Detected Faster than Visual or Acoustic
Ones," Psychology and Perception, 17 (1975), 8.

Garbett, Ann, Ronald Carpenter, Coy Garbett, Winifred
    Keaney, Thomas Klammer, Jessie Lawson, and John
    Odmark. "Annual Bibliography for 1975." Style,
    12 (1978), 211-239.

[11]Frederick Ball et al., "Semantic Targets Are
Detected Faster than Visual or Acoustic Ones," Psychology
and Perception, 17 (1975), 8.

Garbett, Ann, et al., "Annual Bibliography for 1975."
    Style, 12 (1978), 211-239.

FIGURE 14.18 Examples of "Many Names" in Footnote and Bibliography Entries

"Next-to-last name?" at which point we exit from the flow chart and return to our original flow chart. This form is shown in the third group in Figure 14.18.

The next special flow chart enters information about books with 1. a translator, 2. an editor of an author's book, 3. a second or later edition, and 4. more than one volume. This flow chart is given in Figure 14.19, and examples developed from it are given in Figure 14.20. You'll find you can loop quickly through this flow chart to find the information you need.

Two other referencing problems have not been flowcharted. One is the question of referencing an article published in an anthology; the other is the question of citing a book by an author, but also with an editor's introduction. Both are explained, with examples, in Figure 14.21.

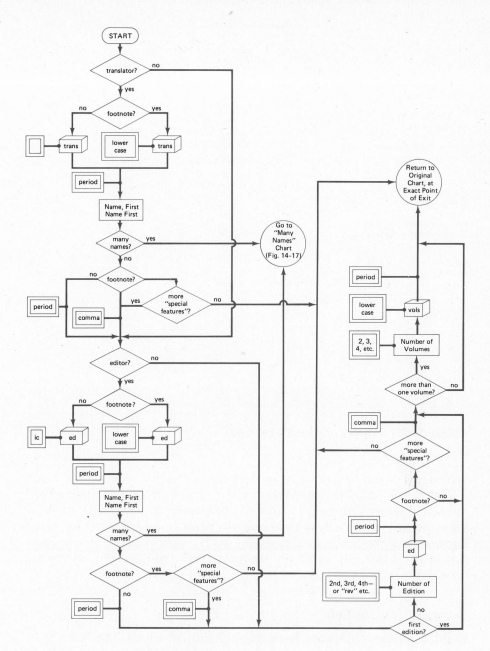

FIGURE 14.19   The "Special Features" Flow Chart for Books

Book with translator—
footnote entry

Book with editor—
footnote entry

Book in revised edition—
footnote entry

Book in more than
one volume—bibliography
entry

Book with translator and
editor—bibliography entry

Hypothetical book in many
volumes and revised edition,
with translator and editor

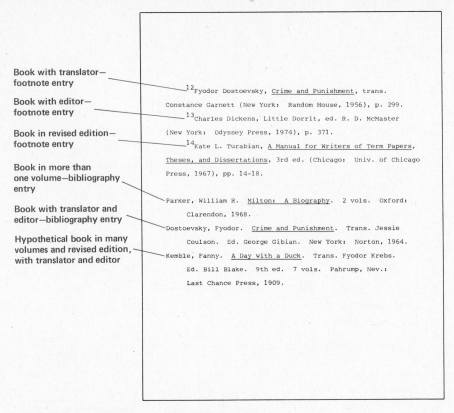

12 Fyodor Dostoevsky, _Crime and Punishment_, trans.
Constance Garnett (New York: Random House, 1956), p. 299.

13 Charles Dickens, Little Dorrit, ed. R. D. McMaster
(New York: Odyssey Press, 1974), p. 371.

14 Kate L. Turabian, _A Manual for Writers of Term Papers,
Theses, and Dissertations_, 3rd ed. (Chicago: Univ. of Chicago
Press, 1967), pp. 14-18.

Parker, William R. _Milton: A Biography_. 2 vols. Oxford:
    Clarendon, 1968.

Dostoevsky, Fyodor. _Crime and Punishment_. Trans. Jessie
    Coulson. Ed. George Gibian. New York: Norton, 1964.

Kemble, Fanny. _A Day with a Duck_. Trans. Fyodor Krebs.
    Ed. Bill Blake. 9th ed. 7 vols. Pahrump, Nev.:
    Last Chance Press, 1909.

FIGURE 14.20 Examples of "Special Features"

There are many other dimensions to footnote and bibliography form—citing government documents, dissertations, films, and so on. Your instructor may ask you to check the *MLA Handbook* (cited in "For Further Reading") for directions for such entries; other instructors may suggest that you construct your own reference, using your common sense.

Second Footnote References

Both co-authors of this text have children in high school, who learn the investigative paper by using out-dated guides for referencing, guides that have little to do with the practice of actual researchers today. In particular, they struggle with an elaborate set of Latin abbreviations—*ibid., op. cit., anon.*—that most scholarly journals no longer recommend.

Once you have given a full footnote reference to a source, you may cite that source in precisely the short form that you've used in your own referencing—most simply, the author's name and the page number. A number of possible shortened forms are given in Figure 14.22.

We should note, in conclusion, that footnotes can do much more than merely cite a source. Footnotes can define, clarify, quibble, cite several references to prove a point, even annoy.[3] We've stressed the form of citation in this chapter; our own footnotes may suggest some of the other uses of footnotes in academic discourse.

Final Typing: Manuscript Form

Writers who have had a series of typing courses are usually drilled in the proper form for a typed manuscript—the need for margins, the proper form of a typed dash, the indentations for paragraphs, and so

FIGURE 14.21   References to Articles in Anthologies and to Editors as Main Source

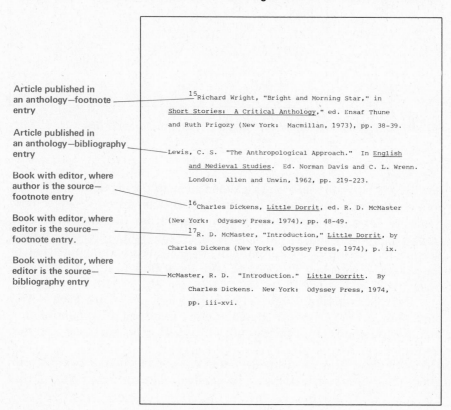

Article published in
an anthology—footnote
entry

Article published in
an anthology—bibliography
entry

Book with editor, where
author is the source—
footnote entry

Book with editor, where
editor is the source—
footnote entry.

Book with editor, where
editor is the source—
bibliography entry

[15] Richard Wright, "Bright and Morning Star," in
Short Stories: A Critical Anthology," ed. Ensaf Thune
and Ruth Prigozy (New York: Macmillan, 1973), pp. 38-39.

Lewis, C. S. "The Anthropological Approach." In English
and Medieval Studies. Ed. Norman Davis and C. L. Wrenn.
London: Allen and Unwin, 1962, pp. 219-223.

[16] Charles Dickens, Little Dorrit, ed. R. D. McMaster
(New York: Odyssey Press, 1974), pp. 48-49.
[17] R. D. McMaster, "Introduction," Little Dorrit, by
Charles Dickens (New York: Odyssey Press, 1974), p. ix.

McMaster, R. D. "Introduction." Little Dorritt. By
Charles Dickens. New York: Odyssey Press, 1974,
pp. iii-xvi.

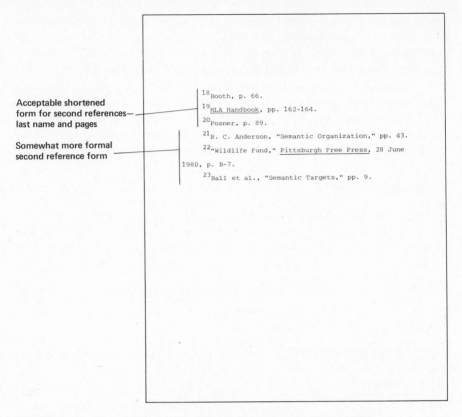

Acceptable shortened
form for second references—
last name and pages

Somewhat more formal
second reference form

```
      18
        Booth, p. 66.
      19
        MLA Handbook, pp. 162-164.
      20
        Posner, p. 89.
      21
        R. C. Anderson, "Semantic Organization," pp. 43.
      22
        "Wildlife Fund," Pittsburgh Free Press, 28 June
1980, p. B-7.
      23
        Ball et al., "Semantic Targets," pp. 9.
```

FIGURE 14.22   Footnote Forms for Citing a Work for the Second Time

on. But such matters are often glossed over in an introductory typing course, and not all students have taken even an introductory course. Thus we print, as Figure 14.23, two pages from the final copy of a research paper, noting in one column the "print code" of a typed manuscript and in the other column the writer's decisions about what to footnote and what not to footnote and about how to introduce quotations.

It's worth examining Figure 14.23 for a few moments, even if you have your papers typed by someone else. The form of a handwritten manuscript should approximate that of typed copy as closely as possible.

Your instructor may well place other restrictions on manuscript form, generally matters of legibility, convenience, and courtesy. We ask that students use a paper clip to gather their pages, for example, rather than stapling them or using unwieldy binders. We ask that students not use "easy-erase" typewriter paper (the ink rubs onto our hands), and that they not submit pages torn from spiral binders (the scraps litter our floor).

SUMMARY

This chapter has discussed two special writing tasks: the essay examination and the investigative paper. In both discussions, we stressed responding to the needs of the reader and the conventions of the writing task. Thus we stressed the notion of responding to the question and forming an answer that displays one's ability in speaking of the essay examination, and we focused on the skills of summary, paraphrase, and skillful quotation in discussing the investigative paper. We presented one of many forms of documenting ideas, and we printed sample pages from an investigative paper.

FINAL WRITING ASSIGNMENTS

I. A Recommendation   Study carefully the product tests in the journal *Consumer's Reports,* noting how the articles decide on criteria for judging products and how they present their findings to their readers. Then think of a product of interest to college students—ball point pens, popcorn, introductory psychology textbooks, student housing—and construct a product evaluation for publication in *Consumer's Reports.* You'll want to think carefully about criteria for judging the product, particularly about the degree to which you can rely on questionnaires as well

---

ms: Manuscript Form   Rewrite or edit your paper to the appropriate form for college manuscripts, illustrated in Figure 14.23 and discussed above.

Most commonly, students neglect to leave adequate margins, making the paper difficult to read and denying the instructor the chance to comment. The marginal comment may also be used to indicate a departure from standard form for footnots and bibliography entries or for punctuation marks.

Most instructors (and most publishing companies) will accept neatly made corrections (in ink) of typed copy.

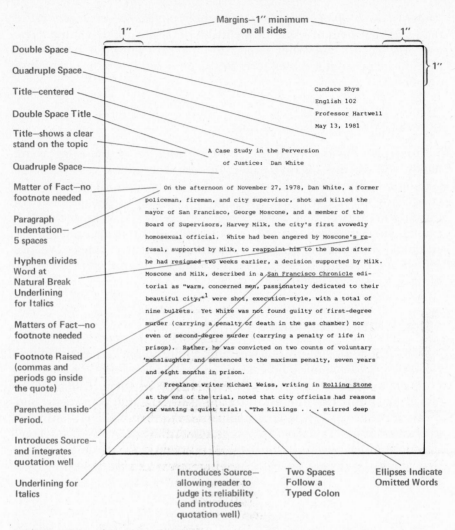

Margins—1″ minimum on all sides

1″

1″

1″

Double Space

Quadruple Space

Title—centered

Double Space Title

Title—shows a clear stand on the topic

Quadruple Space

Matter of Fact—no footnote needed

Paragraph Indentation— 5 spaces

Hyphen divides Word at Natural Break Underlining for Italics

Matters of Fact—no footnote needed

Footnote Raised (commas and periods go inside the quote)

Parentheses Inside Period.

Introduces Source— and integrates quotation well

Underlining for Italics

Introduces Source— allowing reader to judge its reliability (and introduces quotation well)

Two Spaces Follow a Typed Colon

Ellipses Indicate Omitted Words

Candace Rhys
English 102
Professor Hartwell
May 13, 1981

A Case Study in the Perversion
of Justice: Dan White

On the afternoon of November 27, 1978, Dan White, a former policeman, fireman, and city supervisor, shot and killed the mayor of San Francisco, George Moscone, and a member of the Board of Supervisors, Harvey Milk, the city's first avowedly homosexual official. White had been angered by Moscone's refusal, supported by Milk, to reappoint him to the Board after he had resigned two weeks earlier, a decision supported by Milk. Moscone and Milk, described in a San Francisco Chronicle editorial as "warm, concerned men, passionately dedicated to their beautiful city,"[1] were shot, execution-style, with a total of nine bullets. Yet White was not found guilty of first-degree murder (carrying a penalty of death in the gas chamber) nor even of second-degree murder (carrying a penalty of life in prison). Rather, he was convicted on two counts of voluntary manslaughter and sentenced to the maximum penalty, seven years and eight months in prison.

Freelance writer Michael Weiss, writing in Rolling Stone at the end of the trial, noted that city officials had reasons for wanting a quiet trial: "The killings . . . stirred deep

FIGURE 14.23 Manuscript Form

as laboratory tests, and you'll also need to think about the "stance" adopted by the team-written *Consumer's Reports* articles. Include the graphs and visual aids typical of such articles. For some topics, you may want to include "boxed inserts" to discuss products that offer special features or don't fit into the general category being discussed—for example, an evaluation of ball point pens might treat "erasable pens" in a boxed insert.

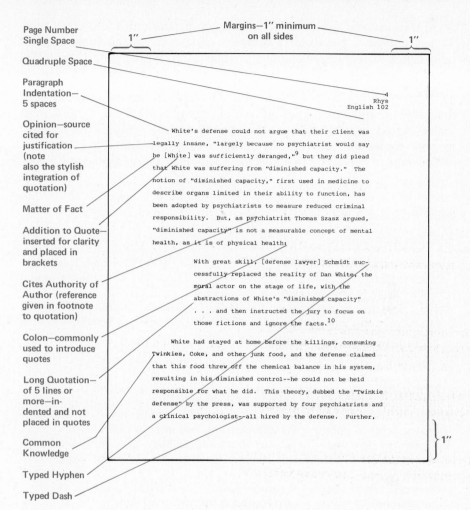

Page Number
Single Space

Quadruple Space

Paragraph
Indentation—
5 spaces

Opinion—source
cited for
justification
(note
also the stylish
integration of
quotation)

Matter of Fact

Addition to Quote—
inserted for clarity
and placed in
brackets

Cites Authority of
Author (reference
given in footnote
to quotation)

Colon—commonly
used to introduce
quotes

Long Quotation—
of 5 lines or
more—in-
dented and not
placed in quotes

Common
Knowledge

Typed Hyphen

Typed Dash

Margins—1″ minimum
on all sides

1″   1″

Rhys
English 102

White's defense could not argue that their client was legally insane, "largely because no psychiatrist would say he [White] was sufficiently deranged,"[9] but they did plead that White was suffering from "diminished capacity." The notion of "diminished capacity," first used in medicine to describe organs limited in their ability to function, has been adopted by psychiatrists to measure reduced criminal responsibility. But, as psychiatrist Thomas Szasz argued, "diminished capacity" is not a measurable concept of mental health, as it is of physical health:

With great skill, [defense lawyer] Schmidt successfully replaced the reality of Dan White, the moral actor on the stage of life, with the abstractions of White's "diminished capacity" . . . and then instructed the jury to focus on those fictions and ignore the facts.[10]

White had stayed at home before the killings, consuming Twinkies, Coke, and other junk food, and the defense claimed that this food threw off the chemical balance in his system, resulting in his diminished control--he could not be held responsible for what he did. This theory, dubbed the "Twinkie defense" by the press, was supported by four psychiatrists and a clinical psychologist--all hired by the defense. Further,

1″

II. The Making of . . . Investigate "the making of" a book, movie, or stage play, using biographies and autobiographies, contemporary newspaper and magazine reports, and other books and articles. This assignment works well with "the making of a movie," particularly with a well-known or controversial movie, and it offers special challenges to your investigative abilities.

III. A Trial Report on a trial, of any kind, focusing on the arguments used and the logical issues involved. You may wish to choose a current, local trial, or you may wish to investigate a national, well-known trial. If you choose a particularly complex case, such as the trial of Julius and Ethel Rosenberg, executed as spies after World War II, you will need to narrow your focus to a specific aspect of the trial.

IV. The Controversy over . . .   Find an area of controversy in your major field, and investigate the arguments presented for various positions. Avoid topics that seem too broad or too complex for a short paper—topics like abortion or religion or the Equal Rights Amendment—and try to come to a specific position of your own on the issue.

FOR FURTHER READING

I. Reference Guides

MLA Handbook for Writers of Research Papers, Theses, and Dissertations. New York: Modern Language Association, 1977. Gives more details on the footnote and bibliography system described in this chapter.

Publication Manual of the American Psychological Association. 2nd ed. Washington, D.C.: American Psychological Association, 1974. Offers a reference system widely used in the social and natural sciences.

II. Indexes

Applied Science and Technology Index. Lists articles on space science, chemistry, physics, mathematics, engineering, and related fields.

Art Index. Lists articles from journals and museum bulletins on art and such related fields as photography, film-making, and interior decoration.

Biological and Agricultural Index. List articles on biology, agriculture, and such related fields as bacteriology, botany, ecology, forestry, and animal husbandry.

Book Review Index. Lists book reviews—and thus a useful source for checking the opinions of professionals about a book you may want to use as an authority.

Business Periodicals Index. Lists articles in such fields as accounting, advertising, banking, economics, and taxation.

Education Index. Lists articles in all areas of education.

Essay and General Literature Index. Lists essays that appear in chapters or sections of books. Valuable in the humanities and such social sciences as history and psychology.

Social Sciences Index. Lists articles in the social sciences—anthropology, criminology, economics, geography, religion, and so on. Particularly valuable.

III. Abstracts

Abstracts of English Studies. Summarizes articles on English and American Literature.

Historical Abstracts. Summarizes articles on political, economic, social, cultural, and intellectual history.

New York Times Index. Summarizes articles and news reports in the *New York Times* (thus an excellent source of background information on any historical topic).

Psychological Abstracts. Summarizes articles in psychology and related disciplines.

Sociological Abstracts. Summarizes articles in sociology and related disciplines.

IV. Other Investigative Tools

Book Review Digest. Summarizes book reviews, noting the length of each review.

NOTES

1. The student may consider a "catchall" note to reference the source of facts: "Details of the life of Charles Dickens have been taken from K. J. Fielding, *Charles Dickens: A Critical Introduction* (Boston: Riverside Press, 1958)."
2. Of course, some books have both an author and an editor—this matter is discussed in Figure 14.21.
3. Like this.

UNIT VI

INVENTION

Analysis:
Thinking with Concepts

METHOD, therefore, becomes natural to the mind which has been accustomed to contemplate not things only, or for their own sake only, but likewise and chiefly the *relations* of things, either their relations to each other, or to the observer, or to the state and apprehension of the hearers. To enumerate and analyze the relations, with the conditions under which they are discoverable, is to teach the science of Method.

SAMUEL TAYLOR COLERIDGE

This four-chapter unit explores the process of *invention* (from Latin *inventio,* literally "a finding"). Invention can be defined as discovering the arguments available for a given issue; put more simply, invention is finding something to say. In this chapter, we'll look more deeply at the process of communicating in print, to develop the notion of *print explicitness,* and we'll develop a special vocabulary to help with the most common college writing assignment, asking the student to respond to the writing of others, a task that our chapter title identifies as "Analysis: Thinking with Concepts."

We will start, however, by noting how much we've already been concerned, in this text, with the nature of invention, and how much your own natural abilities are, in themselves, inventive.

YOU ARE AN "INVENTION MACHINE"

In our view, writing is not a matter of packaging a preconceived idea, but an active process of discovery, of "finding," and thus of invention, at all levels of the writing process. As a result, we've already pointed out a number of techniques for finding ideas:

■ *free writing generates ideas.* The writer can often "write into" a topic by free writing, forcing the hand to move across the page as quickly as possible. One way to find something to write is to write something.

■ *brainstorming generates ideas.* The writer can brainstorm, using the informal process often used by businesses, discussed in chapter One, thereby generating the elusive "something to say."

■ *the rhetorical triangle generates ideas.* The rhetorical triangle, discussed in chapter Two, is a potent device for invention: The writer who knows her reader and her position as writer has solved the most difficult problems of communication. Indeed, for nineteenth-century philosopher Coleridge, cited in our chapter headnote, the analysis of ideas is precisely the interplay of message, writer, and audience:

15.1 . . . but likewise and chiefly the *relations* of things, either their relations to each other, or to the observer, or to the state and apprehension of the hearers.

■ *the commitment-response model generates ideas.* Getting an idea, however silly—"green olives are dangerous to your health"—means getting a commitment, making a promise to the reader that must be supported. The commitment-response model thus generates writing, asking you to fulfill commitments made to readers.

■ *style is an act of discovery.* "Styling" a message is a way of re-seeing, a testing of the possibilities of words, and hence a kind of discovery. Even sentence imitation, we've learned, can be creative.

We can therefore offer a first conclusion. Thinking up ideas is such a natural part of being human that it occurs all the time. It's impossible not to think, and though we'll offer some devices and suggestions to help structure and direct your thinking out through writing, they are simply natural extensions of abilities you now have in abundance. The language animal is an invention machine.

ON READING THIS UNIT

Nevertheless, writing about thinking, as we're doing in this unit, makes for difficult reading. The play of ideas in writing can't be treated like instructions for assembling a bicycle ("put the chain around the sprocket"), and you shouldn't expect the chapters in this unit to offer you step-by-step directions for coming up with ideas for writing. Rather, you want the chapters in this unit to give you:

■ a sense of the suggestions that work best for you, and thus
■ a sense of where you want to return to in this unit for help with future writing assignments.

These learning goals—finding suggestions that work for you and setting up this unit as a reference—are different from the learning goals of most textbooks, and you'll want to adapt your reading strategies to help you achieve those goals. Here are some suggestions:

■ *Watch us.* The business of invention—reading critically, generating ideas, becoming comfortable at analysis, argument, and discovery— is much easier to demonstrate than explain. So much of our discussion in this unit is essentially demonstration. You might think of us as tennis instructors, batting a few balls across the net.
■ *Participate.* It's particularly important that you work with the discovery problems in this unit. After all, you want to find out what works for you, and you can't learn that unless you try.
■ *Question.* You want this unit to serve as a reference for future writing assignments, so read with a pencil in hand, marking, questioning, underlining. Contrary to the usual instructions, please bend, fold, staple, and mutilate this text.
■ *Relax.* This unit discusses a set of strategies for writing, and you'll master those strategies by working with them, not by reading about them. So relax—this unit isn't conventional textbook reading.

PRINT EXPLICITNESS

At points in this text, we've stressed the close relationship of writing and speaking—when we asked you to hear the "sound" of a sentence composed on the page with an "inner ear," and when we discussed the "voice" that writers transmit through the printed page. At other points, we've stressed the differences between writing and speaking—when we discussed the "print codes" of punctuation and spelling, or when we discussed the nature of examination questions as "display questions" in chapter Thirteen. We return to the question again, to develop a notion that we think of as *print explicitness:* Writing must say exactly what it means.

Consider, for example, a sentence that would work fine in any ordinary speaking situation, but which is almost meaningless in print:

15.2 "Meet me here tomorrow with a stick about so big."

Separated from ordinary speech, the words lose their meaning. Writing is separated from time—you as reader share no "here" or "tomorrow"

a. To reach Leisure Village West from New York or northern New Jersey, take Garden State Parkway south to Exit 88, turn right on Route 70 for six months and you'll see the community on your left.—*Newark (N.J.) Star-Ledger*

> A welcome sight it'll be, too!

b. THANK YOU . . .

I am extremely grateful for the expression of trust and confidence shown me on Feb. 22.

I deeply appreciate your vote and will do everything in my power to betray that trust. I will be a commissioner for all the people.

Sincerely,
Ralph Burgess
—*Adv. in the Panama City (Fla.) News-Herald*

> We like your style, Ralph.

c. DEAR LOAN CUSTOMER:

Because of the critical paper shortage and in the spirit of conservation, we have replaced our return envelopes with a set of self-addressed labels. Please affix these labels to your envelopes when mailing your payments to us.—*Letter from Main Line Federal Savings & Loan Association, Ardmore, Pa.*

> That solves *that* paper shortage!

d. A Western sophomore, Stevens possesses an uncommonly creative and passionate feeling for the arts. "I love acting and I love writing," she said, and indeed she obviously does. In a few short years she has written eight complete original plays and twelve short stories, two of which consist entirely of prose.—*Kalamazoo Western Herald*

> We'd have to see them.

e. Although Nicholas Jacques Conté gave his name to this delightful crayon, in fact, he was the inventor of the lead pencil. For the record, lead pencils did not become widely used until Conté invented them in 1799.—*"Drawing for Fun," by Alfred Daniels*

> People were naturally hesitant.

f. SEX DISCRIMINATION

Interior/Secy amends rules concerning sex discrimination by deleting the word "sex" whenever it appears therein; effective 3-3-78.—*Federal Register*

> It'll rear its ugly head anyway.

g. One should strive to keep tea conversation as light and frothy as the fare. And it is terribly important to remember to pour milk

into the cup before adding tea. (Or is it the other way around?)
—*St. Louis Post Dispatch*

> Never mind. The point is it's important.

h. IF YOU WANT FLOWERS ON SUNDAY: The Harbor
Greenery at 117 Atlantic Ave. 523-6131, will take care of you. They
take all major credit cards, telephone orders, and they're open 6
days a week. Closed on Sunday.—*Leisure Guide*

> Well, all work and no play, you know. ■

ARGUMENT: STATING THE CASE
AND FINDING GOOD REASONS

In problem two, below, we present a number of writing assignments
used as placement assignments for freshmen writers. Your instructor
may assign one or more of these topics as a writing assignment; if not,
we'd suggest that you select one or two questions and make a scratch
outline of how you might go about answering it.

Problem Two. The freshman essay examination   Choose one of the following questions, and write a coherent essay in response to it.

a. SAT verbal test scores of high school seniors dropped 32 points
from 1966 to 1975, and there is public outcry over the literacy
crisis in American high schools. One suggestion is that students
should be required to demonstrate certain reading and writing skills
before being allowed to receive a high school diploma. Those who
failed the test would receive instead "certificates of attendance." Do
you agree? Why, or why not?

b. Some people feel that advertisements today are obviously dishonest, while others defend them as examples of effective persuasion. How do you feel about modern advertising?

c. "In order for a society to be healthy it is essential that it employ
capital punishment in certain instances." Agree or disagree, giving
reasons for your opinion. ■

These essay exams all ask for your opinion, but they are also "display"
questions in the sense discussed in chapter Thirteen; they ask you to
"display" your ability to conduct an argument. Questions *a* and *c* explicitly ask the writer to explain a position, and we would recognize
that a bare answer to question *b* would not receive a passing grade:

15.8 I think advertising is obviously dishonest.

Example 15.8 may well reflect the writer's opinion. But it's not fully explicit; the reasons for the opinion are not developed.

Stating the Case

A useful first step in constructing an effective argument is "stating the case." Stating the case is a clear part of legal arguments. The prosecution states the law and argues that the actions of the accused match, "beyond a reasonable doubt," the provisions of the law. The defense, however, has many different ways of stating the case. The defense might deny that the accused performed the actions (by providing an alibi, for example); the defense might admit that the accused committed the actions, but offer a different interpretation ("He didn't mean to shoot him; his finger slipped, and the gun went off by accident"), a different motivation ("He thought the deceased was pulling a gun; he fired in self-defense"), or mitigating circumstances ("We will present expert psychiatric testimony to show that the accused was temporarily insane at the time of the murder").

Each statement of the case makes a different kind of evidence necessary. Witnesses to the crime become important if the facts of the case are to be argued; character witnesses become important for other arguments; and expert testimony is central for other arguments (psychiatric testimony, for example).

The essay questions above would seem to supply their own statement of the case. But a little thought will generate other possible statements, possibly leading to other arguments. Is it possible, in terms of question *a*, to devise a reliable test for literacy? Do the declining SAT scores *prove* a decline in literacy? Could one accept the desirability of such tests but argue for a different group to administer them to—perhaps at the ninth grade, so that students weak in skills could receive help? Similarly, question *b* seems to state the case as, "either all advertising is 'obviously dishonest' or all advertising is 'effective persuasion.' " One might restate the case in different ways. For example, one might discriminate between effective persuasion (advertisements offering "good reasons") and "obviously dishonest" advertising. Or one might distinguish between advertising offered to adult consumers, who should be responsible enough to judge its value, and advertising aimed at children, such as that on Saturday morning children's programs. Or one might take an argument often offered by advertisers, that advertising seems to be a necessary way to inform consumers of new products, and separate necessary advertising (supermarket ads? want ads?) from unnecessary advertising.

Problem Three. Stating the case Return to essay question *c* in problem two, above, and write a short paragraph exploring different ways of "stating the case." ■

Problem Four. Being "Dear Abby" Below are three letters to "Dear Abby," the newspaper advice columnist. Write a short answer to each of these letters, dealing as best you can with the writer's problem. Then check your answers with those of "Dear Abby," given in the answer section at the end of the book. Write a sentence, for each letter, explaining whether you and "Dear Abby" responded to the same "statement of the case."

A DEAR ABBY: My husband just told me he has a chance to drive two middle-aged widows to the mountains next June. He is to be their guide and chauffeur. I am not allowed to go along. He says they know he is married and it doesn't matter to them.

If he drives those widows to the mountains, he will be gone for two weeks.

He met these ladies in a beer joint. I asked him how much they were paying him for his services and he was very evasive and acted as though the money wasn't important. (It is. We can barely make ends meet.) I get madder and madder as time goes on. Does this sound like a legitimate business deal or not? **—STEAMED IN JERSEY**

B DEAR ABBY: My mother is a widow in her 70s who has been dying for the past 20 years. She keeps praying to die, and says she knows she will not live much longer. The doctors tell me there is nothing wrong with her.

It is very depressing to be around her. I want to be a loyal daughter, but I am so tired of hearing her say that she is praying to die, when there are so many people praying to stay alive.

The biggest problem is that she demands so much of my time. I am married and have my own family, Abby, and I just can't run over there and spend every day with her. I feel a responsibility to my mother, but she makes me feel guilty if I don't see her every single day. I have two sisters and one brother who give her very little time, and it doesn't seem to bother them. Please advise. **—STUCK IN CHAMPAIGN, ILL.**

C DEAR ABBY: My husband's boss wants to transfer us to a bigger city about 500 miles from here. It has more advantages for our children and would mean a big promotion for my husband, but every time I think of moving, I burst into tears. I've even put off going there to look for a place to live because I hate the thought of leaving this town.

I've lived here all my life. My family lives here. Our children's friends are here. And we have just built a lovely home. I know I sound selfish, but I can't help it. My husband wants to move. If I need a good lecture, let me have it. **—HATES TO MOVE**

■

The Scope of Argument: Good Reasons

We can't argue about bare facts. Questions like 15.9 or 15.10 are questions of bare fact:

15.9 Did Red China build the Berlin wall?

15.10 Did Alexander Hamilton sign the Declaration of Independence?

These are factual questions, and the answer, normally, is a simple "yes" or "no." Of course, the notion of "fact" is often more complex. It depends, for example, on the use to which the fact is put:

15.11 Is Italy shaped like a boot?

The best answer is, it depends. The answer would probably be "yes" for some people—the statement might be quite useful for a tourist, for example. For a map-maker, the answer would be a resounding "no," for a map-maker needs a more detailed picture of Italy.

In a more complex way, facts are facts only within a system of belief, a model of the world in the mind. One politically conservative mental patient answered "yes" to 15.9, "Did Red China build the Berlin wall?" Psychologists isolated the following belief system behind the answer:

15.12 The Berlin wall damaged American prestige, and Red China will do anything to damage American prestige. They must, therefore, have built the Berlin Wall.[1]

For this patient, historical and geographical facts weren't as important, in creating "facts" for himself, as his overriding fear of communism. If we wanted to argue with this patient, we'd probably forget about the Berlin wall and move back to his more general assumptions. Even so, we might still be unable to reason rationally with the patient. (We explore these matters in more detail in chapter Seventeen.)

At the other extreme, we can't argue about mere questions of opinion:

15.13 Liver is delicious.

15.14 That was a delightful movie.

Here, our counterarguments are limited to stating our own opinion:

15.13A Well, I don't like liver.

15.14A Well, I was bored to death.

Matters of fact	Matters of argument (the realm of "good reasons")	Matters of faith

FIGURE 15.1 The Limits of Rhetoric

Or, we can shift the ground (restate the case), and attack the motives of the speaker:

15.13B You don't really like liver; you're just trying to get out of an awkward situation.

15.14B You didn't really like that movie; you're just trying to make the best of it on a first date.

Most of us, even dogmatic liver-haters, would recognize these as matters of opinion, with each person entitled to his or her own view. Religious belief, however fervently we may try to argue about it, remains fundamentally a matter of opinion, and thus most religions speak more strongly of faith than of argument. (As a result, most instructors ask that students not write on religious topics: While they respect the opinions of students, they find that religion is, finally, a matter of faith rather than of rhetoric.)

We have drawn two extremes, matters of fact and matters of faith or opinion, that are beyond the area of rhetoric, of persuasive writing. That doesn't mean, we hasten to add, that "everything is a matter of opinion," or that "everything is relative." Rather, it suggests what we like to think of as the limits of rhetoric; it marks off the realm of "good reasons." This realm, diagrammed in Figure 15.1, is the realm of argument.

The best example of the realm of argument, again, is the legal system. If Twisty Harry, a known criminal, was filmed as he mugged a little old lady, caught with her purse in his pocket, identified by forty-three witnesses, and has signed a full confession, then we can conclude "beyond a reasonable doubt" that he is guilty of robbery. It becomes a matter of fact.

In most court cases, though, the issues are less clear-cut. We don't expect juries to argue about matters of opinion or belief: Jury members would reject arguments like, "I didn't like the color of his tie," or "You can never trust Italians," as irrelevant to the case at issue; they would not be "good reasons."

Problem Five. Good reasons   Consider each of the brief arguments below in terms of whether or not they offer "good reasons" to support their claim. You are not asked to agree or disagree with the claim, but rather to discuss whether or not the claim is supported with good reasons.

a. I always showed prospective clients the dramatic improvement that followed when Ogilvy, Benson and Mather took accounts away from old agencies—"in every case we have blazed new trails, and in every case sales have gone up."

David Ogilvy, Confessions of an Advertising Man

b. Our position on the manufacture of napalm is that we are a supplier of goods to the Defense Department, and not a policy maker. . . .

Simple good citizenship requires that we supply our Government and our military with those goods which they feel they need whenever we have the technology and capability and have been chosen by the Government as a supplier.

Dow Chemical Company statement, cited in
Don Whitehead, The Dow Story

c. These days, almost everyone seems to be worried about the future of money—a fact that was reflected in a recent *Times* nonfiction bestseller list on which five of the fifteen books, from "Crisis Investing," No. 7, to "Money Dynamics for the 1980's," No. 14, were books about money: how to get it, how to keep it, how to acquire things without having it.

"Talk of the Town," New Yorker

d. The militancy of young people, both white and black, eager for social change is often accounted for by saying they have lost faith in the slow processes of democratic discussion and decision-making. This argument seems to me highly questionable. It is my impression that militant young people, far from being "disillusioned" with democratic processes, are totally unacquainted with them, since they are rarely shown on television.

S. I. Hayakawa, "Who's Bringing Up Your Children?"

e. Plymouth Sapporo is a luxury sports coupe from Japan, just like Celica. Except Sapporo has more luxury, more sports and more coupe.

Chrysler Plymouth advertisement, Motor Trend

f. Regardless of the merits of the arguments on the heritability of intelligence, you could hardly have expected an unbiased evaluation from Leon Kamin, who has been one of the leading opponents of Jensen's work.

Letter to Psychology Today

g. Coal is America's most plentiful natural resource. By developing coal and using more of it to fuel electric power plants and industries, America can reduce its dependence on foreign oil.

Exxon advertisement

h. I notice that whenever we lose, you're always my partner.

Joan Ace, from the 1930s
radio program "Easy Aces"

■

ANALYZING ARGUMENTS

Most arguments, such as those of problem five, lay themselves out as *grounds* for a *claim:*

15.15 *Grounds:* Democratic processes are rarely shown on television. ⇒ [SO]

  Claim: Militant young people are totally unacquainted with them.

15.16 *Grounds:* Five of the fifteen books on the *Times* nonfiction bestseller list are about money. ⇒ [SO]

  Claim: These days, almost everybody seems to worry about money.

15.17 *Grounds:* In every case that we have taken over an account sales have gone up. ⇒ [SO]

  Claim: Your sales will go up if you let us take over your account.

Notice that this way of laying out arguments makes them more explicit; it corresponds to the way we respond to claims in ordinary language.

15.18 "He must be guilty."
"Why?"
"The little old lady positively identified him."

15.19 "It's going to rain."
"How do you know?"
"Farmer's Almanac says that it's rained on this day eight of the last ten years."

15.20 "The New York Islanders can't win the Stanley Cup."
"What makes you say so?"
"No expansion team has won a championship in any professional sport."

Seen this way, questions about claims—"Why?" "What makes you think so?" "How do you know?"—can be restated as "What are the *grounds* that *support* your claim?"

Notice further that we can continue the arguments of 15.18 through 15.20 by introducing a third term, *warrant,* in the conversational sense of "an unwarranted belief":

15.18A "He must be guilty."
"Why?"
"The little old lady positively identified him."
"I think your belief in her testimony is unwarranted."
"Not at all. She has firsthand knowledge of the crime, and she has no reason to lie."

15.19A "It's going to rain."
"How do you know?"
"*Farmer's Almanac* says that it's rained on this day eight of the last ten years."
"Your faith in the *Farmer's Almanac* is unwarranted."
"Not at all. My father used it daily his whole life."

15.20A "The New York Islanders can't win the Stanley Cup."
"What makes you say so?"
"No expansion team has won a championship in any professional sport."
"Your belief that what has happened in the past will happen in the future is unwarranted. After all, the Islanders have been building their team through the draft and trades, and they are now a disciplined and dedicated team."

You might think of the use of the word *warrant* in law, as in, "We have a warrant for your arrest." Here, the warrant is what authorizes us to perform an action. Or you might think of an automobile *warranty,* which allows the owner to have repairs performed. Or you might think of the use of *warrants* in science or mathematics:

15.21 *Grounds:* The rectangle is four feet wide and ten feet long. $\Rightarrow$ $\boxed{\text{SO}}$
   Claim: It has an area of forty square feet. $\Rightarrow$ $\boxed{\text{SINCE}}$
   Warrant: The formula for the area of a rectangle is length times width, or $A = w \times l$.

We plot these relationships in Figure 15.2.

Our examples—both our invented conversations and our actual arguments—suggest that warrants are often not explicitly stated. We need

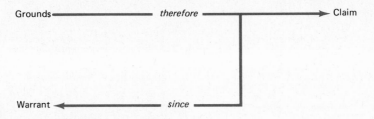

FIGURE 15.2   Warrants Support Arguments

to ask, "Where's the warrant for that belief?" When we do, we often isolate shortcomings in arguments. We outline the implied warrants of 15.15 through 15.17 in Figure 15.3. As you can see, we begin to separate strong arguments from weak arguments by asking, "Where's the warrant?" The question allows us to articulate what's at issue in an argument.

Problem Six. Where's the Warrant? first series   Identify the grounds and the claim in each of the following examples, and provide an explicit statement of the warrant needed to connect grounds with claim. The answers to the first six are given in the answer section at the end of the text.

a. She'll do well in college. She got excellent grades in high school.

b. He'll make an excellent president for the university. Look how successful he was as a banker.

c. Of course the federal government has to balance its budget. After all, no family could live with an unbalanced budget.

d. When Pahrump College introduced the honor system, they almost entirely eliminated cheating. We should introduce the honor system at this college, so we'll achieve the same result.

e. George Washington couldn't have been completely truthful. He was a politician, wasn't he?

f. If the Pope were a woman, he'd favor abortion.

g. It's either a buoy or a shark. It hasn't moved for ten minutes— let's go for a swim.

h. SAT verbal scores have fallen 32 points from 1966 to 1975, so naturally we need to be concerned about a literacy crisis.

i. In order for a society to be healthy it is essential that it employ capital punishment in certain instances.

j. I certainly deserve an "A" on this paper. I worked hard enough on it.   ■

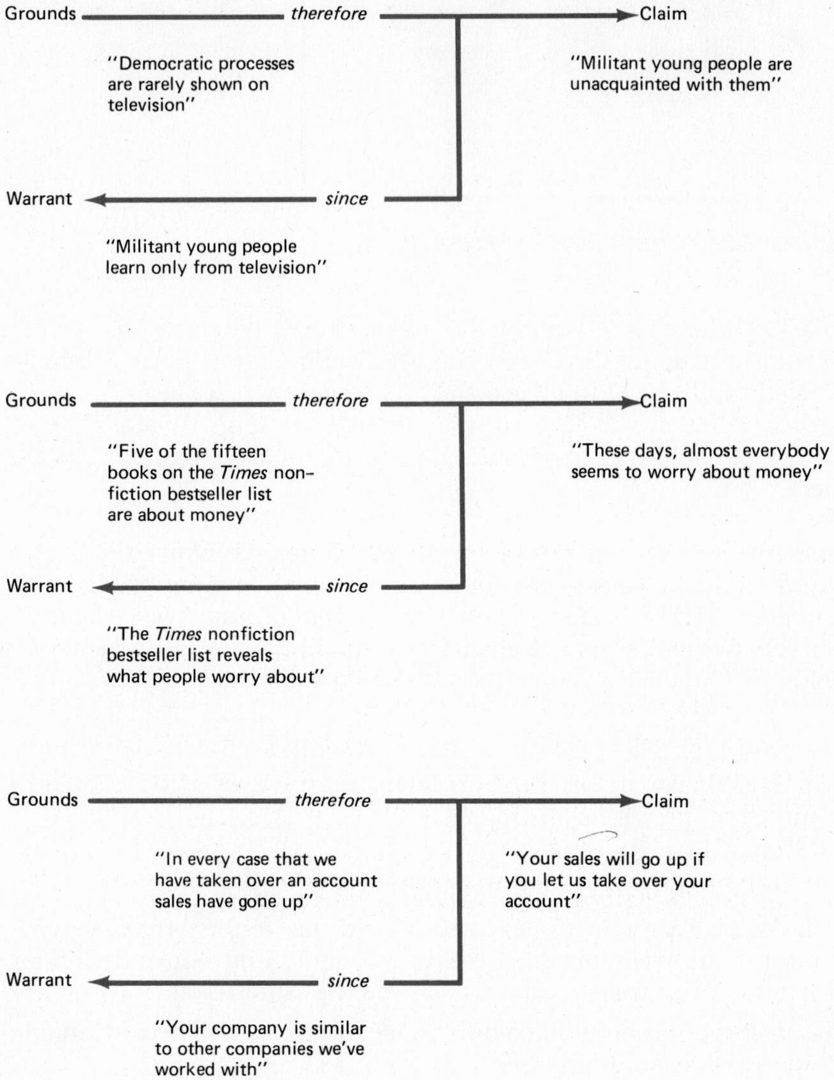

FIGURE 15.3 Discovering Warrants

Grounds ——————— *therefore* ————————→ Claim

"Democratic processes are rarely shown on television"

"Militant young people are unacquainted with them"

Warrant ◄——————— *since* ————————

"Militant young people learn only from television"

Grounds ——————— *therefore* ————————→ Claim

"Five of the fifteen books on the *Times* non-fiction bestseller list are about money"

"These days, almost everybody seems to worry about money"

Warrant ◄——————— *since* ————————

"The *Times* nonfiction bestseller list reveals what people worry about"

Grounds ——————— *therefore* ————————→ Claim

"In every case that we have taken over an account sales have gone up"

"Your sales will go up if you let us take over your account"

Warrant ◄——————— *since* ————————

"Your company is similar to other companies we've worked with"

Problem Seven. Where's the Warrant? second series Identify claim and grounds in each of the following examples, and then provide the warrant that connects the two. Often the warrant will be assumed rather than stated.

a. Clearly, *Playboy*'s astonishing popularity is not attributable solely to pin-up girls. For sheer nudity its pictorial art cannot compete with such would-be competitors as *Dude* and *Escapade*.

Harvey Cox

b. Self-improvement begins with self-expression . . . saying what you think and feel in words that stimulate, motivate, inspire. The ability to write opens worlds of possibilities to you for personal gratification and for the pursuit of a writing career. We've created a unique test to determine your ability to write. Send for our FREE WRITING APTITUDE TEST TODAY.

Writer's Institute advertisement

c. The promise, alas, far surpasses the payoff; in other words, the production values completely outclass the plot. The audience knows almost from the start that gruff general manager Peter Boyle is the villain and that marshal Sean Connery's single-handed victory is anticlimactically simple. . . . Once again, Hollywood's superlative technology has been squandered on an undernourished screenplay.

David Ansen, review of the movie *Outland*

d. The favorite horse, Doggonit Honey, was stepping down in class, from "nonwinners of two races since September" to "nonwinners of three races since September." . . . Kiowa Lou, however, had just won by five lengths against "nonwinners of three races since September." For my friend Mark, who was fully attuned to the importance of class at Barrington, Kiowa Lou deserved an automatic bet because she had already won under today's conditions. I recognized the strength of her credentials, but I also watched the odds board. I saw that Doggonit Honey was getting strong support, opening at 9-5 and dropping to even money. . . . But Kiowa Lou's price was drifting steadily to 8-1. There was no smart money on her. I passed the race. [Note: Kiowa Lou won, paying $18.40 for each $2 bet.]

Andrew Beyer, *Turf and Sport International*

e. J. V. Walker, a National Health officer in England, has suggested that researchers develop a pill that will postpone puberty until after students complete college.

Playboy
[Note: A special challenge]

f. Wondering why is the most rewarding activity of science. Learn to ask yourself questions beginning with "Why?" when you make observations in and out of the chemistry laboratory.

Paul R. O'Connor, *Chemistry*

■

Let us complicate this model of analysis still further, by continuing our imaginary conversations.

15.18B "Not at all. She had firsthand knowledge of the crime, and she has no reason to lie." *[warrant]*
"How can you be sure?"
"Well, we do know that people generally tell the truth, particularly when they are under oath and faced with cross-examination."

[backing for warrant]

"But you should remember that the defense pointed out that the little old lady was related to the victim." *[rebuttal]*
"That's true. *But I'm still sure, beyond a reasonable doubt,* that I can believe the little old lady and therefore find Twisty Harry guilty."

[qualifier]

15.19B "My father used the *Farmer's Almanac* daily his whole life." *[warrant]*
"So what?"
"Well, that demonstrates that the *Farmer's Almanac* has been accepted, for generations, as a reliable guide to the weather."

[backing for warrant]

"But times have changed. We now have weather satellites, infrared photography, and a host of modern scientific measurements. Statistics show that the weather service does a much more reliable job of predicting the weather than does the *Farmer's Almanac.*"

[rebuttal]

"Nevertheless, there's *a good chance* it will rain, and I'm going to take an umbrella." *[qualifier]*

15.20B "Nevertheless, the fact that expansion teams haven't done well in the past suggests that they are so limited by their beginnings that they will never reach the level of ability of the other teams in the league." *[backing for warrant]*
"But I think if you analyze the players, you'll find that the Islanders have the best offense in the league, a solid defense, and a goalie who comes through in clutch situations." *[rebuttal]*
"Maybe so. But I'm *so sure that* the Islanders won't win that I'll bet ten bucks on it." *[qualifier]*

As these arguments continue they introduce three new elements: *qualifier, rebuttal,* and *backing.*

The *qualifier* indicates the strength of a claim. It is commonly expressed by words like "probably," "certainly," "perhaps," or by expressions like, "there is a real possibility that." In our last example, one speaker qualified his belief by offering a bet. In legal cases tried before a jury, the qualifier is a formal one: "beyond a reasonable doubt." In science, a qualifier may be expressed as a statistic; in advertising, it may be a "money-back guarantee."

By looking for a qualifier in an argument, a reader can sense the degree of certainty the writer offers, and a writer is forced to ask herself, "What degree of certainty do I have about the argument I'm making?" Note, of course, that strong qualifiers—"absolutely," "certainly"—are not necessarily the best qualifiers.

The *rebuttal* offers a chance for counterarguments. A rebuttal is thus an "unless" statement:

15.15A Democratic processes are rarely shown on television, so— unless it can be shown that young people learn other than from television—militant young people are totally unacquainted with them.

15.16A Five of the fifteen books on the *Times* nonfiction bestseller list are about money, so—unless it can be shown that this has been true for years and years, or unless the *Times* bestseller list does not represent the interests of people—these days, almost everybody seems to worry about money.

15.17A In every case that we have taken over an account, sales have gone up, so—unless you are untypical of other firms, or unless your sales will go up automatically anyway—your sales will go up if you let us take over your account.

It's this last rebuttal that advertising executive David Ogilvy omits from his sales pitch:

15.22 I always showed prospective clients the dramatic improvement that followed when Ogilvy, Benson and Mather took accounts away from old agencies—"in every case we have blazed new trails, and in every case sales have gone up." But I was never able to keep a straight face when I said this; if a company's sales had not grown more than sixfold in the previous twenty-one years, its growth was less than average.

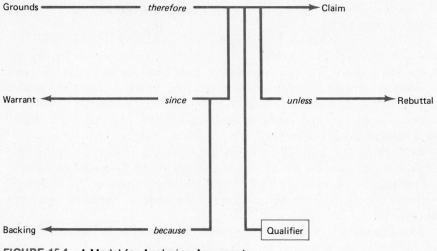

FIGURE 15.4   A Model for Analyzing Arguments

The *backing* of an argument is its final authority—the theory or body of experience that justifies the warrant. In our conversations, our questions about warrants forced our arguers to turn to general statements about courtroom evidence, to explicit statements about the authority of the *Farmer's Almanac,* and to a broad claim about expansion teams in sports. The backing of a legal argument may finally be a statement of a law or precedent. The backing of a formula in science is a statement of the theory and experiments that support the formula. The backing of the opinion of a movie critic may be more imprecise:

15.23   It is a general principle that the story line of a movie should not be predictable.

We insert these elements—qualifier, rebuttal, and backing—into our abstract diagram in Figure 15.4, and we offer, in Figure 15.5, three typical arguments analyzed on the basis of this model.

Of course, few arguments in print are conducted with the full explicitness of this model. Indeed, most arguments in print are a series of claims or grounds or warrants or rebuttals, chaining themselves into a complete argument.

Nevertheless, this model of analysis is a useful one for the critical reader, for it helps to supply assumptions, links, and implications that may be missing from the text. It helps us see the "why" of an argument.

Grounds ——————————— *therefore* ——————→ Claim

"The dancers in the ballet company face various poor working conditions, such poor pay, lack of adequate travel expenses, etc."

"The dancers should form a union"

Warrant ←——————————— *since* ——————— *unless* ——————→ Rebuttal

"Ballet dancers have the right to consider themselves workers, just as any members of a craft"

"One could show that dancers do not meet legal definitions of workers" *OR* "One could show that the disadvantages of forming a union would be worse than the advantages (a loss of jobs, for example)"

Backing ←——————————— *because* ——————— Qualifier : "In my view"

"Workers have the legal right to organize freely, protected under various federal and state laws"

"Perhaps"

"Certainly"

Grounds ——————————— *therefore* ——————→ Claim

"Increasing expenditures for advertising usually leads to increased sales"

"Schroeder Salmon Company ought to increase its advertising budget"

Warrant ←——————————— *since* ——————— *unless* ——————→ Rebuttal

"Schroeder Salmon is typical of such business"

"There are limits on the amount of salmon one can sell" *OR* "The advertising firm will not produce a good campaign" *OR* "The economic situation at this time is not comparable to that of the past."

Backing ←——————————— *because* ——————— Qualifier : "Certainly"

"Businesses have a duty to their stockholders, under the American free enterprise system, to seek all ways of assuring profits"

FIGURE 15.5 Typical Arguments

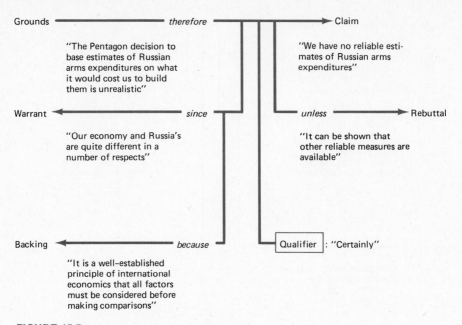

FIGURE 15.5 Typical Arguments (*continued*)

Similarly, it's a useful model for the writer of an argument as well, for it forces the writer to be explicit about warrants and backing, to think of possible rebuttals, and to be aware of the strength of an argument. It is not a formula for writing, but rather a formula for prewriting—for getting one's arguments in order.

Problem Eight. Analyzing an argument   Return to the paper or outline you constructed for problem two, the "freshman essay examination." Examine your arguments by the model of Figure 15.4, and decide where you might strengthen your argument—by a more careful rebuttal or qualifier, for example, or by making explicit for the reader the warrant that supports your claim. Consider whether the model allows you to create other arguments. Revise your paper or outline, and discuss, in a few sentences, how successful the model of analysis is as a prewriting device.   ■

Finally, this model of analysis makes us think about the process of arguing in the different disciplines. Science deals in hard evidence, explicit formulas, and precise "laws" of nature. Literary criticism deals with more subjective reactions, with values, and with questions of quality.

Rhetoric deals with relative notions of "better written," "appropriate for this context," and "effective for this audience." The social sciences fall somewhere in the middle, with backing supplied by notions like "causation" in history, "motivation" in psychology, or "social class" in sociology.

Problem Nine. The process of arguing in your field   Choose a textbook or a current issue of a journal in the field you are majoring in. Use it as the basis for a paper, "Arguing in _____." Pay particular attention to questions like the following:

■ Where does my discipline find its *grounds* for argument? What kind of "evidence for belief" does my discipline use?
■ What kind of *claims* does my discipline make, and how does it make them?
■ What is the degree of certainty in my discipline? What *qualifiers* are commonly used in arguments?
■ Where does my discipline find its *warrants* for beliefs? What form do these warrants take?
■ What is the ultimate *backing* of arguments in my discipline? In what form does such backing appear?
■ How do specialists in my discipline *rebut* each other? What questions do they disagree about? How are *rebuttals* handled in arguments in my discipline?

As an alternate assignment, take a textbook from a course that you don't do well in, particularly a course in which you feel capable of doing better work. Analyze the process of arguing in that field, using the questions above, and, from that analysis, suggest specific ways in which you might improve your performance in that field.   ■

A NOTE ON FALLACIES

A *fallacy* is a "false argument" (the word is ultimately Latin, borrowed from Old French, and related to *fallacious, fallible,* and ultimately to *fail*). The list of fallacies is perhaps endless—there are so many ways of being wrong in argument that it's a wonder we ever get it right. We do list a few fallacies—those that the developing writer commonly commits. But the writer who falls into a common fallacy in argument shouldn't be crushed, since, as the Latin names given to many suggest, these pitfalls in thinking have existed for thousands of years.

The Appeal to Authority

The student, arguing in favor of a literacy test for high school seniors, turns to his outside reading to support his position:

> **15.24** TV journalist Edwin Newman has complained in books such as *Strictly Speaking* of the rising illiteracy.

In doing so, he quietly undermines his position, for he notes that Edwin Newman is a TV journalist, not an educator specializing in literacy. (Indeed, many educators don't feel that a "literacy crisis" exists, noting, for example, that more students are going on to college, thus broadening the test base of the SAT, and perhaps in itself accounting for the drop in SAT scores.) In other words, he appeals to authority but without establishing his authority as a legitimate source.

The appeal to authority (Latin *argumentum ad verecundiam,* "the argument to veneration") is common enough in advertising and politics. In advertising it shows up as a reference to a vague authority, as in "science tells us," or as the use of a popular sports or entertainment personality (Reggie Jackson selling videotape decks, for example). In politics, it shows up in citing remarks by, say, Abraham Lincoln, without demonstrating that those remarks are relevant to the modern world.

Of course, there are legitimate appeals to authority, but only if the writer shows that the authority indeed provides solid grounds to support the claim being made.

Against the Person

The argument against the person (Latin *ad hominem*) attacks the person making the argument, not the argument itself.

> **15.25** No one who would support the death penalty, except in the rarest cases, could be a real Christian. They are callous people, insensitive to the value of human life.

> **15.26** Regardless of the merits of the arguments on the heritability of intelligence, you could hardly have expected an unbiased evaluation from Leon Kamin, who has been one of the leading opponents of Jensen's work.
>
> letter to *Psychology Today*

The first writer makes a claim of insensitivity against a broad group; the second charges a person with bias. Neither provides the grounds necessary to support the claim. Such name-calling is common enough in politics, where a candidate's background—a divorce or a religious belief—may be called into question, without showing that the background is relevant to the political position.

Again, the problem with arguments against the person is that grounds need to be connected with claims. A personal argument is legitimate if it can be shown to be relevant.

The Appeal to Pity

The appeal to pity (Latin *ad misericordiam*) reaches toward our emotions rather than our logic.

15.27 Consider the plight of the poor student given a "certificate of attendance" instead of a diploma. He will find only the lowest paying job, forced to limit himself to manual labor and unable to climb the ladder of life.

15.28 It has more advantages for our children and would mean a big promotion for my husband, but every time I think of moving I burst into tears.

"Dear Abby" letter

Of course, we have a right to be aware of emotional issues, as long as they are relevant to the case in question. But "Dear Abby" rejected the emotional appeal of 15.28, and the student author of 15.27 was led to realize, in a class discussion of her argument, that a marginally literate student with a high school diploma would face the same fate as the "poor student" she envisioned.

The Bandwagon Appeal

The bandwagon appeal flatters the audience (thus, *argumentum ad populum,* an argument to the people). It's a staple of television advertising—all those happy families enjoying canned and frozen meals, all those owners who really love their pets. The warrant is, "Do this because it's the popular (traditional, serious, patriotic) thing to do."

The essay question on capital punishment, since it refers to "the health of society," invites a "bandwagon appeal." Such an appeal becomes a fallacy when it becomes irrelevant to the conclusion, when it offers flattery instead of harmony:

15.29 Surely all decent, right-thinking Americans share a sense of outrage at the random violence, the destructive crime, that infects the health of our society.

Begging the Question

An argument "begs the question" when it assumes that the claim is true, without offering grounds for belief, or when it restates the claim without grounds or warrant (thus Latin *petitio principii,* "petitioning the principle").

> **15.30** Since a literacy test will establish a clear measure of literacy, it should be implemented immediately.

> **15.31** Because the death penalty will deter crime, it will improve the health of society.

Whoa, says the critical reader. You're assuming that what you're supposed to prove is already true—where are the grounds for believing that a literacy test will establish a "clear measure" of literacy, where the warrant for believing in the deterrent power of the death penalty?

False Cause

The fallacy of the false cause connects two events in time without offering grounds for believing that one causes the other (thus the elegant Latin *post hoc, ergo propter hoc,* "after this, therefore because of this").

> **15.32** Deceptive advertising causes Americans to distrust television and other news media, and thereby unravels the fabric of our moral life.

The student author of 15.32 offers a strong argument (clothed, we might say, in an interesting metaphor), but, without grounds or warrant, it is not a convincing one.

The distinction between "true causes" and "false causes" is a rather intricate one. The extremes are clear-cut: It's probably safe to assume that reducing the speed limit from 70 to 55 "caused" the reduction in highway deaths that followed, and it's equally clear that a prediction in the *Farmer's Almanac* doesn't "cause" the rain to fall. At the very least, "true causes" must be defended with grounds for belief.

We might illustrate an extreme example of the *post hoc* fallacy by citing an old joke, thereby ending a fairly serious chapter on a rather light note.

> **5.33** A farmer was traveling with his wife on a train when he saw a man across the aisle take something out of a bag and begin eating it. "Say, Mister," he said, "what's that thing you're eating?"

"It's a kumquat," the man said. "Here, try one."

The farmer took it, peeled it, and just as he swallowed the first bite, the train roared into a tunnel.

"Don't eat any, Maude," he yelled to his wife. "It'll make you go blind!"[2]

SUMMARY

We began this unit on invention by reviewing our earlier discussions of your natural inventive abilities—in voice, development, and style. We then mentioned the special requirements of *print explicitness,* the need to be perfectly clear to the reader. We discussed various ways of "stating the case" and the importance of "good reasons." We then developed a model for the analysis of arguments: A *claim* is supported by *grounds* because of a *warrant* supported by *backing,* offered with a *qualifier* and due care for possible *rebuttal.* In short form: *grounds,* so (*qualifier*) *claim* since *warrant,* because *backing,* unless *rebuttal.* We concluded by mentioning several of the fallacies of argument.

FINAL WRITING ASSIGNMENTS

I. Ways of Arguing   Choose five columns by a newspaper or magazine columnist and, treating them as typical of that writer, analyze that writer's characteristic ways of presenting and supporting arguments. As an alternate assignment, choose five reviews by a single book, record, or movie reviewer.

Deal with the underlying values, assumptions, and procedures of the writer; do not merely summarize his or her opinions. Such an analysis may demand a fairly complex organization, since you will find it difficult to develop your own argument fully by adopting the most obvious organization, an introduction, a paragraph to each column, and a conclusion.

II. Stating the Case   Identify a public issue—a campus problem, a political question, a recent legal decision. Using several different sources— letters to the editor, news reports, editorials—analyze the different ways of "stating the case." You may wish to offer a neutral analysis, aimed at clarifying the issues involved; you may, however, choose to support one "statement of the case" as superior to others. The reference work *Editorials on File* may be available in your college library. (Caution: The issue should be narrow enough to be covered adequately in a short paper—avoid general topics like "abortion" or "American foreign policy.")

III. Print Explicitness   We reprint below two interviews from Studs Terkel's *Working*—tape-recorded interviews which the author has edited into "written down speech." Both speakers, in addition to simply "talking about" their work, offer implied arguments at various points. Choose one of these speakers, and attempt to lay out an implied argument fully, using the model of Figure 15.3. Then, as an experiment in print explicitness, consider how that speaker might wish to restructure that argument in print. Conceive such an argument for a specific audience—perhaps *Glamour* magazine for the model and *Business Week* for the executive secretary—and consider how you might preserve some of the spoken "voice" of the person in a written message.

ANNE BOGAN

We're on the thirty-second floor of a skyscraper, the office of a corporation president. She is his private secretary. The view of the river, railroad yards, bridges, and the city's skyline is astonishing.

"I've been an executive secretary for eight years. However, this is the first time I've been on the corporate end of things, working for the president. I found it a new experience. I love it and I feel I'm learning a lot."

I become very impatient with dreamers. I respect the doers more than the dreamers. So many people, it seems to me, talk about all the things they want to do. They only talk without accomplishing anything. The drifters are worse than the dreamers. Ones who really have no goals, no aspirations at all, just live from day to day . . .

I enjoy one thing more than anything else on this job. That's the association I have with the other executives, not only my boss. There's a tremendous difference in the way they treat me than what I've known before. They treat me more as . . . on the executive level. They consult me on things, and I enjoy this. It stimulates me.

I know myself well enough to know that I've always enjoyed men more than women. Usually I can judge them very quickly when I meet a woman. I can't judge men that quickly. I seek out the few women I think I will enjoy. The others, I get along with all right, but I feel no basic interest. I don't really enjoy having lunch with them and so on.

You can tell just from conversation what they talk about. It's quite easy. It's also very easy to tell which girls are going to last around the office and which ones aren't. Interest in their work. Many of them aren't, they just don't dig in. They're more interested in chatting in the washroom. I don't know if that's a change from other years. There's always been some who are really not especially career-minded, but they have to give a little bit and try a little harder. The others get by on as little as possible.

I feel like I'm sharing somewhat of the business life of the men. So I think I'm much happier as the secretary to an executive than I would be in some woman's field, where I could perhaps make more money. But it wouldn't be an extension of a successful executive. I'm perfectly happy in my status.

She came from a small town in Indiana and married at eighteen. She had graduated from high school and began working immediately for the town's large company. "My husband was a construction worker. We lived in a trailer, we moved around a lot. There's a lot of community living in that situation and I grew pretty tired of it. You can get involved, you can become too friendly with people when you live too close. A lot of time can be wasted. It was years before I started doing this."

I have dinner with businessmen and enjoy this very much. I like the background music in some of these restaurants. It's soothing and it also adds a little warmth and doesn't disturb the conversation. I like the atmosphere and the caliber of people that usually you see and run into. People who have made it.

I think if I've been at all successful with men, it's because I'm a good listener and interested in their world. I enjoy it, I don't become bored with it. They tell me about their personal life too. Family problems, financial, and the problems of raising children. Most of the ones I'm referring to are divorced. In looking through the years they were married, I can see this is what probably happened. I know if I were the wife, I would be interested in their work. I feel the wife of an executive would be a better wife had she been a secretary first. As a secretary, you learn to adjust to the boss's moods. Many marriages would be happier if the wife would do that.

JILL TORRANCE

She is a photographer's model, high fashion. Her face is a familiar one in magazine ads as well as on television commercials. She has been engaged in this work for eight years. She earns the city's top rate: fifty dollars an hour.

I do whatever kind of products anyone wants. This week I had a job for some South American product. They said, "We want you to be sexy, coy, pert, but not too effervescent." It always means the same smile and open eyes. For forty-five minutes they tell you what they want. They explain and explain and you sort of tune out and do the same thing.

There are a lot of people there: the person who has the product, the man from the ad agency, a couple of people from the photography studio, the stylist, who poses your dress to make sure it hangs right . . . suddenly there are a dozen people standing around. Each is telling you to do something else. You know they are even more insecure than you. You pretend you're listening and you do what you'd planned to do in the first place. When you've worked before a camera long enough, you know what they want even though they don't.

At first you work very hard to try to discover different looks and hairdos. After a while, you know them all. Someone once asked me, "Why do high-fashion models pose with their mouths open? They look like they're catching flies." (Laughs.) This look has been accepted for a long time. They want everything to be sexy, subtle or overt. After a while, it's automatic.

Now the natural look is in. Jumping up and down or staring out there . . . What's natural about looking into space? They want you natural but posed. (Laughs.) How can you feel natural with three pounds of make-up, in some ridiculous costume, standing there and looking pretty? What they think of as being natural is very phony.

You never know from day to day. I did a job for a snow blower in Michigan. It's a little machine that ladies are able to push to get snow out of the way. It was ten below. We flew over at five thirty in the morning. I had my long underwear on, but I forgot to wear my heavy shoes and I froze my feet. You're either doing fur coats in 110 degrees in the summer or bathing suits in the winter. I do whatever they ask me. I take the money and run.

Someone will call you at seven in the morning and say be ready at eight thirty. Can you be there in forty minutes? You're a basket case trying to get your wardrobe together and be there on time. You're having a cup of coffee, suddenly the phone rings and you have to run. It's terrible. Somehow you manage to make it on time. I'm very seldom late. I'm amazed at myself.

I'd like to say I'm sick and can't make it, but I seldom turn something down unless I think it's really awful. Usually I'm just rushing and do the job. I feel guilty if I say no. When you're working for one agency, they expect you to be on call. Otherwise the client may think you're too pampered.

You go out of your house with your closetful on your arm. Different colors and shoes to match and purses and wigs. Every time I get a taxi, they think I'm going to the airport. They're upset when I'm going ten blocks away. I've never found one to help me in or out of a cab. And I'm a good tipper. So I've developed these very strong muscles with one shoulder lower than the other from carrying all the wardrobe about. (Laughs.)

In the middle of the winter it's really horrendous, because you're fighting all the people to get a taxi. I have three or four pieces of luggage. It's pretty heavy. Then I struggle out of the cab and upstairs to the studio. You're supposed to look fresh and your hair is supposed to be sparkling. By the time you get there, you're perspiring like crazy, and it's difficult to feel fresh under all those hot lights when you've had such a struggle to get there.

What's your first reaction when the phone rings in the morning and it's a job call?

Oh, crap.

"I hadn't set out to be a model. I worked as a receptionist in a beauty shop during high school. This was in South Dakota. A woman who had worked for Eileen Ford and had been in Vogue *and* Harper's Bazaar *said to me, 'Why don't you go to New York and be a model?' I didn't know what a model was. I thought they were dummies in catalogues. I thought the people in the photographs were just cutouts. I didn't think they were really people. I paid no attention to advertising.*

"I wanted to go to college, but I had saved only three hundred dollars. So I went to New York at eighteen. I had never put anything on but lipstick and had never worn high-heeled shoes. I walked up and down Lexington Avenue for three hours 'cause my room at the Y wasn't ready. I didn't dare turn left or right. I just kept walking. A hamburger in South Dakota was twenty-five cents and in this drugstore suddenly it was a dollar and a quarter."

At Eileen Ford, they told me I was too long-waisted and that maybe I should think about something else, and it was too bad since I had come all the way from South Dakota. I was so green.

I looked in the telephone book. Huntington Hartford had just bought this agency. So I went there. I was so bashful I couldn't even give my name to the receptionist. About a half an hour later, this guy who had just taken over the agency—he'd been a male model—came in. He was the first man I'd seen in New York, close up. I was just staring at him. He said, "You! Come into my office!" I thought I had really been discovered. He probably called me because I was staring at him and he liked himself a lot. (Laughs.)

A week or two later there was a cocktail party. I'd never had a drink in my life. They said you should be there at five o'clock. At five I was the only person there. They asked me what I wanted to drink. I didn't know. I said, "Bourbon and water is really nice." It was awful. The party was for Sammy Kaye. I'd never heard of Sammy Kaye.

The guy just wanted us to be there. He was having fifteen of his favorite models over. You just go. No pay. If there's an opening at a photography studio or whatever you go, because advertising people are there and you should be seen and you should make sure they remember your face. All the ridiculous things . . . That's what happens to a lot of girls who go into modeling. They're very vulnerable. They don't know what they're doing. Usually they come from very poor families. This seems glamorous. Most of the girls I met were from Ohio or Indiana or some place like that.

I had fifty cents left in my pocket when I got my first job. I worked two hours and made sixty dollars. It was absolutely incredible to me. I pinned a corsage on a guy. It was some hotel ad in a trade magazine. It was a very silly shot that was terribly simple. It was getting all this money for smiling and pinning a flower on a guy. It didn't turn out to be that simple.

Most people have strange feelings about standing before a camera. You have to learn to move and make different designs with your body. Some girls know how to puff their nose in and out to make it change or their lips or cheekbones. They practice in front of a mirror.

Usually you're competing with anywhere from thirty to sixty girls. They're cattle calls. Sometimes they take you in ten at a time. You wait from forty-five minutes to an hour before you're called. They narrow it down and ask for three or four to come back. It's like going out on a job interview every day. Everybody is very insecure. You walk into a room and see thirty beautiful girls and say, "What am I doing here?" Immediately you feel you should leave. But you think you might get three out of fifteen jobs, so . . .

There's no training needed, no kind of background. People spend thousands of dollars going to charm schools to learn make-up. It's ridiculous. They just take money from young girls. You learn while you're working. I didn't think it was funny the first few years because I was so nervous. After you relax, you see how absurd it all is.

I've always had a problem gaining weight. I told a photographer I had gained two pounds. I was happy about it. The agency said, "She's too fat, tell her to lose weight." They wouldn't have known if I hadn't told them.

I think the shyest people get into show business or modeling. They were wallflowers in their classes. You never really feel at ease and you force yourself to do things not natural to you. It's always something that you really aren't, that someone else wants you to be.

You feel like you're someone's clothes hanger. One day someone will say you're great. In the next studio, they'll say you're terrible. It changes from minute to minute: acceptance, rejection. Suddenly it doesn't mean anything. Why should you base your whole day on how you look in the morning?

My feelings are ambivalent. I like my life because it does give me freedom. I can have half a day off to do things I like. I couldn't do that if I had a normal job. I could never be a secretary. I make as much money working three hours as a secretary makes in a week. If I had to sit in an office for eight hours a day filing, I would find that more degrading than modeling. I don't look down at secretaries. Most are talented women who could do better jobs than their bosses probably, but will never get the chance—because they're women.

I'd probably join women's lib, but they don't believe in make-up and advertising, so I couldn't very well go to their meetings as I am. At school, where I'm studying photography, they said if I had any interest in women's lib I wouldn't be modeling. I was trying to tell them women are so underpaid that I couldn't earn a comparable wage at any other job. They disagreed, but in the next breath they were talking about something they'd seen advertised and wanted to buy the next day.

I feel guilty because I think people should do something they really like to do in life. I should do something else, but there is nothing I can do really well. I'm established and make a steady living, so it becomes pretty easy. It's not very fulfilling . . . but I'm lazy, I admit it. It's an easier thing to do.

You stop thinking when you're working. But it does take a lot of nervous energy because the camera goes one, two, three very fast, and you have to move very fast. There's a *kind* of thinking about what you're doing. If your left knee is at the right angle . . .

I usually don't tell people that I model. I say I'm an actuary or something. You're a celebrity because your picture is in a magazine or there's the negative connotation. If strippers or whores are arrested, they usually say, "I'm a model." There's also the thing about models being free and easy. I've never had the problem of men making passes at me. I've always managed to maintain a distance. I would never have become a model had I known . . .

Mrs. Paley—what's her name? Babs Paley—said the greatest thing is being very thin and very rich. I'm afraid that turns me off. I don't like to look at my pictures. I don't like to ride by and see some advertisement and tell everyone that's me.

Most models, after one or two years, can't be very interested in it. But they get involved with money, so it's difficult for them to quit. And there's always the possibility of the commercial that's going to make you twenty thousand dollars at one crack. You can work very hard all year on photos and not make as much as you can on two television commercials.

Male models are even worse. They're always talking about that lucky streak. They're usually ex-beach boys or ex-policemen or ex-waiters. They think they're going to get rich fast. Money and sex are the big things in their life. They talk about these two things constantly. Money more than sex, but sex a lot. Dirty jokes and the fast buck. You see this handsome frame and you find it empty.

I go off into my own world most of the time. It's difficult for me to talk with the others, because most people I work with are very conservative and play it safe. I usually get emotional, so since I'm not going to change them and they're not going to change me, we sort of talk about everyday gossip. You end up smiling and being nice to everyone. You can't afford not to be.

POSTSCRIPT: *"When I visit that Baptist family back home, they ask if I drink and what do I drink. When I say, 'Seven-Up,' they don't believe me. When I come home once a year, I try to make my people happy or bring them gifts. Probably like the guilty father who brings gifts for his children . . ."*

IV. An Argument for Analysis   Below are two short arguments that appeared in the *New York Times* in 1977, one supporting standardized tests, the other attacking them. Carefully analyze the arguments, noting the points at which they agree and disagree, the warrants offered for claims, and the final backing of each argument. Analyze the adequacy of the arguments in a short essay titled "Good Reasons."

Standardized Tests: They Reflect
the Real World
Robert L. Ebel

Are standardized tests headed for extinction? To judge from news reports, magazine articles and some popular books the answer might seem to be yes. A variety of charges have been laid against them, and there is substance to some. But the effects are neither so overpowering nor so harmful as the critics imply. On balance the case for standardized tests is persuasive.

A common accusation is that some pupils have, and others lack, a special talent for taking tests and that tests end up measuring this ability rather than academic achievements. Only on a carelessly or ineptly constructed test, though, can a pupil inflate his score by special test savvy. Most widely used standardized tests have been constructed carefully by experts. Unfamiliarity with the item types or response modes employed in a standardized test can indeed handicap a naïve examinee. But that kind of naïveté can be removed quite easily by careful instructions and practice exercises.

Bear in mind that the test score reports only the level of knowledge the pupil possesses, not how frequently or how effectively he makes use of it. It reports what the pupil can do, not what he typically does. What a pupil does, and how well he does it, depends not on his knowledge alone. It depends also on his energy, ambition, determination, adroitness, likableness and luck, among other things. A pupil's knowledge as measured by a standardized or any other test is one ingredient—but only one—of his potential success in life.

The simplicity with which answers to multiple-choice questions can be recorded on an answer sheet, and the objectivity and speed with which correct answers can be detected and counted by modern scoring machines, offends some devotees of the other common type of examination, the written essay. They confuse the simplicity of the process of recording an answer with the complexity of the process of figuring it out. Some of them charge that multiple-choice questions test only rote learning, or superficial factual information. That is clearly not true. Consider this question:

The sides of a quadrilateral having two consecutive right angles are consecutive whole numbers. The shortest side is one of the two parallel sides. What is the area of the quadrilateral in square units? (a) 11 (b) 18 (c) 25 (d) 36 (e) Not given

Answer:

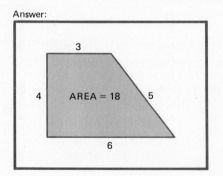

Multiple-choice questions can be trivial or irrelevant. They need not be.

Critics of tests and testing sometimes provide examples of questions that seem to be ridiculously trivial or impossibly ambiguous. In some cases their criticisms are justified. Bad questions have been written and published. But few of these come from professionally constructed standardized tests of achievement. In other cases the criticism is not justified. The objection is based on a possible but unlikely interpretation different from the clearly intended sense of the question. One who sets out to discover how a question might conceivably be misconstrued is likely to find some way to misconstrue it. Language, after all, is not a flawless means for the precise communication of thought.

Another charge is that standardized testing harms children. It is said that the tests threaten and upset pupils, that if a pupil gets a low score he will be seriously damaged and that standardized testing is incompatible with educational procedures designed to support the child.

There is, no doubt, anecdotal evidence to support some of these claims. However, common sense suggests that the majority of pupils are not harmed by testing, and as far as I know there is no substantial survey data that would contradict common sense on this matter. The teachers I talk with seem much more often to be concerned with pupils who don't care enough how well or how poorly they do on such tests, than with the relatively rare instances of pupils who care too much.

It is normal and biologically helpful to be somewhat anxious when facing any real test, regardless of one's age. But it is also a necessary part of growing up to learn to cope with the tests that life inevitably brings. Of the many challenges to a child's peace of mind, caused by such things as angry parents, playground bullies, bad dogs and shots from the doctor, standardized tests must surely be among the least fearsome. Unwise parental pressure can in some cases elevate anxiety to harmful levels. But usually the child who breaks down in tears at the prospect of a test has problems of security, adjustment and maturity that testing did not create and that cannot be solved by eliminating tests.

A pupil who consistently gets low scores on tests of what that pupil has tried hard to learn is indeed likely to become discouraged. If this does happen, the school cannot claim to be offering a good educational program, and the teacher cannot claim to be doing a good job of teaching. Most low scores on tests, however, go to pupils who, for one reason or another, have not tried very hard to learn. In the opinion of the teachers of such pupils, it is the trying rather than the testing that is most in need of correction.

It is sometimes charged that tests distort school curriculums by causing schools to teach to the tests and by thus hampering curricular innovation.

A school that is teaching what the tests test will surely teach many other things besides. Even in the basic areas that the test does sample, there will be time and cause to venture into areas of learning not covered by the standardized tests. Standardized tests can dominate local curriculums only to the extent that school administrators and school teachers allow them to.

There are, of course, some programs of open education that are satisfied merely with maximum pupil freedom, trusting nature alone to do what others employ the art and science of teaching to help nature do. To say that standardized tests of achievement are inappropriate for such programs may imply more criticism of the programs than of the tests.

Standardized tests are also charged with encouraging harmful comparisons of one pupil with another. Let a pupil measure his achievements against his potential, or against his own past performance, say the critics, not against his classmates.

I believe they are wrong. What they should criticize is unwise reactions to comparison, not comparison itself. For those who are interested in excellent education find it difficult to believe that comparisons of educational achievement are irrelevant or unnecessary. No proud parent believes it. No capable teacher believes it. It simply is not true.

The only basis for judging a human performance excellent, acceptable, or inferior is in comparison with other human performances. The only basis for setting reasonably attainable objectives for pupil learning is knowledge of what similar pupils have been able to learn. Of course it is good for a pupil to compare his present performance with his own past performance. But that is no substitute for comparing his present performance with the present performances of his classmates. Surely it is cold comfort to a pupil when his arithmetic teacher says, "For you, five out of ten is quite good."

Only in some eyes have tests lost favor. Quite clearly they are not headed for extinction. They are much too useful to the competent, concerned educator. They are much too essential to the pursuit of excellence in education.

Standardized Tests: They Don't
Measure Learning
Edwin P. Taylor and Mitchell Lazarus

The controversy over achievement testing starts from a simple fact: Achievement tests reward test-taking skills as much as they reward achievement. Different children who know a subject equally well can still receive very different scores on a multiple-choice achievement test.

Some children work fast, not taking time to think deeply: they may make quick conventional guesses on some questions, be tidy and accurate in shading boxes on answer sheets and have suburban, middle-class backgrounds—useful for quickly grasping the words and pictures on most tests. These children get credit, perhaps, for what they know about the subject matter.

Other children may work slowly, think through too many possibilities, be too insecure to guess fast or be sloppy with the answer sheet. Children come from a variety of cultural and linguistic backgrounds. Thus many children's test scores will probably not reflect their grasp of the subject, even if they know the subject well.

And nearly every achievement test is a reading test first, before it is a test of anything else.

Neatness, accuracy, speed and good reading are useful skills, worth encouraging in children. But as long as test scores depend so much on skills that supposedly are not being tested, the results are bound to be inaccurate.

All questions on standardized achievement tests are multiple choice. The child must (1) read the question and (2) think of the answer—but not write it down! Instead, he or she must (3) try to find this answer among those given; (4) and when it is not there, pick one that is; (5) keep track of its number or letter, and (6) shade in the correct little box on the answer sheet. Only two of these six steps concern the subject being tested. The other four help the computer grade the test.

Multiple-choice questions distort the purposes of education. Picking one answer among four is very different from thinking a question through to an answer of one's own, and far less useful in life. Recognition of vocabulary and isolated facts makes the best kind of multiple-choice questions, so these dominate the tests, rather than questions that test the use of knowledge. Because schools want their children to perform well, they are often tempted to teach the limited sorts of knowledge most useful on the tests.

Questions are often badly worded, confusing, or downright wrong. For many questions, the thoughtful or imaginative student can see several acceptable answers among those given.

There is an easy defense against the charge of poor question quality: make the questions better. But after many decades of testing, the proportion of defective questions seems about the same—enough so that missing the defective ones can change a first-rate performance into a mediocre score. For at least two reasons—test secrecy and use of multiple-choice questions—the proportion of defective questions is unlikely to go down in the future.

Aside from the content of the tests, there is the fact that some children are intimidated by the testing procedures—vastly different from ordinary classroom activity—and perform poorly.

"Keep quiet. Sit with an empty row of desks between you and your neighbor. Listen hard to the instructions. Don't mind the teacher stalking up and down between the rows during the test. Remember how much your future depends on your score—but don't be nervous. Imagine what your folks will say if you land in a low percentile. If you tighten up under pressure, you are in real trouble. Hurry. Stay calm. Hurry. Stay calm."

There are many stories of children breaking down during a test or being physically ill the night before. But life is full of trials and fears; why should we protect children? Because they are children; because we want to find out, for example, how well they are learning rather than how well they stand stress, and because those children already hobbled by insecurity, past failure or discrimination will be the most vulnerable in a vicious cycle.

Once the tests are administered and scored, the purpose to which the results are put—comparing children using numbers—is of no use.

Every person is complicated, everyone has unique skills and difficulties. But each test score reduces the pattern of a child's strengths and weaknesses to a single number. Why? To compare the child with others around the country. Why? To tell if the schools are doing their job. But the single numbers and averages carry no hints about how to improve either the schools or individual children.

Healthy competition encourages excellence. But competition in standardized tests encourages intellectual narrowness and triviality.

Society does need to measure people's achievement and school performance, and could do so in much better ways. Imagine school tests set up like the test for a driver's license, each test matched to the skills under test and each child doing "well enough" or not, with a chance for those who did not to try again later. In judging a school, attention would focus on the fractions of its children who passed various tests at various ages.

Your children's future depends in part on tests you are not allowed to see. There is growing expert opinion that this violates your rights and those of your children. It also puts the test publishers beyond public criticism—and that's one reason the tests remain so bad.

The publishers say that the tests must be secret so children cannot prepare for them. But if the tests were good, preparing for them would be a fine idea. Everyone knows the range of questions that will be on the driver's license tests, and by practicing and preparing for them, it is possible to become a better driver. Children could become better thinkers in much the same way if they were given good, open tests.

In the past we developed an unjustified faith in numbers, and then in computers. Objectivity and statistical analysis became major virtues; automatic data analysis often replaced thoughtful evaluation. Now we are learning that numbers can misrepresent children and can lead to wrong decisions about their lives. There can be no true objectivity in a heterogeneous society, and all data analysis is subject to the GIGO principle: garbage in, garbage out.

The task is to find out how well children are learning. The present standardized multiple-choice achievement tests are doing it badly, sometimes destructively. There are better ways to find out, without compressing children into uniform molds that misrepresent their accomplishments.

FOR FURTHER READING

The title of this chapter echoes the title of a short book by English philosopher John Wilson, *Thinking With Concepts* (Cambridge: Cambridge University Press, 1963). It was written for the British equivalent of American high school seniors, who face a college entrance examination asking them to write extended analytic essays.

The model of analysis presented here is adopted from Stephen Toulmin's *The Uses of Argument* (Cambridge: Cambridge University Press, 1958). It is presented, in more detail, in texts such as Douglas Ehninger, *Influence, Belief, and Argument* (Glenview, Ill.: Scott, Foresman, 1974), John O. White, *Legal Reasoning: The Strategy of Persuasion* (New York: St. Martin's, 1976), and Stephen Toulmin, Richard Rieke, and Allan Janik, *An Introduction to Reasoning* (New York: Macmillan, 1979).

There are many popular books on logical thinking. Monroe C. Beardsley's *Writing with Reason* (Englewood Cliffs, N.J.: Prentice-Hall, 1976) is specifically directed at writers. Howard Kahane's *Logic and Contemporary Rhetoric* (Belmont, Cal.: Wadsworth, 1971) offers examples from politics and the popular media. Ronald Munson's *The Way of Words* (Boston: Houghton Mifflin, 1976) is studded with entertaining problems.

NOTES

1. Robert P. Abelson, "The Structure of Belief Systems," in *Computer Models of Thought and Language,* ed. Roger C. Shank and Kenneth Mark Colby (San Francisco: W. H. Freeman, 1973), pp. 287–339.
2. Ronald Munson, *The Way of Words* (Boston: Houghton Mifflin, 1976), p. 277.

16

The Common Places of Invention

> In the first place a man must know the truth about any subject that he deals with, either in speech or writing; he must be able to define it generically, and having defined it to divide it into its various specific kinds until he reaches the limit of divisibility.
>
> PLATO

Every subject-matter has its own ways of going about things. There are secrets about changing fuses, hints on strategy in parchesi, and preferred ways of solving quadratic equations. Rhetoric as such isn't concerned with these special methods; it's concerned instead with "universal" methods of invention, those that can be applied to more than one field, those that deal with writing problems in general. For example, one good strategy for a parchesi player is, "Watch what the other guy is doing." If we make that strategy more general, we come up with useful rhetorical principles: "Examine the arguments available to your opponent"; or "Examine the possibility of rebutting your argument," a strategy built into the model of analysis presented in the last chapter; or "Be aware of your audience," a strategy built into the rhetorical triangle of chapter Two.

Similarly, changing fuses and solving quadratic equations share a general strategy, "proceed with a plan," that's also a good idea for parchesi players. The householder who replaces fuses at random, the math student who attacks a quadratic equation without a sense of order, the parchesi player who moves without purpose—all these lack a strategy to guide their behavior.

A good word for such a guiding strategy is the Greek word *heuristic,* borrowed from the Greek *heuriskein,* "to find." Perhaps the easiest way to master the word is to connect it with *Eureka!*—"I have found it!"— shouted when gold was discovered in California and now the motto of the state. A heuristic, then, is a guiding strategy, a plan for discovery. In this chapter and the next we offer a *heuristic for invention*—a guiding strategy to help writers come up with better ideas for writing. (You may want to re-read the section "On Reading this Unit" on pages 494–495.)

The Greeks had a visual image for the process of invention. They spoke of the *topoi* or "topics" of invention, and they visualized them literally as "places" of invention. Thus they pictured the writer or speaker as walking mentally from one "place" of invention to another, examining each possible argument or idea. This literal sense of the word survives in our word *commonplace,* so that the original meaning of the expression, "a commonplace argument"—now quite negative in connotation—was simply "an argument developed from one of the common places." We've resurrected the original sense of the word in our chapter title, for we'll stroll mentally through four common "places" to look for ideas: definition, classification, illustration, and comparison and contrast.[1]

DEFINITION

A definition can be as short as a word or phrase, explaining a term or a name for the reader.

> **16.1** Horus, *God of the sun,* had as his symbol the human eye.
>
> Hector Chevigny and Sydell Braverman,
> *The Adjustment of the Blind*

Such passing definitions are only a courtesy for the reader; here we're concerned with a more expansive or formative sense of *definition,* with definition as a mode of discovery.

Let's begin with two negative examples. First, the "loaded" definition, one that closes off argument:

> **16.2** When the Supreme Court knocked out state anti-abortion laws six years ago, it made legal killing the nation's most common form of surgery.
>
> Robert Webb, *Cincinnati Enquirer*

The definition implied here—that abortion is "legalized murder"—carries with it its own judgment. Indeed, most arguments about abortion, for and against, show what we would call the "heuristic value" of definition, for they center on one's definition of the term.

A second negative example of definition is the subjective definition, so personal that it makes communication impossible. A classic example is the logic of Humpty-Dumpty in Lewis Carroll's *Through the Looking-Glass,* who claims the right to control the meaning of words:

> **16.3** "There's glory for you."
>
> "I don't know what you mean by 'glory,' " said Alice.
>
> Humpty-Dumpty smiled contemptuously. "Of course you don't—till I tell you. I meant 'there's a nice knock-down argument for you!' "
>
> "But 'glory' doesn't mean 'a nice knock-down argument,' " Alice objected.
>
> "When *I* use a word," Humpty-Dumpty said, in a rather scornful tone, "it means just what I choose it to mean—neither more nor less."
>
> "The question is," said Alice, "whether you *can* make words mean so many different things."

Positive Uses of Definition

Definition serves a fundamental role in courts of law. The final backing of any legal argument is the law itself, an attempt at a fully explicit definition:

> **16.4** Robbery is a crime that consists of the taking of personal property from the possession of another person, through the use of fear or force, against said person's will or desire, without said person's permission, and without full and adequate recompense.

A legal definition provides a standard of judgment, criteria that can be applied, one by one, to a given crime: Was personal property taken? Was fear or force used? and so on.

The weakness of a legal definition—aside from the dullness that grows out of full, impersonal explicitness—is that its key terms are "contestable," so that a defense attorney might focus on an element of the definition to make his case—on "full and adequate recompense," for example. Legal arguments are essentially arguments about definition. Indeed, we write this more than twenty-five years after the Supreme Court, in the case of Brown versus the Topeka Board of Education in 1954, ruled that separate education facilities for blacks were illegal, and ordered the integration of public schools "with all due speed." Cases over school integration still crowd the courts, usually centering on the meaning of the short phrase, "with all due speed."

A legal definition is a formal definition, most commonly called an *Aristotelian definition.* A word or concept is placed in a general class ("robbery is a crime") and then distinguished from other members of that class by one or more differences ("that consists of . . .").

16.5   The roadrunner is a cuckoo that runs on the ground.

An Aristotelian definition can be expanded by elaborating the differences; such elaboration might be the "formative idea" of an essay, just as a prosecuting attorney might build a case around the defining features of a robbery.

Less formally, definitions can be made by example, by pointing to an object. We do this commonly for children—pointing to an object and naming it. The joke is an old one, but it's a good example of defining a difficult term by example:

16.6   He chopped up his mother and father with a hatchet, and then asked the judge for mercy, on the grounds that he was an orphan. That's *chutzpah.*

Definitions by example are of the "happiness is a warm puppy" kind—the example won't tell you the full meaning of the term unless the examples are multiplied:

16.7   We received a letter from the Writers' War Board the other day asking for a statement on "The Meaning of Democracy." It presumably is our duty to comply with such a request, and it is certainly our pleasure.

Surely the Board knows what democracy is. It is the line that forms on the right. It is the don't in Don't Shove. It is the hole in the stuffed shirt through which the sawdust slowly trickles; it is the dent in the high hat. Democracy is the recurrent suspicion that more than half of the people are right more than half of the time. It is the feeling of privacy in the voting booths, the feeling of communion in the libraries, the feeling of vitality everywhere. Democracy is the score at the beginning of the ninth. It is an idea which hasn't been disproved yet, a song the words of which have not gone bad. It's the mustard on the hot dog and the cream in the rationed coffee. Democracy is a request from a War Board, in the middle of a morning in the middle of a war, wanting to know what democracy is.

E. B. White, *The Wild Flag* (1943)

Another form of definition tells how something works rather than what it is, thus an *operational definition*. Here is an operational definition of a roadrunner:

16.8 He doesn't need to fly because he can run faster. He kicks dirt in a snake's face, and then eats the snake. He chases lizards, and watches hawks with one eye.

George E. Hollister, *National Wildlife*

Operational definitions are useful ways of expanding formal definitions, but they have limits in themselves. Government spokesmen in the 1960s and 1970s, for example, defended our involvement in South Vietnam by claiming that we were defending democracy in Southeast Asia. Pressed for evidence, they replied, in effect, "Of course South Vietnam is a democracy; they have regular elections." Regular elections are an operational feature of democracies, but not a defining feature—particularly when opposition parties are banned or controlled.

Finally, a definition may give a special meaning to a word, thus a *stipulative definition*, that "stipulates" a new meaning. Often this means giving a special meaning to a common term.

16.9 A *Game* is an ongoing series of complementary ulterior transactions progressing to a well-defined, predictable outcome. Descriptively it is a recurring set of transactions, often repetitious, superficially plausible, with a concealed motivation; or more colloquially, a series of movements with a snare, or "gimmick."

Eric Berne, *Games People Play*

Eric Berne "stipulates" a new meaning for the word *game*, allowing him to view relations between people as the "games people play."

A Heuristic for Definition

Definition is a master "place" of invention, for it accumulates example, classification, and contrast. Our heuristic for definition asks you to question a topic or concept in terms of how it changes, how it occurs, and where it occurs. In other words, question in terms of *change, sequence,* and *context* (we label the potential topic as X):

16.10 A heuristic for definition. What is X? More precisely, how do I define X in terms of *change, sequence,* and *context?*

Change: How and in what ways can X change? When does it become something different? What was X in the past (months ago, years ago)? What is it likely to become in the future? What could it become? What couldn't it become?

Sequence: When does X occur? What happens before it? Why does X occur? What causes, prompts, or motivates it? What does X cause, prompt, or motivate? If X were the case, then. . . ? What would be true if. . . ?

Context: Where is X typically found? Where is it unlikely to be found? Would putting it in a new setting influence my understanding of it? What is X's relation to its surroundings? Does it fit in? Is it appropriate or consistent with the things that surround it?

Problem One. Definition as discovery We'll ask you to work with our developing heuristic in three ways: as a way to develop responses to essay questions, as a way of responding to reading concepts, and as a way of dealing with objects. You may respond to these tasks in any way suggested by your instructor—by free writing, by taping a small-group discussion, or by writing out short answers to the questions that seem most "formative."

a. Return to the essay questions offered in the previous chapter, in problem two, page 499—on literacy exams, advertising, and capital punishment. Treat each as a question of definition, and use the heuristic of 16.10 to generate ideas for answering the question.

b. Choose one of the following concepts as the focus for a possible essay in definition. Use the heuristic of 16.10 to generate ideas for writing. Possible concepts: wealth, prejudice, worthwhile courses, democracy, freedom, shyness, writing.

c. Choose one of the following objects as the focus for a possible essay in definition. Use the heuristic of 16.10 to generate ideas for writing. Possible objects: a telephone, an eye, a blank sheet of paper, a leaf, an ashtray, a candlestick holder. ■

Here are some responses to the tasks of problem one. One student used the notion of "sequence" to gain a new perspective for an essay opposing literacy exams:

16.11 Once I saw that the test was penalizing the students for what had to been seen as the failure of schools and teachers, I began to get a focus for my argument.

Two professional writers approach much the same topic by means of the notion of "change," arguing that the word "literacy" has taken on a different meaning than it had in the past:

16.12 We think that this nation perceives itself as having an unacceptable literacy level because it is applying a criterion that requires, at a minimum, the reading of new material and the gleaning of new information from that material. We shall argue in this paper that this high literacy standard is a relatively recent one as applied to the population at large and that much of our present difficulty in meeting the literacy standard we are setting for ourselves can be attributed to the relatively rapid extension to large populations of educational criteria that were once applied to only a limited elite.

Daniel P. and Lauren B. Resnick,
"The Nature of Literacy"

The logic of this argument from definition has a strong force: The authors show that "literacy," in the nineteenth century, meant merely the ability to sound out the words of the Bible, regardless of comprehension, and they conclude, therefore, that the "back to basics" movement is unlikely to achieve the goals of current literacy.

Two other writers turn to the notion of "context," and explore the meaning of "literacy" to the Athabaskans of central Alaska, where cultural norms restrict self-display:

16.13 To an Athabaskan, to acquire English essayist literacy is to become smug, boastful, talkative, and arrogant.

Ron and Suzanne B.K. Scollon,
"Literacy as Interethnic Communication"

Two student writers, taping a conversation about "feminism," talk themselves into a surprising approach to a definition:

16.14 **A:** "Let's see . . . change. How has feminism changed?"
B: "Well, it's changed over time . . . in what it tried to do. You know, they were campaigning for the vote back before, and now it's things like abortion and ERA."
A: "What's it likely to become?"
B: "I don't know . . . it could just disappear, I guess, like if women achieved all their rights."
A: "What couldn't it become?"
B: "Well, I don't think it could become something negative, you know, something that put men down . . . like a negative movement."
A: "What about context?"
B: "No . . . let's go back to 'change.' I think the point is—the argument is—that feminism doesn't merely help women. The point is that, if we really got ourselves together on the thing, that fem-

inism would benefit men too, 'cause we'd get rid of all the stereotypes and stuff . . ."

A: "Men ought to be feminists?"

B: "I guess that's the point. . . . Let's see, I could start out by
showing that the goals of the feminist movement have been becoming more and more general, and then I could. . . ."

Here, a heuristic works precisely as it should work, not as a lock-step
procedure, but as a way of guiding the writer systematically toward a
controlling purpose.

CLASSIFICATION

Classification (or often, *division*) means to sort things into groups—"last
names beginning with A to H in this line, the rest in that line." As such,
it seems rather cut-and-dried, rather mechanical. But classification, as
the next problem will suggest, is a powerful, even formative, "place"
for learning.

Problem Two. Experiments in classification   Here are two experiments
in psychology. You are asked to predict the results.

a. In the first experiment, people were divided into three groups,
and each person was given a set of fifty-two cards, each with a
word on it. People in group one were asked to remember as many
words as they could. People in group two were asked to sort the
words into piles—that is, to classify them. People in group three
were asked both to sort the words and to remember them. Each
group was given the same amount of time to examine the cards,
and then each group was asked to remember as many of the cards
as they could. Which group or groups did the best?

b. In a second experiment, people were given thirty cards, each
with a word on it, and they were asked to memorize the words.
They were watched as they went about this task, and they were
classified into two groups: people who alphabetized the cards to
help them remember, and people who sorted the cards into groups
to help them remember. Both groups were tested immediately after
looking at the cards and then again six days later. Which group
did better on each test?   ■

Classification has been a formative principle for use at several points
in this text, most obviously in chapter Eleven, when we explained the
level of abstraction of words by using a simple classification like that of
Figure 16.1.

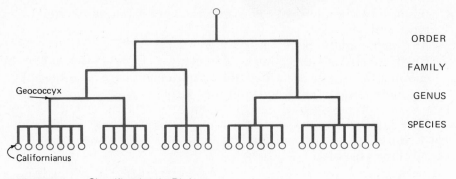

FIGURE 16.1   Classification in Biology

Biology students among our readers will recognize the figure as a simple form of Linnean classification: In biology, all species are arranged in a descending order of generalization, and all animals are named, or classified, by specifying their general class and their specific species:

16.15   Roadrunner: *Geococcyx californianus*

Such a system has a heuristic value to the biologist who finds a new species, for it must be classified, or named, within the system. The periodic table of the chemical elements serves much the same heuristic function in physics—indeed, some elements have been discovered by positing "holes" in the chart.

Classification has this sort of formative value for learners as well. Knowledge that is classified, tagged with a label, is easier to retain. In the first experiment of problem two, for example, people told to memorize the words did less well at remembering than did the other two groups. But the second and third groups—those told to classify and those told to classify *and* remember—did equally well.[2] In the second experiment, which divided people into alphabetizers and classifiers, both groups did equally well on the immediate test of memory, but classifiers remembered twice as many words when they were examined six days later.[3]

Remembering something, we might conclude, means to classify it. In an alphabetized list, a "B" word, *boat,* gives no clue to a "C" word. In a list classified as "things that float," a word like *boat* generates a long list—*canoe, battleship, yacht, rubber ducky,* and so on. A heuristic for classifying asks how things fit together.

16.16   A heuristic for classification. In what ways is X similar to things I know? What does it resemble or remind me of? Is X an instance or example of a larger class of things? How can I label X? How can I group it with other things?

Problem Three. Classification as discovery Return to the topics of problem one and choose one essay question, one concept, and one object. See what ideas or approaches you can generate using the classification as a "place" of invention, asking the questions of 16.16. Report your findings in the form recommended by your instructor. ■

One student, applying classification as a "place" of invention to our question about literacy tests, came up with the formative principle of an essay.

16.17 There are basically two kinds of tests, legitimate tests and illegitimate tests. Legitimate tests perform a necessary screening for society; they test skills that need to be tested. A driver's examination or a lawyer's bar examination or the test given to airline pilots are examples of legitimate tests. Illegitimate tests are unnecessary and often dishonest. The "voter's tests" often used, in the past, to discriminate against black voters is a good example of an illegitimate test. There are many reasons for thinking that a high school literacy exam would be more like an illegitimate test than like a legitimate one.

Another student generated a piece of free writing examining different possible ways of classifying the object "telephone":

16.18 Voices that come into your home. Things that talk to you. Things that ring or buzz. Things that communicate. It's like a bomb, it's like a box, it's like a piece of furniture, it's like a friend. It's an instance or example of modern technology, of invasion of privacy, of interference, of interruptions, of friendship. I can label it a nuisance, a monopoly, a necessity, a hindrance, can't write. I can label it phone, voice box, talking machine, voice transmitter. Now they can type. I'll group it with appliances, nuisances, necessities, gimmicks, and devices for advertising.

There's no "formative idea" that emerges from that hurried catalog. What does emerge is a rather uncomfortable double feeling about the telephone, a feeling the writer sharpened by visiting the next "places" of invention and expanded into a short theme, "The Telephone: A Necessary Nuisance."

Classification seems most formative with marginal cases. Thus, scientists search out experiments that don't confirm accepted theories, because they're much more likely to lead to changes in theory. And the developing writer who classifies college students without considering, say, older people returning to college, night students, and veterans, has missed a chance to turn a boring topic into an interesting one.

Problem Four. An exercise in classification   Here's an interesting problem in classification, designed to focus on "reasons for" classifying. The proverbs listed below were written by either of two writers, Benjamin Franklin or William Blake. Here is a sample proverb by Benjamin Franklin:

■ "Early to bed, early to rise, makes a man healthy, wealthy, and wise."

And here is a sample proverb by William Blake:

■ "The tygers of wrath are wiser than the horses of instruction."

Now sort the proverbs into two piles, a pile labeled "proverbs by Benjamin Franklin" and a pile labeled "proverbs by William Blake." As you do, try to develop the principles of classification that explain your choices. Write up your findings as your instructor directs.

a. A Robin Red Breast in a Cage
Puts all Heaven in a Rage.

b. Sooner murder an infant in its cradle than nurse unacted desires.

c. Eat not to fulness; drink not to elevation.

d. He who desires but acts not, breeds pestilence.

e. Dip him in the river who loves water.

f. Avoid extremes, forbear resisting injuries as much as you think they deserve.

g. Speak not but what may benefit others or yourself; avoid trifling conversation.

h. Always be ready to speak your mind, and a base man will avoid you.

i. The road of excess leads to the palace of wisdom.

j. Let all your things have their places; let each part of your business have its time.

k. Lose no time, be always employed in something useful; cut off all unnecessary action.

l. Rarely use venery but for health and offspring, never to dullness, weakness, or the injury of your own or another's reputation. (Hint: *venery::Venus*)

m. The hours of folly are measur'd by the clock, but of wisdom: no clock can measure.

n. Prudence is an ugly old maid courted by Incapacity.

o. Resolve to perform what you ought; perform without fail what you resolve.   ■

ILLUSTRATION

Illustration gives meaning to concepts, judgments, or generalizations by showing an example:

16.19 "Look—out the window—there's a roadrunner."

Illustrations are a tool for clarifying—so important a tool that, in this text, we have set off and numbered examples that illustrate. A carefully chosen illustration can test, even destroy, a claim—as in the following example, testing the claim that writing must be elegant.

16.20 Finally, according to the Rhetorics, good writing must be elegant (or beautiful, as some of them have it). Let me apply this test to a sentence in *What Price Glory?* There is a passage in which shell-shocked Lieutenant Moore, driven to hysteria by what he has seen and done, lets himself go in an effort to say what he thinks about the war. He had wondered, as his companions must often have wondered, what irony of fate it was that placed *them* in the trenches, while millions of people were safe at home, eating good food, sleeping in soft beds, and valiantly fighting the war from arm chairs. Why were they not all in the trenches too? And now, as he shouts his incoherent denunciation of the war, the injustice of this fact strikes him with unendurable force, and he ends his tirade with a devastating indictment of the whole bloody business: "God damn every son of a bitch in the world who isn't here!" This is clear, it is past all doubt forceful; but is it elegant? The professors of Rhetoric who taught me would not, I feel sure, have thought so. But all I can say is that if all good writing must be elegant, then this is elegant; for no one will persuade me that so true and effective an expression of a profound and genuine emotion is not good writing.

Carl L. Becker, "The Art of Writing"

In 16.20, Carl Becker focuses on the context of his quote, to justify his attack on "elegance," a much-valued concept in rhetoric texts of a generation or two ago.

Thus the writer needs to be aware of the variety of uses of illustration.

16.21   *Test Cases.*   "Dapper George entered the bank with a sawed-off shotgun, ordered everyone to the floor, and took $18,000 from the cashiers' drawers. If that isn't robbery, I don't know what is."

16.22   *Contrary Cases.*   "The little old lady took the handbag away from Dapper George. He chased her and took his handbag back. Clearly, he's not guilty of robbery."

16.23   *Related Cases.*   "Certainly it's justified to punish the person who bilks old people of their life savings by fraudulent insurance schemes. Isn't this the same kind of crime?"

16.24   *Borderline Cases.*   "We would admit that the poor man who steals a loaf of bread to feed his starving children—steals from the company store that offers stale bread at inflated prices—is only technically guilty of robbery. The real crime is the social pressure which forces such an action."

Our heuristic for illustration centers on the notion of *focus;* it asks you to visualize illustration as if you were focusing with the lens of a camera:

16.25   A heuristic for illustration. What is an example of X? How many times can I change the focus—that is, attend to different details or facets of a topic—so as to get the most complete understanding of the topic?

Problem Five. Illustration as discovery   Return to the topics of problem one and choose one essay question, one concept, and one object. See what ideas and approaches you can generate using "illustration" as a "place" of invention. Pay particular attention to the shifting of focus as a device for illustration.   ■

Illustration, as a "place" of invention, provides a way of making concepts or arguments specific. In chapter One we quoted from a book by James Agee, in essence a close examination of the life of one family of southern white sharecroppers, the Grudgers. The book bears the surprising title *Let Us Now Praise Famous Men,* and the argument is a "test case"—to see if the Grudgers are famous men (and women). . . . Studs Terkel's *Working,* cited in the last chapter, is a series of taped interviews with a cross-section of workers; the examples become, in themselves, an analysis of work in American society. A student writes about his process of rewriting a paper, shifting from general to specific.

16.26 I wanted to deal with the special nature of golf as a sport. I wrote, through several drafts, at a pretty general level, about why strength and reflexes weren't particularly important, and thus, why many golfers don't hit their prime until middle age. It was all pretty boring, particularly if you're not interested in golf. Finally I just shifted to examples. I wrote several paragraphs about Arnold Palmer's career, and I wrote several paragraphs about Johnny Miller's career. When I had written the specifics, I cut the general stuff in half. The examples made the points better.

COMPARISON AND CONTRAST

Comparison and contrast is a formal way of setting out likenesses and differences. It can be organized as a chunk of comparison and a chunk of contrast:

16.27 The roadrunner shares the general characteristics of the cuckoo family. Members of the cuckoo family generally inhabit temperate regions; their diet is commonly caterpillars and other insects; and they are slender and long-tailed.

The roadrunner, however, differs from other members of the cuckoo family in several respects. It runs on the ground, and thus its feet are larger and its diet more varied. Roadrunners are heavily streaked in color, in contrast to the solid colors of other cuckoos, and their wings display a white crescent in flight.

An alternate method of organization is to interweave likeness and difference:

16.28 Like other cuckoos, roadrunners inhabit temperate regions, but the roadrunner, as a distinct species, is limited to the American southwest, specifically to Arizona, California, and northern Mexico. . . .

As a "place" of invention, comparison and contrast asks the writer to search out standards. Indeed, some topics seem to demand a clear contrast: One cannot explore the position of women in our society, for example, without some point of reference, perhaps reference to the position of men or reference to the position of women in other societies.

16.29 Why is it when a man buys a suit, his alterations come free, but when a woman buys an outfit of equal or more value, she pays extra?

Erma Bombeck, *I Lost Everything
in the Post-Natal Depression*

Our heuristic for comparison and contrast is given in 16.30:

16.30 A heuristic for comparison and contrast. In what way is X like or different from other things I know? In what ways is X different from what I hoped/expected/feared? What are my feelings or thoughts about X? How do they differ from my feelings or thoughts about Y? How might my feelings/thoughts about X differ from those of other people?

Comparison and contrast might be triggered, as a "place" of invention, by an assignment—an essay assignment in geography, for example:

16.31 Compare and contrast the wet tropics and the wet-dry tropics.

Or it can be triggered by searching for a standard of judgment:

16.32 The Diplomat coupe, built on the same platform as the smaller Aspen series, with transverse torsion bars in front and longitudinal leaf springs in the rear, has a smart, crisp look about it that separates it completely from its bland little brother Aspen and is a big departure from the original Diplomat styling. . . . Overall, the new Diplomat delivered on its promises of 6-passenger capacity, economy and—something the Diplomat never had before—eye-catching style.

Chuck Nerpel, Motor Trend

Here, this automotive review is informed by two comparisons, with the general Aspen series and with the previous Diplomat.

Finally, here is a student writer, free writing, on a blank sheet of paper, about a blank sheet of paper.

6.33 A blank sheet of paper shares qualities with many other things—an empty glass, a paper plate, an ash tray, a trash can. All are objects to be filled. It differs from these objects, however, in that it is to be filled with words. Like these. Trash cans and glasses are full when they are filled to the top. Blank sheets of paper work the other way. They are full when they are filled with words at the bottom. Trash cans and ash trays are washed when they are full; paper plates are thrown away. Sheets of paper filled with words are sometimes thrown away, but they are seldom washed (except when recycled to create more blank sheets of paper). When filled with words, a blank sheet of paper talks to a reader. Empty, a blank

Definition:	*Change:* How and in what ways can X change? When does it become something different? What was X in the past (months ago, years ago)? What is it likely to become in the future? What could it become? What couldn't it become? *Sequence:* When does X occur? What happens before it? Why does X occur? What causes, prompts, or motivates it? What does X cause, prompt, or motivate? If X were the case, then . . . ? What would be true if . . . ? *Context:* Where is X typically found? Where is it unlikely to be found? Would putting it in a new setting influence my understanding of it? What is X's relation to its surroundings? Does it fit in? Is it appropriate or consistent with the things that surround it?
Classification:	In what ways is X similar to things I know? What does it resemble or remind me of? Is X an instance or example of a larger class of things? How can I label X? How can I group it with other things?
Illustration:	What is an example of X? How many times can I change the focus— that is, attend to different details or facets of a topic—so as to get the most complete understanding of the topic?
Comparison and Contrast:	In what way is X like or different from other things I know? In what ways is X different from what I hoped/expected/feared? What are my feelings or thoughts about X? How do they differ from my feelings and thoughts about Y? How might my feelings/thoughts about X differ from those of other people?

FIGURE 16.2 The Common "Places" of Invention

sheet of paper has no voice. It says nothing. Sometimes I am frightened by blank sheets of paper. I stare at them. Other times I welcome them (aha, another blank sheet of paper to battle with).

This isn't finished writing, of course. But it is, at the very least, inventive writing.

More formally, comparison and contrast as a place of invention should have two characteristics.

■ The comparison should be fair and reasonable. It is quite fair to compare the cultural opportunities in Cincinnati with those in Cleveland, but quite unfair to compare those in Cleveland with those in New York, a much larger city. Of course, a more general issue might make a comparison possible—if one were, for example, comparing the "quality of life" in New York and Cleveland—but that would in turn demand that other features be compared. Similarly, it would seem as unfair to argue that community colleges are "better" than four-year universities because they have vocational training programs as it would be to argue that universities are "better" because they have graduate programs.

■ The comparison should be illuminating. It should provide the reader with evidence, standards of judgment, and conclusions that could not have been set out as well in another way.

SUMMARY

Instead of a summary, we reprint the first stage of our heuristic, "the common 'places' of invention," as Figure 16.2. It offers, in essence, the suggestions of this chapter.

IMPLICATIONS FOR THE WRITER

At various points, we've recommended that the student experiment with generating ideas from a heuristic. We'd like to explore that process again, this time in rather practical terms. We list, in the examples below, some actual writing assignments given out in various college departments.

16.34 Write a four-page review of Jane Addams's *Twenty Years at Hull-House* [a social worker's autobiography, covering the years 1889–1909, used as a supplementary text]. Discuss her awareness of the social issues of the period, and evaluate her historical judgments. (American history)

16.35 Discuss the advantages and disadvantages of computer models of human thought. (psychology final examination)

16.36 Each student will submit a review paper, summarizing present research in a well-defined area of biology. The topic must be approved in advance. The paper, of six to ten pages, should include at least eight references to current research. Consider your audience to be classmates, unfamiliar with the specifics of your topic. (biology)

16.37 Describe a small group to which you belong, considering the group's norms, values, subcultural features, role stratification, and social control techniques. (sociology)

16.38 In what way does the philosophy of Immanuel Kant attempt to solve the problems isolated by David Hume? How successful do you think Kant was in his attempt? (philosophy final examination)

You'll be writing assignments like these, in one form or another, throughout your college career. They vary greatly in their level of generality, the biology and sociology assignments (16.36 and 16.37) rather general, the others more specific. Each assignment deals with the subject matter of the discipline, but the form of the assignment is likely to be repeated from course to course. For example, the sociology assignment—to describe a group in terms of the concepts of sociology—might be repeated as a similar assignment in educational psychology, and the comparison of the philosophy of Hume and Kant (16.38) might be framed as a comparison of the psychology of Freud and Jung in an introductory psychology course.

We're not going to attempt answers to these questions (even we quake at the philosophy of Immanuel Kant). But we would like to explore the degree to which the common "places" of invention provide help for the writer faced with such assignments.

All assignments involve the master "place" of invention, definition. That is explicit in assignment 16.36, involving a "well-defined area" of biology. Indeed, the notions of *change* and *sequence* might provide the "formative idea" for a paper exploring gradual advances in science. Similarly, one might use definition as a help in defining "computer models of human thought" ("What could it become?" "Does it fit in?"), in defining "a small group to which you belong" ("What does X cause, prompt, or motivate?"), and in defining the social views of Jane Addams and the philosophy of Immanuel Kant.

Assignment 16.37, the sociology paper, is given as a classification essay, and it asks the writer to connect her personal experience with topics covered in the textbook—thus, "In what ways is X similar to things I know?" Classification might also provide a "formative idea" for responding to the philosophy assignment:

16.39 Kant provides a successful answer to Hume's concerns about personal identity, but he was less successful in dealing with other issues Hume raised.

Classification might lead to a tidy conclusion to the biology assignment (Are the studies I've examined "an instance or example of a larger class of things"?), and it might prove equally formative in sorting out the social views of Jane Addams.

Illustration, of course, would be formative in all assignments—citing examples to support opinions and judgments, shifting the focus to provide specifics. One student, writing the psychology final examination (16.36), made illustration the formative idea of her answer, arguing for the disadvantages of computer models of human thought by pointing to the specific failure of computers to translate from one language to another, concluding that human thought was more complex than computer models could indicate. (In one experiment, a computer translated a biology article containing the phrase *fruit flies* into Russian, and then translated it back into English as "apples aviate.")

Comparison and contrast would be similarly useful in considering a small group ("How is it different from other groups?"), in evaluating the philosophy of Kant ("What are my feelings or thoughts about X?"), and most obviously, in comparing computer models of human thought with other models of human thought. Less obviously, it might lead to a formative approach to the book review assignment from the history class, for evaluating Jane Addams's historical judgments means, or could mean, finding relevant comparisons to evaluate them with.

These common "places" of invention, then, are ways in which the mind works. By formalizing them as a set of questions, we give you a way of proceeding systematically about the business of finding something to write—a heuristic for invention.

FINAL WRITING ASSIGNMENTS

I. Inventing Arguments   Write a persuasive essay on one of the questions below, using the common "places" of invention, from Figure 16.2, to help uncover the arguments you wish to develop.

A. Are the "social sciences" really sciences in the same sense that the "natural sciences" are?

B. What is the difference between an "invention" and a "discovery"? (*Invention* is used here in the general sense of the word, not in our special sense of "rhetorical invention.")

C. Should the study of foreign languages be required in college?

D. Do television and motion pictures reflect the values of American society, or do they mold and control those values?

E. "A poem is a truth about human experience." Agree or disagree with this definition.

II. Two Experiments in Definition   Several different definitions are provided below for two rather important words, *language* and *grammar*. Choose one of those words, and try to sort out, in an analytic essay, the similar senses of the word and the points of apparent conflict or difference. You'll find this process much more complicated than it sounds— some definitions may be too subjective to use, some may be persuasive; and you'll have to decide whether apparent differences are minor matters of vocabulary or substantive differences in definition.

Some starting hints. With regard to *language*, three possible points of conflict are these: Is language strictly learned behavior or is it, in some sense, innate? Is human language distinct from animal communication, or simply an extension of it? Is language creative? With regard to grammar, we might note that a portion of an essay by linguist W. Nelson Francis is often reprinted with the title "The Three Meanings of Grammar," and we might also refer the reader to our discussion of "knowing how" and "knowing about" in chapter One.

Definitions of *language*.

A. Language is any set or system of linguistic symbols as used in a more or less uniform fashion by a number of people who are thus enabled to communicate intelligibly with one another.

Random House Dictionary

B. Language is a system of arbitrary vocal symbols used for communication.

Ronald Wardhaugh

C. Language is a systematic means of communicating ideas or feelings by the use of conventionalized signs, sounds, gestures, or marks having understood meanings.

Webster's Third New International Dictionary

D. Language is a system of arbitrary, vocal symbols which permit all people in a given culture, or other people who have learned the system of that culture, to communicate or to interact.

M. Finocchiaro

E. Language is the ever-repeating working-out of the spirit.

Wilhelm Von Humboldt

F. The American language is the American language and the English language is the English language.

The New Statesman

G. Language is, first of all, an instrument of communication. It consists of an arbitrary system or pattern of sounds by means of which man imparts to others, and shares with others, his thoughts, emotions, and desires. Inasmuch as language is human and non-instinctive, it is raised above the noises made by animals, birds, and insects. . . .

Simon Potter, *Language in the Modern World*

H. Language is a perpetual Orphic Song
Which rules with Daedal harmony a throng
Of thoughts and forms, which else senseless and shapeless were.

Percy Bysshe Shelley, *Prometheus Unbound*

I. Language is a purely human and non-instinctive method of communicating ideas, emotions, and desires by means of a system of voluntarily produced symbols. These symbols are, in the first instance, auditory and they are produced by the so-called "organs of speech."

Edward Sapir

Definitions of *grammar*

A. An adequately formulated *grammar* of a language *is,* in fact, a theory of that language.

Lyle E. LaPalombara

B. This protest against traditional usage and the rules of grammar is merely another manifestation of the unfortunate trend of the times to lawlessness in every direction. . . . Quite as important as keeping undesirables out of the vocabulary is the maintaining of respect for the rules of grammar, which govern the formation of words into phrases and sentences.

Detroit Free Press

C. English Grammar is the art of speaking and writing the English Language correctly.

Gould Brown (1858)

D. The grammar of any tongue is a collection of observations on the structure of it, and a system of rules for the proper use of it.

Joseph Priestly (1772)

E. Grammar, then, is structure; the observation of what people do when they use English words in discourse. Grammar, as here defined, makes no choices, expresses no preferences, takes no sides, creates no standards.

Robert C. Pooley

F. Grammar may be defined as the study of how a language "works"—a study of how the structural system of a language combines with a vocabulary to convey meaning.

Edward P. J. Corbett

G. We can use the term *grammar of a language* ambiguously, as referring not only to the speaker's internalized subconscious knowledge but to the professional linguist's representation of this internalized and intuitive system of rules as well.

Noam Chomsky

H. "I don't want to talk grammar. I want to talk like a lady."

Eliza Doolittle, in G. B. Shaw's *Pygmalion* (1900)

I. Grammar teaches the Art of expressing and communicating our thoughts with verbal propriety.

Caleb Alexander (1792)

FOR FURTHER READING

A fuller treatment of the classical "places" of invention is available in Edward P. J. Corbett's *Classical Rhetoric for the Modern Student,* 2nd ed. (New York: Oxford University Press, 1971), and a popular book on the notion of a "mental walk" is Herbert F. Crovitz's *Galton's Walk: Methods for the Analysis of Thinking, Intelligence, and Creativity* (New York: Harper & Row, 1970).

NOTES

1. Our heuristic is adapted from Lee Odell, "Discovery Through Questioning," *English Record,* 27 (1976), 78–86.
2. George Mandler, "Organization and Memory," in *The Psychology of Learning and Motivation,* ed. Kenneth W. Spence and Janet T. Spence (New York: Academic Press, 1967).
3. Susan P. Lueck, George A. Cicala, and John P. McLaughlin, "Spontaneous Categorizers Retain More than Spontaneous Alphabetizers," *Memory and Cognition,* 4 (1976), 476–82.

The Special Places of Invention

The first act of a teacher is to introduce the idea that the world we think we see is only a view, a description of the world. Every effort of a teacher is geared to prove this point to his apprentice. But accepting it seems to be one of the hardest things we can do; we are complacently caught in our own particular view of the world, which compels us to feel and act as if we knew everything about the world. A teacher, from the very first act he performs, aims at stopping that view.

CARLOS CASTANEDA

Ask not what's inside your head, but what your head's inside of.

WILLIAM H. MACE

The last chapter developed a *heuristic* for writers (a *heuristic* is a systematic way of exploring a topic, a "finding device" for ideas to write about), based on the common "places" of invention, the rational processes of defining, classifying, illustrating, and comparing and contrasting. And you may want to re-read the section "On Reading this Unit" on pages 494–495. In this chapter, we'll explore a heuristic for invention that is based on nonrational processes. A nonrational process is not necessarily an irrational process, of course, and you may find our "strategies for invention" useful in generating ideas for writing.

ASSUMPTIONS ABOUT DISCOVERY

We can begin by offering three assumptions about the general process of creative thinking.

■ First, the creative process is essentially the same regardless of field. That is, poetic creativity and scientific creativity—even rhetorical creativity—all share certain underlying features, a certain common ground, even though the results of that creativity may take quite different forms—a poem or a scientific theory or (would you believe?) a five-hundred-word theme.

■ Second, a useful way to develop creative ability is to exercise it. Thus, this is an activity chapter, studded with games, problems, and paradoxes that may seem, at first, far removed from writing as such. But it's consistently useful to think of the writer as "problem-solver," and the problems we'll examine would seem to have a direct connection with writing problems, whether those problems are large (What do I write?) or small (What do I write next?).

■ Third, this view of writing as "an act of discovery" may demand a fundamental shift from the developing writer, a recognition, to repeat our quotation from Carlos Castaneda, that "the world we think we see is only a view, a description of the world." It's worth beginning, then, with an experiment designed to destroy your confidence in your "description of the world."

Problem One. A confidence-destroying quiz   Identify each of the following statements as *true* or *false*. Label them T for "true," and F for "false." Work quickly.

a. President Grant is buried in Grant's Tomb.

b. Columbus discovered America in 1492.

c. The word *lecture* means reading.

d. The world is round.

e. There is no such thing as a child psychologist.

f. The sun rises in the east and sets in the west.

g. If you call a tail a leg, then a dog has five legs.

h. The zoo has seventy-five creatures, with a total of two hundred legs. It has twenty-five four-legged animals. Therefore, it must also have fifty birds.   ■

As you may have guessed, our confidence-destroying quiz was a series of trick questions, and we hope you've missed them all. Let's examine the correct answers:

■ President Grant is buried in Grant's Tomb. False. Well, of course President Grant *is* buried in Grant's Tomb—but so is Mrs. Grant. And, in technical logic, if a statement is not completely true, it's false.

■ Columbus discovered America in 1492. False. The date of 1492 is the right date for Columbus's visit, but it was hardly a "discovery," except for Europeans. Native Americans had inhabited the continent for thousands of years, and it's possible that others—Danish, Phoenician, or Jewish sailors—may have visited America before Columbus. (A "true" answer, we might argue, reveals an *ethnocentric* attitude—nothing matters but what Europeans do.)

■ The word *lecture* means reading. True—of course it does . . . in French. (You simply assumed the question meant "in English.")

■ The world is round. False. The world is lightly flattened at the poles, and thus departs from true roundness. (You were thinking of "round" as opposed to "flat," but that's a special meaning of *round*.)

■ There is no such thing as a child psychologist. That's true—no child could master the complex training of a psychologist. All psychologists are adults. ("Child psychologist" is ambiguous, meaning either "psychologist who studies children" or "psychologist who is a child." We selected the less likely meaning.) By the way, there is also no such thing as an "animal doctor."

■ The sun rises in the east and sets in the west. False. The sun doesn't "rise" or "set" at all; the earth rotates around it. We've inherited the fossilized metaphors of *sunrise* and *sunset,* but they aren't literally true.

■ If you call a tail a leg, then a dog has five legs. False. Calling a tail a leg doesn't make it one. (Attributed to Abraham Lincoln.)

■ The zoo has seventy-five creatures, with a total of two hundred legs. It has twenty-five four-legged animals. Therefore, it must also have fifty birds. False. This zoo—admittedly not a typical zoo—has twenty-five four-legged animals, forty-nine snakes, and one insect, a centipede.

What's the purpose of this exercise in trickery, double-dealing, and deceit? To suggest that "the writer as problem-solver" may have to go beyond the obvious way of defining a problem. Our next problem presents you with a more troublesome question of "defining a problem."

Problem Two. "Four straight lines" Draw four straight lines (without lifting your pencil or pen from the paper) to cross through all nine circles on page 557.   ■

Problem two proves to be quite difficult for most people. Apparently, people tend to see the problem with built-in limits, as if it were designed as pictured in Figure 17.1.

Many of your mistakes in problem one, as well, came from the same mistake—assuming that ordinary language adequately pictures the world

("the sun rises in the east . . ."), assuming the most obvious meaning of "child psychologist" or that we meant the word *lecture* in English. In each case, you put limits on the problem that weren't really there. The solution to connecting the circles of problem two comes only when one removes the built-in limits around the problem, and sees it in different perspective. The solution—given in Figure 17.2—involves moving outside the limits put around the problem.

FIGURE 17.1   Seeing a Closed Context

Our next problem attempts to force you to go outside of your normal way of defining things by placing them in a totally new setting—placing them on the moon rather than on the earth.

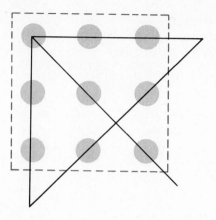

FIGURE 17.2 "Open" Context

Problem Three. Lost on the moon: Thinking in a new context Your spaceship has just crash-landed on the moon. You were scheduled to rendezvous with a mother ship two hundred miles away on the lighted surface of the moon, but the rough landing has ruined your ship and destroyed all the equipment on board, except for the fifteen items listed below.

Your crew's survival depends on reaching the mother ship, so you must choose the most critical items available for the 200-mile trip. Your task is to rank the fifteen items in terms of their importance for survival. Place number one by the most important item, number two by the second most important, and so on through number fifteen, the least important.

_____box of matches
_____food concentrate
_____first-aid kit
_____fifty feet of nylon rope
_____parachute silk
_____solar-powered portable heating unit
_____two .45-caliber pistols
_____one case of dehydrated milk

_____two 100-pound tanks of oxygen
_____stellar map (of the moon's constellation)
_____self-inflating life raft
_____magnetic compass
_____five gallons of water
_____solar-powered FM receiver-transmitter
_____signal flares

You should take the test individually and then join a group of four to seven people to work out a group response. Share your individual solutions and reach a consensus—one ranking for each of the fifteen items that best satisfies all group members. NASA experts have determined the best solution to this task. The answers are given in the answer section at the end of the book. (Adapted from Jay Hall, "Decisions, Decisions, Decisions," *Psychology Today,* November 1971.) ■

The "Lost on the Moon" problem points out how a new context creates new values. A compass is an essential in a "Lost on the Earth" problem; on the moon, with no magnetic field, it's nearly as worthless as a box of matches (the moon has no oxygen to support a fire).

THE MODEL OF THE WORLD IN THE MIND

The first step to creative thinking is to recognize that we do have a "model of the world" in our heads. We see that model developing in the minds of children, as they adapt their verbal categories to correspond to those of the adult world. The word *horsie* might begin as a general term for farm animals, and only later be narrowed to horses—but expanded, on the other hand, to pictures of horses as well as real horses. That developing model of the world may explain why few of us can remember much of life before the age of three or four—one theory holds that the memories are still in our minds, but we can't retrieve them because we no longer code information, or retain it, with the categories of a small child.

A useful word for "the model of the world in the mind" is the Greek word *paradigm*—meaning "pattern" or "model." One use of the word *paradigm* is in the study of foreign languages, where students memorize a single model, such as 17.1:

17.1 *amo,* "I love"; *amas,* "you love"; *amat,* "he, she, or it loves"

This paradigm models the way many verbs work in Latin. Another use of the word *paradigm* is in science, where a particular experiment serves as a model for other experiments. Thus, the experiment becomes *paradigmatic.*

Our use of the word *paradigm* is somewhat more general. We'll suggest that your beliefs, attitudes, and assumptions about the world make a paradigm, a "model of the world in the mind," and we'll ask you, to cite the quotation by William H. Mace used at the beginning of our chapter, to "ask not what's inside your head, but what your head's inside of."

Seeing the World

We can most easily get at what your head's inside of by turning to visual perception. Experimenters have devised hundreds of visual illusions that force us to conclude, to quote psychologist Frank Smith, that "the eyes merely look and the brain sees." Two such visual illusions are given in Figures 17.3 and 17.4. Notice that in both cases, we are forced to see the lines in a way that distorts reality. The lines of 17.3 are parallel; those of 17.4 are of equal length.

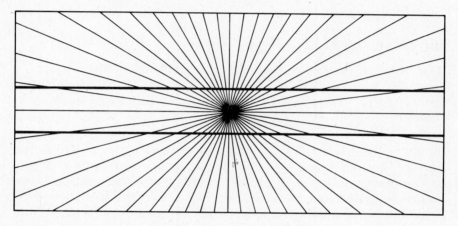

FIGURE 17.3   An Illusion Created by Ewald Hering in 1861

FIGURE 17.4   An Illusion Created by Franz Muller-Lyer in 1889

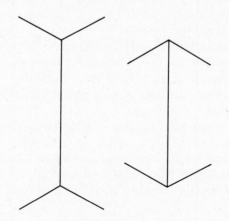

FIGURE 17.5   Reversible Goblet (Introduced by Edgar Rubin in 1915)

Even more interesting are illusions that can be seen in more than one way. Examine, for a moment, the goblet in Figure 17.5. Look at it for a moment, and then, using the narrowest point of the goblet as a reference point, try to see two faces in silhouette. (The narrowest point of the goblet becomes the two noses of the faces.) If you'll look at the illustration, for a few moments, a peculiar effect will occur. It's called "figure-ground reversal." You'll be able to see either the goblet or the faces, but not both at the same time. The best known of such ambiguous figures is the old woman, hunched in her fur coat, shown in Figure 17.6. Glance at the old woman before reading on.

Most of the visual paradoxes we've looked at were developed by psychologists; this one was published as a cartoon, with the title "My Wife and My Mother-in-Law," by W. E. Hill in 1915. If you'll look again, you should be able to see a young woman, her head tilted to your left. (The old woman's mouth is a necklace on the young woman; the young woman's chin is the old woman's nose.)

The curious thing about such paradoxes is that most people find that they must see them as one thing at any point in time; most of us find it impossible to see both the young lady and the old woman at the same time.

Apparently, even simple "seeing" is actually an interpretation. The eye and brain are active interpreters rather than passive receivers. That view is most interestingly shown in cross-cultural studies. We've been told informally that Turkish people shown the old woman/young woman

FIGURE 17.6 "My Wife and My Mother-in-Law"

FIGURE 17.7 Who Is The Man Aiming The Spear At?

tend to see the old woman while Americans tend to see the young woman. The explanation offered is that Turkish people place a high value on age, while our culture values youth. The picture in Figure 17.7 was shown to a number of unskilled African workers with the question, "Who is the man aiming the spear at?" Our answer would be, "Obviously, at the antelope." But the majority of the unskilled workers answered, "The elephant." We have learned to see three dimensions in a two-dimensional drawing; the unskilled workers have not.

The point is not that our perceptions are "correct," while those of the African people tested were "wrong." It's rather that seeing three dimensions of a flat surface is more truly "knowing" three dimensions in two, and therefore seeing it. The picture of an elephant preferred by Western observers is not more truly an elephant than that of the one preferred by unskilled Africans (in Figure 17.8); it's simply a different way of "knowing" *elephant.*

Indeed, one might conclude that multiple ways of seeing might be an effective mode of discovery. What serves well in perception theory serves equally well with concepts. If seeing objects is more properly "knowing" objects, then "seeing" concepts ought to be "knowing" concepts.

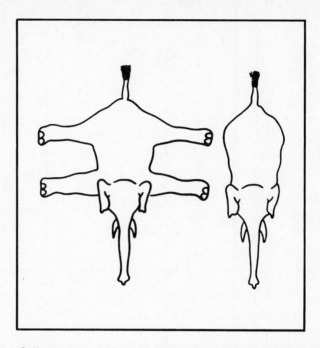

FIGURE 17.8 Split-elephant drawing (*left*) was generally preferred by African children and adults to the top-view perspective drawing (*right*). One person, however, did not like the split drawing because he thought the elephant was jumping around in a dangerous manner.

Problem Four. Knowing baseball   If an anthropologist from Mars were to visit an American sports event, say a baseball game, would it be able to figure out the rules of the game? Let's allow the Martian to watch as many games as it wants; let's assume that the Martian is intelligent; and let's assume that all the games are "normal games"—there are no rained-out games or extra-inning games or games marred with fights, all of which might mislead the Martian.

Think about this problem, and write out your answer in a short paragraph, explaining why the Martian would (or would not) be able to figure out the rules of the game.   ■

Here are two discussions of problems similar to that of the Martian anthropologist above. The first discussion gives an answer more elaborate than the paragraphs of our students, but essentially like them—of course the visitor could figure out the rules of the game:

17.2 Suppose you, as the proverbial visitor from a distant planet, were to land in Yankee Stadium. A baseball game is in progress and, curious about the folkways of earthlings, you follow the action with great attention. At first, the activities seem senseless; you do not understand the reasons for uniforms of two patterns and colors, the crowd of people in the stands, the numbers on the scoreboard, the public-address system, the peculiar behavior of the players. Ignorant of the spoken language, you must rely exclusively on your visual perception of these activities if you are to unravel their meaning. Within a reasonably short period of time, however, you should begin to discern certain regularities. You notice that the men in the dark blue uniforms remain stationary throughout; that the "players" fall into two distinct groups, housed in separate "dugouts"; members of each team alternatively remain each at one place in the field, then take their turns at bat; after about three hours everyone leaves. It would take longer to discern the subtleties of play: the way in which balls and strikes are determined, the rules governing hits, runs, and errors; the system of innings and complete games. And you would have to watch for many months before successfully sorting out the gyrations of the first- and third-base coaches, ground-rule doubles, earned-run averages, pennant races, the unique features of each contest. Eventually, however, given sufficient ingenuity and patience, you should be able to achieve a fairly complete picture of the game, teasing out the merely incidental features (color of uniforms, the seventh-inning stretch, peanut vendors, size of the ball park) from the essential ones (number of men on a team; rules for pinch-hitting; procedure for a double play).

Howard Gardner, The Quest for Mind

Gardner's view is a comforting one, both for the mental powers of his visitor from a distant planet and for our own mental powers. "Given sufficient ingenuity and patience," we'll figure it out. But ingenuity and patience didn't work too well for our confidence-destroying quiz, where we as test-givers could shift the normal meanings of words and the normal use of logic, and ingenuity and patience don't work for illiterate Africans, who have no concept of "seeing three dimensions in two dimensions." And note that Gardner employs a vocabulary that clusters around the concept *game:* If our visitor had no concept of *game,* how could it figure out "uniforms," "players," "runs," and "contest"?

Another writer, John Searle, comes to a more pessimistic conclusion about a problem like that of the Martian anthropologist. Searle separates the world of bare experience, which he calls *brute facts,* from the concepts that give it meaning, which he calls *institutional facts.* A $5 bill, in this view, is simply a piece of paper, usually somewhat rumpled, with green ink on it—a brute fact. But, given the institutional facts of the concept of money, the United States of America, and the Treasury Department, it becomes what we see it as, a $5 bill. For Searle, our Martian observer would not have access to the notion of game, and all it would see would be brute facts. (Searle uses a football game as an example.)

17.3   Let us imagine a group of highly trained observers describing an American football game in statements only of brute facts. What could they say by way of description? Well, within certain areas a good deal could be said, and using statistical techniques certain "laws" could even be formulated. For example, we can imagine that after a time our observers would discover the law of periodical clustering; at statistically regular intervals organisms in like-colored shirts cluster together in a roughly circular fashion (the huddle). Furthermore, at equally regular intervals, circular clustering is followed by linear interpenetration. Such laws would be statistical in character, and none the worse for that. But no matter how much data of this sort we imagine our observers to collect and no matter how many inductive generalizations we imagine them to make from the data, they still have not described American football. What is missing from their description? What is missing are all those concepts which are backed by constitutive rules, concepts such as touchdown, offside, game, points, first down, time out, etc., and consequently what is missing are all the true statements one can make about a football game using those concepts. The missing statements are precisely what describe the phenomenon on the field as a game of football. The other descriptions, the descriptions of the brute facts, can be explained in terms of the institutional facts. But the institutional facts can only be explained in terms of the constitutive rules which underlie them.

John R. Searle, Speech Acts

A HEURISTIC FOR DISCOVERY THINKING

We find Searle's argument more convincing than Gardner's, and it forces us, as we construct a heuristic of discovery thinking, to find ways to explore "what our head's inside of" as well as "what's inside our head."

"Cross-Breeding" Ideas

One "cross-breeds" ideas by taking them out of one context or discipline and putting them in another. One creates something new by combining something old. The invention of bronze, bringing on the "Bronze Age" of early history, came from combining two metals, copper and tin, which had been produced separately for some time. More recently, after Charles Darwin announced his theory of the evolution of the animal kingdom, many scholars in the nineteenth century wanted to find the same pattern of evolution in humankind, creating the assumption commonly called "social Darwinism."

George Eliot's novel *Middlemarch,* called by some one of the six greatest novels in the world, was a piece of writing created by cross-breeding. ("George Eliot," by the way, was the pen name of Mary Ann Evans.) She began the novel in 1869, describing an English village, Middlemarch, but accomplished little for two years. At the end of 1870, she started a different story, "Miss Brooke," noting that she was "experimenting in a story which I began without any serious intention of carrying it out lengthily. It is a subject which has been recorded among my possible themes ever since I began to write fiction, but will probably take new shape in development."

In 1871, the two stories were merged. The character Dorothea Brooke entered the world of *Middlemarch,* and the novel, given the catalyst of cross-breeding, was quickly completed. And notice also that Eliot's phrase, "experimenting in a story," is itself a kind of cross-breeding, bringing the language of science to the writing of fiction. In fact, you'll notice the same principle of cross-breeding at work as we develop our heuristic for discovery, for we will try to cross-breed scientific discovery and artistic discovery to bring them to bear on the writer's problem of invention.

Thus, we turn to a scientific insight achieved by cross-breeding. Alexander Marshack, a journalist, was completing a book on the scientific background of the lunar space program. In April of 1963 he came across a clipping he had filed, without reading, from a 1962 article in *Scientific American.* This article described a small bone, dating back to about 6500 B.C., found in central Africa, with patterns scratched on by humans. The author of the article had been unable to explain the scratches, suggesting only that they might be an "arithmetical game." The rest of the discovery can be explained in Marshack's own words.

17.4   I looked at the photos and drawings of the bone for perhaps an hour, thinking. I got up for coffee, still thinking, and came back. How does one "decode" or translate or interpret scratch marks made 8500 years ago created by a culture that was dead and by a man who spoke a language that was lost? Scratch marks that had been made 2000 to 3000 years before the first hieroglyphic writing? And, besides, what proof could there be of any interpretation? . . .

What went on inside me for that hour was odd. I was churning with the broad, encompassing insights of an unfinished book, and I was disagreeing with an interpretation that seemingly went against what I had written. It was a dull, blackened bit of scratched bone, about three and three-quarter inches long . . . and would one day end up in a museum under glass, with a caption, probably, about the enigmatic, undecipherable activities of prehistoric man.

I decided to try a hunch, based on ideas suggested by the book I was writing. In fifteen minutes I had "cracked the code" of the Ishango bone. Or, at least, I felt I had come close to it. I was dizzied. . . .

I piled my nearly finished manuscript and the notes for the book on a space in a corner of my desk, and for two days I tried to disprove my solution, making graphs, doing computations, going anxiously to the library and searching almost desperately to prove myself wrong. . . .

Much as I tried, however, I could not disprove my too easy "solution." Reading all I could lay my hands on that dealt with the archaeological evidence, and doing computations into the night and morning, the most I could do was retain the possibility that I might be right. And bit by bit, it seemed to me, undecipherable mysteries of the prehistoric past began to fall into line with the "solution."

I realized that if this solution was right or even approached some validity, it would perhaps be necessary to rewrite much in the histories of science, art, religion, and civilization and to reinterpret some of the meaning of man and his intelligence.

The Roots of Civilization

Marshack's solution to the bone was that primitive man organized time like space-age man: The marks recorded a lunar calendar. Marshack's discovery is a sterling example of cross-breeding—an explanation developed to aid a moon launch explains an 8500-year-old carved bone.

Here is a set of heuristic questions to encourage you to cross-breed in order to invent:

17.5 A heuristic for cross-breeding. What bodies of knowledge in other disciplines can I bring to bear on X? What things that I know about other things (X, Y, Z) can help me learn about X? How was X cross-bred? How can I combine two things about X to obtain some new, third, thing?

Problem Five. Exercises in cross-breeding   Here are three problems in cross-breeding. The first two have many possible answers; the last—

taken from an actual business problem of a few years ago—has a specific answer, given in the answer section at the end of the book (and perhaps other possible answers).

a. List the college courses you are now taking, and, for each, list four or five concepts or topics—perhaps "motivation" or "behavioralism" from psychology and "the paragraph" and "invention" from this text. Then attempt to cross-breed these concepts or topics to create some new, third, thing—a concept, a possible theory, an idea for writing.

b. We give at the end of this problem a list of inventions of one kind or another. Add six to eight additional recent inventions to the list. Then see if you can cross-breed among items in the list to create some new invention. (You are obligated, we should think, to send the authors of this text one-third of any profits you may realize from your invention.) Our list, to start you off: a can opener, an erasable ball point pen, a rear windshield wiper on an automobile, cable television, disposable lighters, musical calculators.

c. In the 1960s, work on the experimental B-1 bomber was plagued with engineering delays, production delays, and changes in government plans. At first, a hundred bombers were to be built, then twenty-four, and finally two prototype models were built. The rubber tires for the B-1 bomber were specially made, at a cost of $100,000 each, and, for safety reasons, they were discarded after they had aged six months. With the production delays, tires were sitting for six months and then being discarded before they could be used. How can you save this extra expense? (Hint: Think about tennis.) ■

Think Paradigmatically

Alexander Marshack, in our example above, had the advantage of not being a professional archeologist. Archeologists expected "primitive thought" in "primitive humans"; Marshack expected thought as complex as that used in the space program. Marshack's *paradigm* for primitive man allowed him to cross-breed the lunar exploration with primitive lunar calendars, thereby changing our view of early man.

The discovery of penicillin is an interesting example of how paradigms set limits on what we can and cannot see. In 1928 bacteriologist Alexander Fleming removed the cover on a plate of bacteria he was cultivating, and a spore of the mold *Penicillium notatum* settled on the plate by accident. Fleming noticed that the bacteria around the spore of the mold were being destroyed. The result, with time, was the discovery of penicillin.

"Blind luck," many would say, or perhaps use the more presentable word *serendipity,* "a discovery made by accident." What this view neglects is that Dr. Fleming, working in World War I, had become skeptical of the heavy use of artificial antiseptics, preferring to trust natural protective systems. He was mentally prepared to "see" such systems, where another scientist might not have been.

A negative example of paradigmatic thinking is told of German scientists, just before World War II, performing experiments that demonstrated practical nuclear fusion, the source of the atomic bomb. But the evidence didn't normally show up on their instruments, since it was blocked by a lead shield. One day the shield was forgotten, and the evidence of nuclear fusion appeared dramatically. The scientists decided the missing shield had "ruined" the experiment, and they quickly replaced it. They were not prepared to *see* what they had seen.

Thinking paradigmatically is always difficult, of course, for it's hard to "see" preconceptions, assumptions, and predispositions. But the writer who attempts to think paradigmatically may transform a work-a-day topic into a vehicle for discovery. Here is a heuristic for thinking paradigmatically:

17.6 A heuristic for paradigmatic thinking. What words, categories, and presuppositions are necessary for me to recognize X? What "model of the world" is X part of? What might X be like in other "models of the world"?

Problem Six. Paradigms for spelling research Below are summaries of several educational research projects exploring the teaching and learning of spelling. Each experiment implies a model, or paradigm, of what spelling is. Group together those experiments that seem similar, coming up with perhaps two, three, or four groups. Provide a label for the paradigm implied in each group, and explain your grouping in a paragraph. (As a special problem, review our chapter on spelling, and try to decide which experiments we would find most interesting.)

a. Investigators studied 17,000 common words of American English, hoping to develop rules to connect sounds with letters. (In a report of 1716 pages, they developed about 200 rules, which give the correct spelling of English words about 80 percent of the time.) Paul R. Hanna et al., *Phoneme-Grapheme Correspondence as Cues to Spelling Improvement,* U.S. Office of Education Cooperative Research Project No. 1991 (Washington, D.C.: U.S. Government Printing Office, 1966).

b. Investigators studied the relationship between knowing the meaning of a word and being able to spell it. (They found a significant relationship.) J. N. Mangieri and R. S. Baldwin, "Meaning as a Factor in Predicting Spelling Difficulty," *Journal of Educational Research*, 72 (1979), 285–87.

c. Investigators studied the ability of 2nd-grade black children and white children to spell words that had different pronunciations in "Standard English" and "Black English," expecting that the black 2nd-graders would make more spelling errors. (The investigators felt that the results supported their hypothesis, but other investigators interpreted the results differently.) See Bruce Cronnell, "Black English and Spelling," *Research in the Teaching of English*, 13 (1979), 81–90.

d. Investigators studied spelling patterns in adult aphasic (brain-damaged) patients. (They found that some patients relied on letter-sound relationships while other patients relied on a preserved image of the word's appearance.) Wendy Wapner and Howard Gardner, "A Study of Spelling in Aphasia," *Brain and Language*, 7 (1979), 363–74.

e. An investigator studied the possible differences between students' ability to recognize a misspelled word in a list as opposed to their ability to spell a word from dictation. (He found that there was no relationship between these two abilities.) David H. Russell, *Characteristics of Good and Poor Spellers*, Contributions to Education, No. 727 (New York: Teachers College, Columbia University, 1937).

f. An investigator suggested that the spelling system be changed, so that it accurately reflected pronunciation. (This has been a common suggestion—playwright George Bernard Shaw, in his will, left a substantial fortune to a spelling reform organization.)

g. An investigator compared the effect of one hour of spelling instruction per day in elementary school with the effect of ten minutes of instruction per day. (This classic study found that ten minutes of instruction was as effective as one hour of instruction.) Joseph M. Hinds, *Scientific Management in Education* (New York: Hinds, Noble & Eldredge, 1912).

h. Investigators suggested that children be taught to spell (and to read) using a special alphabet with 42 letters, so that all words could be spelled as they sounded. (This approach—still used in Britain—is called the *i.t.a. method*, for "initial teaching alphabet.") Albert J. Mazurkiewicz and Peter A. Lamana, "Spelling Achievement Following i.t.a. Instruction," *Elementary English*, 43 (1966), 759–61.

i. An investigator studied the spelling of children who invented their own writing systems before starting school. (He found that such children could make "significant generalizations" about sound and spelling, though those generalizations often did not match those of our spelling system. Here, for example, is the writing of one four-year-old: "How r you wan you gad i chans sand is ol i ladr. ad dow gt ane chribls." [*How* and *you* are learned spellings; the rest are invented. The passage reads, "How are you? When you get a chance, send us all a letter. And don't get any troubles."] Charles Read, "Pre-School Children's Knowledge of English Phonology," *Harvard Educational Review*, 41 (1971), 1–34.

j. Investigators studied 5th- and 8th-grade spellers, dividing them into "stronger spellers" and "weaker spellers" and presenting them with pairs of five-letter combinations (like *thrge* and *throp*), asking them to choose the one that "most looked like English." (They found that "better spellers" were much faster at choosing possible English words.) J. Wallace et al., "Spelling Ability and the Probability Texture of English," *Journal of Educational Research*, 61 (1968), 315–19.

k. Investigators listed 27,000 common words in English, dividing them into grade levels from 1st grade through 12th grade. They recommended that the vocabulary of children's reading be limited to words at their grade level. Burdette R. Buckingham and E. W. Dolch, *A Combined Word List* (Boston: Ginn and Company, 1936).

l. An investigator suggested that, even in early elementary school, children be exposed to "irregular" spellings that did not match pronunciation, such as *telegraph::telegraphy::telegrapher*. She stressed that the vocabulary of children's reading should not be artificially limited. Carol Chomsky, "Reading, Writing, and Phonology," *Harvard Educational Review*, 40 (1970), 287–309. [Starting hint: Note that the last two examples, k and l, have entirely different views of how one teaches spelling.] ■

Problem Seven. Paradigms for writing   At the end of chapter One, we print passages by three professional writers, discussing their writing processes. At the end of chapter Three, we print passages from three writing textbooks, explaining to students the "voices" that the authors wish them to adopt. Examine these passages in terms of the models of writing, or paradigms, that they imply. Write a short essay on your findings.

Or, as an alternative assignment, discuss any learning experience, in a classroom or outside of a classroom, that has changed "the model of the world in your mind." We may have challenged that model at several points in this text—for example in sketching a "dynamic model" of rhetoric in chapter Two or questioning your assumptions about paragraphs in chapter Five. ■

Think Analogically

An analogy is an answer to the question "What is it like?" that leaps across the normal boundaries of thought. A car is "like" a bus or a truck, on a literal level; automobile companies encourage us to think analogically by calling their cars Pintos or Sprites, Foxes or Barracudas, even Beetles.

We've found ourselves resorting to analogy as a mode of conceptualization again and again in this text. The analogy of writing to sports is a formative image in chapter One, and the notions of voice and stance in writing are analogies drawn to the printed word from ordinary speech. Our treatment of style developed from a series of analogies— freight trains, firecrackers, teeter-totters—and even our treatment of normal thought was offered with the analogy of a mental walk.

Analogy is a fundamental mode of discovery thinking in science as well. Linguist Michael Ventris had struggled to decipher the written language known as Linear B, left to us only on an ancient stone tablet, probably Minoan, that had not been deciphered in the seventy years since it had been recovered. Ventris "cracked" the code of Linear B with a simple analogy, "What if it were like Greek?" The analogy broke all the rules of prehistory then current, for no known connection existed between the Greeks and the Minoans. But it explained the language of Linear B, and thereby ushered in a new age of speculation about the development of the great civilizations of the past.

Creative writers, of course, find analogy basic to their art—and what is particularly interesting for our purpose is the analogies they offer to explain that art. Here are some examples of creative writers discussing their view of the process; note what a central force analogy has in these samples.

17.7 You go into a book and you're in the dark really . . . you don't know what's going to happen to you between getting on the boat and stepping off.

James Baldwin

17.8 It begins with a character, usually, and once he stands up on his feet and begins to move, all I do is trot along behind him with a paper and pencil trying to keep up long enough to put down what he says and does.

William Faulkner

17.9. I start off but I don't know where I'm going; I try this avenue and that avenue, that turns out to be a dead end, this is a dead end, and so on. The search takes a long time, and I have to backtrack often.

Galway Kinnell

17.10 Each novel is a kind of voyage of discovery.

Margaret Laurence

17.11. Writing poetry is a process of discovery . . . you can smell the poem before you see it . . . Like an animal.

Denise Levertov

17.12. Writing is like exploring . . . as an explorer makes maps of country he has explored, so a writer's works are maps of the country he has explored.

Lawrence Osgood

For these creative writers, writing is following a character, taking a physical voyage, "smelling" a poem, exploring. Here are questions to help you explore the formative power of analogy:

17.13 A heuristic for analogy. How is X like other things? How many ways can I complete sentences like these: "X is as _____ as _____." "X is to Y as _____ is to _____." "X is like _____."

Problem Eight. Forcing analogies   The passages below offer raw material for forcing analogies. For each, select two or three possible analogies—ask, What might this be connected with?

a. Old paint on canvas, as it ages, sometimes becomes transparent. When that happens it is possible, in some pictures, to see the original lines. A tree will show through a woman's dress, a child makes way for a dog, a large boat is no longer on an open sea. That is called pentimento because the painter "repented," changed his mind. Perhaps it would be as well to say that the old conception, replaced by a later choice, is a way of seeing and then seeing again.

Lillian Hellman, Pentimento

b. If you found a watch, having never seen one before, you would be able to make two inferences by careful examination. First, you would decide that the watch had a purpose, even though you might not be able to explain that purpose. Second, you would be able to decide that the watch had a maker. It would be clear, for example, that the parts were too carefully designed, too inter-related in their function, to be purely accidental.

adapted from William Paley, Natural Theology (1802)

c. The Wu Li Masters move in the midst of all this, now dancing this way, now that, sometimes with a heavy beat, sometimes with a lightness and grace, ever flowing freely. Now they become the dance, now the dance becomes them. This is the message of the Wu Li Masters: not to confuse the type of dance that they are doing with the fact that they are dancing.

Gary Zukav, The Dancing Wu Li Masters

d. Suppose it were perfectly certain that the life and fortune of every one of us would, one day or other, depend on his winning or losing a game of chess? Don't you think that we should all consider it to be a primary duty to learn at least the names and the moves of the pieces; to have a notion of a gambit, and a keen eye for all the means of giving and getting out of check?

Thomas Huxley, "A Liberal Education" (1868)

■

Think Visually

The analogies cited by creative writers, above, are all visual analogies—boat trips, walking avenues, trotting behind a character. Often writing problems can be solved by turning them from word problems to problems in visual space.

The act of writing in a line across the page, word after word, may seem to be the most linear of acts (indeed, LINE::LINEar). Writing, laid out on a printed page, has almost minimal visual form—only the indentations of paragraphs block off the printed text.

But that block shape hides an inner movement of ideas, a pattern of movement that can be pictured visually. We've turned again and again in this text to diagrams, illustrations, and various ways of spacing text out visually on the page. Thus we've modeled various ways of "thinking visually."

Visual thinking is common in the sciences. The most instructive example we know of is the discovery of DNA, the protein molecule that carries the "imprint" of life, the basic structure of the genes. In February of 1953, four scientists had the information needed to solve the structure—they knew which earlier experiments had been misinterpreted, and they knew which information needed to be cross-bred from other fields. The scientists were Francis Crick and James Watson, working together at Cambridge University in England, Rosalind Franklin at King's College, London, and Jerry Donohue, also at Cambridge. Donohue, however, was interested in other chemical problems and did not pursue the question of DNA. (We would label this *motivation*—you have to want to do something before you'll be able to do it.) Franklin pursued the problems using two methods: keeping a notebook of analysis—the kind of careful analysis we have discussed in chapters Fifteen and Sixteen—and using microphotography (visual thinking, but here quite literal—the structure, she hoped, would show up on the photographs).

Crick and Watson solved the structure of DNA in the spring of 1953 (and they were awarded the Nobel Prize for their discovery in 1962). They had three advantages over their competitors: 1. They worked as a team; 2. they tried to think visually by experimenting with models of the structure; and 3. they were convinced that the "shape" of DNA must explain its function in transmitting genetic information—they were searching for a shape that would be *formative*.

Here are some questions to help you think visually about a topic:

17.14 A heuristic for visual thinking. How would I make a map of X? How would I make a doodle of X? How would I describe X to someone without words?

SUMMARY

Instead of a formal summary, we reprint, in Figure 17.9, our questions for the "special places of invention."

"Cross-Breed" Ideas:	What bodies of knowledge in other disciplines can I bring to bear on X? What things that I know about other things (X, Y, Z) can help me learn about X? How was X cross-bred? How can I combine two things about X to obtain some new, third, thing?
Think Paradigmatically:	What words, categories, and presuppositions are necessary for me to recognize X? What "model of the world" is X part of? What might X be like in other "models of the world"?
Think Analogically:	How is X like other things? How many ways can I complete sentences like these: "X is as _____ as _____." "X is to Y as _____ is to _____." "X is like _____."
Think Visually:	How would I make a map of X? How would I make a doodle of X? How would I describe X to someone without words?

FIGURE 17.9   The Special Places of Invention

IMPLICATIONS FOR THE WRITER

Problem Nine. Problems for a rhetorician   Answer each of the following problems, writing out your answers if your instructor directs.

a. Many people, in Seattle in the 1950s, began to notice that the windshields on their cars were becoming pitted. As more and more people discovered this, worry mounted, and finally a federal investigative team was sent to the city. They found that two explanations were given for the pitted windshields: One was that the pitting was caused by fallout from Russian atomic tests; the other was that the pitting was caused by a recent state highway construction program. If you were the head of the federal investigating team, which possibility would you investigate first?

b. The Greeks considered Achilles to be the fastest man on earth. But it is told that Achilles was once challenged to a race by a tortoise. In a spirit of fairness, Achilles lets the tortoise reach the halfway point before he begins. As he starts, he realizes that when he reaches the halfway point, the tortoise will have traveled a further distance. When he reaches that point, the tortoise will have traveled further. Achilles continues to reason in this fashion until he realizes that he can never catch the tortoise and gives up in disgust. What advice do you have for Achilles?

c. How do you make a pigeon neurotic? Suggest one possible way.

■

Normal thinking is what we think of as "thinking"—it's rational, linear, step-by-step, the kind of thinking that is demanded in most college classes and the kind we've discussed in the last two chapters. It is thinking that runs down fixed tracks to a known destination.

But there are limits to "normal thinking," limits that we might parody by introducing a friend of ours, a somewhat dotty psychologist.

- Our friend decided to find out where a fly's ears were. He trained a fly to jump when he sounded a bell. Then he surgically removed the fly's wings. When he sounded the bell, the fly jumped. He then removed the fly's probocis (its nose). He again sounded the bell, and again the fly jumped. He then removed the fly's hind legs. This time, when the bell was sounded, the fly did not move. "Aha," he concluded, "a fly's ears are in his hind legs."

- Our friend drank Scotch and soda one evening—quite a bit of it— and, unfortunately, he became rather drunk. He decided to find the cause of this phenomenon. The next evening he drank Bourbon and soda, with the same unfortunate result. Then, the next day, vodka and soda—and the same result. Our friend now refuses to drink soda water, because he has proved that it causes intoxication.

- "A most interesting machine," our friend said, as he watched us insert a quarter and two dimes into a Pepsi machine, push a button, and obtain a shiny can of Pepsi from the bottom. "I will figure out how to make a machine like that."

  After several months he appeared again. "I've built the machine," he announced. You inserted a quarter and two dimes, and the machine melted them down, formed them into a shiny twelve-ounce can, sprayed it with paint, and dispensed it from the bottom.

A real psychologist, B. F. Skinner, found a way to make a pigeon neurotic. The pigeon would receive a bit of food when it pecked a lever. But, the food would be delayed for about ten seconds after the lever was pressed. The pigeon would learn to associate any random action it performed—scratching, waving wings, hopping up and down—with the food it received. It would press the lever and then go into an elaborate, and totally meaningless, routine.

The federal investigators called to Seattle to investigate the pitted windshields were wise to check into context before they tried to solve the "problem." Actually, windows weren't abnormally pitted at all—it was simply that, as their attention was called to it, residents began to look closely at their windshields, finding the small pits that appear on any windshield. They began to notice something that they hadn't been aware of.

And the best advice one might give Achilles is that he change his context of thinking. As long as he worries about catching the tortoise—instead of thinking about winning the race—he'll never win the race.

Our special places of invention—"discovery thinking," as we call it—ask you to be willing to go beyond the obvious.

FINAL WRITING APPLICATIONS

I. Discovery Thinking   Return to the writing assignments at the end of the previous chapter, and use discovery thinking to generate a new approach to a specific topic. Consider possibilities for cross-breeding, for thinking paradigmatically, visually, and analogically, and for approaching the topic from different perspectives.

II. The Martian Perspective   Appoint yourself an anthropologist from Mars. You have been asked to provide an analysis of some aspect of the culture of the United States (or any subgroup within that culture). Select an institution, a tradition, a manner of acting, a mode of training or instruction, a habit of working, a process of making something—any repeatable and describable mode of behavior shared by a group. Write an analysis of the mode of behavior for your Martian audience, providing a complete description of the institution or behavior, a discussion of its origin and development, and a consideration of its stated and unstated relationship to the larger values of the group. Can you, as a Martian, find values or purposes in the mode of behavior that aren't apparent to those within the culture?

III. Paradigms for Belief   We no longer accept any of the beliefs below—most of us, anyway—but they were widely accepted by some people at some time. Using library resources where necessary, explore the "paradigmatic" structure within which the belief existed.

a. The world is flat.

b. Women are inferior to men.

c. Caucasians must bear "the white man's burden" and rule over the colored races of the world.

d. The theory of evolution is contrary to God's law and man's law; it should not be taught in the schools.

e. The Great War (1914–1918) has made the world safe for democracy and established peace for the next century.

f. The Bureau of Indian Affairs should encourage American Indians to leave their reservations and enter urban society. To accomplish this goal, it is best to take children from their families at an early age and send them to boarding schools for eight years. Children will not be allowed to speak their native tongue; English will be the only language of instruction. Visits from relatives will be prohibited, and male Indians will be required to wear their hair short.

IV. Discoveries   Using available library resources, investigate a scientific discovery, using the terms and concepts of this chapter. Or report on the background assumptions behind one of the following technological discoveries.

a. IQ tests

b. Electroshock therapy for mental illness

c. Front-wheel drive for automobiles

d. Computer-assisted instruction

e. The military tank

FOR FURTHER READING

The issues in this chapter branch out into a number of fascinating areas; we can only suggest a few popular introductions to the various topics touched on here. A good starting-point is a novel, Robert M. Pirsig's *Zen and the Art of Motorcycle Maintenance: An Inquiry into Values* (New York: Bantam, 1974), which takes up many of the issues of this chapter in a fictional context—we understand it's becoming an underground campus classic.

Robert Ornstein's *The Psychology of Consciousness* (San Francisco: W. H. Freeman, 1972) explores the thinking process from the perspective of modern brain research; Maya Pines's *The Brain Changers: Scientists and the New Mind Control* (New York: Signet, 1975) is a popular introduction to the same subject.

Modern theories of the nature of creativity are collected in two anthologies, *Creativity: Critical Approaches,* ed. R. B. Cattell (New York: Academic Press, 1968), and *Creativity,* ed. P. E. Vernon (Baltimore: Penguin Education, 1970), and students may also wish to consult Arthur Koestler's masterpiece, *The Act of Creation* (London: Hutchinson, 1964). But we'd suggest starting with the first-person accounts gathered in *The Creative Process,* ed. Brewster Ghiselin (New York: Mentor, 1954).

Several first-person accounts of scientific discoveries are cited in footnotes to this chapter, and A. A. Gerthier's *To Catch a Fly* (San Francisco: W. H. Freeman, 1962) is a witty introduction to scientific thought—it's the source of many of our stories of the "normal" thinking psychologist. Much more challenging are Thomas S. Kuhn's *The Rise of Scientific Revolutions,* 2nd ed. (Chicago: University of Chicago Press, 1960) and Michael Polyani's *The Tacit Dimension* (Garden City, N.Y.: Doubleday, 1966). Our examples of visual paradoxes are taken from an anthology of articles from *Scientific American—Image, Object, and Illusion,* ed. Richard Held (San Francisco: W. H. Freeman, 1974).

There are several popular guides to problem-solving—we'd recommend William J. J. Gordon's *Synectics* (New York: Harper & Row, 1961; Collier paperback 1968), the work of a corporate brainstorming firm, and James L. Adam's *Conceptual Blockbusting: A Guide to Better Ideas* (San Francisco: W. H. Freeman, 1974). Two short textbooks, Richard E. Mayer's *Thinking and Problem-Solving* (Chicago: Scott, Foresman, 1977) and Michael I. Posner's *Cognition: An Introduction* (Chicago: Scott, Foresman, 1973), explore formal experiments in problem-solving.

18

Revising: From First Draft to Final Product

> . . . it may be that problem-solving, constructing theories, and thinking are not simply things that go on in our minds so much as something we construct on paper, much as an artist constructs an image on canvas.
>
> DAVID R. OLSON

> In writing, our sense of physically creating an artifact is less than in any other mode except perhaps composing music; thus, the literal act of writing may provide some sense of carving or sculpting our statements, as in wood or stone.
>
> JANET EMIG

We were talking with a group of writing teachers one afternoon, and it occurred to one of us to ask them, "When can you recall learning something about writing?" We received several answers; one, in particular, intrigued us.

18.1   When my freshman composition instructor showed us the second draft, the tenth draft, the forty-seventh draft, and the fifty-third and final version of an eight-line poem.

This seemed an interesting suggestion, letting students in on the complexity of the writing process, and one of us went back to his files to find earlier versions of a six-page essay he'd recently published. He found three hundred pages of drafts, false starts, notes, fragmentary outlines, paragraphs, and pages that ended up in quite different articles, even mere doodles, stretching back over four years—far too much to ask a class to read, even if it could be put in some reasonable order.

We can't expect students to make fifty-seven drafts or to take four years to complete an essay. A writing course is tightly bound to the limits of a college schedule, and time for writing has to compete with time for studying physics, time for working, and time for the myriad other activities that make up our lives.

All we'll attempt in this chapter, therefore, is the following:

■ A few general hints about revising, based on our own experience, what we've learned from our students, and what we've learned from the professionals who've written on or spoken on the subject; these are offered under the heading "A dynamic model of revision."

■ An example of our own revising of a chapter for this text.

■ Two check-lists for revising, and some student examples to practice on.

■ A complete college-level writing situation, from assignment to essays to evaluation. This material moves us from revision to the final written product and the reader's judgment of its value.

We should also note that we've been concerned, implicitly, with revising throughout this text, particularly in our discussion of the writing process in chapter One, in our discussion of sentence chunking in chapter Six, and in our discussion of specific writing tasks in chapter Fourteen (where we offer suggestions about writing essay examinations).

A DYNAMIC MODEL OF REVISION

Here's the last part of a student paper in which the writer has explained his process of writing:

18.2 The rough draft is the most difficult part of the paper. It's difficult because one has to pluck ideas concerning the subject and set them down on paper, all the time making sure they are grammatically correct and sensible.

Then the student must write a final copy. A final copy is the easiest of the parts. All the student has to do is copy the rough draft and correct sentence and spelling errors.

Here's another student's discussion of rewriting; note how much harder it is for this student:

18.3 I spend a lot of time just looking at my first draft, worrying about it, worrying about what my reader will think. I tinker with bits and pieces, and sometimes I give up and start over again from scratch. Often, when I begin to type the final draft, I find myself still changing sentences, even adding whole paragraphs. I have trouble "letting go." If it weren't for due dates, I don't think I'd ever finish anything.

These two students have distinctly different ways of going about revising, the one concerned with correcting "sentence and spelling errors," the other unable to stop tinkering. We might say that they have different models of the writing and revising process, and we might draw, from our discussion of models of rhetoric in chapter Two, the terms "static" and "dynamic" to describe them:

■ a static model of revision is *writer-centered;* the biggest problem in writing is putting the first draft on paper. This often involves conscious steps: choosing a topic, narrowing the topic, and writing an outline.

■ a dynamic model of revision is *reader-centered.* The biggest problem comes after the first draft, when one has to begin, in our student's words, "worrying about what the reader will think."

Some professional writers assert that they write in a structured way implied by the static model—about ten percent who responded to one survey.[1] Most professional writers, though, report that their own process is closer to that of our second student's dynamic model; in this view, a written product is not formed in the mind and then committed to paper; rather, the "committing to paper" is indistinguishable from the "forming in the mind." Again, to echo the point made in our discussion of invention, writing is a special form of thinking. Thus we're particularly taken by the analogies offered by David R. Olson and Janet Emig in our chapter headnotes: Writing can be seen as being like creating a painting or a sculpture, something that can be refined again and again. The analogy that we're most fond of is also a physical one. We like to compare the writer and the blank page to a potter with a lump of clay: We've seen masterworkers in clay refine and refine a shape, then disgustedly lump it together and recreate, from the same materials, a finished product.

This reshaping, in writing, demands a reader's eye, not a writer's eye. That is, it demands a wholly different perspective—not, What can I do with this draft, but rather, What will my reader do with this? The suggestions that follow, then, grow out of this dynamic, reader-centered view of writing.

Free Write a First Draft as Soon as Possible

We've all been stumped by some writing tasks, unable to complete a first draft until, at the last minute, the paper almost writes itself. Professional writers have told of similar experiences (we print some examples at the end of chapter One), and many of our students have similar stories. At the same time, however, when we ask our students to tell us the worst writing experience they've had, the most common response is, "Having to write a paper from scratch the night before it was due." A good hint, then, is to get something on paper before the last minute.

After all, our suggestions about revision will be of little value unless there's something to revise. You can't foresee the problems that will arise in writing a paper until you've run into them, and you can't predict stopping points until you've been stopped. Moreover, revising asks that you shift from writer-centered behavior to reader-centered behavior, and that different perspective is much easier to achieve if one's first draft has been sitting in a drawer for a few days. Our advice, then, is that you use free writing—the nonstop writing discussed in chapter One—as a way of generating a more or less complete first draft.

That is, you might give yourself, say, forty-five minutes to dash off a first start on a five-hundred-word paper assignment. Or you might decide to take a first shot at an eight-page sociology paper by numbering sheets in advance and writing until you fill them. In free writing, you write as quickly as possible, skipping a few lines and starting at a new point if you're stuck. (We leave out a word if we can't think of one, and rather than pause to rethink a problem paragraph, we mark it with a question mark.) Above all, keep writing. Your first draft may well be partly wheel-spinning—we feel lucky if we salvage fifty percent of most first drafts—but at least it will be there on paper to work with. Free writing, you'll remember, is a sort of thinking out on paper, and you may find that you come up with ideas that you didn't know you had.

Some related matters: a time to write, a place to write, and a method for going about writing. Doing that last-minute late-night paper is such a job in part because it's done late at night, when you're most likely to be physically tired, emotionally worried, and hardly at a mental peak. Writing is hard work in part because student writers make it hard work: Try writing in the early morning, or find a convenient chunk of time between classes.

If possible, have your own desk to write at. As one writer noted, having a writing desk makes you a writer when you sit down at it. All the other roles you carry in life—football player, television fan, husband, mother—can be left aside when you assume the role of writer. If you don't have a desk, you can create a metaphorical desk—from a kitchen table or a table in the college library, for example. One of us, as an undergraduate, used to do his first drafts in the Music Library—it had nothing that he was interested in, and he was certain not to be interrupted by friends; moreover it was uncrowded and quiet (since the music majors listened with headphones). He could find an empty desk and create a writing place.

We'd suggest also that writers develop a conscious method of "getting ready to write." Novelist Ernest Hemingway used to sharpen two dozen pencils as a ritual before beginning to write. We ritually clean off all the old projects from our desk before beginning a new project. One student tells us that she takes a ten-minute walk before beginning to write. The co-authors of this text share one common way of working out of writer's blocks. Both of us normally compose on the typewriter, but when stuck we shift to pen and paper.

Read All Drafts Aloud

Problems in sentence chunking, emphasis, even punctuation, simply sit there quietly on the written page, and the writer, approaching them silently, perhaps word-by-word, may let them slip by just as silently. Reading drafts aloud raises these problems to the ear as well as the eye; they become heard problems. The connection between reading and writing is one we've insisted upon in this text, but it's very difficult for the writer to become his or her own reader—the writer has too much investment in what's written to approach it as an outsider, too much knowledge of what's being said to see it as a reader might.

The best method for getting that critical distance needed to become reviser instead of writer is to read aloud into the tape recorder. You may be slightly aware of reading difficulties or false signals on a first reading; listening to a tape recorder will pin down those false signals and difficult parts precisely.

Revise Structurally, from the Top Down

The rhetorical model in this text works from the top down, from the primacy of voice, audience, and strategy to questions of structure, style, and detail. That's a good model to use in revising as well. Questions of sentence style can be resolved by looking at style in context, and questions of paragraph structure or development can be solved by looking at their contribution to the paper as a whole.

Another way of putting this point might be, "revise with scissors and Scotch tape." In fact, an excellent method of testing overall structure is to cut paragraphs apart and lay them out on a desk, exploring different ways of ordering them.

An example may clarify this point. We were asked to consult with probation officers in a certain city. Judges had complained that the probation reports on convicted criminals—an important part of determining the sentence—were hard to understand. We agreed to talk with the probation officers, but first we asked to see some sample reports and learn how they were actually written. It turned out that they weren't written at all. The probation officers were so overworked that they had time only to dictate their reports, which were later typed by a clerical staff and sent to the judge. The probation officers dictated from their notes, which were naturally enough chronological—first I did this, then I did this, and so on down to a conclusion at the end. When we met with the probation officers, we gave them one such report, with each piece of information on a separate slip. As we moved the slips around on a table, a certain organization appeared. The final recommendation, which usually came at the end of the taped report, had to be placed first, since that was the judge's purpose in reading. Other pieces of information—the data to support the recommendation—were best organized topically, the criminal's job record, his home life, his finances, his schooling—even though the data under each topic had been gathered at quite different times. And the data under each topic had to be introduced by, and related to, some controlling judgment.

We had simply helped these writers invent the normal discursive paragraph of chapter Five, of course, but we did so by working from the top down—why exactly does a judge want to read your report? We heard later that the gain was a clear improvement in communication—and an unexpected change in method as well, for the officers switched from note-taking in large notebooks to using small slips of paper that they could then sort out into topics (thereby inventing the research paper notecard).

Find Ways To "Re-See" Your Drafts

The awkwardness of the word *re-see* is there to heighten the fossilized metaphor still present in *re-vision,* to see again. (And you'll recall from chapter Fifteen that entities can indeed be seen in different ways.) Many of our suggestions above are designed to help the writer re-see his writing—tape recording it; putting it away for days; viewing it analogically as clay. An even better suggestion—type your second draft.

It's quite clear, from a number of research studies, that people read handwriting differently than they read typescript or printed material. They read typescript faster, more impersonally, and more neutrally.

The typescript is read as printed material, in large chunks, as meaning units rather than words. Writers at the London University have experimented with writing by hand in a situation where the writer can't see what he's written. Writers report that the situation is unnerving, that they can't write coherently. We and our students have had the same feeling in similar experiments—you simply lose the thread of what you're saying when you can't see it. Curiously enough, that doesn't happen when we've had writers who are good typists compose on the typewriter. Skilled typists seldom look at the paper or keyboard when copying a manuscript, and we find that they are able to compose when the manuscript is hidden from them without any of the discomforts found in writing. The message is, as it were, transcribed from the mind, without fingers and lines and ink smudges and undotted "i's" getting in the way.

Thus typing a second draft is a solid way of "re-seeing" one's draft, and it's a process that most professionals find automatic—poet-novelist (and writing teacher) Donald M. Murray, for example:

18.4   Most writers have superstitions about their favorite writing tools, and most of them vary their tools at different stages of the writing process. I write early drafts of poems in longhand . . . but in a stage central to the process of internal revision, I shift to a typewriter so I can see the poem in print.

"Internal Revision: A Process of Discovery"

We'd like to go even further, to suggest that students make a conscious effort to master the difficult task of composing first drafts on the typewriter. Not all professionals do compose on the typewriter, and it's not an easy skill to master. But we'd suggest giving it a try (as long as you have reasonable typing skills, so that you're not hunting for each new letter)—you may find that you become more conscious of audience as you move away from your own handwriting.

Save Surface Detail for Final Revision

By *surface detail* we mean spelling, punctuation, grammar, and usage— all the features of the "surface" of written language that can hinder the reader's attempts to read through the surface to find the meaning underneath. We consider surface detail important, important enough to have devoted three chapters to it, and to have interspersed other specific comments throughout the text—these are identified inside the back cover and listed in the index.

We'd suggest, however, that you leave such matters until a final revision. We do so partly to save time—why look up the spelling of *di-chotomy* if a later revision will delete it, and why sort out the difference between "difference between" and "difference among" if the paragraph containing the questionable phrase will be cut in a later revision? But more important in our minds is to keep the emphasis in writing where it belongs, on the primacy of purpose, message, and audience.

Some hints, then, on revising a final draft for surface correctness before typing it up:

■ translate written problems to heard problems. This suggestion draws on our "reading aloud" suggestion above; if possible, find a way to "re-see" the problem as a sound problem. Some problems simply can't be treated this way—spelling, for example, and some kinds of punctuation; thus our notion of a *print code* of surface detail. But others can. The *-ed* past tense system, for example, can be keyed exactly to the sound of *worked, noted, veered*.

■ use sight recognition for spelling problems. Most misspelled words sound fine if you read them aloud. You can read "the none tolled hymn she had scene bear feat in our rhuem" if you pay attention only to sound. With spelling, it has to look right (or should we say, as a figure of speech, *look write*?). This approach is a skill that goes against the "sound-it-out" approach that many of you were taught as a reading device, and, to that extent, reading and writing are quite different. And it's also a special skill that takes time to develop.

■ zero in on specific problems. If you tend to confuse *its* and *it's,* for example, why not devote a reading of the final draft to that problem alone? In fact, why not become your own writing teacher by transfer-ring your instructor's marginal comments to the problem chart on the inside back cover, thereby giving you a sense of what problems are random, which need to be zeroed in on.

Treat the Final Draft as Printed Copy

You're irritated when the local newspaper misspells your name, when typographical errors confuse the high school basketball scores, when the weather summary has transposed the temperatures so that it's 32° below in Blythe, California, and 110° in Anchorage, Alaska. Your reader has a similar right to be annoyed when you futz the obvious into the absurd, simply by not treating the final version as "printed copy." "Printed copy" simply means that you take reasonable care to avoid mistakes in spelling, punctuation, proofreading—mistakes that inevitably distract and annoy your reader. There are standards of adult written communication, and your instructor has every right to expect you to meet those standards (just as you have the right to expect that your work will be graded by institutional standards of acceptability).

Solution: Read the final copy again, slowly, aloud, one last time.

AN EXAMPLE OF THE REVISION PROCESS

We can explore these suggestions more concretely, by examining our own revisions to one of the chapters of this text. We've chosen chapter Twelve, "Your Vocabulary and Your Dictionary," because it illustrates the range of changes that a full revision can involve. We won't try to list every revision, and we'll ignore the complexities of shared authorship.

The final ordering of the chapter (or, since we're still in the process of revising the manuscript as we write this, perhaps we should say, the current ordering) is as follows: a joking discussion of vocabulary-building books leads to a discussion of building vocabulary by using a standard college dictionary; a section on dictionaries follows, followed in turn by a section on the history of the English language, designed to explain the sources of borrowed words; we then note that it's more common to broaden the meaning of an existing word than to borrow from another language, and we illustrate the changes words can undergo with the word *hackney*. The chapter is somewhat longer than most of our chapters; the typed manuscript runs about fifty pages.

The chapter began with a draft of about thirty pages; almost nothing remains of that draft except the first part of the paragraph following the subtitle, "The Fallacy of THE Dictionary," several sentences scattered through the chapter, and the first dictionary assignment at the end of the chapter. We gradually built up a second-draft chapter of about seventy manuscript pages, built up actually through a series of drafts: Some parts were written from note slips, as a term paper would be written (the history of the language section, for example); other parts were drafted at top speed and rewritten (the section on vocabulary-building, for example). This draft version had the following order: It began with a long history of the English language, explaining in much more detail how scholars are able to reconstruct languages and offering exercises in changes in the grammar and sound of the language as well as its vocabulary; it then discussed changes in word meanings and the standard college dictionary; and it concluded with advice on vocabulary building.

This version of the chapter was submitted to several reviewers (authors, like students, must answer for their words). The comments of two reviewers are given below:

18.5   Again we're rather far away from questions of student writing. The chapter needs a more explicitly transitional paragraph, and the writing required in the problems needs to be lengthened. Let the reader know why he's learning about language and the dictionary. Certainly the discussion of the history of the language is useful and interesting, but it seems somewhat tangential and certainly needs considerable trimming. The dictionary section and the stress on language roots are commendable. As a kind of radical proposal, the authors might consider cutting all or most of the language history and integrating the dictionary discussion with an edited version of the previous chapter.

18.6   I would suggest that you cut about one-third of the examples, especially in the first forty pages. The discussion in this chapter needs to be connected to the notion of register, dialect, etc., in the previous chapter: how to match words to meanings and audiences.

Note that both reviewers focus on our lack of concern, in the draft version, with the needs of our readers. That is, we'd been writer-centered rather than reader-centered. With these comments in mind, we began revising again. It involved all of the following steps.

Major Changes in Structure

The discussion of vocabulary-building was moved from the end of the chapter to the beginning; it introduced the section on the dictionary instead of following it. Our history of the language was moved from the beginning of the chapter to the middle; it was drastically shortened, with the emphasis shifted to why that history was needed to make sense out of dictionary abbreviations. In our earlier draft, we had been thinking only of "topics to be covered"; now we began to ask, "What should our reader do with this information?" In doing so, we began to follow our advice above, and started revising with scissors and paste. These revisions were mapped out in a conference with two other reviewers.

(And, on the subject of "major structural changes," what is now "chapter Twelve" was variously numbered, in drafts, as chapter Three, Four, Nine, and Eleven.)

Revising Central Claims

The commitment sentence of the original version was a promise to explore a subject-matter:

18.7   This chapter explores a paradox. Every child who learns to speak the English language can be said, in a very real sense, to recreate the language anew. Yet at the same time, the language that the child creates is centuries, even millennia old, and we speakers of English carry with us, embedded in our language, the history of our culture.

In revising the chapter, we realized that this abstract promise, however true, offered no benefit to the reader. Thus we began with an issue that the reader had a stake in, building up his vocabulary, and the commitment was revised to promise a more direct benefit:

18.7A Thus our second suggestion: Master the use of a standard college dictionary. The dictionary is our access to a secret history of words—a "secret" history because of a fascinating paradox. Every child who learns to speak English can be said, in a very real sense, to recreate the language anew. Yet at the same time, the language that the child creates is centuries, even millennia old, and we speakers of English carry with us, embedded in our language, the history of that language. The dictionary is our access to the second part of that paradox, the secret history of words.

Smaller revisions were made to claims throughout the chapter. Our treatment of vocabulary books was (quite properly) trimmed; our estimate of the size of one's vocabulary was checked against authorities; our claims in the history of the language section were consistently modified. Each rethinking demanded new support and clarification.

Elaborating Paragraphs

As an example of responding to this need to elaborate and clarify for the reader, consider the original and final versions of this paragraph sequence.

18.8 Point four is that "breaking words into parts" is generally good advice, but it tends to be advice that works only if you already know the answer. It's nice to be able to break *unfriendly* into *un* + *friend* + *ly,* but you probably already knew the meaning of *unfriendly.*
Thus we'd suggest that you try to swallow words whole. . . .
18.8A Even the common advice, "Break words into parts," is not quite as useful as it would seem. It tends to work only when you already know the answer. It's nice to be able to break *unfriendly* into *un-* plus *friend* plus *-ly,* but you already know the meaning of *unfriendly.* If you can break *bicycle* into *bi-* plus *cycle, tricycle* into *tri-* plus *cycle, unify* into *uni-* plus *fy,* and *unicorn* into *uni-* plus *corn*

(Latin *cornu,* "horn"), you'll be able to understand *unicycle.* But that procedure will confuse you when you meet *epicycle* and *cyclamate,* which depend on quite different senses of the Latin root *cycle,* "circle." Of course, you'll naturally break words into parts when you need to, as you did with *uncounted* and *uncountable,* or as you might do with a scientific term such as *psychophysiology.* Our criticism is with instructions that make the advice too mechanical, changing reading into puzzle-solving, and that offer long lists of prefixes and suffixes to be memorized, instead of relying on the mind's natural filtration system for words.

(We then follow with an additional paragraph on "pullet surprises.") Here the need to elaborate in order to make sure our reader understands leads us to shift conclusions: We no longer suggest that students "swallow words whole" (rather unappetizing advice). Rather we lead to the point that had eluded us in the preliminary draft: That's why the college dictionary is important. Note also that we replaced a rather mechanical pattern ("point four is . . .") with a more natural progression. The mechanical sequence of "point one . . . point two . . ." helped us to work the material out in draft form, but it was no longer necessary when we adopted a reader's perspective and provided tighter transitions.

Shortening Paragraphs

We might summarize this range of revisions with a problem for the reader. Given a need to shorten and to focus on why the history of English explains dictionary abbreviations, how would you revise the following version of our preliminary draft? (You'll note, if you compare your version with our final version (beginning on the bottom of p. 344, continuing on p. 345) that revision also clarifies sentence structure, even verb tense.)

We suspect that Indo-European was spoken in Northern Europe, perhaps between 10,000 and 3000 B.C. Our guess at the location can be supported by examining cognates in existing Indo-European languages: there are shared words for <u>snow</u>, <u>beech</u>, <u>bear</u>, and <u>wolf</u>, but not for <u>olive</u>, <u>palm</u>, <u>elephant</u>, or <u>lion</u>. Our guess at the date has much less support, although we do know, from cognates again, that IE speakers farmed (<u>corn</u>, <u>weave</u>, <u>sow</u>), used gold and silver, but not copper and iron, and used wheeled vehicles (<u>yoke</u>, <u>axle</u>, <u>wheel</u>).

In the course of thousands of years, IE speakers migrated across Europe, through the Near East, and into Northern India. Figure 9.5 offers a simplified chart of the Indo-European language family. It includes all the languages spoken in Europe (except Basque, a language spoken in

Northern Spain), Russian and the slavic languages, and, through Sanskrit, Modern Hindi.

ENGLISH AS LANGUAGE

English developed from the Germanic branch of Indo-European. English was not the first language spoken in England—that appears to be
Celtic, a language that has now disappeared. Julius Caesar invaded England in A.D. 43, subjugating the Celtic-speaking natives, and Roman
soldiers remained in England until A.D. 410, when they were removed to
protect the collapsing Roman empire. Angles and Saxons, Germanic-
speaking tribes from Northern Europe, had already been looting coastal
towns, and with the departure of the Romans, England was again ripe for
conquest. Three or perhaps four tribes from northern Europe invaded England in the middle of the fifth century—Angles, Saxons, Jutes, and
Frisians. All spoke West Germanic dialects, and these merged to become
the earliest form of English, called either Anglo-Saxon (AS) or as here,
Old English (OE). By A.D. 600, speakers of Old English have been converted to Christianity, incidentally adopting the Roman alphabet, and
written records begin to appear.

By such revisions, we reduced a seventy-page manuscript chapter to
a fifty-page manuscript chapter, even though about fifteen pages of
new material are added.

Revising Sentences and Word Choices

We've given examples of our sentence revisions in chapter Six and of
our revisions in word choice in chapter Eleven. Certainly such revisions
made up a large part of our changes to chapter Twelve. Here our goals
were straightforward—clarity, precision, truth of detail, and ideally a
certain stylishness in presentation.

But in revising that chapter (and the manuscript as a whole) we found
our primary emphasis drawn to the larger issues discussed above: Whole
paragraphs and whole pages, quite effective in themselves, were discarded because they didn't contribute to the overall structure of our
presentation to the reader, as it developed in revision.

Two Check-Lists for Revision

Astronauts work through a check-list of items as they prepare for
launch; it's a way of systematizing the complex task of getting everything
together for a spaceflight. Our check-lists won't guarantee the reliability

of a NASA space launch, but they will test your perception of your writing against what your reader might perceive.

The First Check-List This one is designed for in-class use, with peers or a group of peers reviewing your draft. This one will work best if you fill it out first, listing what you expect your readers' reaction to be, and then compare their reactions with yours.

1. Read the first paragraph aloud and stop. Write down what you think the paper is going to do.
2. Circle what you think the strongest point of the paper will be:

          interest   purpose   voice   complexity

3. Circle what you think the weakest point of the paper will be:

          interest   purpose   voice   complexity

4. Finish reading the paper aloud. If you are in a group, one person should read while the others follow the text, placing a check in the margin at points that seem to be going well, a vertical line at points that seem to need revision. The group should arrive at a group decision on checks and lines.
5. Rank the paper in terms of its strengths using the five terms below—the strongest point is one, the next two, and so on.

       purpose   interest   voice   organization   complexity

6. Review the paper sentence by sentence, marking those that seem under-chunked, or too thin, with *SUB* (consider subordinating or combining ideas), and those that seem overchunked, or too clogged with ideas, with COORD (coordinate or expand statements for clarity). Use the following abbreviations after each sentence, if relevant.
SW: So what? We see what you're saying, but we don't see why it's important.
Why: Why are we as readers being given this information?
How: How? Add more explanation or detail.

The Second Check-List This is designed for your own use in revising drafts.

1. *Prerevision.* List below the areas that you most want to improve in, under the two headings *rhetoric* (voice, main idea, style, organization, development) and *surface detail.* Make your list as specific as possible.
2. Read the paper aloud, noting those places where the text is hard to "chunk" naturally, places where your meaning doesn't come across clearly, and places where the reading takes on a mechanical, tick-tock quality.
3. Number the paragraphs of the paper and spread the pages out on a desk. Look for mechanical patterns of development, each paragraph the same length, developed the same way, and look for possibilities for rearrangement or reweighting of ideas.
4. Review the paper sentence by sentence, as a reader might read it. Consider adding transition words, explanations, and other helps for the reader.

5. Now divide the notes you made on surface detail into two groups—those that will be picked up by the ear (such as an *-ed* ending) and those that must be picked up by the eye (such as spelling). Read the paper twice more, checking for surface detail, the first reading silent, watching for "eye" problems, the second reading aloud, listening for "ear" problems.

FOUR STUDENT PAPERS FOR REVISION

We've printed four student papers below to allow you to work with revision using actual student writing. The papers range in quality from a solid final version, an "A" paper, to one that we would consider a decent first draft, a start on a topic. The first two papers respond to the dictionary assignment at the end of chapter Four; the third paper is also an out-of-class paper; the fourth was a response to a forty-minute in-class assignment, "Choose one thing that makes you mad, and write a coherent essay about it."

As a start on revising, you might list comments on each paper at random. Not all of the comments will be valid; you are simply trying to generate as many alternatives as possible for the writer to consider.

Paper One

The Politician Becomes A Statesman

How many times have you heard someone say "Ronald Reagan is nothing but a common politician"? But when he successfully resolves a national issue he becomes a "true statesman," and when he is the intermediary in the Middle East he immediately escalates to a "diplomat." Just what is the difference between *politician, statesman,* and *diplomat*? Any answers you come up with will probably show only a slight resemblance to their dictionary definitions. In fact, the explicit meanings of these three words have changed very little over the centuries. Yet their connotations—both in England and in America—have changed greatly.

Politician, adopted from *politics,* has its origin in the Greek words *polis* (city) and *polites* (citizen). The French derived the word *politicien* from the Greeks, and, in turn, the English transformed it into *politician.* Thus, considering its origins, *politician* originally implied a person who was concerned with safeguarding the interests of his city and its citizens. Although the Statesman's job is as old as that of a politician, *statesman* is a comparatively new word, primarily coming from the French *homme d'etat,* "man of the state." It was translated into the English *state's,* plus *man.* Literally, *statesman* meant a man who was concerned with the affairs of the state. To cover politics on an international level, the French adopted *diplomate,* a back-formation from *diplomatique* (diplomatic) which was transferred into English as *diplomatist.* Then, over a period of centuries, it was shortened to *diplomat*—the form most widely used in America.

Through the eighteenth century, the connotations of these three words remained relatively stable and universal. That is, if you wrote to your cousin in England, you might safely refer to King George III as a politician without fear of being called a traitor. For at this time, *statesman* and *politician* were exact synonyms of each other. *Diplomat* was rarely used in government, but when it was used it always referred to international representatives. It does show up in some early English satire. There it is synonymous with *politician*—"a crafty or shrewd person" (*OED*).

By the mid-nineteenth century, the American connotations of *politician* and *statesman* had begun to move away from their original suggestions. *Politician* had gained its present negative connotation of a man without principles—scheming and conniving for his own or his party's good. This view is shown in a passage written in 1879: "The word 'politician' is used in a bad sense in America, as applied to people who make politics a profession, and are skilled in the art of 'wire pulling' and such practices" (*OED*). The negative connotation was even carried over to animals after the discovery of the small white-eyed Vireo. A New York Zoo publication explained how the bird got its nickname: "From its habit of using bits of newspaper in the construction of its nest . . . it is sometimes called the Politician; intending thereby a sly allusion to feathering its nest by the use of even the commonest materials" (*OED*). In contrast, *statesman* has retained its positive associations. It emphasizes sound judgment, far-sightedness and skill in dealing with national affairs—qualities usually coming only after wide and varied training and experience. You can easily see why most political operators shun the label *politician*, much preferring to be called *statesman*.

Despite the changes in America, the British still see the politician and statesman on equal footing. They are both "versed in the theory of science of government and the art of governing" (*OED*). The only difference (as in their original meanings) is that the statesman operates on a national level and the politician operates on a local level. On the other hand, *diplomat* or *diplomatist* has carried with it a slightly negative meaning. An English history book describes diplomatists as being "more distinguished by their address . . . than by generous enthusiasm or austere rectitude."

This view of diplomats was prevalent in America until about the latter half of this century. The image was improved with the emergence of such distinguished diplomats as Clare Booth Luce and Henry Kissinger. They are thought of as being one step higher than a statesman, but were more than all talk and no action. More than likely, *politician, statesman* and *diplomat* will continue to change in connotation. There may come a time when, through the overuse of *statesman*, it will take on a negative meaning, and *politician* will be back in favor. Who knows, one day we may call Aaron Burr a statesman.

Paper Two

The Hand-Me-Downs

Are the names of things just made up out of the clear blue sky? No, words and parts of words are hand-me-downs from years and cultures gone by. This paper will show how the word *car, coupe* and *sedan* have been handed down.

The word *car* is not as new to our language as the vehicles we've been driving for the past 85 years or so. According to *The Oxford English Dictionary,* the word *car* was first found in the Middle English period. Back then it was spelled *carre.* The word was used and spelled differently in many other languages. Old Northern French, for example, used the same spelling as the English, but the late Latin spelling for the word was *carra.*

In the early days the word *car* meant, according to the *Webster's Third New International Dictionary,* "a vehicle moving on wheels." This definition is not far from what we think of today when the word is mentioned. The chariot was also referred to as a car. I must not forget to mention that vehicles that were adapted to rails, as well as early elevators, were also known as cars.

There are many different words describing cars, but I will talk of only two. First, let me talk about the *sedan.* The word, as it is used today, means a type of automobile that is enclosed and has two or four doors, according to the *Webster's New Encyclopedic International Dictionary.* The word *sedan* goes back to the early 1600's, but its origin is unknown. There is a town in Northern France by the name of Sedan, but this does not seem to be the likely origin of the word. According to the *O.E.D.,* "In 1634 the exclusive right of supplying 'covered chairs' was granted to Sir Sanders Duncombe; the word *sedan* does not occur in the grant, but the index to the patent of the year has covered chair (called *sedans*). The statement of Evelyn that Duncombe brought the sedans from Naples may be correct, as the thing had long been in use in Italy." Yet there still isn't any real knowledge of the origin of the word.

As was mentioned before, the first usage of the word was as a portable covered chair to carry one person. The chair was borne on poles carried by two people at either end. This is not far from what we now refer to as a sedan; all we did over the years is make it larger, smoother riding, and most likely a little faster. Today it still remains a form of transportation.

The third word is another old word, *coupe. Coupe* is of French origin and means "to cut." In ballet, dancing a quick sharp cut, finishing with an extension, is called a *coupe* (according to the *W.N.E.I.D.*). In the old days, the cutting down of a full-sized carriage to a two passenger coach produced a *coupe,* where the driver and the luggage were on the outside. Well, the automobile industry picked up on another old word and modernized it again. This time they cut the full size car down to a two-seater and made the luggage compartment separate. It was then referred to as a *coupe.*

Coupe, car and *sedan* were not words that were made up because the auto industry needed to name the products they produced. The words have come a long way from their origins, but are basically the same. Do I dare think what products will carry the same names years from now?

Paper Three

The Wall

The "generation gap" exists as a wall, only because the children of today will not listen. They will not attempt to communicate with their parents; and, therefore, they have built this "wall" separating themselves from their parents.

Today, children are constantly "downgrading" their parents, because, to them, their parents take too long to get accustomed to the new ideas and philosophies of the world. Children can't seem to understand that, to their parents, all the ideas and philosophies of today are changes, whereas, to the children, they are their ways of life; not changes, and changes take time to get accustomed to.

Children often forget that their parents were once children, also. This can be easily visualized since children only see their parents as adults. Children often feel their parents never experienced a child's world—from infancy through adolescence—so, as a result, they feel that their "growing-up" is a totally strange experience to their parents.

It is true that today's children are being brought up in a different environment and way of life from that of the one their parents were brought up in; but, too, children must realize that their parents were brought up in a totally new environment and way of life from that of their parents. Communication difficulties were obviously experienced by the children's parents, and differences of opinion were most likely expressed and discussed, so the children's problems are not all so new. Children should realize this fact and think about it.

The whole trick to parent-child communication is to listen and learn. No harm has ever been done by this. Children still have the freedom to either chew up what they hear, and spit it out, or chew it up and store it. The children will be surprised to find that what their parents have been through, and what they've learned is common to what the children are experiencing now. Parents, they'll (children) find, are not "another breed of animal"; but the same breed as themselves, only a little older and a lot wiser.

A little listening and trying will prove to be a rewarding experience. Soon that brick wall, preventing communication, will crumble, and be recognized as a child-made disaster.

Paper Four

What Makes Me Mad

When you try to sit down and write about all the things that make you mad or just one thing. It doesn't seem to me that it wouldn't be that easy. Some people could write forever on this seemingly simple subject. I can't really sit down and say there's just one thing that makes me mad out of all the things that are going on in the world.

I would guess one of the first things I can say that makes me mad is the subject of conventions. I can't understand why so many networks have to carry them. Why couldn't just one network carry it, and the others would then be able to continue with their regular programs that are already scheduled. I mean there are a lot of people who could care less about the stupid conventions, and even those people who do care can still watch the conventions if they were just shown on one channel.

One of the many other things that really make me mad is the subject of pollution. Pollution is one the biggest problems that this country along with the rest of the world has to learn to stop before it is too late to do anything about it. Many people are worrying about what is going to become of our environment with factories and their smoke stacks smoking away, dirtying the air we breathe. Everyone must help; the government can't do everything.

The crime rate is something that really makes me mad. I think there should be stricter laws concerning the punishments of crimes. I think this would discourage a lot the crimes committed in this country. Just compare Europe and our crime rate. Europe's rate is much lower because of more severe penalties for committing even small offenses so severe penalties help to discourage people in committing crimes, although somebody will always be around to break laws.

Another one of the things on my list of things that makes me mad is when you have to do something you don't want to. Many things fall in this category; a few of them are mowing the yard, pulling weeds, shoveling snow and homework—most likely the biggest one on every kid's list at this time of year. I realize now each year more and more that these things have to be done, but at first when you start having to do them you think should be able to do nothing but the fun things you want to do. So it always used to make me mad when I had to do these things.

One of the things that has to be toward the top of my list of things that makes me mad is my brothers messing things up. I like things to be neatly arranged, not just thrown all over the place. The reason my brothers do mess things up around home I believe is just to make me mad, and I think they do a pretty good job of it most of the time.

I think the thing that makes me the most mad is my car, I have only had it since May 15 and already have had several minor repairs done to it. One of the good things about the car is its good gas mileage and that's important, since I do a lot of driving. Of course six-cylinders should get better gas mileage. A few of the things that have needed to be replaced already are the battery, front brakes, rear brakes and three drums ground. The real reason this makes me mad is I don't know the first think about working on cars and it is a big mess getting things taken care of. I think I'm going to have to learn a little about cars; my mechanic friends aren't always going to be around unfortunately.

PUTTING IT ALL TOGETHER: A COMPLETE WRITING SITUATION

This section explores an actual writing and grading situation. You'll have a chance to write an essay (or at least outline one), then to read a discussion of the problems presented by the assignment, to look at explicit grading standards developed by the readers, to rate answers written by students, and then to see readers' evaluations of those essays. In other words, we'll present a complete classroom writing situation, from question to evaluation.

The writing and grading situation we've chosen is a part of the 1977 Advanced Placement Test in English Composition and Literature. The Advanced Placement (or AP) test allows high school seniors to take a special course in English (usually called an "AP course") and to earn college credit by achieving at a certain level. Many colleges award advanced standing credit in the Freshman English requirement for a certain level of performance on the test.

We choose this example for several reasons. The question itself is an interesting one. It asks the student to "write about literature," and thus it explores a common theme assignment in English classes. It was given as an "in-class" essay (students were given a one-hour multiple-choice test and then asked to write three essays in two hours; this question is one forty-minute segment), and thus it also expands our discussion of taking essay tests. The question itself deals with revising: a poet's revision, literally a re-seeing, of a poem. Finally, we choose the example because the Educational Testing Service, which administers the test, has been quite successful on two counts: They've been able to establish reliable grading standards and to explain them to the public; and they've been able to do long-term studies which show that the test is successful in measuring academic performance in English. In other words, this is a "real" writing situation, which had direct pay-offs for those who took the test; it's not a made-up example for a textbook.[2]

Your first task, then, is to write a timed forty-minute essay. The question is given in problem one. (If your instructor does not ask you to write the essay, you should at least read the question carefully and make notes on how you would go about answering it, so that you'll benefit from the discussion that follows.) Your audience is the 1977 AP grading team, made up of college and high school English instructors from across the country.

Problem One. An Advanced Placement question   Below is question two from the 1977 Advanced Placement Test in English Composition and Literature.

Question 2
(Suggested time—40 minutes)

Printed below are two poems by D. H. Lawrence titled "Piano." Read both poems carefully and then write an essay in which you explain what characteristics of the second poem make it better than the first. Refer specifically to details of both poems.

(I)

Piano

Somewhere beneath that piano's superb sleek black
Must hide my mother's piano, little and brown, with the back
That stood close to the wall, and the front's faded silk both
  torn,
And the keys with little hollows, that my mother's fingers had
  worn.

Softly, in the shadows, a woman is singing to me
Quietly, through the years I have crept back to see
A child sitting under the piano, in the boom of the shaking
  strings
Pressing the little poised feet of the mother who smiles as she
  sings.

The full throated woman has chosen a winning, living song
And surely the heart that is in me must belong
To the old Sunday evenings, when darkness wandered outside
And hymns gleamed on our warm lips, as we watched mother's
  fingers glide.

Or this is my sister at home in the old front room
Singing love's first surprised gladness, alone in the gloom.
She will start when she sees me, and blushing, spread out her
  hands
To cover my mouth's raillery, till I'm bound in her shame's
  heart-spun bands.

A woman is singing me a wild Hungarian air
And her arms, and her bosom, and the whole of her soul is
  bare,
And the great black piano is clamouring as my mother's never
  could clamour
And my mother's tunes are devoured of this music's ravaging
  glamour.

(II)

Piano

Softly, in the dusk, a woman is singing to me;
Taking me back down the vista of years, till I see
A child sitting under the piano, in the boom of the tingling
        strings
And pressing the small, poised feet of a mother who smiles as
        she sings.

In spite of myself, the insidious mastery of song
Betrays me back, till the heart of me weeps to belong
To the old Sunday evenings at home, with winter outside
And hymns in the cozy parlour, the tinkling piano our guide.

So now it is vain for the singer to burst into clamour
With the great black piano appassionato. The glamour
Of childish days is upon me, my manhood is cast
Down in the flood of remembrance, I weep like a child for the
        past.

Problems Presented by the Question

The author of the 1977 AP report, C. F. Main, offered an extended
commentary on the demands posed by the question. You might note
three features of his commentary. First, the problem of organization
seemed central—and that's a rhetorical problem rather than a problem
of "reading literature," as such. An answer was downrated if the author
did not find a way to organize his understanding of the poems for his
readers, even if the answer showed indirectly an understanding of the
two poems. Second, better answers were structured around what we
call a *formative idea* (Main's term is *significant generalization*); weaker essays tended to wander or to tie themselves to what we've called "dead-
level fact." Third, better answers seemed better able to manipulate the
vocabulary available for discussing poetry. That is, they are better as
"display answers" in the sense used in chapter Fourteen; they demonstrate the ability to "do poetry" better than do the weaker answers.
Main's commentary on the question is in part printed as example 18.10.

18.9 *Commentary.* This question tells the candidates that the second
poem is better than the first and asks them to explain why. The
question is a rarity: it required literary judgments but did not en-
gender controversy. The Readers agreed on scoring standards in
a short time, and they read the responses with remarkable agreement and efficiency.

The question was also successful in providing the candidates with a topic which a vast majority of them could discuss. All but a small percentage of the candidates understood the task that was set, and the best candidates found interesting ways of organizing their discussion of details in the poems around significant generalizations. "The main difference," one student remarked, "between the two versions is that the first is cluttered with mixed and irrelevant facts, imagery, diction, and events which confuse and detract from the experience the poem is attempting to communicate." This clear-minded reader of verse then went on to marshal details from the two poems as evidence of the second's superiority.

One conspicuous virtue of the question was that it called on the candidates to muster whatever organizational powers they possessed. The question required them to deal with both poems at once; a close reading of one and then of the other—as most people saw at the outset—simply could not be accomplished in the allotted time. And so one efficient way of distinguishing the essays was according to how well they were organized. Organization at an AP Reading is always regarded as an aspect of writing, and it can therefore, according to the rubric, either increase or diminish a score. The best papers handled superlatively the problem of organization—not by "reading" the two poems through consecutively or simultaneously, but by locating certain points, such as the relative unity and economy of the second or the superior coherence of its imagery, on which to base detailed comparisons.

Some of the middle-range papers resorted to overstatement and strained imagery, as did for instance the essay which remarked, rather opaquely but in a sentence admirable for its rhetorical strategy, "When an accomplished poet denies his thoughts the full thrust of his poetical devices, it becomes criminal; when he later animates the same matter to aspiring proportions, it is refreshing." Fortunately this was the only high flight in an otherwise down-to-earth essay. Other middling papers went to the opposite extreme, away from fancy notions to dutiful counting of the number of words in each and concluding, as one candidate did, that the second poem "follows Strunk and White's advice not to use ten words where one will do." This rather literal-minded student (whose rule would be the death of certain kinds of poetry) is certainly to be preferred to his low-scoring fellow aspirant to advanced placement who found that in the second poem "Lawrence uses *less* words."

Neither poem is particularly difficult or obscure, though indeed the diffuse first one may have provided many candidates with a handy introduction to the more concentrated second, in which the two times—the past and the present—are conflated. An essay failing to perceive that both poems deal with a concert in the present which arouses memories of music in the past recieved a low score, as the rubric indicates it should, because such a failure suggests that the candidate could not read the poems and therefore had no real basis for an opinion on their relative merit.

In conclusion, it is impossible to resist pointing out another virtue of the question—a virtue which resided in the poems themselves. These poems express feelings and emotions that most people have experienced: nostalgia for the innocent pleasures of childhood, maternal love, moist eyes at concerts. Without intending any denigration of other kinds of poetry, it can be said that these poems do speak more directly to the "general reader" than do the typical ironical, complex, and ambiguous modern poems that appear over and over again in the textbooks and on national examinations.

Standards for Grading

Readers graded each essay on a nine-point scale, with nine as the highest score and one as the lowest. (Scores on the three essays and the multiple-choice section are later weighted by computer to arrive at a final overall score of from one to five.)

The reliability of individual readers is checked often during the reading of the essays, and general standards—called a *rubric*—are developed for each question. The rubric for this question is given in 18.10 below. You'll note that there's no preconceived, single "right" way of answering the question, but that there are clear general expectations at each point level.

18.10 *Rubric for Scoring Responses: General Directions:* Reward the essays for what they do well in response to the question. A very well written essay may be scored a point higher than it would be scored on the basis of content alone. A poorly written essay should be scored a point lower. A very poorly written essay must be scored in the lower half of the scale.

Possible Scores on the Nine-Point Scale

9-8-7 The best papers present a careful and detailed comparison of the two poems and use details from both to argue for the second's superiority, making some points *like* the following but not necessarily these particular ones:

a. the greater subtlety and complexity of the feeling expressed in poem 2.

b. the greater economy (elimination of the sister, e.g.) of poem 2.

c. the superior technique (rhythm and imagery) of poem 2, resulting in greater coherence and unity of effect.

d. the speaker's greater self-awareness in poem 2 ("In spite of myself . . .").

e. the irony (e.g., *glamour* applied to past childhood rather than to the present concert) of poem 2, tempering its sentiment.

6-5 These scores are for essays that use both poems but use them less well than the best essays do. Essays that argue well for the superiority of poem 1 may receive a score no higher than 6.

4-3 These scores are for essays that:

a. are vague and general.

b. merely respond in a gushy, sentimental way to the poems.

c. distort or misread the poems (e.g., fail to see that past and present are contrasted in both poems).

d. discuss only one poem. Such an essay may receive a grade no higher than 3.

2 This score is for essays that compound the faults of those in the 3-4 range.

1 This score is for an on-topic response that has no redeeming qualities.

Examples for Evaluation

Now let's examine three actual student responses to the question given in problem one, offered as representative of high (9, 8, or 7 points), middle (6, 5, or 4 points), and low scores (3, 2, or 1 point).

Problem Two. Grading student responses Rank the three student responses below as "high," "middle," or "low" in quality as answers to the question given in problem one. Base your judgments on the standards set out in the rubric for the question (18.10 above), and be prepared to defend your judgments by explicit reference to the rubric. (Your instructor may ask you to defend each judgment in a short paragraph.)

Essay A

The second poem entitled "Piano" is better than the first because the second employs better word choices, is more tightly constructed, and contains a clear statement of theme with which to conclude. While it is true that both poems are meant to illustrate the same emotional feeling for a thing of the past and in places contain identical phrases, the second appears more artistically conceived. Word choice is more carefully developed in the second poem. This is best illustrated in the image of the child sitting under the piano which is present in both poems. The "boom of the shaking strings" is not as figurative as "the boom of the tingling strings." Lawrence is attempting to recall the beauty of a past experience and the word "shaking" is harsh and fails to convey the same subtle emotional sense provided by the word "tingling." The figurative nature of the latter word is further supported by the contrasting nature of "tingling" and "boom." This artistic combination of loud and soft, strong and weak is not conveyed by the comparable wording in the first poem. In each poem this image is illustrated in two lines. In the second poem word choice and tighter construction has allowed for a more even rhythm. In the first poem these two lines dangle, almost as run-on lines. But through the use of word changes such as shaking to tingling and little to small and by the use of a comma in the second line, the second poem takes on a more rhythmic quality. In the first poem Lawrence goes to great lengths to create multiple images of his childhood experiences with the piano. These images are merely repetitious illustrations of the theme and are not as well constructed as the single, briefly described picture of the second poem. The repetition of "clamour" in the second to the last line of the first poem takes away much of its rhythmic quality. Nowhere in the first poem is to be found a line which clearly suggests a theme. The overall intent of the poem must be gathered from the images. This poem also lacks an ending line which sums up the purpose. Within the careful organization of the second poem the thematic idea is used as the foundation of the verse. The reminiscent theme is stated at the beginning ("Taking me back down the vista of years . . .") and at the end ("Down in the flood of remembrance, I weep like a child for the past") of the poem, thus adding additional emotional feeling to the image presented and, thus, creating a natural ending to the poem. Therefore, on the basis of word choice, structure, and statement of theme, the second poem is better than the first.

Essay B

In both poems, Piano (I) and Piano (II) by D. H. Lawrence, a man's temporary return to his youth is treated, yet the second poem preserves and intensifies this odyssey into the past, and through that, conveys greater and truer feeling.

Being longer, the first poem is more cumbersome, and the images are far less pure and concise. Several lines seem forced, as "And hymns gleamed

on our warm lips, as . . . glide," and "and blushing, spread out her hands
. . . bands." There is no indication of Lawrence's effort in the second
poem, in terms of constrained rhymes and thoughts, for the lines flow,
and the rhyme and rhythm are natural and melodic. Many lines are similar,
yet the incorporation of images into tightly packed lines is far more notice-
able in the second. The line that begins "To the old Sunday evenings . . ."
and ends "piano our guide" is a startling example of Lawrence's compres-
sion of an entire stanza in the first poem into two *better* lines in the second.

Many irrelevant details are left out of the second as well, such as the
entire first stanza of Piano (I) and the fourth stanza. For, while these stanzas
give a feeling for the appearance of the piano, and give an indication of a
family episode, they have no bearing on the basic thematic idea.

Lawrence's slight shift in his treatment of this basic idea is, by far, the
most significant improvement in the second poem. One notes a shallowness
of feeling in the first, and the image of a base, passion-led existence is
connoted in Piano (I). This is evidenced in the persona's violent shift after
four stanzas of reminiscences to the description of a "wild Hungarian air,"
of "her arms and her bosom," and of the "clamouring" of the black piano.
The tender remembrances of his youth are pushed aside violently, loudly,
and passionately, by an almost wanton presence.

This presence is seldom mentioned in the second, and therein lies the
beauty and purity of it. The persona is led, "softly, in the dusk," by the
"insidious mastery" of song, to seek the past and lay aside his manhood
for a time. The persona acquiesces with some resignation at first, for it is
"in spite of" himself that he returns to his youth, and the song "betrays"
him back; and yet he senses the necessity for a return, and goes. As the
journey progresses, he is more and more certain of his choice, and "now
it is vain for the singer to burst into clamour" because his "manhood is
cast/Down the flood of remembrance" and he belongs to his childhood
again.

A truer representation of a man's yearning for his youth is the second
poem. The theme is followed through with far more clarity, as is the sen-
timentalism that accompanies these journeys into the past.

Essay C

Upon reading both these poems, the second was better than the first because
I could feel more readily the tenderness experienced by the poet.

The second poem also has quite a few less lines. This is the result of
packing more meaning into a single word, instead of using a group or
phrase of words. For example in the first poem the poet refers to "the
heart that is in me" and in the second poem, "the heart of me." He cut
down on unnecessary words.

In the second poem the poet also uses personification. For example "till
the heart of me weeps to belong." The rhythm of the poems is very different. The second poem is slower, more thoughtful and meditative. It is
almost like a melody, the melody of the song the poet hears.

Comments on the Sample Essays

We print below, as example 18.11, Professor Main's comments on the three sample essays. We have added to his comments bracketed identifications of the ranking of the essays.

18.11 *Comments on the Sample Essays.* The high score response [Essay B] strikes a nice balance between literary means and literary ends. Its author knows that criticism of a poem must always take into account matters of technique—rhyme, rhythm, imagery, structure—yet the essay also shows throughout an awareness that discussion of technique is pointless unless it is informed with concern for what the poem expresses. Some of the essays answering this question got so bogged down in minute comparisons between the language of "Piano I" and "Piano II" that they lost sight of what that language was saying. Of course both the *how* and the *what* must be treated, and this candidate earned a high score by dealing with both in a competent fashion.

The essay does well all of the things listed for 9-8-7 papers in the rubric except (e), which was not at all a requirement for the top scores. Of course the actual wording of the essay doesn't correspond completely with the wording of the rubric, but that is hardly to be expected. Candidates must have the freedom to express their ideas in their own words. And of course this particular high score paper isn't perfect; one might pick at individual sentences or cavil with minor points. But to do so would be to violate the first injunction of the rubric, which is to "reward the essays for what they do well."

The middle score sample [Essay A] proceeds according to a plan, with a two-sentence beginning, a many-sentence middle, and a one-sentence ending. This commendably tidy if somewhat mechanical organization is the strongest feature of the essay. The body of the essay also pays rewardably close attention to details in both poems, though here and there it labors, as when it draws a tedious, unconvincing distinction between *tingling* and *shaking*. At this point, some recollection of onomatopoeia might have been useful. The candidate seems to have good impressions but insufficient language in which to express them. All in all, the middling essay does pretty much what the high-score essay does, but with somewhat less clarity, conviction, control, and intelligence. And it operates on some dubious assumptions: for instance, that a poem with an explicit theme is superior to one with an implicit theme. Here, probably, the candidate is groping towards the idea that everything in the second poem supports its theme, while certain details in the first are in conflict with it. In the very best papers, this sort of reworking of the ideas to make sense of them isn't at all necessary. In the middling papers, a candidate's verbal medium is often not quite equal to the message being transmitted, and so translation is needed.

The low-score response [Essay C] errs in being vague and general rather than in being distorted or confused. Its author quotes three times from the two poems, but the details so cited are not used to support an interesting or important argument. While it is better to cite than not to cite, citation alone is not enough. However, the paper does not lack what the rubric calls "redeeming qualities": the syntactically distorted first sentence contains a kernel of truth about the relative "tenderness" of the two poems, and the statement that the second poem is shorter than the first, though itself not made economically, is correct.

While amusing misinterpretations of the two poems might have been included in this report, such samples would hardly be useful because misreading is an individual and fortunately a rare problem, while being unable to say much of anything on paper is, unfortunately, very common. The particular low-score paper included here is not so much wrong as weak, both in thought and expression.

Problem Three. Ranking your essay   Either individually or as a class project, rank the essay you've written for problem one. Base your standards on those of the committee's rubric, and provide a short paragraph defending your judgment. (AP grading standards, we might note, appear to be higher than those of some freshman English programs.)

FINAL WRITING ASSIGNMENTS

I. The Interview   Make an appointment to interview a professional in the field you plan to enter about the kind of writing that is required of those in the profession. You should prepare questions in advance—based on a hypothesis about your results—and you should also think in advance about the form of your final essay (a "feature" report for a newspaper, an interview format like that of *Playboy* magazine or the more subjective format of a *Rolling Stone* interview). Several options are possible: You may wish to interview a professor on campus, someone who's written a good deal, about his or her writing process; you may wish to shift the focus from writing to teaching, and interview two or three instructors who are regarded as good teachers.

II. The Self-Analysis   A good way to round out a writing course is to go back through papers you've written and look at them in the light of what you've learned, attempting to summarize your strengths and weaknesses in a short paper.

III. The Writing Process of a Professional   You may wish to take on, as a research topic, the writing process of a professional writer whose work you admire. You're best off choosing a writer who is fairly well known, and you'll find more letters, manuscripts, and other material available for deceased writers.

FOR FURTHER READING

The best source of information on how writers—creative writers at least—go about writing and revising is the regular series of interviews in the *Paris Review.* These have been collected in five volumes, *Writers at Work: The Paris Review Interviews,* ed. Malcolm Cowley and George Plimpton (New York: Viking).

We'd particularly recommend that the student look at Peter Elbow's *Writing Without Teachers* (New York: Oxford University Press, 1973), a writing teacher's discussion of his own process of writing. And one textbook focuses entirely on the process of revising, with useful examples and suggestions—Richard A. Lanham's *Revising Prose* (New York: Scribner's, 1979).

NOTES

1. Janet Emig, *The Composing Processes of Twelfth Graders* (Urbana, Ill.: National Council of Teachers of English, 1971), ch. 1.
2. All the material in this section is reprinted from *Grading the Advanced Placement Examination in English Composition and Literature, 1977 and 1978,* a report by C. F. Main (Princeton, N.J.: College Entrance Examination Board, 1979).

Appendix A

A BRIEF GLOSSARY OF USAGE

Note: This glossary presents an alphabetical list of common usage issues. We've tried to keep our discussion short and to the point, but that means we inevitably simplify the complexities of many usage issues. For more discussion of these issues, see the reference works cited at the end of chapter Eleven, p. 367.

- *accept/except.* Connect *except* with *exception* and *exceptional.* "Everyone left except John"::"John was an exception." The verb form is *accept:* "They accept credit cards."
- *affect/effect.* *Affect* is usually a verb: "Her letter affected me greatly." *Effect* is usually a noun: "He wanted to have a definite effect on his reader." Connect *effect* with *effective, affect* with *affection,* "a mannerism." *Affective* has a special meaning in education and psychology, meaning "emotional," as in "the cognitive and affective domains"—areas of thinking and emotion.
- *allusion/illusion.* The words are pronounced nearly alike in most relaxed pronunciations, but they have different print forms. An *allusion* refers to something; it's related to the verb *allude:* "She made an allusion to the defendant's background"::"She alluded to the defendant's background." An *illusion* is a false mental image; it's related to a different root: "An illusion illustrates an illusory quality."
- *alot/a lot.* The print form *a lot* always uses two words; *alot* is a misspelling.
- *alright/all right.* *Alright* began as a misspelling of *all right,* but is now listed in many dictionaries. Most writers will prefer the older form; they might remember it with a comparison: "all wrong::all right."

■ *bad/badly.* See text, pages 391–392.

■ *can/may.* The textbooks of a hundred years ago placed much emphasis on the distinction, arguing that *may* indicates permission and *can* indicates ability to do something. Thus, the child who said "Can I go to the bathroom?" was corrected to "May I go to the bathroom?" Most of us now feel that a grammar lesson is not a particularly good idea when someone needs to go to the bathroom, and the distinction has left the spoken language of most of us. You can use either form . . . (or is it, you may use either form?).

■ *choose/chose.* This related pair of words presents a common spelling problem (as do other pairs, like *loose/lose*). Putting the words together can force you to get a visual sense of the sound/spelling connections. "I had to choose a new college because I didn't like the one I chose last year." "The spectator was holding me, but I had to get loose; I couldn't lose the race."

■ *cite/sight/site. Cite* is usually the unfamiliar word. *Cite* is related to *citation* ("a traffic citation"); it means "to refer to": "The text cites many professional writers." *Site* is related to *situation;* it means "location": "The site of the new library has been determined." *Sight* is the common word, meaning "vision."

■ *cloth/clothe.* These words are also common spelling problems. Again, the solution is to force a "visual sense" of their spelling: "I used some cloth to make some clothes to clothe my doll."

■ *could of/could have; might of/might have; would of/would have. Could of,* and similar spellings, reflect the sound of speech, but not the underlying grammar. The correct spellings are *could have, might have,* and *would have.* A model may lock in the verb "have" behind our relaxed speech: "I have gone to the party"::"I could have gone to the party"::"I might have gone to the party"::"I would have gone to the party."

■ *data is/data are.* The engineer turns to a co-worker and says "The data is impressive." Yet, when he writes up his findings, he writes "The data are impressive." In print, then, he thinks formally of *data* as the plural of Latin *datum.* Thus, *data are* is generally preferred in scientific and technical writing.

■ *develop.* The word *develop* does not have a "silent e" at the end. Connect it with a related word, "develop::development."

■ *effect.* See *affect/effect.*

■ *except.* See *accept/except.*

■ *fewer/less.* Here, formal usage departs radically from much of the language of advertising and media. Formally, *fewer* refers to items that can be counted: "We have fewer customers this month." *Less* refers to group nouns or to qualities: "We grew less wheat than last year." "What we need is more foresight and less hindsight." Advertisers, however, delight in ignoring the distinction, announcing gleefully on packages,

"Contains fewer calories." You may want to try out both alternatives, deciding whether you wish to sound like advertisers or like more formal writers.

■ *formally/formerly. Formally* is from *formal;* it means "properly." *Formerly* is from *former;* it means "before": "She was formerly the president of the club."

■ *good/well.* See text, pp. 391–392.

■ *it/there.* Speakers of some dialects use *it is* where other speakers use *there are:* "It's three things I want to talk about." "There are three things I want to talk about." *There are* is the only accepted "print code" form in such sentences. *It is,* of course, is appropriate in other contexts: "It is the car I want." (No one would consider, "There are the car I want" as an alternative.)

■ *less.* See *fewer/less.*

■ *like/as.* We find some students oversensitive to *like,* avoiding it even as a verb (writing "He had a strong emotional regard for her" instead of "He liked her") and using *as* for *like* where *like* would be more natural: "She looks like a dancer" is much preferable to the awkward, "She looks as a dancer." *Like* is a usage problem only when it introduces a verb: "He cooks like his father does," or, "Winston tastes good, like a cigarette should." In this single case, writers may prefer to avoid advertising talk.

■ *loose/lose.* See *choose/chose.*

■ *might of/might have.* See *could of/could have.*

■ *one . . . they/one . . . he or she.* We heard a national figure in the teaching of English, widely admired for her prose style, open a meeting by saying, "If everyone will take their seats, we'll begin." This is considered an error, the argument being that *anyone* (and other such words— *someone, one,* and so on) is singular, while *their* is plural. Technically then, she should have said, "Will everyone take his or her seat." But we're aware of using the "anyone . . . their" idiom in our classes ("Will everyone turn in their papers"), and we suspect that few of us now maintain the "correct" forms in speech. But the code of print is much more restrictive than the codes of speech, and the standards of most college writing demand "anyone . . . he or she."

■ *prepositions to end a sentence with.* This issue was invented by John Dryden in 1686. He was translating the writings of a Roman poet, and it occurred to him that it is impossible, in Latin, to use a preposition to end a sentence with. He decided that English ought to adopt the same rule, so as to be more like Latin. Few modern authorities accept Dryden's argument. British prime minister Winston Churchill, chided for ending a sentence with a preposition, replied, "That is nonsense up with which I will not put." (And notice how often, in this discussion, we have been able to use prepositions to let sentences finish up with.)

■ *pronouns.* Speakers of some dialects say "He and I went to the store." Speakers of other dialects say "Him and me went to the store." We would all recognize the first version as the written form, and speakers of the "him and me" dialect have no problem shifting, in writing, to "he and I." The problem comes in a different area. Speakers of both dialects above would naturally say, "between you and me" and "send it to me and her." But speakers of the second dialect can overgeneralize their strategy for writing, producing the incorrect forms "between you and I" and "send it to I and she." A related problem with pronouns is the choice of "it is I" and "it is me." Both are now widely accepted, and the choice between them is more a matter of how the writer wants to present himself or herself than a matter of correctness.

■ *reason is because/reason is that.* "The reason I came to college is because I want to get a good job." Spoken, this sentence seems fine. Written down, open for reinspection, it seems less successful. Alternatives are the more formal "reason . . . is that" construction ("The reason I came to college is that I want to get a good job") and, still better, turning to a more emphatic subject-verb combination: "I came to college because I want to get a good job."

■ *split infinitive.* An infinitive is a verb with the word *to:* "to eat," "to cogitate," "to connect." One splits an infinitive by putting a word between the two words, as in "to boldly go where no man has gone before," from *Star Trek.* Split infinitives were invented as a usage problem by analogy with Latin. A Latin infinitive is a single word, such as *amare,* "to love," and cannot be split, and English, it was argued, should be like Latin. Split infinitives are now quite common in business and industry—"to quickly deliver the orders," "to carefully implement the plan"—and, in some sentences, the meaning changes if the infinitive is not split: "To really get to know someone you have to live with him." On the other hand, split infinitives are still avoided in most scholarly writing, and the developing writer may decide, at the least, to split carefully, if at all.

■ *unique. Unique* originally meant "only" or "single." With that original meaning, the word cannot be modified, as in "a very unique program." (The word *perfect* still functions in this way; one would be suspicious of a sentence like, "It was not just a perfect party; it was a very perfect party.") Some speakers, hearing "very unique," have created a new meaning, "uncommon," which would allow the word to be modified. The prejudice against "very unique" remains strong, however, and most careful writers avoid it.

■ *well/good.* See text, pages 391–392.

■ *would of/would have.* See *could of/would of.*

Appendix B

ANSWERS TO SELECTED PROBLEMS

Note: Not all problems are answered in this section. Some problems are writing assignments, with many possible answers; other problems have no single correct answer.

CHAPTER ONE: WRITING FLUENTLY

Problem Seven. Exercising competence Most native speakers of English identify sentences d, f, and l as "not sounding right."

Problem Eight. Kinds of nonsense Sentences a, d, h, and j are "nonsense A"; b, e, g, and k are "nonsense B"; c, f, i, and l are "nonsense C."

Problem Nine. A proverb from Trinidad Don't give up so easily. "T'ief t'ief t'ief" is a complete sentence; which word is the verb? (If you must have an answer, you may wish to do some library research. We found the proverb in J. L. Dillard, *All-American English* [New York: Random House, 1975], p. 257.)

CHAPTER TWO: THE DIMENSIONS OF RHETORIC

Problem One. The word *Rhetoric* The positive sense of "true rhetoric" is used in sentences c, e, f, g, and i. Sentence g may have presented a problem, since you were not given the full context of the quotation.

CHAPTER THREE: VOICE, TONE, AND THE WRITER'S STANCE

Problem Four. Reading the bureaucratic voice   **a.** You can't teach an old dog new tricks. **b.** Dead men tell no tales. **c.** A rolling stone gathers no moss. **d.** A word to the wise is sufficient. **e.** Sticks and stones may break my bones, but words will never hurt me. **f.** Beginner's luck! **g.** Don't cry over spilt milk. **h.** All that glitters is not gold. **i.** Where there's smoke, there's fire. **j.** Beauty is only skin deep.

Problem Eight. Recognizing parody   Passages b, e, f, and g are parodies—you might notice the names given to these dancers.

CHAPTER FOUR: FROM TALK TO WRITTEN DISCOURSE

Problem One. Creating coherence   The original passages are printed below, with the missing words in italics.

Passage A   Richard Petty didn't want to *be* a stock car driver when *he* was growing up. He got into it because, as *he* says, "When your old man is winning every *race* in sight, people kind of expect you to *follow* in his footsteps."

Petty climbed into his first *race* car when he was 21 years *old*. He finished sixth in that first *race*, in Columbia, S.C., in July 1958. Eight years *later*, he had *won* 55 *races*, eclipsing his father's record of 54 *races*, the most ever won before *by* a stock *car* driver. *Time* (1975)

Passage B   Willie Sanders was taking a day off. In a waterfront bar called The Hatch, across the *street* from the Todd Shipyards in San Pedro, Calif., Willie, a 37 *year*-old riveter, sipped *his* beer. "You get to the point," he *said*, "where you stare at the rivets and to make *them* mean something you start counting them like *counting* sheep. When you *do* that, you better watch *out*. Some guys tell you that means you're *going* crazy. So when it happens to *me*, I just go home and watch *television* until I can come back and face it *again*. My kid looks at me and says, 'dad, what're you doing *home* again?' I tell him, 'Listen, kid, you're going to *college* one day. You just won't understand *it*.' I can never explain *to* him. You just can't get the feeling of *what* it's like there until *you* get behind a riveting gun and begin blasting away. Some *guys* like to think they're fighting a war. It makes *them* feel good." *Newsweek* (1975)

Problem Three. An exercise in incoherence   This problem is particularly difficult because of the lack of full context for the quotations. Passages a, d, and f are by mental patients; they are taken from André Roch Lecours, "Methods for the Description of Aphasic Transformations of Language," in *Foundations of Language Development,* ed. Eric H. and Elizabeth Lenneberg (New York: Academic Press, 1975), II, 75–94. Passage b is from a poem by Emily Dickinson ("The Soul Selects Her Own Society"—1862). Passage c is a typical bit of nonsense from Joseph Heller's *Good as Gold* (New York: Pocket Books, 1980), p. 22. Passage e is from Gertrude Stein's *Tender Buttons* (1914). Passage g is from the conclusion of D. H. Lawrence's *The Rainbow* (1915). Passage h is from Joan Didion's *Slouching Towards Bethlehem* (1968).

Problem Five. Repetition in Word and Sentence Pattern   **a.** "Nobody wants to be dull. But if the alternative to dullness is dishonesty, it may be better to be dull." **b.** "The prose of Huckleberry Finn established for written speech the virtues of American colloquial speech. This has nothing to do with pronunciation or grammar. It has something to do with ease and freedom in the use of language. Most of all it has to do with the structure of the sentence, which is simple, direct, and fluent, maintaining the rhythm of the word-groups of speech and the intonations of the spoken voice." **c.** "A dollar don't do as much buying for me as it used to do, so I don't do as much for a dollar." **d.** "Words should count, they should make sense, and the great enemy of counting sensibly is wordiness."

CHAPTER FIVE: THE DISCURSIVE PARAGRAPH

Problem One. When Is a paragraph?   Passage A begins new paragraphs with sentences d and g. Passage B begins new paragraphs with sentences g and l.

Problem Four. The three-sentence paragraph   (Note: Other readings are often possible.) **a:** 1], 2], 3]. **b:** 1], 2], 2]. **c:** 1], 2], 3]. **d:** anomalous: 1], 1], 1]. **e:** anomalous: 1], 1], 1]. **f:** 1], 2], 3]. **g:** 1], 2], 3].

CHAPTER SIX: SENTENCE CHOICES: CLARITY AND DIRECTNESS

Problem Eight. Predication choices   (Note: Other answers are possible.) **a** and **b.** answered in problem. **c.** "Accountants use several methods to calculate periodic depreciation." **d.** "Ruth St. Denis, a mystic who was interested in the dances of the Orient, built the foundations of modern American dance." "Ruth St. Denis was a mystic, interested in the dances of the Orient, who built the foundations of modern American dance." **e.** "Michael DeBakey achieved a major breakthrough in heart surgery by successfully implanting the first artificial heart in 1966." **f.** "The darter is a small, freshwater fish that takes its name from its swift, darting movements while swimming." **g.** "There are two kinds of metabolic reactions, anabolism and catabolism." **h.** "Monorails, vehicles suspended from a single rail, are usually powered by electric motors." **i.** "The persistence of minority groups may be attributed to their desire to retain their particular traditions."

Problem Nine. Improving predication   (Note: Other answers are possible.) **a.** "Historians offer a number of explanations for the Civil War." **b.** "He remembered the event clearly." **c.** "I wish to explore the origin of language." **d.** "The Fine Arts Committee implemented the program." **e.** "Hamlet also reveals his character in his soliloquies." **f.** "Antigone asserts her character most forcefully when, before her death, she meets Creon face to face." **g.** "The official must establish probable cause before searching a person or possessions." **h.** "However, the rest of Europe respected Prussia's armies, and so they raised Prussia to a position of power." **i.** "Margaret Mead does not view American culture with the same neutrality with which she views other cultures, and so her views have more problems than they can resolve." **j.** "I would like to develop better flexibility and variety in expression." or: "I would like to express myself more flexibly, and with greater variety, in writing."

CHAPTER SEVEN: STYLE IN DESCRIPTION AND NARRATION

Problem Two: Recognizing free modifiers   **a.** After the accident his face had a long time healing. [left-branched free modifier] **b.** But along with their scars, black people have a secret. [left-branched free modifier] **c.** Jargon, the sublanguage peculiar to any trade, contributes to euphemism when its terms seep into general use. [embedded free modifier] **d.** New Jersey has nearly a thousand people per square mile—the greatest population density of any state in the Union. [right-branched free modifier] **e.** Moving beyond a first draft, McPhee generally picks up speed. [left-branched free modifier] **f.** Now that it has more central heating and fewer mouldering gibbets, the countryside is more pleasant than it was. [left-branched free modifier] **g.** The babies were all under one year old, very funny and lovable. [right-branched free modifier] **h.** I remember sitting behind him, rubbing the shoulder and hoping he would always think it was rheumatism and remember only the autumn hunting days. [right-branched free modifier.] **i.** He had grown up, one of the ten children of Russian Jewish immigrant parents, on tough Notre Dame Street in Montreal, where the major sports were craps, poker, and petty larceny. [embedded free modifier and right-branched free modifier— we assume that "on tough Notre Dame Street . . ." would not be separated by punctuation if the embedded free modifier was removed: "He grew up on tough Notre Dame Street. . . ."] **j.** After the lions had returned to their cages, creeping angrily through the chutes, a little bunch of us drifted away and into an open doorway nearby, where we stood for a while in semidarkness, watching a big brown circus horse go harumphing around the practice ring. [two left-branched free modifiers and two right-branched free modifiers]

Problem Three: Creating free modifiers (Note: Other free modifier positions and other grammatical constructions may be equally correct.) **a.** The children looked at the clown, their eyes wide with wonder. **b.** The Chinese factotum, with a quick movement of his hand, grabbed the microfilm. **c.** As a student and the mother of four students, I speak with authority. **d.** The winners celebrated, forming a tight huddle and giving a loud cheer. **e.** The duck waddled across the farmyard, quacking loudly. **f.** The hockey player raced down the sideline, the puck cradled in his stick, his eyes on the net. **g.** The wheat fields spread out before them, the grains rustling softly in the breeze, as if brushed by a gentle hand. **h.** The mackerel banged its head against the side of the tank, banging again and again, with quick, darting movements. **i.** The woman, tall and well-dressed, looked at the elephant playing in the water. **j.** We stood there quietly, holding hands, our heads together, watching the sea gulls.

Problem Four. Identifying free modifiers **a.** He carries a briefcase, lobbies Congress for environmental causes, builds an empire in Utah, appears organized and on the move, but he's still a fogbound romantic, easily slipping into memories of foreign ports, the diaries of his youth, in which he was just another Edgar Allan Poe. [A series of three right-branched free modifiers, following two sentence bases linked by *but*, the first with four verbs coordinated.] **f.** After that we rode on in silence, the traces creaking, the hoofs of the horses clumping steadily in the soft sand, the grasshoppers shrilling from the fields and the cicadas from the trees overhead. [The first two words are "free by position," left-branched; the sentence ends with three right-branched free modifiers.] **g.** Here beside me on the table as I write, occasionally running a tentative paw through the littered sheets of manuscript and notes, is Hobie Baker, a tawny yellow tomcat, named for the great hockey player. [An embedded free modifier, between subject and verb, and two right-branched free modifiers.] **h.** Most of the time she simply rode in a standing position, well aft on the beast, her hands hanging easily at her sides, her head erect, her straw-colored ponytail lightly brushing her shoulders, the blood of exertion showing faintly through the tan of her skin. [The first four words are "free by position," left-branched, and the sentence ends with a series of five separate free modifiers, right-branched.]

Problem Six. Annotating free modifiers (Note: Other answers—in essence, other ways of reading each sentence—are possible.)

a   1] It is a winter day,
           2] overcast and still,
~and~   1] the town is closed in itself,
           2] humming and muttering a little,
             3] like a winter beehive

b   1] The planes dive soundlessly,
           2] like toys on strings,
           2] all but hitting the five-foot trees as they pull out of their dives and simultaneously drop their payloads in the target area,
             3] usually with a concerted accuracy / / that is almost unbelievable.
                4] /—plane after plane after plane—/

c   1] Crane sat up straight.
           2] smiling shyly,
           2] looking pleased,
             3] like a child who has just been given a present.

d   2] Now   ("free by position")
   1] she ran to the bundle, picked it up, and scuttled to the black mouth of the alley a few feet away—
           2] a rather tall woman,
             3] bent,
             3] and in dark clothes from head to feet.

e   1] There were no shops on this wide street that he was walking along,
           2] only a line of tall houses on each side,
             3] all of them identical.

f   1] Connie sat out back in a lawn chair and watched them drive away,
           2] her father quiet and bald,
             3] hunched around so that he could back the car out,
           2] her mother with a look that was still angry and not at all softened through the windshield,

    2] and in the back seat poor Jane all dressed up as if
       she didn't know what a barbecue was,
      3] with all the running yelling kids and the flies.

g   1] The grandmother / / had been occupied once more in
     losing a son.
    2] /, muffled down in the back seat in the corner of
      the old carryall,
      3] in her worn sealskin pelisse,
        4] showing coffee-brown at the edges,
    2] her eyes closed,
    2] her hands waving together,/

h   2] To the right,
   1] the clustered lights of the village spread thinner,
    2] becoming a line along the valley floor and finally
      disappearing in the distance.

i   1] He lumbered into the city room,
    2] a big guy in his middle twenties,
      3] wearing a suit too dark for the season,
      3] and [wearing] the disconsolate frown of a hunter
       who has seen nothing but warblers all day.

j   1] He could bear to think of her only after she overpassed
    the common life of everything and lay in her bed,
    2] on her back,
    2] her narrow heels close together in a painful preci-
      sion,
    2] her face calm,
      3] eyes closed,
      3] preferably with moonlight falling across her face,
    2] her right arm flung back on the pillow,
      3] crooked over her head,
    2] her left arm laid across the mound of her breasts.

Problem Seven. Mastering the free noun phrase   **a.** They had a child, a little girl. (A William Faulkner sentence.) **b.** The obvious leader of the party was an old man, Loren Pierce. (Adopted from a Harold Frederic sentence, "The obvious leader of the party, Loren Pierce, a rich quarryman, was an old man of medium size and mean attire, with a square, beardless face that was as hard and impassive as one of his blocks of limestone.") **c.** I was born in 1927, the only child of middle-class parents. (Adopted from a John Fowles sentence, "I was born in 1927, the only child of middle-class parents, both English, and themselves born in the grotesquely elongated shadow, which they never rose sufficiently above history to leave, of that monstrous dwarf, Queen Victoria.") **d.** The moderator, an "award-winning aerospace journalist" for *Chicago Today,* stepped in occasionally. (Adopted from a Timothy Ferris sentence, "The moderator, Peter Reich, an 'award-winning journalist' for *Chicago Today,* stepped in occasionally to mangle elementary concepts of radio astronomy, relativity and plate techtonics.") **e.** Tina, the Jamaican girl, had given a fishing line to the American, Kennedy. (Adapted from a V. S. Reid sentence, "Tina, the Jamaican girl, had given a fishing line to the American, Kennedy, but for a long time, nothing happened.") **f.** He is the child and product of the disrupted times, a perfect specimen of his generation. (Adapted from a Thomas Mann sentence, "He is the child and product of the disrupted times, a perfect specimen of his generation, follower of the revolution, Bolshevist sympathizer.") **g.** He was my sister Mimi's crazy husband, a mystical child of darkness, a bright, talented, sheepish, tricky, curly-haired man-child of darkness. (Adapted from a Joan Baez sentence, "He was my sister Mimi's crazy husband, a mystical child of darkness, blatantly ambitious, lovable, impossible, charming, obnoxious, tirelessly active—a bright talented sheepish tricky, curly-haired man-child of darkness.") **h.** By the end of the week they all knew him—the hungry mouth, the insufferable humorless eyes, the intense ugly blue-shaved face. (A William Faulkner sentence.)

Problem Nine. Mastering the free verb phrase (Note: Many other versions are possible.) **a.** They were coming for him, walking in step like a tap-dance team returning for a third encore. (Adopted from a Ralph Ellison sentence, "They were coming for him, walking in step, slowly, like a tap-dance team returning for a third encore.") **b.** Father, pleased with himself, was stepping out like a boy. **c.** He mounted the steps and went through the screen door, hearing it bang behind him. (A Richard Wright sentence.) **d.** Next to the child's mother was a red-headed youngish woman, reading one of the magazines and working on a piece of gum. (Adapted from a Flannery O'Conner sentence, "Next to the child's mother was a red-headed youngish woman, reading one of the magazines and working on a piece of chewing gum, hell for leather, as Claud would say.") **e.** Annie came to the door, trying to smile and curtsy, tidying her hair, wiping her hands on her pinafore. (A Dylan Thomas sentence.) **f.** A bicyclist was riding near him on gleaming wheels, cupping his fist to his mouth like a megaphone, cheering him on as they do at races. (A Vladimir Nabokov sentence.)

Problem Eleven. Mastering the free absolute phrase   (Note: Many other versions are possible.) **a.** She's flushed and silent, her mouth half open. (A Robert Coover sentence.) **b.** The priest stood transfixed, his jaw slack. **c.** And then the duck skidded across the surface of the lake, its wings flapping nervously, its legs breaking the water into a series of silvery arcs. (Adopted from a Michael McLaverty sentence, "It circled the lake twice, thrice, coming lower each time, and with a nervous flapping of wings it skidded across the surface, its legs breaking the water into a series of silvery arcs.") **d.** The boys split up, some of them taking the subway down to Greenwich Village, others heading for the Empire State Building. (Adapted from a Lillian Ross sentence, "The boys split up, some of them taking the subway down to Greenwich Village, others heading for the Empire State Building, where they paid a dollar-thirty for tickets to the observatory, and once up there, found that fog and rain blotted out the view completely.") **e.** Then these melodies turn to ice as real night music takes over, the pianos and vibes erecting clusters in the high brittle octaves and a clarinet wandering across like a crack on a pond. (A John Updike sentence.) **f.** He watched the stage-coach go by, the four horses spanking along as the driver flicked them, the polished metal gleaming in the sun, the body swaying as the wheels rose and fell in the rough trail.

Problem Thirteen. Mastering free prepositions and adjectives   **a.** He went to speak to Mrs. Bean, tiny among the pillows. (Adapted from a Murial Spark sentence, "He went to speak to Mrs. Bean, tiny among the pillows, her small toothless mouth open like an 'O,' her skin stretched thin and white over her bones, her huge eye-sockets and eyes in a fixed, infant-like stare, and her sparse white hair short and straggling over her brow.") **b.** She was by the bedside now, very deliberate and very calm. **c.** My fingers, strong and sensitive from their long training, were well adapted to this kind of work. (Adapted from a James Weldon Johnson sentence, "My fingers, strong and sensitive from their long training, were well-adapted to this kind of work, and within two weeks I was accounted the fastest tobacco 'stripper' in the factory.") **d.** She stood before him, with a relaxed dignity, like a priestess at the top of some immensely long stone staircase. **e.** Rose was different today, more tense and more careful. **f.** The students finished the sentences, confident and alert, like dutiful apprentices.

CHAPTER EIGHT: STYLE AS CRAFT

Problem Twelve. Parody   Passage b is taken from Jack Kerouac's *On the Road* (New York: Grove Press, 1957); passage c is a parody of that novel by John Updike titled "On the Sidewalk." Passage d is the opening of J. D. Salinger's *The Catcher in the Rye* (Boston: Little Brown, 1951); passage a is a parody by Dan Greenberg, "Catch Her in the Oatmeal," *Esquire,* February 1958.

CHAPTER NINE: THE PRINT CODE: PUNCTUATION

Problem Two. The Great Punctuation Game, first version (Note: The answers give the punctuation used by the author. Many other answers are equally correct.) 1. semicolon, 2. semicolon, 3. colon, 4. parentheses: "Now the bridge is officially named for him, an action inspired by an 'outsider' (no one who has lived in Chepachet less than thirty-five years is considered a native)." 5. dash, 6. dash, 7. semicolon, 8. colon, 9. semicolon, 10. semicolon, 11. semicolon, 12. colon, 13. semicolon.

Problem Five. The Great Punctuation Game, second version (Note: The answers give the punctuation used by the author. Many other answers are equally correct.) 1. dash, 2. parentheses, 3. dash, 4. dash, 5. comma, 6. parentheses, 7. comma, 8. commas, 9. comma, 10. commas, 11. dash, 12. parentheses, 13. comma, 14. comma, 15. comma, 16. parentheses, 17. dash.

Problem Six. The Great Punctuation Game, championship version (Note: The answers give the punctuation used by the author. Many other answers are equally correct.) 1. dash, 2. comma, 3. comma, 4. semicolon, 5. comma, 6. comma, 7. colon, 8. comma, 9. comma, 10. semicolon, 11. comma, 12. comma, 13. comma, 14. parentheses, 15. comma, 16. comma, 17. comma, 18. comma, 19. comma, 20. comma, 21. comma, 22. colon, 23. comma, 24. parentheses, 25. comma, 26. comma, 27. comma, 28. comma, 29. comma, 30. comma, 31. semicolon, 32. comma, 33. comma, 34. parentheses, 35. comma, 36. comma, 37. comma, 38. semicolon, 39. comma, 40. comma.

CHAPTER TEN: WORDS, WORDS, WORDS

Problem One: Problems in word choice (Omitted words are in italics.) **a.** This *magnificent* heirloom library will *consist of* 50 great books by the *giants* of American literature. The books will be *impeccably crafted.* Sumptuously bound and decorated with *graceful* golden accents. **b.** The American Heritage Dictionary of the English language is a *completely new* dictionary, new in content, new in format, new in the *wealth* of information it *offers.* It *presents* not only words and their meanings but also *extensive* notes on how to *use* them. These *illuminating* notes are prepared with the *assistance* of a *select* panel of more than a hundred of America's most *notable* writers, editors, and public speakers. **c.** *Yuck!* Morning breath, the *worst* breath of the day. You know that *pasty* film that covers your mouth, teeth, and gums while you're *asleep?* And then, when you wake up, your breath is really *gross?* Well, Scope does a *great* job of *fixing* all that. Use it first thing, and your mouth will feel *clean and fresh.* Not even the mediciney antiseptic cleans your mouth better than Scope. And *best of all,* when you leave the house to meet your *friends,* your breath will be *minty-fresh,* not *mediciney.*

Problem Eleven. Jargon   Students should be able to explain the jargon of passage a (on high fidelity) and d (on art), and passage c (on linguistics) will be beyond the ability of all but a trained linguist to explain. Passage b (from horse racing), however, may need an explanation, since students (and instructors) may be unfamiliar with racing jargon. Here is the passage again, with bracketed explanations: "The Proudest Roman [the name of the horse] filly [a female horse under five years old,] conditioned [trained] by Jimmy Picou, broke her maiden [won a race for the first time—a *maiden* is a racehorse, male or female, that has not won a race] at first asking [in her first race], topping [beating] Daisy Miller [the horse who finished second] by slightly more than a length [a *length* is 'the length of a horse,' a measure of distance in racing].

"Sun Valley Sally [another horse] also scored [won a race] her first time out [in her first race], beating Tuvalu, but wound up [finished] fourth against Heavenly Lass [the winning horse] in her most recent [race]."

CHAPTER TWELVE: THE PRINT CODE: SPELLING

Problem Two: Spelling and meaning   (Note: Other answers are possible.) **c.** musCular, **d.** desiGnation, **e.** condemNation, **f.** goverN, **g.** maliGnant, **h.** sofT, **i.** paradiGmatic, **j.** contemPtuous.

Problem Three. Spelling and meaning **c.** figure::figurative, **d.** really::reality, **e.** playwright::shipwright, **f.** copyright::birthright, **g.** birthright::copyright, **h.** penal::penalty, **i.** eternal::eternity, **j.** copywriter::screenwriter.

Problem Five. Finding the schwa vowel   **d.** democratic::demOcracy, **e.** president::presIde, **f.** repetition::repEat, **g.** precedent::precEde, **h.** comparable::compArison, **i.** composition::compOse, **j.** janitor:: janitOrial, **k.** manager::managErial, **l.** illustrate::illUstrative, **m.** industry::indUstrious, **n.** immigrate::mIgrate, **o.** consolation::consOle, **p.** abolition::abOlish, **q.** competent::compEte.

Problem Six. Homonyms   **a.** The horse is hoarse because the course is coarse. **b.** If you sight the right site, cite the right law. **c.** You're on your toes. **d.** Who's going to drive whose car? **e.** It's too bad it's too late to save the chicken from its inevitable fate. **f.** Get your council from the counsel. **g.** I'd advise you to get some advice.

Problem Seven. The missing -ed hunt   "Toss salad" is a mistake for "tossed salad." "Shatterproof bottles," now the common spelling, were originally "shatterproofed." "Unfinish furniture," "bake potato," "use car," and "skim milk" are still mistakes for "unfinished furniture," "baked potato," "used car" and "skimmed milk." But "can goods," "corn beef," "condition reflex," and "oversize load," though not all are recognized by dictionaries, are now common, and "incline plane" and "wax paper" have replaced the original "inclined plane" and "waxed paper." "Business bribe," "creme rinse," "contact lenses," "labor relations," and "home run" did not ever have -*ed* endings.

Problem Eight. A special problem in subject-verb agreement   **a:** is, **b:** is, **c:** is, **d:** points, **e:** are.

CHAPTER FOURTEEN: TWO WRITING TASKS

Problem Two. A true/false test on essay tests   **a:** false, **b:** true, **c:** false, **d:** false, **e:** false, **f:** false (at least for most instructors), **g:** true, **h:** false, **i:** true, **j:** false, **k:** false.

Problem Eight. Thinking like a librarian   **b.** This writer invented the *New York Times Index,* which summarizes news stories in the *New York Times,* with helpful cross-references. It is thus a useful first source for "dating" a research problem—that is, finding the dates which one wants to use in searching other indexes. **c.** This writer invented the *Consumers' Index,* an index to over 100 journals dealing with the well-being of consumers. **d.** This writer invented the *Biological and Agricultural Index,* dealing with biological science and its applications, and, by following the cross-references in the card catalog, he came upon several book references. **e.** This writer invented the *Social Sciences Index,* which uses the same format as the *Reader's Guide,* and she also discovered *Historical Abstracts,* which prints brief summaries of articles. She began, of course, by using the *New York Times Index* to find the dates of the events. She followed two subject entries in the card catalog, those relating to President Truman and to "Atomic Weapons."

Problem Nine. Creating a reference work   **b.** This writer also created the *New York Times Index.* **c.** This writer created *Editorials on File,* a loose-leaf file of newspaper editorials. **d.** This writer created a special source, *Language and Language Behavior Abstracts,* which provides abstracts on a number of topics, including "the origin of language." **e.** This writer created some helps that proved to exist at one of our libraries: first, a computerized print-out listing journal holdings in the library by subject-matter, and second, a separate "Nursing Library," with all the journals displayed on racks. Failing these helps, the student might have used a recent nursing textbook, both to find references to journals and to find a controversial topic.

CHAPTER FIFTEEN. ANALYSIS: THINKING WITH CONCEPTS

Problem Four. Being "Dear Abby." (Answers were written by Abigail Van Buren, in the "Dear Abby" column of the *Cincinnati Enquirer* on the dates noted.) **a.** DEAR STEAMED: Is your husband a professional guide and chauffeur, or did he agree to be the one to accommodate these ladies? It's not a legitimate business deal unless he has some kind of contract or agreement with them. If he hasn't, it sounds to me like a lot of hot air that came out of a lot of cold beers. —January 14, 1979 **b.** DEAR STUCK: If you've heard her praying to die story for 20 years, you should be used to it by now. You should also realize that she probably doesn't mean it, and she could be a little sick. Handle her as you would a demanding child. Be compassionate and patient, but firm. Give her what time you can, and don't feel guilty about the rest. Your problem is not your mother. It's your inability to accept a situation which you can't change. —January 14, 1979 **c.** DEAR HATES: You rattled the right cage. If a man is to succeed in business, his greatest asset is a wife who is always in his corner. Let him accept the promotion. You and your children will make new friends. Help your husband climb the ladder of success by being supportive and you will have another lovely home that his "Jack" built. —November 19, 1977

Problem Six. Where's the Warrant? first series (Note: These warrants can be phrased in other ways.) **a.** College is the same kind of educational experience as high school. **b.** Presiding over a university takes precisely the same skills as being a successful banker. **c.** The federal budget is exactly comparable with a family budget. **d.** Our college is exactly comparable with Pahrump College. **e.** No politician is completely truthful. **f.** All women favor abortion.

CHAPTER SEVENTEEN: THE SPECIAL PLACES OF INVENTION

Problem Three. Lost on the moon: Thinking in a new context The rankings of NASA scientists, with their reasoning given in parentheses:

1. two 100-pound tanks of oxygen (most pressing survival need), 2. five gallons of water (replacement for tremendous liquid loss on lighted side), 3. stellar map (primary means of navigation), 4. food concentrate (efficient means of supplying energy requirements), 5. solar-powered FM receiver-transmitter (for communication with mother ship; but FM requires light-of-sight transmission and short ranges), 6. 50 feet of nylon rope (useful in scaling cliffs, tying injured together), 7. first-aid kit containing injection needles (needles for vitamins, medicines, etc., will fit special aperture in NASA space suits), 8. parachute silk (protection from the sun's rays), 9. self-initiating life raft (CO_2 bottle in military raft may be used for propulsion), 10. signal flares (distress signal when mother ship is sighted), 11. two .45 caliber pistols (possible means of self-propulsion), 12. one case of dehydrated Pet milk (bulkier duplication of food concentrate), 13. solar-powered heating unit (not needed unless on dark side), 14. magnetic compass (magnetic field on moon is not polarized; worthless for navigation), 15. box of matches (no oxygen on moon to sustain flame; virtually worthless).

You can score yourself by subtracting the difference, for each guess, between your ranking and that of NASA's scientists (if you ranked something 1 that NASA ranked 8, you would list that as 7 penalty points). A score of 0 to 15 is excellent, 26–32 is good, 33–45 is average, 46–55 is fair, and over 56 is poor.

Problem Five. Exercises in cross-breeding   **c:** An engineer solved this problem by cross-breeding from a game of tennis to Air Force bombers. He stopped to open a new can of tennis balls during a weekend game, and when he heard the hiss of air as he opened the vacuum-packed balls, he realized that the tires could be protected by placing them in large vacuum-packed cans. A game of tennis (and an alert mind) saved the government several hundred thousand dollars.

Problem Six. Paradigms for spelling research   There are many possible ways of classifying these studies. The one that seems most useful to us is to group those studies that assume that spelling merely reflects sound (or should reflect sound) with those that assume that spelling can be taught mechanically. We might label this group "mechanical approaches to spelling," and in it we would place items a, c, f, h, and k. The other studies seem to view spelling more complexly; we might label this group as "generative" or "formative" approaches to spelling, as in studies b, d, e, g, i, j, and l.

Problem Eight. Forcing analogies   You might be interested in the original analogies forced from these passages—though you will have forced quite different analogies, of course. Passage a, from an autobiography by Lillian Hellman, is used as an analogy for human memory. Passage b, in the 1804 original, is used as an argument by analogy for the existence of God. Passage c, the dancing Wu Li masters, is used as an analogy for the work of modern physicists. Passage d is used as an argument for the study of science.

Index

Absolute phrase, 224–26
Abstraction levels
  in paragraphs, 136–55
  in sentences, 215–19
  in words, 296–301
Abstracts, reference work, 456–60
Acronyms, 357
Adjective form, 391–92
Adjective phrase modifiers, 226
Adverb form, 369, 391–92
Adversative structure, as form,
    424–26
Agee, James, 7–8
Albersheim, Peter, 130–31
Allen, Woody, 33–34
Allusions, writing stance, 67
Ambiguity in sentences, 171–73
American Heritage Dictionary, 295,
    337
Analogy
  and creative thinking, 572–76
  uses of, 306
Analyzing arguments, writing,
    505–12
"And" linkages, 116–18
Annotation and free modifiers,
    218–19
Anthologies, bibliographic form, 472,
    480, 483

Antithesis in sentences, 246–47
Argument
  analysis of, 505–15
    model for, 512
  fallacious appeals, 515–19
  scope of, 502–5
  stating the case, 499–501
Aristotelian definition, 535
Auden, W. H., 11
Audience, writing, 40–42, 50
  and voice, 57–80
  and writer's stance, 57–89
Authority, appeal to, 516
Authors, bibliographic form for, 468,
    478–80, 483

Backing in argument, 510–14, 525
Bacon, Francis, 243, 254
Balanced sentence, 245–46
Bandwagon appeal and argument,
    517
Base clause and separation, 274, 278
"Because" linkages, 113, 118
Becker, Carl L., 543
Begging the question, argument, 518
Beginning point, writing, 4–5
Bell, Quentin, 85–86

Bibliography
  cards for, 455, 458
  definition, 452
  form of, 467–76
Blends and word meaning, 357
Books
  and bibliographic records, 455
  footnote form, 476–82
  form for, bibliographies, 468–72
    sample entries, 471
  reviews, indexes to, 458
Bound modifiers
  and meaning changes, 206
  and punctuation, 211, 274
  recognition, 206–19
  and texture, 203–5
Brainstorming and invention, 9–10,
    494
Brand, Norman, 440
British Simplified Spelling Society,
    372
Bronowski, Jacob, 146
Brown, Claude, 146–47
Brute facts and meaning, 565–66
Bubblegum voice, writer's stance,
    59–62
Bureaucratic voice, 69–74
Business letter and fixed form,
    416–17
"But" linkages, 114, 118

Card catalog, library, 452–54
Carpenter, Edmund, 99
Carroll, Lewis, 240–41
Castaneda, Carlos, 554
Catalog card, library, 452–54
Cause and effect, as form, 425–26,
    428
Caxton, William, 350
Celtic language, 345
Central commitment, writing, 602
Chace, Howard, 395–96
Christensen, Francis, 230–31
"Chunking"
  and ambiguity, 171–73
  effective use, 190–94

fused sentences, 175–77
  and meaning, 170–78
  pronoun reference, 175–77
  and the reader, 173–77, 194
  and sentence base, 180
Claims and grounds, argument,
    505–15, 525
Clarity and writing, 167–94
Classification, as form, 539–43, 547
Close imitation and style, 241–42
Closed context, creativity, 557
Closing an essay, 427–29
Code of print. *See* Print Code
Coherence
  complexities of, 94–101
  creation of, 120–24
  evaluation of, 107–10
  framework for, 122–24
  implications for writer, 107–24
  and incoherence, 98–101
  linkages, 118
  as pattern of meaning, 95–128
  in speaking, 101–2
  in writing, 101–2
College dictionaries, 335–39, 362
College paper. *See* Investigative paper
Colon and sentence connectors, 116,
    118, 269
Comma
  and free modifiers, 210–11, 213–14
  importance of, 262
  purposes in sentences, 210–11
  as sentence connector, 266
  as series connector, 278–79
Comma plus connector, 266, 268
Comma splice, 271, 273
Commitment-response model, in-
    vention, 494
Commitment-response sentences,
    133–36, 154, 160
Committed personal voice, 77–80
Communication codes, 45–46
Comparison and contrast, as form,
    545–48
Complexity, figurative language, 305
Compound sentences and coordi-
    nation, 185–86

Compounding and word meaning, 355–56
Concluding sentences, paragraphs, 152–53
Concrete words, 300–301
Conjunctions, 271
Connectors
 and discursive patterns, 106
 sentences, 186, 264–74
 series, 278
Connotative meaning, 295, 301–3
Context
 and creativity, 557–58
 of rhetoric, 35–45
Contrast and invention, writing, 545–48
Cookbook principle, narration, 231–33
Coordination
 paragraphs, 142–47, 153, 215–19
 sentences, 185–86, 217–18
Corporate authors, bibliographic form, 473
Craftsmanship and style, 237, 261
Cramming, exams, 440–41
Creativity. *See also* Invention in writing
 and language, 18
 process of, 554–59
Cross-breeding, ideas, 566–69, 576
Cumulative sentences, 230–31

Dale, Edgar, 70
Dangling modifier, 227
Danish influence, language, 348, 354
Dash
 versus hyphen, 275
 and sentence connectors, 267–69
 as separator, 275
de Mille, Agnes, 234–35
Dead metaphors, 307–10
Definition
 Aristotelian, 535
 change in, 536
 context, 537

heuristic for, 536–39
and invention, writing, 533–39, 547
positive uses, 534–36
sequence in, 537
Deloria, Vine, 86
Denotative meaning
 Latin influence, 351
 and work choice, 295, 301–3
Description
 and style, 199–236
 texture in, 202–19
Detached discursive voice, 74
Detail in narration, 232–33
Development of claim, paragraphs, 140–42
Dialects, 320–23
Diary, as writer's aid, 7–9, 22–23
Diction
 dimensions, 293–327
 and prose style, 167–68
Dictionary
 fallacies of, 335–40
 information in, standard college, 336–39
 as knowledge source, 338–40
 manual of, 335–67
 as vocabulary builder, 333
Didion, Joan, 8, 86–87
Dillard, Annie, 217
Directness, writing, 167–94
Discovery thinking
 and analogy, 572–75
 assumptions about, 554–59
 cross-breeding ideas, 566–69
 heuristic for, 566–76
 and paradigms, 569–72
 visual aspects, 575–76
Discursive paragraph, 129–64
Discursive pattern
 linkages, 117–19
 speaking, 104–5
Doctorow, E. L., 99–100
Drafts and paper writing, 464–67
 first draft, 584–85
 revision model, 582–89
Dumb reader, 173–77,
Dynamic model, writing, 31–48

Ebel, Robert, 525–28
-ed system and misspelling, 384
Editor, book, bibliographic form,
    472, 478–80, 483
Effect/cause and writing structure,
    425–26, 428
Elaboration
    and figurative language, 305
    of paragraphs, 591–92
Elasticity, sentences, 247–51
Elbow, Peter, 25
Eliot, George, 567
Embedded words, 230
Emotional argument, rhetoric, 37–39
English, history of the language,
    341–55
Enumeration, as form, 424–25
Essays
    closing, 427–30
    examinations, college, 436–46
    opening, 427–30
    purpose of, 439–40
    stating the case, 500–501
    studying for, 440
Ethical appeal, rhetoric, 37–39
Etymology
    definition, 333
    dictionary presentation, 336–39
    of English spelling, 376–79
    and spelling errors, 369
Euphemistic language, 316–18
Euphuistic style, 243
Examinations, essay. See Essays
Expansion and sentence style, 249–51
Explanatory model, rhetorical
    triangle, 36–39
Explictness, writing, 493, 495–97
Exploding sentence, 253–55
Expressive writing, 46

Fallacies of logic, 515–19
False cause, argument, 518–19
Fifty-star theme, 412, 427–28
Figurative language, 303–10
Final draft, writing, 587–88
First draft, writing, 584

First-person voice, 85
Fixed form, 411–20
    business letter, 416–17
    opening and closing, 427–29
    résumé, 418–19
Flow charts, bibliographic form, 469
    books, 470, 476, 479, 481
    journals, 474–75, 477
Fluency, 4
Focus and invention, writing, 544
Footnotes
    form, 467–69, 476–85
        authors, books, 478–80
        books, 476
        journals, 477–78
        special features, 478–82, 484
    guidelines, 464
Form, writing. See also Writing
    grasping of, reading, 405–11
    and message, 402
    and writing, 401–35
Formal language, 313–15
Formal outlines, readers, 161–63
Formative idea, writing, 412, 421–30,
    445
Formative principle, 401–35
Fossilized metaphors, 308
Fragments, sentence, 180–84
Frameworks of meaning
    coordinates, 142–47
    and writing, 122–24
Free absolute phrase, 224–26
Free imitation and style, 241–42
Free modifiers
    grammar of, 219–28
    implications for writers, 228–35
    movement of, 207, 212
    and punctuation, 207–8, 211,
        274–78
        commas, 213–14
    recognition of, 206–19
    and texture, 203–5
Free noun phrase, 219–22
Free verb phrase, 222–23
Free writing, 5–7, 23, 494
French influence, English language,
    348–50

Fries, Charles Carpenter, 102–3
Fudge factors, paragraphs, 152–54
Funk & Wagnalls Standard College Dictionary, 338
Fused sentence, 175–77

Gardner, Howard, 564–65
Generality levels
   paragraphs, 136–42
   sentences, 215–19
   and word choice, 294, 297–300
Generalization
   language learning, 19–20
   and word meaning, 356
Generative model, rhetorical triangle,
   39–43
Germanic languages, 345, 347–48
Gibson, Walker, 88–89
Grading, standards for, 604–5
Grammar
   comma splice/run-on sentence,
    272*b*
   dangling modifiers, 227*b*
   definitions of, 552
   of free modifiers, 219–28, 277*b*
   introductory modifiers, 277*b*
   versus logic, sentences, 179
   of metaphor, 304–10
   parallelism, 244*b*
   predicate, 180*b*
   quotes and italics, 284*b*
   sense of, and language, 19, 21
   and sentence base, 178–84
   sentence fragments, 182–83*b*
   series constructions, 280*b*
   and style, 191
   subject, 180*b*
   and subordination, 186–87
   tense shifts, 466*b*
   verb, 180*b*
   and word choice, 322*b*
Grammar of coherence, 118–19, 122
Greek model, writing, 52
Greenburg, Dan, 259
Gross, Ronald, 403

Grounds and claims, argument,
   505–15
Guess vocabulary, 331

Hackneyed expressions
   avoidance of, 308
   history, 357–58
Hall, Donald, 87–88
Harmony, writer's goal, 47
Hays, David G., 404
Hellman, Lillian, 574
Hemingway, Ernest, 202–4, 255–56
Hering, Ewald, 560
Heuristic. *See* Discovery thinking
Homonyms and spelling problems,
   369, 382–83
Huxley, Thomas, 575
Hyphen
   versus dash, 275
   as separator, 275
   uses of, 286

Illusion and creativity, 560–66
Illustration, 543–45, 547
Imitation and style, 240–42
Incoherence, 94
   as measure of coherence, 98
   and reading, 97–98
Incomplete sentence, 180–84
Indexes and investigative papers,
   455–60
Indo-European language family,
   347–48
Informal language, 313–15
Informal outlines, 161
Institutional facts and meaning,
   565–66
Internalization, writing process,
   12–13
Introductory modifiers, 277–78
Introductory sentences, paragraphs,
   152–53
Invention in writing
   classification in, 533–39
   common "places" of, 547

Invention in writing (*continued*)
  and communication process,
    493–530
  comparison and contrast, 545–48
  and creative process, 554–59
  definition in, 534–39
  guiding strategy, 533, 547
  illustration, 543–45
  revision process, 581–612
  and rhetoric, 52
  special places of, 554–79
Inverted sentence, 252–53
Investigative paper
  bibliography and footnotes, 452,
    467–82
  drafting of, 464–85
  goals of, 446
  indexes and abstracts, 455–60
  manuscript form, 483–87
  process of, models, 449–50
  reading and notetaking, 460–64
  resources for, 451
  steps in writing, 448–51
Irony, 82
Italics, 282–86

Jargon, 319–20
Journal
  bibliographic features, 468
    form, 473–75
  footnote form, 477–78
Journal keeping, 7–9, 22–23
Journalistic voice, writing, 62–66
Joyce, James, 296
"Jumps" and linkage, 118–19

Kelly, Lou, 88
Kennedy, John F., 238–40
Kerouac, Jack, 259
King, Martin Luther, 143–44

Labov, William, 420–21
Lakoff, Robin, 75–76

Language. *See also* English language
  chunks in, 171
  competence in, 17–20
    sentence base, 178–84
  definitions, 551–52
  figurative, 303–10
  general characteristics, 13–22
  Indo-European family, 347
  knowing how and knowing about,
    14–17
  learning of, 19–20
  levels of, 313–16
  and writing, 13–20
Latin roots
  helpfulness, 332
  influence, 347–48, 350–54
Lawrence, D. H., 601–2
Lazarus, Mitchell, 528–30
Lead sentence, journalism, 64
Left-branched modifiers, 230, 274
Levels of generality
  paragraphs, 136–42, 155
  sentences, 215–19
Levels of language, 313–15
Lexicon, definition, 333
Library of Congress catalog card, 453
Library resources, 451–60
  catalog card, 452–53
  mapping of, 451–53
Linkages, word, 113–25. *See also*
    Transition
Lish, Gordon, 250–51
Literal words, 295, 303–10
Literature, writing about, 600–609
Logic
  versus grammar, sentences, 179
  versus rhetoric, paragraphs, 153
Logical argument, rhetoric, 37
Logical connection, sentences, 96–
    101. *See also* Transition
  discursive patterns, 106
  sentences, 96–101
  transition, 113–19

Macrorie, Ken, 52
Mailer, Norman, 255

Main, C. F., 602–4
Malcolm X, 334
Manners in writing, 50
Manuscript form, 483–87
Mapping, approach to reading,
    126–27, 162
Marshack, Alexander, 567–68
Master paragraph, 151–52
Master sentence, 234–35
McKerrow, R. B., 414
Meaning
    changes in, and words, 355–59
    and chunks. *See* "Chunking"
        and meaning
    creation of, writing, 411–21
    and cumulative sentences, 230–31
    explosiveness of, 251–55
    and punctuation, importance, 264
    and reading, 408
    and spelling, 373–76
        word forms, 383
Media, 45–46
Message, writing, 40
Metaphor. *See also* specific types
    and analogy, 306
    grammar of, 304–10
    new journalism, 67
    revitalization, 309
    and simile, 305
Middle English, 346, 348–51
Middlemarch, 567
Mischunking. *See* Ambiguity in sen-
        tences
Mixed paragraph frameworks,
    147–52
Mixed metaphor, 308
Models
    and creativity, 559
    of revision, 582–89
    of writing, 31–48
        rhetorical triangle, 36–43
Modern English, 346, 351–53, 387
Modifiers, 206–7, 277–78. *See also*
        specific types
Momaday, N. Scott, 237–38
Morris, William, 251–52
Muller-Lyer, F., 560

Narration
    cookbook principle, 231–33
    showing versus telling, 233–34
    and style, 199–236
    texture in, 202–19
Narrative pattern, 104–5, 119
Neutral voice, writing, 62–66
New journalism, 66–69
"New novelists" and style, 256
New York Times, 66, 316
New Yorker, 234, 246, 280–81
Nonrestrictive modifiers, 277–78
Norman influence, English lan-
        guage, 348–50
Notebooks, writer's aid, 7–9, 22–23
Notetaking, 460–64
Noun modifiers, 219–22
Nurnberg, Maxwell, 71, 263

Old English, 346–48, 387
Open context, creativity, 558
Open form, 412, 421
Opening an essay, 427–29
Operational definition, 536
"Or" linkages, 116
Order, paragraph construction,
        140–42
Outlines, 161–63
Oxford English Dictionary, 340
Oxymorons, 253
Ozick, Cynthia, 253·

Paley, William, 574
Paradigm
    and creativity, 559
    and thinking, 569–72, 576
Paragraph
    anomalies, 154
    commitment sentence, 133–36
    conclusion, 152–53
    discursive, 129–64
    elaboration, 591–92
    generality levels, 215–19
    introduction, 152–53
    levels of generality, 136–42

Paragraph (*continued*)
  mixed frameworks, 142–47,
      215–19
  punctuation, 155–57
  rhetoric versus logic of, 153
  shortening of, 592
  subordinate frameworks, 144–47
  topic sentence, 131–32
Paragraph barrier, 158–61
Parallelism, 242–45
Paraphrase, paper writing, 461–65
  draft stage, 465
  notetaking stage, 461–64
  and plagiarism, 463–64
Parentheses as separator, 275
Parody, 82–83, 258–60
Parts of speech, dictionaries, 336–40
Passive sentences, 188–90
Past tense and misspelling, 369,
      384–85
Paste predication, 192
Pattern of meaning, sentences, 95–
      101, 104
Periodic sentences, 251–52
Persona. *See* Voice
Personal argument, rhetoric, 37–39,
      41
Personal attack and argument,
      516–17
Phonetics
  code of, 373
  and misspellings, 378–79
  and spelling, 372–76
  vowel symbols, 371
Pity appeal and argument, 517
Plagiarism, 463–64
Plurals and misspelling, 369, 386–88
Poetic writing, 46
Poetry
  central commitment, 602–4
  and coherence, 98–99
  power of form, 403
  and repetition, 110–11
Possessives and misspelling, 389–91
Pound, Ezra, 98
Predicate
  choice of, 184–94
  and sentence base, 179–80

Preliminary topic, 448–51
Prepositional phrase, modifiers,
      226–27
Prewriting, 10
Print Code, 49–50
  origin, 350
  and punctuation, 262–89
  and spelling, 368–98
  and style, 239–61
Print explicitness
  and argument, 520–25
  definition, 493, 495–99
  versus speech, 495–97
"Private" style, 237–39
Problem/solution structure, as form,
      424–26
Pronouns and "chunking," 175–77
Pronunciation
  dictionary presentation, 336–39
  and spelling, 375
Proper names and word meaning,
      357
Prose style, 167–68
"Public" style, 237–39
Publisher, bibliographic form, 472
Punctuation. *See also* specific types
  control of meaning, 264
  free modifiers, 207–8, 211–14,
      274–78
  major uses, 262–88
  and speaking, relationship, 262
  and the Print Code, 262–89
Puttenham, George, 249

Qualifiers in writing, argument,
      510–14
Question, approach to reading, 125
Question/answer, as form, 424–26
Quinn, Jim, 409–11
Quotation, 461–64
Quotation marks
  bibliographic form, 468–69
  special uses, 282–86

Random House College Dictionary, 333,
      371

Reader-centered revision, 583, 591–92
Reader-centered writing, 42
Reader's Guide to Periodical Literature, 455–58
Reading
  active nature, 97
  ambiguity, interpretation, 173–78
  approaches, 124–27
  for college papers, 460–64
  and commitment sentence, 135
  and form, grasping of, 405–11
  and meaning, 408–9
  plan, importance of, 405–7
  for tone, 80–83
Reading vocabulary, 331, 353
Rebuttal in writing, argument, 510–15
References, 468–69. *See also* Bibliography; Footnotes
Regional dialects, 320–23
Register (social standing of words), 310–24
Repetition
  and discursive patterns, 105
  uses of, 110–13
Research journal, 448
Research paper. *See* Investigative paper
Résumé and fixed form, 418–19
Revision
  checklists, 593
  dynamic model, 582–89
  example of, 589–90
  paragraphs, 591–93
  sentences, 593
  and the writing process, 11
Rewriting. *See* Revision
Rhetoric
  and cumulative sentences, 230–31
  definition, 27–30
  dimensions, 27–55
  limits of, 503
  versus logic, paragraphs, 153
  and manuscript revision, 593
  uses of, 30–31
Rhetorical choice, 34–35
Rhetorical contexts, 35–45

Rhetorical triangle, 36–43, 494
Rhythms of writing, 242–47
Right-branched modifiers, 228, 230, 274
Robbe-Grillet, Alain, 256–57
Rolling Stone, 66–67, 77–80
Romance languages, 345, 347
Rubin, Edgar, 561
Run-on sentence, 271–73
Russell, Bertrand, 23–24, 154, 159–60

-s systems and misspellings, 386–88, 390
Salinger, J. D. 259
Satire, 82
Scholarly journals, bibliographic form, 474–75
Schools and writing, 51–52
"Schwa" vowel
  finding of, 381–82
  and spelling errors, 369, 379–82
Searle, John R., 565–66
Selven, Samuel, 20–21
Semicolon
  and sentence connectors, 266–69
  series connector, 279
Sentence
  balancing, 245–47
  base. *See* Sentence base
  choices of, 167–98
  and "chunking," 170–78, 190–94
  combining. *See* Sentence combining
  connectors, 186, 264–74
  coordination of, 185–86
  elasticity, 247–51
  expansion of, 249–51
  exploding, 253–55
  fragments, 180–84
  fused, 176–77
  introductory and concluding, 152–53
  inverted, 252–53
  meaning of, and predication, 184–85
  outline, 162–63
  passive, 189–90

Sentence (*continued*)
  patterns. *See* Sentence patterns
  response to, and grammar, 179
  run-on, 272–73
  separators, 274–78
  style, 167–68, 199–236
  subordination, 186–87, 193
Sentence base
  and grammar, 178–84
  and texture, 203–5
Sentence combining
  free modifiers, 219–28
  and style, 168–70
Sentence patterns
  and meaning, 93
  and paragraph construction,
    140–42
    coordinates, 142–43
  repetition, use of, 111–13
  sentence-to-sentence connections,
    119–20
Separators
  bound modifiers, 274
  commas, 275–77
  dashes, 275
  free modifiers, 274
  parentheses, 275–76
Series connectors, 278
Seventeen, 295–96
Seventeenth century, writing, 254
Sexism in language, 323–24
Shakespeare, William, 352
Shaler, Nathaniel Southgate, 201–2
Shape. *See also* Form
  and formative ideas, 421–22
  principles, 424–26
  and reading, 405, 407–8
Shaw, Irwin, 228–29
Shoptalk and words, 319–20
Shortening, word meaning, 357
Shulman, Max, 81
Simile
  grammar of, 304–5
  and metaphor, 305
Simple coordinate framework,
    143–47, 153
Slang, 323

"So" linkages, 115, 118
Social dialects, 320–23
Social register of words, 310–15
Social sense, language, 57
Sociolinguistics, 51
Sound. *See* Phonetics
Speaking
  coherence in, 101–2
  elements of arrangement, 93–128
Speaking vocabulary, 331, 353
Specialization and word meaning,
    356
Specialized appeal, writing, 41
Specificity and word choice, 294,
    297–300
Speech versus print, explicitness,
    495–97
Spelling
  etymological basis, 376
  improvement of, 376–94
  and phonetics, 372–75
  and print code, 368–98
  problems in, classification, 369
  research in, paradigms, 570–72
  system of, 369, 372–76
    and misspelling, 392–94
  systematic patterns, 368–98
Spelling log, 376–77
SQRRM and reading, 124–27
Stance, writer's, 57–89
Standard for grading, 604–5
Starting point, writing, 4–5
Static model, writing, 31–33, 583
Stating the case, writing, 499–501
Stein, Gertrude, 195–96
Stephens, Martha, 215
Stipulative definition, 536
Studying, essay exams, 440–41
Style
  and craftsmanship, 237–61
  in description and narration, 199–
    236
  imitation and, 240–42
  and invention, 494
  lack of, 255–57
  potential of, sentences, 199–236
  in prose, 52, 167–68

reading, implications, 258–60
sentence combining, 168–70
Subject headings, card catalog, 453–54
Subject-verb agreement, 388–89
Subject-verb combinations
    choice of, 184–85
    implications for writers, 187–93
    improvement, 190
Subjects and sentence base, 179–80
Subordination
    in paragraphs, 144–47, 216
    in sentences, 186–87, 193
Subtitles, bibliographic form, 472
Summary in writing, 461–65
Surface detail and revision, 587–88, 594
Survey approach, reading, 125
Syntax
    and prose style, 167–68
    sentence combining, 168–70

Taylor, Edwin P., 528–30
Tense
    patterns in, 465–67
    and spelling errors, 369, 384–85
Tests. *See* Essays
Texture, narration and description, 202–19
"That is to say" linkage, 118
Thesis sentence, 161–62, 421
Thinking and discovery, 566–79
Thomas, Dylan, 235
Three-sentence paragraph, 138–42
Titles, bibliographic features, 468
Tolkien, J. R. R., 255
Tone, 80–83, 85–89
Topic outlines, 161–62
Topic sentences, 131–32
    versus commitment sentences, 134
    in "fifty-star theme," 413
    in magazines, 157–61
    and paragraph barrier, 158–61
    and paragraphs, 131–32
Transactional writing, 46
Transfer and word meaning, 355

Transition, 113–25
    "and" in, 116–18
    "and then" in, 117–18
    "because" in, 113, 118
    "but" in, 114, 118
    colon, 115–16, 118
    "jumps" in, 118–19
    "or" in, 116, 118
    paragraph construction, 140–42
    "so" in, 115, 118
    "yet" in, 114
Trilling, Lionel, 112
Trite expressions, 308
True versus mere rhetoric, 27–31
Truth, writer's goal, 47–48

Universal audience, 40, 50, 447
Updike, John, 259–60
Usage. *See* Word Usage

Verbs
    Phrase modifiers, 222–23
    and spelling, 385, 387
Visual thinking, 575–76
Vocabulary
    building of, rules, 328–30
    sources, 354
    types of, 331
Voice
    bubblegum type, 59–62
    bureaucratic, 69
    committed personal, 78
    definition, 80
    detached discursive type, 74
    ideal types, 74–80
    journalistic, 62–66
    neutral, 62–66
    new journalism, 66–69
    and writer's stance, 57–80, 83–89
Vowel symbols
    misspellings, 379–82
    phonetics, 371
Vulgar language, 313–15

Warrant, in writing, 506–15, 525
Watson, James, 575–76
Weasel words, 316–18
Webster's International Dictionary,
    362–63
Webster's New World Dictionary, 336
Webster's Seventh New Collegiate Dictio-
    nary, 339
Whitman, Walt, 49
Williams, Martin, 130
Williams, Raymond, 74–75
Williams, William Carlos, 402
Wolfe, Tom, 24, 157–58
Word choice, 293–327
Word endings and misspelling, 384
Word ladders, 296
Word linkage, 113–19
Word order and sentences, 178–79
Word patterns and repetition, 112
Word usage, 611–14
    jargon, 319
    shoptalk, 319–20
    slang, 323
Words
    abstract, 300–301
    concrete, 300–301
    connotation, 301–3
    denotation, 301–3
    general, 297–99
    shifts of meaning in, 355–59
    specific, 297–99
    weasel, 316–18
World English, 353–54
Writer-centered revision, 583
Writer-centered writing, 42

Writer's stance, 57–89
    and tone, 80–83, 83–89
    and voice, 59–80, 83–89
Writing. *See also* specific types
    analysis of argument, 505–12
    "chunking" in, 170–71
    coherence in, 101–7
        implications for writer, 107–24
    and craftsmanship, 257–58
    creating meaning, 411–24
    descriptive and narrative, 199–236
    dynamic model, 31–48
    elements of arrangement, 93–128
    fixed form in, 411–21
        business letter, 416–17
        résumé, 418–19
    fluency, 3–25
    form in, 401–35
    formative idea in, 421–30
    learning process, 12–13
    open form, 421–26
    paradigms, 572
    process of, 10–13, 23–25
    purposes and goals, 45–48
    rhythms of, 242–47
Writing process, 10–13
    examples, 23–25
    and fluency, 10–13
Writing vocabulary, 331

"Yet" linkages, 114

Zukav, Gary, 574

Guide to Handbook Materials

Sentence Sense (Chapters 6–8)
    Sentence Base   pp. 167–190
    Sentence Fragment   pp. 180–184
    Comma Splice, Run-on Sentence   pp. 264–273
    Expanding Sentence Patterns   pp. 199–260
Punctuation (Chapter 9)
    Sentence Connectors   pp. 264–273
    Modifiers   pp. 274–278
    Series Constructions   pp. 278–282
    Quotes and Italics   pp. 282–286
    Hyphens   pp. 286–288
Diction (Chapters 10–11)
    Word Choice   pp. 293–325
    Vocabulary Building   pp. 330–334
    Dictionary Use   pp. 334–359
Spelling (Chapter 12)
    Etymological Basis of Spelling   pp. 368–379
    Spelling the Schwa Vowel   pp. 379–382
    Homonyms   pp. 382–383
Word Forms (Chapter 12)
    The -*ed* System (tense)   pp. 384–386
    The -*s* Systems (subject-verb agree-
       ment, plurals, possessives   pp. 386–391
    Adjective and Adverb Forms   pp. 391–392
    Systems of Word Formation   pp. 392–394
Manuscript Form   pp. 483–487
Usage (Appendix A)   pp. 611–614

The Basics

Getting Started   Ch. 1
Writing to an Audience   Ch. 2
Adopting a Stance as Writer   Ch. 3
Writing Coherently   Ch. 4
Developing Paragraphs   Ch. 5
Writing Clearly   Ch. 6
Expanding Sentences   Ch. 7–8
Choosing Words   Ch. 10–11
Developing Ideas   Ch. 13–14
Analyzing Arguments   Ch. 15
Finding Ideas   Ch. 16–17
Revising   Ch. 18